ROYAL HORTICULTURAL SOCIETY

PRUNING
& TRAINING

Warwickshire County Council

Ath			
10/11/18			
4/7/22			

This item is to be returned or renewed before the latest date above. It may be borrowed for a further period if not in demand. **To renew your books:**

- **Phone the 24/7 Renewal Line 01926 499273 or**
- **Visit www.warwickshire.gov.uk/libraries**

Discover ● Imagine ● Learn ● *with libraries*

Warwickshire County Council

Working for Warwickshire

ROYAL HORTICULTURAL SOCIETY
PRUNING &TRAINING

CHRISTOPHER BRICKELL
DAVID JOYCE

DK | Penguin Random House

Revised Edition
Senior Editor Alastair Laing
Art Editor Anne Fisher
Cover Design Nicola Powling
Pre-Production Producer Catherine Williams
Senior Producer Ché Creasey
Managing Editor Stephanie Farrow
Managing Art Editor Christine Keilty

Consultant and Additional Text Guy Barter
New Illustrations Debbie Maizels

Royal Horticultural Society
Editor Simon Maughan
Publisher Rae Spencer-Jones
Head of Editorial Chris Young

DK India
Project Editor Janashree Singha
Editor Sugandh Juneja
Managing Editor Soma B. Chowdhury
Managing Art Editor Navidita Thapa
Pre-Production Manager Sunil Sharma
Senior DTP Designer Pushpak Tyagi
DTP Designers Manish Upreti, Umesh Singh Rawat

First Edition
Project Editor Louise Abbott
Project Art Editor Stephen Josland
Managing Editor Francis Ritter
Managing Art Editor Derek Coombes
Photography Peter Anderson
Illustrations Karen Cochrane
Additional artwork Sarah Young, John Hutchinson

This edition published in Great Britain in 2017 in
association with The Royal Horticultural Society
by Dorling Kindersley Limited, 80 Strand, London WC2R 0RL

First edition published in Great Britain in 1996

Contents

Introduction

Ornamental trees

Tree fruits

Climbing plants

Ornamental shrubs

Roses

Soft fruits

Introduction

Understanding how plants grow and appreciating their individual needs and responses to pruning makes it easier to choose the correct pruning and training techniques for each one.

At the simplest level, the purpose of pruning and training is to ensure that plants are as healthy and vigorous as possible, free of structural weakness and at the least risk of being infected by disease. The effects of expert pruning, however, go beyond this straightforward aim. With additional knowledge of how pruning and training influences the way in which plants grow and perform, the gardener can not only improve their natural appearance, but also enhance ornamental features such as flowers and foliage, increase crops, and create striking plant features and combinations. Understanding the principles of how and why plants respond to pruning is the key to realizing their potential.

"How do you prune it?" is one of the most commonly asked questions about plants. There is often more than one correct answer, because many can be grown and pruned in different ways to produce different effects. While pruning is often a complex subject, for many plants pruning can be kept very simple, since they require little more than the removal of dead, diseased or damaged wood to keep them in good health.

There are special considerations that will influence the type and degree of the pruning that you undertake. Some people prefer immaculate, formal gardens in which each plant is neatly and symmetrically shaped, while others prefer to allow

natural, sometimes unexpected growth habits to develop. In some situations pruning to restrict size may be important – to increase the range of plants that can be grown in a limited space, or under glass, for example.

But in most cases, the aim is simply to ensure a healthy, soundly structured and pleasingly shaped plant. Remember that sound early training lays firm foundations for a fine mature specimen, and that, at any stage in its life, pruning causes some stress to a plant, so should never be done without good reason. If you choose the right plant for the right situation and desired effect, the need for remedial pruning will be avoided.

Mop-head fuchsia
Many small ornamental plants lend themselves to novel training and pruning methods. The technique of pinch pruning can be used to produce brilliant flowering displays.

◀ **Classic lines**
A formal double row of pleached lime trees provides an attractive, regimented allée leading to the informality of the hidden garden beyond.

How Plants Grow

For plants to grow, they must have food, water, light and a suitable climate. Plants have adapted to a vast range of habitats, and their needs regarding climate (*see facing page, below*) are correspondingly diverse. However, provided that individual needs are met, most plants grow in a similar way.

Plants have the ability to modify the structure and function of their cells throughout their lives, so that not only can they reproduce sexually, they are also able, given the right conditions, to regenerate as entire plants from, for example, a small section of stem, root or leaf separated from the parent plant. This ability is exploited by gardeners every time a plant is propagated.

The most active site of cellular activity in plants is at soft, green shoot tips, where hormones are manufactured that stimulate and control the plant's growth. Extension growth is made principally from just below the topmost (apical) bud – the growing point or "leader". The apical bud imposes what is called "apical dominance", whereby the hormones move down the stem and inhibit the growth of the side buds ("lateral" buds). These buds will break into growth to form branches only once the growing tip has grown away strongly. If the apical bud is damaged, a single sideshoot may grow up strongly and re-impose apical dominance, but in some cases, two or more growing tips share apical dominance and form dual or multiple leaders (*see p.24*).

The second area of intense cellular activity is in the cambium layer, which surrounds the plant stem just beneath the tough, outer skin, or bark. It is this area of activity that enables plants to be grafted; if genetically compatible, the cambium tissue of two stems fuses when pressed closely together. The growth at the cambium layer increases the stem girth. Not only does the stem thicken, it also becomes more robust, as specialized strengthening tissue develops. In woody plants, this process is known as lignification ("becoming woody"). The build-up of strong, woody stems is stimulated by stem movement, such as that caused by flexing in the wind. This is why low stakes are preferable during a tree's early years – they allow stem flexing, and this helps to produce strong trunks (*see* Staking, *p.21*).

HOW PLANT GROWTH ADAPTS
The main objective of a plant is to grow to maturity then reproduce, usually by means of setting seed. Some plants fulfil this function quickly, and then die – the plants we call "annuals" and "biennials". Woody and herbaceous perennial plants take longer to reach

Parts of a plant

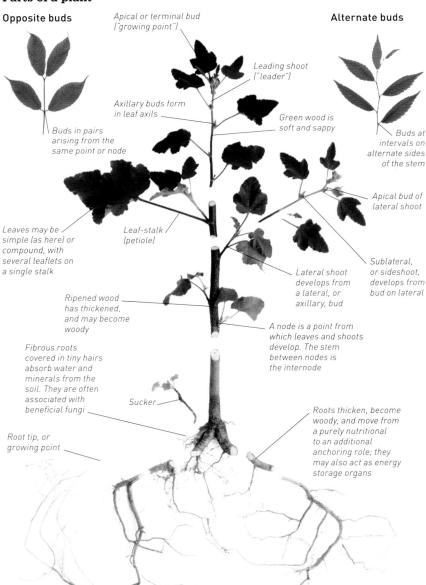

Opposite buds

Apical or terminal bud ("growing point")

Axillary buds form in leaf axils

Buds in pairs arising from the same point or node

Leaves may be simple (as here) or compound, with several leaflets on a single stalk

Leaf-stalk (petiole)

Ripened wood has thickened, and may become woody

Fibrous roots covered in tiny hairs absorb water and minerals from the soil. They are often associated with beneficial fungi

Root tip, or growing point

Sucker

Leading shoot ("leader")

Green wood is soft and sappy

Alternate buds

Buds at intervals on alternate sides of the stem

Apical bud of lateral shoot

Sublateral, or sideshoot, develops from bud on lateral

Lateral shoot develops from a lateral, or axillary, bud

A node is a point from which leaves and shoots develop. The stem between nodes is the internode

Roots thicken, become woody, and move from a purely nutritional to an additional anchoring role; they may also act as energy storage organs

Cross-section through a plant stem

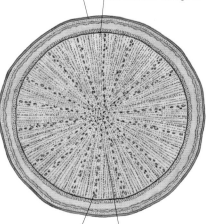

Tough outer skin, or bark, minimizes water loss from the stem surface and protects the soft tissue within

In the cambium layer, cells divide and diversify to create vascular bundles of transporting tissues and increase stem girth

Vascular bundles in stem tissue carry water, nutrients, sugars and growth hormones up and down the stem

Pith is a connecting matrix for other tissues. It dies, is lignified, and forms the heartwood

"Stagheaded" dieback
Oaks protect the main body of the tree by isolating entire branches suffering from dieback with "natural barriers". The dead wood will be shed without harming the tree.

Natural barrier has isolated dead wood

Cut straight across here

Clear demarcation between dead and live tissue

Replacement shoots have grown

Stem dieback
A stub left by incorrect pruning has died back to the next active buds, which, protected by the barrier the plant has formed to halt the dieback, have produced healthy shoots.

Renewal growth from base
Continual renewal growth from the base of the plant acts as insurance for this rose, in case any of its main stems are damaged, become diseased or simply die of old age.

maturity, but then gain the advantage of being able to repeat the reproductive process many times. These plants must develop tissue that is cold- and weather-resistant in order to survive from year to year. Trees and shrubs produce hard, woody tissue that resists winter cold. In harsher climates, the soft top growth of some shrubs may be killed by cold, but the plant is still able to regenerate, producing new shoots from buds on its woody base that will grow and flower in a single season. Deciduous plants also shed their most vulnerable parts, the leaves, and become dormant in winter. Many plants, such as roses (*see above right*) combine these strategies.

Plants adapt in many other ways to their environment. They grow towards

sunlight and develop a branched habit to expose the maximum leaf area to the sun and optimize photosynthesis (*see p.13*), and extend their roots to maximize anchorage and exploit the soil for moisture and nutrients. They can adapt their growth to adverse conditions, for example, by developing shorter, stubbier, stronger growth on the side of the plant buffeted by a prevailing wind (producing distorted "wind-pruned" crowns).

ADAPTATIONS TO DAMAGE AND DISEASE
Plants are often able to limit the spread of disease, which usually attacks the vulnerable, soft upper growth. By the actions of certain chemicals, they form a "natural barrier" across the stem, isolating the diseased portion from the main body

of the plant. When the barrier is complete, the isolated portion dies, becomes dry and brittle and eventually is shed. This defence mechanism is most pronounced – and most clearly understood – in trees, but can be observed in many woody plants. The plant responds to wounding by transporting protective chemicals to the site of the wound to create a natural barrier that isolates the damaged tissue and defends the body of the tree from colonization by wood-rotting organisms.

Over time, the tree reinforces this barrier by forming an air- and watertight seal over the wound. This process originates in the cambium layer, where cells divide rapidly to form scar, or callus, tissue, which extends from the edges inwards over (*continued on p.10*)

THE INFLUENCE OF CLIMATE
Climatic influence on plant growth is profound and is not limited simply by the range of average seasonal temperatures. Climate also influences length of growing season, the way plants flower and ripen wood, and whether they become dormant.

Glossary of climatic terms
CONTINENTAL Found at the centre of large land masses: has clearly defined seasons, with hot summers, when growth is rapid, ripens well, and becomes more able to withstand the very cold winters. Rainfall all year, often highest in summer.
MARITIME A climate warmed by the nearby presence of a sea mass, which evens out seasonal temperature fluctuations. Wood may not ripen well in summer and be less winter-hardy; mild springs induce early growth, susceptible to late frost.
MEDITERRANEAN Has hot, dry summers, with most rain falling during the mild,

almost frost-free, winters. Mediterranean plants dislike wet, cold winters.
MICROCLIMATE Describes local conditions encountered in a specific site. A "frost-pocket" is a localized, very cold microclimate. Artificial microclimates include sunny walls; plants benefit from reflected heat and light that helps to ripen wood and increase hardiness and flowering potential.
SUBTROPICAL Highest temperatures in summer, with a definite cool season in which plants may become dormant. May have seasonal or evenly distributed rainfall.
TEMPERATE Climates with a relatively narrow range of temperatures, having warm summers and cool winters (warm temperate) or cooler summers and cold winters (cool temperate), linked by intermediate spring and autumn conditions. Rainfall occurs year-round.
TROPICAL Has high temperatures year-round; may have high rainfall, seasonally or throughout the year. Growth may be

continuous without a distinct dormant season. Arid tropics have low rainfall; plants grow immediately after seasonal rains, which can be unreliable.

Plant hardiness
FULLY HARDY (H4–H7) MINIMUM -15°C (5°F); plants survive all but unusually hard winters in cool climates.
FROST-HARDY (H3–H4) Minimum -5°C (23°F); plants do not usually survive hard or prolonged frost.
HALF-HARDY (H2) Minimum 0°C (32°F); after long, hot summers when wood is well ripened, plants may survive light frost.
FROST-TENDER OR TENDER (H1A–H2) Needing minimum temperatures of at least 5°C (41°F). Plants are unlikely to survive even light ground frosts. Many plants are frost-tender when young but fully hardy when mature; the same applies to ripened and unripened wood.

(continued from p.9) several years to close the wound. The more damage there is to the cambium tissue – by a torn wound or a rough cut – the slower this process will be. The use of wound paints interferes with this process, and is no longer recommended *(see also p.20)*.

The intervention of the gardener can help a plant to recover from damage or disease. If a plant has already formed a natural barrier between live and dead wood, never cut below it, or the plant will have to expend energy needlessly by forming either scar tissue or another barrier further down the stem. It is always best to remove the dead wood; it may be colonized by harmful organisms, becoming a source of infection.

In some situations, pruning cuts must be made back into live, healthy wood *(see near right)*. Diseases like coral spot spread so rapidly that the plant has no time to build defensive barriers, and may die unless the affected portion is swiftly "amputated". Where a plant is damaged, a clean cut beyond all damage will heal far more quickly than the rough wound.

Never make a larger cut than is necessary. The term "target pruning" describes the process of making the smallest, cleanest wounds possible, at points where the plant's own defence mechanisms are most active. When removing woody branchlets or branches, even if they are completely dead, do not cut into the main branch or trunk or even flush with it, or you will breach the plant's defences, and cause structural weakness by allowing in wood-rotting organisms. The point at which a branch forks from a main stem develops

Life-threatening disease and damage

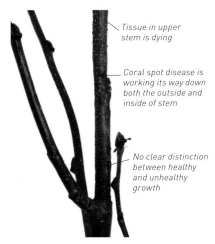

Tissue in upper stem is dying

Coral spot disease is working its way down both the outside and inside of stem

No clear distinction between healthy and unhealthy growth

Diseased wood Coral spot spreads rapidly, and affected growth must be cut well back to where both the surface and interior of the stem are completely healthy and clean.

structurally in a complex way *(see below)*. As it thickens, cylinders of strengthening tissue form a seamless "sleeve" from the main stem along the "arm" that is the shoot. At the junction, a thickened, reinforcing "branch collar" forms that takes the strain caused by branch's increasing weight and by wind. The branch collar is also the most active site of the tree's natural defences. Always cut just beyond it *(see below)*.

Some wounds are so large and jagged that they never seal completely, and remain vulnerable to infection. If the plant has several stems, the damaged

Split branch crotch Wind has split this narrow-angled branch away from the trunk, causing serious damage. The branch should never have been allowed to develop.

one may be cut out at the base. If the damage has occurred at a large branch crotch on a single-trunked tree, neither plant nor gardener may be able to remedy it, and professional advice should be sought; it may be necessary to remove the tree. Such damage often occurs because branches make too narrow a crotch angle with the main stem. Removing shoots likely to develop into such branches is the best way to minimize the risk of later damage. The preventative aspect of correct pruning and training is just as important as its corrective role later in a plant's life.

Cross-section through a branch crotch

The position of the branch collar and bark ridge indicates where to make the least harmful cut. Make the cut on the branch just beyond the branch collar, at an equal and opposite angle to that made by the bark ridge on the main stem.

Branch crease, where internal structures of branch and trunk merge, is visible externally as the "bark ridge"; never cut into it

Target pruning
A small, clean cut beyond the branch collar closes up (occludes) rapidly and keeps the plant's natural defence barriers intact.

Angle branch makes to trunk is known as "crotch angle", "V-angle" or "angle of attachment"

Best place to make cut (see left)

Thickened ring or "branch collar"; cut just outside it

Bark ridge is visible at branch crotch, or fork

Frost damage It is correct to prune frost damage back into completely healthy wood, cutting to a bud, but not when more frosts are likely; the cut will expose buds previously sheltered by the (albeit damaged) upper stem and foliage, and further frosts may damage them too.

Principles of Pruning and Training

The foundations of good gardening lie in good cultural practice (*see p.13*), ensuring that plants' basic needs for food, water and light are met. The foundations of good pruning lie in two primary principles. The first should be always to assess the whole plant before making any cuts, and the second is never to cut without good reason. There are, however, many good reasons for pruning.

The most important, and the most routine, pruning tasks are the removal of any dead, diseased and damaged tissue. Prompt action helps plants to remain healthy, and appropriate pruning cuts improve their chances of recovery from damage and disease (*see facing page*). Additional pruning and training will be used for a host of other good reasons: to produce safe, structurally sound specimens; to create pleasing shapes that best display plants' ornamental qualities; to stimulate vigorous growth and encourage other desirable habits (for example, dense, bushy growth in hedging plants); and, last but not least, to enhance flowering and fruiting.

The key fact underlying the techniques used for all of these objectives is that when material is removed from a plant, either through natural causes or by a pruning cut, the plant will usually respond by making new growth elsewhere. Gardeners can prune to induce growth where and when it is wanted, and vary the direction, quantity and vigour of this growth as desired.

BREAKING APICAL DOMINANCE

When a stem is broken or cut, and the sap flow is stopped, the apical dominance of the terminal bud is also broken. Shoots then sprout from buds immediately below the wound, and from lower down on the stem, sometimes where no buds were visible. These latent or dormant buds remain concealed beneath the bark until stimulated into growth. Many trees, including conifers such as *Abies* and *Araucaria*, have strong apical dominance, and are best allowed to develop their natural habit without pruning in this way.

Because apical dominance is strongly associated with vertical growth, it may also be broken by pulling a vertical shoot down and tying it in horizontally. This reduces the sap flow so that the terminal bud loses much of its dominance. A number of sideshoots then develop from buds along the stem; all will grow upwards with similar vigour, and are much more likely to flower and fruit. This technique is ideal for climbing and other long, flexible-stemmed plants, and for cordon or espaliered fruit trees, to increase flowering and fruiting displays and crop yields. (*Continued on p.12*)

Breaking apical dominance by cutting through a stem

Before With the terminal bud intact and maintaining apical dominance, vigour is primarily directed into further upward growth. Lateral buds on the stem may be slow to develop into shoots.

Upward growth

After Removing the topmost bud induces lateral shoots to break. The topmost remaining bud will grow most strongly, but because it does not have absolute dominance, shoots will also grow from buds lower down the stem.

Lateral growth

Pinch pruning (coleus)

Nipping out the main terminal bud of this cutting, and those of its lateral shoots, with finger and thumb results in dense, bushy growth, rather than a single vertical stem.

Before: single stem grown from cutting

After: growth when shoot tips have been regularly pinched out

Cutting back to older wood

Suitable plants can be cut back to areas where no buds are visible. Dormant buds, clustered at the base of the plant, are stimulated by hard pruning to "break" through the bark that conceals them, resulting in a mass of shoots.

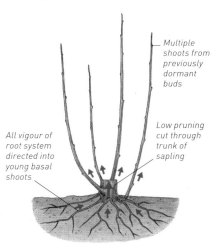

Multiple shoots from previously dormant buds

Low pruning cut through trunk of sapling

All vigour of root system directed into young basal shoots

Horizontal training (rose)

Upward growth

Vertical stem (left) The main emphasis of growth is vertical, seen in this main stem and in its sideshoot.

Horizontal stem (below) Tying down the sideshoot has induced buds in its leaf axils to break into shoots. All will grow vertically and the majority should bear flowers.

Upward growth from horizontal stem

HOW PLANTS ARE GROUPED

In botanical classification the grouping of most importance to gardeners is the "genus", which includes a variable number of "species"; species may be interbred to create "hybrids", indicated by the prefix "×". Within a species there may be natural variants (for example, with a different flower colour), and cultivated varieties, or "cultivars", maintained to perpetuate a distinctive quality. Thus *Lonicera* is a genus, while *Lonicera japonica* and *L. nitida* are species (*see below*) and *L × heckrottii* is a hybrid. *L. nitida* 'Baggesen's Gold' is a cultivar, selected for its golden leaves.

Plants are grouped in genera according to shared characteristics such as flower form and petal number, whereas pruning and training needs depend on growth habit and flowering season, so the requirements of species within a genus may vary considerably.

Same genus, different habit

***Lonicera nitida* 'Baggesen's Gold'**
This evergreen, dense shrub species has branched, rigid stems and small glossy leaves, and is often used as a hedge.

Lonicera japonica This is typical of the climbing species we know as honeysuckles, with long, slender, twining stems and a profusion of flowers.

INFLUENCING VIGOUR OF REGROWTH

Restricting shoot growth by pruning stimulates the production of new growth elsewhere on the plant. In general, the harder the pruning, the more vigorous the regrowth will be – provided that the individual plant is healthy and tolerant of hard pruning. Conversely, pruning lightly, or not at all, results in limited regrowth. So if, for example, the growth of a shrub becomes unbalanced, prune the weaker side back hard, and either leave the other side alone, or trim it back very lightly to shape.

Pruning hard will not necessarily limit a plant's size – quite the reverse – unless it is regularly repeated, as with such special techniques as coppicing. For many shrubs and trees, repeated hard pruning to restrict size merely weakens the plant. It is always best to choose a plant that fits the available space, rather than have to cut it back continually.

TIMING OF PRUNING

The timing of pruning is critical and is directly related to the age and type of flowering wood. Late summer- and autumn-flowering shrubs, for example, flower on the current season's growth, and are pruned in spring to encourage vigorous shoots that will flower later in the same year. Spring and early summer-flowering shrubs flower on the previous season's growth and are pruned after flowering, to permit new wood to grow and ripen, then bloom in the following year. In some cases, flowers are borne on

Same genus, different training

Free-standing buddleja Many buddlejas can be cut back hard each year, producing tall, vigorous, arching stems that may grow to 2m (6ft) and flower in a single season.

spurs arising from a framework of old wood; the spur wood is pruned back to the framework at the appropriate season, depending on flowering time. With some plants, other factors must also be taken into account; plants that "bleed" when cut, for example, should not be pruned in spring, when the pressure of rising sap will cause profuse bleeding. If evergreens are pruned too early in spring or too late in summer, they produce soft new growth that may be damaged by frost or cold wind.

Same plant (*Syringa meyeri* 'Palibin'), different training

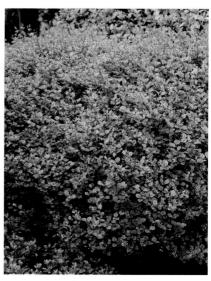

Near-natural form (above) *Syringa meyeri* 'Palibin' naturally forms a neat, bushy shrub clothed with growth to the ground.

Trained form (left) Special training as a standard results in quite a different effect.

Wall-trained buddleja Species that require only moderate pruning can, because much growth is retained each year, be wall-trained as a permanent feature.

PRUNING TO DIRECT GROWTH
Pruning to direct growth may be as simple as cutting to a bud that faces in the desired direction. It is, however, usually combined with training shoots in the required direction, either to form a framework, or to replace branches or fill in gaps in an established framework.

PRUNING FOR SPECIAL EFFECTS
Plants may be pruned to produce a number of special effects, such as topiary (see p.48), or by using special techniques such as coppicing or pollarding (see p.34), which can produce brilliant winter stems or larger, more colourful leaves, or perpetuate a display of attractive juvenile foliage, as with many *Eucalyptus*. With more complex pruning and training, some plants that make attractive natural specimens can be trained in controlled forms such as standards. Wall-training a tree or climber displays the flowers to great effect, although it may take many years and require annual maintenance.

Many plants respond well to a variety of pruning techniques, but it is vital when choosing plants for special treatment to be sure that they will respond in the desired way. Do not assume that all plants in the same genus respond in the same way to pruning – they often do, but they may equally well vary widely in the way that they grow, and thus in their pruning and training needs. *Clematis viticella*, for example, is cut back almost to the base every year in spring, while *C. alpina* needs minimal pruning. Plants within a genus may also differ in their tolerance of pruning, so while one is stimulated by hard pruning, another may respond with poor growth or no flowers, or may even die of shock.

CARE AND CULTIVATION
While removal of dead, diseased and damaged wood is always positively beneficial to the plant, other types of pruning inevitably remove material that was actively providing the plant with its source of energy. The process by which plants manufacture energy, photosynthesis (see right), takes place in the leaves. Green chlorophyll traps the energy of sunlight and uses it to convert water and carbon dioxide into a food source that takes the form of carbohydrates. Oxygen is a by-product, and is released into the atmosphere. The more contrived the garden effect – annual cutting down to a framework, for example – the more you deprive the plant of useful material. Stimulating more abundant flowering or fruiting also makes considerable demands on the plant's energy. In general, the more material you remove, and the more frequently you do it, the greater will be the plant's needs for nutrients. If a plant is to remain in good health and to be stimulated, rather than stressed, by pruning, it is essential to provide the plant with sufficient nutrients and water to fuel its new growth. The plant needs a complete fertilizer that contains a balanced formulation of nutrients, including nitrogen, phosphates and potassium, along with essential trace elements.

FEEDING AND MULCHING
Apply a balanced fertilizer at the manufacturer's recommended rate in spring. Use only recommended quantities; too much will scorch or burn, or otherwise damage, the plants. If repeated applications are required, in cool climates feed until no later than midsummer, as soft growth produced late in the year will be more vulnerable

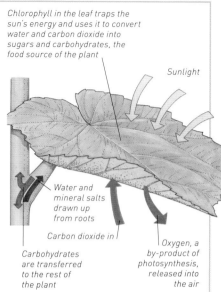

Chlorophyll in the leaf traps the sun's energy and uses it to convert water and carbon dioxide into sugars and carbohydrates, the food source of the plant

Sunlight

Water and mineral salts drawn up from roots

Carbon dioxide in

Carbohydrates are transferred to the rest of the plant

Oxygen, a by-product of photosynthesis, released into the air

Photosynthesis
The leaf is the primary site of photosynthesis; stomata (pores) on the underside open and close to control the exchange of gases.

to damage by winter frost. Apply a mulch after fertilizing on to moist soil in spring (see below right). Avoid the immediate area around the base of the plant. Mulching regulates soil temperatures, conserves soil moisture and, by blanketing the ground, helps to control weeds that will compete with the ornamental plants for water and nutrients. To be effective, a mulch needs to cover the entire area beneath the leaf canopy. Where specimen shrubs or trees are grown in lawns or rough grass, it is essential to keep an area at least 1m (3ft) in diameter free of grass and weeds, at least during the establishment period.

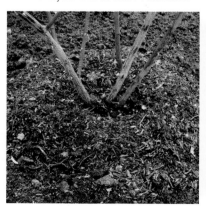

Mulching
Apply a mulch 7.5–10cm (3–4in) deep after fertilizing in spring, avoiding the immediate trunk or stem base.

Feeding
Apply a balanced fertilizer on to moist soil in spring. Spread it evenly over the root zone and rake it in lightly.

Tools and Equipment

It is well worth investing in the best garden equipment you can afford. The ideal is to have an appropriate tool to hand for every task. You will achieve the best result by using the correct tool. This is particularly important with cutting tools. Using secateurs to cut over-thick stems can damage both plant and tool, as well as making the job uncomfortable and, over time, tiring.

Make sure, before you buy, that you find the tools comfortable to use; feel their weight and check that they fit into your hand well, are easy to grip, and can be used without strain.

CUTTING TOOLS
Secateurs are the most useful of pruning tools, and can be used for all soft growth and on woody stems of up to 1cm (½in) in diameter. Do not try to exceed their capabilities; use a pair of loppers to cut through thicker branches.

Many people do not realize that there is a "right way up" for each cut when using secateurs. The thinner blade (the upper blade, when holding the secateurs normally) should always be nearer the bud or stem junction to which you are cutting. To achieve this, it is often necessary to turn your hand so that your palm is facing downwards (*compare above right and below*).

Never cut wire with the blades of secateurs; it will damage them. There is sometimes a wire-cutting notch that can be used on the outer edge of the blades.

A saw has several uses: cutting thick, woody growth; cutting away stubs from the bases of roses; and thinning old,

The "wrong" and "right" way to cut with secateurs

Incorrect use When secateurs are held normally (thin blade uppermost), this lateral (*above left*) cannot be cut off correctly; the thick blade is nearer the trunk and thus determines the cut's position The cut is made too far from the main stem (*above right*), leaving a stub that may die back.

Correct use By turning the secateurs over, the thin blade is nearer the trunk and the cut can be made precisely where it is required.

knobbly spur systems. Choose a special pruning or Grecian saw designed for garden use; household saws clog up quickly when cutting green wood. Double-edged saws often damage nearby growth, and amateur gardeners rarely need to, and in most cases should not, tackle jobs large enough to require a bow saw.

Always have a garden or pruning knife to hand, for smoothing cuts and nipping out soft growth. Do not use it to cut string; it will blunt the blade.

Shears can be used on plants such as lavenders and heathers that need regular clipping over, and for hedges and topiary. Wavy-edged shears that trap shoots as they are cut, so that they are not pushed out with the scissor action of the blades, are useful for precise topiary work. Other

pruning tools include long-handled tree pruners, which often have saw or fruit-picking attachments. They can be used for trees and climbing plants to which access by ladder is impossible. It is, however, difficult to make precisely positioned cuts. A half-moon lawn edger can also be used, to chop at the edges of thicket-forming plants; chopping through and removing the roots when cutting out peripheral stems restricts their spread far more effectively than pruning above ground. A sharp-edged spade can be used to do the same job.

TOOL MAINTENANCE
Always clean and dry tools thoroughly after use, particularly those with cutting blades. A final wipe with an oily rag will keep blades rust-free and in good

Using cutting tools correctly

Using secateurs correctly A sharp pair of secateurs will cut quickly and easily through small, woody stems of no more than, approximately, the thickness of a pencil.

Using secateurs incorrectly Tugging and wrestling to cut this over-thick stem is tearing and bruising plant tissue, and also blunting the secateur blades.

Using loppers correctly A stem whose girth will fit entirely within the bite of the loppers is easy to cut. The long handles exert extra leverage, so little effort is required.

Fruit ladder
This useful ladder has a prop, or "back leg".
Its tapering top can reach well into the tree.
It is ideal for pruning branched-head trees
with no trunk against which to prop a ladder.

condition. If you have been pruning out
diseased plant material, disinfect tools
before moving on to prune other growth,
or before putting them away. Dip them
in a dilute disinfectant recommended for
garden use, and dry carefully. Always keep
cutting blades sharp. This is not only
important for making clean cuts; working
with inefficient tools is frustrating and
makes gardening a chore rather than a
pleasure. Working with shears that need
sharpening, oiling or tightening is
particularly irksome.

DISPOSAL OF PRUNED MATERIAL
Soft prunings can be composted, but
woody material takes too long to break
down, unless you have access to a garden

shredder. Never compost or shred diseased
plant material. Though the heat within
a compost heap can kill certain pathogens,
there is no guarantee that all will be
completely destroyed. Burn it or dispose
of it as waste.

SAFETY
Accidents are rare when the right tool
for the job is used correctly, provided
that you do not attempt tasks that are
beyond your capabilities. Tree-felling
and the removal of large branches must
always be carried out by professionals
(*see* Major tree surgery, *p.33*).

Ideally, never work up a ladder alone,
and be careful not to overstretch to reach
growth while up a ladder.

Remember that stems that you are
pushing or pulling in order to tie in or
cut more conveniently can spring back,
especially when cut. In addition to gloves,
plastic goggles are recommended when
working with thorny stems at head height.

Some plants exude sap when cut
whose irritant effects can range from
a mild rash to dizziness and vomiting.
The hairs on certain plant stems are also
irritant. *Euphorbia*, *Fremontodendron* and
Rhus species are particularly notable for
their harmful effects.

TETANUS
The tetanus bacterium is carried in soil
and enters through breaks in the skin.
It is highly advisable for gardeners to
ensure their tetanus "jabs" are up-to-date.
If you have cut yourself on a plant or got
soil or manure in an open wound and have
not been inoculated, or cannot remember
when your last inoculation was, visit
a doctor's surgery. If you develop severe
muscle stiffness or spasms go immediately
to your nearest casualty department or
call 999 for an ambulance.

POWERED TOOLS
Powered tools are invaluable for some
pruning tasks, provided that they are
used with strict attention to safety.
A nylon line trimmer can be used
to prune back large expanses
of some ground-cover
shrubs, such as
Hypericum calycinum.
Many types of hedge
trimmer are available:
in general, small, light,
single-edged,
double-action
models with
narrowly-spaced
teeth are the best
for controlled
clipping and shaping.
Electrically powered,
rather than petrol-
driven, trimmers are
lighter and more convenient to use.
For any trimmer that is supplied with
mains electricity via flex, use a plug or
adaptor fitted with a residual current
device (RCD or "circuit breaker") to
protect you should you inadvertently
cut through the flex. Never trim wet
plants, or in wet weather.

Ear defenders

Goggles

Protective goggles are essential
when trimming with powered tools,
and earplugs or ear defenders are also
recommended. If using a trimmer for
the first time, obtain a demonstration
of its correct and safe use.

Chainsaws are potentially very
hazardous. No-one should use one
without suitable training, and no
reputable agent will hire you one if
they know you to be inexperienced
in its use; they may offer training.

Using loppers incorrectly A stem that
is too wide for the blades to admit strains the
loppers; it is unlikely that the branch can be
cut cleanly with a single cutting action.

Using a pruning saw A small, curved
pruning saw is ideal for cutting thick wood
and stubs, and can be used without damaging
other growth in confined or awkward places.

Using a knife On cuts big or small, rough
edges should be smoothed with a knife. Use
a garden knife or a special pruning knife; its
blade is curved for a more controlled cut.

Ornamental trees

A tree can be the most striking single feature in a garden, and careful training and pruning to ensure an attractive form and a sound branch structure will be amply repaid over many years.

In most gardens, trees are the element of greatest structural importance. Their potential size and longevity demand that careful thought must be given, before planting, to the choice of species and the forms in which they are to be grown.

A wide range of trees is available to suit most growing conditions, and this includes a good selection of small trees that can be accommodated in today's relatively small gardens. The techniques of grafting, pruning and training all have roles in making the most of trees of ornamental value.

The characteristic growth pattern of a tree in the wild – its natural form or "habit" – may be affected by many factors, among them disease, damage, drought or the proximity of other plants. These can result in trees of unusual appearance that, although often attractive in the wild, are undesirable for the garden or street. In these contexts a tree needs not only to be pleasing to the eye, but also to have a sturdy, well-balanced branch structure that will ensure a long and healthy life.

Formative training in a tree's early years is essential, either to make the best of a natural habit or to produce one of a number of trained "forms". Most trees need very little pruning and training once they are established, but the future of a mature tree is often determined by the way it is trained when young. All is not necessarily lost when a tree has been neglected. Many trees can be successfully rejuvenated by skilful renovation. This may call for the use of powered equipment and the removal of large branches. These operations, along with tree felling, are potentially dangerous and they should be undertaken only by professional arboriculturists.

Pollarded *Catalpa bignonioides*
Many trees lend themselves to special training and pruning techniques such as pollarding, which produces a tree with a compact, bushy crown on a clear trunk.

◀ *Acer palmatum* 'Osakazuki'
Requiring only minimal initial pruning to create a well-balanced basal structure, this elegant Japanese maple has developed into a small, multi-stemmed tree.

Tree Forms

A well-grown tree is trained when young into one of several broad categories of tree forms. In many cases, training will have been aimed simply at producing a well-shaped example of a natural habit. Some tree forms are, however, produced and maintained solely through pruning and training methods. In the nursery industry, standardized descriptions are used, often not only of the tree's form but also of its measurements, to help buyers make their choice; in addition, a tree should never be purchased without its eventual size and spread being known, or it may outgrow its situation, entailing tree surgery or even removal.

As trees mature and develop, some of the rigid form distinction created in the nursery may be lost. Unless the tree's safety is threatened, this is rarely a problem requiring action; the tree will be no less pleasing for a less formal habit of growth. Some of the more strictly trained and manipulated forms, however – particularly those involving grafting – require careful control to ensure that the ornamental effect is not lost. Conversely, it is often possible to modify the form and development of a bought tree – clearing a trunk of lower branches to turn it into a standard, for example – if a different effect is desired.

Branched-head standard

These have a single, clear trunk that divides and branches to form an open-centred crown. A common natural form (for example, of horse-chestnuts), it can also be produced at the formative stage, either by top-grafting (as for some *Prunus*) or by cutting back a young tree's main stem (*see p.27*) to stimulate branching at a given height.

Half-standard

Growers use several terms to describe young standard trees of varying heights and proportions. A "half-standard" should have a clear trunk of 75–125cm (30–40in) and a small crown. The form is often lost with age; some trees can be pruned to retain the proportions of a half-standard, such as *Laurus nobilis* (bay).

Feathered tree

The natural form of most young trees, with trunks clothed in lateral branches almost to ground level. Though many shed their lower branches as they develop naturally into standards, a number retain this form into maturity with minimal training (*see p.25*) – for example, many conifers and some eucryphias.

Central-leader standard

The tall, strong trunk of these trees persists all the way through the crown, terminating in a distinct leading shoot. This is a very common form in nature – for example, *Quercus rubra* and *Corylus colurna*. It can also be produced (*see p.26*) by gradually removing the lower branches from a young feathered tree to leave a clear trunk of about 1.5–2m (5–6ft).

Fastigiate tree

These narrow, columnar trees have light, upswept branches, usually virtually from top to bottom, from central trunks that often fork narrowly into two or more stems some way into the crown. It is a wholly natural growth habit that cannot be developed by pruning and needs no pruning to maintain. Many conifers grow in this way, as do *Populus nigra* var. *italica* and *Fagus sylvatica* 'Dawyck'.

Bush

Some trees – for example, medlars – develop naturally in a bush form, with a rounded head of branches on a very short trunk. However, bush trees are more commonly produced by fruit growers, using pruning and training to form cropping trees that are not too tall, and therefore easy to harvest.

Multi-stemmed tree

These trees resemble very large shrubs, with several distinct main stems, or trunks, emerging at the base or from a short stem. These may be slender, upright and clear of branches, as with many birches, or clothed with branches to form a dense thicket. The form may be created by pruning (*see p.28*).

Weeping standard

A weeping standard (*see p.26*) is often formed by top-grafting a weeping cultivar onto a stock plant with a clear stem. The branches weep either straight down from a central point or, like *Fraxinus excelsior* f. *pendula* (weeping ash), cascade outwards to form a mushroom-shaped head.

Basic Techniques

Trees are trained and pruned chiefly to keep them vigorous, healthy and, by forming a strong, well-balanced branch framework, stable. Pruning can also influence shape and size, and enhance features such as bark or flowers.

Pruning and training are most important in the early years, laying the foundations of a well-shaped mature tree. Once a tree is established, pruning is more often than not confined to the removal of dead, diseased, damaged or wayward growth, directing energy into maintaining a strong, shapely

specimen. The younger a tree is when pruned, the more active the healing process, and the younger the growth that is cut, the faster it heals: prune shoots, where necessary, before they become woody, and twigs before they develop into branches.

As with all plants, hard pruning stimulates a more vigorous response than light pruning. Unless using special techniques such as pollarding and coppicing (*see p.34*), pruning hard in order to restrict a tree's size is counterproductive, so choose trees that will not outgrow the space

available. The removal of large branches should always be a last resort – as a response to damage or disease, or to renovate a neglected or unsafe tree. Never remove healthy branches at random in an attempt to improve or alter a mature tree's form: it is risky for the amateur "surgeon" and the tree itself may be left not only disfigured, but also vulnerable to disease and possibly dangerously unstable. Major pruning that needs to be done from a ladder, or involves the removal of large limbs, should always be undertaken by professional arboriculturists.

Making cuts

Every cut, large or small, should be cleanly made so that plant tissue is not torn or bruised. Slanting cuts are usually preferable, since rain cannot collect on the surface as with a horizontal cut; trapped moisture encourages fungal rots. Cuts should ideally be made either close to a bud, at a fork on a branch or just beyond a branch collar – the slight swelling just before it joins its main branch or the trunk (*see also p.10*).

WHEN TO PRUNE
The time at which a tree is pruned is important. It is usually best carried out at the same time as wood is shed in nature. In winter, snow, ice and wind break off dead wood and weak branches on trees that are fully dormant. The wounds heal swiftly once strong growth begins in the spring.

However, most trees tolerate moderate pruning to correct localized problems at any time. Key exceptions are trees that "bleed" sap profusely from pruning wounds, such as birches and walnuts, which normally should never be pruned when the sap is, or is about to start, rising (from mid- to late winter to midsummer), and trees that are susceptible to disease at certain times of the year; cherry trees, for example, are usually pruned in summer, when there is the least risk of silver leaf infection. The *Dictionary of Ornamental Trees* (*see pp.52–91*) gives timings for pruning individual trees.

CUTTING TO A BUD
Select a strong, healthy bud that is pointing in a direction that will give the new shoot room to develop without crossing or crowding other growth. This is normally an outward-facing bud. On trees with opposite buds, the bud facing in to the centre of the tree can be rubbed off to encourage outward growth of the remaining bud. (*Continued on p.20*)

Thin blade of secateurs nearer the bud

Bottom of cut just above top of bud

Cutting to an alternate bud
Make a slanting cut at a point about 5mm (¼in) above the bud. The gentle slope will allow moisture to roll off the cut surface, discouraging the development of disease.

Thin blade of secateurs nearer the buds

Blade well clear of the tips of both buds

Cutting to opposite buds
Cut squarely across the shoot above a healthy pair of buds, as close as you can without grazing and damaging the buds. A pair of healthy shoots should then develop.

Effect of clean and rough cuts on the healing process

Clean cut A clean cut encourages protective new wood – callus or scar tissue – to form most rapidly. The visible cut surface gradually shrinks and is finally "occluded".

Cavity is forming

Diseased tissue

Rough cut Fungal spores that cause fast-spreading rots can easily invade torn and jagged tissue. This infected wound on the trunk may endanger the whole tree.

(Continued from p.19) Never make a cut half-way between buds or branches. It will leave a stub that, without active buds, will wither and die. The normal healing process may be disrupted, allowing disease to penetrate.

Sometimes a cut must be made at a point where there are no visible buds – for example, when coppicing a tree *(see p.34)*. The pruning cut should stimulate a dormant bud: cut away any stub left when the new shoot appears.

MAKING LARGER CUTS

Large pruning cuts, which may take many years to heal, are potential entry points for disease. It is important to make cuts that heal with maximum speed. If the cut is smooth and made in the correct position, the callus, or scar tissue, grows uninterruptedly from around the edge of the wound to its centre, sealing it and preventing the entry of harmful organisms. Once the process is under way, do not further trim or tidy wound edges, as this may disrupt the production of callus tissue.

If a sawn surface is rough, it should immediately be smoothed, especially round the edge. A curved pruning knife is the best tool, though professionals often use a chisel. Care must be taken not to enlarge the wound. Gouging into a main branch or trunk may interrupt sap flow and kill tissue.

CUTTING OFF BRANCHES

The general practice in the past was to remove larger branches with a "flush" cut, right up against the stem. It is now recognized that the branch collar – the ring of slight swelling at its base *(see also p.10)* – should be left intact. This means making a very gently angled cut, slightly away from the main branch or trunk but without leaving a distinct stub. If the branch collar is difficult to find, start the cut on the top of the branch 2–3cm (½–1in) away from the crotch, then cut downwards at a slight outward angle using an appropriately sized pruning saw for the cut required. Smaller folding saws are adequate to remove smaller branches.

WOUND PAINTS

Proprietary wound paints used to be widely applied to cuts to provide an artificial barrier against infection while they healed, but research has shown that they do not assist the healing process much – and some may even hinder it. Exposed tissues are never sterile before the treatment is applied; moreover, some micro-organisms are dormant in healthy wood and only develop when the tissue just under the bark is damaged. In both cases, therefore, harmful organisms will effectively be sealed in behind the paint. At present, no paint has proved totally

Cutting off a branch

Trees recover most rapidly from large cuts if they are smooth and do not damage the branch collar. If the branch is large, remove the bulk of it first (always in small, manageable sections), to minimize the weight of what will fall last. Then support, or first make an undercut on, what remains to be cut away, because if it falls under its own weight before the final downward cut is completed, it may tear the bark and damage the tree.

Cutting to the branch collar

Second, top cut

First undercut

Branch crotch

Final cut

Branch collar

1 *Reduce the weight of the branch to make the final cut more controllable. Some 30cm (12in) away from the trunk, saw a quarter of the way into the branch from the underside. This partial cut stops the bark tearing down the trunk if the branch accidentally breaks.*

2 *Cut squarely down from the top of the branch about 5cm (2in) beyond the undercut (further away from the trunk) until the branch falls away. The undercut ensures that you do not need to support the weight of the branch, provided the area beneath is clear.*

3 *If the remaining stub is still heavy or awkward to support securely, make another undercut 5–8cm (2–3in) from the trunk. Then make the final cut following the line of the branch collar from top to bottom (see Cutting to the branch collar, top of page).*

Finished cut *The final cut downwards must be completely smooth; if an undercut was first made, ensure that the final cut is either closer to the trunk or meets the undercut exactly. Smooth any rough edges with a pruning knife, without enlarging the wound.*

impermeable to air and water – the two principal carriers of plant diseases. The fungicidal properties of wound paints are also of dubious benefit; copper naphthenate, for example, prevents the plant's "natural barrier" against disease *(see p.9)* forming. They may also kill non-harmful organisms such as sugar fungi, which can inhibit wood rot.

While fruit growers with large orchards, through which disease could spread rapidly, may be reluctant to give up their use, wound paints are now considered neither necessary nor advisable. Future research in the area of biological control may perhaps provide new paints for which there is a role in the garden.

Staking

A newly planted tree will usually need initial support for at least two years. The purpose of the stake is not to hold up the tree, but to allow it to establish with a straight, vertical stem. The method used depends on the planting site and the type and size of the tree. While trees used to be staked rigidly, research now shows that a little free movement helps to strengthen the trunk. Low stakes and looser ties that allow the tree to flex in the wind are now recommended, except in special cases. Two low stakes, with flexible bands between them and the tree (*see bottom left*) are ideal. When planting a bare-rooted tree, insert the stake into the hole first, then spread the roots around it without damaging them; never drive a stake through a dense root system, nor force roots round the stake. Position the stake on the side of the prevailing wind. Stakes must be treated with fungicidal preservative and driven at least 60cm (24in) into the ground.

USING TREE TIES

Ties should hold the plant securely but not rigidly. Even with short stakes, it helps to position the ties as low down as possible. Always use padding or a spacer so that ties do not rub directly against the bark: abrasions may affect the future health of the tree. Ties must be checked and adjusted as the tree's girth expands. Ties that are never loosened as the tree grows will cut into the bark and stop food from reaching the branches.

Low stake

A stake that is less than one-third of the tree's height enables the tree to flex and its stem to increase in thickness and strength. Using a spacer keeps the stake clear of the trunk, so that its roughly sawn top does not chafe and damage the young tree's tender bark.

Angled stake

A short, angled stake can be placed clear of a containerized tree's rootball and can be inserted into the ground after planting. Lean the stake at 45° into the prevailing wind. Use a belt tie in a figure-of-eight, or padding, to stop the stake chafing the bark.

Tall stake

A tall stake does not allow the trunk to build up strength. However, tall stakes (preferably one on each side) are occasionally useful: for trees that are top-grafted or have heavy, pendulous branches; in very exposed sites; or if a new leading shoot needs to be trained in.

Two stakes

A pair of short stakes, driven into the bottom of the planting hole on either side of the rootball, can be used for all trees, but particularly for those bought as rootballed or containerized specimens. Flexible ties allow the trunk to flex and strengthen in the wind.

Guy-ropes

If planting a large tree, support it with guy-ropes until its roots have grown sufficiently (usually in about two growing seasons) to stabilize the weight of the crown. Take strong wire through low, sturdy forks in the crown. Lengths of hosepipe threaded on to the wire will stop it cutting into the tree (*see inset left*). Use angled pegs fitted with wire tension adjusters (*see inset right*) so you can ensure that the trunk is trained vertically. Mark small pegs clearly so that they are not a hazard to people or machinery.

Initial Training

The chances of a tree developing a sturdy, well-balanced framework and being long-lived are greatly enhanced if it gets a good start. The requirements of all trees in the first and second growing seasons (a period often referred to as the "nursery" stage) are much the same. More specific training into the various tree forms (*see pp.25–28*) does not normally begin until the second winter.

Gardeners often buy young trees ready-trained (*see facing page*) but it is possible to start with a tree you have propagated yourself, a young sucker lifted from around an existing tree (provided it has not been grafted), or a bought tree that has not yet been trained (these may only be available from a specialist grower, and will possibly have to be purchased by mail order). Very young trees consisting only of unbranched, upright stems are known as "maiden whips", or simply "whips". When a good complement of laterals has developed (usually after two growing seasons, though growth is occasionally very vigorous in the first year) they are referred to as "feathered" trees.

When selecting trees and deciding how they are to be trained, consider carefully your requirements and the limitations of your site. Ensure that the tree you have in mind is suitable for training into the form you would ideally like (and vice versa). Always ascertain its maximum height and spread, and whether special pruning to restrict size, using such techniques as pollarding, is an option. The Dictionary of Ornamental Trees (*see pp.52–91*) provides detailed information for individual trees.

If the tree is not to be planted in its final site from the start, use a small patch of ground as a "nursery bed" to care for young plants together.

RAISING YOUNG TREES

Plants raised from seed, root cuttings or softwood cuttings will grow, initially, as a single, upright shoot with a terminal bud. A hardwood cutting usually produces its new leading growth from the uppermost side bud: if a multi-stemmed tree is required, lower buds on the cutting are allowed to grow, while if only one trunk is required, the lower buds are rubbed out.

Many tree cultivars are produced by grafting: joining the scion – the selected cultivar (in the form of a bud or buds, or a length of stem) – to a rootstock from a compatible plant. The point at which the two tissues are fused (the graft union) is usually visible as a slight swelling, near the base of the trunk on "bottom-grafted" trees. "Top-grafting" – joining the scion

at the top of a clear trunk grown from the rootstock – is mainly used nowadays to produce weeping standards. These are rarely sold until they are several years old, and have special pruning and training needs (*see p.26*). While bottom-grafting is a technique that can be practised by the amateur, top-grafting is rarely practicable except for the professional grower. Trees that you have bottom-grafted yourself will need to be trained and pruned using the same techniques followed in the nursery industry.

A tree produced by bud-grafting will grow away from the graft point as a single shoot. Any growth from the stock plant, either from the stem below the graft point or from the roots, must be removed completely as seen.

Where a short section of the scion's stem is grafted on to the stock plant, the topmost side bud will grow into the new leading shoot. (*Continued on p.24*)

Cane is vertical and extends above the stem it is supporting, so leader can be tied in as it grows

Growing point

Vigorous, straight, single leading shoot, well-clothed by (compound) leaves

Pot size is in proportion to size of tree

Well-trained young tree

At the end of its first growing season, this ash seedling is upright, vigorous and healthy. Its pot is large enough to accommodate, without constriction, a root system capable of supporting the top growth.

Top growth is too extensive to be supported by rootball, which is constricted by small pot

Competing leaders have been allowed to develop

Stem is not supported by a cane, and is growing at an angle

Neglected young tree

Lack of care in the first two years results in a young tree that already stands little chance of becoming a well-shaped mature specimen. Without remedial action, this *Gleditsia* will grow to be badly shaped and lop-sided.

Shoot from terminal bud will grow to extend leader, continuing the main stem

Side buds will develop into lateral shoots unless rubbed off

Graft union, still covered with protective tape

Any growth from below graft will be of stock plant and must be removed

Young grafted tree

A recently grafted tree can be staked with a split cane, not only to keep the leading shoot growing straight, but also to protect it from stress and breakage at the graft point.

Buying young trees

Purchased trees may suffer more problems than those propagated and trained in the garden. Actual physical defects are rare where growers take pride in their good reputation, though shoots may have been removed for propagation, spoiling the form. There may, however, be "hidden" tissue damage, perhaps caused by roots drying out, insufficient hardening off or acclimatization or stress during transportation. If you can, select and collect young trees personally, so that you can assess nursery conditions and look trees over for potential problems. Transport them carefully: many trees are killed between nursery and garden. Containerized trees quickly desiccate or scorch if left to stand in hot sun or on hot tarmac or concrete. A tree transported on an open truck or roof rack, with its foliage buffeted in the slipstream, suffers considerable stress.

SELECTING PARTLY TRAINED TREES
There is an obvious, time-saving advantage in purchasing three- or four-year-old trees, but there are disadvantages too. Most problems are caused by root-to-shoot imbalance – top growth that is far too large for the rootball to sustain once the intensive nursery feeding and watering has stopped. The spread of a container-grown tree should not be more than three or four times the width of the container. Laterals that are overlong compared with the rest should be pruned to a single bud.

A common problem is that the tree has been made to look almost too attractive to the prospective buyer – allowed to flower or fruit when energy would be better spent on growth; or fed heavily to stimulate lush green shoots that may not survive frosts. Small, sturdy trees that have been "grown hard" nearly always make the best mature specimens.

ROOT PRUNING ON PLANTING
Bare-rooted trees are particularly vulnerable to damage during lifting and transporting. As soon as they are exposed to the air, the fine feeder roots begin to dry out and die. To minimize the area of cut surface, cleanly cut away roots with abrasions and ragged, broken ends. Prune to even up overlong, mis-shapen or lop-sided roots so that there is a good spread emanating from the stem. Roots should never be so long, nor the planting hole so small, that they have to be wound around the hole. Generally, container-grown or rootballed trees should not have their roots pruned

when transplanting. Roots that are tightly packed will be very slow to penetrate the surrounding soil, so where roots are constricted, tease them out. Cut back only any roots that have been damaged – for example, by growing through the bottom of the container.

TRANSPLANTATION SHOCK
Young plants thrive in nurseries, grown close together. When their environment suddenly changes – to isolation and exposure to strong winds, hot sun and hard frosts – their growth rate may be set back. Some trees are remarkably resilient; others, no matter how carefully they are moved, suffer considerable post-planting shock. The older the tree when moved, the more serious the problem. The second most common reason why

newly planted trees fail to "grow away" well is that their top growth is too large for their root system: the roots, struggling to sustain the over-large tree, cannot absorb the extra nutrients and moisture necessary to make new growth. If the problem continues into the second growing season, the only remedy is to prune to redress the balance. In the dormant season, reduce the top growth by half by thinning, removing some shoots to the point of origin but leaving the rest intact and unshortened (the terminal buds are thought to aid growth). Feed lightly, and mulch and water the tree well during the following growing season. The treatment may have to be repeated for a further year if the tree does not respond with strong growth.

Selecting trees for purchase

Good example
This short, sturdy, well-trained young crab apple shows a good balance between top-growth and rootball.

Poor example
This birch is an extreme example in combining virtually all of the faults caused by neglect of early training. Never buy a tree that resembles it in any respect.

Light staking will straighten strong terminal shoot

Lateral branches spaced out to admit air and sunlight, yet profuse enough to provide good foliage density in summer

Laterals make wide V-angles with main stem

Main stem is clear

Substantial rootball is able to support top growth

Original leader has failed and its replacement has not been trained vertically

Weak shoots within crown will increase wind resistance and make young tree unstable

Lack of staking has caused main stem to grow at an angle

Long, spindly branches may snap in wind

Main stem has forked and so may weaken and eventually split

Roots protruding from pot will have dried out; tree may never recover from being completely pot-bound

(*Continued from p.22.*) If a single stem is required, other lower buds should be rubbed out. Remove growth from the stock plant as for a budded tree.

FIRST-YEAR TRAINING

During the first growing season, leaves and sometimes small shoots will appear along the length of the main stem. Do not remove these unless they become damaged or diseased: the tree needs every leaf possible to manufacture food for further growth.

During the following winter, a strong, healthy young tree should not need much pruning, but at this stage any weak or wayward-growing shoots may be cut out. If the leading shoot is growing poorly, replace it by cutting it back to a strong bud or young shoot, if a suitable one has been produced; this should then develop into a vigorous shoot to train vertically as a new leader during the next growing season.

To ensure straight, vertical growth, stake the main stem or stems using a cane to which extension growth can be tied as it develops. Do not damage the roots when inserting canes, and let ties allow some movement to strengthen the stem. Any laterals that compete with the leader should be removed.

COMPETING LEADERS

A vigorous lateral that threatens the dominance of the leader must be shortened or removed. If the leading shoot of a tree with opposite buds has been damaged and a pair of dual leaders has grown, select only one (*see below right*). If neither is suitable, cut lower down the stem to a pair of buds, rubbing out one of the new shoots that develop.

SECOND-YEAR TRAINING

As the young tree develops strong laterals along its main stem or stems, remove only growth that is dead, diseased or damaged, or any competing leaders. It is essential to maintain strong main or leading shoots that will form either the single, central trunk, or the several trunks of a multi-stemmed tree. If competing leaders are not dealt with, there are likely to be problems arising from crossing branches and an unsound framework.

BROKEN LEADER

If the leader is "lost" – it dies back, is damaged by frosts or is broken – prune it back to the nearest sound, strong lateral that can be trained vertically to take its place. If there are as yet no laterals, prune to a healthy bud, and then train the resulting shoot. On a tree with opposite buds, remove the weaker shoot or one of the pair of buds in order to direct all energy into the new leader.

Competing leaders

On this young tree, competing leaders have been neglected and now form an upright cluster at the tree's apex. Further training into a structurally sound and well-shaped form will be impossible unless a single leader is selected and the rest removed. With a pair of sharp secateurs, cut out any competing leaders.

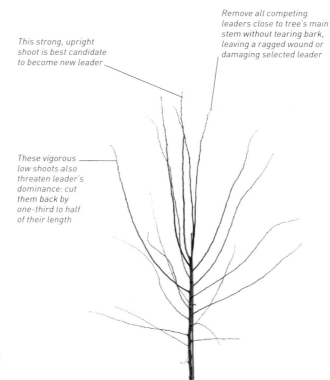

This strong, upright shoot is best candidate to become new leader

Remove all competing leaders close to tree's main stem without tearing bark, leaving a ragged wound or damaging selected leader

These vigorous low shoots also threaten leader's dominance: cut them back by one-third to half of their length

Selecting a leader

Where competing leaders have been allowed to develop, the topmost shoot may now not necessarily be the best choice as the new leader. Here, the lower shoot has grown stronger and straighter.

Broken leader

Cut a damaged leader back to a strong, healthy shoot that is growing almost vertically. Attach a cane to extend the original support until the new leader is growing strongly. If there is no suitable shoot, cut back to a strong bud and tie the new growth to the cane as it develops.

1 *Tie in the new leader securely but not tightly, at intervals of 15–30cm (6–12in).*

2 *Prune back the damaged leader, making a clean, angled cut above a strong bud.*

Dual leaders

On trees with opposite buds, the loss of the leader will, if the tree is neglected, result in a pair of new leaders. Here, although the shoot on the left is stronger, the other may be easier to train in the line of the original main stem.

Form training

If not already in their final site, two-year-old trees can be planted out and form training can continue in *situ* without further disturbance to the root system. They can be pruned and trained into a variety of tree forms. Some trees are only suited to one way of growing, while with others there is more choice. Evergreen trees (*see below*) are usually trained as feathered trees, with a single stem clothed with laterals to near-ground level. There is more scope for training deciduous trees in the various ways shown on the following pages, although in many cases the soundest structure is simply a well-shaped version of the habit the tree would naturally adopt. The Dictionary of Ornamental Trees (*see pp.52–91*) gives advice on suitable forms for individual trees.

FEATHERED TREE

This is the easiest tree form to produce. All that is necessary is to remove dead, diseased or damaged wood, together with any laterals that cross another shoot or form too narrow an angle of attachment with the main stem. Where the crotch angle is narrow, the junction is potentially weak; heavy branches may break from the trunk at this point. Take care that a prevailing wind, shade or competition from other plants do not cause lopsided growth: it is better to remedy the cause than correct the effects.

Training a feathered tree

Aim to maintain a straight main stem and remove any laterals that are not well-spaced and positioned to ensure a balanced, well-shaped tree. If laterals grow more vigorously on one side, tip-prune the branches on the weaker side to stimulate their growth.

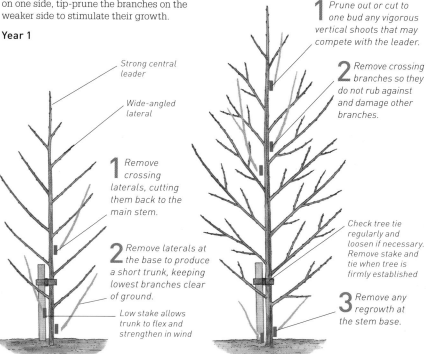

Year 1

Strong central leader

Wide-angled lateral

1 *Remove crossing laterals, cutting them back to the main stem.*

2 *Remove laterals at the base to produce a short trunk, keeping lowest branches clear of ground.*

Low stake allows trunk to flex and strengthen in wind

Years 2 and 3

1 *Prune out or cut to one bud any vigorous vertical shoots that may compete with the leader.*

2 *Remove crossing branches so they do not rub against and damage other branches.*

Check tree tie regularly and loosen if necessary. Remove stake and tie when tree is firmly established

3 *Remove any regrowth at the stem base.*

Shaping a young evergreen

Cut out competing leader

Shorten lanky branches that spoil symmetry of tree

Stake leader in an exposed site

Remove badly placed lateral branches

Thin dense bushy growth to allow air into centre of plant

EVERGREEN TREES

The crowns of broadleaved evergreen trees, as opposed to conifers (*for which see p.38*), are heavy with foliage even in winter and offer a great deal of resistance to strong winds. It is not advisable, therefore, to grow the majority of evergreen trees with tall clear trunks as the weight of snow or the force of gales could snap the trunk, particularly of grafted specimens. Most evergreens are, therefore, best treated as feathered trees (*see above*) with a strong central leader. The majority naturally form a compact, conical shape. If the leader is lost, a new one must be trained in, and any competing leaders should be removed (*see facing page*). If a long leader has grown and laterals are not developing, as occurs with some hollies, shorten by half the section that is bare of branches. Pinching out the tips of sideshoots also encourages a dense habit from an early age, desirable for evergreens intended to become hedges or topiary.

Bushiness is only desirable for certain evergreens. An open framework of branches suits some large-leaved species, such as the evergreen magnolias. This may entail thinning growth, targeting first any shoots that are unhealthy, weak or poorly placed. Prune growth when young, as large wounds on evergreens are slow to heal, particularly in tropical climates. Despite retaining their foliage, evergreens have a dormant and a growing season just like deciduous trees. It is strongly recommended that evergreens should be pruned as growth begins in spring, wherever practical.

STANDARD TREES

Standard trees have a length of clear trunk, surmounted by a crown through which the leader persists (a central-leader standard) or which divides into several main branches (a branched-head standard). Many standards develop naturally, their lower branches dying off and being shed as upper laterals develop and cut off the light (a process known as "shading out"). However, in order to produce or enhance the effect of a clear trunk, lower branches can be pruned from feathered trees. This should be done early in a tree's life to reduce the size of the pruning scars.

Although the crowns of central-leader and branched-head standards develop in different ways, their trunks are cleared in the same way, gradually over several years. Stripping the trunk of its laterals all at once will cause dormant buds low down on the stem to produce further growth and inhibit top growth. In some cases, removal of all foliage from a stem hitherto shaded by leaves may lead to sun scorch or frost damage. Another reason for removing laterals in stages is that their foliage helps to provide the tree with energy, enabling the main stem or stems to grow thick and strong. The laterals temporarily retained are often described as "stem builders".

CENTRAL-LEADER STANDARD

For a central-leader standard, pruning and training is directed into maintaining a main stem that extends through the crown. The principal danger is that the leader will be lost, either through damage or because another vigorous shoot overtakes it. However, both problems can be rectified (*see* Broken leader *and* Competing leaders, *p.24*). A long, stout cane lashed to the tree's stake can be used to support a new leader and ensure vertical growth.

BRANCHED-HEAD STANDARD

Branched-head standards do occur naturally (for example, many oaks) but the habit may take years to develop, the leader gradually losing apical dominance (*see p.8*) to a number of strong lower framework branches.

However, pruning is commonly used to form a branched head on trees that would otherwise grow with a central leader to a considerable height. As the tree may naturally tend to revert to upward growth, a branched-head standard can sometimes only be maintained by pruning, although this becomes less necessary or possible with old trees. A well-trained young tree, with problems promptly dealt with, will not need much attention in maturity; a neglected one may eventually require major surgery.

Central-leader standard

As a guide to clearing the trunk in stages, each year divide the length of the tree's main stem from the ground to the topmost lateral into approximate thirds.

Year 1, winter

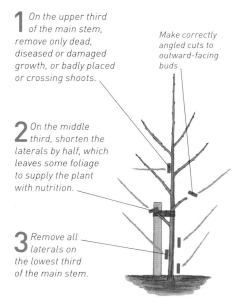

1 *On the upper third of the main stem, remove only dead, diseased or damaged growth, or badly placed or crossing shoots.*

Make correctly angled cuts to outward-facing buds

2 *On the middle third, shorten the laterals by half, which leaves some foliage to supply the plant with nutrition.*

3 *Remove all laterals on the lowest third of the main stem.*

WEEPING STANDARDS

There are two forms of weeping standard: natural and grafted. If naturally weeping, the habit is vertical (provided that it is well-staked), then arching at a height that varies with the tree. Do not cut away any branches growing upwards: they will eventually arch over, raising the height of the tree and producing the characteristic and attractive tiered effect.

In other cases, a prostrate cultivar is grafted on to the clear stem of a stock plant. Because the branches all grow away in the same horizontal plane they can become congested, and sideshoots crossing the centre at awkward angles should be removed early on. On most top-grafted trees, upward growth will spoil the weeping form and should be removed.

Shoots growing on the clear stem should always be removed. As trees mature, shorten branches nearing the ground to a bud or sideshoot.

Staking is often required for some years after the head develops. A tall, strong stake may be needed as the head of a weeping tree often develops rapidly and may prove too heavy to be supported by the trunk until this has increased considerably in girth.

Top-grafting

A short length of stem may be grafted on to the clear stem of the stock plant; shoots then develop from its several buds, as here. The alternative is budding: two or even three buds may be inserted to ensure that the standard will have a balanced head, important for the stability as well as the look of the tree.

Young weeping standard

Keep the trunk clear of lateral growth, particularly on top-grafted trees, ideally by pinching off the entire shoot while the growth is still soft. The more mushroom-shaped (cascading as opposed to weeping) the crown, the more likely it is that growth will become congested. Suppressed growth will die, and should be regularly removed to prevent a build-up of debris.

On top-grafted trees, cut out at once any branch that reverts to vertical growth

Prune out weaker shoots, especially where growth is crowded

Remove any shoots on main stem as soon as possible, rubbing them out if still soft or pruning flush with trunk

Years 2 and 3, winter

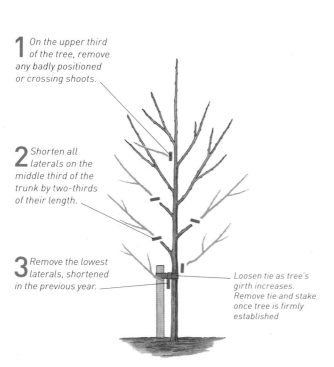

1 *On the upper third of the tree, remove any badly positioned or crossing shoots.*

2 *Shorten all laterals on the middle third of the trunk by two-thirds of their length.*

3 *Remove the lowest laterals, shortened in the previous year.*

Loosen tie as tree's girth increases. Remove tie and stake once tree is firmly established

Year 4, winter

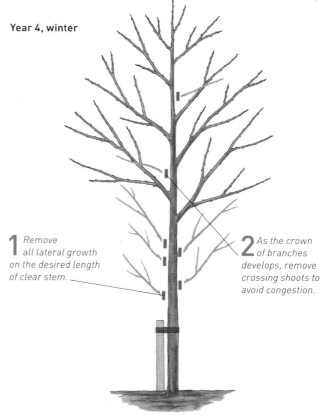

1 *Remove all lateral growth on the desired length of clear stem.*

2 *As the crown of branches develops, remove crossing shoots to avoid congestion.*

Branched-head standard

In the first two or three years, train as for a central-leader standard, above. When three or four strong laterals have developed above the desired height of clear trunk, the leader can be pruned to form the branched head. The selected laterals will become the framework branches of the crown.

Year 3 or 4, winter

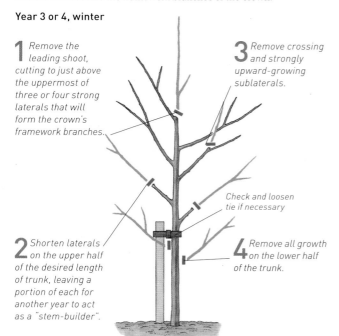

1 *Remove the leading shoot, cutting to just above the uppermost of three or four strong laterals that will form the crown's framework branches.*

3 *Remove crossing and strongly upward-growing sublaterals.*

Check and loosen tie if necessary

2 *Shorten laterals on the upper half of the desired length of trunk, leaving a portion of each for another year to act as a "stem-builder".*

4 *Remove all growth on the lower half of the trunk.*

Year 4 or 5, winter

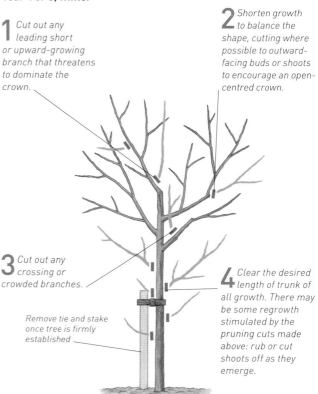

1 *Cut out any leading short or upward-growing branch that threatens to dominate the crown.*

2 *Shorten growth to balance the shape, cutting where possible to outward-facing buds or shoots to encourage an open-centred crown.*

3 *Cut out any crossing or crowded branches.*

Remove tie and stake once tree is firmly established

4 *Clear the desired length of trunk of all growth. There may be some regrowth stimulated by the pruning cuts made above: rub or cut shoots off as they emerge.*

MULTI-STEMMED TREE

This form occurs naturally in trees that sucker – produce shoots from the base – or branch very low down, though pruning can enhance this effect by controlling the number and spacing of the trunks. A similar effect can be achieved by planting several single-stemmed trees close together. The multi-stemmed form can also be created by cutting a tree hard back (*see below*) so that several new stems develop. The cut stimulates low dormant buds, which should shoot strongly the following year. Only certain species (*see pp.52–91*) respond well to this treatment. Never apply it to grafted cultivars.

The several trunks of multi-stemmed trees can either be left clothed with lateral branches, giving a thicket-like appearance, or cleared to show off attractive – perhaps silvery, coppery or textured – bark. The latter option is more popular in a garden context, and for best effect the number of main stems should be restricted by selecting the required number of strong, well-spaced shoots early in the tree's life and cutting out any weak or surplus shoots. Clear the stems of lower branches as for a central-leader standard (*see p.26*).

Trees that have a naturally suckering habit may produce more shoots from the base as they mature. This growth must be removed to maintain the desired number of stems unless a replacement for a damaged or diseased trunk is needed. Conversely, new basal stems growing

CORKSCREW TREES

Certain cultivars of hazel and willow produce twisted twigs and stems. They are usually multi-stemmed, with main branches springing from a short trunk. Let them develop naturally, removing only dead, diseased, damaged or crossing growth. Once the tree is established, however, the erratic habit will disguise light pruning to restrict size or to thin growth. These trees tend to become congested and thinning reduces stress on the twisted, load-bearing branches. Branches with sharp bends may crack along the grain under stress. A small crack on a healthy stem will heal quickly, but the branch will have been weakened and, ideally, should be removed.

Corkscrew hazels and willows are ungrafted, and tolerate complete renovation; they can be cut to the ground in winter. The already extensive root system will sucker freely as a result: select only the best of the new stems (or only one if a single trunk is desired), and prune out those that are weak or badly placed.

Salix matsudana 'Tortuosa'
These extravagantly twisted stems are decorated by catkins in spring.

from regularly cut back, or coppiced, trees (*see p.34*) tend to become sparser as the years go by.

Inward-growing branches on a multi-stemmed tree may need to be thinned to avoid congestion and to maintain the ornamental appearance of the group of trunks. If too much growth is removed,

however, one or more stems may be left isolated and may splay out from the group, possibly breaking. If this happens it may be necessary to cut isolated stems to the base as they will spoil the ornamental effect. Well-spaced young shoots from the base may then be allowed to develop as replacements.

Producing a multi-stemmed form from a single-stemmed tree

Year 1, winter
Cut the main stem of a two-year-old tree straight across at the desired height – at lowest, as here, 8cm (3in) from the ground. Trim the wound so there are no rough edges.

Year 2, winter
Select three or four strong, well-spaced shoots, preferably of equal vigour to encourage even development. Remove all other shoots, cutting them back to the base.

Year 3, winter
Let laterals develop, only removing the lowest if clear stems are desired. Remove any new suckers. These cuts in turn may stimulate basal regrowth; remove in subsequent years.

Pruning Established Trees

Although established trees do not need the regular pruning required by many shrubs and climbers, all benefit from regular checks and routine maintenance throughout their lives, no matter how natural their manner of growth. Some, such as trees with variegated foliage and top-grafted weeping standards, need extra attention. The safest times for non-essential pruning are given in the Dictionary of Ornamental Trees (*pp.52–91*). However, it is always safer to correct the problems outlined on these pages as soon as they are seen; check large, older trees, which are not easily pruned frequently, in midwinter and late summer for defects that should be corrected.

DEAD AND DISEASED WOOD

All plants have natural defence mechanisms that must be taken into account when cutting away dead and diseased wood. Once diseased, tree tissue never becomes healthy again; instead, the tree forms a natural, chemical barrier (*see also p.9*) between diseased and healthy wood. In most cases, provided the disease is not too widespread, the diseased part – deprived of nourishment by the barrier – eventually dies and is shed.

The presence of unshed dead wood, host to fungal rots as it decays, poses a health hazard to the tree. Cutting the dead portion out completely – that is, cutting back into live wood – will force the tree to waste energy healing a wound where an efficient barrier already existed. Cut dead wood out, therefore, just above the line (usually quite distinct) between live and dead wood.

If an entire main branch seems dead right up to the trunk or large limb, cut it off just as you would a healthy branch

Branch could alternatively be cut to this node

Damaged branch
Remove the branch (*inset*) or, if replacement growth at this point is greatly desired (*see over*), cut straight across below all damage, to a node if visible. If shoots do not develop in the following growing season, remove the stub.

(*see p.20*). Do not attempt to excise dead wood from the live trunk or limb, or you will create a channel in the barrier between dead and live wood through which disease can spread back into the whole plant.

If disease is still active, however, there will be no clear demarcation between dead and live wood. Therefore, when cutting off diseased wood, it is essential to cut well below the signs of infection and inspect the cut surface carefully – if disease or discoloration is still visible, more wood must be cut away.

STAG-HEADED TREES

Old trees often become "stag-headed", with gaunt, dead branches sticking out of the top of the crown. The cause is usually deep-seated disruption to

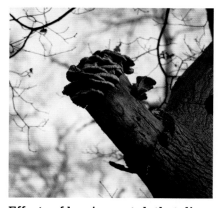

Effects of leaving a stub that dies
If new shoots do not develop from a stub, it dies and may become diseased. This bracket fungus indicates serious rotting. Prune back to clean wood. If the cut surface still shows rot at the crotch or main trunk the tree cannot be saved.

surrounding land: possibly adjacent building development, soil compaction or fluctuations in the local water table. Trees can survive for many years in this condition; however, if you find them unsightly, have their condition assessed by a professional arboriculturist.

TORN BRANCHES AND BARK

Branches that are partially broken, for example by lightning damage, the weight of snow or the action of vandals or grazing animals, rarely mend if tied back in position. It is usually better to cut them right out or shorten them to a suitable replacement shoot below the damage. Bark that has been knocked or torn off is most unlikely to reunite with the cambium layer. (*Continued on p.30*)

Torn bark on the trunk of a tree

Damage at the branch collar This injury often results from vandalism. The only course is to remove the branch and trim and smooth the wound with a pruning knife. Keep the area of cut surface as small as possible.

Abraded bark Incorrect staking and tying is a major cause of bark grazes. Here the tie has been pushed up, and with time has chafed the bark and pulled the tree over. Reposition the tie correctly and trim any rough edges.

Effects of torn bark This badly damaged ginkgo is not thriving. The new shoot that has developed below the damaged area shows that the passage of food and growth-inducing substances up the trunk is barred by the wound. In addition, the orange markings show that the disease coral spot has taken hold. There is little that can be done for this tree.

(*Continued from p.29*) The wound is best opened and allowed to dry, after you have pared any rough edges with a knife. Major damage to bark at the base of a tree is a serious problem that could affect the tree's safety. It is therefore important to avoid causing damage with garden machinery such as lawnmowers.

EPICORMIC SHOOTS

Epicormic shoots are those produced from dormant buds, often completely invisible under bark until stimulated into life. This stimulus may be a pruning cut: many trees have a tendency to produce fast-growing epicormic shoots – known as "water" shoots – around the site of pruning wounds. These must be rubbed out as they emerge, or they will proliferate and divert energy from the rest of the tree. On some species, strong shoots may be kept – to replace a broken branch, for example – provided that others are removed (*see right*). On other trees, this type of growth is so sappy and rapid that it will never become robust enough to make a safe new branch. These trees are identified in the Dictionary of Ornamental Trees (*pp.52–91*).

SUCKERS

Trees such as *Populus tremula* (aspen) naturally develop shoots, or suckers, from their root systems, while some species, such as *P. nigra* (black poplar), produce them only when a root is damaged. Suckers do not harm a tree, though they may sap its energy. The easiest way to control them is to grow the tree in a lawn, where the suckers will be regularly sheared off by mowing. Otherwise, suckers must be cut off at the point of origin, paring away the surrounding tissue to remove dormant buds nearby. Simply digging or pulling suckers up will stimulate these buds into growth. Never

Growth from adventitious buds

Suckers and epicormic shoots This willow tends not only to produce occasional shoots on its clear trunk, but also sends up suckers from underground. Both types of growth should be removed as soon as seen.

Thinning regrowth from a lopped branch

Last shoot will be shortened to this bud

All surplus and wayward shoots have been removed. Rub out any subsequent regrowth from these pruning sites

Before This damaged branch has been lopped, initially giving a clumsy appearance. However, many strong new shoots have now appeared, from which, by careful selection, balanced regrowth can be developed.

After A strong shoot has been selected at each of the four "compass points", to give each plenty of room. Cut them back by at least half, varying lengths so that sideshoots will not develop in an unnatural "mophead".

use systemic herbicide on suckers, as it will be taken up by the tree's roots.

The rootstocks of grafted trees (particularly some *Prunus*) also tend to shoot from below the ground. Suckers from below a graft point must always be removed at the point of origin, as above, as swiftly as possible. If they are left, the stock plant, often more vigorous than the grafted tree, will take over from it.

Beware of planting naturally suckering species where suckers may spread beyond the boundaries of your property. *Ailanthus* (tree of heaven), *Robinia* and *Gleditsia triacanthos* are notorious "fence-leapers", the latter so much so that its cultivation is prohibited in certain parts of the world.

"Water" shoots
A pruning cut may stimulate dormant (sometimes called "latent") buds into life. Shoots that develop where they are not wanted must be rubbed out or cut off as soon as possible.

REVERSION

Many trees have variegated cultivars, with splashes or edgings of gold or silver on their leaves. These cultivars are vegetatively propagated from sports – naturally occurring mutations – of the original, green-leaved tree, and just as the tree mutated to produce this effect, so it may partially revert back to plain foliage. Any shoots with green foliage on a variegated form should be cut out immediately. The same problem may arise with cultivars that have been developed for their unusual "cut" or feathery leaves; shoots bearing leaves of the plainer, "normal" shape should also be removed. When a tall tree reaches maturity, removing reverted shoots is easier said than done, but while they are not harmful to the tree, they will rise to dominance if left.

PROPPING AND BRACING

Extra-long and picturesque branches or reclining trees may need to be propped or braced to stop them breaking. Forked posts made of wood or stone or purpose-built metal supports are suitable, but do not use wrought ironwork, which may cut into the branch. With all supports, it is advisable to place some padding between the crutch and the branch, so that slight movement does not result in chafing of the branch. Sacking or old carpet are both suitable materials.

The support needs to take the weight of the branch without forcing it upwards, which will create other stresses at the point where it joins the trunk. Commonly grown trees that frequently require propping

Reverted shoots

On variegated or fancy-leaved cultivars, remove at their point of origin entire shoots that have reverted to plain foliage as soon as they are seen.

Witch's broom

Clusters of twiggy growth such as this are harmless, but may be removed if found unsightly. Remove the branch at its point of origin, or shorten it to a replacement shoot below the affected area.

are *Cedrus libani* (cedar of Lebanon), *Cercis siliquastrum* (Judas tree), *Morus* (mulberries) and *Catalpa bignonioides* (the Indian bean tree).

CAVITIES AND HOLLOW TRUNKS

Tree cavities, usually in the trunk, are caused by damaged or old tissue decaying and eventually rotting away. They rarely cause problems in an otherwise healthy tree, and should never be cleaned out, enlarged or drained, nor plugged with any artificial material such as concrete. Research has now shown that water filling a cavity actually reduces harmful fungal activity.

A tree trunk that is split by lightning must immediately be inspected by a professional arboriculturist. However, old hollow or even split trunks are not necessarily unsafe, especially if they are short and broad. A hollow trunk of live wood can be very strong, protected from disease by a natural barrier (*see p.9*) between live tissue and the rotting heart wood. A large tree should be inspected by a professional for health and safety: if its branches are unsafe, it may still be salvageable by pollarding (*see p.34*).

WITCHES' BROOMS

Trees can develop dense clusters of stunted twigs and foliage on their branches. These witches' brooms, as they are known, are the result of attack by certain fungi, insects or mites. They do not harm the rest of the tree, so they can safely be left. If they are unsightly, as they often are on silver birches, the entire branch may be cut back below the affected area at a suitable point, such as a junction with a main branch.

ROOT-PRUNING ESTABLISHED TREES

Many trees make excellent container plants, providing they are well cared for and fed. The reduction in vigour that results from restricting the size of the root system, either in pots or with barriers, enables many tender species to be grown under glass. Container-growing is often combined with hard pruning (*see* Coppicing and pollarding, *p.34*) to restrict further the tree's size. Most trees dislike being pot-bound, and will occasionally require root pruning, as for a container-grown shrub (for step-by-step illustrations, *see p.154*).

In open ground, root pruning by digging and making spade cuts into the ground around an established tree is sometimes recommended to restrict growth, most particularly for fruit trees (for step-by-step illustrations, *see p.101*). It is vital to use the correct method, and cut the roots well away from the trunk, or the tree's stability may be affected.

Crutches for low branches

Prop low branches if they add to a tree's picturesque appeal. A crutch of old wood or driftwood gives a natural effect.

FELLING A SMALL TREE

Never fell a large tree yourself (*see pp.32–33*). Small trees, however, may need removing simply because they are no longer wanted, or because they have grown up as suckers or seedlings in a neglected garden. Cut the trunk about 1m (3ft) from the ground, so that the stump can be used to lever the roots out of the ground. If you need professional help, and provided that the site is accessible, winching with chains or stump grinding are options for removing the stump. If it must be left, cut it flush with the ground. It may, however, become a site for honey fungus, which can affect other plants. Seek specialist advice about chemical stump killers.

1 *From the side on which you want the tree to fall, make a downward cut one-third of the way through the trunk, using a sharp bow saw.*

2 *Make a horizontal cut below the first cut until they meet. Then take away the small wedge of wood between the two cuts. This should ensure that, with the final cut, the tree falls in the right direction.*

3 *From the opposite side of the tree, about 4cm (1½in) above the base of the wedge cut, saw horizontally until the wood splits downwards and the tree topples over.*

Renovation

There are many situations in which more extensive tree pruning than that outlined on the previous pages will be necessary – to renovate a neglected tree, or one that has grown lopsided or become unsafe; to bring an overgrown tree back under control; or to fell an unwanted or unsound tree. Much tree renovation work is potentially dangerous. Major tree surgery (*see facing page*) and the felling of large trees should never be undertaken by the amateur gardener. Even for minor renovation, assessment by a professional arboriculturist is often advisable.

SAFETY MEASURES
The specialized tools and equipment designed for tree surgery should never be used by untrained personnel. Chainsaws are particularly dangerous: amateurs should never use them from within the crown of a tree, nor attempt, when standing on the ground, to cut a branch that is above waist height.

Felling trees with trunks more than 15cm (6in) in diameter, or lopping main branches and lowering them safely to the ground, are arduous tasks that should not be undertaken by anyone not accustomed to strenuous physical exercise. Sawing, lifting and guiding long lengths of wood may strain rarely used muscles, particularly if the body twists to work in awkward positions.

If at all possible, work from the ground. A ladder propped up in a tree is likely to be unstable. The higher the ladder is climbed, the more branches will lean away as they take the weight: stepping off the ladder into the tree may make a branch spring back alarmingly. If you are climbing even part-way into a tree, always wear a hard hat with a chin-strap, and safety glasses. Never work when bark is wet and slippery. Never work alone, and ensure your companion remains on the ground. Clear the area of garden furniture, equipment and other tools before you begin, and keep children and pets well away.

LEGAL PRECAUTIONS
Before any work is done, check whether the tree is legally protected; if so, permission from the appropriate organization may be necessary for felling or even the removal of branches. Check whether the work you intend could threaten overhead wires or underground piping or cabling: if so, you must bring in a trained professional to do the job and inform the relevant authority.

The most bitter disputes between neighbours often result from misunderstandings over boundaries. It is both courteous and wise to advise neighbours of your intentions if your tree borders their

Correcting uneven growth on a small tree

Year 1 Do not be tempted to cut the stronger side back harshly. Instead, tip-prune its branch leaders, which will result in limited regrowth, and prune the growth on the weaker side hard, stimulating a vigorous response that will balance the tree's form.

Year 2 and after Strong new shoots should have developed on the weaker side. In this and subsequent winters, remove only those that cross other shoots, or that will spoil the symmetry of the crown as it develops. Patience is needed while the tree regrows.

property, and most particularly if you wish to prune a tree growing in a neighbour's garden that encroaches on your property.

MINOR RENOVATION OF SMALL TREES
A tree may have its growth stunted on one side through suppression by a neighbouring tree or structure. If the factor causing the lopsided growth – suppression by a neighbouring larger tree, or shade cast by an outbuilding, wall or fence – is to remain, there is no point in remedial pruning. However, if it is removed, it is possible to prune correctively over several years to restore a more even shape (*see above*).

Neglect may cause any number of minor problems to accumulate – dead, diseased, and damaged wood, crossing or obstructing branches, overcrowding, wayward shoots, or new growth obscuring a previously clear trunk. If branches have become very low and spreading, they must be removed or propped (*see p.30*), as they may be placing considerable strain on the trunk. If the trunk splits, air, water and decay fungi may gain entry: a hollow trunk may develop, or the tree die.

To renovate a small tree, in the first year, improve its general condition: remove all unhealthy and dead wood, suckers and

crossing branches that are damaging bark by rubbing. In the second and, if necessary, the third year, reduce overcrowding (some of which will have been caused by regrowth from the previous year's cuts), and remove or shorten other branches as necessary to enhance the shape. Remove only one or two entire branches in any one year, cutting them out in sections to reduce the risk of tearing the bark.

TIMING AND AFTERCARE
It is best to tackle any renovation work during the dormant season, with certain exceptions (see *pp.52–91*); with deciduous trees, the form will be seen more clearly, and work be made much easier, in the absence of foliage.

After minor renovation, apply a top-dressing of balanced fertilizer according to the maker's instructions. Many old trees may not have received supplementary feeds for a long time – if at all – so it is better to apply a thin mulch of well-rotted manure, since a rich feed could stimulate too much soft new growth too rapidly. Never spread a thick layer of soil under an old tree, because this may alter the finely balanced supply of oxygen to the tree's roots and adversely affect its health.

Major tree surgery

Trees that have been neglected or have grown too large for their position should either be cut down or, if still fundamentally healthy, they may be renovated. Except in a confined space or sensitive urban situation, felling a tree is easier and cheaper than renovation and also allows a more suitable tree species to be planted in its place. In urban areas in particular, tree surgery is almost always best carried out by a qualified arboriculturist – often referred to as a "tree surgeon".

Major tree surgery covers not only felling but also crown reduction, lifting and thinning. Crown reduction, or more drastically pollarding (*see p.34*), reduces the overall size of a mature tree's canopy. Crown lifting increases the height of clear trunk by removing large lower branches, and is most often necessary where branches overhang a street or driveway. Crown thinning removes congested growth: this may be done simply to benefit the tree's health, but it is also a valuable option where a tree is casting heavy shade or blocking a view. Thinning branches to let in dappled light can often mean that an area of garden, or a window view, is reclaimed without the loss of a fine tree being necessary.

It must be emphasized that none of these jobs is by any means straightforward, but requires crucial decisions about the tree's structure based on specialist

Tree made unsafe by damage
Storm or lightning damage within the crown of a large tree must be assessed and dealt with using expert knowledge and techniques.

knowledge and experience. Without this knowledge, pruning may result in a dangerously unstable tree.

Amateur work has additional pitfalls. Mistaken or misguided attempts to improve a tree by cutting off branches are, of course, impossible to rectify,

whereas skilful tree surgery should result in a tree that is pleasing to the eye for many years to come. This should not only further deter the amateur, but also highlights the importance of using reputable, preferably recommended professional firms or individuals: shoddy work nearly always entails more expense and risks the loss of the tree.

Skilfully performed tree surgery is never cheap, but the outlay is repaid by much more than the actual labour. Before the work is undertaken, an arboriculturist will advise on what should be done (and whether any alternatives are feasible), how long it will take, what the effects will be, as well as what future work might be needed and when. As well as being qualified to carry out specialist work, the arboriculturist should undertake to dispose of all lopped or felled wood.

The services of a consultant tree surgeon can also prove invaluable when local authorities have an interest in legally protected trees. A site visit can sort out numerous other minor problems, and alert an owner to such factors as subsidence and soil heave, details that would perhaps not occur to a lay person.

The real cost of using a professional arboriculturist should be assessed in the light of all of these benefits, but be sure to check before work begins that any liability for damage or compensation claims is the responsibility of the firm or individual.

Crown lifting
Sections or all of some lower branches are removed to create more room below the tree, for example to allow a bus to pass freely below, or to expose a street light that has become hidden in the branches.

Crown thinning and reduction
These operations are often combined to reduce the size of a tree and allow more light and air to penetrate through the crown, reducing wind resistance and stress from wide-spreading, heavy branches.

Coppicing and Pollarding

Some trees (and many shrubs) tolerate hard pruning on a regular basis and respond by producing vigorous new growth that is often of considerable ornamental value in the garden. The techniques of coppicing and pollarding used in this kind of pruning are among the most ancient horticultural practices.

Coppicing is the regular, sometimes annual, cutting back of a tree to ground level to obtain vigorous young stems. These were traditionally cut in winter, to be used for firewood, basketwork and hurdles and as poles. There is evidence of coppicing dating back to Neolithic times; in England and northern France, where this type of woodland management was popular, coppice survives that is at least 600 years old. Coppicing can prolong tree life apparently indefinitely when the cuts are clean and fast-healing, as produced by ancient implements such as billhooks and axes. Roughly sawn coppice is unlikely to be so long-lasting.

A similarly renewable supply of wood was produced by pollarding, but here the shoots arose from the head of a clear tree trunk, from which all branches had been cut away. This elevated form of coppicing freed the land below to provide pasture for grazing animals – a very early form of dual land use.

PRUNING FOR ORNAMENTAL STEMS

Today, gardeners use coppicing and pollarding mainly for ornamental effect, and also to grow trees in less space than is normally necessary. Only a limited number of trees will tolerate such hard treatment: disease resistance is crucial to enable continual recovery from wounds.

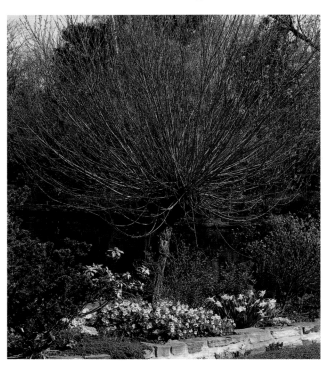

Coppicing and pollarding are chiefly used to produce, either on the ground or at eye level, crops of young stems that, when bare in winter, bring a welcome splash of colour to the garden. Willows (*Salix*) and dogwoods (*Cornus*) are the woody plants most commonly managed in this way as their young stems are often vividly coloured, from yellow through scarlet to dusky purple. The stems are not cut back until early spring in order to have the longest possible display.

Developing a pollard (left)

Buy or train a suitable young tree (such as this willow) with a well-branched head on a clear stem of about 2m (6ft). Once established in its planting site, but before its stem has a diameter much greater than 10–13cm (4–5in), in late winter or early spring saw through the main stem just above the lowest cluster of branches. Cut these back to within 2.5–8cm (1–3in) of the main stem. Treat the resulting mass of shoots as an established pollard.

Established pollard (right)

To maintain the effect, prune every one to three years. In late winter or early spring, shorten all stems to within 1–2cm (½–¾in) of the main stem. Ensure that the enlarged head of the pollarded main stem is not damaged. As the tree matures, when growth begins again the new shoots may be overcrowded: thin them out to leave the remainder evenly spaced. Remove as seen any shoots that appear on the main stem or at the base of the tree.

Colourful young stems

This pollarded willow with its bright new shoots brings winter and early spring colour into the garden. Pollarding on a low trunk produces a plant of shrub-like proportions, but developing a clear trunk, as here, of 1.2–1.5m (4–5ft) raises the new stems well above other border plants.

PRUNING FOR ORNAMENTAL FOLIAGE

Unusual foliage effects can be achieved by coppicing trees such as *Ailanthus* and *Paulownia*. The directing of all energy into new shoots results in lush, enlarged leaves, giving some plants an almost tropical character. Sometimes the leaf shape and colour of this juvenile foliage is markedly different, as with eucalyptus. However, any flowers will be lost, since most trees flower on mature wood.

PRUNING TO RESTRICT SIZE

Coppicing and pollarding greatly restrict the size of a tree: a full-size *Paulownia*, for example, can easily reach 25m (80ft), whereas coppicing will confine it to the space necessary for a large shrub (although it can still grow to 3m/10ft in a single season). Bear in mind, though, that the tree will still have a full-sized root system. However, provided there is sufficient space for their root run, trees such as *Catalpa* and *Morus alba* can be grown as small, attractively mop-headed, lush-leaved specimens. Pollarded trees – planes and limes in particular – are popular for street use, although they are often not completely pollarded, to the head of the trunk, but lopped: their main branches are shortened to form a larger framework from which new shoots will grow. This leaves a larger crown, more in proportion with the tall trunks necessary if traffic is to run beneath. Lopping often looks clumsy in a garden setting; crown reduction (*see p.33*) is usually more suitable.

PRUNING TO REJUVENATE

Pollarding and heading back can be used to save a tree that is far too large either for safety or for its situation. Some English oaks are estimated to have lived for over 400 years since losing their original limbs through natural "branch drop". Yew trees, too, rejuvenate remarkably well after severe pruning. Pollarding or coppicing may be the solution for a tree

Hazel coppice

In late winter or early spring, cut all growth to a few inches above ground level; never sever shoots below the soil surface or injure the swollen, woody base of the tree. It is from here that new shoots will develop. The new growth springs from the outer edges of the coppice "stool". The new shoots can be thinned if they are too dense. Cut stems out at the base, rather than shortening them, to maintain a natural effect.

After pruning (*below*)

Regrowth in spring (*right*)

that has been left an eyesore through losing much growth to wind damage. Sometimes, after coppicing, a single stem can be selected and grown on to form a replacement leader from which a new crown can be developed (*see Eucalyptus, p.64*). When used on large established trees, these techniques should only be undertaken by a

professional arboriculturist (*see also* Major tree surgery, *p.33*).

Coppicing also makes it possible to protect some trees from winter damage – in cold climates, cutting back trees such as bay and eucalyptus to the basal stumps (often called the "stool") before hard weather sets in makes them easy to cover, for example with straw.

Pruning for foliage effect

Instead of forming a tall tree, this *Acer negundo* 'Flamingo' lights up the border with its fresh, cream-splashed variegated foliage, an effect created by pollarding to a very low stem. The leaves of many trees are at their most attractive on the newest growth.

SUITABLE ORNAMENTAL TREES

Acer pensylvanicum 'Erythrocladum' Produces attractive young red stems.
Ailanthus Restricts size, and produces larger leaves (*see p.53*).
Carpinus betulus, Corylus Coppicing produces multi-stemmed plants for hedging.
Catalpa bignonioides, Castanea sativa Pollarding can be used to retain an overgrown or damaged tree (*see p.57*).
Cercis Pollarding restricts size and brings flowers down to eye level (do not cut back every year).
Eucalyptus Many respond by producing attractive juvenile foliage and a shrubby habit.
Fagus sylvatica Coppicing can be used to produce multi-stemmed plants for hedging.
Morus alba Pollarding keeps crown small.
Paulownia Restricts size and produces attractive large leaves (*see p.78*).
Platanus × acerifolia Pollarding reduces size of crown (*see p.80*).
Quercus Prolongs life of unsafe trees.
Salix Many species produce attractively coloured young stems (*see p.86*).
Taxus baccata Rejuvenates old trees, or produces multiple stems for hedging.
Tilia Pollarding restricts crown size; coppice red-twigged limes such as *Tilia platyphyllos* 'Rubra'.
Toona sinensis 'Flamingo' Produces attractive pink juvenile foliage.

Pleaching

Pleaching is the weaving together of the branches of a row of trees. Combined with formal trimming, it produces a hedge with an intricate branch structure on a free-standing row of clear trunks. It is a horticultural art with a long history: in Tudor England, pleached avenues were status symbols, showing off the number of gardeners the landowner was able to employ.

Pleached rows and avenues are enjoying a revival today, despite requiring almost constant attention throughout their lives. The trees traditionally used for this most labour-intensive form of tree pruning are limes, hornbeams, beeches and hollies, though most trees that tolerate clipping are suitable. A strong and well-constructed framework will be needed until the row is fully established: for hornbeam and beech, this may be about 15 years.

BUILDING THE SUPPORT
The main support posts for each tree's trunk must be driven at least 60–90cm (2–3ft) into the ground, and be as tall as the intended finished hedge. For the best effect, spacing between posts should be about 2.5m (8ft). Endposts will be needed a short distance from the first and last tree, so that the framework can support the entire extent of their growth. Horizontal battens or, for a less obtrusive effect, wires, fixed or tightly stretched between the posts, form the horizontal framework to which the lateral branches will be tied.

FORMATIVE PRUNING AND TRAINING
Start with three- or four-year-old trees with strong, straight central leaders, already partially cleared as for a standard (*see p.26*), and with laterals at or near the height of the lowest wire. These laterals

Traditional pleaching
Lime, hornbeam and beech are the most commonly pleached deciduous trees. The woven branches (*below*) have ornamental value in winter. Using beech cultivars with varying leaf colours (*left*) creates a tapestry effect.

need to be growing in as flat a plane as possible. Plant in late autumn or early winter, pruning away any shoots below the bottom wire or batten, and those growing at right angles to the framework that cannot be tied in. Tie the remaining laterals along the battens or wires.

Throughout the following and subsequent growing seasons, pinch or rub out shoots that appear on the clear trunks, or that will grow away from the framework. Tie in the leader as it extends, and weave and tie in suitably placed shoots as they grow to form an evenly spaced network. Weave along

the battens or wires; as growth develops, the gaps between will narrow. In winter, remove badly placed growth and shorten long shoots to encourage branching.

ESTABLISHED PLEACHED TREES
When a densely woven screen has been established it can be clipped just as an ordinary hedge (*see p.44*). Keep rubbing out shoots on the trunks and remove dead, diseased or damaged growth as seen, always taking the opportunity to weave and tie in laterals wherever there are gaps. Feed the trees well in spring to compensate for removing so much foliage and keep them in good condition.

PLEACHED ARCHES AND TUNNELS
The upper parts of two trees can be intertwined to create an arch, free-standing or spanning a gap within a hedge. Attach a hoop of thick wire to tall stakes supporting the trees. Gently pull over and tie in the leaders; suitable laterals and sideshoots are then woven together and pruned to develop a solid bridge. More elaborately, pairs of young trees may be trained over a series of arched supports and their branches pleached to form a tunnel (*see also Laburnum, p.70*). Supports must be permanent, so the framework must be solid and of a long-lived material that is either unobtrusive or decorative – iron is the traditional choice. Pruning may be time-consuming, shoots above the top of the arch being especially difficult to reach.

A "PLEACHED" EFFECT
For a labour-saving alternative to pleaching, once the framework has been covered, prune the previous season's growth by at least half each winter to encourage branching (*as left*), tying in awkward growth. This will form a "hedge on stilts" that can be clipped (*see also Hedges, p.44*).

Formative training, pleached trees

Pruning on planting, winter

1 Having constructed a strong framework, plant a three- or four-year-old tree in front of each post, aligning as many laterals as possible parallel to the framework. Tie in the leader, adding extra ties during the subsequent growing season as it develops.

2 Tie suitably placed lateral branches securely along their adjacent wire or batten.

3 Remove any laterals that are growing outwards and cannot readily be secured to a wire or batten.

4 Cut back to the main stem any laterals that are growing below the bottom wire or batten.

Year 2, winter

1 Once the leader reaches the top wire or batten, start to train it horizontally. Train a suitably placed lateral along the top batten on the other side. For even development, train all leaders in the same direction.

2 Shorten any long laterals back to a strong sideshoot, and sideshoots back to two or three buds to encourage new, vigorous growth to cover the framework.

3 Throughout the growing season, pinch out all new shoots except those that are growing sideways or can be pulled across and trained sideways. While still pliable, intertwine and tie these laterals within the framework so that all the spaces are filled in.

4 Remove any new growth on the clear trunks.

Year 3, winter

1 Cut back to a bud all new shoots that extend beyond the limits of the supporting framework, at the edges or at the top. For the best formal effect, keep the line of cuts perfectly straight.

2 Start to weave together and tie in suitably placed shoots. As the gaps between the tiers narrow, shoots from above and below can be drawn and tied together.

3 Where shoots are growing away from the horizontal surface of the row (that is, sticking out at the front or back) cut back to a sideways-facing bud.

Conifers

Conifers do not generally respond well to pruning and it is best to choose carefully one whose rate of growth and ultimate size are consistent with the space available. There are situations, however, where careful pruning can be effective and, especially if started at the juvenile stage, the tree can be contained and its appearance enhanced. Shortening unbalanced sideshoots and reducing the number of leading shoots will produce a good shape from the outset.

Columnar conifers can spread if left unpruned, which is often undesirable as such trees are chosen for their limited width. To avoid undue spread, the number of leading shoots can be reduced and shoots on the sides of the tree shortened, but without cutting into the brown wood that does not carry growing needles. In some cases, it may be possible to trim or shear to control width and thicken growth, in the same way that conifer hedges are trimmed to restrict spread (see p.47).

Mounded conifers tend to turn pyramidal with age and if this is disliked they can be trimmed in spring to retain their shape. Low growing, spreading conifers also often benefit from having their strongest shoots shortened in spring, to thicken coverage for ornamental effect and weed control.

DEALING WITH LARGE TREES

The shape and size of larger conifers can be controlled, and appearance enhanced, by removing or thinning larger branches. No regrowth is likely to occur from limbs that are removed close to the trunk, and growth

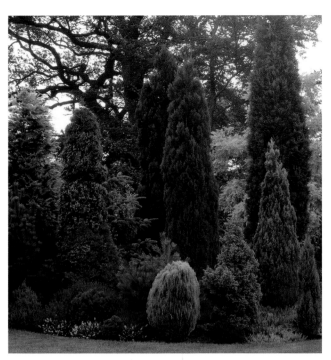

will continue from the untouched outshoots on the remaining limbs.

If all upward growing shoots are removed, conifers will not significantly develop upwards, and in conjunction with shortening lower, horizontally growing shoots, a mounded conical shape will result. Such trees offer shelter and privacy

or block nearby eyesores, and this strategy is often used where replacement of a tree and subsequent lack of tall foliage is inconvenient. A qualified tree surgeon or arborist will often be able to undertake this work on even very large mature trees. As severe damage to mature trees is possible, an arborist's advice should be sought.

Conifer planting scheme

As a group, conifers require little pruning or training. They offer a wide range of shapes and sizes, often with a dense, compact habit that enhances their clean outlines. With careful selection, they prove invaluable in creating low-maintenance plantings with strong contrasts of form, texture and colour.

GINKGO BILOBA

Ginkgo biloba is a very uncharacteristic, elegant, deciduous conifer with bright green, veined, broadly fan-shaped leaves that turn butter-yellow in autumn. The tree has several variants, with either upright or semi-pendulous branches: all are grown as central-leader standards. Ginkgos form two kinds of shoot; slow-growing, short growths with leaves at the tip, and rapidly growing, long shoots with well-spaced, alternate branchlets, that become upright or nearly so once established. A healthy tree maintains a balance between these two types of growth; a tree under stress may produce unbalanced growth (see right).

Prune young trees only to remove competing leaders, when dormant between autumn and early spring. Established trees dislike pruning, and shortened shoots often die back. Poorly shaped trees can rarely be improved by remedial pruning, but feeding in spring with a balanced general fertilizer may improve growth.

Profusion of slower-growing, stubby shoots

Upright stem has only one long lateral

CONIFERS SUITABLE FOR HEDGING

These conifers can be used as hedging but need regular clipping to maintain them as formal hedges; the majority are upright cultivars.

CHAMAECYPARIS
  LAWSONIANA
    'Allumii'
    'Bleu Nantais'
    'Columnaris'
    'Columnaris
      Glauca'
    'Ellwoodii'
    'Erecta Aurea'
    'Erecta Viridis'
    'Grayswood Pillar'
    'Green Hedger'
    'Green Spire'
    'Kilmacurragh'
    'Pembury Blue'
    'Wisselii'

CUPRESSUS
  ARIZONICA
    'Fastigiata'
    'Glauca'
  MACROCARPA
    'Goldcrest'
    'Golden Spire'
  SEMPERVIRENS
    'Stricta'
    'Totem Pole'

× CUPROCYPARIS
  LEYLANDII cultivars
  inc. 'Castlewellan Gold'

TAXUS
  BACCATA
    'Fastigiata'
    Fastigiata Aurea
      Group
    'Fastigiata
      Aureomarginata'
    'Fastigiata Robusta'
  × MEDIA
    'Hicksii'

THUJA
  OCCIDENTALIS
    'Brabant'
    'Holmstrup'
    'Smaragd'
  PLICATA
    'Atrovirens'
    'Fastigiata'

TSUGA MERTENSIANA
  'Blue Star'

Training and pruning

Many conifers are very resinous and "bleed" copiously when cut. Bleeding is most profuse during active growth, which begins in early spring, often with a second flush in summer. There is no reason to avoid pruning at these times, however, as the resin helps to seal wounds and protect trees from infection.

TRAINING A LEADER

Most conifers produce a strong central leader, and many naturally reform a leading shoot if damaged in juvenility or early maturity. If damage occurs, select and train in a replacement leader as soon as possible (*see below*). In most species, it is unusual for dual leaders to form in response to damage when young. A leader lost later in life, however, often results in the formation of dual leaders, particularly as many conifers produce shoots in "whorls" – clusters of three or more, arising at about the same point on the stem. Many pines produce dual leaders in response to damage, even when young. Remove one (*see right*) to produce a single-stemmed tree and to avoid dangerous narrow forks at maturity.

Not all conifers have a single main stem. *Metasequoia glyptostroboides* often develops multiple leaders but continues to form an upright tree without intervention. Some shrub-like conifers, including many junipers, are grown for their tight, upright habit. If they develop a loose upper canopy with several leaders, tie these in with rubber tree ties or with netting to maintain a dense habit, and to protect them from snow or wind damage. (*Continued on p.40.*)

DWARF CONIFERS

Dwarf conifers are propagated vegetatively from sports (natural mutations) of the "normal" tree. Sports are often selected for a prostrate, congested or fastigiate habit, or, in many dwarf conifers, for the retention of soft, needle-like juvenile foliage that differs markedly from the more scale-like leaves of the adult plant. Pruning is usually unnecessary. Sometimes, however, the plant produces growth that reverts to the normal habit – strongly upright shoots on a prostrate plant, for example (*see right*) – which spoils the form and may eventually become dominant. All such reverted growth must be cut out to maintain the distinctive shape and habit for which the plant has been selected.

Removing reverted growth
Cut out at the point of origin any shoot that exhibits atypical growth, masking the cut within the remaining foliage.

Competing leader
To maintain a single-stemmed, central-leader tree, it is essential to remove competing leaders as soon as possible. Cut out the weaker or more crooked shoot cleanly at its base.

Replacing a broken leader

Damaged tree *On young plants, a broken leader can be replaced with a strong lateral that, even if growing horizontally, can be tied in to assume the dominant, vertical role.*

1 *Remove all damaged growth, cutting it back cleanly to a strong shoot, preferably of upright habit, that can be trained to replace it. The resulting small wound will heal quickly.*

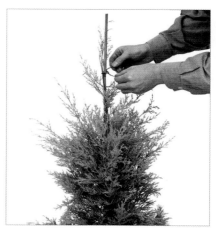

2 *Insert a cane carefully through the centre of the tree, or tie it to the main stem. Tie in the replacement shoot. Remove the cane once the new leader is growing strongly upwards.*

(*Continued from p.39.*) Some conifers, such as *Cedrus deodara*, produce a pendulous leading shoot, known as a "dropper". During rapid growth the terminal bud is "lowered" and protected by several lateral buds. At the end of the growing season, the shoot straightens and the leading bud resumes its place at the top of the vertical shoot. Do not prune or straighten a dropper; in most cases, this will suppress growth.

CLEARING THE TRUNK
Before clearing the trunk, consider the ultimate shape, size and habit of the mature tree. This will dictate the extent and height of trunk clearance. Most members of the Cupressaceae, and species such as *Abies lasiocarpa* that produce a skirt of foliage to the ground, are best with lower branches retained. Conifers such as *Picea bungeana* have beautiful bark, but make unattractive "lollipop" trees if cleared too high. Thin the lowest whorls of branches so that the bark can be seen without spoiling the overall form of the tree at maturity. Conifers with a semi-pendulous or pendulous habit, such as *Picea smithiana* and *P. breweriana*, need the lowest whorls of branches removed so that the remaining foliage is just clear of the ground. Many others need a taller clear trunk to show off their form. Once the tree is growing strongly, clear the first 1m (3ft) as the tree reaches 2.5–3m (8–10ft) tall, cutting branchlets cleanly back to the trunk to leave small scars that will heal quickly. Over the next several years, clear the trunk to 2m (6ft), then proceed according to the height of the mature tree; one that reaches 20m (70ft), for example, looks well with a trunk of 4–6m (12–20ft).

HARD PRUNING
Conifers that respond well to pruning back into older wood include:
Cephalotaxus
Cryptomeria
Cunninghamia
Sequoia
Taxus
Torreya
and young specimens of:
Araucaria
Metasequoia
Taxodium
Most of the Cupressaceae, including *Chamaecyparis*, *Cupressus* and *Thuja*, respond well to regular trimming of young growth, and can be trimmed as formal hedges (*see p.45*), provided that training and pruning is initiated from the start; as with most other conifers, they will not break from older wood.

Dealing with splayed-out growth

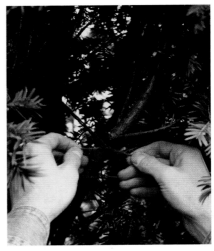

1 *Wind, heavy snow or ice, or occasionally the weight of an upright branch, may cause growth to splay out. Check that the branch has not split; if undamaged, it can be tied back in.*

2 *Tie the growth in, using soft material in case the tie is forgotten as growth extends. Use soft tarred twine, a rubber tree tie or, ideally, nylon tights or a stocking.*

Dealing with dead patches

1 *Remove completely all shoots bearing dead or scorched foliage (inset). Unless the damage is very minimal, this will leave an unsightly hole, especially in formally shaped trees and hedges.*

2 *Insert a cane into the body of the tree, tying it securely to a main stem or branch, then draw neighbouring branches over and tie them in. Though the cane may be temporarily visible, new growth will soon disguise it and the hole.*

Thinning
To thin congested growth, first clear away dead matter and other debris, then remove crowded shoots cleanly at their bases, thus disguising the cuts within the foliage. Avoid exposing bare, brown inner branches, since they seldom produce new shoots.

With maturity, many conifers lose their lowest whorls of branches naturally by "shading out". All dead or dying branches should be removed as seen.

CONGESTION

Many conifers accumulate dead wood, produce congested growth and trap leaf litter within the canopy. This is often unattractive, and may increase the risk of winter damage by trapping heavy snowfall. In highly resinous species, the accumulation of debris can pose a fire risk in hot summers, especially in hot climates. All dead material should be removed regularly. Where branch whorls are very congested, judicious thinning (*see facing page, below*) will reduce the risk of snow damage. On mature trees, however, this is best done by a professional arboriculturist.

SNOW AND WIND DAMAGE

Conifers grown for their tight form can be damaged by the effects of wind and snow. Remove lying snow to avoid the risk of damage and splaying out of branches. Splayed-out growth can be tied in (*see facing page, above*). If the branch is broken, remove it, and, to disguise the gap, reposition adjacent branches and tie them in using rubber tree ties or soft tarred twine. This avoids exposing internal branches only partially clothed with foliage, which seldom re-sprout. If damage is confined to the extremities of the branch, remove only the affected growth and allow unaffected branches to grow out to restore the shape. Patches of dieback or wind scorch can be remedied in a similar way (*see facing page, centre*), but can be more difficult to deal with, as damage occurs (and may recur) on the colder, more exposed side of the plant. Cold and exposure inhibit the regrowth that is necessary to restore the canopy. Young trees may be best moved to a more sheltered situation. Alternatively, provide extra wind protection, perhaps by planting shelter plants or erecting a temporary screen, as they regrow.

RENOVATION

With a few exceptions (*see* Hard pruning, *facing page*), conifers do not regenerate freely from old wood and, in most cases, renovation is limited to the removal of dead or dying branches. Where trees have become too tall for their situation, removal and replacement is the best option. Removal of the top usually results in an ugly, mutilated appearance. Many of the *Cupressaceae* tolerate hard clipping of young growth, and new growth will rapidly mask the cuts. Yew (*Taxus baccata*) does tolerate hard pruning, but then needs careful shaping to restore its form.

Dictionary of Conifers

A

ABIES *SILVER FIR*

Hardy, evergreen conifers with dense, glossy, rather soft, dark green needles and strongly pyramidal forms. The species are usually large forest trees that may be grown in very large gardens and parks. *Abies koreana* is the most common species found in bigger gardens. Pruning is seldom required, but where it is needed to control shape, remove damaged branches, or replace doubled or damaged leaders, it should be carried out in early spring.

 A. nordmanniana is the "Christmas tree" species sometimes planted in domestic

Abies koreana
The Korean fir bears dark green leaves and violet-blue cones, and is suitable for gardens.

gardens. Since trees can eventually reach up to 40m (130ft) they must be regularly clipped or will quickly need replacing.

ARAUCARIA

Hardy, evergreen conifers, mostly native to warm tropical climates with a dry season. All have spirally arranged leaves and elegant sculptural forms that seldom require pruning. *Araucaria heterophylla* is a common indoor plant and is best replaced rather than pruned in domestic situations.

Araucaria araucana
Male cones of the monkey puzzle are oblong-shaped and drooping; female cones are ovoid.

A. ARAUCANA

CHILEAN PINE, MONKEY PUZZLE

Suitable for growing outdoors in cool climates, the monkey puzzle tree bears sharp, leathery, pointed leaves on a conical juvenile form where branches extend to ground level. With age, the tree becomes spreading and mop-headed, shedding its lower branches.

■ **WHEN TO PRUNE** Pruning is best undertaken in spring before growth starts. Substantial oozing of resin from pruning cuts is normal and actually protects the tree from infection.

■ **TRAINING AND PRUNING** Remove competing leading shoots to retain the characteristic shape. Side branches may also be removed to allow access beneath the tree, or if they are damaged or diseased. Plants damaged by weather may regrow and selective pruning can be used to produce an attractive crown.

C

CEDRUS *CEDAR*

Hardy, evergreen conifers with medium-sized, slower growing garden forms. Young trees are conical and graceful, becoming broadly spreading with age. Broad boughs can be vulnerable to weather damage.

■ **TRAINING AND PRUNING** Cedars bear clusters of needles on sideshoots that have the potential to sprout, and pruning to a green sideshoot is effective. Competing leaders may need to be removed in young trees. Prune leading shoots and shorten sideshoots to control the size and shape of smaller trees. Bushy trees and hedges can be achieved by shortening green shoots by half in the spring, starting when young.

 Regrowth from old wood is unlikely, so heavy pruning is not effective. Crowns can, however, be reduced by pruning off the upper parts, which results in an ungainly but long-lived tree. Branch breakage after snow can lead to wounds that are slow to heal; action by a qualified tree surgeon can reduce the chances of further loss.

 Cedrus atlantica f. *glauca* is commonly grown in gardens for which it is too small. Replacement is the best option, but annual clipping and trimming is possible.

CHAMAECYPARIS
FALSE CYPRESS

Evergreen conifers with scale-like leaves on long, attractive shoots. Juvenile leaves are larger and less scale-like, and are retained on some of the many valuable dwarf or slow-growing cultivars, such as *Chamaecyparis lawsoniana* 'Ellwoodii'. Tall forms are best suited to growing as specimen trees in large gardens and parks. To keep trees small and bushy or to make a high-quality hedge, shoot tips can be trimmed or shortened to a green sideshoot. Dwarf or slow-growing cultivars seldom require pruning. Heavy pruning into brown, leafless wood is highly unlikely to result in regrowth.

CUPRESSUS *CYPRESS*

Evergreen conifers with scale-like leaves. *Cupressus* are highly unlikely to regrow after heavy pruning into brown, leafless wood, but it is possible to shorten shoot tips for bushier growth or to make a hedge, and the removal of competing leaders is advisable. *Cupressus macrocarpa* 'Goldcrest' has particularly dense, golden foliage and is widely sold as a small tree that rapidly becomes too large and a little scraggly; these inexpensive trees are better replaced and not really worth the pruning.

J–L

JUNIPERUS *JUNIPER*

Hardy, evergreen coniferous shrubs and trees, originating in dry, mountainous and forested areas, and well adapted to garden use. Adult plants bear scales but juvenile plants, including many dwarf cultivars, carry attractive, awl-shaped needles. There are many spreading ground-cover cultivars and dwarf bushes, often used in rock gardens.

■ **TRAINING AND PRUNING** Juniper growth is very neat and the trees seldom require pruning. However, to keep them small and bushy or to enhance the ground-hugging properties of the low-growing cultivars, shoot tips can be trimmed or shortened to a green sideshoot. Regrowth from old wood is possible in some species, particularly those that bear scales, but is not reliable.

LARIX *LARCH*

Hardy, deciduous conifers grown for their graceful forms, delicate whorls of needles, and autumn colour. Little pruning is required other than reducing to a single leader, where necessary, and pinching or shortening young stems for bushier growth. Larch is unlikely to sprout from old, brown, leafless wood.

P–T

PICEA *SPRUCE*

Hardy, evergreen conifers with dense, sharp, glossy, dark green needles borne on "pegs". Some dwarf cultivars are available but spruce is generally better suited to estates and forestry. Regrowth from old, brown, leafless wood is highly unlikely, but size and shape can be controlled by trimming and shortening in spring, which is also the time to prune to a single leader, if necessary. Norway spruce (*Picea abies*) is the traditional "Christmas tree" sometimes planted in domestic gardens; as it can grow to 40m (130ft) it will require early replacement unless regularly clipped.

PINUS *PINE*

Hardy, evergreen coniferous trees that carry long needles in bunches, pines make one flush of growth each year early in summer.

■ **TRAINING AND PRUNING** Many pines grow into large trees suited to forestry and estates and pruning these is unnecessary and impractical. Smaller pines, such as *Pinus mugo* and dwarf cultivars, are picturesque plants suited to small gardens and pruning to enhance their qualities is often worthwhile. Shortening branches to sideshoots in spring will enhance their density. Where bushier growth is required, in spring the soft "candles" formed at the tips of branches can be cut off or snapped with finger and thumb to produce sideshoots. Regrowth is highly unlikely from older leafless areas of branches.

Pinus mugo 'Slowmound'
Dwarf mountain pines make attractive, compact conifers that are perfect for small gardens.

TAXUS *YEW*

Hardy, evergreen coniferous shrubs and trees, yews respond exceptionally well to formal and informal pruning, and will reliably and vigorously re-sprout from old wood as latent buds are common in old leaf axils. Where pruned to the trunk, however, recovery can be patchy.

Taxus baccata 'Icicle'
Variegated cultivars of yew are available, with yellow or cream margins to the leaves.

■ **WHEN TO PRUNE** Very heavy pruning is best done just before growth commences in late winter or early spring, to allow a whole growing season for new leaves to be produced. Hedges require annual pruning in late summer.

■ **TRAINING AND PRUNING** Shoot tips can be cut or sheared to produce a denser canopy, or where an open canopy is desired whole branches can be removed. If hedges need renovating, the top and one side can be reduced as much as is required in late winter or early spring, and when the cut areas have re-sprouted the remaining side can be renovated in turn. Spreading and narrow (fastigiate) forms can be spoilt by pruning and are best tied or trained where shape and habit need modifying.

THUJA *ARBORVITAE*

Hardy, evergreen conifers with scale-like leaves and often with a strongly defined, narrow, pyramidal shape. *Thuja* are generally large forest trees, by nature they make excellent hedges and there are many desirable dwarf or slow-growing forms.

■ **TRAINING AND PRUNING** Although a single leading shoot is usual, some species can divide into several leading shoots from the outset; this is their natural habit and they do not need to be thinned to a single leader. *Thuja* is sometimes said to regrow from older wood after pruning but this cannot be relied upon. Shoot tips can be trimmed or shortened for bushier growth and to restrict size.

TSUGA *HEMLOCK*

Hardy, evergreen conifers with narrow, needle leaves, *Tsuga* make good specimen trees for larger gardens and can be used for hedging. Routine pruning is unnecessary, but loss of branches or leaders can result in numerous replacement shoots, which must be thinned to restore a single leading shoot.

Palms AND PALM-LIKE PLANTS

Palms need minimal training, and little or no pruning. They grow from the centre of their single or several stems, and if the growing tip is removed, the palm dies; there are no growth buds lower down on the stem. It is, therefore, difficult to restrict size by pruning. In cool climates, many palms are grown as young plants in the home or conservatory. If they become too large, they are usually discarded; new plants are easily grown from seed. With suckering palms, such as *Chamaerops*, height and spread can be controlled removing very tall or excess suckers. Some, such as *Chamaedorea elegans*, produce aerial roots on the stem. Reduce height by air-layering the stem, then re-planting the rooted top.

GROOMING PALM TRUNKS

Most palms benefit from "grooming" to remove dead leaves. In cool climates, this is done mainly for cosmetic effect. In hot climates, it is more important, as an accumulation of dead leaf bases can form a fire hazard. Where dead leaves persist, cut them off close to their base, at any time of year, leaving the stubs to create a neat pattern. Do not cut them right back to the stem; a naked stem is ugly and more susceptible to damage. Wear stout gloves, especially for those with spiny leaf bases, such as *Livistona australis*. Many palms produce a protective fibrous covering on the trunk which is also best left in place; it will be shed naturally as the plant matures.

Cutting back dead palm leaves
Cut dead leaf bases back almost to the stem to leave a neat stub. Do not overclean the stem by removing all vestiges of the leaf.

PALM-LIKE PLANTS

A number of plants resemble palms in that they bear their leaves in rosettes, either basally or at the tips of stems. They include aloes, agaves, cordylines, phormiums and yuccas. They do not, however, produce all growth from a single growing point, and often possess dormant buds that produce shoots after damage or pruning, forming new rosettes lower on the stem. In general, they need pruning only to remove dead leaves, or to cut out faded flower stems.

Cordylines and yuccas sometimes suffer frost damage when grown at their limits of hardiness. When any danger of hard frost has passed and new growth begins to appear in spring, cut damaged branches back to just above the newly formed shoots. Apply a balanced fertilizer and a mulch to help produce vigorous new growth. Both genera respond well to hard pruning and renovation; cut back to suitable sideshoots or basal shoots, or even to ground level, if necessary. To create a multi-branched specimen, remove the growing point before growth begins, then feed and mulch.

Rosette-forming plants such as agaves and aloes readily produce new offsets to replace damaged growth. Remove over-large or damaged offsets carefully to avoid breaking the new shoots that are growing underneath. Alternatively, root young offsets as cuttings and discard the mother plant.

The pruning of slow-growing plants, such as the cycads, *Pandanus* and *Xanthorrhoea*, is best restricted to the removal of dead leaves and spent flower stems. They may produce new growth, but recovery is very slow.

Removing spent yucca flower
Remove spent flower spikes in spring, cutting them back close to their point of origin in the centre of the rosette.

PRUNING HARDY PALMS

Hardy palms are increasingly grown in cooler climates as part of exotic tropical displays. In winter, these are either brought indoors or left in situ if hardy enough. If left outdoors, the evergreen leaves, apex, and trunk will still need to be wrapped with horticultural fleece.

Brahea armata (Blue fan palm) Dead leaves can be removed but the fibrous leaf bases that clothe the stem should be retained.

Butia capitata (Jelly palm) Removal of dead leaves is usually kept to a minimum as the leaves are spiny. Fruits can be used to make jam but worthwhile crops are unlikely in cool climates.

Chamaerops humilis (Mediterranean dwarf fan palm) Older, lower leaves can become unsightly and are best removed. Most likely palm to succeed outdoors in cool climates.

Cordyline australis (Cabbage palm, Torbay palm) A small evergreen tree from New Zealand, rather than a true palm, and as such it will re-sprout freely after pruning.

Jubaea chilensis

Jubaea chilensis (Chilean wine palm) Trimming is not required as the leaves fall when they die.

Phoenix canariensis (Canary Islands date palm) As fronds fall quite soon after dying there is no need for rigorous trimming, and any trimming should be kept to the minimum required.

Rhapidophyllum hystrix (Needle palm) Removing dead stems is difficult due to the very spiny nature of these palms and they are best left alone.

Sabal minor (Dwarf palmetto palm) A short palm that is useful for understorey planting. Dead fronds can be removed.

Trachycarpus fortunei (Chusan palm) Older leaves can be unsightly and are best removed, but living leaves should be retained.

Washingtonia robusta (Mexican fan palm) Tall, fast-growing palm often carrying a "petticoat" of dead foliage. As the skirt of dead foliage can look scruffy it can be removed, but living fans should be retained.

Hedges

Hedges and screens play an important role in the structure and character of a garden, as well as having a variety of practical uses. Hedges provide privacy, create boundaries, and screen unsightly views. They can provide shelter from wind or strong sun, and filter out noise and dust from nearby roads. Hedges may also provide food and shelter for wildlife. The types of plants you choose will depend on the style of the garden, and the size, position and purpose of the planned hedge. Is it to be informal or formal, evergreen or deciduous, flowering or not? A hedge is a long-term project, so it is vital to make the right choice from the wide range of suitable trees and shrubs. Make sure that your chosen species is suited to your climate, site and soil, and keep plants growing vigorously and evenly by good soil preparation and cultivation.

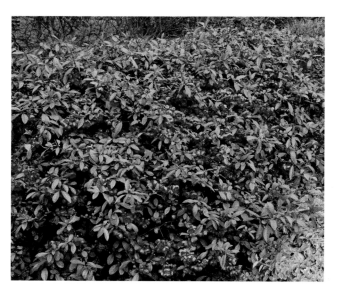

Flowering hedge
This attractive *Chaenomeles* bears flowers and fruit on lateral shoots from old wood. Trimming to shape the hedge encourages the production of more flowering and fruiting spurs. In some cases, as with holly (*Ilex*), berries will be sacrificed by pruning.

Initial training

Consider the desired height and spread of the hedge, and the speed of growth of your chosen species. Fast-growing plants provide rapid results, but in general slow-growing plants live longer, make dense hedges and, when established, do not need such frequent clipping.

Evergreen hedges eventually provide privacy, shelter and a uniform backdrop to other plantings throughout the year. However, although a deciduous hedge may be bare and leafless in winter, most species will still "filter" wind, providing a degree of shelter. In very exposed sites, this filtering effect can have advantages over dense, thick evergreens, which may cause strong

winds to "jump" the hedge and swirl violently beyond it.

Deciduous species offer a changing display throughout the year, attractive in spring and summer when in full leaf, perhaps with the additional ornamental value of flowers and fruit. Some hedging plants, such as *Fagus sylvatica*, have leaves that change colour in autumn and do not fall, persisting through the winter. A number of deciduous species, such as fuchsia, can be used to provide temporary or seasonal hedging. In cold areas they may die back in winter, but will produce long flowering displays throughout the spring and summer.

Starting a hedge
Buying plants in bulk usually entails accepting a "mixed bag" of young specimens. Do not try to prune each for balanced regrowth; simply alternate weaker plants with strong ones. If possible, do not stake hedging plants; if in a very exposed, windy site, use posts and wires (*see left*), positioned on the windward side of the plants, so that they are not blown against the wire, risking damage to the bark.

PRUNING ON PLANTING
Prepare the ground to a width of 60–90cm (2–3ft). Space plants 30–60cm (1–2ft) apart, depending on the vigour of the chosen species. For dwarf hedges, intended for parterres and knot gardens, space plants about 10–15cm (4–6in) apart. Plant in straight lines: staggered double rows are not now generally recommended, because growth becomes crowded and dead wood can accumulate.

The degree of pruning on planting depends very much on the chosen plants and the desired effect. Flowering shrubs for an informal hedge can be pruned lightly as for free-standing specimens (*see p.155*). Most evergreens also need only minimal pruning; shorten only overlong lateral shoots in the first few years (*see also* Evergreen trees, *p.25*). Let leaders grow on to the desired height.

Prune plants such as beech (*Fagus*) and hornbeam (*Carpinus*) moderately to stimulate balanced regrowth. Do not simply "even up" young plants; you are likely to induce the reverse effect. Prune strong shoots lightly and weak ones hard. Shorten vigorous leaders and laterals by no more than one-third, and weaker growth by up to two-thirds of its length.

Vigorous plants with a strongly upright habit, such as privet (*Ligustrum*) and hawthorn (*Crataegus*), need hard pruning to encourage growth to bush out at the base. Cut them back to within 15–30cm (6–12in) of ground level in late spring, and clip back laterals again in late summer. During the second winter or early spring, cut back hard again, removing at least half of the previous season's growth.

Establishing and maintaining hedges

Once hedging plants are established, regular pruning or clipping must be initiated and maintained to form a balanced outline and to keep growth dense and healthy. The frequency, timing and degree of pruning depend mainly on the style of hedge and the species chosen.

INFORMAL HEDGES
An informal hedge is basically a screen of small trees or, more commonly, shrubs. The timing and techniques of pruning, if required, are much the same as for individual specimens. The main difference is that regular pruning should be accompanied by gentle shaping of the outline. Remove misplaced growths, and trim back annually to keep within bounds. For flowering and fruiting hedges, the timing of pruning is critical if the next season's display is not to be spoiled.

SEMI-FORMAL HEDGES
Evergreens suitable for semi-formal hedges, such as *Prunus lusitanica*, *Aucuba* and *Garrya*, need only minimal pruning (*see* Evergreen trees, *p.25*, and Evergreen shrubs, *p.157*) to create solid, but natural-looking shapes and outlines. Many have large glossy leaves that are spoiled by cutting with hedge trimmers or shears; the cut leaves will turn brown and become unsightly. In these cases, prune with secateurs (*see right*) and, if necessary, a pruning saw.

For flowers and fruit, choose shrubs such as *Pyracantha*, *Forsythia* and *Chaenomeles*, which bear their flowers on laterals or spurs from older wood, rather than terminally on growth that will be removed by trimming.

FORMAL HEDGES
Plants used for formal hedges must have a dense habit of growth, and be tolerant of close clipping. The aims of pruning and training are to ensure dense growth from the base to the top, and to produce a neat outline.

From the early stages, the hedge sides should be cut at a slight angle (known as the "batter"), with the base as the widest point. The aim is to produce a tapered outline, with a flat or gently rounded top, which will be less vulnerable to damage by snow or strong winds. Snow will fall away down the sides of a tapered hedge; high winds will be deflected down its sloping sides, thus causing minimal damage to the hedge. In addition, a batter permits more even distribution of light from the top to the bottom, reducing foliage loss at the base from "shading out". Dwarf hedges and parterre plantings do not need a batter and look best with vertical sides. (continued on p.46)

Informal hedge
This fuchsia hedge will provide colour throughout summer, but offers little interest when it dies back in winter. Many gardeners are willing to accept a dull winter appearance in order to enjoy the changing seasonal displays offered by flowering deciduous hedges.

Semi-formal hedge
Hedges with large, shiny leaves, such as laurel, should be pruned with secateurs. Ideally, individual shoots should be cut back to within the foliage canopy to disguise the pruning wounds. Pruning with a hedge trimmer or shears will damage the leaves and cause unsightly browning. Since the foliage is the main feature of many formal evergreen hedges, it is important to keep it neat.

Formal hedge shapes

This hornbeam hedge has been pruned to taper at the top, ensuring that light reaches its lower flanks.

This yew has been cut into a classic formal A-shape, tapering gently to a neat, flat top.

Sloping sides and a rounded top give this conifer hedge a softer, but still very neat, outline.

(continued from p.45) A level top is achieved by cutting to a straight-edge or garden line stretched between canes. It is important to use a guide when clipping low hedges too, since unevenness is just as visible when looking down as when viewing from eye level. Conifers and many evergreens increase their height only by means of their apical shoots, so in most cases, only the laterals are pruned in the formative years. Do not shape the top until the desired height is reached.

MAINTENANCE

Once the size and batter have been achieved, the hedge simply needs trimming to shape, using a straight-edge or garden line as a guide. Most formal hedges are trimmed twice annually: when dormant and in midsummer for deciduous hedges; in late spring and late summer for evergreens. Yew (*Taxus*) needs only one summer clipping. For most conifer hedges, this regular trimming is particularly important to maintain a dense surface, since shoots seldom break freely from older wood.

Most formal hedges are cut with shears or an electric trimmer. Ensure that electric trimmers are fitted with a residual current device (RCD or "circuit breaker"), and do not use them in damp conditions. Avoid lifting an electric trimmer above shoulder height; use a sturdy stepladder or staging when cutting tall hedges. Always wear gloves and goggles (*see also* Tools and equipment, *p.15*).

To maintain strong, even growth, all hedges need an annual application of balanced fertilizer and mulch in spring.

Trimming hedges

Using shears When using shears to trim a hedge, always keep the blades parallel to the line of the hedge to ensure that the surfaces of the top and sides are cut level and flat.

Using a trimmer If you use an electric trimmer, keep the blade parallel to the hedge and use a wide, sweeping action so that you do not cut into the hedge and damage the outline.

Shaping a hedge

Using a line To achieve a level top, stretch taut string horizontally between two upright posts to act as a guideline for the highest point of the hedge, then cut the top of the hedge along this line.

Using a template To taper the top, cut a template of the required shape. Place the template on the hedge and cut, following the line of the template, moving it along as you proceed. Then cut the sides.

Changing display
Once the catkins fade, *Garrya elliptica* can be formally clipped.

RECOMMENDED HEDGING PLANTS

Evergreen, formal
CARISSA *p.182*
ELAEAGNUS *p.190*
ESCALLONIA *p.192*
EUONYMUS *p.192*
GRISELINIA *p.196*
ILEX *pp.66, 201*
LAURUS *p.69*
LONICERA NITIDA
　p.205
OSMANTHUS
　DELAVAYI *p.208*
PHILLYREA *p.211*
PRUNUS
　LAUROCERASUS,
　P. LUSITANICA
　pp.212–13
For conifers, *p.38*

**Evergreen,
semi-formal**
ACACIA *p.52*
ACALYPHA *p.173*
ATRIPLEX *p.175*
AUCUBA *p.175*
BERBERIS DARWINII,

B. × STENOPHYLLA
　p.176
BOUVARDIA *p.176*
BRUNFELSIA *p.177*
CARISSA *p.182*
CASSINIA *p.183*
CEANOTHUS *p.183*
COTONEASTER
　LACTEUS,
　C. STERNIANUS
　p.188
DESFONTAINEA *p.189*
DURANTA *p.190*
GARRYA ELLIPTICA,
　G. × THURETII
　p.195
MURRAYA *p.207*
NANDINA *p.207*
OLEARIA *p.208*
PIERIS *p.211*
TAMARIX *p.220*

Deciduous, formal
ACER CAMPESTRE *p.51*
CARPINUS *p.54*
FAGUS SYLVATICA *p.63*
LIGUSTRUM *p.204*

**Deciduous,
semi-formal**
ALNUS *p.52*
CORYLUS *pp.58, 187*
COTONEASTERS *p.188*
PRUNUS × BLIREANA,
　P. CERASIFERA
　'PISSARDII' and
　VAR. 'NIGRA' *p.80*

Flowering hedges
BERBERIS *p.176*
CAMELLIA *pp.180–1*
CHOISYA *pp184–5*
ESCALLONIA *p.192*
FORSYTHIA *p.194*
FUCHSIA *pp.194–5*
IXORA *p.202*
GREVILLEA *pp.65,195*
HIBISCUS *p.199*
MYRTUS *p.207*
NERIUM *p.207*
RIBES *p.215*
ROSA *pp.298–325*
TAMARIX *p.220*
VIBURNUM *p.222*

Fruiting hedges
ARONIA *p.174*
PYRACANTHA *p.213*
ROSA RUGOSA *p.314*
SYMPHORICARPOS
　p.220

Barrier hedging
BERBERIS *p.176*
CHAENOMELES *p.184*
ILEX *pp.66, 201*
PONCIRUS *p.213*
PRUNUS SPINOSA *p.81*
PYRACANTHA *p.213*
ULEX *p.221*

**Dwarf hedges/
edging**
BUXUS *p.179*
DAPHNE MEZEREUM
　p.189
LAVANDULA *p.189*
RHODODENDRONS
　(dwarf) *p.214*
ROSMARINUS *p.215*
SANTOLINA *p.217*
SARCOCOCCA *p.217*

Renovation

Given regular maintenance and feeding, most hedges will remain healthy and in good shape for many years. In time, however, hedges may gradually edge their way beyond bounds, obscuring pathways, encroaching on a border or becoming too tall and casting shade on to other parts of the garden.

A number of hedging plants respond very well to hard renovation pruning, even when they have been neglected and become severely overgrown. They include beech (*Fagus*), hawthorn (*Crataegus*), hornbeam (*Carpinus*), holly (*Ilex*), Lonicera nitida and yew (*Taxus baccata*). The renovation of most conifer hedges (*see right*) is limited to the tying-over and patching of holes (*see p.39*), and in the long term it may be better to consider removing and replacing them with young plants.

RENOVATING CONIFER HEDGES

Conifers (*see pp.38–41*) are ideal plants for hedging in many ways. However, they may pose problems if they are neglected. Initial training followed by regular trimming is especially important to maintain a dense, even surface. If neglected, the usual result is a bare, woody, open centre with a fringe of foliage at the extremities. The hedge then becomes prone to splitting or collapse in heavy snow or strong winds. A few conifers, especially yew (*Taxus*), respond well to hard pruning, but many do not readily produce shoots from old wood. Branches can be tied over to conceal holes (*see p.40*), but in the long term, replacement may eventually become necessary.

Section through conifer hedge
Regularly trimmed conifers have a dense, even surface, but are leafless within; most will not produce new shoots from this old, bare wood.

WHEN TO RENOVATE

For best results, deciduous hedges should be renovated in midwinter, and evergreen ones in mid-spring. Where drastic renovation is necessary, renovate each side of the hedge in different years (*see below, left* and *centre*) to avoid overstressing the plants. Reducing height (*see below right*) should also be a separate operation; allow a complete growing season for recovery. In the growing season before first pruning, feed and mulch well in spring, to encourage vigorous growth. Follow each pruning operation by a further application of fertilizer and mulch, to replenish the plants' food reserves and ensure strong regrowth. The surfaces that are not subjected to hard renovation pruning should be pruned in the usual way.

RESTORING THE OUTLINE

To recreate a dense, even surface, both the top and sides of the hedge need to be cut back to at least 15cm (6in) less than the final desired width and height. Where hedges are very thin and patchy, it may be necessary to cut back almost to the main stems to stimulate more vigorous regrowth. When reducing the height of very long hedges, it may be easier to paint on an indicator line that identifies where to cut, using whitewash or a proprietary white-line marker that will not damage the plants, and which will be removed during pruning. In most cases, a straight-edge or garden line should be used as a guide to reinstate the hedge's new, clean edge. When re-shaping the sides, do not forget to taper them, restoring the batter (*see p.45*). To recreate a uniform surface, it is essential that each plant in the hedge is cut back to the same width. Check this at regular intervals.

Renovation pruning inevitably results in ugly, bare areas and wounds, but, provided that you feed and mulch the hedge well, regrowth should be sufficiently rapid to hide these wounds within one or two growing seasons.

Reducing the width of an overgrown hedge

This side pruned normally

This side now cut back hard

Reducing hedge height

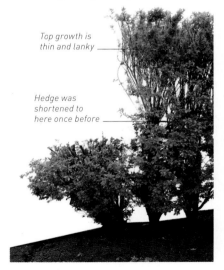

Top growth is thin and lanky

Hedge was shortened to here once before

First year In the first year, cut one side of the hedge back hard, almost to the main stems if necessary (*right side*). Prune the other (*left*) side as is usual for the plant.

Second year In the second year, the renovated surface has produced dense regrowth. Cut the unrenovated surface back hard, by the same amount as the other side.

To recreate a dense, uniform top, reduce the height to at least 15cm (6in) below the desired height. Cut back harder where upper portions are open and patchy.

Topiary

A form of training to create living garden "sculpture", topiary is a garden art that has been popular since Roman times. Traditionally used to produce strongly architectural and geometric shapes in formal gardens, it has been developed to include birds, animals and unusual, even whimsical, features such as giant chess-pieces and trains.

Different styles of topiary may be used to create a variety of effects. Imaginative forms express personal style and add a humorous or bizarre touch to a garden. Using topiary for geometric shapes such as cones, obelisks and columns provides a strong, structural element in a design. This type of topiary has uses both in formal gardens, perhaps to frame a vista or form an avenue, and in informal gardens, as a contrasting foil

for less structured planting. A hedge top can be used for topiary, clipping it into birds, spheres or cubes, for example. Topiary is also effective in containers; use a single container plant as a centrepiece, a pair to flank a doorway, or several to line a path.

Many plants are suitable, including traditional, long-lived evergreens such as yew (*Taxus*), bay (*Laurus nobilis*) and box (*Buxus*), and less common ones like *Osmanthus*, *Berberis* and *Phillyrea*. Simple, short-lived shapes can be created using *Artemisia abrotanum* or *Santolina chamaecyparissus*. The impatient gardener can achieve almost instant topiary effects by training climbers, such as ivy (*see p.272*), on wire forms.

Topiary shapes and effects

Basic design
Simple geometric forms, such as a cone, obelisk or pyramid, lend a formal elegance to the smallest garden or courtyard. They are easy and economical to produce, since they require no intricate training, and can usually be created by clipping single young specimens. Use small-leaved plants, such as box or conifers, to achieve a dense surface and neat, sharp outline.

Poodle
More complex symmetrical shapes, such as the traditional tiered "cake-stand" or "poodle" topiary form, are also relatively simple to create if you have a steady hand and eye. The easiest way is to "carve" the tiers out of a bushy young shrub. A fixed-length line attached to the central stem is used as a compass, to ensure that each tier has an even circumference.

Spiral
A spiral effect is formed in two stages, and will take several years to complete. First train the shrub against a central cane, and clip to form a vertical cylinder. In the third year, using secateurs and a wire spiral as a guide, begin shaping the spiral from the bottom up. The canes and wires are removed when the spiral reaches its full height.

Stem effects
Eyecatching effects can be created using a combination of simple training and pruning techniques. This shrub has been trained as a standard (*see p.165*), but its young, flexible leader was first trained around a stout cane, so that it grew up in a spiral (*see p.51*). The formal "mop" or "lollipop" head is then shaped and kept compact by regular trimming with secateurs.

Novelty animal
This hunting hound is one of any number of unusual designs that can be created using topiary techniques. It is formed around a permanent guide frame of chicken wire and metal laths, anchored in the ground at the hedge base, that provides both strong support and a shape to which to work. A bundle of strong shoots is left unclipped to grow out from the hedge top. While still flexible, they are trained and tied in to the frame (*see also p.50*), and encouraged to cover the wire so that, eventually, the wire is completely disguised. The form is clipped with shears and secateurs.

Clipping to create shapes

Plants used for topiary must have a dense habit, produce pliable growth and respond well to clipping. If a close, dense surface and crisp outline is required, they should also have small leaves. It is essential to check that the species selected is suitable for your soil type and that it is completely hardy in your climate. Precise forms and close-textured surfaces are quickly spoiled by dieback caused by frost and wind damage or unsuitable soil conditions.

TRAINING AND SHAPING

Topiary requires precise clipping using techniques that are slightly different to those used for normal hedge cutting. It is important that tools are kept perfectly sharp at all times. Complex forms need a combination of clipping and training and tying in to a guide frame, preferably with tarred soft twine that will eventually rot. Take time when clipping and shaping, especially in the formative stages, and stand back frequently to check for discrepancies. Do not cut too much in one place, as it may spoil the symmetry of a design for a whole season, or until replacement growth appears. Work from the top downwards and from the centre outwards, moving from side to side to ensure balance and symmetry.

Rounded topiary pieces are easier to produce and maintain than sharp-edged, geometric shapes, and are usually cut freehand. To produce a sphere, first trim the top of the plant and then cut a channel down both sides around the circumference. Cut a second channel at

Simple geometric shape

The simplest topiary design is one that is closest to the natural shape of the plant. This young box tree is first clipped roughly into shape. In the following year, the bush is clipped into a neat cone, using canes and wire as a guide. The finished plant needs clipping two or three times a year, depending on growth rate, to retain a crisp outline.

90° (at a right angle) to the first to leave four distinct quarters to be trimmed. Use the tips of the shears rather than the flat of the blades to cut curved surfaces.

Geometric topiary should have precise symmetry, flat, even surfaces and sharp, angled or squared edges, and such perfection is more difficult to form and maintain than rounded shapes. Even if you have a good eye, you will need to use

levels, straight-edges, guide lines and a plumb line for vertical surfaces, to ensure the precision of a cut. Clipping, with the flat edges of the shear blades held parallel to the surfaces, needs to be accurate to maintain a well-defined shape. Adjusting discrepancies may entail clipping the entire surface again. Use shear tips, secateurs or single-handed trimmers to shape intricate niches and corners.

Detailed geometrical shape using a frame

1 *Make frameworks for large topiary pieces from strong materials, as they will be in place for several years or even permanently. Clip a young plant (a yew is shown here) as necessary to keep it within the framework.*

2 *Pinch out shoot tips until the entire frame is filled with bushy growth. Then clip to shape in late summer, following the outline of the framework and pinching shoots that do not yet extend beyond it to encourage density.*

3 *When mature, the plant will form a dense bush and cover the framework. It needs regular clipping, at least twice during the growing season, following the lines of the frame to maintain the precise outline of the design.*

Training to produce irregular shapes

The forming of complex designs is limited only by the gardener's patience and imagination. Intricate forms need a combination of clipping and intensive training, and may take several years to complete. It is, however, very rewarding to watch the gradual growth and development of the final form.

Irregular topiary designs need a sturdy framework that will be used as a guide form to train and tie in to, as a template for clipping, and as a support for the finished sculpture. Use strong materials such as metal laths or heavy-duty fencing wire to

form a "skeleton", and chicken wire and finer gauge wire to form more precise detail. For free-standing or hedge-top forms, anchor the framework firmly into the ground. Use temporary canes and lines as necessary during formative shaping. To tie in shoots, use tarred soft twine that will eventually rot away. Avoid using wire to tie in since it may eventually constrict stems as they increase in girth. For intricate clipping, use shear tips, secateurs, or single-handed trimmers.

Whether working to a design from scratch, or adding to an existing hedge

top, the shoots to be trained should be young and sufficiently pliable to bend around the framework. Tie them in regularly throughout the growing season, and check previous ties to make sure that they are not rubbing or constricting growth. As shoots reach the desired length, pinch out their tips to encourage branching. Use the resulting sideshoots to fill in the body of the design. It is best to select only well-placed young shoots to fill in, and to cut or rub out the remainder at an early stage. If left to develop, they may have to be pruned out at a later stage, thus leaving awkward gaps or holes.

Creating a topiary bird

Finished bird *Topiary birds and animals are most successful if the outline is stylized and simple, since this makes clipping more practicable. Aim to produce a characteristic pose rather than fine detail.*

1 *In the first year, insert a fan-shaped cane support at an angle to form the tail. Select well-placed shoots and train and tie them in to the canes with soft twine. Tip back weaker shoots to stimulate their growth.*

2 *During the growing season, prune back the trained-in shoots by up to one third of their length, cutting to a leaf, to encourage dense, compact growth that will form a solid mass of foliage without holes or gaps.*

3 *In the second year, insert a supporting cane for the head. Select three strong shoots, and tie them to the cane to start forming the head. Trim the tail and pinch out shoots on the body. Unwanted shoots can be removed, as here, or (right) brought across to bulk out the tail.*

Using wire *As an alternative method, the plant can be trained using wire. Thread the wire carefully through the plant to create an approximate form. Train shoots onto the wire, then trim or "carve" out the finished shape as the plant grows.*

4 *In the third year, tie down the strongest shoot at the head to form the curve of the beak. Continue trimming to gradually shape the body more precisely and to keep the tail growth dense. Once the shape is formed, clip regularly, at least twice during the growing season.*

ORNAMENTAL STEM EFFECTS

A "mop-head" standard, such as those made of box, bay (*Laurus nobilis*), or weeping fig (*Ficus benjamina*), can be enhanced by special stem effects. These add a novel dimension to plain, formal heads of foliage. Attractive forms, like the spiral "barley-sugar" stem or plaited stems shown right, are easily created using simple training techniques on flexible young stems. To form a barley-sugar stem, train one or two young shoots around a strong cylindrical pole. Plaited stems are formed simply by plaiting three young stems together. They will eventually form a strong natural graft, fusing where they touch, but will need the support of a stout cane until growth hardens sufficiently to support itself.

Producing trained stem effects

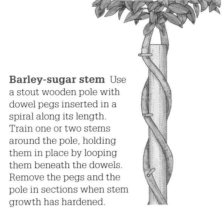

Barley-sugar stem Use a stout wooden pole with dowel pegs inserted in a spiral along its length. Train one or two stems around the pole, holding them in place by looping them beneath the dowels. Remove the pegs and the pole in sections when stem growth has hardened.

Plaited stem Form a plaited stem simply by braiding together three flexible young shoots. Select the strongest three on a multi-stemmed young plant, and remove the remainder. Single-stemmed plants can be cut back hard to produce multiple stems (*see p.28*).

Maintaining topiary

Once a topiary feature is established, it will need frequent routine clipping during the growing season. The time between cuts will depend on the rate of growth, and on the vigour of the species. An intricate, geometric design in box may need to be cut at four- to six-week intervals. Trim as soon as any new growth begins to appear uneven.

If a perfect finish is not required throughout the year, two cuts during the growing season are usually sufficient for a shaped effect, depending on the plant used. Yew, for example, needs to be cut only once a year, box (depending on the cultivar) usually needs to be cut twice and *Lonicera nitida* three times.

Clip plants at the appropriate time of year. Do not clip bushes after early autumn, as any young shoots produced in response will not ripen sufficiently to

withstand low winter temperatures. In warm climates where growth may be almost continuous, regular trimming will be needed throughout the year.

Feeding, watering and mulching are vital to keep topiary in good condition. Since clipping is intensive, it is important to apply balanced fertilizer two or three times during the growing season to ensure vigorous regrowth.

In regions that experience regular snowfall, topiary forms should be netted in winter to prevent splaying out and breakage of branches under the weight of snow. Brush snow off all flat surfaces to take its weight off the plant.

RENOVATION

With regular attention to clipping, feeding, mulching and watering, most problems can be avoided. Where

renovation becomes necessary, however, it will only be successful for species that regenerate freely from old wood, such as box (*see below left*).

If topiary specimens have been left unclipped for one or two years, regular clipping should restore the original form within the season. Where topiary has been neglected for several years, the shape may have been lost. Prune hard in the first spring to restore the outline, and clip more precisely in the following two or three seasons to restore a dense, even surface. Feed with a balanced fertilizer and water the plant thoroughly to aid its recovery.

DAMAGED GROWTH

If a leader, a section, or a branch has been damaged or broken, cut it back cleanly with secateurs. Alternatively, it may be possible to manipulate nearby shoots by tying them in to fill the gap (*see* Conifers, *p.40*). Where damage is severe, and the shape has been badly disfigured, it may take several years before regrowth is sufficient to repair the damage. In this case, especially where designs are abstract or free-form, it may be possible to form a new design out of the remains of the old one, thus avoiding the problem of gaps in the original shape.

The foliage of some evergreens may be scorched or die back in hard winters. The new growth in spring will usually disguise the damage, but trim it back if it is unsightly, carefully following the outline of the shape as closely as possible. Occasionally, shoots will not regenerate to fill gaps. If growth is poor or slow, check for pests or diseases and take appropriate action, or consider whether damage to the root system is being caused by poor drainage or other unsuitable cultural conditions.

Restoring box topiary

Damaged growth If dead patches appear in established topiary forms, they must be cut back hard to healthy living wood. Check that pests, diseases or unsuitable soil conditions are not the cause; if so, they must be rectified.

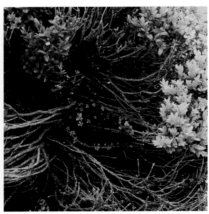

Replacement growth Provided that the plant is well fed and watered, new shoots emerge on old wood when cut back hard. It will take several years to restore the original form if damage is extensive, as shown here.

Dictionary of Ornamental Trees

A

Acacia flowers
Deadheading a young acacia with secateurs after flowering directs the plant's energy into the production of compact, branching growth.

ACACIA *MIMOSA, WATTLE*

Trees or large shrubs that are valued for their delicate foliage and fragrant clusters of soft, fluffy, usually yellow flowerheads, mostly borne in late winter and early spring on wood formed in the previous growing season. In frost-free climates acacias are used as specimen plants and as hedges and windbreaks. In cool temperate zones no acacia is totally hardy, although *A. dealbata* and *A. baileyana* can be grown outdoors in the shelter of a warm sunny wall. Acacias are also excellent conservatory plants.

■ **WHEN TO PRUNE** Soon after flowering. Remove frost-damaged growth in late spring once prolonged frosts are past.

■ **TRAINING AND PRUNING** Train as central-leader standards (*see p.26*), clearing the trunk to 1–2m (3–6ft). Vigorous species (*A. longifolia, A. dealbata*) may be cut hard back when young to form multi-stemmed trees (*see p.29*), suitable for growing in the shelter of a wall. Prune young plants after flowering, cutting to a sideshoot or to two or three buds beyond the spent flowered shoot to encourage compact, branching growth.

Keep pruning of established plants to a minimum. *A. cultriformis, A. saligna* and *A. verticillata*, however, tolerate moderate clipping and may be used as informal hedges (*see p.44*). Most acacias resent hard pruning and cannot be renovated successfully. Suckering species, which include *A. dealbata* and *A. melanoxylon*, may regenerate.

ACER *MAPLE*

Fully to frost-hardy trees valued for their autumn foliage colour and delicate flowers. Many of the smaller maples branch low, a habit that is also induced by pruning. Those with attractive bark are usually grown with clear trunks. *Acer griseum* and the snakebark maples are prone to coral spot; affected growth must be cut out as soon as seen.

■ **WHEN TO PRUNE** Winter, when fully dormant; maples "bleed" sap badly at other times. Small cuts, to remove reverted shoots, for example, may safely be made in late summer/early autumn.

A. DAVIDII

PERE DAVID'S MAPLE, SNAKEBARK MAPLE

Hardy, deciduous tree with white-striped green or purplish bark and handsome foliage, colouring orange and yellow in autumn.

■ **TRAINING AND PRUNING** Train as a central-leader standard (*see p.26*), then let the tree branch naturally at 1–1.5m (3–5ft), or prune to form a multi-stemmed tree on a low trunk (*see below*). Clear the trunk or trunks to about 1.5m (5ft) to display the bark. As the crown develops, remove crossing shoots and twiggy growth that obscures the bark on the trunk and main branches. Established trees need minimal pruning. Renovation is rarely successful: hard pruning seldom produces shoots that are strong enough to form a new branch framework.

A. NEGUNDO

BOX ELDER, ASH-LEAVED MAPLE

Hardy, deciduous tree with yellow-green or reddish flowers. Golden-leaved or variegated cultivars may be coppiced or pollarded for larger leaves (*see facing page and p.34*).

■ **TRAINING AND PRUNING** Train as a central-leader standard (*see p.26*) with a clear trunk of 1.5–2m (5–6ft). As the crown develops the leader will naturally lose dominance. No further special pruning is required. Remove any green shoots on variegated cultivars. If epicormic shoots develop where wind-damaged branches are removed, retain only one or two to develop into replacement branches.

A. SACCHARINUM

SILVER MAPLE

Hardy, deciduous tree with a graceful habit. Its brittle branchlets may be damaged by strong winds.

■ **TRAINING AND PRUNING** Train as a central-leader standard (*see p.26*) with a clear trunk of 2–2.5m (6–8ft) to display the bark and allow the branches to form pendulous "skirts" around the trunk. It is important to retain the leader for as long as possible, removing any competing shoots. Prune established trees only if necessary. Renovation is rarely successful.

Pruning to form a multi-stemmed tree on a low trunk (*Acer davidii*)

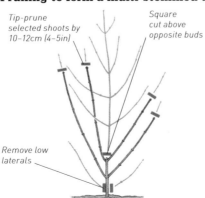

Tip-prune selected shoots by 10–12cm (4–5in)

Square cut above opposite buds

Remove low laterals

Year 1, winter Prune a young feathered tree to about 50cm (20in), above two pairs of strong shoots. Remove lower laterals and prune the selected shoots to induce branching.

Remove shoots affected by frost damage and dieback

Prune weak laterals to a bud at 2.5–5cm (1–2in)

Year 2, winter Young maples are prone to dieback and frost damage; cut it out, pruning to healthy buds or to the shoot's point of origin. To stimulate weak stems, prune hard.

Pollarded *Acer negundo*
Cut back to a framework in winter for larger leaves and a shrubby habit. Variegated cultivars grown from cuttings may be less prone to reversion than grafted plants.

OTHER MAPLES
A. CAMPESTRE Training should consist only of staking and the removal of badly placed or crossing shoots. When established, keep pruning to a minimum.
A. CIRCINATUM As for *A. campestre*.
A. GRISEUM As for *A. davidii*.
A. JAPONICUM As for *A. campestre*.
A. OPALUS As for *A. saccharinum*.
A. PALMATUM As for *A. campestre*.
A. PENSYLVANICUM As for *A. davidii*.
A. PLATANOIDES Although seedlings develop naturally as central-leader standards, train grafted garden cultivars to form compact branched-head standards (*see p.26*) with clear trunks of 1.35–2m (4½–6ft). When established, keep pruning to a minimum. Remove green shoots on variegated cultivars. Renovation is rarely successful.
A. PSEUDOPLATANUS As for *A. platanoides*.
A. RUBRUM As for *A. saccharinum*.
A. RUFINERVE As for *A. davidii*.
A. SACCHARUM As for *A. saccharinum*.
A. SEMPERVIRENS As for *A. campestre*.
A. TATARICUM SUBSP. GINNALA As for *A. campestre*.

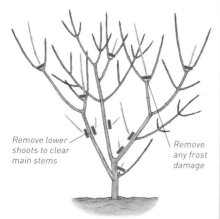

Year 3, winter Remove low laterals on main stems to display the bark. If necessary, remove inward-pointing laterals from main stems to prevent overcrowding in the centre.

Remove lower shoots to clear main stems

Remove any frost damage

AESCULUS *HORSE-CHESTNUT, BUCKEYE*

Deciduous, fully to frost-hardy, large trees and big, shrubby, suckering species. The trees are trained as central-leader standards, from seedlings or grafted cultivars. Early training is crucial to form a strong structure that will support the heavy, spreading branches. Allow plenty of space for larger species; they are often lopped, ruining their form, having been misplaced in small gardens.

A. HIPPOCASTANUM

COMMON HORSE-CHESTNUT

Fully hardy, heavy-branched tree with yellow- or red-centred white flower "candles" in early summer, followed (except in the double-flowered 'Baumannii') by lustrous nuts (conkers) in spiny casings.

30 | 100

m | ft

■ **WHEN TO PRUNE** After leaf-fall, from autumn until mid-winter. Minor pruning may be carried out in summer.

■ **TRAINING AND PRUNING** Train as a central-leader standard (*see p.26*), with a clear trunk of 2–3m (6–10ft) or more to accommodate the downward-sweeping lower branches when mature. Maintain the central leader for as long as possible to produce a tall trunk with evenly spaced framework branches.

Keep pruning of established trees to a minimum. Epicormic shoots that develop around pruning wounds will not make sound replacement branches. Cut or rub them out as soon as seen. On older trees, cut out any vigorous vertical shoots on horizontal branches as soon as possible to avoid unbalanced, heavy growth. Hard pruning should always be undertaken by a professional.

OTHER AESCULUS
A. × CARNEA As for *A. hippocastanum*. When training, remove all laterals making narrow V-angles with the main stem (*see p.10*) as this hybrid is prone to structural weaknesses. Mature trees may produce unsightly burrs (corky, cankerous growths) on the bark. Do not remove them, as they will not heal well.
A. INDICA As for *A. hippocastanum*, but clear the trunk to about 1.5–2m (5–6ft). The cultivar 'Sydney Pearce' is grafted.
A. × NEGLECTA As for *A. indica*.
A. PARVIFLORA Large, suckering shrub to 3m (10ft) forming a dense thicket that may be thinned, if desired, as for the shrub *Amelanchier stolonifera* (*see p.173*).
A. TURBINATA As for *A. hippocastanum*.

Terminal flowers

Pair of opposite buds

Opposite buds
All horse-chestnuts have opposite buds; if the leader is lost and a pair of shoots develops, select one to train vertically and remove the other as soon as the new leader is established.

AILANTHUS

Ailanthus altissima (syn. *A. glandulosa*) is a pollution-tolerant, very hardy, upright deciduous tree that may reach 30m (100ft), with bold leaves, grey bark and, on female trees, red-brown fruits. Suckering and, in continental climates, self-seeding may cause problems. Train seed-raised plants or suckers as central-leader standards (*see p.26*), pruning when dormant to produce a clear trunk of 2–3m (6–10ft).

If the leader is lost or cut out, the resulting suckers can be thinned to develop a multi-stemmed tree. Keep pruning of mature trees to a minimum.

A. altissima responds vigorously to annual or biennial coppicing (*see p.34*), producing new shoots 2m (6ft) or more in height with large, striking leaves. To renovate, coppice and then select a single stem to train as a central leader.

OTHER ORNAMENTAL TREES
ADANSONIA Training is generally unnecessary. Established trees have no special pruning needs.

AGONIS Leader may need training upwards when young, otherwise pruning when established is best kept to a minimum.

ALBIZIA *SWAMP WATTLE*

Large, mainly semi-deciduous trees, with feathery foliage and pink, yellow or white "powder-puff" flowers. Most commonly grown species are fast-growing trees. In frost-prone climates with hot summers *A. julibrissin* f. *rosea* will grow and flower well provided the young wood has been ripened the previous year.

■ **WHEN TO PRUNE** Spring, as growth begins.

■ **TRAINING AND PRUNING** Train as branched-head standards, letting the leader divide, or pruning it if necessary to induce branching (*see p.26*), at 1.2–2m (4–6ft). Established trees generally do not need pruning, although in cool climates frost-damaged growth may need removing in spring. *A. julibrissin* tolerates pruning to restrict size: cut back last year's growth to four or five buds, or 7–10cm (3–4in), of the old wood. It can also be pollarded (*see p.34*); if renovating using this method, new shoots must be carefully selected to recreate a branch framework.

ALNUS *ALDER*

Hardy trees grown for their catkins and foliage, and for their tolerance of a wide range of soil conditions. Most alders are pyramidal in habit, naturally developing straight trunks with well-spaced branches. Although usually trained with a central leader, many species, including *Alnus incana* and *A. japonica*, will naturally develop as multi-stemmed trees, a suitable form for informal plantings. *A. glutinosa*, the common alder, is a familiar waterside tree of narrowly pyramidal habit but often multi-stemmed and spreading. *A. incana*, the grey alder, is similar but with grey-downy leaves. Its cut-leaved cultivar 'Laciniata' and the yellow-leaved 'Aurea' may be grown from cuttings or grafted.

■ **WHEN TO PRUNE** After leaf-fall in autumn until mid-winter. Minor pruning may be carried out safely in summer.

■ **TRAINING AND PRUNING** To form a central-leader standard (*see p.26*), clear the stem to 1.5–2m (5–6ft). Lower laterals are often shed naturally by *A. cordata*, *A. firma* and *A. rubra*. With species (such as *A. incana* and *A. japonica*) that tend to branch from the base, if a standard is required, train a single main stem as early as possible, or let them develop naturally as multi-stemmed trees – if necessary, prune them to the base (*see p.28*) to produce this form. Established trees have no special pruning needs, but respond to hard pruning if necessary.

Amelanchier, *see* Dictionary of Ornamental Shrubs, *p.173*

ARBUTUS

Evergreen trees with dark foliage, warm-toned bark, panicles of white flowers and red strawberry-like fruits. Though they tolerate pruning, none transplants well, so plant as young as possible, with shelter from cold, dry winds; *Arbutus* are frost-tender when young (but regenerate well after frost damage). They generally need minimal training. *A. menziesii*, *A. andrachne* and *A. × andrachnoides* need firm support until well established, or they may lean over with age.

A. MENZIESII

MADRONA

One of the most attractive species, with large flower panicles and smooth, peeling, red-brown bark. It forms a tall, spreading tree with a branched head, although it often retains a central leader some way into the crown.

■ **WHEN TO PRUNE** Spring, as soon as any danger of frost is over.

■ **TRAINING AND PRUNING** Stake newly planted trees well, and allow to develop naturally, removing low laterals as for a standard tree (*see p.26*) to display the bark on the trunk, if required. Cut frost-damaged growth hard back once live growth is clearly distinguishable.

Established pruning is best kept to a minimum, though the careful removal of low branches is tolerated if a taller trunk is desired. As the tree matures, small branches within the canopy die off naturally and should be cut out as seen.

OTHER ARBUTUS

A. ANDRACHNE, A. × ANDRACHNOIDES As for *A. menziesii*.
A. UNEDO (strawberry tree) Commonly a tall shrub (which can be allowed to develop naturally), but can make a small tree in favourable climates. To produce a tree, train and prune as for *A. menziesii*.

B

BETULA *BIRCH*

Hardy, deciduous trees, popular in cool regions for their graceful habit, autumn colour and ornamental bark. They are vulnerable to bracket and rot fungi, and hard pruning is not recommended.

■ **WHEN TO PRUNE** Birches bleed heavily; prune only when fully dormant, from late summer to before mid-winter.

B. ALBOSINENSIS

CHINESE RED BIRCH

An elegant tree, spreading and open with age, whose zig-zag shoots droop at the tips. It has clear yellow autumn colour and warm-toned peeling bark.

■ **TRAINING AND PRUNING** Train as a feathered tree (*see p.25*), or as a central-leader standard (*see p.26*) with a clear trunk of 2m (6ft). Once established, little pruning is needed. In autumn, remove twiggy shoots on the trunk and main branches that obscure the bark.

B. PENDULA

SILVER BIRCH

Semi-weeping tree with delicate foliage and silvery, peeling bark, upright when young and spreading with age, the tips of branchlets usually pendulous. The leaves turn a fine clear yellow in autumn.

Raising the height of a naturally weeping standard (*Betula pendula* 'Tristis')

It is essential to keep the leading shoot firmly staked until the wood has hardened sufficiently for the stem to remain rigid. As the tree grows, tie the leading shoot to a vertical cane attached to the main stake. Continue tying in as growth proceeds until the leader reaches the required height. The weeping crown may then be allowed to develop naturally. Remove any low laterals that develop on the main stem.

Draw the leader up gently but firmly

Bamboo cane lashed to stake

■ **TRAINING AND PRUNING** Train as a central-leader standard (*see p.26*), clearing the trunk to 2m (6ft), or as a feathered tree (*see p.25*). To create a multi-stemmed tree, cut back either close to ground level (*see p.28*), or to about 30–60cm (1–2ft) from the ground, as for *Acer davidii* (*see p.52*). Established trees have no special pruning needs; as for all birches, hard pruning is not recommended.

B. PENDULA 'TRISTIS'

WEEPING BIRCH

Narrow-crowned, elegant, strongly weeping tree, usually top-grafted at a height of about 2–2.2m (6–7ft). It is also possible to grow the tree on its own trunk, from softwood

25 80

m ft

cuttings or low-grafted stocks, in which case very careful vertical training of the main stem to the required height is essential to overcome its naturally pendulous habit.

■ **TRAINING AND PRUNING** Train and, when established, maintain as a weeping standard (*see p.26*), removing any shoots below the graft union. If a taller tree is desired (*see above*), in the early years the leading shoot, which is flexible when the wood is young, may be trained to extend the height of the trunk up to 3–4m (10–12ft).

OTHER BIRCHES
B. CALCICOLA, B. NANA Dwarf shrubs that need no pruning.
B. ERMANII, B. 'INVERLEITH', B. 'JERMYNS', B. PAPYRIFERA, B. PLATYPHYLLA, B. SZECHUANICA, B. UTILIS VAR. JACQUEMONTII (including 'Grayswood Ghost' and 'Silver Shadow') As for *B. albosinensis*.
B. MEDWEDIEWII Naturally densely branched: no special training or pruning.
B. NIGRA As for *B. albosinensis*, although the stem frequently divides naturally at 60–90cm (2–3ft) into two to four stems, forming a multi-stemmed tree on a short trunk.
B. PENDULA 'YOUNGII' Deciduous, mushroom-shaped tree, commonly sold as a weeping standard top-grafted at 2–2.2m (6–7ft). Train as a weeping standard (*see p.26*). This cultivar has a strongly weeping habit and, left to develop naturally, may form a squat dome that is broader than it is tall. Its height can be extended up to 8m (25ft) by vertical training of one of the leading shoots (there may be several bud-grafts), as for *B. pendula* 'Tristis' (*see above*).
B. PUBESCENS As for *B. pendula*.

Betula nigra
Birches with coloured, peeling bark are striking in winter when grown with clear trunks, as multi-stemmed specimens (*as left*) or in small groups. For a group planting, place three seedlings, evenly spaced, in the same, large planting hole, and train each as a central-leader standard.

BRACHYCHITON
BOTTLE TREE, FLAME TREE

Large, fast-growing, evergreen or summer-deciduous trees (sometimes with swollen trunks) that require frost-free conditions, though mature plants of some species withstand short periods of light frost. In subtropical regions, they are grown as central-leader standards and used as shade and street trees. In cold areas, they can be grown under glass, although they need careful shaping and pruning to keep within bounds. Some flowers will be lost, as they are borne only on older wood.

■ **WHEN TO PRUNE** After flowering. Plants grown under glass may also be pruned when dormant, soon after leaf-fall.

■ **TRAINING AND PRUNING** Brachychitons usually form a naturally strong central leader, making them easy to train. They can be trained as a feathered tree (*see p.25*) or as a standard (*see p.26*), clearing the trunk gradually to about 3m (10ft). Once established, specimens grown outdoors need little further pruning. Plants grown under glass will need, and will tolerate, regular pruning as necessary to restrict their size.

OTHER ORNAMENTAL TREES
ALECTRYON Training and pruning are generally unnecessary.
ALLOCASUARINA *See Casuarina, p.57.*
AMHERSTIA Train as a central-leader standard (*see p.26*). Keep pruning thereafter to a minimum.
ANGOPHORA As for *Eucalyptus* (*see p.64*).
BANKSIA Tree species have no special needs, though tolerate shaping when young. For shrub species, *see p.175*.
BARKLYA (BAUHINIA) SYRINGIFOLIA As for *Albizia julibrissin* (*see facing page*) but prune after flowering.
BAUHINIA As for *Albizia julibrissin* (*see facing page*) but prune after flowering. *See also* Dictionary of Climbing Plants, *p.263.*
BOLUSANTHUS Allow *B. speciosus* to develop either as a single-stemmed or as a multi-stemmed tree. Low laterals may be removed to clear the trunk. Pruning when established is generally unnecessary.
BOMBAX Train as a standard, allowing the leader to branch at about 2m (6ft). Established trees tolerate but generally need little pruning.
BROUSSONETIA As for *Morus* (*see p.76*).
BROWNEA As for *Albizia julibrissin* (*see facing page*), but prune after flowering.
BUCKINGHAMIA Train as a central-leader standard (*see p.26*). Keep pruning thereafter to a minimum.
BUTEA *B. monosperma* is best left to develop its untidy, congested habit naturally. Tolerates hard cutting back to the swollen rootstock if required.

C

CARPINUS *HORNBEAM*

25 | 80
m | ft

Hardy, deciduous trees with year-round interest: catkins in spring, winged fruits and foliage colour in autumn, and silvered bark in winter. *Carpinus betulus*, the common hornbeam, is the most often grown. The cultivar 'Fastigiata' is conical when young, but assumes a flame-like outline with age. Hornbeams are usually grown as feathered trees or central-leader standards. Easily trained and very responsive to pruning, they are also ideal for pleaching and hedging. *C. caroliniana* branches freely from the base, so while it is ideal as a hedge, choose *C. betulus* or *C. orientalis* for pleaching or for hedges "on stilts".

■ **WHEN TO PRUNE** From late summer to mid-winter, to avoid severe bleeding.

■ **TRAINING AND PRUNING** Train and prune either as feathered trees (*see p.25*) or central-leader standards (*see p.26*). Established trees need little attention. To use as a hedge, *see p.44*. To pleach, *see p.36*. *C. betulus* 'Fastigiata' looks best as a specimen central-leader standard: clear the stem to 1–2m (3–6ft).

Hornbeams tolerate hard pruning, if necessary, but this may result in twiggy growth that, while ideal for hedging, will not develop into strong replacement branches for a tree unless thinned to strong, well-spaced shoots.

***Carpinus betulus* 'Fastigiata'**
This upright tree should be trained and pruned as for the common hornbeam.

CARYA *HICKORY*

5 | 15
m | ft

Relatively slow-growing, elegant trees that naturally develop long, straight, single trunks and shapely crowns, usually conical but sometimes broad and spreading.

Autumn foliage colour varies from golden yellow to rusty-red in different species. *Carya illinoinensis*, the best nut-bearing species (*see* Pecan, *p.148*), does not grow well in cool maritime climates (as in the British Isles). Ornamental hardy hickories include *C. cordiformis*, *C. glabra* and *C. ovata*.

It is important either to sow seed or to plant out seedlings as young as possible in the final position. Hickories rapidly produce long taproots and do not transplant well from containers unless long pots have been used that allow the root to develop naturally. If the taproot is damaged or pruned on planting, trees are likely to form weak, unstable root systems.

***Carya* flowers**
Even if the climate is too cool for nuts to develop, hickory trees have great ornamental value.

■ **WHEN TO PRUNE** Hickories bleed heavily if pruned in spring, so prune only when fully dormant in autumn or early winter.

■ **TRAINING AND PRUNING** Grow as feathered trees (*see p.25*), or as central-leader standards (*see p.26*) with a clear trunk of 2m (6ft). Little pruning or training is necessary, as most species adopt these forms naturally. Keep pruning of established trees to a minimum. Renovation is seldom effective.

CASSIA *SHOWER TREE*

A huge genus of trees, shrubs and sub-shrubs, of which only a few are grown in gardens, mainly for their flowers. Some are hardy, but most will grow outdoors only in completely frost-free climates.

C. FISTULA

GOLDEN SHOWER, INDIAN LABURNUM

15 | 50
m | ft

Deciduous or semi-evergreen tree, suitable for outdoor cultivation only in tropical areas, where it is valued as a street tree and lawn specimen. In spring, the tree bears pendent racemes of small, fragrant, cup-shaped, bright yellow flowers, followed by dark brown pods to 60cm (2ft) in length. Grown as a central-leader standard, it develops an ovoid crown.

■ **WHEN TO PRUNE** Prune young plants when dormant, and established trees after flowering, if necessary.

■ **TRAINING AND PRUNING** Train as a central-leader standard (*see p.26*), clearing the trunk in the early years to about 2–3m (6–10ft). Established specimens need little pruning other than to remove shoots that will grow to cross others. Cassias tolerate hard pruning well, but are so easily raised from seed that replacement is a preferable option.

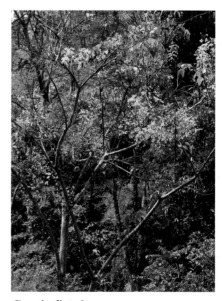

Cassia fistula
Tree species of *Cassia*, such as *C. fistula*, look best trained with a tall clear trunk, echoing their natural habit in their native forest environment.

OTHER CASSIAS
C. CORYMBOSA (syn. SENNA CORYMBOSA)
See Dictionary of Ornamental Shrubs, *p.182*.
C. GRANDIS As for *C. fistula*.
C. JAVANICA As for *C. fistula*.

CASTANEA *CHESTNUT*

The trees in this summer-flowering, deciduous genus form spreading, increasingly stately, domed canopies. Their creamy flowers are followed by spiny fruits that may enclose edible nuts. Though chestnuts are mostly fully hardy, only *C. sativa* will thrive in areas with cool summers.

Chestnut trees are grown as central-leader standards. Some species sucker freely, and respond vigorously to hard pruning. Chestnuts were traditionally coppiced for fencing poles; today, coppicing has largely saved *C. dentata* (the American chestnut) from extinction by chestnut blight, which only attacks mature growth; the continually renewed young stems are resistant to the disease.

C. SATIVA

SWEET CHESTNUT,
SPANISH CHESTNUT

Broad, imposing tree with toothed leaves and attractive grey-brown bark. In cool temperate climates, its nuts ripen to edibility only in mild regions, or after very good summers.

20 ‖ 70

m ‖ ft

■ **WHEN TO PRUNE** When dormant, in autumn or winter. Minor pruning may safely be carried out in late summer.

■ **TRAINING AND PRUNING** Train as central-leader standards (*see p.26*), gradually producing a clear trunk of 2–3m (6–10ft). It is important to ensure a balanced, evenly spaced branch system when young, since a lopsided framework of heavy branches is liable to wind and storm damage. Established specimens need little pruning. Remove reverted shoots from variegated cultivars in late summer. Mature trees may lose large limbs, and crown thinning (*see p.33*) or reduction may be needed. Any such work on these heavy-limbed trees should be carried out only by a professional arboriculturist.

OTHER CHESTNUTS
C. ALNIFOLIA, C. PUMILA Shrubby, suckering species best allowed to develop their thicket-like habit naturally. Tolerate thinning as for *Amelanchier stolonifera* (*see p.173*).
C. DENTATA As for *C. sativa*.
C. MOLLISSIMA Resistant to chestnut blight. As for *C. sativa*.
To grow *C. sativa* for its nuts, *see also* Chestnuts, *p.148*.

CATALPA *BEAN TREE*

Hardy, deciduous trees with spreading crowns and handsome large leaves, and erect panicles of purplish-pink or white blooms in summer, followed by long, dark brown pods that persist through the winter. Catalpas prefer a sheltered site. In cool climates, *C. bignonioides* does not flower well; *C. speciosa*, the western bean tree, is more reliable. Catalpas are usually trained initially as central-leader standards, though the crown usually branches naturally as it develops. They are best planted at one or two years old: older specimens may develop large heads, out of proportion to the rootball. Catalpas respond well to hard pruning and make good pollards.

C. BIGNONIOIDES

EASTERN CATALPA, INDIAN BEAN TREE

A handsome tree bearing white flowers with yellow-striped and purple-spotted throats in late summer. The foliage, often purple-tinted when young, is particularly attractive in the golden-leaved cultivar 'Aurea', which is often pollarded to increase the size of its leaves. In cool climates, unripened wood may die back following poor summers.

18 ‖ 60

m ‖ ft

■ **WHEN TO PRUNE** When dormant, between autumn and late winter. Prune out frost-damaged growth in spring.

■ **TRAINING AND PRUNING** Train as a central-leader standard (*see p.26*), clearing the stem to 1.2–2m (4–6ft). The leader can then be allowed to branch and produce a low, open, spreading crown, mature specimens often being broader than tall. If you have purchased a ready-trained tree whose head seems too large for its rootball the crown should be thinned on planting (*see also p.23*) to leave a strong framework of only four or five main branches. Established trees need little pruning, although heavy branches may need shortening or removal to balance the framework. This should be done by a professional arboriculturist.

Catalpas respond to very hard pruning (to no lower than 30–60cm/1–2ft); to redevelop a branch framework, retain only the strongest, best-placed new shoots from the regrowth. To maintain as a pollard, cut back annually or every two years (*see p.34*) in late winter.

OTHER CATALPAS
C. SPECIOSA As for *C. bignonioides*.

Pollarded *Catalpa bignonioides*
This tree, suffering from dieback, was pollarded to a framework at about 1.2m (4ft) and has regenerated well, responding with a mass of vigorous young growth that has been carefully thinned (*see p.30*).

OTHER ORNAMENTAL TREES
CALODENDRUM *C. capense* needs little pruning other than to cut back over-long shoots after flowering to maintain its naturally neat outline *See* also Evergreen trees, *p.25*.
CALPURNIA Treat *C. aurea* as for *Albizia julibrissin* (*see p.54*), but prune after flowering, if required.
CARRIEREA Train *C. calycina* as a feathered tree (*see p.25*), pruning soon after leaf-fall in autumn as necessary. Established trees have no special pruning needs.
CASUARINA Pine-like evergreens that develop as feathered trees but may be pruned to clear the trunk (*see* Central-leader standard, *p.26*). Otherwise, little pruning is necessary. *C. stricta* and *C. glauca* tolerate clipping, and make good hedges (*see p.44*).
CEDRELA *See Toona*, *p.90*.
CEIBA *C. pentandra* naturally forms an upright, single-stemmed tree with no special training or pruning needs. It will tolerate fairly severe pruning if required.

CELTIS *HACKBERRY, NETTLE TREE*

Hardy, small to medium-sized deciduous trees with alternate leaves and well-spaced, horizontal branches that droop at the tip. Most are best grown as single-stemmed, central-leader trees. Poor growing conditions and transplantation shock often result in the loss of the leading shoot, which may be difficult to replace. If possible, purchase seed-raised specimens, as these are easier to train than grafted plants. Plant as young as possible, in a site sheltered from frost and wind, and use only a low-nitrogen fertilizer. The trunk must be cleared of laterals while the tree is young, as, with the exception of *C. occidentalis*, hackberries are very prone to decay and to form cavities, which large wounds made later in the tree's life will encourage.

C. AUSTRALIS

MEDITERRANEAN HACKBERRY, SOUTHERN NETTLE TREE

Deciduous, spreading tree with pointed, sharply toothed, lance-shaped leaves and insignificant flowers that are followed by purple-black fruits.

■ **WHEN TO PRUNE** When dormant in winter, before growth resumes in early spring.

■ **TRAINING AND PRUNING** Train as a central-leader standard (*see p.26*), aiming to clear the stem to about one-quarter of the young tree's overall height after the first two growing seasons. In exposed areas or northern climates, retaining the leader is difficult, but possible with patience. Once the required length of stem has been cleared, little further pruning is needed. Rub out water shoots (*see p.30*) that develop around pruning wounds when they are young, to avoid having to make future unnecessary cuts.

Mature trees may produce vigorous, vertical shoots which, if allowed to develop, increase the load on the horizontal branches, leading to possible breakage. Cut them out to the base as soon as possible: if upright branches have become well established, however, they are best left in place to avoid large pruning wounds. For this reason, too, renovation is rarely successful.

> **OTHER CELTIS**
> C. CAUCASICA, C. OCCIDENTALIS, C. LAEVIGATA As for *C. australis*.

Celtis occidentalis
Celtis are best trained as standards, with a clear trunk to raise their near-horizontal, spreading lower branches above ground level.

CERCIDIPHYLLUM

Cercidiphyllum japonicum (katsura tree) is a graceful deciduous tree, usually forming a conical crown with evenly spaced, upright branches, and sublaterals that become pendulous towards the tips. Its paired, heart-shaped leaves are noted for their autumn colour (which is best on acid soil). Although fully hardy, *C. japonicum* does better in a sheltered site in cool climates. It grows naturally as an upright multi-stemmed tree or, equally attractively, with a single central leader. Individual trees determine their own growth habit from a very early age; do not attempt to train or prune them into a different form. *C. japonicum* f. *pendulum* is treated as for the species.

■ **WHEN TO PRUNE** Autumn to late winter, when dormant. Remove dead wood and frost-damaged growth in late spring.

■ **TRAINING AND PRUNING** Trees that naturally adopt a multi-stemmed habit begin to branch at or near ground level at an early age, and need little formative pruning. Remove the lowest laterals when young only where access is necessary – for example, for underplanting. If young plants naturally produce a central leader, train as a central-leader standard (*see p.26*) and clear the lowest two or three whorls of branches to about 1.5m (5ft), to enhance the tree-like character. Established trees need little further pruning. They do not respond well to hard pruning.

Cercidiphyllum japonicum
Allow young trees that branch early to develop naturally as multi-stemmed trees. Use a short angled stake (*see above*) to support very low-branching specimens.

CERATONIA *CAROB, LOCUST BEAN*

Ceratonia siliqua is an evergreen tree bearing long, leathery pods that have a variety of culinary uses. It prefers a Mediterranean-type climate and is very drought-tolerant. There are grafted cultivars selected for their potential to bear heavy crops of pods. Carobs are usually trained with a short trunk to make harvesting easier. While top growth is slow in the first year, carobs quickly develop a long taproot. Young trees sold in long pots or bags that let the root grow naturally will establish more quickly than older, pot-bound ones.

■ **WHEN TO PRUNE** Winter to early spring.

■ **TRAINING AND PRUNING** Prune to form a multi-stemmed tree on a 60–90cm (2-3ft) trunk as for *Acer davidii* (*see illustrations, p.52*). Young trees will tolerate shaping cuts if growth is uneven and straggly: remove branch leaders and shorten sideshoots to make a more compact, bushy crown. Mature trees tolerate trimming to restrict their size, but do not remove too much growth in any one year: the pods are borne on new sideshoots springing from older laterals.

CERCIS *REDBUD*

Deciduous trees and shrubs with alternate leaves, grown for their purplish-pink or white flowers and foliage that colours well in autumn. *Cercis canadensis* 'Forest Pansy' has dark red-purple leaves. The pea-like flowers appear on older wood before or as the leaves emerge. All thrive and flower most freely in areas with long, hot summers. Judas trees develop long taproots and are very susceptible to transplant shock, which may cause the leader to die back, so plant as young as possible, preferably in spring as the buds begin to break. Weak or damaged wood is vulnerable to coral spot; cut affected growth well back into healthy wood in late summer.

C. SILIQUASTRUM

JUDAS TREE

Deciduous, often multi-stemmed, bushy tree with purple or pink flowers and heart-shaped leaves, beautiful as a specimen tree. Old trees tend to lean, and may need propping or renovation.

■ **WHEN TO PRUNE** Prune and remove any frost-damaged shoots in early summer.

■ **TRAINING AND PRUNING** Train and, if necessary, prune to create a multi-stemmed tree on a trunk of 60–90cm (2–3ft), as for *Acer davidii* (*see p.52*). Select three to five strong laterals, well-spaced around the main stem, to form a framework. The natural tendency is for stems to cluster, forming tight, V-shaped crotches that are easily split by strong

Early flowers
Cercis are unusual among hardy trees in flowering directly on bare branches.

wind. The resulting damage renders the tree susceptible to rot.

Established trees need no special pruning, but can be completely renovated by cutting back close to ground level and once again selecting, at most, five strong, young stems to form a frame-work. This is best done during clear, dry weather in late spring or early summer to deter the entry of decay organisms.

> **OTHER CERCIS**
>
> C. CANADENSIS Train as a feathered tree (*see p.27*) or clear the stem to about 90cm (36in). For a small garden, can also be trained as a multi-stemmed tree as for *C. siliquastrum*. Established trees have no special pruning needs; they do not respond well to renovation.
> C. CHINENSIS Shrubby species; needs no special training or pruning. Frost-tender, it may be wall-trained (*see Magnolia grandiflora, p.74*) in cool climates.
> C. OCCIDENTALE As for *C. siliquastrum*.
> C. RACEMOSA As for *C. canadensis*. Thrives only in areas with hot summers and mild winters.

CLADRASTIS

Hardy, deciduous trees and shrubs grown for their form, flowers and autumn colour, usually clear yellow; both this and the wisteria-like flowers are produced most reliably in areas with long, hot summers. Cladrastis rapidly develop long taproots, and must be planted young.

C. LUTEA SYN. C. VIRGILIA

VIRGILIA, YELLOW WOOD

A deciduous tree with alternate leaves and white flowers, forming a broad, flattened, dome-shaped canopy with heavy branches. Formative pruning is vital: it is essential to avoid creating a low-branching or multi-stemmed structure that will become unsafe. The wood is brittle, and narrow, V-shaped crotches, especially those with included bark (*see p.11*), frequently split. The resulting damage usually lets in decay, eventually leading to the decline of the tree. Because of the potential for structural weaknesses, do not plant this species close to buildings or busy thoroughfares.

■ **WHEN TO PRUNE** Midsummer.

■ **TRAINING AND PRUNING** Train as a central-leader standard (*see p.26*), clearing the trunk to about 1.5–2m (5–6ft). Select only evenly and well spaced laterals to form branches, and remove any that grow at narrow angles to the main stem. Established trees have no special pruning needs. They do not respond well to renovation: the timber is prone to splitting, and damaged branches are best removed by a professional.

> **OTHER CLADRASTIS**
>
> C. PLATYCARPA As for *C. lutea*, but is less prone to structural weaknesses. Makes a much smaller tree in cool areas.
> C. SINENSIS In continental climates and mild maritime climates, as for *C. lutea*. In cooler regions, it forms a much smaller tree that is best allowed to develop naturally.

CINNAMOMUM

The evergreen, frost-tender camphor tree, *Cinnamomum camphora*, grows to 12m (40ft) or more. Its single trunk usually branches early, resulting in a low canopy formed by competing, near-upright limbs. Prune in summer, after the first flush of rapid growth. Train as a central-leader standard (*see p.26*), with a clear trunk of

about 2m (6ft). If branching is allowed before this length of trunk is cleared, crown lifting (*see p.33*) may be necessary in later years to allow access beneath the tree. Established trees have no special pruning needs, though they renovate well. To restrict size under glass, treat as for *Camellia* (*see p.180*).

> **OTHER ORNAMENTAL TREES**
>
> CHORISIA Train as a central-leader standard (*see p.26*), with a clear trunk of 2m (6ft) to accommodate the spreading branches. Renovates well.
> CITHAREXYLUM Train as a central-leader standard (*see p.26*), with a clear trunk of 1.5–2m (5-6ft). When established, little pruning is required. May be tip-pruned in
>
> summer to restrict growth and will tolerate harder pruning if necessary.
> COCCOLOBA No special training or pruning required.
> COLVILLEA Train *C. racemosa* as a central-leader standard (*see p.26*), with a clear trunk of 1.35–2m (4½–6ft). Maintain the leader through the crown for as long as possible.
>
> CORDIA Train as a central-leader standard (*see p.26*) with a clear trunk of 1.35–1.5m (4½–5ft). Established trees have no special pruning needs.
> CORDYLINE See Palms and palm-like plants, *p.41*.

CORNUS *DOGWOOD, CORNEL*

Trees in this mainly deciduous, fully to half-hardy genus are grown for their form and foliage, and for the pale, papery bracts that surround the summer flowers.

C. CAPITATA

BENTHAM'S CORNEL

Tiered, evergreen or semi-evergreen tree with dark leaves, pale yellow bracts and strawberry-like fruits. In cool climates it usually grows as a smaller, multi-stemmed tree or large shrub; wall-training will give extra frost protection.

■ **WHEN TO PRUNE** Autumn to early spring.

■ **TRAINING AND PRUNING** In mild regions, can be grown as a feathered tree with a single trunk (*see p.25*). In cold and exposed areas, it is best allowed to develop naturally as a multi-stemmed tree, thinning if necessary to ensure a well-spaced framework of branches. To wall-train, *see p.74*. Keep pruning of established trees to the minimum.

C. CONTROVERSA

Hardy, deciduous tree with a tiered habit, white bracts, red-purple autumn colour and red shoots in winter. Needs a sheltered site, as it is prone to canopy distortion by prevailing winds.

■ **WHEN TO PRUNE** Autumn to early spring.

■ **TRAINING AND PRUNING** Train as a central-leader standard (*see p.26*), with a clear trunk of one-quarter to one-third of the young tree's height. Little other pruning is needed. Does not respond to hard pruning; wind-pruning is hard to rectify.

C. KOUSA

Hardy tree best allowed to develop as a central-leader or branched-head standard with minimal attention.

■ **WHEN TO PRUNE** Autumn to early spring. Remove dead wood after flowering.

■ **TRAINING AND PRUNING** Clear a short trunk, to 60–90cm (2–3ft), then keep pruning to an absolute minimum. When removing dead wood, take care not to damage the twiggy flowering growth. Does not tolerate hard pruning.

Cornus controversa

Most dogwoods make beautiful free-standing small trees. Those that develop a tiered habit with age, such as *Cornus capitata*, *C. controversa* and *C. florida*, can be fan-trained on a preferably sunny wall (*see also Magnolia grandiflora, p.74*).

OTHER DOGWOODS

C. ALTERNIFOLIA Equally attractive allowed to develop as a multi-stemmed feathered tree, or trained as a standard as for *C. controversa*, clearing the trunk very slowly to 1–1.5m (3–5ft). In the first two or three years, limit pruning to the removal of competing leaders and strong low laterals.
C. 'EDDIE'S WHITE WONDER' Best left to develop naturally with minimal attention. Also recommended for wall training (*see Magnolia grandiflora, p.74*).
C. FLORIDA As for *C. kousa*, clearing a short trunk (*see p.26*) to 60–90cm (2–3ft) if desired. Shading and frost damage may spoil the form, resulting in an untidy, multi-stemmed tree that should not be pruned in an attempt to improve it.
C. NUTTALLII As for *C. controversa*, with a clear trunk to about 1.5m (5ft). A short-lived tree, and prone to dieback; does not respond well to hard pruning and is best replaced.
See also Dictionary of Ornamental Shrubs, *p.186*.

CORYLUS *HAZEL*

While the shrubby hazel species are valued for their nuts, trees in this hardy, deciduous genus are grown for their foliage and erect habit, and for the yellow, male catkins borne in late winter and early spring on bare branches with attractively rugged bark. The tiny female flowers fringe the trees in a red haze in early spring.

C. COLURNA

TURKISH HAZEL

Conical tree with spreading, rather twisted branches, best grown with a clear trunk to display the bark.

■ **WHEN TO PRUNE** Winter, when dormant.

■ **TRAINING AND PRUNING** Train as a central-leader standard (*see p.26*), gradually clearing the trunk to about 2m (6ft). Always remove competing leaders as soon as possible. Established trees need little pruning other than to remove occasional suckers at the base. They respond well to hard pruning.

OTHER HAZELS

C. AVELLANA, C. MAXIMA See Dictionary of Ornamental Shrubs, *p.187*. Grown for edible nuts, see Cobnuts and Filberts, *p.149*.
C. AVELLANA 'PENDULA' Weeping cultivar usually top-grafted onto a clear stem at about 2m (6ft) to form a weeping standard. To maintain this tree form, *see p.26*. Prune in winter.
C. JACQUEMONTII As for *C. colurna*.

Corylus colurna

A pleasing tree structure, with a straight trunk and well-spaced branches, makes the most of the ornamental value of shaggy hazel bark in winter.

+ CRATAEGOMESPILUS *BRONVAUX MEDLAR*

This tree is a hardy, deciduous graft hybrid between *Crataegus* and *Mespilus,* grafted on to *Crataegus* stock. It is grown as a branched-head standard, forming a round-headed tree bearing clusters of white flowers in profusion during late spring and early summer, followed by medlar-like fruits.

■ **WHEN TO PRUNE** Autumn to early spring. Summer pruning may also be necessary.

■ **TRAINING AND PRUNING** Train with a clear trunk of no more than 2m (6ft) (*see p.26*), then allow the crown to branch naturally. Pruning of established trees should be minimal, since it can create an imbalance between the two genetically distinct tissues of which the tree is composed. Shoots occasionally develop comprising tissue of only one of the parent species. These need not be removed unless very vigorous, when they should be cut back by up to one-third in summer, so that they do not become dominant. Does not respond well to renovation measures.

× CRATAEMESPILUS

Crataemespilus grandiflora is a vigorous, deciduous hybrid valued for its weeping habit, profusion of white flowers in late spring, and autumn colour. Grown as a central-leader standard, it makes a beautiful specimen, up to 8m (25ft) tall.

Train as a central-leader standard (*see p.26*), pruning when dormant. Although the laterals are horizontal when young, they will become increasingly pendulous with age, so clear the trunk to about 2m (6ft) so that they do not form an unsightly skirt of foliage around the base. Does not respond well to hard pruning.

CRATAEGUS

Deciduous, usually thorny, hardy trees, often with a congested branch structure, useful as barrier hedging that may be clipped after leaf-fall, or pruned more informally on a two- or three-year cycle to obtain more flowers and fruits, which are borne on older wood (*see* Hedges, *p.44*). Tree-forming species tend to branch from the base, but are easily trained as standards (which may be trimmed into formal "lollipop" shapes).

■ **WHEN TO PRUNE** Between autumn and early spring.

C. CRUS-GALLI

COCKSPUR THORN

Small tree with a widely spreading, often flat-topped crown, white flowers and red fruits. The leaves turn orange in autumn. It is an ideal standard tree for a small garden.

■ **TRAINING AND PRUNING** There is usually a strong central leader that can be allowed to lose dominance as the crown develops. Clear two or three whorls of lower branches (*see p.26*) as the tree reaches semi-maturity, to give a clear trunk of about 2m (6ft). Established trees need little pruning.

C. MONOGYNA

COMMON HAWTHORN, MAY

Round-headed tree, with fragrant white flowers and red haws. It is best trained as a central-leader specimen, but can also be left to develop more naturally as a multi-stemmed tree. The cultivar 'Pendula'

Crataegus blossom
The flowers are followed by fruits ("haws") that may be orange, red, yellow, blue or black.

is usually sold as a top-grafted weeping standard (*see p.26*). It sometimes occurs among seed-raised plants, however, and these should be trained with a clear trunk to about 2.5m (8ft) to accommodate the weeping branches.

■ **TRAINING AND PRUNING** *C. monogyna* has a strong tendency to branch from the base. To obtain a tree-like form, it is best to purchase a whip (*see p.22*) and feed in the first three years with nitrogenous fertilizer in early spring to encourage vigorous, more upright growth that is easier to train. Do not start to remove any laterals until after planting in the final location, then clear the trunk gradually (*see p.26*) to about 1.5–2m (5–6ft). Mature trees need little pruning. Crown congestion is natural; only remove badly rubbing branches. Over-thinning may cause branches to twist and tear in high winds. Responds well to hard pruning.

OTHER CRATAEGUS
C. DOUGLASII, C. OXYACANTHA, C. TANACETIFOLIA As for *C. monogyna*.
C. × DUROBRIVENSIS Shrubby in habit, with no special pruning needs.
C. × PERSISTENS As for *C. crus-galli*. In cool climates, thin young trees on planting to reduce the risk of frost damage.
C. × PRUNIFOLIA (syn. C. PERSIMILIS 'PRUNIFOLIA') As for *C. crus-galli*.

CYPHOMANDRA

Cyphomandra betacea (tamarillo, tree tomato) is a small, evergreen tree with waxy, pink-tinged flowers borne on new growth, followed by egg-shaped, fleshy red fruits, edible only when fully ripe and cooked. Grown widely in tropical to warm temperate regions, in cool climates it needs a heated conservatory or glasshouse. Seedlings develop an erect, sparsely branched habit, while trees grown from cuttings are more bushy and spreading.

■ **WHEN TO PRUNE** In early spring, just before new growth begins.

■ **TRAINING AND PRUNING** Over the first two or three years, aim to create an open, branched crown on a clear stem to a height of about 50–75cm (20–30in). Let the leader break at this height to form a broad, open head. Young trees grow fast; if they reach 1.5m (5ft) before producing laterals, prune back to a strong bud at about 90cm (3ft) from the ground to stimulate branching.

To promote the production of flowering wood, and contain tree size if necessary, prune established trees annually, cutting back one in three of the fruited laterals to the main branches. Take care as branches are brittle. Mature trees may require staking or bracing since the root system is fibrous and relatively shallow. Tamarillos have a productive life of only about eight years, so replace rather than renovate old trees.

OTHER ORNAMENTAL TREES
CORYNOCARPUS Evergreen (*see p.25*) with no special needs; if desired, the trunk may be cleared to 2m (6ft).
CYDONIA See Quince, *p.121*.

D

DAVIDIA *HANDKERCHIEF TREE*

Davidia involucrata
is a fully hardy,
deciduous tree of
elegant habit with
graceful, pendent
white bracts that
are produced from late
spring on the previous year's growth.
The growth habit is very distinctive,
with long terminal shoots and very short,
almost spur-like sideshoots. It is the longer
growths that must be used to create the
branch framework. Davidias are best
grown as central-leader standards with
quite a tall trunk, so that the bracts hang
down, and formative training is vital
during the first five or six years. A multi-
stemmed tree cannot be transformed by
pruning into a central-leader standard.
Trees may naturally lose their leaves
unevenly in autumn: this should not
be mistaken for dieback or disease.

■ **WHEN TO PRUNE** Autumn to early spring.

■ **TRAINING AND PRUNING** Train as a
central-leader standard (*see p.26*) with
a clear trunk of 2–3m (6–10ft). The tree

Davidia involucrata
Davidia is also known as the ghost tree
or dove tree; all of its common names are
inspired by its striking large, white bracts.

naturally forms a strong central leader
surrounded by strongly upright laterals.
These can usually be allowed to grow
without check unless very vigorous,
upright laterals overtake the leader.
If these are allowed to develop, they
result in an undesirable multi-stemmed
crown; remove them, or tip back by up
to one-quarter. If the leader is damaged,
select and train in a long lateral as a
replacement (*see p.24*).
     Established trees need no special
attention. They do not respond well
to hard pruning and are reluctant to
branch, so a poor form is hard to rectify.

*Regrowth after last
year's pruning cut*

*Cut made
previous year*

*Lateral now being
completely removed*

Clearing the trunk
Davidia looks best trained with a clear
trunk, tall enough to allow access
below the lowest branches to view the
bracts from beneath. As for most trees,
remove laterals in stages, shortening
them in one year and then cutting
them back to the main stem the next.

DELONIX *FLAME TREE, ROYAL POINCIANA*

Delonix regia is
a deciduous tree
widely grown in
subtropical and
tropical regions for
its showy red flowers.
Its broad, flat-topped
crown makes it an ideal shade tree. Plant
as young as possible: if the long, stout
taproot is damaged, the tree may be
unstable when mature.

■ **WHEN TO PRUNE** Late winter, before
the new flush of growth begins in spring.

■ **TRAINING AND PRUNING** Train initially
as a central-leader tree, with a clear trunk
to a height of about 2m (6ft). The leader
quickly loses dominance and cannot be
maintained. To support the spreading
crown, main framework branches must
be well spaced around the trunk. In the
early years, select about five strong
laterals arising from different, evenly
spaced points, and remove the remainder.
Provided that formative pruning is
carried out early, little further pruning
is necessary. *Delonix* will respond to
renovation, but replacement is preferable.

DIOSPYROS

Elegant, spreading
trees, fully to frost-
hardy, grown for
their attractive
form and foliage
that often colours
well in autumn. In
warm climates, some species are grown
for their fruits (*see Persimmon, p. 131*).
     Train as central-leader standards
(*see p.26*) with the trunk clear to a height
of 1.2–2m (4–6ft) to allow the semi-
pendulous branches to sweep almost
to ground level. Prune between autumn
and early spring. In cool maritime
climates, where trees need a well-lit site
to develop a good form, the leading shoot
of *D. virginiana* is sensitive to frost damage
when young. Plant in a sheltered site; if
the leader is damaged or lost, select and
train in a new leader as soon as possible.
When established, *Diospyros* need little
pruning (remove any dead wood when
in full leaf) and do not respond well
when cut back hard.

DOMBEYA

Small, fast-growing, bushy trees, bearing
pendent flower clusters in winter or early
spring, on wood made the previous year.
They can only be grown outdoors in
warm, frost-free climates, where they
are best allowed to develop naturally as
feathered trees (*see p.25*), needing little
pruning. Make any shaping cuts in early
summer. Specimens grown in a warm
conservatory tolerate pruning to restrict
size. Grow as a tallish pollard (*see p.34*)
to display the flowers at eye level (*see also
Brugmansia, p.177*). Cut back flowered
shoots by about one-third in spring or
early summer. Most dombeyas respond
vigorously when hard pruned.

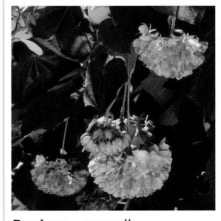

Dombeya × cayeuxii
Though dombeyas tolerate pruning to restrict
size, grow them tall enough to display the
appearance and fragrance of the flowers.

E

EMBOTHRIUM

Embothrium coccineum
(Chilean firebush)
is a small, evergreen
or semi-evergreen
tree grown primarily
for the abundance
of vivid red flowers
produced along its branches in late
spring or early summer. Often suckering
in habit, it is usually grown as a multi-
stemmed tree, but in mild, damp,
maritime climates may also be trained
with a central leader. It tolerates frosts
and coastal conditions, but must have
shelter from cold, dry winds.

■ **WHEN TO PRUNE** Late summer, after
flowering. Remove dead wood in spring.

■ **TRAINING AND PRUNING** In most areas,
E. coccineum is best allowed to develop
naturally with little or no pruning,
resulting in a multi-stemmed specimen
with each stem arising from below
ground. In mild, damp climates, where

growth is rapid, to avoid congestion
at maturity, select three to five strong
stems to provide a framework that is left
clothed with laterals to ground level. On
exposed sites, also thin out young stems,
by about one in five, to reduce wind
resistance. To grow as a single-stemmed
specimen, train as a central-leader tree
(*see p.26*) with a clear trunk to a height
of about 1.5m (5ft). Newly planted trees
need initial staking but root growth is
vigorous and plants stabilize quickly.
Remove basal suckers as seen.

Because of the suckering habit, multi-
stemmed trees may develop into a mass of
vertical stems sparsely furnished with thin
horizontal laterals, and overcrowding may
result in dieback and rot. Remove dead
stems with a sharp spade, cutting them out
from below ground, thus leaving room for
new, replacement growth that will emerge
from the roots. It is also possible to grub
out old plants, leaving young stems to
regenerate from the periphery of the
original plant.

**Embothrium
coccineum**
The previous year's
wood flowers at
the same time as
extension growth
is being made from
the shoot tip.

EMMENOPTERYS

Emmenopterys henryi
is a deciduous tree
of open habit with
slender branches
and rough, attractive
bark. Its terminal
clusters of white
flowers are produced freely only in
areas with long, hot summers. In cool
climates, provide a warm, sheltered,
sunny site.

■ **WHEN TO PRUNE** Between autumn and
early spring.

■ **TRAINING AND PRUNING** Train as
a central-leader standard (*see p.26*). If
the leader is damaged by frost, it is difficult
to train in a replacement, though not
impossible with patience. Once established,
pruning is best kept to a minimum. Young
plants tend to put on extension growth at
the expense of an increase in girth, giving
a rather spindly appearance. Pruning will
not improve this habit; the tree naturally
becomes less spindly with maturity. It
does not respond well to hard pruning,
tending to produce a proliferation of
soft, frost-sensitive growth.

ERYTHRINA

Half-hardy to frost-tender, usually
thorny trees bearing racemes of
brilliantly coloured, pea-like flowers.

E. CRISTA-GALLI

COCKSPUR CORAL TREE

Deciduous, upright,
small, bushy tree,
grown in warm
climates as a
spreading, heavy-
branched, central-
leader standard. In cool climates it is best
planted against a warm, sunny wall. It may
die back to ground level in winter, regrowing
as a rounded, untidy shrub that nevertheless
produces brilliant crimson flowers.

■ **WHEN TO PRUNE** When fully dormant,
between autumn and early spring.

■ **TRAINING AND PRUNING** In warm
climates, train as a central-leader standard
(*see p.26*). Once established, little pruning
is needed except to remove dieback. In
cool climates, the inevitable loss of the
leader results in shrubby growth that
is best cut back annually (*see* Coppicing
and pollarding, *p.34*) when dormant.
Mulch to protect the base from frost.

OTHER ERYTHRINAS
E. CORALLODENDRON In warm climates,
as for *E. crista-galli*. In cool conditions
grows naturally as a lax shrub with no
special pruning needs.
E. VARIEGATA (syn. **E. INDICA**) Needs
minimal training and pruning.

Erythrina crista-galli
In cool climates, cut all stems back to a low
framework each spring, before growth begins.

OTHER ORNAMENTAL TREES
DILLENIA Develops naturally as a
branched-head standard, similar to
Catalpa bignonioides (*see p.57*).
DOCYNIA As for *Malus baccata* (*see p.75*).
Tolerates pruning well.
EHRETIA Train with a clear trunk to about
1.2m (4ft), then let the crown branch.
Responds well to hard pruning.
ELAEOCARPUS *See* Evergreen trees, *p.25*.

EUCALYPTUS *EUCALYPT, GUM TREE*

A huge genus of evergreens, ranging in habit from large forest trees to shrubby "mallees" that produce slender stems from a tuberous rootstock (lignotuber). They are grown for their habit, the often fragrant flowers (rarely produced in cool climates), aromatic foliage and peeling, mosaic bark in shades of cream, grey-pink and soft green. Most thrive only in frost-free climates; *E. gunnii*, *E. dalrympleana*, *E. parvifolia* and *E. pauciflora* are fully hardy if sheltered from cold, dry winds and given a deep winter mulch. Some species naturally form attractive, informal multi-stemmed trees. Others are trained as central-leader standards, although the leader may lose dominance as the tree matures. Many develop crooked trunks even if staked when young; poorly formed trees can be cut back hard and retrained (*see below*). This treatment is also the best course for trees that have suffered damage or extensive dieback, often caused by frost or strong, particularly salty, winds. All eucalypts tolerate hard pruning, and several are often grown as pollarded or coppiced, shrub-like specimens for their attractive juvenile foliage.

■ **WHEN TO PRUNE** Winter to spring, when new growth begins, after any danger of late hard frosts in cool climates.

E. DALRYMPLEANA

MOUNTAIN GUM

Fast-growing eucalypt with grey-green leaves that are bronze-tinted when young, and mosaic bark that gradually turns white.

■ **TRAINING AND PRUNING** Train as a central-leader standard (*see p.26*) with a clear trunk to about 2m (6ft). Many specimens grow naturally as central-leader trees; lower limbs can be removed just as they start to die back. Maintain a strong leader up to early maturity.

Established trees need little attention; even large, heavy, horizontal branches are usually sound. If necessary, new branches can be developed by hard pruning, and then thinning the dense regrowth to reduce wind resistance and the likelihood of breakage. *E. dalrympleana* can be pollarded or coppiced when young, but other species are better suited to regular cutting back.

E. GUNNII

CIDER GUM

Can be grown as a central-leader standard, or as a pollard or a coppiced shrub with perpetually juvenile, round, silver-blue leaves. A row of coppiced shrubs, with alternate specimens cut back each year, makes an attractive hedge.

■ **TRAINING AND PRUNING** Train as a tree as for *E. dalrympleana*. Poorly formed or damaged trees should be replaced or completely renovated (*see below*), rather than having individual branches removed. To produce and maintain a pollarded or coppiced specimen, *see p.34*. Cut back all new growth annually or every other year in early spring. Pollarding or coppicing is best initiated from the start, rather than used on overlarge or damaged mature trees.

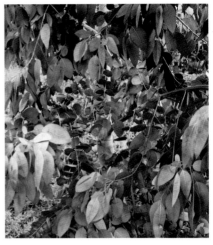

Eucalyptus foliage
Many eucalypts have juvenile (*centre*) and adult foliage that is quite different in form.

OTHER EUCALYPTS

E. CAESIA SUBSP. MAGNA (syn. E. 'SILVER PRINCESS'), E. CITRIODORA, E. FICIFOLIA, E. GLOBULUS, E. LEUCOXYLON, E. PARVIFOLIA, E. URNIGERA As for *E. dalrympleana*.
E. CINEREA, E. EREMOPHILA, E. LEHMANNII As for *E. gunnii*.
E. COCCIFERA As for *E. dalrympleana*, to display the bark well. In cooler climates, may adopt a stunted or shrubby habit.
E. KRUSEANA Small shrubby species needing minimal pruning; frost-hardy, ideal for conservatories.
E. MACROCARPA, E. TETRAPTERA Best allowed to develop a multi-stemmed, lax habit with minimal pruning.
E. PAUCIFLORA As for *E. citriodora*.
E. PAUCIFLORA SUBSP. NIPHOPHILA As for *E. gunnii*.
E. RUBIDA As for *E. dalrympleana*.

Retraining a central leader (*Eucalyptus gunnii*)

Before pruning (spring)
Eucalypts often grow crooked and may need staking for support. It is better to renovate, a process best repeated every five or six years.

Reducing top growth first for safety, saw stem straight across here (see Felling a small tree, p.31)

Year 1, summer

1 *Select and stake a strong stem for vertical growth. Ties must be secure but allow some movement.*

2 *Cut all other new stems back to the ground or the stump.*

Vigorous regrowth has typical vertical habit

Year 3, summer

1 *Let a crown of branches develop at the desired height, removing only crossing shoots or laterals making narrow V-angles with the trunk.*

2 *Remove shoots on the desired length of clear stem (new growth can be rubbed out as breaking buds), and any further basal growth.*

EUCRYPHIA

Elegant trees, some upright, some multi-stemmed, grown for their glossy foliage and beautiful, four-petalled flowers. Frost- to fully hardy, in cool climates they benefit from a sheltered site. They generally need little pruning or training, and do not respond well when cut back hard. In cool climates, however, pruning may be necessary to counter the effects of frosts and cold winds.

E. × NYMANSENSIS

Columnar, evergreen tree with slender, upright branches and few laterals. The form develops naturally, but is difficult to maintain if the tree is exposed to prolonged cold; even mature trees may be extensively damaged by hard frosts or cold winds. Careful pruning and feeding (*see p.13*) may restore the form.

■ **WHEN TO PRUNE** Spring, if required.

■ **TRAINING AND PRUNING** Little or no formative pruning is required. To restore winter damage, cut back dead and damaged growth into living wood just above a suitable lateral. If possible, reduce all other branches to the same height. New growth quickly adopts the upright habit and requires little further attention except to thin if overcrowded.

OTHER EUCRYPHIAS
E. CORDIFOLIA, E. LUCIDA, E. MOOREI Columnar evergreens; may develop a shrubby habit in cold regions and need an open but sheltered site. Need minimal attention. Remove dead wood in spring.
E. GLUTINOSA Needs little training, usually growing naturally with a central leader and lower branches that may sweep down and then grow upwards as they touch the ground. On windy sites, the crown may become distorted; corrective pruning in spring (*see p.32*) will restore the form if the tree is still young. Avoid pruning mature trees.

OTHER ORNAMENTAL TREES
EUCOMMIA Elm-like tree (*see Ulmus, p.91*) best trained as a central-leader standard (*see p.26*). It is hard to replace a lost leader. Prune when dormant, keeping cuts as small as possible. Does not renovate.
EUPTELEA Usually develops naturally as a multi-stemmed tree (*see p.28*); trunks may be cleared to 75–90cm (30–36in) if desired, as for a birch (*see Betula, p.57*). When established, sparse-leaved older wood can be removed in the dormant season to encourage new growth.

F

FAGUS *BEECH*

Fully hardy, deciduous trees with dense, spreading crowns and long, straight, smooth-barked, silver-grey trunks, grown for their habit, fresh green leaves (some cultivars have rich purple foliage) and copper and golden autumn colour. They make fine specimens for parkland, avenues and large gardens, and *F. sylvatica* is ideal for formal hedging.

F. SYLVATICA

COMMON BEECH, EUROPEAN BEECH

Stately tree with pendulous lower branches and dense foliage, conical when young and domed with age. It is shallow-rooted, and trees must be well trained to avoid instability in high winds. Can be grown as a clipped hedge (*see p.44*).

■ **WHEN TO PRUNE** Autumn to early spring. Prune hedges in winter, or midsummer if they show any signs of disease.

■ **TRAINING AND PRUNING** Allow young trees to develop initially as feathered trees (*see p.25*). The lower laterals protect the young bark of these forest natives from sun scorch. Removing laterals early may also encourage dual leaders. When the tree is six to eight years old, growing with a strong, distinct central leader, clear the trunk (*see p.26*) over four or more years, ideally always removing laterals before they reach 6cm (2½in) in diameter. Small wounds seal quickly, leaving no obvious stem blemish. A clear trunk of 2.5–3m (8–10ft) lets the pendulous lower branches fall to just above ground level. As the crown develops, remove any strongly upright laterals that may compete with the leader. Pruning of mature trees (rarely necessary) should be carried out only by a professional.

Fagus sylvatica 'Pendula'

This strongly weeping cultivar may already, when purchased, have developed laterals to below soil level. Shorten them to an outward-facing bud.

OTHER BEECHES
F. JAPONICA, F. ORIENTALIS As for *F. sylvatica*.
F. ENGLERIANA Multi-stemmed tree (*see p.28*), often dividing just above ground level. Needs no special pruning.
F. GRANDIFOLIA As for *F. sylvatica*. More effort is required to maintain a central leader. Planting as young as possible and extra feeding will help.
F. SYLVATICA 'DAWYCK' Fastigiate form (*see p.18*), needs no pruning.
F. SYLVATICA 'PAGNYENSIS' Usually sold grafted; keep pruning to a minimum.
F. SYLVATICA 'PURPUREA' (Purple or Atropurpurea group) As for *F. sylvatica*, but where possible remove any shoots that revert to green foliage.
F. SYLVATICA 'ZLATIA' Train as a standard (*see p.26*) with a clear trunk to 2–3m (6–10ft), then let the broad, multi-stemmed crown develop naturally.
F. SYLVATICA 'PENDULA' The weeping beech may adopt two habits. If young trees have stout, horizontal branches with slender, pendulous laterals, treat as for *F. sylvatica*. The other form (*see above*) has a distinctive narrow crown, with stems that ascend, then droop, clothed in long, pendent laterals. These laterals will root on touching the ground to produce a distinctive and unusual mature form of great size (*see below*); to encourage this habit, the trunk should not be cleared and pruning should be kept to a minimum.

Mature weeping beech

In time, the narrow-crowned form of *Fagus sylvatica* 'Pendula' may form a monumental specimen with several generations of layers radiating from the parent tree.

FICUS *FIG*

Ornamental tree species in this large and varied genus (for climbers, *see p.271*) are often used as shade trees in warm to tropical regions, or, in cool temperate climates, as foliage plants for the house or heated conservatory. *Ficus carica*, which will tolerate cool-climate conditions, makes a handsome tree but is more commonly grown for its edible fruits (*see* Figs, *p.138*). While tropical species grow into giant trees with a buttressed trunk and a tangled mass of aerial and surface roots, when grown under cover they are far less vigorous, and their size can be restricted by pruning. Young plants benefit from training, but the naturally erratic, congested branch structure, and the bleeding of latex sap, makes pruning of mature trees very difficult. In warm climates *F. benjamina* is used for hedges (*see p.44*) and is wall-trained (*see p.74*).

■ **WHEN TO PRUNE** Late winter, or at any time in frost-free regions.

■ **TRAINING AND PRUNING** In tropical climates, train initially as central-leader standards (*see p.26*) and maintain the leading shoot for as long as possible, clearing the trunk to 2–3m (6–10ft). The leader is often lost early, and is difficult to replace. Allow ample space for growth, and keep pruning of established specimens to a minimum. Remove any plain green shoots on cultivars with variegated or marbled foliage. Under glass or in the home, prune only to confine to the allotted space. Ficus respond well to hard pruning, and even relatively large wounds are soon hidden by new growth.

Ficus benjamina
When grown as a small house or greenhouse plant, trunks can be braided for an ornamental effect (*see* Topiary, *p.48*).

FRANKLINIA

Franklinia alatamaha is a small, deciduous tree grown for its large white flowers and scarlet autumn colour. It grows and flowers best in areas with long, hot summers and mild winters, reaching 6m (20ft) in eastern North America. It grows naturally as a single-stemmed, sparsely branched central-leader standard, and needs little formative pruning. Any that is necessary should be carried out when the tree is dormant, between autumn and early spring. As the tree matures, lower branches may eventually form secondary leaders. Do not shorten them: they will form a broad, structurally sound crown. Once established, prune only to remove any dead wood in summer and carry out other routine tasks (*see p.29*). Does not respond well to hard pruning.

FRAXINUS *ASH*

Mostly hardy, deciduous trees grown for their attractive foliage and impressive stature. Some, notably *F. ornus*, have attractive flowers or, like *F. americana*, colour well in autumn.

■ **WHEN TO PRUNE** Between autumn and early spring, when dormant.

F. EXCELSIOR

COMMON ASH

A large tree with heavy branches, attractive in winter when the youngest bark is flushed yellow. It must have a strong central leader that persists through the crown: forked trees may be unsafe.

35 | 120

m | ft

■ **TRAINING AND PRUNING** Needs little formative pruning, naturally forming a vigorous leader that remains dominant as the crown develops. Train with a clear trunk (*see p.26*) of about 3m (10ft). Prune mature trees only to remove wind damage. Mature ashes produce fast-growing water shoots (*see p.30*) from wounded tissue, especially around large cuts. Rub out as soon as seen; if allowed to develop, they are prone to breakage. Does not respond well to hard pruning.

F. EXCELSIOR 'PENDULA'

Weeping standard, top-grafted onto a clear trunk of, usually, 1.5–2m (5–6ft) in height. The growth habit is congested and, unless checked, crossing or rubbing branches may fuse, concealing structural defects and rot within ripples of bark. Framework branches must be carefully selected when young.

15 | 50

m | ft

■ **TRAINING AND PRUNING** Train and maintain as for any weeping standard (*see p.26*). Does not respond well to hard

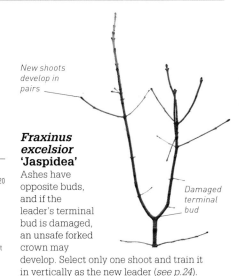

New shoots develop in pairs

Fraxinus excelsior 'Jaspidea'
Ashes have opposite buds, and if the leader's terminal bud is damaged, an unsafe forked crown may develop. Select only one shoot and train it in vertically as the new leader (*see p.24*).

Damaged terminal bud

pruning. In the early years, remove crossing branches, and also the weaker of any two that twine together, since one or sometimes both may die from suppression. Aim to achieve evenly spaced branches around the graft union. Do not over-thin as gaps in the canopy will spoil the outline.

OTHER ASHES

F. AMERICANA As for *F. excelsior*.
F. ANGUSTIFOLIA (syn. *F. OXYCARPA*) 'RAYWOOD' Popular as a street tree, and so usually trained as a central-leader standard. However, is equally attractive as a feathered tree (*see p.25*). Otherwise, as for *F. excelsior*.
F. EXCELSIOR 'MONSTROSA' Fasciated form, needs little pruning.
F. EXCELSIOR 'PENDULA WENTWORTHII' Clone that forms a strong, upright central leader with naturally pendulous branches; can thus be bottom-grafted, avoiding ugly graft unions at eye level and suckering on the trunk. Remove laterals as for a central-leader standard (*see p.26*). Once the tree is allowed to branch and weep, maintenance is as for any weeping standard (*see p.26*). Does not respond well to hard pruning.
F. ORNUS Naturally forms a clear trunk and needs minimal pruning and training.

G

GLEDITSIA

Deciduous, spiny trees, grown for their elegant form and divided foliage that often turns yellow in autumn. Although hardy, they often make soft growth late in the season that is vulnerable to frosts. They grow best in sun and shelter.

G. TRIACANTHOS

HONEY LOCUST

In its native North America, may reach 55m (180ft) in height. There are many forms and cultivars.

■ **WHEN TO PRUNE** Late summer to midwinter.

■ **TRAINING AND PRUNING** Train as a central-leader standard (*see p.26*), with a clear trunk to a height of about 2m (6ft). *G. triacanthos* naturally produces a vigorous leader and needs little formative pruning. Established trees tolerate light pruning, but this is rarely necessary.

Most cultivars, such as the golden-leaved 'Sunburst' (less vigorous and, with its tiered habit, a fine specimen for a small garden) are treated as for the species. The slow-growing 'Nana', which eventually forms a medium-sized tree, is trained as for the species, but the leader usually branches early, producing a broad crown. 'Bujottii', with white-mottled leaves, is a weeping standard (*see p.26*). 'Elegantissima', which is shrubby in habit, will not form a central leader and needs minimal pruning.

> **OTHER GLEDITSIAS**
> G. CASPICA, G. JAPONICA As for *G. triacanthos*.

GREVILLEA *SPIDER FLOWER*

Half-hardy to frost-tender evergreens (*see also* Dictionary of Ornamental Shrubs, *p.195*) grown for their habit, foliage and spidery flowers, produced reliably only in warm conditions. *G. robusta* (silky oak), which can attain a height of 35m (110ft) or more, is widely grown: in cool areas in pots under glass; wall-trained as a foliage plant in mild smaritime climates; or as a street tree or garden specimen in warm temperate or subtropical climates.

■ **WHEN TO PRUNE** Early summer as growth slows down (in mature trees, after flowering).

■ **TRAINING AND PRUNING** In warm temperate areas, grow as feathered trees (*see p.25*) or as central-leader standards (*see p.27*), with a clear trunk to a height of 2–3m (6–10ft). It is difficult to train in a replacement for a damaged leader, and without a leader a tree is likely to develop an unsound branch system. To wall-train, *see p.74*. Avoid pruning mature trees unless

Grevilleas as pot plants
Tree species of *Grevillea* can be grown from cuttings to make short-lived potplants under glass in cool climates. They will not flower, but the young, fern-like leaves are attractive.

absolutely essential. Large pruning wounds are disfiguring and are seldom disguised by new growth. If crown lifting becomes necessary (*see p.35*), remove complete limbs rather than shortening branches.

H–J

HALESIA

SILVER BELL, SNOWDROP TREE

Fully hardy, deciduous small trees and shrubs grown for their snowdrop-like flowers and winged fruits. Most colour well in autumn. Although they can be allowed to develop naturally into multi-stemmed trees, they display their flowers and sweeping branches better with a short trunk. Despite a naturally untidy habit they generally require little pruning.

H. CAROLINA SYN. H. TETRAPTERA

CAROLINA SNOW BELL

Halesia carolina is a small tree with spreading, even slightly pendulous lower branches that furnish the tree with foliage to the ground. It prefers a sunny position.

■ **WHEN TO PRUNE** Autumn to early spring.

■ **TRAINING AND PRUNING** Several stems often develop from the base: it is best if the strongest, most upright stem is selected and trained as a single trunk that can then be allowed to branch low, at about 50–75cm (20–30in).

Established trees have no special needs. If they are poorly formed or do not flower well, prune out some older wood in early spring to stimulate new growth that will bloom in the following year. On old, congested plants, thin out the oldest flowered growth immediately after flowering. Never attempt to lift the crown of established specimens, since this will spoil the graceful outline.

> **OTHER HALESIAS**
> H. DIPTERA No special pruning needs.
> H. MONTICOLA Forms a much taller tree than *H. carolina*. Until four years old, prune only to remove competing leaders, then train as a central-leader standard (*see p.26*), with a clear trunk of about 1.5m (5ft). Routine pruning of established trees is unnecessary. Poorly formed or poorly flowering trees can be treated as for *H. carolina*. Lower branches can be removed from older trees (*see also* Crown lifting, *p.33*).

> **OTHER ORNAMENTAL TREES**
> FIRMIANA Train as a central-leader standard (*see p.26*).
> GEIJERA Maintain *G. parviflora* as a weeping standard (*see p.26*). Laterals can be pruned back, when dormant, to pendulous sublaterals to enhance the weeping form.
> GINKGO See Conifers, *p.38*.
> GORDONIA Related to *Camellia* and needs similar treatment (*see C. japonica, p.180*)
> whether grown outdoors or under glass.
> GYMNOCLADUS Train as a central-leader standard (*see p.26*) with a clear trunk of about 2m (6ft). Established trees have no special pruning needs.

HOHERIA

Small evergreen or deciduous trees with attractive, alternate leaves, bearing a profusion of large white flowers on the current season's growth in late summer or early autumn. They are generally quite hardy, but in cold areas the evergreens in particular are best grown in the shelter of a warm, sunny wall. If protected at the roots, deciduous species badly damaged by frost often regenerate from the base in spring.

H. POPULNEA

LACEBARK

Spreading ever-
green with narrow,
glossy, dark green
leaves and white
flowers and, when
mature, brown and
white flaking bark.
Grows naturally as a multi-stemmed tree,
branching freely from the base.

12 | 40
m | ft

■ **WHEN TO PRUNE** In late spring.

■ **TRAINING AND PRUNING** Needs little, if any, formative pruning. Restrict growth of trees against walls, if necessary, by removing over-long branches to well within the tree to maintain an informal outline. This species responds well to hard pruning: old, ragged or poorly formed specimens can be rejuvenated by severe cutting back.

> OTHER HOHERIAS
> **H. GLABRATA** Grows naturally as a bush tree needing minimal pruning. Hard cutting back, in early summer, is tolerated but it is better to replace plants than to attempt renovation.
> **H. LYALLII** Train as a central-leader standard (*see p.26*) with a clear stem of 1–1.5m (3–5ft), pruning in early summer. Established trees need little further pruning, other than routine removal of dead wood.
> **H. SEXSTYLOSA** As for *H. populnea*.

IDESIA

Idesia polycarpa is a small, hardy tree (it grows much taller in Mediterranean-type climates) grown for its red, pea-like fruits and its tiered, open crown – a habit it only achieves on fertile, slightly acid soil in an open, yet sheltered, sunny site. Grow as a feathered tree or as a central-leader standard (*see p.26*) with a clear trunk to a height of 1–2.5m (3–8ft). Prune, if necessary, when the tree is dormant. Do not cut back hard; the water shoots that result will not make sound replacement branches.

ILEX *HOLLY*

Mostly fully hardy, evergreen and deciduous trees and shrubs grown for their glossy foliage and berries, borne on female trees when males grow nearby. Variegated cultivars of *Ilex aquifolium* and *I. × altaclerensis* have gold or silver markings either around the leaf margins or as a central blotch. The second type (*see right*) is more prone to reversion. The evergreens are widely grown as formal hedges (*see p.44*) and in clipped shapes (*see* Topiary, *p.48*), though berries will be lost as they are borne on two-year-old wood. Even informal, free-standing specimens benefit from the occasional shaping cut, though overzealous pruning spoils their form.

I. AQUIFOLIUM

COMMON HOLLY, ENGLISH HOLLY

Evergreen, densely
branched pyramidal
tree, with usually
spiny, glossy dark
foliage and bright
red berries. The
smaller cultivars of
shrub-like proportions
can be pruned as for the larger ones.
The weeping 'Pendula' is a bottom-grafted tree that, unlike many pendulous trees, is compact and dome-forming, naturally producing more height at its centre: it is easy to select and train in a central leader, which is best cleared to display the habit to advantage.

20 | 70
m | ft

■ **WHEN TO PRUNE** Mid- to late summer. Clip hedges and shaped trees in late summer, when new leaves are firm and glossy, but before the shoots have fully ripened and become hard to cut. If pruned before midsummer, a second flush of uneven regrowth may occur, thus spoiling the clean outlines created by pruning.

***Ilex × altaclerensis* 'Lawsoniana'**
The foliage of variegated holly cultivars may have either coloured blotches or edges.

■ **TRAINING AND PRUNING** Train as a feathered tree or central-leader standard (*see* Evergreen trees, *p.25*). Young hollies are vigorous, frequently forming competing leaders. Rapid extension growth sometimes fails to ripen fully before the onset of winter and is susceptible to frost damage – cut back to live wood in spring. Maintain or improve the natural pyramidal shape by removing any vigorous, protruding branches, cutting back to well within the crown to hide the cuts, or by clipping.

Train 'Pendula' with a clear trunk to about one-third of the height of the young tree, so that the branches will weep to just above soil level. Maintain as for any weeping standard (*see p.26*). Common holly responds vigorously to hard pruning, even into old wood. Thin regrowth if necessary.

> OTHER HOLLIES
> Most evergreen hollies, including
> **I. × ALTACLERENSIS** and **I. LATIFOLIA**, are pruned as for *I. aquifolium*.
> **I. × ATTENUATA** (and other American hybrids) See *I. opaca*, Dictionary of Ornamental Shrubs, *p.201*.

JACARANDA

Very vigorous,
frost-tender,
evergreen or semi-
deciduous trees
grown for their
fern-like foliage
and vivid blue
flowers produced in spring (at the same time as leaf-fall) and sometimes in autumn. They form tall trees with branches so widely spaced that they look vulnerable to wind damage, but in fact this rarely occurs. Unlike many fast-growing trees, they produce strong, flexible wood and are long-lived. Outdoors, they look best with a clear trunk and well-spaced

50 | 160
m | ft

branches. Jacarandas grown under glass form smaller trees that are best left feathered, allowing flowers to be appreciated at close quarters.

■ **WHEN TO PRUNE** Winter, when dormant.

■ **TRAINING AND PRUNING** Train as central-leader standards (*see p.26*), clearing the trunk up to 6m (20ft) as desired, or under glass as feathered trees (*see p.25*). Remove any vigorous, vertical laterals. If allowed to develop, they will form narrow crotch angles that are prone to splitting. Respond well to hard pruning.

JUGLANS *WALNUT*

Large deciduous trees grown for their stately habit, beautiful bark and big, pinnate leaves that, in some species, emit a sweet scent when crushed. *J. regia* is also grown for its edible nuts (*see p.149*), which ripen well only in long, hot summers. If a walnut tree is not to be cultivated primarily for its nuts, *J. nigra* is an easier tree to grow, particularly in cool climates.

Though hardy when mature, young trees are very easily damaged by frost and desiccating winds, and need a sheltered site. They are intolerant of root disturbance and pruning and must be planted young, as one- or two-year-old trees, with as large a rootball as possible, to minimize check when transplanting. Do not purchase pot-bound, container-grown specimens as these are very difficult to establish.

Young walnut wood is made up of hollow compartments of very soft pith. If incorrectly pruned, this tissue is very prone to dieback and, in severe cases, cavities may form (*see p.31*). When pruning, it is very important not to leave stubs that will die back. Walnuts also bleed profusely, so pruning must be kept to a minimum. Certain species should not be pruned at all.

■ **WHEN TO PRUNE** Midsummer to before midwinter. Do not prune in late winter or spring as the sap rises early and will bleed profusely.

J. NIGRA

BLACK WALNUT

A large tree that naturally forms a central leader, giving it a distinctive pyramidal habit when young. It spreads widely in maturity, with lower branch tips that are more or less pendulous, furnishing the tree with foliage almost to ground level.

■ **TRAINING AND PRUNING** Train as a central-leader standard (*see p.26*). It is important to remove laterals from the trunk when the tree is young to reduce the risk of cavities and stem blemish. Keep pruning of established trees to a minimum (*see also J. regia*). Does not respond well when cut back hard.

New shoots develop in pairs

Frost-damaged terminal bud

Juglans nigra
Walnuts are prone to losing their leaders; because they have opposite buds, dual leaders (*see p.24*) will develop unless one bud or shoot is removed.

J. REGIA

PERSIAN WALNUT, ENGLISH WALNUT

Naturally forms a rounded canopy with heavy branches and little twiggy growth, giving a solid appearance. It is valued for its timber, and for edible nuts that ripen reliably only in warm climates. Most cultivars are treated as for the species. Thin the crown of *J. regia* 'Pendula', a weeping standard (*see p.26*), when young to avoid congestion in maturity.

30 | 100
m | ft

■ **TRAINING AND PRUNING** Train as a central-leader standard (*see p.26*). In cool climates, the leader is easily lost to frost damage: cut back to a healthy shoot in summer and train it in. It is vital when removing frost damage to cut well into healthy, solid wood. Clear the trunk early in the tree's life to reduce the risk of cavities forming. Pruning of established trees should be kept to a minimum. If a damaged branch must be removed, it is imperative that the branch collar is left intact (*see p.11*). The tree does not respond well to hard pruning.

OTHER WALNUTS
J. AILANTHIFOLIA, J. CINEREA As for *J. regia*. *J. CALIFORNICA, J. HINDSII, J. MICROCARPA* Best allowed to develop naturally into small, shrubby, multi-stemmed trees. *See also* Walnuts, *p.149*.

K

KALOPANAX

Spiny, deciduous, stout-trunked tree that grows naturally with a central leader and short, well-spaced, near-horizontal branches. Young trees are prone to frost damage. New shoots flower terminally, then develop spur-like sublaterals with whorls of leaves. Plant young, as transplant stress may cause dieback. Trees may take two or three years to produce laterals. Train as a central-leader standard (*see p.26*), clearing the trunk to 2–3m (6–10ft) by rubbing out shoots as they emerge. This avoids stem blemish and reduces the risk of decay entering the soft, pithy wood. Keep pruning of established trees to a minimum.

KOELREUTERIA

10 | 30
m | ft

Deciduous, sun-loving tree prone to dieback in shade. A lax, open habit that lets in light is to be encouraged. Always choose a lanky, open young tree. Koelreuteria is fast-growing and short-lived, and the pithy wood is susceptible to rots, especially coral spot. Do not feed on planting in fertile soils; the resulting sappy growth will be susceptible to disease and frost damage. Train as a central-leader standard (*see p.26*), pruning when dormant, but do not remove laterals until they begin to die back as a result of shading. Never tip-prune to encourage dense growth. Keep pruning of established trees to a minimum; they do not respond to hard pruning.

Koelreuteria paniculata
The foliage turns butter-yellow in autumn, especially after a long, hot summer. In warm climates, the flowers are followed by distinctive bladder-like fruits.

OTHER ORNAMENTAL TREES
HOVENIA Train as a central-leader standard (*see p.26*). Established trees need minimal attention.

HYMENOSPORUM Train *H. flavum* with a clear trunk initially (*see p.26*), then allow the crown to branch naturally.

KIGELIA As for *Brachychiton* (*see p.55*). KNIGHTIA As for *Hovenia* (*see left*).

L

+ LABURNOCYTISUS

Small, fully hardy, deciduous graft hybrid between *Cytisus* and *Laburnum*, often unstable due to poor root formation. Plant as young as possible, and use a short stake to strengthen the stem (*see p.21*). Use guy ropes on established specimens with weak stems. Train as a central-leader standard (*see p.26*), with a clear stem to 1.5–2m (5–6ft), then

allow the leader to lose dominance, letting a branched head develop naturally. Prune during the dormant season or very lightly in mid- to late summer and, once the tree is established, only if necessary. Promptly remove suckers and uncharacteristically vigorous shoots within the canopy, as these will be pure laburnum and, if allowed to develop, will suppress the hybrid. Renovation should be avoided: hard pruning upsets the tissue balance and may lead to a proliferation of pure laburnum growth.

+ *Laburnocytisus adamii*

Two genetically distinct tissues form a single plant that bears three types of flower at once: yellow laburnum, purple broom and these pink flowers that are a mixture of both. The foliage is mostly laburnum-like, but branches of *Cytisus* may occur within the canopy.

LABURNUM *GOLDEN RAIN*

Small, hardy, deciduous trees, grown for their pendent racemes of bright yellow flowers. They respond well to training and regular pruning to maintain trained forms. Although usually grown as free-standing specimens, laburnums are exceptionally beautiful trained to form an arch. They are fast-growing when young, but tend to be short-lived. They resent transplanting, so plant as young as possible. Check containerized plants for root restriction and do not purchase if pot-bound. All parts are poisonous.

L. ANAGYROIDES

COMMON LABURNUM

Vigorous, spreading tree that flowers profusely in late spring and early summer. Named cultivars, such as *L. anagyroides*

'Aureum', with golden leaves, and 'Erect', with ascending branches, are grafted, and are treated as for the species; rootstocks may sucker.

■ **WHEN TO PRUNE** Late summer to before midwinter, to avoid bleeding of sap.

■ **TRAINING AND PRUNING** Grow as a feathered tree, or train as a central-leader standard (*see p.26*) to show off the pendulous flowers to best effect. Aim to create a balanced head and a clear stem of about 1.5m (5ft) by the third year, since the removal of larger laterals usually leads to the formation of cavities. Avoid pruning established specimens except for spur-pruning (*see below*) of trained forms. If removal of dead wood is necessary, try to avoid cutting back to living tissue, since this will breach the tree's natural defences (*see p.9*). On grafted or budded cultivars, rub out immediately any

buds that break below the graft union. Renovation is seldom successful; replace old or poorly formed specimens.

Training of laburnums to walls and arches (*see below*) is relatively easy but must be maintained and combined with both renewal and spur pruning each year to encourage free flowering.

OTHER LABURNUMS
L. ALPINUM As for *L. anagyroides*.
L. ALPINUM 'PENDULUM',
L. ANAGYROIDES 'PENDULUM'
Maintain as top-grafted weeping standards (*see p.26*).
L. × WATERERI 'VOSSII' Voss's laburnum, usually sold as a grafted, central-leader standard; choose young trees with neat, sound graft unions. Train and prune as for *L. anagyroides*. Remove suckers or buds that appear below the graft union.

Forming a laburnum tunnel

Formative training
Plant one- or two-year-old feathered trees in two rows along the structure at 2–3m (6–10ft) intervals. Train over the framework of the arch, tying in early in the season whilst the wood is still supple. Where insufficient laterals are produced to fill in the sides of the framework, tip back the leading shoot to encourage laterals to break. Trees pictured right are shown at various stages of development.

First-year tree
Second-year tree
Third-year tree
Fourth-year (established) tree

Established pruning
Once the basic branch framework is established, prune annually at the end of the growing season to reduce the density of growth and allow the production of flowering spurs. Remove dead or badly placed branches, and select replacement shoots where possible to fill in gaps. Reduce the remainder of the current year's shoots to two or three buds of the framework branches; this will encourage spur production.

LAGERSTROEMIA

Deciduous and evergreen multi-stemmed trees or shrubs grown for their terminal panicles of large pink, red, purple or white flowers that are produced from mid- to late summer on the current year's growth. The leaves colour well in the autumn (shortly after flowering is over) but may drop quickly if the weather is cold. Although *L. indica* tolerates several degrees of frost, in general lagerstroemias thrive and flower well only in areas with long, hot summers and mild winters. In cooler zones, they can be grown in a well-lit cool greenhouse or conservatory.

■ **WHEN TO PRUNE** Autumn to early spring.

■ **TRAINING AND PRUNING** Train as a multi-stemmed tree (*see p.28*), selecting three to five strong shoots to form main stems arising at or near ground level. These will support a proliferation of slender, flowering laterals and sublaterals if desired. Once the framework is established, annually, in early spring, prune one in three of the laterals and sublaterals back to the framework. This stimulates new growth that ripens to bear flowers from mid- to late summer. Plants grown in frost-free climates need little further pruning. In cooler areas and under glass, especially in northern areas with short growing seasons, thin to allow light and air into the centre of the tree to promote ripening of the wood.

LAURELIA *CHILEAN LAUREL*

L. serrata is a small, evergreen tree grown mainly for its attractive foliage, which is spicily scented when crushed. Although the mature tree is quite hardy, young growth is not. The densely leafy older branches are prone to break in strong winds, so plant in a warm, sheltered site. It grows naturally with a strong leader and is best grown as a feathered tree (*see p.25*), pruning in summer, after flowering.

Laurelias need little training or pruning. If necessary, restrict spread by cutting back branch leaders by up to one-third of the season's growth. They are suitable for training against a sunny wall (*see Magnolia grandiflora, p.74*). They regenerate well if pruned hard, but the dense regrowth may need thinning to reduce wind resistance. If branches are broken by winds, cut back to sound wood. Crown thinning (*see p.33*) may be needed to reduce future wind resistance.

LAURUS

Slow-growing evergreens with aromatic foliage, sometimes grown as dense shrubs and as hedges. Bay trees are grown both for their culinary use and for their formal ornamental value.

L. NOBILIS

BAY, BAY LAUREL, SWEET BAY

A dense, low-branching tree with leathery leaves used in cooking. It grows naturally as a central-leader tree, looking best with branches retained almost to ground level. It is hardy, although the foliage is susceptible to wind scorch by cold, dry winds. Bay lends itself to topiary, responding well to pinch pruning and clipping, and is popularly trained as cones, pyramids or "lollipop" standards. In cool climates, except in very mild areas, these need winter protection.

■ **WHEN TO PRUNE** Train young plants in spring, just before new growth begins. Clip or trim shaped plants in summer.

■ **TRAINING AND PRUNING** Train as a feathered tree (*see p.25*). Upper laterals rarely compete with the leader, eventually forming near-horizontal branches. Once established, pruning is best kept to a minimum. Clip formally-shaped specimens (*see Topiary, p.48 and also Hedges, p.44*) with secateurs, not shears. If wind scorch or dieback occurs, wait until late spring, when defoliated branches often leaf up again. If they do not, cut back to live wood, concealing cuts within the canopy. New shoots will develop to fill in gaps. Although tolerant of severe pruning, bays are slow to recover and regrow. Large wounds are therefore very obvious and heavy pruning should be a last resort. Occasionally, strong winds cause trees to develop unevenly. In early summer, prune correctively (*see p.32*), but as lightly as possible, to restore a balanced shape. Thereafter, trim lightly and regularly in summer to encourage a dense habit.

> **OTHER LAURUS**
> *L. azorica* As for *L. nobilis*. Hardy in mild areas that experience only light frosts, if given the protection of a sheltered, sunny wall.

Year 1

Stem cleared of shoots

Year 2

Remove basal suckers

Laurel topiary
To form a small standard, prune a young straight-stemmed plant back to a cluster of laterals, shortening these to outward-facing buds. As new shoots develop, tip-prune each to a bud facing in the direction in which growth is desired, building up a compact head.

LEUCADENDRON

Leucadendron argenteum (silver tree) is a frost-tender, columnar, evergreen tree (or large shrub in less favourable areas) grown for its silver-grey foliage and tiny yellow flowers with silver bracts, produced from autumn to spring and followed by curious, cone-like fruits. In cool climates, it is suitable for the conservatory. Good air circulation is essential for successful growth. Trees are usually short-lived, but easily raised from seed. In warm climates, train as a feathered tree (*see p.25*), leaving laterals almost to ground level. Prune, as necessary, in early summer. For established specimens and for those grown under glass, pruning should be kept to an absolute minimum, since this tree is prone to infection and dieback.

> **OTHER ORNAMENTAL TREES**
> Lagunaria Train as a central-leader standard (*see p.26*). Tolerates pruning if required, for example to restrict size when grown under glass.

LINDERA *SPICE BUSH*

Aromatic trees and large shrubs grown for their form and foliage. Although frost-hardy, they prefer a sunny, sheltered site, and can be wall-trained. Young growth may be frost damaged, but linderas usually regenerate well.

L. PRAECOX

Small deciduous tree that can also be coppiced for attractive large leaves (but few flowers).

■ **WHEN TO PRUNE** Autumn to early spring.

■ **TRAINING AND PRUNING** In mild climates, train as a central-leader standard (*see p.26*) with a clear trunk to 1.2–1.5m (4–5ft). In cool climates, it will develop naturally as a multi-stemmed tree (*see p.28*). To wall-train, create a multi- stemmed form if necessary by pruning to within 30cm (12in) of the ground when dormant (*see p.28*). Select three to five well-placed, upright shoots from those that develop to form the main stems. If wall-training, tie these in (*see p.74*), fanned out over the allotted space, as growth proceeds. The slender, flowering laterals need little pruning other than, if wall-training, to remove long outward-growing shoots. This will stimulate water shoots (*see p.30*): rub them out as they emerge. Remove shoots from the base promptly or train in if needed to replace an older branch. Linderas respond well to hard pruning if needed. Cut coppiced trees (*see p.34*) back to 30–50cm (12–20in) every other year in early spring.

OTHER LINDERAS
L. BENZOIN, L. OBTUSILOBA Shrubby species that need little pruning. Respond well to renovation if carried out over two or three years (*see p.160*).

LIQUIDAMBAR

Deciduous trees with maple-like leaves, grown for their autumn colour and attractive bark. All are intolerant of root disturbance, so plant ideally at two or three years old. Older trees are usually ready-trained, central-leader standards (although some species look equally attractive as feathered trees). They establish more successfully if the lower laterals are removed before transplanting to reduce water loss through transpiration. Avoid pot-bound, container-grown specimens; plants are intolerant of root pruning, especially if planting in autumn. No liquidambar responds well to hard pruning in cool climates.

L. STYRACIFLUA

SWEET GUM

Broadly pyramidal tree with drooping branches at maturity, grown for its glorious autumn colours of scarlet, crimson and purple. It is the hardiest and most widely grown liquidambar.

■ **WHEN TO PRUNE** When dormant, from late autumn to early spring. Remove dead wood in late summer.

■ **TRAINING AND PRUNING** Train as a central-leader standard with a short trunk (*see p.26*). Young trees naturally form a strong central leader; any competing leaders must be removed

Liquidambar styraciflua
Brilliant autumn foliage colour makes this variegated cultivar a striking specimen tree, particularly against a dark background.

as soon as possible. Remove lower branches to no more than 5m (15ft) to allow the drooping branches to descend to eye-level, so that the autumn colour can be appreciated at close quarters.

OTHER LIQUIDAMBARS
L. FORMOSANA, L. ORIENTALIS Prone to frost damage and competing leaders when young: train as a feathered tree (*see p.25*) until at least 6m (20ft) tall. Only then clear the trunk, if desired, by about 30cm (12in) each year over four or more years.

LIRIODENDRON

Hardy, deciduous trees grown for their pale green, tulip-like flowers in mid-summer, and for their foliage, which turns to deep gold in autumn.

L. TULIPIFERA

TULIP TREE

Fast-growing, vigorous tree; in its native eastern North America, some authorities regard it as a weed species. In cool temperate climates, it is ideal for medium-sized gardens, seldom growing taller than 30m (100ft) and forming a dense, more rounded crown; it may also lose the characteristic semi-pendulous nature of mature branches.

■ **WHEN TO PRUNE** When dormant, from autumn to early spring. Remove dead wood when the tree is in full leaf.

■ **TRAINING AND PRUNING** *L. tulipifera* usually forms a strong central leader, and little formative pruning is required. In continental climates, remove laterals gradually in the early years to clear the trunk (*see p.26*) to about one-third of the overall height of the young tree. In cool, maritime climates, delay the removal of laterals until the tree is well established. Aim to clear the trunk to about 2–3m (6–10ft).

Keep pruning of established trees to a minimum as the wounds are vulnerable to wood-rotting organisms. If branch removal becomes necessary, seek professional advice.

OTHER LIRIODENDRONS
L. CHINENSE Plant as young as possible. Train and prune as for *L. tulipifera*.
L. TULIPIFERA 'FASTIGIATUM' Fastigiate form (*see p.18*) best left branched to the ground. Needs little or no pruning.

LOMATIA

Small to medium-sized evergreen trees, frost-hardy, although frost often nips terminal buds, resulting in bushier growth. They are pruned after flowering. Let *L. ferruginea* form a multi-stemmed tree (*see p.28*). *L. hirsuta* looks best as a single-stemmed, feathered tree (*see p.25*) but if the leader is damaged, it cannot be replaced; allow a multi-stemmed form to develop, with five to seven main stems. These trees have no special pruning needs once established. They can also be wall-trained, as for *Lindera* (*see above*).

LUMA

Luma apiculata (syn. *Myrtus luma*, *M. apiculata*, *Myrceugenia apiculata*) is a frost-hardy evergreen tree or

shrub of variable habit, but usually with upright laterals that droop at the tip with maturity, and elegant, pendulous sublaterals. It is grown for its aromatic, leathery, glossy green leaves and small, cup-shaped white flowers, borne from late summer to early autumn. Its attractive, cinnamon-coloured bark peels to reveal a creamy-grey inner surface. In mild, almost frost-free areas it is grown as a central-leader standard, but in cooler regions, where it seldom reaches more than 6m (20ft) in height, it is more successful, and equally attractive, as a multi-stemmed tree.

■ **WHEN TO PRUNE** Spring, before new growth begins.

■ **TRAINING AND PRUNING** In mild areas, train as a central-leader standard (*see p.26*), removing lower branches progressively to about 1.5m (5ft). The leader is not strongly dominant, so remove competing shoots as soon as

Luma apiculata
Cup-shaped flowers are followed by spherical, red fruits, darkening to purple. Both are set off well by the dark, glossy foliage. A cultivar with yellow-splashed leaves, 'Glanleam Gold', is also available.

possible. In cool climates, allow to develop as a multi-stemmed tree (*see p.28*), branching at the base or from a low trunk; if necessary, select only three to five of the strongest shoots to form a well-spaced framework of main stems. Once trees are well established, thin laterals within the crown to produce an open-centred canopy that will reveal the bark. Mature trees rarely require attention. If needed, thin branches of established specimens better to display the bark and drooping habit; however, this is unlikely to be necessary provided that trees have been well trained.

LYONOTHAMNUS *CATALINA IRONWOOD*

Lyonothamnus floribundus is an exceptionally graceful evergreen tree that is frost-hardy, though it prefers frost-free

conditions and is usually quite small in cool climates. It is grown for its fern-like foliage, terminal panicles of small white flowers and shredding, chestnut-brown bark. Usually grown as a central-leader specimen tree, it is also suitable for wall-training.

■ **WHEN TO PRUNE** Spring, before new growth commences.

■ **TRAINING AND PRUNING** Train as a single-stemmed, feathered tree (*see p.25*), leaving well-spaced branches to ground level. These produce both upright and pendulous, whippy sublaterals on the same branch. Prune only to thin

congested branches. Removal of too much growth stimulates vigorous water shoots (*see p.30*) that spoil the crown. Once the framework is established, little further pruning is required.

These trees do, however, tolerate drastic pruning and respond well. Cut neglected or overgrown plants back almost to the ground in spring. As for eucalyptus (*see p.64*), select the strongest of the resulting shoots as a new leader and remove the rest of the shoots. Repeat formative pruning as described above.

The most effective way of growing lyonothamnus against a wall is, once the central leader and main, horizontal laterals are trained in (*see Magnolia grandiflora, p.74*), to allow only those sublaterals that have a pendulous habit to develop, thus creating a curtain of foliage. Remove any upright laterals annually in mid- to late summer, after flowering.

M

MAACKIA

Small, fully hardy, deciduous trees grown for their pinnate foliage and spikes of small, white pea-flowers borne in late summer.

M. AMURENSIS

A spreading tree often grown as a multi-stemmed specimen. It can also be trained as a standard with a short clear trunk and an open, rather sparse crown.

■ **WHEN TO PRUNE** Autumn to early spring.

■ **TRAINING AND PRUNING** If left to develop naturally, *M. amurensis* will form an attractive multi-stemmed tree that needs little or no pruning. To produce a more tree-like form, select and train a central leader, removing lower branches (*see p.26*) to a height of at least 75–90cm (30–36in). If the leader is lost, the crown will open out quickly, providing little opportunity for selecting and training a replacement. Established trees do not respond well to hard pruning.

> OTHER MAACKIAS
> **M. CHINENSIS** As for *M. amurensis*. If forming a central-leader tree, tip-prune any competing leaders.

MACLURA *OSAGE ORANGE*

Maclura pomifera is a spiny, round-headed, hardy deciduous tree with very hard wood, bearing pale yellow, orange-like fruits. It is grown as a central-leader tree or as impenetrable, informal hedging or barrier plantings. Its milky sap is potentially harmful: wear gloves when pruning. Prune when dormant, from autumn to early spring. Train as a feathered tree (*see p.25*). Little pruning is needed. The leader loses vigour early and a broad, naturally congested crown develops that should not be thinned. For a hedge or screen, plant close, 50–90cm (20–36in) apart, to restrict height and width. If necessary, shear back hard in winter. (*See also Hedges, p.44*.)

OTHER ORNAMENTAL TREES
LITHOCARPUS As for *Quercus ilex* (*see p.84*).
LITSEA See *Neolitsea, p.77*.

LOPHOMYRTUS As for *Luma* (*see above*).
LOPHOSTEMON Treat *L. confertus* (syn. *Tristania conferta*) as for *Luma* (*see above*), training

as a central-leader standard. Withstands hard pruning well.

MAGNOLIA

Large genus of trees and shrubs grown for their showy, often fragrant flowers. They are fully to frost-hardy; most need protection from strong winds. Early-flowering species may be marred by late frosts. Plants grown on poor soil seldom make well-shaped specimens.

In general, avoid pruning established magnolias unless essential. Many species bleed and should only be pruned from summer to before midwinter. Where light pruning (making cuts no more than 2cm/½in in diameter) is necessary to shape young plants or restrict growth, prune in midsummer those that flower before or with the new leaves in spring, and prune the late-flowering species, that bloom after new leaves are produced, in spring as new growth begins. Many magnolias break from old wood and respond well, if necessary, to hard pruning at the correct season. Recovery is slow: trees usually direct their energy into wound healing in the first year, producing new growth only in subsequent years. The more vigorous may produce sappy water shoots (*see p.30*) around cuts, which must be removed.

M. CAMPBELLII

Deciduous, hardy tree, bearing usually pink flowers from late winter to mid-spring. It is sometimes low-growing and sprawling, but more commonly a well-branched, pyramidal tree with a strong central leader. Grafted plants (usually cultivars) tend to branch earlier than seedlings, and often develop lower, broad crowns.

■ **WHEN TO PRUNE** Early to midsummer, when the leaves have expanded fully.

■ **TRAINING AND PRUNING** To train a single, straight-stemmed, pyramidal tree, select a vigorous, unbranched whip (*see p.22*). It is important that the leader grows without check for the first four or five years. Remove only damaged growth and competing leaders: harder pruning will stimulate vertical shoots that rise up through the centre of the tree, spoiling its form. Grafted plants tend to branch low in the early years; if low laterals become overlong, particularly if the central leader is weak, shorten them by two buds (these are on stubby "pegs").

Once the central leader is well established, remove lower branches over two to four years (depending on vigour). Little further pruning is required. To fill a gap if a branch is lost, select a suitable shoot from the cluster that arises around the wound. Remove the rest, and rub out new buds as they emerge. Tip-prune the new shoot in early spring to promote

Training against a wall (*Magnolia grandiflora*)

Year 1, first summer after planting

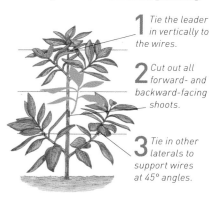

1 *Tie the leader in vertically to the wires.*

2 *Cut out all forward- and backward-facing shoots.*

3 *Tie in other laterals to support wires at 45° angles.*

Year 2, summer

1 *Continue to tie in new laterals at 45° when long enough.*

2 *Laterals that were previously tied in at 45° are now growing vigorously and can be lowered and tied in horizontally.*

Year 3 and thereafter, summer

1 *Continue to tie in tiers of branches, first at an angle, then horizontally. Cut out shoots on the main stem that cannot be trained to the left or right of the main trunk.*

2 *Tie in shoots where possible to fill in the framework. Once the allotted space is filled, pinch out shoot tips.*

3 *Shorten sublaterals growing away from the wall or across other shoots to one or two leaves, unless they bear flower buds. Delay pruning these shoots until after flowering.*

Magnolia kobus

branching, and in the following spring cut back the vertical portion of the shoot to the best-placed, outward-growing side-shoot, and remove others. Rub out unwanted shoots as they emerge.

To renovate completely, cut back all branches to a main framework (but preferably over two or three years). Select and train in new shoots as above.

M. GRANDIFLORA

BULL BAY

Frost-hardy evergreen with large leaves and creamy-white late summer flowers. In its native southern United States, where it may reach 25m (80ft), it is a dense, conical tree. In cool climates it has a lax, shrub-like habit, and is usually trained against a wall (preferably sunny and sheltered), where a central leader can be retained to a good height.

■ **WHEN TO PRUNE** Spring, as growth begins, and in summer if wall-training.

■ **TRAINING AND PRUNING** In areas with long, hot summers and mild winters, it forms a strong central leader and needs little pruning other than to shorten lanky young branches, if necessary, to maintain the conical outline. To wall-train in cooler climates, *see facing page*. Renovate as for *M. campbellii*.

> **OTHER MAGNOLIAS**
> M. DELAVAYI As for *M. grandiflora*.
> M. DENUDATA (syn. M. HEPTAPETA) As for *M. grandiflora*, which it resembles, though it is better suited to cool climates.
> M. KOBUS Spring-flowering; pyramidal when young, then spreading to form a broad-crowned tree. Grows naturally with a strong leader; little training is needed. Prune lightly after flowering in midsummer if necessary. Older trees sometimes produce water shoots within the canopy: remove as seen. Renovate as for *M. campbellii*.
> M. SALICIFOLIA Prune lightly after flowering in midsummer. Train as a central-leader standard (*see p.26*) with a clear trunk to about 1–1.5m (3–5ft). Needs little or no pruning once established. Renovate as for *M. campbellii*. For other species, *see* Dictionary of Ornamental Shrubs, *p.206*.

MALUS *CRAB APPLE*

Fully hardy, small to medium-sized deciduous trees grown for their spring blossom, their foliage and fruits, and, in some cases, autumn colour. They are noted for the strength of their wood. *Malus* look equally attractive as standards or feathered trees. Bottom-grafted cultivars such as 'Golden Hornet' and 'John Downie' are usually purchased as pre-trained, branched-head or occasionally central-leader standards.

■ **WHEN TO PRUNE** Autumn to early spring.

M. BACCATA

SIBERIAN CRAB

Spreading tree with heavy branches, with white flowers followed by red or yellow fruits. It is best grown on its own roots: grafted specimens, even if well trained, often lean over with age.

■ **TRAINING AND PRUNING** Grow initially as a feathered tree (*see p.25*). The tree usually sheds lower branches naturally. If not, remove only a single whorl in each year. Harder pruning stimulates vertical shoots within the canopy: these should be removed as they will form an unattractive secondary crown.

Once established, try to avoid hard pruning: it often leads to branch dieback due to infection by paperbark fungus.

M. FLORIBUNDA

Spreading tree with a dense natural branch structure, grown for its profuse pale pink flowers. Some forms have a shrubby habit, whilst others grow naturally with a strong central leader.

■ **TRAINING AND PRUNING** Specimens that exhibit shrubby growth at an early age cannot be trained as trees. Let them develop naturally with several main stems clothed to the ground with branches. Train those that produce a leader with a clear trunk (*see p.26*) to 1–1.5m (3–5ft), then allow the crown to branch, removing only badly placed or crossing branches to form a well-spaced framework and alleviate the naturally congested habit that develops with age. Once the tree is five years old little further pruning is required. It does not respond well to hard pruning.

Malus **'Butterball'**
Crab apple cultivars bear fruits in a range of colours, all attractive to foraging birds.

M. TSCHONOSKII

A beautiful specimen tree for smaller gardens, with a distinctive pyramidal habit, white flowers, greenish-yellow fruits and vibrant autumn foliage colour.

■ **TRAINING AND PRUNING** Field-grown trees tend to produce insubstantial root systems and a short stake is essential to build this up (*see p.21*). The tree grows naturally with a central leader and semi-upright or upright branches, needing little formative pruning. If the leader is lost and a new one is trained in, shorten vigorous upper laterals by four buds so they do not compete. Low branches can be retained or cleared to a height of 1.5–2m (5–6ft). No other pruning is needed. Does not respond well to hard pruning.

> **OTHER MALUS**
> M. 'GOLDEN HORNET', M. 'JOHN DOWNIE', M. 'DARTMOUTH' As for *M. baccata*. Occasionally produce water shoots in the crown, and suckers from below the graft union. Remove as seen.
> M. HUPEHENSIS A natural central-leader standard; treat as for *M. tschonoskii*.
> M. IOENSIS Small, grafted branched-head standard, needs minimal pruning.
> M. × PURPUREA Train as a central-leader standard as for *M. tschonoskii* or, where access beneath the tree is unnecessary, let it branch low to give a more natural appearance. Pruning will not correct the natural ungainly habit, and is not recommended; hard pruning induces a mass of water shoots.

MELALEUCA *HONEY MYRTLE, PAPERBARK*

Medium-sized evergreens with dark, glossy foliage and "bottle-brush" flowers. Half-hardy to frost-tender, they need a sunny site. They benefit from shaping when young but little further attention is necessary. They do not respond well to hard pruning and are better replaced than renovated.

■ **WHEN TO PRUNE** Late winter or early spring. Shrubby melaleucas such as *M. hypericifolia* tolerate trimming to shape and to limit size after flowering.

■ **TRAINING AND PRUNING** Most are best left to develop a multi-stemmed form with minimal pruning. They make attractive semi-formal hedging or screening if regularly trimmed; shoots will not break from old, bare wood. *M. linariifolia* may be left to grow naturally, but displays its erect habit and flowers better when only three strong main stems are selected (*see p.28*). Remove any laterals that show strong horizontal growth to encourage an upright profile. Grow *M. styphelioides* as a single-stemmed, feathered tree (*see p.25*); once established, remove low branches, if desired, to about 1.5–2m (5–6ft) to display the papery bark.

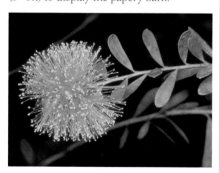

Melaleuca nesophila
These pinky-mauve flowers are borne terminally in spring on last year's shoots.

MELIA

Melia azedarach (bead tree, Chinaberry) is a round-headed, deciduous tree bearing panicles of star-shaped, lilac-pink flowers in spring, followed by orange-yellow fruits. Train as a central-leader standard (*see p.26*), pruning between autumn and early spring. Maintain the leader for as long as possible and aim to clear the trunk to a height of about 2m (6ft). Young trees produce well-spaced branches with long internodes and few sublaterals, creating an open, spindly habit. Clearing the trunk in the early years encourages closer branching higher on the trunk.

MELIOSMA

Slow-growing, deciduous trees and shrubs, bearing pyramidal clusters of small, honey-scented flowers in early summer. Tree species – *M. alba* (syn. *M. beaniana*), *M. oldhamii* and *M. veitchiorum* – are grown as central-leader standards. They are fully hardy, but soft growth made late in the season may suffer frost damage.

■ **WHEN TO PRUNE** In spring, as growth begins, or lightly in early summer.

MICHELIA

Frost-tender evergreen trees related to *Magnolia*, grown for their fragrant flowers in late winter or early spring.

M. DOLTSOPA

Evergreen or semi-evergreen tree with a broad, rounded crown, attractive as a standard or multi-stemmed tree. It is suitable for outdoor cultivation only in sheltered gardens in mild climates. Flowers open in early spring from buds set the previous autumn, which can be damaged by hard winter frosts.

■ **WHEN TO PRUNE** Prune new plants in the spring and, once established, switch to pruning after flowering.

MORUS *MULBERRY*

Fully hardy, deciduous trees, grown for their foliage, edible fruits and bark, but mainly for their gnarled, picturesque habit. With age, they form a broad, open crown of great character. Mulberries have brittle, fleshy roots; plant with care.

■ **WHEN TO PRUNE** When fully dormant, from autumn to early winter, to avoid bleeding of sap.

M. ALBA SYN. M. BOMBYCIS

WHITE MULBERRY

The white mulberry forms a wide, rounded head of heavy branches supported on a stout trunk, often of impressive girth. Although a less attractive tree than the black mulberry (*M. nigra*), the fruits do not stain paving as they drop in autumn. The most picturesque specimens often have structural defects, usually the result

■ **TRAINING AND PRUNING** Train as central-leader standards (*see p.26*) with a clear trunk to 1.5–2m (5–6ft). Even when young, *M. oldhamii* is very slow-growing, characteristically forming a single stem and short, stubby laterals that may take several years to develop as proper branches. The sparse habit that results is natural and will not be improved by pruning. Established trees need little pruning and do not respond well when cut back hard.

■ **TRAINING AND PRUNING** Minimal formative pruning is needed to produce a multi-stemmed specimen (*see p.28*); the young tree will branch naturally from ground level. To train as a central-leader tree (*see p.26*), remove competing stems and clear one trunk to a height of about 75–90cm (2½–3ft). As the tree matures, the leader loses dominance, resulting in a multi-stemmed crown with upright, then spreading branches.

Keep pruning of established trees to a minimum; they do not respond well when cut back hard.

> OTHER MICHELIAS
> M. FIGO As for *M. doltsopa*. Will tolerate light trimming in spring to shape or restrict size.

of neglect in their formative years. A "prematurely aged" specimen can be deliberately created by pruning (*see below*) so that the tree will almost certainly develop weak lower limbs that will eventually require propping.

'Pendula' is a bottom-grafted, naturally weeping tree that will not form a central leader unless a shoot is specifically trained for the purpose.

■ **TRAINING AND PRUNING** Train as a central-leader standard (*see p.26*) with a clear trunk to about 1.5m (5ft). To create a prematurely gnarled, spreading crown, remove the leader when the tree is four or five years old and allow the tree to develop its own form without further pruning. To produce a structurally strong specimen, it is essential that the leader is maintained for as long as possible, preferably to a height of about 6m (20ft). No further pruning is needed. As the tree matures, the growth of lateral branches will naturally exceed that of the leader, forming a characteristic

N–O

NOTHOFAGUS *SOUTHERN BEECH*

Fully to frost-hardy trees grown for
their botanical interest and fine-textured
foliage. They usually grow rapidly and may
be damaged by high winds.

N. DOMBEYI

Frost-hardy, evergreen
tree with toothed,
glossy, dark foliage and
an elegant, horizontally
branching habit.

20 | 70
m | ft

■ **WHEN TO PRUNE** Late spring, after the
first flush of rapid spring growth.

■ **TRAINING AND PRUNING** Train as
a central-leader tree (*see p.26*) with
a clear trunk to a height of 1.5–2m
(5–6ft).If lower branches are retained,
the result is a skirt of foliage around the
base of the tree that restricts access
beneath. The tree tends to form dual
leaders and often continues to do so into
early maturity. If allowed to develop,
these will form weak crotches. Remove
the weaker of the two leaders as seen.
Established specimens need little
pruning. Lower branches that reach
ground level may begin to grow
upwards, thus forming a skirt of foliage.
Remove the lowest branches, if necessary,
to permit access beneath.

N. OBLIQUA

ROBLÉ BEECH

Vigorous deciduous
tree with horizontal
branches, pendulous at
the tips. The silver-grey
bark becomes furrowed
and reddens with age,
and the leaves colour
well in autumn. Although fully hardy,
N. obliqua is not suited to exposed sites:
the fast-growing crown creates a wind-
resistant "sail" that cannot be supported
by the roots, and trees often blow over.

30 | 100
m | ft

■ **WHEN TO PRUNE** Autumn to early spring.

■ **TRAINING AND PRUNING** Train as a
central-leader standard (*see p.26*) with a
clear trunk to a height of 3m (10ft). It is
vital to maintain a single strong leader.
The rapid growth and weight of mature
branches create a high risk of dangerous
structural weakness if narrow forks are
allowed to develop. With maturity,
lower branches become very heavy and
produce long, pendulous sublaterals,
usually to ground level. If access
beneath the tree is necessary, reduce or
remove the sublaterals. Because of their
weight, entire lower branches should
only be removed by a professional.

***Nothofagus
procera***
The branchlets of many southern beeches
make a distinctive herringbone pattern.

OTHER SOUTHERN BEECHES

N. ANTARCTICA Grow as a feathered tree
(*see p.25*). Trees often lose their central
leader early but this is not a problem.
N. BETULOIDES As for *N. dombeyi*,
except that the tree can be left clothed
with laterals to the ground.
N. PROCERA (syn. N. ALPINA, N. NERVOSA)
Fully hardy but needs shelter from cold,
dry winds or a misshapen tree will result
that pruning or training cannot rectify.
Train as for *N. obliqua*, but with a clear
trunk to about 4m (12ft). Support with
a short stake (*see p.21*). Ties may need
several adjustments during the growing
season. If the leader is lost, it is usually
replaced naturally by vigorous growth
from a lateral branch. If not, train in a
replacement (*see p.24*). Established trees
need little pruning and do not respond
well to hard pruning.

---

*Leader must be
trained vertically*

*Laterals shortened
to outward-falling
shoots*

***Morus alba
'Pendula'***
If growing this
strongly weeping
tree in a
container, prune
to restrict size
and enhance the
cascading effect:
shorten branches
to an outward-
growing lateral.

broad crown. Keep subsequent pruning
to a minimum. Remove any epicormic
shoots (*see p.30*) periodically. Trees are
not easily renovated by drastic cutting
back; they respond by producing a mass
of water shoots (*see p.30*). Prop lower
branches (*see p.31*) if necessary.
   To train *M. alba* 'Pendula', insert
a stout stake on planting and tie in a
flexible young shoot to form a leader.
Extension growth will be strongly
arching. Towards the end of the growing
season, before the wood is fully ripe,
straighten the leader and tie in to the
support. Repeat over several years, until
the tree reaches a height of about 5–6m
(15–20ft). During this period, gradually
clear the trunk to a height of about 1.5m
(5ft). Thereafter, the crown can be
allowed to weep naturally. Keep pruning
of established trees to a minimum.

OTHER MULBERRIES

M. NIGRA, M. RUBRA See Mulberries,
p.137.

OTHER ORNAMENTAL TREES

MANGLIETA Treat *M. insignis* as *Magnolia
campbellii* (*see p.74*). Do not prune hard.
MAYTENUS Plant young. For a multi-
stemmed tree (*see p.28*), remove the
central stem when young. For a single-
stemmed feathered tree (*see p.25*), select
the strongest stem and remove others.
When established, pendulous growth may
rest on the ground or become congested.
Thin lateral branchlets only. Hard
pruning encourages water shoots and may
result in a shrubby, less attractive habit.
MELICYTUS *M. ramiflorus* can be grown
in a cool greenhouse or conservatory.
Needs little pruning other than to tip
back laterals, when dormant, to shape.
MESPILUS See Medlar, *p.120.*
METROSIDEROS Usually grows as a
large-limbed, multi-stemmed tree.
Little pruning is required.
MYRTUS *See* Luma, *p.73*, and Dictionary
of Ornamental Shrubs, *p.207.*
NEOLITSEA (syn. LITSEA) Train with a
clear trunk of about 1m (3ft) (*see p.26*)
then allow the tree to branch to form a
broad, usually structurally sound crown.
Established trees need little pruning and
do not respond well to renovation.

NYSSA *TUPELO*

Deciduous trees with attractive foliage and spectacular autumn colour. Climate influences their growth habit and form: in warm climates with hot summers it is possible to grow them as central-leader trees; in cool, temperate climates the leader is frequently lost, and it is best to train from the start as multi-stemmed trees on short trunks.

N. SYLVATICA

BLACK GUM, SOUR GUM

Deciduous tree grown for its form and for its stunning autumn colour. It is extremely

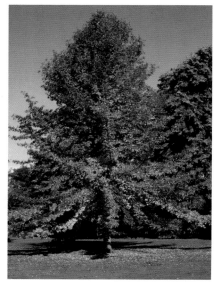

Nyssa sylvatica
A clear trunk allows lower branches to spread, creating a striking "starburst" effect, particularly in autumn.

intolerant of transplanting, so plant only one- or two-year-old trees. Transplant shock may be fatal and older trees that survive it seldom form good specimens. Shelter young trees from wind and frost. They become hardier as they mature.

■ **WHEN TO PRUNE** When dormant, between autumn and early spring.

■ **TRAINING AND PRUNING** In warm climates, train as a central-leader standard (*see p.26*), but do not start to clear the trunk until the second year; then remove laterals gradually over four or five years to a height of 2m (6ft). Hard pruning too early may induce early branching in the crown. To create a tree-like form it is vital that the leader remains dominant in the early years. Reduce any vigorous laterals that compete with the leader by up to one-third of their length. If the leader is lost or damaged, it is very difficult to replace; it may be better to allow the tree to develop as a multi-stemmed specimen (*see below*).

In cool climates, create a multi-stemmed form on a short trunk by tip-pruning a newly-planted whip to promote branching. Select four or five strong laterals to form framework branches. Remove the lowest laterals so that the trunk is clear to 60–90cm (24–36in).

Little further pruning is needed. The spreading limbs of semi-mature and mature trees sometimes produce fast-growing upright shoots that grow through the canopy, spoiling the form of the tree (especially in winter). Remove as seen. *Nyssa* tolerate pruning when necessary to tidy growth, restrict spread or thin a congested canopy (*see* Renovation, *p.32*).

> OTHER NYSSAS
> N. SINENSIS As for *N. sylvatica*.

OXYDENDRUM *SOURWOOD, SORREL TREE*

Oxydendrum arboreum is a deciduous, fully hardy tree grown for its slender terminal panicles of greenish-white flowers in late summer, and brilliant scarlet autumn colour. Tree-like growth occurs only in areas that experience hot summers, where it is grown as a central-leader specimen. In areas with cool summers, it will naturally develop as a bush or multi-stemmed tree. Plant trees in their final location as young as possible; transplant shock often results in the loss of the leading shoot. They prefer an open, sunny site. Shade and competition from other vegetation will produce a distorted or offset canopy,

which is best accepted; the sourwood is generally intolerant of pruning.

■ **WHEN TO PRUNE** When dormant, between autumn and early spring.

■ **TRAINING AND PRUNING** Plant a young, well-feathered tree. In areas with hot summers, grow as a feathered tree (*see p.25*), removing only the lowest laterals. It is seldom possible to replace a lost leader, and if loss occurs, trees are best allowed to branch and grow naturally. Once established, pruning is best kept to a minimum. Does not respond well when cut back hard.

PARROTIA

Parrotia persica (Persian ironwood) is a deciduous tree grown primarily for its spectacular gold and crimson autumn colour. It is variable in habit, being either tree-like or shrub-like. It is very hard to determine which form of growth will be adopted. In shrub-like forms, the leader is quickly lost and laterals adopt a horizontal or even pendulous habit. This results in a wide-spreading specimen, seldom more than 4m (12ft) in height and usually broader than it is tall. This form resists all attempts to train an upright leader. In tree-like forms, which may reach 12m (40ft) in height, the leading shoot continues to grow, apparently suppressing short laterals that become increasingly stout with age. Parrotias do not transplant well and

PAULOWNIA

Fast-growing, deciduous trees grown for their handsome foliage and foxglove-like spring flowers. All need long, hot summers to ripen the pithy stems, increasing hardiness and reliability of flowering. Even in continental climates, young plants are best raised under glass, or protected for at least the first winter. In cool climates, young growth and flower buds, which develop in autumn, are often lost to frost; paulownias can alternatively be grown as foliage plants by cutting hard back to produce vigorous shoots with very large leaves. These are best overwintered under glass.

P. TOMENTOSA SYN. P. IMPERIALIS

FOXGLOVE TREE, PRINCESS TREE

Broadly columnar tree with fragrant, pink-lilac flowers, grown as a central-leader standard (although climate usually dictates growth habit) or as a coppiced or pollarded non-flowering shrub.

■ **WHEN TO PRUNE** Spring or early summer.

■ **TRAINING AND PRUNING** Train from an early age as a central-leader standard (*see p.26*), but clear the trunk, to a height of about 1–1.5m (3–5ft), where possible by rubbing out buds before they shoot rather than by removing laterals: their branch

Parrotia persica

Parrotias have a curious self-grafting habit: branches that touch will in time fuse together, adding interest to the tree in winter, when its attractive patchwork bark can also be clearly seen.

their habit does not become apparent until specimens are three or four years old. They are best planted in a site where either form will be acceptable.

■ **WHEN TO PRUNE** Autumn to early spring.

■ **TRAINING AND PRUNING** Shrub-like specimens need no formative pruning. Do not thin or shorten laterals, as this

will lead to congested growth. With tree-like forms, train as a naturally branched-headed standard (*see p.26*), clearing the trunk to about 1.5m (5ft), then allowing the crown to branch. If necessary, shorten pendulous tips to allow access beneath and display the bark. Established specimens need no regular pruning and are better replaced than renovated. Older trees may be grafted: remove any suckers (*see p.30*).

---

collars (*see p.12*) are often poorly formed and even if left intact, may not prevent the onset of decay. The leader is ften lost – not always to cold – and the crown branches early. In areas with hot summers, the leader can usually be replaced with a vigorous lateral. In areas with cooler summers, numerous lateral buds produce competing leaders, resulting in shrubby growth that is best accepted. Once established, prune only to remove

dead wood or frost damage. Paulownias tolerate hard cutting back but are then best maintained as coppiced or pollarded specimens (*see below and p.34*); cut back annually in early spring.

OTHER PAULOWNIAS
P. fargesii, **P. fortunei** As for *P. tomentosa*.

New shoots will grow up to 2.5m (8ft) in height

Smooth and bevel edges of cut with a pruning knife

Pruning encourages large leaves

Paulownia tomentosa

Paulownias can be grown as foliage plants, with much larger, "tropical"-looking leaves, by cutting hard back each year; this also enables them to be grown in containers in cool climates, either in glasshouses or conservatories, or as summer bedding plants.

PHELLODENDRON

Small to medium-sized deciduous trees with a broad crown of well-spaced, spreading branches; most have rugged, corky bark. The leaves, golden in spring, assume striking yellow tints in autumn. Young trees need moist, loamy soil and an open yet sheltered site to produce a good form; fine specimen trees are rare in cool climates. Prune when dormant. Train as a central-leader standard (*see p.26*) with a clear trunk to about one-third of the young tree's height. Take care not to damage the leader; it is very difficult to replace. The crown branches early, forming a flattened dome. Prune mature trees only to remove dead wood; they do not respond well to renovation.

PHYTOLACCA

Phytolacca dioica is a vigorous evergreen that will grow outdoors only in frost-free climates. Train as a central-leader standard (*see p.26*), with a clear trunk of 2–3m (6–10ft). Prune in winter or early spring, before growth begins. The leader often branches early, and by early maturity the crown usually increases more rapidly in spread than in height. Established trees need little pruning.

PISTACIA

In warm climates, *P. chinensis* forms a tall tree with a long, straight trunk and a broad, domed crown, but in cool climates is often more shrubby: a sheltered site may help to produce a tree-like form. Train as a central-leader standard (*see p.26*) with a short, clear trunk, pruning in winter. A lost leader is difficult to replace, and the resultant shrub-like habit is best accepted. Established trees need little pruning and do not respond well to hard pruning. Drying winds may cause die-back that in turn results in a proliferation of growth, which should be thinned. To grow *P. vera* for its nuts, *see p.148*.

OTHER ORNAMENTAL TREES
Olea *See Olive, p.146*.
Ostrya As for *Carpinus* (*see p.56*).
Parkinsonia No special pruning needs.
Peltophorum Train as a central-leader standard (*see p.26*). Established trees have no special pruning needs.
Persea *See Avocado, p.147*.
Picrasma *P. quassioides* grows naturally as a multi-stemmed tree (*see p.28*). Needs little pruning, other than to clear low laterals, in the early years, to about 60cm (24in).
Planera As for *Ulmus* (*see p.91*).

PLATANUS *PLANE*

Large, stately, deciduous trees with dense foliage, popular in urban areas throughout the cool temperate world: they thrive in polluted environments. Planes develop heavy branch structures, and even if well-trained they may become unsafe. However, most respond vigorously to hard pruning. Planes grown as street trees are often pollarded, giving them a compact crown atop a tall, clear trunk that allows for traffic below.

■ **WHEN TO PRUNE** Autumn to early spring.

P. × ACERIFOLIA SYN. P. × HISPANICA

LONDON PLANE

Platanus × acerifolia (syn. *P. × hispanica*, *P. × hybrida*) attains huge dimensions in continental climates, but is often of only medium height in temperate regions. Young trees are vigorous, with a strong central leader and short, well-spaced laterals. The tree looks equally attractive with foliage to the ground or with a tall, clear trunk. Variegated cultivars may revert (*see p.30*); remove any plain green-leaved shoots.

■ **TRAINING AND PRUNING** For a central-leader standard (*see p. 26*), clear the trunk to up to 3m (10ft). To produce a tree clothed to the ground, remove laterals below 1.2m (4ft) and allow downward-pointing sublaterals to develop. Because branches grow heavy, it is essential to maintain a strong leader and develop a sound framework. Badly damaged young trees are better replaced. Occasionally, horizontal branches produce upright shoots that will become structurally dangerous "secondary leaders", so remove strongly upright sublaterals as seen.

Established trees need little further pruning. Planes in need of renovation must be dealt with only by a professional.

P. ORIENTALIS

ORIENTAL PLANE

Similar to *P. × acerifolia*, but has a more spreading habit, with very heavy branches and deeply lobed leaves.

30 | 100
m | ft

■ **TRAINING AND PRUNING** Train as a central-leader standard (*see p.26*) with a clear trunk to 2–3m (6–10ft). As the crown develops, keep only evenly and well-spaced laterals: if they arise at or near the same point on the trunk, the mature tree will be unsound. Old specimens with congested branches need crown thinning and careful crown reduction, which must be performed only by a professional. Over-thinning results in a mass of vigorous growth that increases wind resistance and thus instability. Crown lifting is not generally successful; nor is using cable braces to support large limbs: it leads to decay and potential cavity formation.

OTHER PLANES

P. OCCIDENTALIS Broadly columnar in continental climates, but rarely achieves a good form in temperate zones. Prune as for *P. × acerifolia*.

Crown reduction
The crown of a plane that has outgrown its situation, or is casting too much shade, can be reduced by professional tree surgeons (*see also* Major tree surgery, *p.33*).

Lopping
Street planes are frequently disfigured by crude pruning techniques. Full pollarding, taking all branches back to the head of the trunk, is more attractive in a garden setting.

PLATYCARYA

Platycarya strobilacea is a small deciduous tree with catkin-like flowers followed by cone-like fruits. A member of the walnut family, its wood has soft pith. Although hardy, young growth is often damaged by late spring frosts, and since it is seldom possible to replace a lost leader, a sheltered site is essential. Train and prune as for *Juglans* (*see p.69*).

PLUMERIA

Tropical, deciduous trees with fleshy branches and fragrant, waxy flowers. In cool areas they may be grown in a greenhouse or conservatory in full light.

P. RUBRA

FRANGIPANI

A multi-branched tree (or shrub, to about 3–4m/10–12ft under glass). Its upright shoots bear terminal clusters of foliage, and branch to produce an open, flat-topped crown. The soft wood is prone to rot, and shrinks at the site of cuts, hampering wound sealing. Pruning is therefore best kept to a minimum.

6 | 20
m | ft

■ **WHEN TO PRUNE** Early spring.

■ **TRAINING AND PRUNING** Train initially as a central-leader standard (*see p.26*) with a clear trunk to 1m (3ft). The leader is rapidly lost as the naturally branched head develops, and pruning will not aid its retention. Established trees need little further attention. Replace trees rather than attempt major renovation. When grown under glass, size may be restricted by cutting back to a shoot or branch junction.

OTHER PLUMERIAS

P. ALBA As for *P. rubra*.

POLIOTHYRSIS

Deciduous tree that, although hardy, grows and flowers best in areas with long, hot summers. Train as a central-leader standard (*see p.26*) with a clear trunk of 1–1.5m (3–5ft). The leader is easily lost; in the first year or two, a spring feed of high-nitrogen fertilizer, which induces vigour and inhibits branching, makes training easier (though it increases the risk of frost damage). Mature trees need no special pruning. Avoid cutting back hard into old wood.

POPULUS *POPLAR*

Usually fast-growing, hardy, deciduous trees, grown for their stature and foliage and for their tolerance of a wide range of conditions. Although often considered brittle, most poplars are very wind-resistant. The wood is flexible and well-trained trees rarely split. The exceptions are those susceptible to bacterial poplar canker, such as *P. wilsonii* and *P. × canadensis* 'Eugenei'. Canker is untreatable but there are resistant clones. Prune poplars vulnerable to canker, which gains entry through wounds, in summer when wounds seal most quickly. Prune suckering species in summer also, to check the regrowth of suckers and water shoots (*see p.30*). Prune other poplars in autumn, as many begin growth in late winter or very early spring and bleed badly if pruned then.

P. ALBA

ABELE, WHITE POPLAR, SILVER-LEAVED POPLAR

Short-lived tree grown for its foliage and autumn colour, best as a central-leader standard or in barrier plantings, where it may also be allowed to develop its natural suckering habit. 'Pyramidalis' is best trained as a feathered tree (*see p.25*); train 'Globosa' initially with a central leader, which will soon be lost as the crown begins to spread; it needs little further pruning.

■ **WHEN TO PRUNE** Late summer or early autumn.

■ **TRAINING AND PRUNING** To train as a central-leader standard (*see p.26*), clear the trunk to a height of about 1.5–2m (5–6ft). Remove any basal growth and suckers in late summer. Trees grown as standards do not respond well to severe pruning. To grow as barrier plantings, leave suckers to develop; a proportion usually die before the clump becomes congested. Suckering clumps are easily regenerated by hard pruning.

P. × CANADENSIS

CANADIAN POPLAR

Group of hybrids, including some with golden leaves ('Aurea'), and columnar types such as 'Eugenei', 'Robusta' and 'Serotina', the black Italian poplar. All are potentially very large trees, and neglect of formative pruning will ultimately result in a dangerous tree.

Populus × candicans 'Aurora'
This variegated poplar, with cream-blotched leaves, makes an attractive foliage plant when coppiced or pollarded.

■ **WHEN TO PRUNE** As for *P. alba*.

■ **TRAINING AND PRUNING** Aim to produce a straight-stemmed tree with light, even branching. Train as a central-leader standard (*see p.26*) with a clear trunk of 2–3m (6–10ft). The leader must be maintained at least into early maturity; never allow competing leaders to develop. Remove laterals that are not evenly and well spaced and shorten any upright growth that develops at branch tips by about one-third. Established trees need little pruning. It is rarely worth renovating an old tree; they are susceptible to rot and respond to hard pruning by producing a mass of water shoots that do not form sound branches.

P. LASIOCARPA

CHINESE NECKLACE POPLAR

Grown primarily for its attractive habit and heart-shaped leaves with downy undersides. Young trees naturally produce a strong central leader surrounded by stout, vigorous, upright shoots; with maturity, the lower branches become almost horizontal, creating a round-headed tree.

■ **WHEN TO PRUNE** As for *P. alba*.

■ **TRAINING AND PRUNING** Train as a central-leader standard (*see p.26*), with a clear trunk of 1.5–2m (5–6ft). Little further pruning is required. The leader is strongly dominant, and despite their vigorously upright habit, the topmost laterals seldom form competing leaders, so do not shorten or remove them. Does not respond well to renovation.

P. NIGRA VAR. ITALICA

ITALIAN POPLAR, LOMBARDY POPLAR

Probably the best known fastigiate tree (*see p.18*), widely planted as a windbreak or visual screen in the open landscape. The cultivar 'Plantierensis' is similar, branching lower and with a denser, slightly broader crown. It makes a more effective screen and is less prone to canker.

■ **WHEN TO PRUNE** As for *P. alba*.

■ **TRAINING AND PRUNING** Grow as a feathered tree (*see p.25*). Although little formative pruning is needed, cutting young laterals back to 10cm (4in) results in bushier growth that is useful for a screen. Although the leading shoot always appears to be under threat from competing laterals, actual dual leaders are very rare. Avoid pruning established trees; they cannot be renovated.

OTHER POPLARS

P. BALSAMIFERA (syn. **P. TACAMAHACA**) As for *P. trichocarpa*.

P. × BEROLINENSIS As for *P. nigra* VAR. *italica*.

P. × CANDICANS 'AURORA' Commonly grown as a central-leader or branched-head standard (*see p.26*). Remove suckers regularly during summer. Can also be coppiced annually or biennially, in late winter (*see p.34*), to produce a large-leaved, multi-stemmed shrub.

P. × CANDICANS 'GILEADENSIS' (syn. **P. × JACKII 'GILEADENSIS'**) As for *P. trichocarpa*.

P. × CANESCENS As for *P. × canadensis*.

P. MAXIMOWICZII As for *P. trichocarpa*.

P. TREMULA, P. TREMULOIDES Need little, if any, training or pruning.

P. TRICHOCARPA Easily trained as a central-leader standard (*see p.26*) with a clear trunk to a height of 2–3m (6–10ft). Prune in late summer or early autumn. In summer remove suckers at the base of the trunk. Little further pruning is required. Does not respond well to renovation.

P. WILSONII Very susceptible to canker: do not prune unless absolutely essential. To clear the trunk, to about 1.5m (5ft), rub out buds on the lower stem before they shoot. The upright habit of the laterals can lead inevitably to weak branch crotches and breakage. Remedial pruning is best done by a professional, but carries the risk of infection by canker and the loss of the tree.

PRUNUS

A huge and complex genus of deciduous
and evergreen trees and shrubs, grown
variously for attractive bark, foliage,
fruits and flowers, and for crops such
as plums, cherries and almonds. The
pruning of nearly all ornamental *Prunus*
is best kept to an absolute minimum.
Where formative pruning is necessary,
it should be done as early as possible,
aiming to create well-formed trees that
will need little further attention in later
life. Keeping pruning wounds small, and
pruning in midsummer, reduces the risk
of diseases such as silver leaf (*see p.123*).
In common with the stone fruits,
ornamental *Prunus* are sometimes
affected by gumming (*see p.123*).

P. AVIUM

GEAN, MAZZARD, WILD CHERRY

Hardy, deciduous
tree grown for its
white spring
flowers. With the
exception of the
dwarf 'Nana',
which needs no
pruning, cultivars, including 'Pendula',
are treated as for the species. Most
produce surface roots that sucker freely.

■ **WHEN TO PRUNE** Summer is best but not
essential. Remove dead wood in summer
and suckers in early spring.

■ **TRAINING AND PRUNING** Train as a
central-leader standard (*see p.26*) with
a clear trunk to a height of 1.5–2m
(5–6ft). Remove suckers by rubbing
out while young. Established trees
need little further pruning and do not
respond well when cut hard back.

Rootstock shoots on *Prunus* 'Ukon'
The growth of epicormic shoots (*see p.30*) on
clear trunks (here below a top-graft union) is
a common problem with *Prunus*.

P. CERASIFERA

CHERRY PLUM, MYROBALAN

Fully hardy,
deciduous tree
grown for its
profuse white
flowers, followed,
in areas with warm
summers, by red
cherry plums. It is grown as a branched-
head standard, but also makes an attractive
flowering hedge.

■ **WHEN TO PRUNE** In midsummer. Prune
established hedges after flowering.

■ **TRAINING AND PRUNING** Train initially
as a central-leader standard (*see p.26*) with
a clear trunk to a height of at least 1.5m
(5ft). Horizontal branches often throw up
vigorous, vertical shoots. Remove these or
reduce by one-third to avoid competition
with the leader. The leader breaks by early
maturity, resulting naturally in a dense,
congested crown. Pruning of established
specimens is best kept to a minimum, as it
stimulates the growth of epicormic shoots
that spoil the crown. They do not respond
well to renovation.
  To grow *P. cerasifera* as a hedge, plant
young trees or whips at 1m (3ft) spacings
during the dormant season. Tip back
the leading shoots in midsummer
to encourage branching. In subsequent
growing seasons, clip back the new growth
by about one-quarter to one-third in
midsummer until the required dimensions
have been achieved. Once established, clip
annually in early summer, immediately
after flowering. Overgrown hedges respond
well to renovation by hard pruning,
preferably spread over three years (*see
Hedge renovation, p.47*).

P. DULCIS

ALMOND

Hardy, deciduous
tree, valued in cool
temperate gardens
for its mass of white,
pale pink or rose-
pink flowers in late
spring. The nuts
(almonds) ripen
fully only in Mediterranean-type climates.
The lightly branched crown casts only
dappled shade, permitting underplanting.
Single trees look splendid against a
dark background, and group plantings
make an exceptionally beautiful garden
feature. Trees are usually raised by budding
on to plum rootstocks, and are often sold as
whips (*see p.22*). Rootstock suckering can
be a problem. Almonds are susceptible to
peach leaf curl (*see also Peaches, p.132*).

Top-grafted Japanese cherry
Always choose young trees with neat, sound
graft unions: never cut or pare graft points
that have become unsightly with age.

■ **WHEN TO PRUNE** Prune and remove
dead wood in midsummer. Remove
suckers in early spring.

■ **TRAINING AND PRUNING** Train as a
central-leader standard (*see p.26*) with
a clear trunk to a maximum height of
1.5m (5ft). Remove suckers from the
rootstock in early spring, by rubbing
out or, if necessary, paring with a
sharp pruning knife (*see Suckers, p.30*).
Established trees need little further
pruning. They commonly produce
twiggy growth in early maturity,
usually resulting in increased flower
production. Thinning of the crown
is unnecessary and usually spoils the
tree's habit. To wall-train, *see Peach
fan, p.134*.

P. SATO-ZAKURA GROUP

JAPANESE FLOWERING CHERRIES

These complex hybrids, probably all
derived from *Prunus serrulata*, form
one of the most important groups of
flowering trees in the temperate world.
They vary enormously in growth, habit
and character. They include fastigiate
forms such as 'Amanogawa'; weeping,
mushroom-shaped domes such as 'Kiku-
shidare' (syn. 'Cheal's Weeping'); the stiffly
ascending, vase-shaped 'Kanzan' (syn.
'Sekiyama'), and the largest-flowered of
all, the broadly spreading 'Taihaku', the
great white cherry. All are grafted and,
depending on the cultivar, are grown
variously as central-leader, branched-head
or weeping standards. Most need little, if
any, pruning.

■ **WHEN TO PRUNE** Early to midsummer.

Young *Prunus* 'Amanogawa'
To encourage strong, upright branches and reduce the risk of wind damage, in the first year loop them loosely around a cane or stake with strips of hessian or netting, or soft twine.

■ **TRAINING AND PRUNING** In general, do not prune unless absolutely essential. If removing, for example, dead wood or crossing or rubbing branches, the tree's natural habit, whether fastigiate, spreading, weeping and so on, should be enhanced, and not compromised, by pruning operations. All pruning must be undertaken early in the tree's life. *P*. 'Kanzan' will naturally form a short trunk, displaying its bronzed young foliage and pink flowers at eye level. Where access beneath the tree is necessary, train early with a clear stem to a height of 1.5–2m (5–6ft).

P. 'Amanogawa' is strongly upright, but the branches can be lax when young, and will benefit from support (*see left*).

On established trees, prune only to remove any dead, diseased and damaged wood, and any suckers that appear below graft unions, pruning in summer. Drastic pruning to renovate a tree is seldom successful.

P. SERRULA

BIRCH-BARK TREE

A fully hardy, deciduous tree grown for its smooth, glossy, mahogany-red bark that peels with age. Small white flowers in spring are followed by red fruits in autumn.

20 | 70
m | ft

■ **WHEN TO PRUNE** Early to midsummer. Pruning in spring results in gumming (*see p.123*) that may cause bark dieback.

■ **TRAINING AND PRUNING** Train as a central-leader standard, ensuring well-spaced laterals. Remove unwanted laterals by rubbing out buds before they shoot, to prevent stem blemish at maturity. Train with a clear trunk no taller than 1.5m (5ft); excessive clearing will spoil the crown. To enhance the bark effect on the lower limbs, clear sub-laterals to within 30–45cm (12–18in) of the main trunk, again by rubbing out buds. Do not prune established trees: it creates wounds that seldom seal fully and results in atypical growth.

OTHER PRUNUS
P. CORNUTA As for *P. padus*.
P. MAACKII Train as a central-leader standard, clearing the trunk to about 2m (6ft) as for *P. serrula*, rubbing out buds before they shoot. Established trees need no special pruning and do not respond well to hard cutting back.
P. PADUS As for *P. avium*, but must be trained early: soon produces vigorous upright growth. Plant ideally at only two or three years old. Older specimens tend to produce dual leaders.
P. SEROTINA As for *P. padus*.
P. SERRULATA See *P*. Sato-zakura group.
P. SPINOSA Suckering shrub or small tree. Transplant stress (*see p.23*) increases suckering. Prune in mid-summer. To grow as a tree, train a field-raised whip initially as a central-leader standard (*see p.26*). Remove basal suckers and clear the trunk to one-quarter of the young tree's height by rubbing out buds before they shoot. A branched head will develop naturally. Once established, little further pruning is needed other than the annual removal of suckers. If grown as a shrub, needs little pruning; control spread by annually removing surplus basal growth. To grow as a hedge, plant 45–60cm (18–24in) apart and treat as for *P. cerasifera*.
P. SUBHIRTELLA Grown as branched-head standards or multi-stemmed specimens needing little or no pruning. A strong central leader is seldom formed. Clear the stem (*see p.26*) to about 1.5m (5ft), or allow branching from the base.
For other species, see Dictionary of Ornamental Shrubs (*p.212*) *and* Hardy Fruits (*pp.122–136*).

Correcting uneven growth, top-grafted *Prunus*

Year 1

1 Lightly tip-prune branches on the stronger side.

2 Shorten weak growth by two-thirds to stimulate vigorous regrowth.

3 Remove any shoots on the clear trunk.

Year 2

1 Shorten vigorous laterals, but leave branch leaders unpruned.

2 Prune vigorous growth by one-half, and weaker shoots harder, to one or two buds.

3 Remove any shoots on the clear trunk. The pruning cuts above may have stimulated their growth.

Year 3

Head of branches now more evenly balanced

1 Remove any vigorous shoots that spoil the balanced shape of the head.

2 Remove any shoots on the clear trunk.

PTEROCARYA *WING NUT*

Deciduous trees grown for their catkins and slender-winged nuts. Though fully hardy when mature, they can be frost-tender when young. All develop heavy, spreading branches with pendulous sublaterals. *P. × rehderiana* and *P. fraxinifolia* tend to sucker.

■ **WHEN TO PRUNE** Late winter. With young trees, delay removing any frosted growth until there is no further danger of cold winds or late frosts. Never prune them in autumn; the cambium of the pithy wood shrinks, leading to frost crack.

PYRUS *PEAR*

Hardy, deciduous trees with white blossom and alternate-leaved foliage that often colours well in autumn. *P. communis* is grown for its fruit. Some species also have attractive bark. Fireblight (*see p.117*) may be a problem: cut out affected growth and disinfect tools.

■ **WHEN TO PRUNE** Autumn to early spring.

P. CALLERYANA

CALLERY PEAR

Valued for its white spring blossom, russet-brown fruits and, especially in areas with long, hot summers, autumn colour. *P. calleryana* 'Bradford' has a distinctive pyramidal form; although often recommended as a street tree, the branches frequently form weak crotches that may break. 'Chanticleer' seems less prone to structural weakness.

■ **TRAINING AND PRUNING** Train as a central-leader standard (*see p.26*) with a clear trunk of 1.5–2m (5–6ft). For 'Bradford' and 'Chanticleer', retain only laterals that are evenly and well spaced around the trunk to reduce the risk of branch failure at maturity. Established trees need little further pruning. They do not respond well to drastic pruning.

P. SALICIFOLIA

WILLOW-LEAVED PEAR

Grown for its pure white flowers that coincide with new, silvery leaves. Its spreading crown of horizontal branches bears semi- or, in the widely grown cultivar 'Pendula', fully pendulous sublaterals, creating a curtain of willow-like foliage. Loss of the leader

■ **TRAINING AND PRUNING** Train as central-leader standards (*see p.26*). Clear the trunk to one-third of the young tree's height by rubbing out buds before they shoot. It is important to maintain a clear trunk of this height until early maturity. Remove suckers from the base or roots as seen; if a mass build up, removing all simultaneously will stimulate many more to grow. The crown of mature trees may need lifting (*see p.33*) to stop the pendulous sublaterals reaching ground level and rooting to form an unsightly mass of congested growth.

Pyrus salicifolia
The zigzag habit of shoots and sideshoots will disguise light thinning or trimming cuts.

may be due to poor soil or transplant shock. Plant as young as possible.

■ **TRAINING AND PRUNING** Train as a central-leader standard (*see p.26*), with a clear trunk to 1–2m (3–6ft), depending on whether foliage to the ground is required (bear in mind that the pendulous habit only develops with maturity). 'Pendula' needs a trunk of at least 1.5m (5ft) to accommodate its fully weeping habit. To avoid congestion at maturity, thin laterals in the early years to create an evenly spaced, balanced framework. Established trees need little further pruning. Though light thinning or trimming is tolerated, trees do not respond well if cut back hard. If growth is vigorous, established specimens may need crown thinning (*see p.33*); take great care not to create gaps in the curtain of foliage since older trees rarely produce replacement growth.

OTHER PYRUS
P. COMMUNIS See Pears, *p.117*.
P. USSURIENSIS As for *P. calleryana*.

Q

QUERCUS *OAK*

An enormous and varied genus of frost- to fully hardy, evergreen and deciduous trees, generally slow-growing and noted for their strength and longevity. They are usually grown as central-leader specimens, producing a spreading crown of large, heavy limbs that support smaller, often bushy sublaterals, thus producing the characteristic billowing outline.

Q. CERRIS

TURKEY OAK

Broadly domed, deciduous tree with fissured bark, eventually stately in form, with a trunk of 2m (6ft) or more in diameter. It is distinguished by its variably cut and lobed leaves, the twisted whiskery growths that surround the buds, and the acorns enclosed in mossy cups.

■ **WHEN TO PRUNE** When dormant, between autumn and early spring.

■ **TRAINING AND PRUNING** Train as a central-leader standard (*see p.26*) with a clear trunk to 2.5m (8ft). In areas with short, cool summers, as in northern Britain, the leading shoot may lose dominance at an early age, resulting in shrubby growth of poor form. To preserve the leader, clear the trunk gradually over three to five years, reducing each limb progressively in two or three stages. Apart from the regular removal of dead wood, established trees need little further pruning. Renovation of these large trees, including the removal of large dead branches within the canopy, should be undertaken only by a professional arboriculturist.

Q. ILEX

HOLM OAK

One of the finest of evergreen oaks, forming a broad, rounded canopy well-furnished with dark, glossy leaves that are grey-fawn beneath. Young trees, best planted as young as possible, vary in habit from pendulous to fastigiate (usually somewhere in between), often resembling shrubs when young. All, however, produce a central leader. The holm oak tolerates clipping if trained early as a hedge (*see p.44*) or as a large, formally shaped tree.

■ **WHEN TO PRUNE** Mid- to late summer, after the first flush of rapid growth.

■ **TRAINING AND PRUNING** Train as a feathered tree (*see p.25*), allowing lower laterals to be shed naturally through shading out. The leader only just retains dominance, but do not shorten laterals that appear to compete; these will ultimately form framework limbs. Old specimens often form asymmetrical crowns, but restoration is seldom successful: holes in the crown rarely fill in. Only prune established specimens if essential: for example, to deal with storm damage. This should be dealt with by a professional. The pendulous growth of low branches is attractive, and crown lifting should only be undertaken if essential for light penetration or access.

Q. ROBUR

COMMON OAK

Deciduous tree with a broad canopy of strong, heavy framework branches arising from a trunk that becomes gnarled and massive with age. Grown as a central-leader tree, it is suitable for large gardens and open parkland. The cultivars 'Cristata' and 'Filicifolia' and the fastigiate form are best left to develop naturally. *Q. robur* f. *pendula* should be trained as for the species.

■ **WHEN TO PRUNE** When dormant, between autumn and early spring.

■ **TRAINING AND PRUNING** Train as a central-leader standard (*see p.26*), aiming to clear the trunk to about one-quarter of the tree's overall height by the third or fourth growing season. Little further formative pruning is required. Old specimens may accumulate dead wood, and if extensive this should only be removed by a professional arboriculturist. A proliferation of epicormic shoots on the main stem and lower laterals usually precedes dieback. This does not necessarily herald the end of the tree's life; the English oak can take as long to die as it does to reach maturity. Pollarding (*see p.34*) is an option for renovation.

Q. PALUSTRIS

PIN OAK

Elegant tree with often brilliant red autumn colour. Although hardy, it is much less vigorous in cool climates. It should always be trained as a central-leader standard to show off its light branching habit.

20 | 70
m | ft

Quercus robur
Mature oaks can often become "stag-headed", their "antlers" resulting from the dieback of upper branches. They may yet survive for years, protected by the natural barriers (*see p.9*) that plants form between live and dead wood.

■ **WHEN TO PRUNE** As for *Q. cerris*.

■ **TRAINING AND PRUNING** Train as a central-leader standard (*see p.26*) and maintain a clear trunk to approximately one-quarter of the young tree's height until early maturity. In hot-summer climates, retain the leading shoot for as long as possible. In cooler climates the crown usually soon branches but this does not cause problems. Established trees need little further pruning.

OTHER OAKS

Q. AGRIFOLIA As for *Q. ilex*.
Q. ALBA As for *Q. palustris*.
Q. CANARIENSIS As for *Q. robur*.
Q. COCCINEA As for *Q. palustris*.
Q. FRAINETTO A very attractive habit: at maturity, lower laterals produce semi-pendulous sublaterals that contrast with the upward sweep of all other branches. Develops naturally as a central-leader standard and needs little pruning (if necessary, prune while dormant). It is vital, however, that damage to the leader is avoided; if lost, it cannot be replaced.
Q. × HISPANICA 'LUCOMBEANA' (syn. *Q. × LUCOMBEANA*) All pruning is best carried out in mid- to late summer. Train as a central-leader standard (*see p.26*) with a clear trunk to about 1.5m (5ft) at early maturity, thus allowing the pendulous sublaterals to form an elegant curtain of foliage. Established trees need little pruning other than the regular removal of dead wood, easily seen in summer; branches that defoliate completely in winter often leaf up again in spring.
Q. MACRANTHERA Train as for *Q. palustris*. Established trees need little pruning.

Q. PETRAEA In temperate climates can be treated as for *Q. robur*, which it resembles. In colder regions, as in the western escarpment oak woods of northern Britain, trees grow gnarled and stunted, showing clearly the dwarfing effects of low summer temperatures. In these conditions, such climate-trained trees make interesting specimens and need no pruning.
Q. RUBRA As for *Q. robur*. It is essential to select a straight-stemmed, evenly feathered young tree; the growth pattern, often influenced by climate and site, is set early and pruning cannot change it. Young trees need shelter during their first two winters and will only form a balanced crown where there is no competition from other trees.
Q. SUBER In Mediterranean and warm temperate climates, train as a central-leader standard (*see p.26*) with a clear trunk to about 2m (6ft), pruning in mid- to late summer. Established trees need little further pruning. In cool climates, although a leader is relatively easily maintained, vigour is poor and pruning can do little to improve the form; *Q. ilex* is a better choice.

OTHER ORNAMENTAL TREES

PTEROCELTIS As for *Ulmus carpinifolia* (*see p.91*). Grows best in areas with long, hot summers, reaching 12m (40ft). In cooler regions seldom retains a central leader and is best allowed to develop naturally, producing twiggy, shrubby growth.

R

RHUS *SUMACH*

Trees and shrubs, many toxic, grown for their architectural form and foliage that often colours well in autumn. Dense panicles of flowers give rise in some species to conical clusters of fruits.

R. VERNICIFLUA

VARNISH TREE

Hardy, glossy-leaved tree that only achieves its full potential height in areas with warm summers. When cut, it oozes a resin that can cause severe contact dermatitis and vomiting. Avoid skin contact when pruning. Do not burn prunings since the smoke may also cause skin reaction.

■ **WHEN TO PRUNE** Late summer.

■ **TRAINING AND PRUNING** Train as a central-leader standard (*see p.26*), clearing the trunk to about 1m (3ft). The leader is lost relatively early and a broad crown soon develops. Little further pruning is required.

> **OTHER RHUS**
> *For other species, see* Dictionary of Ornamental Shrubs, *p.217.*

ROBINIA

Deciduous, often spiny, hardy trees and shrubs grown for their foliage, flowers and, in some cases, rugged bark. Nearly all grow vigorously and on rich soil may produce overvigorous shoots prone to wind damage. In exposed areas, many are tender when young: plant in spring and do not feed, as fertilizers stimulate soft growth vulnerable to frost.

R. PSEUDOACACIA

FALSE ACACIA, LOCUST

Grown for its fragrant flowers in summer, and for its delicate leaves. In continental climates, usually makes a sound tree, but in cool maritime climates the wood is brittle and susceptible to wind damage, so good training is essential. Plant as young as possible. Treat most cultivars, including the fastigiate 'Pyramidalis', as for the species. They may be grafted, and may sucker. The cultivar 'Inermis', the mophead acacia, naturally branches densely and needs no thinning.

■ **WHEN TO PRUNE** Mid- to late summer.

■ **TRAINING AND PRUNING** Train as a central-leader standard (*see p.26*) with a clear trunk to about 2–2.5m (6–8ft). It is vital to maintain the leader until early maturity, so remove any competing leaders as soon as possible (*see p.24*). Ensure that laterals are evenly and well spaced, and remove any upright growth close to the trunk. Narrow crotch angles are invariably structurally weak.

Pruning of established trees is best kept to a minimum. Remove any suckers as early as possible. Large pruning cuts seldom heal well and are prone to rot. In addition, the tree responds with vigorous vertical growths, which may become dangerous if allowed to develop. Do not renovate, but fell the tree and, if ungrafted, use as a replacement one of the vigorous suckers that grow from the roots after felling.

> **OTHER ROBINIAS**
> R. BOYNTONII, R. ELLIOTTII, R. HARTWEGII, R. HISPIDA All have a multi-stemmed, shrub-like growth habit and need little or no pruning. *R. hispida* can be wall-trained, but has brittle branches; tie in while young and pliable.

***Robinia pseudoacacia* 'Frisia'**
This cultivar produces a changing foliage display, the leaves turning from clear yellow through lime green to orangey-gold in autumn.

S

SALIX *WILLOW*

A large and diverse genus of frost- to fully hardy, mainly deciduous trees and shrubs, grown variously for their habit, catkins, stem colour and foliage (with alternate leaves). Willows are generally very responsive to pruning and many species may be coppiced or pollarded to obtain brightly coloured young stems.

■ **WHEN TO PRUNE** Autumn to early spring. Remove dead wood in summer. Coppice or pollard suitable species in mid-spring, just before new growth begins.

S. ALBA

WHITE WILLOW

Hardy, strongly growing tree, often with a rather unshapely crown comprising upright branches with horizontal sublaterals that bear more or less pendulous shoots. Although it naturally produces a strong central leader, structural weakness is common in mature trees, since vigorous shoots tend to arise from the same point on main stems, leading to congested branches with included bark. It is essential, therefore, that early training establishes a well-spaced branch system. A number of plants in this group, including *S. alba* 'Britzensis' and 'Vitellina', and *S. alba* var. *sericea*, are popularly coppiced and pollarded for their stem effect.

Willows pruned for stem effect
Coppicing and pollarding at various heights has produced a striking display of coloured stems, welcome in winter.

■ **TRAINING AND PRUNING** To grow as a tree, train as a central-leader standard (*see p.26*) but rub out lateral buds before shoots emerge until the trunk is clear to about 2m (6ft). To ensure a balanced branch framework, rub out excess lateral buds to produce evenly spaced, alternate branches as opposed to congested whorls of growth. Once a sound framework is established, little further pruning is needed.

To grow for stem effect, coppice or pollard (*see p.34*) annually or every other year. The length of main stem for pollards can be between 60 and 150cm (2–5ft) depending on the desired effect. This pruning pattern should be established from the start: mature trees respond badly if large wounds are made. Being very susceptible to decay, they rapidly form cavities. The reduction of dangerous limbs on mature trees should be carried out by a professional arboriculturist, but since problems will recur, the best option is to remove and replace old specimens. This is true of most vigorous willows.

S. CAPREA 'KILMARNOCK'

KILMARNOCK WILLOW

Hardy, compact, slow-growing, weeping tree forming an umbrella-shaped crown and bearing a profusion of male catkins in spring. Plants are usually sold as weeping standards, top-grafted onto a clear stem of about 1.5m (5ft). Although they need little further formative pruning (*see also p.26*), they require annual regulative pruning to prevent the crown becoming congested, with a mass of branches growing stiffly downwards to ground level.

■ **TRAINING AND PRUNING** The aim of annual pruning is to remove about 50 per cent of the branches to create a light, airy curtain of foliage that will just reach the ground by the end of the growing season. Thin out branches from within the crown to form an open, umbrella-like framework, and then thin the outermost sideshoots, removing them completely. Shorten the remaining branches by approximately half, cutting back to an outward-facing bud. In spring, the new flush of growth quickly disguises pruning wounds, and by midsummer the

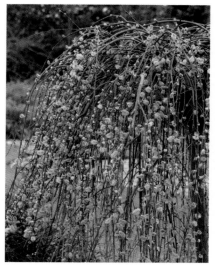

Kilmarnock willow
Salix caprea 'Kilmarnock' is valued for its weeping habit, compact form and profusion of catkins that are first grey, then turn to yellow. Unlike many weeping standards, it benefits from an annual pruning programme.

tree is once again clothed to the ground. Remove regularly suckers arising below the graft union.

S. × SEPULCRALIS

WEEPING WILLOW

Hardy, broadly domed, strongly weeping deciduous hybrid between *S. alba* and *S. babylonica*, valued for its habit and for the brilliant green of its foliage that contrasts well with the yellow-tinted young shoots.

■ **TRAINING AND PRUNING** Young plants typically form a strong leader with short, almost stubby, horizontal laterals. Train initially as a central-leader standard (*see p.26*), with a clear trunk to 1.5–2m (5–6ft). As growth proceeds, the leader will eventually be lost so that the crown broadens and assumes its weeping habit. The tree then increases in height by means of a single, upright, whippy shoot that rises above other laterals during the growing season before

OTHER WILLOWS

S. ALBA 'TRISTIS', S. × PENDULINA As for *S. × sepulcralis*.
S. BABYLONICA As for *S. × sepulcralis*. Needs a site sheltered from frost when young.
S. BABYLONICA VAR. PEKINENSIS 'TORTUOSA' (syn. *S. MATSUDANA* 'TORTUOSA') Noted for its contorted branches (*see also p.28*) clothed in narrow, twisted, bright green leaves. It grows naturally as a multi-stemmed tree with a short bole, needing little formative pruning, but remove about one in three inward-growing laterals to avoid later crown congestion. Once established, occasional thinning by removing badly placed or crossing laterals stimulates new growth and perpetuates the curious growth pattern. Old trees respond well to hard pruning, but as young trees grow more vigorously, replanting is preferable.
S. CAPREA, S. EXIGUA Shrubby, multi-stemmed habit, branching from the base; best left to develop naturally. They respond well if cut back to the base.
S. DAPHNOIDES Naturally forms a well-shaped multi-stemmed tree, or can be pruned hard for increased stem interest: young growth has purple bark with a plum-coloured bloom. Develop as a pollard or coppice as for *S. alba*, then cut back one in three stems every year.
S. FRAGILIS Train as a central-leader standard (*see p.26*), maintaining the leader for as long as possible: the crown will eventually divide and branch naturally.
S. HOOKERIANA Similar to *S. caprea*; may also be trained as a standard as for *S. alba*.
S. UDENSIS 'SEKKA' (syn. *S. SACHALINENSIS* 'SEKKA') Deciduous tree grown for its contorted stems, best cut back annually to a framework of branches to stimulate fresh growth with this curious habit. *For other species, see* Dictionary of Ornamental Shrubs, *p.216*.

adopting a weeping habit the following year: this shoot should never be pruned because of its seemingly atypical early growth habit. In subsequent years, new leading shoots develop on an annual basis, creating a layered crown. Established specimens need little pruning, although occasional crown thinning allows light and air into the centre, strengthening branches that support laterals that become heavy with age. Trees do not respond well to hard pruning.

OTHER ORNAMENTAL TREES

REHDERODENDRON *R. macrocarpum* is best as a feathered tree (*see p.25*) but needs little, if any, pruning. Will not renovate.
ROTHMANNIA Train as a central-leader standard (*see p.26*), pruning after flowering or fruiting has finished. Established trees need minimal attention.
SAMBUCUS *See* Dictionary of Ornamental Shrubs, *p.217*.
SAPINDUS Train as central-leader standards (*see p.26*). Established trees need minimal attention.
SAPIUM Train as a central-leader standard (*see p.26*). Established trees need minimal attention.

SASSAFRAS

Sassafras albidum is a deciduous tree that seldom achieves its potential height of 30m (100ft) in cool climates, where its growth is usually shrubby. In continental climates, it is fully hardy and easily trained as a central-leader standard (*see p.26*) with a clear trunk to a height of about 1.5–2m (5–6ft). To attain this form in mild maritime climates, shelter from winter winds and frost for the first two or three years. Remove frost-damaged growth in early summer. If the leader is lost, it is best to allow the tree to develop as a multi-stemmed, suckering shrub. Otherwise no special attention is required.

SCHEFFLERA

The ivy or umbrella trees are tropical and subtropical evergreens grown for their striking leaves and large clusters of flowers. The recently introduced *S. taiwaniana* is a very cold-tolerant species valued for its handsome foliage. Most need little or no pruning. Plants grown under glass will tolerate hard pruning to limit size: cut back growth to a shoot or main branch in early spring before growth commences.

SCHIMA

Evergreens similar to camellias, needing frost-free or, given a warm site and wall protection, almost frost-free conditions. *S. wallichii* can be grown in tubs in a cool greenhouse or conservatory, as for camellias (*see p.180*). Schimas need little or no formative pruning, but tolerate even hard pruning if necessary. Removing frost-damaged growth usually causes shoots to break from old wood and these can be trained to replace damaged portions of the crown.

SCHINUS

Evergreen, often spiny trees or shrubs grown for their aromatic foliage, small white or yellow flowers and ornamental fruits. Most need a frost-free climate, but in cooler regions are easily grown in a cool greenhouse or conservatory. *S. polygamus* tolerates light frosts. In warm climates, it needs little pruning or training, growing naturally as a multi-stemmed shrub or small feathered tree. It may also be trained against a warm, sunny wall (*see Magnolia grandiflora, p.74*). Under glass, it will tolerate cutting back to confine to bounds. Prune during midsummer when the first flush of new growth has ceased.

SOPHORA

Trees and shrubs grown for their foliage, pendent flowers and, in some tree species, ruggedly handsome bark. Most grow best in warm climates with hot summers. *S. japonica*, the pagoda or Chinese scholar tree, is widely grown as a street tree. Sophoras that tolerate cool maritime climates may not flower in these conditions. They resent root disturbance, so plant as young as possible.

■ **WHEN TO PRUNE** Summer; many species bleed if pruned in late winter or spring.

■ **TRAINING AND PRUNING** Train as central-leader standards (*see p.26*) with a clear trunk to a height of 1.5–2m (5–6ft). In continental climates, they produce a vigorous central leader, naturally shed lower limbs and form a sound branch system, so need little formative pruning. In temperate climates, the leader is usually lost early and an open crown develops, with large, heavy, contorted branches arising from near the same point low down on the main stem. These branches may break in strong winds, so it is essential to maintain a leader for as long as possible, and to select laterals in the early years that will form a balanced framework. If the leader is lost, select and train in a replacement (*see p.24*). This is difficult, but possible with perseverance, and is important since the dominant shoot inhibits the production of weak, contorted branches. Established trees need little pruning, and do not respond well to renovation.

SORBUS

Small to medium-sized deciduous trees and shrubs, grown for their form and foliage, spring flowers and autumn fruits and, often, foliage colour. They are generally undemanding and need little pruning. They prefer cool climates: *S. alnifolia* and *S. commixta* are better suited to areas with hot summers. Most are ideally planted as unbranched whips (*see p.22*) and trained young. This reduces transplant stress and helps to maintain a strong central leader. Semi-mature trees also establish easily; the intermediate (and most widely sold) tree sizes appear to suffer most transplant check. Some cultivars may be grafted. Fireblight (*see p.117*) can cause dieback.

■ **WHEN TO PRUNE** Autumn to early spring. Remove dead wood in summer.

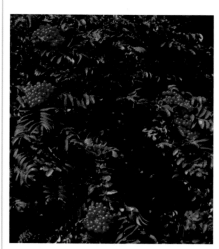

Sorbus aucuparia
The rowan or mountain ash is noted for the profusion of red berries it bears in autumn.

S. ARIA

WHITEBEAM

Dome-shaped tree with upswept branches bearing leathery leaves, white-felted below, and red berries. The canopy often develops an irregular shape on exposed sites; pruning can do little to correct it.

■ **TRAINING AND PRUNING** Train initially as a central-leader standard (*see p.26*), removing laterals so that the trunk is clear to a height of 2m (6ft) by early maturity. The crown can then be allowed to branch. Little further pruning is needed. Cannot be renovated as a tree, but if cut to the ground will regrow as an attractive shrubby thicket.

S. AUCUPARIA

MOUNTAIN ASH, ROWAN

Usually, a broadly conical central-leader standard, ideal for urban plantings and for small to medium-sized gardens. Prune all cultivars as for the species.

■ **TRAINING AND PRUNING** Train as a central-leader standard (*see p.26*) with a clear trunk to a height of 1.5–2m (5–6ft), depending on vigour. Ensure that laterals are alternately and evenly spaced around the trunk, aiming to produce about five main framework branches. This is especially important on fastigiate cultivars such as 'Sheerwater Seedling'. Closely spaced branches often constrict the main stem and result in crotches with included bark that are structurally

Sophora japonica
Cool climates inhibit flowering, but the attractive foliage has great ornamental value.

weak. 'Xanthocarpa' tends to lose its leader early: it should be retained at least until the stem has been cleared. Restrict pruning of established trees to the removal of dead and damaged wood, and of suckers that appear below the graft union on grafted cultivars. Poorly formed specimens are difficult to restore, and are better replaced.

OTHER SORBUS
S. AMERICANA As for *S. aucuparia*. Young trees produce ascending laterals: if any compete with the leader, rub out their terminal buds.
S. CASHMIRIANA As for *S. americana*.
S. COMMIXTA As for *S. aria*.
S. DOMESTICA Train as a central-leader standard (*see p.26*) with a clear trunk to 2m (6ft) so that the horizontal branches, with semi-pendulous sublaterals, clothe the tree with foliage to the ground. Little further pruning is required. Remove accumulated dead wood from old trees.
S. HUPEHENSIS As for *S. aucuparia*, with a clear trunk of 2m (6ft): with age, lower branches adopt a semi-pendulous habit.
S. 'JOSEPH ROCK' Select young, lightly branched specimens. The form is often spoiled by an overlong trunk. Aim to create a short clear trunk of 1m (3ft), and maintain a central leader until early maturity, when the crown will begin to open up slightly. Little further attention is necessary.
S. REDUCTA *See* Dictionary of Ornamental Shrubs, *p.219*.
S. VESTITA (syn. *S. CUSPIDATA*) Train as a central-leader standard (*see p.26*), clearing the trunk to 1m (3ft) by the fourth growing season. Established trees need little pruning.

STYRAX

Deciduous and evergreen trees and shrubs with alternate leaves, grown for their graceful habit and pendent clusters of white flowers in summer. Most cultivated species are tender when young but hardy once established. They dislike pruning, and are best left to develop naturally and informally: they are ideal for woodland gardens and other sheltered sites.

S. JAPONICUS

JAPANESE SNOWBELL

Small, hardy deciduous tree, occasionally a large shrub, with a dense, rounded crown of more or less horizontal branches supporting slender twiggy growth. It dislikes pruning. Training to produce a good leader relies mainly on the prevention of any check in growth during the early years. Plant as young as possible, in a site sheltered from late spring frosts. Avoid exposure to early morning sun to reduce the risk of frost damage.

■ **WHEN TO PRUNE** Autumn to early spring.

■ **TRAINING AND PRUNING** Aim to produce a central-leader tree (*see p.26*) with a short clear trunk. As the dense crown develops, the lowest laterals begin to die back naturally through shading out. Remove the dying limbs by cutting back to the branch collar (*see p.10*) in early spring. Established specimens need little further pruning and do not respond well when cut back hard.

OTHER STYRAX
S. HEMSLEYANUS, S. OBASSIA In warm climates, as for *S. japonicus*. In cool climates, young plants need an open, sunny site. Grow as multi-stemmed trees (*see p.28*); despite narrow crotch angles, the strongly upright branches, which rapidly equal the leading shoot in vigour, are structurally sound at maturity. Established specimens need little pruning. The vigorous growth produced in response to hard pruning is likely to be damaged in hard winters.

SYZYGIUM *LILLY PILLY*

Evergreen trees and shrubs needing a moist, warm temperate to tropical climate, cultivated both as ornamentals and for their edible fruits (most commonly known as water or water rose apples, or jambolans), which can be used in cooking and preserves. Tree-forming species tend to branch low and form a broad, dense, sometimes irregular crown. Though often left to grow naturally as multi-stemmed trees (most have a tendency to branch from the base), they are very tolerant of pruning, which can be used to stimulate fruit production. If a more manageable, heavier-cropping tree is desired, create a multi-stemmed tree on a short leg of 60–90cm (2–3ft), as for *Acer davidii* (*see p.52*), pruning in early spring. Tip-prune any over-vigorous shoots to encourage balanced development. Most species will continue to produce lateral shoots low on the trunk and these and any water shoots should be removed at an early stage, preferably by rubbing them out by hand as they emerge. When trees are established, remove only crossing, diseased or dead wood at regular intervals. Root pruning (*see p.101*) or bark-ringing (*see p.106*) are sometimes used to increase the production of vigorously growing but low-yielding trees.

OTHER ORNAMENTAL TREES
SCHOTIA Train *S. brachypetala* as a central-leader standard (*see p.26*). Established trees tolerate pruning to thin and improve the shape if necessary.
SESBANIA As for *Cassia, p.56*.
SINOWILSONIA As for *Hamamelis, p.196*.
SPATHODEA Train S. *campanulata* (syn. *S. wrightii*) as a central-leader standard (*see p.26*). Established trees have no special pruning needs.
STENOCARPUS Evergreen tree (*see p.25*), needs minimal training as a central-leader standard. Established trees have no special pruning needs.
STERCULIA Train as a central-leader standard (*see p.26*). Established trees have no special pruning needs.
STEWARTIA (syn. STUARTIA) Need little or no formative pruning, and are best allowed to grow naturally so that plants produce flowering shoots more or less to ground level. In continental climates the leader is maintained, but in cool areas trees will branch low and become broadly tiered with age. Planting as young as possible in a sheltered site encourages more tree-like growth.

T

TAMARINDUS *TAMARIND*

Large evergreen with a dense, spreading, rounded crown, grown for its pods in tropical regions. In subtropical areas it is used as a roadside shade tree. It tolerates a range of warm-climate conditions including drought. Young trees are frost-sensitive but older trees are more resistant. Young trees grow slowly, and seedlings rarely fruit until at least five to seven years old. Grafted cultivars are preferable, flowering three or four years after planting. They normally require little training or pruning when established. Renewal pruning is carried out as a matter of course as pods are harvested. To restrict size or renew less productive fruiting growth, cut back fruited wood to a well-placed sideshoot. Trees usually respond well to crown reduction (*see p.33*) if necessary.

TILIA *LIME, LINDEN*

Deciduous, usually long-lived trees grown for their stature, habit, foliage and sweetly scented flowers. Some are very tolerant of pruning and training and are often pollarded (*see p.34*) or pleached (*see p.36*); heavily pruned trees often sucker freely. Several species produce large burrs that give rise to a mass of upward-growing epicormic shoots. Sometimes these shoots add character, but they usually need removing since they can spoil the crown if allowed to develop. At maturity, many limes accumulate and shed dead wood. Dieback tends to occur from the tips downwards, producing a "stag-headed" effect (*see also Quercus, p.84*).

■ **WHEN TO PRUNE** Midsummer to midwinter; limes bleed if pruned in spring.

T. PLATYPHYLLOS

Stately, deciduous tree with a narrow crown of large, heavy, strongly upright branches. Despite very tight crotch angles with included bark and water pockets, it rarely sheds branches. It is prone to cavities but seldom produces burrs or epicormic shoots.

■ **TRAINING AND PRUNING** Train as a central-leader standard (*see p.26*), retaining the leader for as long as possible. Clear the trunk to a height of 2–3m (6–10ft) to allow sublaterals to hang down. As the tree matures, upper laterals begin to grow vigorously, frequently resulting in multiple leaders. These are safe in a well-balanced crown. Trees grown in exposed sites may develop distorted crowns, with branches that are prone to breakage. These are dangerously heavy and should be removed only by a qualified arboriculturist. Provided that trees are free from cavities, the crown of over-mature or declining trees may be reduced by a professional (*see* Major tree surgery, *p.33*) to remove heavy dead wood and extend the safe life of the tree.

T. TOMENTOSA

EUROPEAN WHITE LIME, SILVER LIME

Deciduous tree with a dense, regular crown of ascending branches, its dark leaves felted silver-white beneath.

■ **TRAINING AND PRUNING** Train as a central-leader standard (*see p.26*). The tree grows vigorously when young, and although it produces upright upper laterals, these seldom compete with the leader, so do not reduce or remove them. Aim to clear the trunk to a height of 2.5–3m (8–10ft) by early maturity. If allowed to branch low, this species may produce heavy limbs that form sub-canopies which spoil the otherwise regular outline. It will not respond well to renovation.

TOONA

Toona sinensis (syn. *Cedrela sinensis*) is a handsome, deciduous tree grown for its large leaves, unusual habit and ornamental bark. In warm climates, it also flowers. Train initially as a central-leader standard (*see p.26*) with a clear trunk of 2m (6ft), pruning when dormant, between autumn and early spring, then allow the crown to branch and the irregular habit to develop naturally. Established trees need little further attention and do not respond well to hard pruning. The cultivar 'Flamingo' has striking juvenile pink foliage.

OTHER LIMES

T. AMERICANA, **T. CHINENSIS**, **T. × EUROPAEA** (syn. **T. × VULGARIS**), **T. INSULARIS**, **T. MONGOLICA** As for *T. cordata*, though easier to train.

T. CORDATA Planting young in fertile soil in a sheltered site aids training, essential for a sound tree. Train very gradually as a central-leader standard, with a clear trunk to 2–3m (6–10ft). Delay the removal of laterals until the second or third year, then remove over three or four years, maintaining the leader. Established trees need little pruning (though always remove any shoots on the clear trunk) and do not respond well to hard pruning.

T. × EUCHLORA Readily forms a strong central leader and needs little pruning. Retain the lower laterals to encourage branching to ground level. Established trees naturally begin to exhibit irregular growth that pruning can do little to improve. They do not respond well to hard pruning.

T. OLIVERI Train initially as a central-leader standard (*see p.26*) with a clear trunk of 1.5–2m (5–6ft), then allow to branch to form its broad, domed crown.

T. 'PETIOLARIS' As for *T. tomentosa*. Rub out shoots below the graft union.

Pleached limes

Limes usually grow away well after planting, showing little transplant shock; it is therefore possible to buy and plant semi-mature specimens to hasten the finished result if planning a row of pleached trees.

U–Z

ULMUS *ELM*

Large, mainly deciduous trees, grown for their stature and habit. Since the 1960s, many have succumbed to the fatal Dutch Elm Disease; elms are now rare in Europe and North America. Some species are prone to branch drop, for reasons that are unclear, usually on warm, still days at the height of summer.

■ **WHEN TO PRUNE** Autumn to early spring.

U. CARPINIFOLIA SYN. U. MINOR

EUROPEAN FIELD ELM, SMOOTH-LEAVED ELM

Distinguished by its toothed, shiny, bright green leaves and narrow, domed crown of upright branches that arch at the tip, with long, pendulous branchlets.

30 | 100

m | ft

■ **TRAINING AND PRUNING** Train as a central-leader standard (*see p.26*) with a clear trunk of 2–3m (6–10ft). It produces a strong central leader that is easily maintained into maturity. Mature specimens require little, if any, pruning. They do not seem prone to branch drop.

U. GLABRA

SCOTCH ELM, WYCH ELM

Deciduous tree with a billowing canopy that may produce burrs and epicormic shoots but rarely suckers. 'Camperdownii' (the

35 | 120

m | ft

Camperdown elm) is a top-grafted weeping standard (*see p.26*) noted for its congested, tortuous branch system. 'Pendula' is a straight-stemmed tree, its weeping branches sporting a herring-bone fan of sublaterals.

■ **TRAINING AND PRUNING** Train as a central-leader standard (*see p.26*) with a clear trunk to about one-quarter of the young tree's overall height. Remove all laterals that are not evenly and well spaced around the stem. Tip-prune any that compete with the leader. Older trees accumulate dead wood, which can be heavy and should be professionally removed, particularly where there is public access beneath the tree. *U. glabra* 'Camperdownii' defies training and pruning. The pendulous sublaterals can be tip-pruned if necessary. Weaker limbs are often strangled by competitors. It is usually only possible to remove the extremities of dead branches. Little further

pruning is needed other than to remove any suckers on the clear stem. *U. glabra* 'Pendula' is also impossible to train or prune; let it grow naturally.

U. PARVIFOLIA

CHINESE ELM

Native to Asia, the Chinese elm is resistant to Dutch Elm Disease. It is frequently shrubby when young.

20 | 70

m | ft

■ **TRAINING AND PRUNING** Usually best left to grow naturally; it resists formative training and pruning. In continental climates it can be trained as a central-leader standard (*see p.28*) with a clear trunk to about one-quarter of the young tree's height. Established specimens need little, if any, further pruning. Any shoots that grow on the trunk and mask the attractive bark are best removed.

OTHER ELMS

U. AMERICANA Train as a central-leader standard (*see p.26*), clearing the trunk very gradually to about 4m (12ft) by early maturity (can be increased to 6m/20ft at maturity, depending on vigour). Mature trees need little pruning, except to remove epicormic shoots from the trunk. Where they appear within the crown, they should be dealt with by a professional, as should any damaged, heavy branches.
U. ANGUSTIFOLIA VAR. CORNUBIENSIS (syn. U. CARPINIFOLIA 'CORNUBIENSIS'), U. PLOTII As for *U. carpinifolia*.
U. × HOLLANDICA Hybrids developed for their resistance to Dutch Elm Disease, but not without drawbacks: tend to produce heavy, upright branches with narrow crotches; prone to epicormic shoots, root suckers and branch drop. Train as central-leader standards (*see p.26*), clearing the trunk to 2–3m (6–10ft). It is vital to maintain the leader for as long as possible and to reduce or remove any shoots that compete with it. Retain only laterals that are evenly and well-spaced around the trunk. Remove epicormic shoots on the trunk as for *U. procera*.
U. PROCERA Suckers profusely and is notorious for branch drop; unsuitable for urban environments. Train as a central-leader standard (*see p.26*), but do not remove lower limbs until they begin to die back naturally. Remove any shoots on the trunk using secateurs: tearing increases the risk of infection. Dead wood that accumulates should be removed by a professional to avoid branch drop.
U. PUMILA As for *U. parvifolia*.

ZELKOVA

Hardy, deciduous trees with smooth or flaking bark and alternate, toothed, rough-textured leaves. They look best as specimen central-leader standards.

Z. SERRATA

JAPANESE ZELKOVA

Large, broad-crowned tree with heavy, spreading branches. Though hardy when mature, it may be prone to frost damage when young. The leaves turn orange, pink and yellow in autumn.

35 | 120

m | ft

■ **WHEN TO PRUNE** Late winter. May be lightly pruned if necessary in summer.

■ **TRAINING AND PRUNING** Train as a central-leader standard (*see p.26*) with a clear trunk to 3m (10ft) and well-spaced framework branches. The lower branches of established trees are often semi-pendulous and the crown may need to be raised to allow access beneath. Cut back branch tips to a suitable lateral when the tree is in full leaf. Because they are so heavy, the removal of entire mature branches is best left to a professional.

OTHER ZELKOVAS

Z. ABELICEA (syn. Z. CRETICA) Grows naturally as a multi-stemmed tree (*see p.28*); remove only badly placed branches.
Z. CARPINIFOLIA Train with a clear trunk of 2–3m (6–10ft), then let the stem divide to form an egg-shaped, multi-stemmed crown. Thin the crown carefully when trees are young or semi-mature to reduce the risk of later defects: mature specimens do not respond well to drastic pruning.
Z. SINICA As for *Z. serrata*. Susceptible to coral spot, so keep pruning to a minimum.

OTHER ORNAMENTAL TREES

TABEBUIA Train as central-leader standards (*see p.26*). Established trees have no special pruning needs.
TECOMA Usually develop naturally as multi-stemmed trees. Under glass, limit size by shortening the current season's growth by half after flowering. Respond well to hard pruning; thin regrowth.
THEVETIA As for *Nerium* (*see p.207*).
UMBELLULARIA In warm climates, train as a central-leader standard (*see p.26*) with a clear trunk to 2m (6ft). In cool climates, grow as a feathered, multi-stemmed tree (*see p.28*) in a sheltered site. Branches may have narrow crotches but rarely break. Established trees need little attention.

Tree fruits

Whether grown primarily for their cropping potential or for their combined productive and decorative value, tree fruits need careful pruning and training to maintain high-quality yields.

There has been a revival of interest in growing fruit trees in the garden, due to an increasing desire not only for fresh, fully flavoured fruit, perhaps of more unusual cultivars than those usually found in the shops, but also for produce whose culture is known to have been free of interference from the application of chemical or preservative treatments. With this revival has come a rediscovery of the traditional pleasures of fruit-growing, and of the enormous decorative potential of fruit trees. Nearly all belong to genera that contain trees grown solely for their ornamental value. The choice of a tree that is both attractive and productive well justifies the extra attention needed to realize its cropping potential.

Pruning and training play major roles in fruit tree cultivation. Careful shaping and routine maintenance will maximize yields of high-quality fruit. Many of the tender fruits that crop only in tropical and subtropical climates need little more than basic care and for this reason have been grouped separately (*see pp.140–147*). However, the hardier fruits have always been the focus of great interest in creating more specialized trained forms. But while gardeners' aims in developing training methods have been to afford their trees more protection from harsh weather, or to create a more formal and decorative effect, commercial fruit growers have been more interested in

developing tree forms that are small, compact and easily managed. To meet these growers' needs, new rootstocks with a "dwarfing" effect were introduced, and these have made perhaps the most significant contribution to the wider growing of fruit trees in the domestic garden. With smaller trees, fruit growing is no longer the preserve only of those with large gardens or orchards. When less vigorous trees are grown in compact trained forms, two or even three cultivars can be accommodated in – and make a great ornamental contribution to – a small garden.

◀ Versatile apples
Apples may be grown in a diverse range of tree forms. Where space is restricted, many cultivars can be trained as cordons, espaliers or fan forms on fences or walls. In larger gardens, pyramid or bush forms on dwarfing rootstocks should be considered.

Peach in blossom
Although a major orchard crop only in warm-climate countries, in temperate zones peaches can be trained and pruned to make attractive small fruiting trees that can be grown in containers and brought under cover for winter protection.

Fruit Tree Forms

Most fruit trees can be trained into almost any shape, but several recognized forms have been developed to suit different situations and the habits of individual trees. Some forms are free-standing; others need permanent staking, or the support of a wall or wires. Some are freegrowing, with no restriction on shoot growth; on others, new shoots are pruned to maintain a shape or silhouette. When selecting a form, there are three main factors to consider. First, growth habit; if you want to grow an apple tree against a wall, for example, the espalier form ideally suits the way most apples fruit, on short shoots (spurs). Secondly, consider the space available, and the number of trees required for pollination purposes; several cordons can be sited in the space needed by one fan. Thirdly, estimate how much attention you are prepared to devote to your tree. Free-growing forms such as the bush and spindle bush are quite easy to shape and only need pruning once a year, in winter. More elaborate forms, such as the cordon and espalier, need precise training and need extra maintenance with a pruning programme that may stretch over several weeks in summer.

Bush

A very productive and widely used form, suitable for nearly all tree fruits where space for its considerable spread permits. Framework branches radiate from a trunk that is only 75–90cm (2½–3ft) tall; the leader is pruned to give a branched-headed, open-centred tree. The branches are evenly and well-spaced around and along the upper third of the trunk to give structural strength.

Half-standard

A half-standard is basically the same as a bush tree but with the crown growing above a taller, clear trunk. A vigorous rootstock is required to grow such a large tree. Because the extra height makes maintenance and harvesting more difficult, this form is rarely seen in modern orchards or fruit gardens. However, it provides a fine specimen tree of increased stature that would look well in an ornamental garden.

Standard

With a clear trunk of 2–2.1m (6–6½ft), standards can only be grown on the most vigorous rootstocks. The crown is formed as for a bush tree, though its spread will be far greater. In most gardens standards are too big to be practicable. They are, however, in demand for filling in gaps in old orchards to preserve old and valued non-commercial cultivars in traditional form.

Pyramid

Mainly used for plums, because the maintenance pruning required suits their fruiting habit, pyramids have branches that grow largely outwards. The tree tapers, allowing fruits on the lower branches to receive plenty of sun. These are small, compact trees, no more than 2–2½m (6–8ft) tall, easy to site in a small space because they can be planted closely.

Dwarf pyramid

Modern rootstocks with a very dwarfing effect enable many cultivars of apples and pears to be grown in this small, compact form, no more than 1.5–2m (5–6ft) tall and requiring only the same spacing distance if planted in rows or blocks. The strict pruning needed to restrict growth and spread suits apples and pears, fruiting on short spurs.

Spindle bush

A productive form popular in commercial apple production, the spindle bush – named after the tree's silhouette – has low main branches, creating a broad-based, conical form. The branches are trained horizontally for heavier cropping. Spindle bushes are grown with a stout stake, to which strings may be attached to support branches when they become heavy with fruit.

Cordon

A convenient form for apples and pears as several cultivars can be grown in a small space, on posts and wires or against a wall. For its size, an oblique cordon is very productive. It is a form widely used to produce fruits of exhibition quality, combining maximum sun exposure with all the vigour of a large root system directed into top growth restricted by pruning.

Double ("U") cordon

This variation on the single cordon is more usually grown upright, though it often grows most strongly at the top of its two main arms, so needs careful corrective pruning. A double cordon is easier to site against a narrow area of wall than two single, oblique cordons. It is also an ideal form for soft fruits that are spur-pruned, such as redcurrants.

Multiple cordons

Cordons with three, four or even more vertical arms need intricate training and maintenance, but the result is as decorative as an espalier. They are suitable for apples and pears. Three-armed (triple) cordons are inadvisable for certain cultivars because all the vigour is directed into the central arm. A four-armed ("double-U") cordon is preferable.

Fan
A decorative, heavy-cropping form, suitable for many tree fruits but particularly for stone fruits such as plums and peaches, and for figs. Correctly trained, the main stem is short, and the ribs of the fan originate from two low, angled arms.

Palmette
A variation on the espalier (*below*) in which staggered tiers of branches are angled upwards rather than sideways. It is easier to disguise a slight lack of symmetry with this less rigid form.

Espalier
This form is ideal for apples and pears, but does not suit stone fruits. Its decorative impact lies in its formal symmetry: the pairs of branches should be as nearly opposite as possible, and of equal length.

Stepover
This is a cordon bent almost at right-angles and then trained horizontally. Stepovers are usually free-standing, supported by strong wires. They can form an attractive low edging to a bed.

Rootstocks and tree size

Fruit trees will not usually breed true from seed nor grow satisfactorily from cuttings, so propagation has for centuries been by budding or grafting. Because the tree's growth rate and ultimate size are largely dependent on the rootstock, it has a significant bearing on pruning and training. Traditional vigorous rootstocks produced large, long-lived trees that needed little pruning to crop year after year. Modern rootstocks produce much smaller trees that need more careful pruning and training.

These new rootstocks are clonally reproduced, so all with the same name or number will produce trees of near identical size. The more "dwarfing" their effect, the quicker the tree will crop. In most cases they are special selections of the same fruit, although they can be of a different genus.

To overcome incompatibility between a cultivar and its proposed rootstock, an intermediate length of stem of a cultivar compatible with both may be used: there are thus two graft unions, and these trees are described as being "double-worked".

Never buy a fruit tree without ascertaining that the rootstock used is suitable for its intended site and form. Otherwise, you may end up with a tree that never fulfils your expectations. In particular, a vigorous tree can never be made or kept small by pruning: it will simply respond with more growth and little or no fruit.

How different rootstocks affect tree size
The same cultivar may be available in a range of tree sizes if compatible with several different rootstocks. Rootstocks are often given names or code numbers that refer to the place where they were developed: the "M" series for apples, for example, originated at the horticultural research station at East Malling in southern England.

FAMILY TREES
It is possible to produce a fruit tree made up of several cultivars growing on a single root system. These "family" trees have much more than novelty value: the cultivars may pollinate each other, or may have been selected to crop in sequence to supply ripe fruits over a long season. The rootstock must be carefully chosen, and the cultivars should be of approximately similar growth habit so that the tree is well balanced. Three cultivars is usual for a bush tree.

Fan-trained family tree

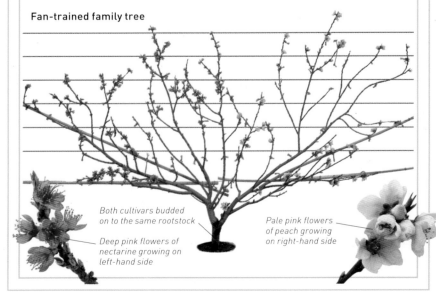

Both cultivars budded on to the same rootstock

Deep pink flowers of nectarine growing on left-hand side

Pale pink flowers of peach growing on right-hand side

Basic Techniques

There are three primary aims when pruning and training fruit trees: to influence the direction of shoot growth, ensuring structural strength and the desired tree form; to remove promptly dead, diseased or damaged wood and prevent crowded or crossing branches, protecting the tree's health; and to maintain a good balance between cropping and growth. Fulfilling these aims should result in a tree that crops evenly and regularly, with well-spaced branches that bear sound, ripe fruits.

Further aims, secondary to the tree's health, are of first importance to the gardener. The amount of space and the site available will influence the choice of cultivar and rootstock, and the tree form that is chosen. And in most gardens,

visual appeal will almost certainly be a factor; the extra work demanded by an espalier, for example, is handsomely repaid by its decorative impact.

DIFFERENT APPROACHES TO PRUNING
Choice of tree form dictates a training programme that can range from simple to intricate. When pruning mature trees, too, there is a clear distinction between the treatment of free-growing tree forms (bushes, standards and spindle bushes) and those where shoot growth has to be restricted (such as cordons, pyramids and fans). With free-growing forms, pruning is used simply to maintain the balance between the number of fruit buds that develop and the amount of growth (which represents future crop

potential) that is made. With restricted forms, pruning must also maintain size, shape and branch structure.

The techniques used will also need to be varied at different times of the year and at different stages in the tree's life. The key is to understand and respond to the growth and fruiting habit not only of fruit trees in general (the "composite tree" below, based on an apple, illustrates some of the terminology), but also of how the chosen fruit and cultivar is affected by your soil, site and climate.

Fortunately, with tree fruits pruning mistakes can usually be corrected within a year or two. Even a tree that has previously been pruned badly or has been neglected may be restored to years of fruitful life by careful renovation.

Different parts of the fruit tree

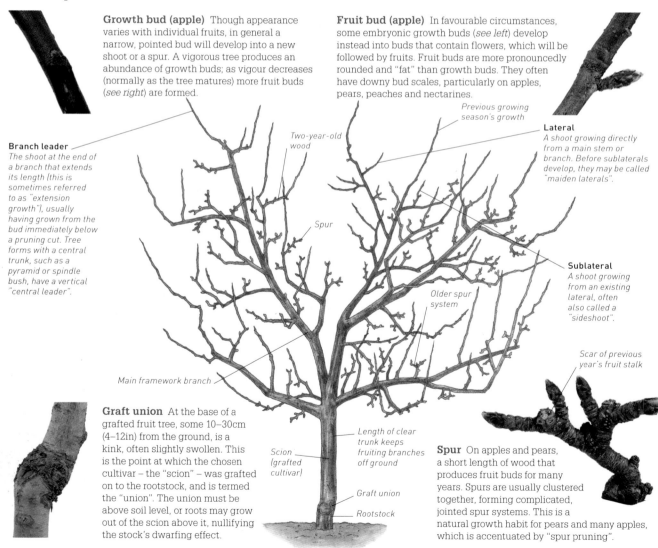

Growth bud (apple) Though appearance varies with individual fruits, in general a narrow, pointed bud will develop into a new shoot or a spur. A vigorous tree produces an abundance of growth buds; as vigour decreases (normally as the tree matures) more fruit buds (*see right*) are formed.

Fruit bud (apple) In favourable circumstances, some embryonic growth buds (*see left*) develop instead into buds that contain flowers, which will be followed by fruits. Fruit buds are more pronouncedly rounded and "fat" than growth buds. They often have downy bud scales, particularly on apples, pears, peaches and nectarines.

Previous growing season's growth

Lateral
A shoot growing directly from a main stem or branch. Before sublaterals develop, they may be called "maiden laterals".

Two-year-old wood

Branch leader
The shoot at the end of a branch that extends its length (this is sometimes referred to as "extension growth"), usually having grown from the bud immediately below a pruning cut. Tree forms with a central trunk, such as a pyramid or spindle bush, have a vertical "central leader".

Spur

Older spur system

Sublateral
A shoot growing from an existing lateral, often also called a "sideshoot".

Scar of previous year's fruit stalk

Main framework branch

Graft union At the base of a grafted fruit tree, some 10–30cm (4–12in) from the ground, is a kink, often slightly swollen. This is the point at which the chosen cultivar – the "scion" – was grafted on to the rootstock, and is termed the "union". The union must be above soil level, or roots may grow out of the scion above it, nullifying the stock's dwarfing effect.

Length of clear trunk keeps fruiting branches off ground

Scion (grafted cultivar)

Graft union

Rootstock

Spur On apples and pears, a short length of wood that produces fruit buds for many years. Spurs are usually clustered together, forming complicated, jointed spur systems. This is a natural growth habit for pears and many apples, which is accentuated by "spur pruning".

Making cuts

Pruning fruit trees may involve cutting into all types of growth – branches old and new, shoots and spurs. Sharp tools are, as always, essential to making clean and precise cuts that do not leave torn and bruised tissue that invites disease.

PRUNING YOUNG GROWTH

The simplest way of pruning young shoots, and one that is frequently needed with fruit trees, is to pinch out new growth, either to a leaf or to its point of origin, while it is still young and soft. If ripened (woody) shoots need cutting, correct positioning above either a bud or sideshoot is vital; most hardy fruits have alternate buds, so unless cuts are to be made back to a main branch or trunk, they should slope gently.

The loss of buds through pruning damage or dieback is particularly serious in the training of young trees because shoots will not then develop where they were needed. The compromises that are then necessary may make shaping the tree much more difficult.

PRUNING OLDER WOOD

Professional fruit growers use a technique whereby wood up to 2.5cm (1in) in diameter can be cut using secateurs only. Holding the secateurs in one hand, use the other to grasp the stem above the blades and very gently push or pull it away from the cutting blade as it begins to bite into the wood. This helps to open up the cut, making the progress of the blades through the wood much easier.

To remove larger sections of branches and old overgrown spurs, use a pruning saw or sharp loppers. Removing whole branches needs a special technique to prevent the bark from splitting (for step-

Good and bad cuts

Correct cuts are made at a gentle angle just above the bud, sloping down away from it. Leaving a stub of "blind" wood *(centre right)* is particularly undesirable: if infection travels down the stem, you may lose the selected bud, and possibly the whole shoot.

Cut does not extend below level of bud

Large cut surface is slow to heal

Rainwater rolls off gently sloping cut

Cut below bud leads to structural weakness

Water will collect on flat surface

Crushed tissue may become diseased

Stub will die back, endangering selected bud

Correct cut   **Cut too sloping**   **Cut too high**   **Rough cut**

by-step illustrations, *see p.20*). The use of wound paints is not now normally considered necessary *(see also p.20)*.

WHEN TO PRUNE

Timing of pruning depends not only on the fruit in question but on the form, trained or otherwise, in which it is grown. In general terms, the pome fruits (those with a core of pips – apples, pears, quince and medlar) are pruned when dormant in winter, to remove older and less productive wood in favour of new growth and fruiting wood.

However, because of a risk of disease if winter-pruned *(see p.123)*, the stone fruits (plums, cherries, peaches and apricots) must be pruned in summer. While young trees are being trained, pruning to influence growth before it begins can be done in early spring.

TRAINED FORMS

Any fruit tree grown in a controlled, trained form, such as a cordon, pyramid or fan, will also require additional summer pruning. Whereas the aim of routine pruning is to stimulate growth, this extra pruning consists largely of restricting it, to prevent the season's new shoots shading the developing fruits and to maintain the size and shape of the trained form. Summer pruning also encourages the tree to produce new fruit buds for the following year.

Emerging sideshoots are in some cases pinched out as they develop to prevent overcrowding. Later in the summer, new shoots are shortened – possibly removing as much as 80 per cent of the tree's foliage – to maintain the trained form and to create spurs on which fruit buds will develop.

New replacement shoot

Old, worn-out wood

Branch collar

Healed wound

Cutting to a bud

Always try to approach with the secateurs from the opposite side to the selected bud. This reduces the risk of the bud being damaged by the closing blades.

Cutting to a replacement shoot

Choose a strong, healthy shoot growing in a direction that will enhance the shape of the tree, and cut in line with this direction of growth. You will be able to make a more controlled, and thus a cleaner, cut if you approach from the opposite side to the shoot.

Cutting back to a main stem

Use more powerful tools for thicker wood, such as a lopper or pruning saw. Cut back to the raised ring, or collar, at the base of the branch *(see p.10)* so that the wound does not interfere with sap flow up the main branch or trunk.

Training Techniques

In the first years of a fruit tree's life, the development of new growth is of prime importance. If formative training is neglected in favour of obtaining a quick crop, a tree can quickly lose its shape, especially if on a dwarfing rootstock. The chosen cultivar's growth habit – with upright, spreading, or even drooping branches – may also become so well established that form-training becomes problematic. In the past, when only those rootstocks inducing vigorous growth were available, seven or eight years could be spent in building up the framework of a tree before fruiting. Today, with dwarfing rootstocks, trees may begin cropping in their third year. However, if a complex form is still being created, it is better to remove any flowers to channel energy into growth.

BUYING YOUNG TREES

Always buy fruit trees from specialist fruit nurseries. They will supply strong, healthy stock that has been well trained from the start, and can offer advice about pollination requirements – whether the cultivar you would like to grow needs another cultivar growing nearby in order to set fruit – and the suitability of your intended planting site. Try to match the choice of tree form to the natural habit of the cultivar, and use the same criteria to select good specimens as you would for ornamental trees (see p.23). A sturdy, robust young tree is preferable to a lanky one. The position and direction of growth of any laterals is also crucial. A one-year-old fruit tree will either be a clear, upright stem – a "maiden whip" – or will have developed sideshoots to become a "feathered maiden". Pruning back the leader and using techniques such as nicking and notching (see p.107) can be used to promote well-shaped growth and encourage laterals to develop where they are needed. Laterals that develop on an unpruned whip may be badly spaced, upright-growing and crowded, giving less scope for the training of a well-shaped

Young fruit trees (apple)

In its first growing season, the tree develops initially as a single stem, or "maiden whip" (see below left), on which laterals may form (when it is known as a "feathered maiden"). Some may be suitable for training as main branches. A two-year-old feathered tree (see right) will have plenty of laterals from which to make a selection.

The lower part of the stem is well furnished with growth

Single shoot

Graft point

Stock plant

Maiden whip

Strong leading shoot is retained for some tree forms, or may be removed

This shoot should be removed: it makes too narrow a "V-angle" of attachment with the main stem, and crosses other shoots

This weak shoot, and the one below it, should be removed; all fruit trees need at least a short length of clear trunk

Well spaced, wide-angled lateral is ideal for a framework branch

Feathered tree

tree. Note that so-called "pre-trained fans" offered for sale are usually palmettes and will need to have their central leader removed, ideally only leaving one or two pairs of arms.

CREATING THE FRAMEWORK

The first few years are spent establishing the branch framework of the chosen form. First, remove or shorten all shoots that are unwanted. For example, as all fruit tree forms have a length of clear trunk, sometimes just tall enough to keep fruits on the lowest branches off the ground, laterals below this height

are always removed. Remove, also, any laterals forming a narrow V-angle (see also p.10) with the stem. If left they will almost certainly break later under the weight of a crop. Even on a mature tree, shoots that form a narrow fork at the point of origin are best removed.

For free-growing forms – bush, standards and spindle bush – the shoots selected to form the framework must be well spaced, originating over a length of trunk rather than in a cluster. Select the best of what is already there, pruning to enhance their direction of growth. Some trees produce ample shoots, making

Correcting uneven development (fan)

Canes are tied to wires

Shoots are tied to canes

1 Here, one lateral is much stronger than the other, which, particularly at this early stage, reduces the chances of obtaining a symmetrical trained form from the young fruit tree.

The canes, not the shoots, are untied and retied to the wires

2 The more vigorous shoot can be lowered towards the horizontal to slow its growth. The weaker shoot can also be raised towards the vertical to increase its vigour.

3 Once the two shoots are of equal length (usually by the end of the growing season) they can be returned to their original positions and training can continue.

selection easy; others, such as tip-bearing apples, do not, and it may take a year or two longer to establish a basic framework of well-placed branches.

For more complex forms, the first shoots have to fulfil more precise requirements and their position and direction of growth should be controlled from the start: more cuts are made that will stimulate shoot growth where it is needed. Surplus shoots are removed, or can be pinched back to two or three leaves; should a selected shoot fail, through damage or disease, the buds left on the pinched shoot may provide a replacement shoot to take its place.

PROVIDING SUPPORTS
Young fruit trees must usually be supported at least until established. For free-standing forms, use a tall stake for pyramids and spindle bushes; these supports will be permanent. Use low stakes, preferably one on each side, with looped ties (*see p.21*), for bushes and standard trees. These can be removed once the tree is established in its final site: usually, after about three years, more if the site is very exposed.

Fruiting branches on free-standing forms, especially the spindle bush, may need extra support if the weight of a good crop threatens to break them. They can be looped up – "maypoled" – with soft twine or ribbons cut from soft plastic netting, which will not damage young bark, either tied around a robust upper branch or nailed to the tree's supporting stake.

Equip walls and fences with horizontal wires held at least 5cm (2in) from the surface, allowing air to circulate behind the tree. Tie shoots to bamboo canes attached to the wires at the desired angle. These act like splints, keeping the tied-in shoots straight and preventing them from rubbing on the thin wire. Once shoots are hardened and woody, tie them directly to the wires and remove the canes.

UNEVEN DEVELOPMENT
On fruit trees, an occasional shoot often develops far more quickly and strongly than others. When training free-growing forms, and on all mature trees, remove over-vigorous upright shoots completely in summer. Where removal of a shoot would set back training for which shoots are desired at precise points (for example, to form the arms of an espalier), correct uneven development (*see facing page, below*) by lowering the vigorous shoot to an angle nearer the horizontal. This will slow its growth, enabling the others to catch up. When they have done so, return the lowered shoot to its original position. Conversely, raising a weak shoot will encourage it to put on more growth. Shoots on canes and wires are easily adjusted; on free-standing trees, use soft twine or plastic netting strips, attached to the stake or pegged into the ground with wire bent into hoops.

TRAINING FOR FRUITING
While horizontal growth is less vigorous than upright growth, it is more fruitful, and should always be encouraged. Some trained forms were developed specifically

Tied-down branch released
Tying down the branch to a more horizontal angle has encouraged fruits to form all along the length of this branch. When the branch does not spring back, but stays naturally at its lower angle, the tie can be removed.

Previously upright branch was pulled down by tie

Fruits all along branch

to exploit the principle of horizontal training – for example, the espalier and spindle bush. On the latter, in particular, upright shoots are best tied down by late summer, before they ripen and become rigid, to increase fruit bud formation (*see also* Apples, *p.110*). On some young trees with very whippy long growths, particularly plums, all long shoots can be pulled down by ties attached to the stake or main stem, a process known as "festooning". This technique, producing good crops on small trees, was in use long before dwarfing rootstocks became available.

Knock a nail into the cane to keep strings from slipping down

Maypoling
The central stake, or, as here, a stout cane lashed to the stake, forms an anchor point for loops of string or netting that support branches heavily laden with fruit.

Sideshoots have developed all along length of branch

Branches once tied down by their tips now remain in position

Festooned plum
Whippy branches are carefully arched over and tied in below, using soft twine, in late summer. In early spring the ties are released but the branches stay bent, conferring the advantages of horizontal training.

Pruning Techniques

Mature fruit trees can expend energy in two ways – in putting on more growth, and in producing fruit. Trees in the wild usually achieve a natural balance, but those that have been grafted onto different rootstocks, or are being grown in a less than natural form, may have this equilibrium disrupted. The skill of fruit tree management lies in using pruning and training to restore and also to influence the balance between growth and the formation of fruit buds. This routine pruning usually takes place in winter (in summer for stone fruits), and is applied to all fruit trees; the additional pruning necessary to maintain restricted trained forms is explained in their individual entries (*see pp.104–139*).

HARD VERSUS LIGHT PRUNING

To maintain the size and balanced shape of a mature tree, the most important rule is to prune weak growth hard, and stronger growth lightly. After hard pruning, the root system has far fewer buds to feed, so these have a much greater growth potential, resulting in strong new shoots. Little or no pruning will leave a smaller ration of nutrients per bud. Hard pruning overall will result, therefore, in strong new growth but few fruits; general underpruning may be followed by an abundance of small fruits, exhausting the tree at the expense of the young growth that would bear future crops.

ADJUSTING THE BALANCE

The degree of pruning must be varied: pruning weak growths hard will encourage them to grow into worthwhile shoots; while pruning vigorous shoots lightly, or not at all, results in little growth, encouraging, instead, their buds to develop into fruit buds. The exact mix and severity of pruning is entirely dependent upon the state of the tree – whether it is lacking in vigorous new growth, or is growing vigorously but cropping lightly – and on where new growth is needed to replace older wood nearing the end of its useful life.

FRUITING HABIT

In general, younger wood produces finer fruits, but tree fruits vary in the age at which a shoot begins to bear fruit, and in the length of time it remains useful. Some, such as acid cherries, peaches and nectarines, fruit only on the young shoots of the previous summer; others, such as apples and pears, fruit mainly on two-year-old and older shoots and spurs. (Year one produces the shoot, year two should initiate some fruit buds on the shoot, and these then flower and fruit in year three; this wood from then on produces more fruit buds.) Plums, sweet cherries and apricots fruit mainly on two-year-old and

older wood, but also bear a few fruits at the base (the oldest part) of one-year-old shoots. For all fruits, routine pruning must be tailored to give a good mix of useful wood of different ages.

GROWTH PROBLEMS

If growth is poor, check the tree thoroughly, taking all possible factors into consideration. A disease such as canker (*see p.102*), competition from grass and weeds or lack of feeding are common causes. If new apple trees are planted where old ones grew, for example, poor growth may be due to a soil problem known as Specific Apple Replant Disease. (Exchanging

planting-hole soil at planting time with soil from another area of the garden helps to prevent it.) Once the problem has been resolved, hard pruning can be used to encourage strong new growth.

Conversely, if growth is very strong and the tree seems reluctant to produce a crop of fruit, consider whether it might have been supplied with too much feed, or has been pruned too severely. Lighter pruning may help to curb over-vigorous trees, as may grassing over the area around the tree to give it some competition. Vigour can also be limited by pruning a tree's root system (*see opposite*), which has the effect of reducing the amount of nourishment the tree is capable of absorbing.

Response to pruning – weak shoots

With light or no pruning, weak shoots develop fruit buds but do not grow much longer. Moderate pruning encourages growth while also allowing some fruit buds to develop, while hard pruning stimulates strong growth.

Light pruning   **Moderate pruning**   **Hard pruning**

Response to pruning – strong shoots

Left unpruned, or at most lightly tip-pruned, strong shoots produce some extension growth and several fruit buds; moderate pruning will increase branching and reduce the fruit-bud count, while hard pruning induces still stronger growth at the expense of fruit buds. Hard pruning can be used to encourage growth on young trees or, on mature trees, to stimulate replacement growth that will fill a gap caused by, for example, removal of a diseased branch.

Light pruning   **Moderate pruning**   **Hard pruning**

ROOT PRUNING

Young trees are most easily root pruned by being lifted and replanted in winter. Dig a trench around the tree, 60–75cm (2–2½ft) from it, and carefully undermine and undercut the root system. Strong tap roots must be cut with a pruning saw, but try to leave fibrous roots undamaged. Replant and stake the tree securely, firming the soil around it well. Mulch the following spring.

On large trees, root pruning in situ (*see right*) is a major operation that should be spread over at least two years. Staking afterwards is helpful, but is rarely possible: guy ropes (*see p.21*) pegged outside the trench may be useful.

If a tree is persistently over-vigorous despite any or all of these measures, there may be a simple explanation – that it is on a more vigorous rootstock than at first thought, and still attempting to grow into its final, mature size before starting to fruit. Provided that you can accommodate a larger tree, this will not pose problems; if you cannot, replace it.

FRUITING PROBLEMS

Poor crops may be caused by any of the factors responsible for poor growth (or by the lack of a suitable pollinating cultivar), or they may result from over-pruning that has suppressed the development of fruit buds in favour of vigorous new shoots. Adjusting the degree of pruning should help. Birds may also be to blame: smaller trained forms, such as the pyramid, and wall-trained trees are much easier to net. Heavy crops of small, unsatisfactory fruit can again be countered by adjusting the pruning level, but an important aid to this is fruit thinning, which will not

Root pruning a fruit tree

To avoid taxing the tree too much, only half of the root system is pruned each year. In the first winter, mark a half-circle about 1.2m (4ft) from the tree and dig a trench 30–45cm (12–18in) deep along it.

Saw through large roots you encounter when digging, taking out the section that crosses the trench. Replace the soil, firming it well, and mulch in spring. Repeat the operation on the other side of the tree the following winter.

only produce a better crop of fewer but finer fruits, but also helps to prevent, in apples and pears, the onset of a problem known as biennial bearing.

BIENNIAL BEARING

An over-heavy crop, frost damage to buds, disease or underfeeding can all trigger biennial bearing, particularly in apples and pears: the alternation of a heavy crop – "on" years – with a light crop, or even no crop at all – "off" years. To counter the problem, in the winter following an "off" year, prune as normal but leave unpruned as many one-year-old shoots as possible. These will not fruit the next year, but will develop plenty of

fruit buds for the following one – the next expected "off" year. The following winter (that is, after the heavy-cropping, "on" season), again leave these shoots (now two years old) unpruned, but prune one-year-old shoots severely, so that two years later (in the next expected "on" year) these will bear only moderate rather than heavy crops, breaking the biennial cycle.

Another cure for biennial bearing is blossom thinning. The number of flowers must be drastically reduced in the year of expected heavy cropping to break the cycle completely. If a tree is very large, thinning can be done on one or two branches only, and should be repeated over the years.

Blossom thinning

To counteract biennial bearing, within a week or 10 days after flowering, remove nine out of every 10 blossom trusses. Pinch or cut out the open flowers with scissors, leaving the rosette of leaves intact.

Fruit thinning

Before thinning If all of these crowded fruits are allowed to develop, they will be small and poorly flavoured. The weight of such a heavy crop may also break the branch, so future crops will also be affected.

After thinning The thinned fruits are large and well-ripened. A moderate crop will also ensure a balance between the formation of new fruit buds and growth for future regular cropping.

Renovation

Neglect is the chief cause of a fruit tree requiring renovation. However, a fruit tree can also need renovating because it has been overpruned, stimulating a mass of vigorous, congested growth that, if allowed to develop, tends to be unfruitful and prone to disease. Always, therefore, resist the temptation to prune neglected trees hard. Renovate carefully and gradually, over several years.

First, decide whether the tree is worth keeping. Even if its crop is of no interest, a fruit tree that is sound and healthy may well, once renovated, be an attractive garden feature. You could also seek expert advice about the possibility of "grafting over" – converting the tree, by specialized grafting, to another cultivar. However, if it is riddled with disease, especially canker, it should be grubbed out and burned. Do not plant another fruit tree on the site.

The same strictures concerning safety apply as when renovating ornamental trees (*see p.32*). Never use a chainsaw without the correct training, or attempt a job yourself if you doubt your ability to complete it safely. Renovate at the same time as you routinely prune the fruit in question: winter for pome fruits; late spring or summer for stone fruits.

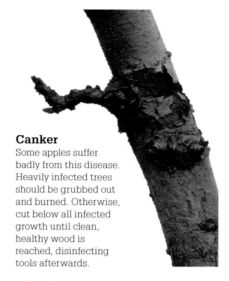

Canker
Some apples suffer badly from this disease. Heavily infected trees should be grubbed out and burned. Otherwise, cut below all infected growth until clean, healthy wood is reached, disinfecting tools afterwards.

Although many growers still use wound paints to "seal" large cuts, recent research has shown them to be unnecessary and often counterproductive (*see also p.20*).

NEGLECTED TREES
Some problems due to neglect are common to all trees, while others are more specific to certain fruits; an apple,

Crowded and crossing branches
Overcrowding causes a build-up of stagnant air and, where branches touch, rubbing can lead to damage and an entry point for disease. Of the crossing pair, retain the younger or healthier growth, if possible.

for example, may have overgrown spur systems. Tackle problems systematically over two or three years. Removing too much growth in one season stresses the tree and leads to excessive regrowth; many large cuts also attract infection. No more than a quarter of the crown should be removed each year. The number of years renovation will take

Renovating a neglected fruit tree (apple) over two years

Before renovation In the first year, remove all dead, diseased and damaged wood. Remove, or shorten to a strong replacement shoot, crowded and crossing branches. In the second year, improve fruiting potential: shorten overlong and unproductive growth to a strong replacement shoot, and thin regrowth from previous cuts. On apples and pears, reduce congested spur systems (*see* Spur thinning, *p.105*).

After renovation Two years later, the tree has a well-spaced crown of strong framework branches on which fruiting growth has plenty of room to develop. Routine pruning for the fruit can now be introduced: on this apple, long, young shoots now need shortening to start the formation of fresh spur systems. To keep new growth balanced, prune weak shoots hard, and vigorous shoots lightly.

Crown is crowded with twiggy growth, some dead and damaged, cutting out light and restricting air circulation

Growth has been allowed to cross, rubbing and chafing bark

Well-spaced growth along branches leaves plenty of room for development

Centre of crown is open, letting in light and allowing free air circulation

Trunk and lower parts of framework branches are clear of growth

Broken branch

Branches broken by wind or weight may split length- or widthways. Here, on the cut surface, water penetration is still visible, but this is as far back as the cut can safely be made without damaging the branch collar.

will vary depending on the tree's size and condition. Concentrate first on restoring health rather than obtaining a crop. As well as dead, damaged or diseased wood and crowded, crossing growth, there may be low, spreading branches that are best removed. Always remove branches correctly (*see p.20*), and never tackle over-large jobs yourself. Once unwanted and unproductive wood has been removed, the normal annual pruning routine can be re-established.

Sappy "water shoots" (*see also p.30*) may emerge in profusion around large pruning cuts. Check the tree, perhaps fortnightly, in summer, and rub these shoots off by hand as they sprout.

OVERPRUNED TREES

A tree whose branches are severely lopped will have produced a mass of shoots that must be thinned over several years (*see right*) to develop worthwhile fruiting branches. Careful treatment is necessary to restore a balance between wood of different ages, so that the normal cycle of pruning can be resumed. Always err on the side of underpruning, or the problem will recur.

RESTRICTED TRAINED FORMS

The more specialized the trained form, the more difficult to rescue, particularly if on a dwarfing rootstock: these trees are far less able to withstand neglect. If the framework can still be discerned, it is worth attempting to reduce growth and thin any congested spur systems until the condition of the main branches can be properly assessed. If they seem sound, and the response in the following growing season is good, routine pruning can be resumed. If not, replace the tree.

Renovating an overpruned tree (pear) over three years

Year 1 Hard pruning has stimulated a mass of over-vigorous shoots, growing vertically without branching as they compete for light. Remove approximately one in two, leaving the remainder evenly spaced. Tip-prune the longest remaining shoots to induce branching.

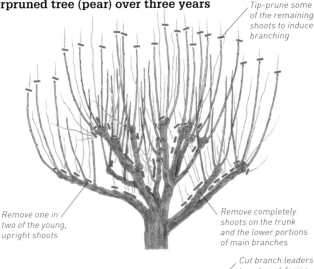

Tip-prune some of the remaining shoots to induce branching

Remove one in two of the young, upright shoots

Remove completely shoots on the trunk and the lower portions of main branches

Year 2 Remove half of the upright growth again, leaving, as in Year 1, well-spaced, well-positioned young branches. Prune these to encourage further outward-facing growth. If the tree still seems overcrowded, remove larger sections of wood from the centre of the crown, being careful not to damage branch collars.

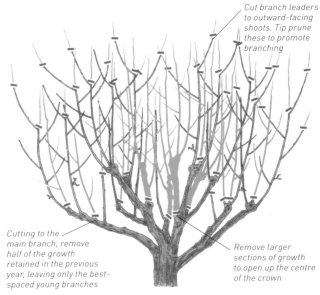

Cut branch leaders to outward-facing shoots. Tip prune these to promote branching

Cutting to the main branch, remove half of the growth retained in the previous year, leaving only the best-spaced young branches

Remove larger sections of growth to open up the centre of the crown

Year 3 Continue to make pruning cuts to correct and balance the new growth. Some fruit buds should be forming; from this stage onwards, slowly introduce routine pruning in the correct season to suit the fruit in question (and the tree's form). This pear standard is being winter-pruned systematically to start fresh spur formation.

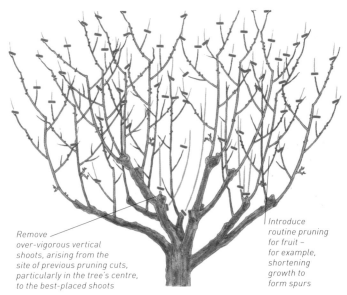

Remove over-vigorous vertical shoots, arising from the site of previous pruning cuts, particularly in the tree's centre, to the best-placed shoots

Introduce routine pruning for fruit – for example, shortening growth to form spurs

Hardy Fruits

Tree fruits that can be grown outdoors in most cool temperate climates are divided into those that are fully hardy, such as apples, pears and plums, and those that require, ideally, the protection in winter of a sheltered wall or greenhouse – for example, peaches and figs. While the latter grow and crop well in hot climates, the fully hardy fruits need a period of winter cold to flower and hence set fruit. This "chilling requirement" is usually expressed as a number of hours below a given temperature. Another important requirement may be for another cultivar to be grown nearby, to act as a pollinator. However, fruit trees can now be grown in a range of sizes and forms. Even a small garden has room for two or three cordons; alternatively, a "family tree" (*see p.95*) could be considered.

Regular and correct pruning and training is essential for all of these trees, to maintain their health and shape, and to ensure quality crops. Their fruiting habits vary, and this has a significant bearing on both timing and techniques.

APPLES

MALUS SYLVESTRIS VAR. *DOMESTICA*

The apple, with its variety of colours and flavours, long season of ripening, culinary and preserving potential, tolerance of different climates and ease of training, easily ranks among the most popular and widely grown hardy fruits. Its fresh green leaves, spring blossom and handsome bark and fruits give it enormous decorative value too, and it is probably the top choice as a single fruit tree in any ornamental garden.

It is also a major commercial crop, and this has had enormous benefits for the gardener. The apple has always been at the forefront of fruit research and development, resulting in a wide range of rootstocks, tree forms and cultivars. Popular cultivars are available as bushes and trees that will grow to anything from two to five metres (5–15ft) or more. Recent interest in traditional cultivars, and in conserving old orchards of large, standard trees,

Apple rootstocks

M27   M9   M26   MM106   MM111

is increasing the availability of older cultivars, considered by many to have the best flavours.

GRAFTING AND ROOTSTOCKS

Choice of rootstock will determine not only the size of the apple tree, but also the forms into which it can be trained: it would be very hard, for example, to grow a tree on the vigorous MM111 stock into a cordon, while the dwarfing M27 will never make a tree of much more than head height. It is vital to decide first in what situation and form you want your apple to grow, next to

Modern apple orchard
Apple trees are grafted in the nursery: during the past 70 years, primarily British research into the dwarfing effects of various rootstocks has had an enormous influence on their cultivation. With the advent of tree forms suitable for ever smaller spaces and closer planting, new formative training and annual pruning systems have had to be developed to create and maintain them.

ascertain the best rootstock, and only then to look at the choice of cultivars (and their pollination requirements) available on those rootstocks. Any good specialist fruit nursery will offer advice.

FRUITING HABIT

Most apples are "spur-bearers", fruiting on wood that is in its third year or older, in the form of short fruit-bearing shoots known as spurs. Their main branches are fairly evenly and well clothed with fruit buds, spurs and new shoots. However, a minority of cultivars tend to produce, instead, clusters of fruit at or near the tips of longer shoots, with far fewer spurs and greater lengths of bare wood between the buds and shoots. These are known as "tip-bearers"; some cultivars are markedly tip-bearing, others partially so. It is crucial to determine whether your apple is tip- or spur-bearing, and to vary the pruning regime in favour of the fruiting habit. This fruiting habit also influences the forms in which the apple may be trained: tip-bearers do not make good cordons or espaliers, where a closely and evenly distributed crop along a fairly short length of main branch is required.

All apple trees vary in the vigorousness of their growth and in their fruitfulness, and the pruning regime needs to be tailored to suit the individual tree. Only experimentation and experience will determine what degree of pruning and which combination of methods gives the best results for your trees.

TIME OF PRUNING

Apples start into growth early in the year, flowering from mid- to late spring. The main pruning season is mid- to late winter, ideally after the harshest of the weather is over. Trained forms need extra pruning in summer, to maintain their shape by restricting new growth.

WINTER PRUNING

Once apple trees and bushes have reached fruit-bearing size, usually after three seasons of growth on dwarf rootstocks and five years' growth for trees on more vigorous rootstock, pruning is undertaken to keep trees productive, to control shape and size, and to promote continuous and plentiful fruit cropping.

REGULATED PRUNING

Regulated pruning uses the natural habit of the tree where fruit is borne on new shoots and short spurs. All dead, diseased, and crossing branches are sawn out. To make an open centre within the canopy, strong branches are removed, but the weaker fruit-bearing shoots and spurs are retained. Over time, branches become too long and should be removed, ideally to a lower side branch that is not too vertical, faces outwards, and has a diameter about one third of the severed branch. No more than 10 to 20 per cent of the canopy should be removed in any one winter.

Older trees can lose vigour, leading to small fruit; this can be remedied by thinning and shortening some branches. They may also bear an excessive number of spurs and these should also be thinned.

Established apple tree or bush, regulated pruning

This pruning technique is suitable for both spur- and tip- (including partial tip-) bearing apple trees, as sections of the branch framework are removed rather than individual shoots. Prune anytime from leaf fall to late winter, when the tree is dormant.

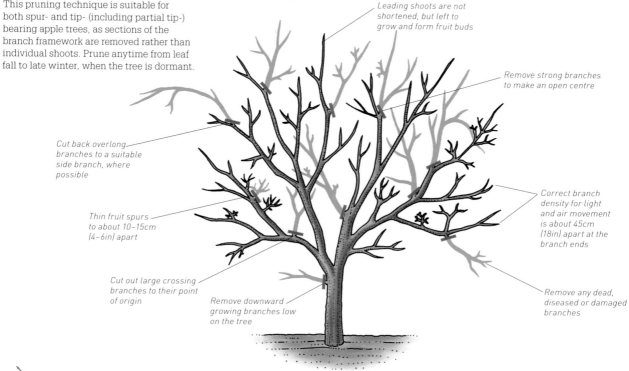

Leading shoots are not shortened, but left to grow and form fruit buds

Remove strong branches to make an open centre

Cut back overlong branches to a suitable side branch, where possible

Correct branch density for light and air movement is about 45cm (18in) apart at the branch ends

Thin fruit spurs to about 10–15cm (4–6in) apart

Cut out large crossing branches to their point of origin

Remove downward growing branches low on the tree

Remove any dead, diseased or damaged branches

Young growth with better fruiting potential

Shoot has fruited for several years

Renewal pruning

Renewal pruning can be carried out on large and congested spur-trained trees by cutting back older fruited shoots to a strong, upward (but not vertical) sideshoot, or, failing that, a well-placed bud. Tip-bearing cultivars can be routinely pruned by the renewal method, which induces a succession of new shoots that carry fruit on the extending branches.

Spur pruning

Close management of spurs and leading shoots can be carried out to keep fruit production near to the main branches, particularly useful for crowded and weak-growing trees. Lateral shoots are shortened each year to build up knobbly spur shoots that carry flowers and fruit *(see p.109)*. Only the most vigorous leading shoots are left unpruned, as pruning would encourage excessively vigorous extension growth. Tip- or partially tip-bearing cultivars do not respond well to spur-pruning and are best pruned by the regulated method described above.

Spurs eventually get so congested that they have to be thinned

Weak spur system has been removed completely

SUMMER PRUNING

The more formally trained ("restricted") apple tree forms, such as cordons, fans and espaliers, must be pruned in summer to restrict growth and encourage fruit buds to form. The technique used is known as the Lorette system. In warm climates, the full system is used. All new shoots 15–22cm (6–9in) long are shortened to 5cm (2in) as their bases become woody. Pruning continues throughout summer, not only of shoots produced in the first flush of growth, but also of the shoots stimulated by the first round of cuts ("secondary growth"). These are shortened to 2cm (³⁄₄in).

In cool climates, such as that of northern Europe, the Lorette system is modified to discourage secondary growth, which may be vulnerable to frost damage. Pruning does not start until the basal third of a new shoot has turned woody, and growth is slowing down. Timing will depend largely on the weather. The shoots will become ready for pruning over a two- to three-week period. Leave unpruned any shorter than 22cm (9in) long.

To further discourage secondary growth, a few vigorous shoots may be left unpruned to act as "sap drawers": any nourishment still travelling up the tree late in the season will be drawn into these shoots, rather than causing any more buds to develop into shoots. Shorten sap-drawers in the spring. If secondary growth does occur, prune it back to a bud at the base in mid-autumn.

Other measures that may need to be undertaken during the growing season are blossom thinning (see p.101) to counteract biennial bearing, and fruit thinning (see p.101) if a heavy crop sets. Bark ringing (see below) may also be used as a last resort in mid-spring to discourage a tree that always makes excessive summer growth at the expense of flowers and fruits. It *must* be done correctly, or the tree may be damaged, even killed. If it has to be repeated, wait a few years.

Summer pruning

Before pruning
New laterals have grown rapidly on this espalier, and are now ripening from the base upwards. If the new growth is not shortened, trees can rapidly outgrow their site, and the trained form will be lost. The foliage on new shoots also tends to shade the fruits from the ripening sun.

1 Shorten new shoots growing directly from the trunk or main branches to three leaves above the basal cluster of leaves.

2 Prune sideshoots from existing laterals or spurs back to one bud above the basal cluster of leaves.

Basal cluster

After pruning
The espalier branch is visibly restored, and more sun can reach the ripening fruits. Pruning cuts made in summer also stimulate the development of future fruit buds.

Bark ringing

Strip of tape used as guide

1 With a sharp knife, encircle the trunk completely with two parallel cuts 6mm (¹⁄₄in) apart, up to 12mm (¹⁄₂in) on larger trees (use tape as a guide). The incisions should penetrate through the cambium layer down to the wood.

2 Carefully and cleanly remove the band of bark, levering it up and out with the blunt edge of a pruning knife. Completing the circle restricts the flow of nourishment to the crown of the tree, hence restricting its growth.

3 Bind insulating tape around the wound to stop it drying out and to assist healing. Seal the wound completely, but do not poke the tape in so that it adheres to the cut surface. Remove it when scar tissue begins to form.

Formative training

Ready-trained young apple trees are available, but they are also relatively simple to train yourself into a range of forms (*see following pages*). Buying young trees is much cheaper if, for example, a row of cordons is required. In addition, one- or two-year-old trees are quick to establish, suffering less of a growth setback caused by transplant shock.

BUYING MAIDEN WHIPS

Starting with one-year-old trees is the most economical option. If you can visit a specialist nursery to select your own trees, so much the better. A well-feathered maiden (already furnished with strong laterals) gives a head start, but if you choose to buy whips (single stems), select good, straight specimens; it is usually worth sacrificing height in favour of a stout stem with plenty of healthy buds. Professional training techniques can be used right from the start to influence the position and direction of shoot growth to suit the intended trained form.

In order to build up a good, thick trunk, whips are often cut back in their first year, and, if the intended tree form is to have a central trunk (for example, a pyramid), a new leader is trained in. However, many more forms require no central leader, but well-positioned, strong low branches. When a whip is cut back, the natural result is for the upper buds to develop into vigorous upright shoots, competing to become the new leader. These are not ideal for branches because they will be growing at a narrow V-angle to the stem, and may split when mature and heavy. Fruit growers use nicking (*see above*) to counteract this

Nicking and notching

Small crescent-shaped piece of bark removed just below bud

Small crescent-shaped piece of bark removed just above bud

Nicking Removing a small wedge of bark below a bud weakens its growth by restricting the supply of nutrients; it may develop into a fruit bud or a small shoot. Energy is directed instead into shoots in more desirable positions.

Notching Notching – cutting above the bud – stimulates a shoot's growth. It is used mainly to encourage shoots to grow low down on a stem, or to obtain shoots in positions desirable for form-training.

undesirable growth habit. Nicking below the two topmost buds once the leader is cut back (*see below*) allows only weak growth from them. Lower buds grow strongly to compensate, and at wide angles, because of shading by the stub of stem above them. Any growth that does develop from the two top buds can be pinched back. The stub can be cut back to just above the topmost lateral in the following winter.

The result is a short trunk well furnished with evenly-spaced laterals, of equal vigour, that make wide angles to the stem, desirable both for strength and for the structure of many tree forms.

Notching – nicking above the bud – is a similar technique that can be used to encourage a shoot to break where it is needed – for example, to fill a gap in a fan. If shoots are not wanted in a

particular place, an alternative to nicking is to keep pinching back to two leaves any growth that develops.

BUYING FEATHERED TREES

A year's advantage can be gained by buying feathered trees, either maidens or two-year-olds (*see p.98*). Choose strong, straight stems with plenty of wide-angled laterals to give scope for training. Less ideal specimens should be pruned to redress any imbalance: prune weaker growth hard, and strong growth less. If one shoot is markedly stronger, it is always best to cut it out completely to avoid any imbalance in future growth. Where only one or two laterals exist, or laterals are spindly or unequal in size, it is better to cut them hard back to one or two buds from their bases and virtually start again, treating the tree as a whip.

Using nicking to produce low, wide-angled laterals for fan-training (apple)

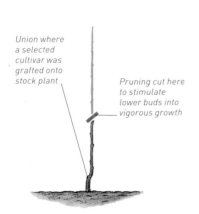

Union where a selected cultivar was grafted onto stock plant

Pruning cut here to stimulate lower buds into vigorous growth

Maiden whip pruned Young apple trees grow away from the graft point as a single stem. For many tree forms, this is cut back to thicken the main stem and encourage lateral shoots to grow from low buds.

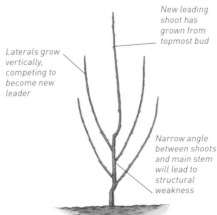

New leading shoot has grown from topmost bud

Laterals grow vertically, competing to become new leader

Narrow angle between shoots and main stem will lead to structural weakness

Two-year-old tree without nicking Laterals grow during the following spring and summer, but naturally tend to adopt a vigorous, vertical habit, undesirable for structural safety and for many trained forms.

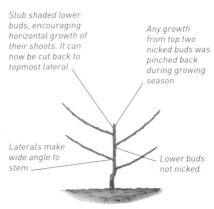

Stub shaded lower buds, encouraging horizontal growth of their shoots. It can now be cut back to topmost lateral

Any growth from top two nicked buds was pinched back during growing season

Laterals make wide angle to stem

Lower buds not nicked

Two-year-old tree with nicking When the leader is removed and the top two buds are nicked, the young tree develops well-positioned, wide-angled laterals, ideal for framework branches of forms such as a fan.

APPLE BUSH

The bush is one of the most useful apple tree forms and one of the easiest to train and maintain. A wide range of rootstocks is available for different heights, though to accommodate their spread, even on the most dwarfing rootstocks they need to be planted at least 2m (6ft) apart.

FORMATIVE TRAINING
The aim is to create a branched, open-centred crown, with eight to ten branches radiating from a short trunk, about 60–75cm (24–30in) tall. Start in winter with a young feathered tree (see p.107) that has three or four strong, wide-angled laterals between 60cm (2ft) and 90cm (3ft) from the ground. The laterals should be as well-spaced as possible both along the length of the trunk and around it, to give the bush strength and symmetry.

The leader is pruned back and the laterals shortened to encourage branching. The next winter, the strongest and best-placed of these shoots are selected and shortened to build up the main branch framework. At this stage, cut to outward-facing buds to give the bush an open centre.

In the third winter, tip-prune branch leaders to encourage the bush to fill out. Adjust other pruning depending on whether the cultivar is a spur-bearer or tip-bearer (see p.104). Spur pruning to create a system of stubby fruiting spurs can be useful on weak trees that may not make sufficient new growth under regulated pruning (see opposite).

ESTABLISHED PRUNING
As the bush becomes established and begins to crop, pruning thereafter is necessary only in winter, and should complement the fruiting habit of the tree, whether spur- or tip-bearing. Some trees vary between the two; experimentation may be necessary to see which method, or combination of methods, is most successful.

An open centre to the bush is still desirable, as it allows air, light and sunshine to penetrate. However, as the bush matures, branches will gradually become lower and more spreading under the weight of cropping. Some pruning cuts should encourage the development of a few strong, more upright growths eventually to replace them, or the bush will splay out and the spreading branches may eventually break.

Apple bush, pruning on planting, winter

1 Prune back the leader to just above the topmost of three or four strong laterals.

2 Shorten laterals by two-thirds of their length. Cut to upward-facing buds on more horizontal shoots, and outward-facing buds on upright shoots.

Well-spaced lower laterals radiate outwards like spokes of a wheel

Short trunk will keep lower fruiting branches clear of ground

Short stake

Year 2, winter

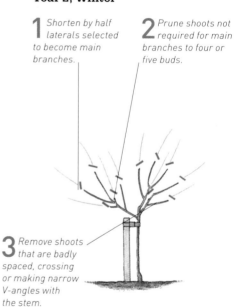

1 Shorten by half laterals selected to become main branches.

2 Prune shoots not required for main branches to four or five buds.

3 Remove shoots that are badly spaced, crossing or making narrow V-angles with the stem.

Year 3, winter (spur-bearers)

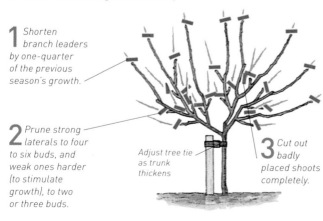

1 Shorten branch leaders by one-quarter of the previous season's growth.

2 Prune strong laterals to four to six buds, and weak ones harder (to stimulate growth), to two or three buds.

Adjust tree tie as trunk thickens

3 Cut out badly placed shoots completely.

Year 3, winter (tip-bearers)

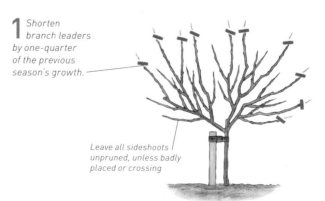

1 Shorten branch leaders by one-quarter of the previous season's growth.

Leave all sideshoots unpruned, unless badly placed or crossing

Established apple bush, spur pruning (for spur-bearers) in winter

Year 1

Shorten a proportion of lateral shoots to four good buds. This will induce two new lateral shoots and also spurs (short fruiting stems) to grow.

Year 2

In the second year, cut back to a fruit bud. If there is room for a bigger side-branch, shorten last year's growth to four buds again.

Year 3

In year three, a stubby branch will develop more small spurs bearing fruit buds.

Year 4

From the fourth year, fruiting spurs develop until eventually they become more congested and require thinning (see right).

Thinning spurs
As the bush matures, shorten or remove any weak or overcrowded spurs (see also p.105).

Established apple bush, renewal pruning (for tip-bearers) in winter

2 Tip-prune branch leaders, or they will be bowed down by fruits that develop at the tip.

Replacement growth resulting from pruning in previous winter

1 Cut back a proportion of older fruited wood to a young shoot or a basal bud to give room for fresh growth to develop.

Longer stem length between shoots typical of tip-bearers

Larger, old branch removed to reduce overcrowding in the bush centre

STANDARD APPLE TREES

The height and spread of standard and half-standard trees, and the relative difficulties in pruning, spraying and picking them, means that they are hardly ever grown in domestic gardens, though they are occasionally required to fill gaps in older orchards. Vigorous rootstocks are used, and the trees may take up to eight years to bear fruit: creating the clear stem takes two years alone.

Beginning with a young feathered tree (see p.107), the leader is not pruned but staked, grown on and gradually cleared of laterals just as for an ornamental

standard tree (see p.26). Standards (above left) need a clear trunk of at least 2m (6ft), and half-standards (above right), 1.35m (4.5ft).

Once the desired length of clear stem is achieved, the leader is pruned back and the crown of the tree built up exactly as if it were a bush (see facing page). The tree's

extra vigour, derived from the rootstock, will produce a crown of a size proportionate to the height of the tree. Because the branches will be larger and heavier, it is extremely important for the tree's safety that they make wide angles to the trunk, so choose laterals carefully to develop the main branch framework.

Once established, these trees are, because of their vigour, usually better served by regulated pruning (see p.105) – the removal of large portions of branches – than by spur or renewal pruning. However, if the tree is sluggish in making new growth, spur or renewal prune in the same way as for a bush.

APPLE SPINDLE BUSH

The spindle bush is a small tree form that was developed in Holland as a way of maximizing crops while minimizing labour costs. Although popular with commercial growers, it is rarely seen in gardens, perhaps because of its rather ungainly appearance. It requires careful formative training and, when established, both winter renewal pruning and a little work in summer, but it does repay this attention with a heavy, early-ripening and easily harvested crop in a very small space.

The basic spindle bush framework consists of a central trunk 2–2.2m (6–7ft) tall with, about a third of the way up, four main branches, or arms, radiating out like the points of a weathervane. The silhouette is thus broadly conical, something like that of an old-fashioned spinning top.

Upper branches on the central trunk above the arms are not permanent, but are pruned hard after carrying one or two crops and replaced by younger shoots so that they never grow large enough to overshadow the lower fruits.

All lateral growth – the main branches and their sideshoots, and those growing from the trunk – is pruned and trained so that it is as near horizontal as possible.

FORMATIVE TRAINING

Young spindle bushes are rarely offered for sale outside the wholesale trade, so it is more than likely that you will have to train one yourself. The starting point is, ideally, a feathered maiden (see p.107) with four good, strong laterals of equal vigour between 60 and 90cm (24–36in) up the stem. (An effective spindle can be made with three arms, but a proportion of the potential crop is lost.) It is essential that the laterals make as wide an angle as possible to the main stem. The tree will need a robust, permanent 2m (6ft) stake.

Initial training concentrates on the development of the arms: pruning cuts will often need to be made to downward-pointing buds, to encourage near-horizontal growth. Tying down (see also p.99) in summer also plays an important role. Use thick string, or strips of plastic netting, that will not cut into the young bark. The ties should not be removed until the branches show no tendency to spring upwards when the tension is slackened.

While the tree is developing, the central leader is shortened each winter, alternating the side on which the bud or shoot that is cut to faces, so that a

Apple spindle bush, winter pruning on planting

1 Prune the leader to a bud at about 90cm (3ft), 7–10cm (3–4in) above the topmost selected lateral.

2 Shorten by half the three or four laterals chosen to form branches, cutting to downward-facing buds.

3 Remove completely any additional weak and low-growing laterals.

Year 1, late summer

New leader has been tied in

1 Cut out completely any excessively vigorous upright shoots.

2 Tie down the main arms at an angle of about 20° to the horizontal.

Tie around shoot should not constrict

Pegs or wire hoops anchor ties to the ground

Year 2 onwards, late summer

1 Tie down laterals on trunk to near horizontal, keeping them straight rather than arched if possible.

Leader was shortened in winter by one-third of the previous season's growth

2 Remove over-vigorous upright shoots on competing laterals.

3 Check ties on the main arms – if the stem does not spring upwards when they are loosened, they may be removed.

straight trunk is achieved. A leader is retrained and tied in until the tree reaches a height of 2–2.2m (6–7ft). Then, delay pruning the leader until late spring to discourage regrowth.

ESTABLISHED PRUNING AND TRAINING

Tie down laterals on the trunk and main branches each summer so that they grow horizontally. Staples hammered into the tree's stake make convenient anchor points, as do lower branches. Remove completely any vigorously upright growth that resists tying down, as it will shade the developing fruits and spoil the tree's shape.

Once cropping begins, the young fruiting branches on the upper length of the trunk are also winter-pruned, using the renewal system, as for a tip-bearing bush (*see p.105*). These branches should never get too big; they should ideally have no more than a three- or four-year lifespan. Growth along the lower, permanent arms is managed with a combination of renewal pruning and spur-pruning (*see p.105*) in winter. To maintain a constant height, cut the new leading shoot at the top of the tree back to one or two buds each year.

Established apple spindle bush, winter pruning

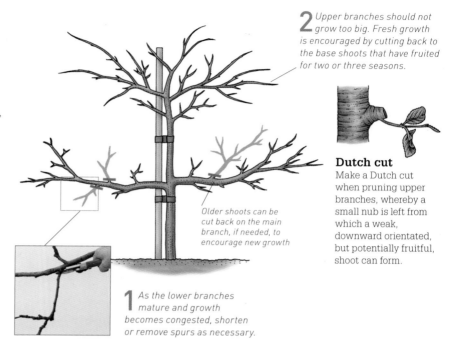

2 *Upper branches should not grow too big. Fresh growth is encouraged by cutting back to the base shoots that have fruited for two or three seasons.*

Older shoots can be cut back on the main branch, if needed, to encourage new growth

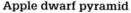

1 *As the lower branches mature and growth becomes congested, shorten or remove spurs as necessary.*

Dutch cut

Make a Dutch cut when pruning upper branches, whereby a small nub is left from which a weak, downward orientated, but potentially fruitful, shoot can form.

APPLE DWARF PYRAMID

The dwarf pyramid is a small tree whose compact form is made possible by dwarfing rootstocks, and maintained largely through regular summer pruning. Branches are progressively shorter from the bottom to the top of the tree, and radiate from a central trunk to form a narrow, pyramidal shape. Because so much shortening of growth is needed to restrict size and prevent overcrowding, the dwarf pyramid is a form best suited to spur-bearers (*see p.104*). It is also an ideal compact form for pear trees.

FORMATIVE TRAINING

As for a pear dwarf pyramid (*see p.118*), starting with a well-feathered young tree (*see p.107*).

ESTABLISHED PRUNING

As for a pear dwarf pyramid (*see p.118*). When summer pruning, follow the Lorette system (*see p.106*); it is particularly important, with this form, to check the growth of vigorous upright shoots high up on the central stem. Winter pruning largely consists simply of shortening leading shoots at the top of the tree, if necessary, and reducing or removing old, crowded growth.

Apple dwarf pyramid

Provided that they are well maintained, dwarf pyramids are suitable for close, almost hedge-like planting at 1.2m–1.5m (4–5ft) apart. They need permanent staking or, if to be grown in a row, a robust system of posts and wires.

APPLE CORDON

A cordon consists of a single main trunk, along which laterals are both summer- and winter-pruned to form fruit-bearing spur systems. The form is best suited to spur-bearing cultivars (*see p.104*). Cordons are ideal for a small garden; they can be spaced at only 75cm (2½ft) from each other in rows 2m (6ft) apart.

The more oblique the angle at which they grow, the better, and more evenly along their length, cordons will fruit. If vertical growth is preferred, consider training a double cordon (*see facing page*). There are apples advertised to grow in single-stemmed, columnar form, often sold as patio or container trees under a variety of names. It is often said that they require no pruning, but they have been shown to be capable of reaching heights of up to 5m (15ft), with vigorous lateral growth. They may require just as much pruning as a traditional cordon, and are available only in a limited range of cultivars.

FORMATIVE TRAINING
Cordons require strong horizontal support wires, either held by vine eyes or battens 10–15cm (4–6in) clear of a wall or sturdy fence, or strung tautly (using straining bolts) between 2.2m (7ft) concrete posts. Start with a feathered maiden or

Apple cordon, pruning on planting, winter

Central leader and short laterals left unpruned

3m (10ft) bamboo cane tied to wires

60cm (2ft) between wires

Lowest wire 30cm (12in) from the ground

Feathered tree planted at 40–45° angle to ground

Prune laterals longer than 10cm (4in) to three or four buds from the base.

Year 1, summer (modified Lorette system)

1 As they ripen, prune new laterals from the main stem to three leaves above the basal cluster of leaves.

Basal third of shoot has turned woody

2 Prune sideshoots from existing laterals to one leaf to begin forming fruiting spur systems.

Established apple cordon, summer (modified Lorette system)

1 Prune new laterals to three leaves above the basal cluster of leaves.

Leader is pruned to a weaker shoot in late spring when it reaches maximum height

Basal third of shoot has turned woody

Before pruning

After pruning

2 Prune sideshoots from laterals and spurs to one leaf above the basal cluster of leaves.

two-year-old tree with plenty of well-spaced laterals (*see p.107*). Plant it at a 45° angle, tying its main stem on to a bamboo cane, which in turn is lashed diagonally to the wires, so that the bark is not damaged. The first stage in developing fruiting spurs is to shorten long laterals, and this is repeated over subsequent summers. The central leader is not pruned until it reaches the top wire; then, cut it back to a weaker shoot, pruning in late spring to discourage regrowth.

ESTABLISHED PRUNING
The laterals, including the leading shoot, are summer pruned following the Lorette system (*see p.106*), either full or modified depending on climate. As the cordon matures and spur systems become more complicated, they will need simplifying and thinning in winter (*see also* Spur thinning, *p.105*). Conversely, if by late spring a length of the cordon remains bare, notching (*see p.107*) above an eye, or latent bud, may stimulate the bud into growth.

Established cordon, winter

Remove older or unproductive sections of congested spur systems. Occasionally, remove an entire older system altogether to relieve congestion and allow for new growth.

Before pruning

After pruning

APPLE, MULTIPLE CORDONS

Double ("U") and four-armed (double-"U") cordons need careful training but look attractive, and are very productive. Triple cordons, with three arms, are not recommended for apples: the central arm tends to grow much more vigorously than the outer two. Achieving a good shape depends on having laterals develop precisely where they are needed to form the main arms, so it is easiest to start with a maiden whip, using nicking and, if necessary, notching (*see p.107*)

to produce shoots in the required positions. All multiple cordons require horizontal wires with bamboo canes tied in diagonally and vertically on which the arms can be trained. Multiple cordons need a more vigorous rootstock than single cordons.

TRAINING AND PRUNING
A double cordon is formed as below (*see also* Redcurrant cordons, *p.236*). From its third summer, growth on the vertical arms is pruned as for a single cordon.

For a four-armed cordon, first create a double cordon, but do not train the arms vertically until they are at least 60–75cm (2–2½ft) apart. The following winter, cut both arms back to the lowest pair of good buds facing to the left and right on the vertical part of the stem. From each, a pair of arms can then be grown on and managed as for a double cordon.

Double apple cordon, formative training

Upper wires 60cm (2ft) apart

Leader pruned to 25cm (10in)

Lowest wire 30cm (12in) from the ground

Year 1, winter

Vertically trained portion of shoot tied onto cane

Sidearms trained near-horizontally for 15–17cm (6–7in)

Trunk about 22cm (9in) tall kept clear of shoots

Year 2, summer

Leading growth tied in as it extends

Laterals ready for shortening to three leaves

Year 3, summer

APPLE ESPALIER

Espaliers need firm support: a wall or strong fence, or concrete posts, with horizontal wires 45–60cm (18–24in) apart (*see also* Apple cordon, p.112). Since much of an espalier's charm lies in its formal symmetry, it must be trained and maintained with care. Always use a spur-bearing cultivar (*see* p.105).

Two-tiered espaliers can be used as low, fruit-bearing "fences"; for more than three tiers, a vigorous rootstock must be used.

FORMATIVE TRAINING
Precise early training is easiest from a whip (*see* p.107), though a feathered tree with one or even two pairs of nearly opposing laterals will have a head start (if it also has a strong upper shoot, cut to it and train it in as the new leader).

Each winter, the central leader is cut back to just above where the next tier of branches is wanted, to direct energy into laterals that will break from buds just below the cut. The topmost shoot – the

new leader – is tied in vertically. The two below it are first trained diagonally on canes to keep them growing strongly. (The two laterals that will form the top tier will need longer canes, lashed to the lower wires, that extend at an angle above the top wire.) At the end of the growing season, cane and shoot are lowered to the horizontal. If one of a pair of laterals is growing less strongly than the other, raise it again temporarily (*see* Correcting uneven development, p.98), or shorten it to stimulate its growth.

When the espalier has filled its allotted space, cut back the central leading shoot and branch leaders to one bud in late spring or summer to discourage regrowth.

Apple espalier, year 1, winter

Year 1, summer

Cut the leader back to a good bud 5–7cm (2–3in) above the first wire. This bud will produce the new leading shoot.

Angled cut

Shoots from buds below wire will form first tier of branches

1 Tie in the new leading shoot.

To protect bark from damage, main stem and shoots are tied onto bamboo canes lashed firmly to wires

2 Train two strong laterals of equal vigour, one on each side, on canes tied to the wires at 40° to the ground. At the end of the summer, lower canes and shoots to the horizontal and tie the canes to the wire.

3 Prune or pinch back any other laterals to two or three leaves.

Year 2 until all tiers are formed, winter

1 Prune the new leader to a good bud just above the next wire, preferably facing in the opposite direction to that below last year's cut.

2 If growth is weak, prune lateral back by a quarter of its length.

3 Completely remove laterals shortened in the summer, cutting back to the main stem.

ESTABLISHED PRUNING

An espalier establishes gradually: on a three- or four-tiered tree, the lower branches are likely to be fruiting before the topmost limbs are fully formed. As each tier is being created, those below will be producing sideshoots that are summer-pruned (*see p.106*) to form fruiting spurs. As spur systems develop and become more complex, use winter pruning to relieve overcrowding (*see below*). Regular summer pruning is vital, otherwise the central stem will direct energy into strong upper growth at the expense of the lower tiers. If the top tiers tend to be more vigorous in spite of summer pruning, thinning shoots on their spurs after growth has started will restore a balance.

Year 2 until all tiers are formed, summer

1 *Train in new leading shoot vertically.*

2 *Select and train laterals to form the next tier as in Year 1.*

3 *Prune shoots on the lower branches back to three or four leaves.*

4 *Shorten any other laterals on the stem by two-thirds of their length.*

Established apple espalier, summer (modified lorette system)

1 *Prune all new laterals from the main arms to three leaves above the basal cluster.*

2 *Shorten all sideshoots to one leaf.*

Once all tiers have been formed, leading shoot is removed

3 *Remove completely any overvigorous, upright shoots on the arms and especially on the main stem.*

Growth on lower arms tends often to be less vigorous than on top tier

Basal third of new shoots has ripened

ESTABLISHED ESPALIER, WINTER

By the time the top tier of an espalier is fully established, lower arms will also have begun to need winter pruning (*see also p.105*) to thin congested spur systems built up by spur pruning. This thinning should subsequently be carried out where necessary every year.

Prune away old or unproductive sections of overcrowded spur systems. If spur systems themselves are too close together, remove one or two completely.

Before pruning

Unproductive old growth

Crowded fruit buds

After pruning

Space between fruit buds will allow fruits to develop

Older spurs have been removed in favour of younger wood

APPLE FAN

The fan form was traditionally used to wall-train plums and other stone fruits. Stone fruits are not suitable for training as espaliers, because such a rigid, closely-pruned form does not exploit their fruiting habit well. However, apples are just as well suited to more informal training, and a fan, if well-formed, does not need quite such rigorous attention to pruning as does an espalier. It may also be more productive.

Fans can sometimes be bought ready-trained, but avoid purchasing one whose branches radiate outwards from a central stem, rather than upwards from two low arms: a central trunk draws the tree's energy upwards so that the top growth in the centre of the fan grows much more vigorously than the rest.

FORMATIVE TRAINING

As for a peach fan (*see p.134*), but because there is no risk of silver leaf as with stone fruits, the pruning can be carried out in winter as for an apple

Fan-trained apple
Fans can be grown on free-standing systems of posts and wires, but these must be very well built to withstand the considerable wind resistance offered by such large, flat trees.

espalier. Use string tied vertically between wires to provide plenty of attachment points for shoots.

ESTABLISHED PRUNING

Once the framework has been formed, growth on the ribs of the fan is summer- and winter-pruned as for a single cordon (*see p.112*). Remove excessively vigorous

shoots that develop during the summer, unless they can be used in the following winter to replace a worn-out branch. Overgrown spur systems will need thinning as for a cordon (*see p.112*).

Fans can carry heavy crops, and efficient and well-timed fruit thinning (*see p.101*) is essential to avoid the onset of biennial bearing (*see p.101*).

APPLE STEPOVER

These are low, horizontal cordons, most often seen grown in series (usually along the edge of a bed or path), reaching to touch the trunk of the next tree in line. Use spur-bearing cultivars (*see p.104*), as they are more suited to the necessary regime of summer and winter pruning. It is essential to start with a very young maiden whip, so that the young stem has the necessary flexibility to withstand

being bent over. This must be done gradually and very carefully, flexing and tying the stem further down (with twine to a peg in the ground) in stages over the entire first growing season.

As laterals develop, shorten them to three leaves from the basal cluster to start building up fruiting spur systems. When the leading shoot attains the desired length, shorten it to a bud. The shoot that develops can be treated as any other lateral.

Established stepovers are summer- and winter-pruned as for a single, oblique cordon (*see p.112*). Growth may be more bushy and vigorous at the "trunk end" of the stepover, and may require more thinning in winter.

Apple stepover
To give support to a row of stepovers, space robust 60cm (2ft) posts approximately 1.5m (5ft) apart and tightly stretch strong wire horizontally between them, fixing it about 5cm (2in) below the post tops.

APPLE PALMETTE

The palmette is a variation on the espalier, with tiers of branches trained at a 40° angle to the ground. It is often seen in commercial orchards in southern Europe where, once formed, it is allowed to grow quite freely, but in cooler climates summer pruning is necessary to allow more sun to reach the lower parts of the tree.

These trees are very rarely offered for sale, but can easily be trained. Both formative and established pruning and training is exactly as for an espalier (*see p.114*), with one crucial difference: the laterals trained to form branches are never lowered from their initial, angled position to the horizontal, but are left to grow permanently at a 40° angle. Remember to check and, if necessary, loosen ties as the girth of the branches expands. A wall or fence with supporting horizontal wires, or posts and wires in the open, will be necessary.

PEARS *PYRUS COMMUNIS*

Although they are cool-climate fruits requiring cold winters, pears generally prefer warmer, more sheltered conditions than apples. As pears flower earlier than apples, harsh weather at flowering time can cause pollination problems and consequently a smaller crop.

For shelter, pears are often grown in wall-trained forms such as cordons, fans and espaliers. Ready-formed young trees are widely available, but pear forms are easily trained in the same way as apples. Cordons are doubly popular because they allow two or more cultivars – essential for pear pollination – to be grown in a small area. Wall-training also displays to good effect the decorative qualities of pear trees – furrowed bark, a stubby, gnarled habit with age, showy clusters of blossom, autumn leaf colour and fruits that vary as greatly in shape and colour as they do in flavour. Bushes and dwarf pyramids – small, compact trees ideal for a sheltered spot – are also popular forms.

ROOTSTOCKS AND GRAFTING

Like apples, pear cultivars do not come true from seed, and are propagated by grafting. Selections of quince are widely used, largely because they produce small, manageable trees that crop from an early age. 'Quince A' is moderately vigorous, 'Quince C' less so; the latter is preferable for growing vigorous cultivars. The choice of trained form may also dictate the rootstock to be used. The disadvantage of quince rootstock is that it is incompatible with a number of pear cultivars. The solution is a form of grafting known as double-working (*see also p.95*), in which two grafts are made using an intermediate length of a mutually

Pear in fruit

Pears are among the most attractive of fruit trees, their profuse white blossom followed by fruits that may develop yellow or red tints as they ripen. The foliage, too, often displays bright autumn colour. Even if its fruits are of little interest, an old pear tree, with its furrowed bark and gnarled habit, is a valuable ornamental feature.

Pear rootstocks

'Quince C' 'Quince A'

compatible cultivar to bridge the gap between the stock and the scion.

The 'PyroDwarf' pear rootstock is intermediate in dwarfing between 'Quince A' and 'Quince C', making a small, neat tree of ornamental as well as fruiting value.

'Kirchensaller' is a vigorous pear rootstock suitable for large trees such as perry pears. Unlike quince stocks, both pear rootstocks are tolerant of chalky soils and there are no graft incompatibility issues.

GROWTH AND FRUITING HABIT

Pears grow in a similar way to apples, and also fruit on two-year-old and older wood. However, a typical pear tree has a rather more upright growth habit than most apples, and usually also has a marked natural tendency to form spur systems. Without regular pruning, these tend to become crowded. Some cultivars, such as 'Doyenne du Comice' and 'Beurré Hardy', are very vigorous and their longer shoots need only light pruning in their early years, at least until cropping has started. Trees that do not grow well, developing nothing but congested, short growths, are usually suffering from a cultivation problem (often nitrogen deficiency).

There are very few tip-bearing, rather than spur-bearing, pear cultivars (*see p.104*); if one of these is chosen, follow the advice given for pruning tip-bearing apples (*see p.105*).

TIME OF PRUNING

All pears need winter pruning. For highly trained forms, summer pruning to restrict growth and maintain the tree's shape is also essential. Winter pruning consists largely of spur thinning, perhaps with the occasional removal of larger portions of branches in favour of younger growth (*see Regulated pruning, p.105*). Pears often set a large crop, and blossom- and fruit-thinning (*see p.101*) are often advisable. (*Continued on p.118.*)

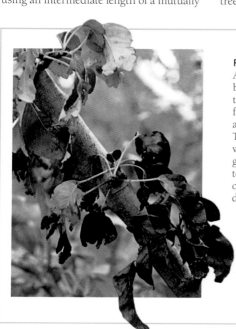

FIREBLIGHT

Additional pruning of pears may be necessary if they are attacked by the potentially fatal bacterial disease fireblight, to which all *Pyrus* (and, to a lesser extent, some *Malus*) are prone. The symptoms of fireblight need watching for in summer; affected growth must be pruned back to at least 60cm (2ft) below any signs of disease, and tools dipped in disinfectant afterwards. Blossom wilt symptoms are similar to fireblight, with which it can be confused.

Pear with fireblight

Blackened, scorched leaves, as if a fire had been burning under them, are the main indication of fireblight. The affected growth must be cut out completely as soon as possible.

(*Continued from p.117.*) Summer pruning of trained trees is identical to that for apples, following, depending on climate, either the full or modified Lorette system (*see p.106*), though usually timed a week or two earlier.

SPUR THINNING

Spur systems build up both naturally and with pruning, becoming more complex with age. Without regular thinning, they become congested and encroach upon neighbouring systems on the branch, crowding the fruits. On older trees, the removal of an entire system, with a saw or loppers, is the best way to start opening up growth on the branch. Then use secateurs to thin the remaining spur systems.

Pears require greater levels of nitrogen than apples, so feeding in the spring following pruning may be necessary.

Spur thinning, pears

Before thinning Start by removing obviously dead, weak or worn out, budless spurs, then continue by thinning wherever growth is crowded.

After thinning Spur pruning shortens and thins growth until only strong, productive spurs remain and there is space for fruits to grow and receive plenty of ripening sunlight.

PEAR DWARF PYRAMID

The pear's fruiting habit (it naturally forms spurs on which fruits are borne) makes it ideal for this neat, small form. As with apples, pear dwarf pyramids can be planted quite closely, with only 2m (6ft) needed between trees. When trees are planted closely, good formative training and regular summer pruning is even more essential to prevent this compact tree form getting out of hand. Use 'Quince A' rootstock, or 'Quince C' for more vigorous cultivars.

FORMATIVE TRAINING

While the shape is being formed, pruning concentrates on overcoming the upright growth habit to reduce vigour and form an open branch structure around a strong central trunk. Choose or train a young feathered tree (*see Apples, p.107*) with good, wide-angled laterals, and encourage this growth habit by cutting to outward-facing buds on the undersides of the shoots. Establishing strong lower branches is the first priority; dominant vigorous shoots on he upper part of the stem should be removed. The tapering pyramid shape ensures that all parts of the tree receive sun and air, with no overshadowing.

ESTABLISHED PRUNING

Summer pruning follows the full or modified Lorette system, depending on climate, as for apples (*see p.106*), but usually timed a little earlier. Winter pruning consists of spur pruning (*see p.105 and above*), and also of shortening the leading shoot, if necessary.

Pear dwarf pyramid
Close planting helps to keep these trees small through root competition. Hedge-like planting is attractive, but pears should not be used as a windbreak, or cropping will suffer.

Pear dwarf pyramid, year 1, winter

1 Cut the main stem to a bud 50–75cm (20–30in) above ground, ideally 10cm (4in) above the topmost lateral.

Dwarf pyramids need permanent staking, so insert a robust, 2m (6ft) post on planting that will support tree in maturity

2 Shorten each lateral to an outward-facing bud approximately 12cm (5in) from the main stem.

3 Remove any low or crossing laterals, and any that make narrow V-angles to the main stem.

Year 1, summer

Prune back to one bud vigorous upright shoots, particularly on the upper part of the tree

If new leader does not grow straight and vertical, tie it to stake

Year 2, winter

1 *Shorten the central leader to a bud, to leave about 25cm (10in) of the new growth. Repeat each year until the tree reaches the desired height.*

Bud faces in opposite direction to previous year's cut to help keep trunk straight

2 *Prune new maiden laterals and branch leaders to 15–20cm (6–8in), cutting to a downward- and outward-pointing bud to create an open branch structure.*

3 *Prune sideshoots to two or three buds to begin the formation of fruiting spur systems.*

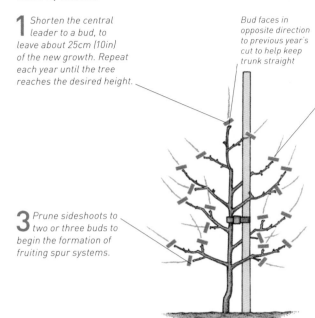

Year 2 and onwards, summer (modified lorette system)

1 *Prune new growth on branch leaders back to five or six leaves.*

Leading shoot left unpruned

2 *Prune new shoots arising directly from the trunk or main branches to three leaves beyond the basal cluster.*

Basal cluster of two or three leaves

3 *Prune sideshoots from winter-pruned laterals (spurs) to one leaf beyond the basal cluster.*

Basal third of shoot has ripened

Year 3 and onwards, winter

1 *To maintain the desired height, shorten leader to one bud of the summer's growth. (This pruning can be delayed until mid-spring to discourage regrowth.)*

2 *Reduce overgrown spurs and as trees mature, thin out spur systems where overcrowded.*

Other pear tree forms

PEAR BUSH

This is the most commonly grown unrestricted pear form. Formative training is as for an apple bush (*see p.108*). Many pear cultivars are more upright in habit than apples, and may need more encouragement to form open-centred bushes. Cutting to outward-facing buds, or tying down young shoots into a more horizontal position with twine pegged into the ground (*see also p.99*), will help. It is important to train shoots when young, as pear wood becomes inflexible as it ages. If the chosen cultivar is growing too vigorously for a compact, bushy shape to be achieved, prune more lightly or not at all to curb regrowth.

Established bushes wwill form spurs naturally, but this can be encouraged by spur pruning. Considerable spur thinning (*see p.105*) and occasional regulated pruning – removing older sections of branches where young growth exists to develop in its place (*see also p.105*) – will be necessary in winter.

STANDARD

These are trained and pruned as for apple standards (*see p.109*), though established trees will, like pear bushes, need more spur thinning. As with apples, these large trees are rarely practicable in a domestic garden, but they may be required as specimen trees or in an older orchard. Only a pear rootstock would provide the necessary vigour; a specialist fruit nursery should be able to offer advice.

CORDON

A pear cordon can easily be sited in a sheltered position, and is trained and pruned as for an apple cordon (*see p.112*). Pears are difficult to train as stepovers – low, horizontal cordons – because pear wood lacks the flexibility of apple wood, which can be bent at a 90° angle.

ESPALIER

A pear espalier is trained and pruned as for an apple (*see p.114*), although it will probably need more spur thinning in winter. On a sheltered wall, pear espaliers can be extremely productive. For two or three tiers, choose 'Quince C' rootstock; for more, 'Quince A'.

FAN

Pear fans, trained and pruned as for an apple fan (*see p.116*), are rarely seen but can be very successful and decorative. 'Quince A' rootstock will be necessary.

MEDLAR *MESPILUS GERMANICA*

The medlar makes a handsome tree and bears odd but highly prized fruits that are only edible once "bletted" or almost rotten.

Medlars are fully hardy, and are self-fertile, so only one tree is necessary for a crop. The fruits are borne on spurs from older wood, but these form naturally and spur-pruning is unnecessary.

The natural habit is spreading, even pendulous in some cases, and a strong, straight clear trunk is needed to support the spreading crown. Training is as for an ornamental branched-head standard (*see p.26*), with a clear trunk of at least 1–1.2m (3–4ft). If buying a partly trained standard or half-standard, tie the stem to a short stake at planting. If starting with a maiden, support the stem with a long stake for the first three or four years. If the stem of the partly trained tree appears weak, use a long stake. Once a strong, well-spaced branch framework has been established, however, only minimal pruning is required thereafter, removing a small proportion of older fruited wood in winter if growth is overcrowded. Medlars do not renovate well: hard pruning stimulates a mass of vertical shoots that spoil the tree's appearance.

Medlar tree and fruit
The fruits need to be fully ripened on the tree, then picked and stored, stalk upwards, in a cool, dark place until the flesh turns soft and yellowish-brown. The correct term for such fruit is not rotten, but "bletted".

QUINCE *CYDONIA OBLONGA*

The quince, with its downy, intensely aromatic apple- or pear-shaped fruits, is normally grown as a large bush, but may be trained as a fan or palmette, as for apples (*see p.116*), for wall protection in cooler areas. Cultivars grown for fruit are usually grafted onto either the 'Quince A' or 'C' rootstocks used for pears (*see p.117*). Although the quince is self-fertile it is claimed, though not proven, that growing two cultivars ensures better cropping.

Growth habit is rather untidy, and suckering quite common. Fruits are produced on naturally forming spurs and at the tips of one-year-old shoots.

QUINCE BUSH

Left to its own devices, a quince will form a multi-stemmed tree that will gradually become more dense and thicket-like; it will need constant thinning if it is to continue to fruit well. A well-trained bush form with a short, clear trunk and strong, well-placed and well-spaced main branches is a much more easily managed tree, needing only minimal routine attention.

Starting with a young feathered tree, the branch framework is developed along the same lines as for an apple bush (*see below and p.108*). As the tree matures, growth will become untidy and crowded; vigorous shoots can be shortened (*see below*) to prevent congestion building up, or more informal regulated pruning, removing some older wood (*see also p.105*), can be used to relieve congestion and keep the centre of the bush open. Never prune too hard in any one year, or vigorous regrowth will be stimulated. Congested spur systems should also be thinned, and suckers from the base or on the clear trunk should be removed.

Quince bush, year 1, winter

1 *Making an angled cut just above a healthy bud, prune back the central stem to a bud about 90cm (3ft) from the ground.*

2 *Prune upper laterals by two-thirds of their length, cutting just above an upward-facing bud.*

3 *Remove any laterals arising from the stem less than 60cm (2ft) from the ground.*

Year 2, winter

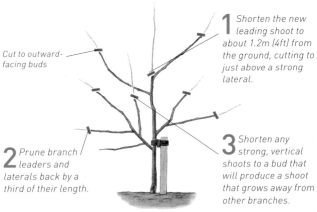

Cut to outward-facing buds

1 *Shorten the new leading shoot to about 1.2m (4ft) from the ground, cutting to just above a strong lateral.*

2 *Prune branch leaders and laterals back by a third of their length.*

3 *Shorten any strong, vertical shoots to a bud that will produce a shoot that grows away from other branches.*

Year 3 until established, winter

The quince's growth habit is erratic: remove any growth that crosses other shoots or develops in unwanted directions

Fruiting spurs start to form naturally

Established quince bush, winter

1 *Thin congested spur systems, removing older, less productive sections to make space for younger growth.*

2 *Remove up to a quarter of the oldest branches by cutting back to the point of origin or a strong replacement branch.*

3 *Remove any dead, diseased, crowded, crossing, or overly vigorous branches to thin out the canopy.*

4 *Look particularly to remove older branches that are low down or in the centre of the tree, to relieve canopy congestion.*

PLUMS *PRUNUS* SPP.

The superior flavour of fresh-picked plums, the huge variety of fruits and the decorative qualities of the trees make plums a popular garden choice. For cool climates there are European plums, gages, bullaces and damsons (*P. domestica* and *P. domestica* subsp. *insititia*), while warmer regions suit the earlier-flowering types – the mirabelle, and the Japanese or salicine plum (*P. salicina*, syn. *P. triflora*).

Although plums have complex pollination requirements, they also make excellent small trees with less rigid pruning requirements than apples or pears, making the siting and planting of two or even three compatible pollinators easy even in a small garden.

Plums flower early in the year, and so are vulnerable to late frosts; the early buds are also appealing to birds, which can cause severe damage. A small and easily netted tree in a sunny position is therefore the ideal. As with apples, the bush is the most productive and widely grown form, though pyramids are also popular. The spindle bush is a similar compact form that requires less maintenance pruning. Wall-training, for extra shelter and sun, may be advisable in cooler areas. The growth and fruiting habit of plum trees is unsuited to the pruning required to maintain cordons and espaliers, so the fan form is used.

Fans grown flat against walls or on open posts and wires are easy to net against birds, as are compact tree forms such as pyramids. This is an important factor in areas where birds are a nuisance; the damage they cause to unnetted trees may necessitate removing branches and rebuilding tree frameworks.

The risk of disease may also be a factor in choosing tree forms. Plums are susceptible to serious infections (*see* Plum problems, *facing page*) that gain entry through pruning wounds, especially if made in winter (*see* Time of pruning, *right*). Forms that require only light pruning, such as the bush and spindle bush, therefore run less risk of being affected by disease.

Plum in fruit
Trees in the plum group, such as this 'Shropshire Damson', fruit all along the length of young shoots, so these are not spur-pruned as they would be on apple and pear trees. On restricted forms, such as the pyramid and fan, some shortening of growth (summer pruning) is necessary to maintain the form and expose the fruits to light.

Plum rootstocks

'Pixy' 'St Julien A' 'Brompton' 'Myrobalan B'

ROOTSTOCKS AND GRAFTING
All plum trees are grafted, and suckering (*see p.30*) may be a problem. For small gardens, rootstocks such as 'St Julien A' or the dwarfing 'Pixy' are suitable, particularly for compact trained forms. 'Brompton' and the cherry plum rootstock, 'Myrobalan B', will produce a large tree or extensive fan. On all rootstocks, damson cultivars develop into smaller trees than other plums.

Stake all free-standing plum trees for the first two years, and those on 'Pixy' permanently. It is vital that the stake and ties do not chafe and damage the stem, creating an entry point for disease.

FRUITING HABIT
Plums fruit at the base of one-year-old shoots, and along the length of two-year-old and older stems. This young growth is therefore not routinely pruned back as on apples and pears, since the newest, most vigorous stems will bear a good crop. Once a strong framework has been formed, therefore, free-growing trees such as the bush or spindle bush require minimal pruning. More pruning is necessary on trained forms simply to maintain their shape.

Plums can fruit heavily, and thinning (*see p.101*) is often needed. A single fruit requires 7–10cm (3–4in) of branch space, depending on the cultivar, to expand fully.

TIME OF PRUNING
Pruning plums in winter is dangerous because silver leaf and cankers may gain entry through the wounds. Pruning tasks usually performed in winter for other fruits are therefore delayed until early spring for young trees requiring training, and until midsummer for older established trees. It is, on balance, safer to remove diseased and damaged wood as seen. Remove dead wood in late summer or autumn, while the tree is still in leaf and it can easily be identified.

The techniques of nicking and notching used for apples and pears should not be used on any stone fruit, because the wounds formed may allow the entry of disease. For most plum tree forms, it is advisable therefore to start not with a whip, but with a feathered maiden trained by a specialist nursery.

Plant plum trees before midwinter, before they start into growth. Do not make pruning cuts until the buds break.

Pinching plum shoots
Pruning wounds on plums should be as small as possible, reducing the cut surface area that is exposed to possible infection. Whenever possible, control growth at an early stage by pinch-pruning, using finger and thumb to nip out the soft tips of shoots. If plums are inspected regularly (once every week or two during the growing season), unwanted growth can be pinched out promptly, rather than being allowed to become woody and require cutting with secateurs.

PLUM PROBLEMS

No plum is immune to the disease silver leaf, though some cultivars are more resistant than others. It appears patchily (if an entire tree's leaves are silvered, the cause may be a nutritional deficiency). Affected growth must be cut back as soon as seen, until the cut surface is perfectly clean. Burn prunings and disinfect pruning tools. Like all stone fruits, plums are also susceptible to gumming; a gum-like substance oozes from the bark, and is sometimes found around the fruit stones. The gum itself is harmless, but is a sign of stress caused by disease, damage or adverse soil conditions. Gumming on one branch probably indicates a local infection; the branch should be removed. Gumming on the trunk or in the crotch of main branches indicates a more serious problem: seek professional advice to cure it. Elongated, flattened cankers that exude gum, accompanied by distorted growth, indicate bacterial canker. Cut back to healthy wood, burn prunings and disinfect tools.

Silvered foliage
These plum leaves are affected by silver leaf disease.

PLUM BUSH

Starting with a well-feathered maiden, the aim is to produce a well-spaced, open-centred crown with three or four main branches on a clear trunk of at least 75cm (2½ft). Once established, no routine pruning regime in either spring or summer is required. Instead, in early summer, remove twiggy, damaged, unproductive, crossing or crowded growth, cutting back to a replacement shoot or to the point of origin. With naturally spreading cultivars (such as 'Victoria'), such cuts should be made to upward-growing shoots; horizontal branches will start to droop, and may break, under the weight of fruit.

Plum bush, year 1, early spring

1 Shorten three or four well-spaced laterals by two-thirds, to an outward-facing or, on more horizontal shoots, upward-facing bud.

3 Shorten low or narrow-angled laterals to two buds. Pinch back any subsequent growth to two leaves throughout the season.

Angled cuts

Check ties regularly to avoid damage through chafing

2 Cut the leader back to the highest of the selected laterals, ideally about 90cm (3ft) from the ground.

Year 2, early spring

1 On each lateral, shorten two or three strong sub-laterals by half to a bud pointing in a direction that will produce a balanced, open-centred crown.

2 Remove completely any weak, badly placed or narrow-angled shoots.

Well-placed shorter growth can be left unpruned

3 Remove completely low laterals pruned and subsequently pinched back in the previous year.

If further shoots emerge on trunk, rub them off

60cm (2ft) stake does not chafe lowest branches

Year 3, spring to early summer

1 Prune branch leaders that are weak or growing horizontally by a quarter in early spring, cutting to a bud facing in the direction where new growth will fill in gaps in the branch framework.

2 Remove any badly placed, over-vigorous new shoots that develop.

PLUM PYRAMID

No more than 2.5m (8ft) tall (2m/6ft if the dwarfing 'Pixy' rootstock is used), the plum pyramid is ideal for a small garden. Although it needs regular pruning to keep the compact form, a tree that is well-trained from the start is easy to maintain. This form, in which numerous branches radiate from a central stem, suits all types of plums, although those of very upright habit are more difficult to control, because the lower branches must remain dominant and not be shaded by growth above. If you are planting several trees, space those on 'Pixy' 2.4–3m (8–10ft) apart (these trees must be staked permanently) and on 'St Julien A', 3–4m (10–12ft) apart.

STARTING WITH A MAIDEN WHIP

Maiden whips should be cut to a strong bud 1.5m (5ft) from the ground. Let the top bud grow to extend the central leader, but rub out the two or three immediately below, as they will develop at too narrow an angle and tend to be too vigorous, so competing with the leader. At the end of the first year the tree should have a good complement of laterals and be equivalent to a feathered maiden: formative training can begin.

FORMATIVE TRAINING

Although it is possible to start training a pyramid from a maiden whip, it is easier to begin with a feathered tree, since all but its lowest laterals can immediately be used in the first stage of branch formation. Trees will also fruit sooner. Because so many laterals are retained, there is no need, as on a bush, to shorten and then remove unwanted growth, in order to retain foliage to assist stem thickening.

The aim, when developing the branch framework, is to create a "Christmas tree"-like shape, so cut to buds whose direction of growth will achieve this structure and outline. While the tree is being formed, encourage branching by shortening the

Plum pyramid, year 1, early spring

1 Cut back the leader, making a sloping cut above a strong bud about 1.5m (5ft) from soil level.

2 Prune laterals that will form main branches by half their length, cutting to an outward-facing bud if habit is upright, upward if spreading. Any less than 22cm (9in) long can be left unpruned.

Robust, 2m (6ft) stake will be permanent

Angled cuts to outward-facing buds

Check tree ties regularly to avoid damage through chafing

Ties secure but not tight

3 Remove completely any laterals less than 45cm (18in) from soil level.

Year 1 until maturity, summer

1 New laterals forming too narrow an angle with the main stem should be removed (preferably pinched out when very young).

Central leader left unpruned

2 Shorten the new branch leaders to about 20cm (8in) from the base of the new growth.

3 Prune strong sideshoots to about 15cm (6in), cutting to a leaf, once the basal third of the shoot has ripened.

4 Rub or pinch off any shoots emerging on the clear trunk.

Year 2 until maturity, early spring

Until the pyramid reaches the desired height, each year, in early spring, shorten the central leader to leave about one-third of the previous year's growth central leader each spring until the desired height is reached. Meanwhile, summer pruning of all sideshoots, once the bases of the shoots have become woody, produces a compact shape and promotes fruitfulness.

ESTABLISHED PRUNING

Once the tree reaches the desired height, delay the annual pruning of the leader until late spring to discourage regrowth, shortening it to 2.5cm (1in) of the previous season's growth. Summer pruning must be carried out annually, or the pyramid form will be swiftly lost. It is particularly important to control growth strictly on the upper part of the tree, or it will shade fruit on the lower branches. Very vigorous upright shoots on the upper branches are best removed completely. The annual shortening of growth will inevitably lead to overcrowding in the centre of the tree: thin out less productive wood to ease congestion.

Fruit thinning (*see p.101*) may be necessary, but even so, pyramids can bear heavy crops for their size. If the weight of fruit is dragging a branch downwards, prop it with a cleft stick, or use maypoling (*see p.99*) to give the branch support. Shorten this branch to an upward-facing shoot after fruiting.

Established plum pyramid, summer

1 *When the bases of new shoots have ripened, shorten branch leaders to 20cm (8in) and strong sideshoots to 15cm (6in).*

Weak regrowth from leader shortened in spring

2 *Where growth is congested, remove some older unproductive sections, cutting back to strong young shoots.*

3 *Remove overvigorous upright growth completely.*

4 *Remove completely any dead or unhealthy looking growth, cutting back to a sound shoot or to the point of origin.*

PLUM SPINDLE BUSH

Spindle bushes, particularly of plums, are more often seen in commercial orchards than in gardens. However, once correctly trained, the basic spindle shape – a broad-bottomed cone, with three or four permanent low branches and a central stem, along all of which short, fruiting branches are renewed from time to time – is easy to maintain. This form therefore combines the compact form of a pyramid (although spindles need a little more space than pyramids) with the less formal pruning requirements of a bush.

FORMATIVE TRAINING

Start with a young feathered tree (preferably on 'St Julien A' rootstock) that has three or four well-spaced laterals making wide angles to the main stem, between about 60cm (2ft) and 90cm (3ft) from soil level. Neither these nor the central leader are cut back in the first spring pruning after planting. Instead, remove any laterals below 60cm (2ft), any that make narrow angles to the main stem, and any upper shoots that are more

vigorous than the selected shoots or threaten to crowd them.

Formative training then continues as for an apple spindle bush (*see p.110*). Pruning and tying down branches to form the spindle shape largely takes place in summer, which is a safe time to prune plums. However, whereas for apples the leading shoot is cut back in winter, delay pruning a plum's leader until spring, to minimize the risk of silver leaf infection entering the wound.

ESTABLISHED PRUNING

Routine pruning and the tying down of branches is broadly as for an apple spindle bush (*see p.110*), but for a plum all cuts should be made only in early summer. Growth on a plum will be more vigorous: as the trees become more mature, the removal of quite substantial sections of growth will become essential, particularly on the upper part of the central trunk. If branches here, which are trained to grow out horizontally, extend too far they may snap under the weight of fruit, so it is safer to shorten them to a sound but less vigorous replacement shoot. Maypoling – supporting branches with ties of twine or strips of netting nailed to the top of the stake (*see also p.99*) – to take the weight of the crop is an alternative.

STANDARDS AND HALF-STANDARDS

A full standard plum tree is not recommended for a domestic garden since the height makes maintenance very difficult. A half-standard is preferable if a tree form is desired. Both will require an area 6m (20ft) in diameter. To provide the necessary vigour to produce a taller tree, use 'Brompton' or 'Myrobalan B' rootstock; on very rich soil, 'St Julien A' is possible for a half-standard.

The trunk is cleared of branches as for an ornamental tree (*see p.26*), though formative pruning must not take place until buds break. As the trunk is cleared to the desired height (about 1.2m/4ft for a half-standard, 2m/6ft for a standard), the crown of branches is developed as for a plum bush (*see p.123*), except that in the first spring, the laterals selected to become framework branches should be shortened by one-third, not half. Subsequently maintainance is as for a plum bush.

PLUM FAN

2.5 | 8

m | ft

Fan-training on a sunny wall is an ideal method, in cool climates, for growing fine dessert plums and gages. They will be less susceptible to spring frost damage, and the ripening fruits are protected from poor weather conditions. Equip walls with horizontal wires about 30cm (12in) apart, threaded through vine eyes (see p.246). Trees on 'St Julien A' rootstocks will need an area 3.6m (12ft) wide by 2.5m (8ft) in height, those on 'Pixy' about 60cm (2ft) less each way. In warm areas fans can also be trained on open post-and-wire fences. Remember that suitable pollinating cultivars should be planted nearby. Even self-fertile cultivars crop better with cross-pollination.

FORMATIVE TRAINING

Plant a young feathered tree with two strong, low laterals, preferably of equal vigour, growing in a horizontal plane. Tie the laterals onto angled bamboo canes secured to the horizontal wires at 40–45°. The angle of either cane can be adjusted if one lateral is more vigorous than the other (see Correcting uneven development, p.98). These two initial "arms" are cut back to stimulate the growth of sublaterals, and from these shoots a selection can be made to form the "ribs" of the fan. All unwanted shoots are pruned out or, preferably, pinched back when young to one or two leaves; these help to feed the tree and are possible reserve sources for new shoots should the chosen shoots be damaged.

When selecting the ribs, aim for even development on each side. Choose a shoot to continue extending each arm, at least two on the upper side of each arm, and at least one from below. These lower ribs are crucial: without them, you will not achieve full coverage of the fan's base, since natural growth is always vertical. To encourage

branching, and thus establish the framework quickly, shorten the ribs in the early spring of the second and third years (see also Peach fan, p.134) to leave 60–75cm (24–30in) of the previous year's growth.

ESTABLISHED PRUNING

Once the fan's framework is filled out, the emphasis of pruning changes, from stimulating growth to controlling it, and avoiding overcrowding. Initially this is done by pinching shoots out when very young with thumb and forefinger. First, pinch those growing directly out and away from, or towards, the wall. Others should be thinned in spring to about 10cm (4in) apart. Later in the season they are shortened (see right), and again once the fruits have been picked.

On older trees, areas of the fan will become crowded and can be thinned in spring or early summer. Spread this work over the years to keep cuts to a minimum in any one season. As the tree achieves full cropping potential, fruit thinning (see p.101) will be necessary.

Training from a whip

If the young tree has no, or only weak or badly placed, laterals, cut it back to a bud about 45cm (18in) from ground level to stimulate vigorous laterals. When a suitable pair are 45cm (18in) long, proceed as right.

Plum fan, year 1, early spring

Young feathered tree with several strong laterals

1 *Cut back the leader to the higher of two selected laterals at about 25cm (10in) from the ground.*

2 *Shorten the selected laterals to an underside bud about 40cm (16in) from the main stem, and, using figure-of-eight knots, tie them to 2m (6ft) bamboo canes attached at a 45° angle to the wires.*

3 *Prune or pinch all other laterals to two buds.*

Young tree planted 20–25cm (8–10in) from wall

Year 1, midsummer

1 *Tie in selected ribs, and, where necessary, fan out and tie in well-spaced, well-placed sideshoots.*

2 *Cut or pinch back surplus sideshoots to one leaf.*

Canes are long enough to support extending leaders

New leading shoot tied in to continue direction of main arm

Well-spaced sideshoots tied in where they cross wires

3 *Remove any growth below the lowest ribs completely.*

Established plum fan, spring

Thin new growth by pinching out shoots until the remainder are 10cm (4in) apart (see also Peach fan, p.134).

New shoots in narrow branch forks are particularly likely to cause congestion

(see also Peach fan, p.134)

Late spring to summer

As the new growth develops, remove badly placed young shoots growing out from the horizontal plane, or inwards towards the wall. Shorten to a bud or shoot any that grow across other stems, or any branch leaders that exceed the allotted space.

Established plum fan, summer

1 *Tie in laterals, using soft twine tied in figures-of-eight, to fill gaps in the framework.*

2 *When they have 9–12 leaves, cut or pinch back laterals not required to fill in the framework to five or six leaves, later pinching out any regrowth.*

3 *Cut out any worn-out wood, and any badly placed, unhealthy or excessively vigorous and upright new shoots.*

Pruning after fruiting

In early autumn, after harvesting, prune back to three leaves all the shoots that were shortened to five or six leaves earlier in the summer.

SWEET AND DUKE CHERRIES *PRUNUS AVIUM* HYBRIDS

Sweet cherries are hardy, but in cool climates crops will not ripen fully unless trees are trained against a sunny wall. In warm regions, sweet cherries make excellent bushes, formed and pruned as for a plum bush (*see p.123*). Most cherries need another compatible cultivar nearby to ensure pollination.

Duke cherries, probably hybrids between the sweet and acid cherry (*see facing page*), have the growth and fruiting habit of a sweet cherry and are trained and pruned in the same way.

GRAFTING AND ROOTSTOCKS

'Gisela 5' is a semi-dwarfing rootstock that produces small (to 3m/10ft) pyramid or bush trees or compact fans, which are suitable for limited space and can be netted against birds. 'Krymsk 5' is another semi-

dwarfing rootstock comparable to 'Gisela 5' but more tolerant of wet soils. While not dwarfing, 'Colt' rootstock can also be used to grow sweet cherries in domestic gardens. Even so, a bush will be too big to net easily against birds, and a fan will need a wall or fence 2.5m (8ft) high by 5m (15ft) wide.

GROWTH AND FRUITING HABIT

Like plums, cherries fruit at the base of the previous season's shoots and on older wood. Fruit thinning is never needed. Cherry branches are robust and are rarely weighed down by fruit; bushes do not, therefore, splay out as they age – so it is important, when pruning, to maintain an open centre. Heavier branches are also liable to break if they make narrow V-angles (*see p.10*) with the main stem or branch. Remove shoots that fork narrowly from the stem.

TIME OF PRUNING

As with other stone fruits, winter-pruned cherries are susceptible to silver leaf (*see* Plums, *p.122*), so pruning must be delayed until bud-burst in spring when training a young tree, and until summer for established trees. Remove dead, diseased or damaged growth as soon as seen.

SWEET CHERRY FAN

A fan on a sunny wall gives excellent results in cool climates, and is also easy to net against birds. Formative pruning is carried out at bud-burst in spring, and the form is maintained by summer pruning in two stages: once in late spring to early summer, and again after fruiting. The framework is built up as for a plum fan (*see p.126*), on a support system of wires and canes. It may be possible to select not two but four laterals on a feathered maiden, and develop the framework more quickly.

Once the framework is established (*see below*), pruning is also as for plums. Shorten growth to stimulate fruiting and keep the fan flat against the wall, thin crowded growth, occasionally remove old growth in favour of young shoots, and, where the fan exceeds its allotted space, cut leaders back to sideshoots.

Cherry rootstocks

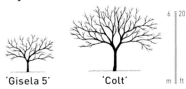

'Gisela 5' 'Colt'

Sweet cherry fan, early summer

1 *Tie in some new shoots where they can fill spaces in the framework. Tying string vertically between wires provides more attachment points.*

Leave branch leaders unpruned until allotted space is filled

2 *Shorten all other new shoots: once they have 8–12 leaves, pinch or cut them back to six or seven leaves, pinching any subsequent growth on them to one leaf. After fruiting, shorten these shoots again, to three leaves (see also Plum fan, p.126).*

ACID CHERRIES *PRUNUS CERASUS* HYBRIDS

The pruning requirements of the acid cherry differ from those of the sweet cherry, and are rather more demanding and complicated than for sweet cherries. However, acid cherries are much easier to grow in cool climates and in small gardens. The trees are less vigorous and mostly self-fertile, and even if the fruits do not ripen to finest quality in a poor summer, they are always excellent for culinary and preserving purposes. In cool climates, a good crop can be obtained from a bush in a sunny position, or from a fan trained on a wall – not necessarily one receiving full sun. 'Morello' is the most popular and widely available cultivar; there are inferior variants of this cultivar, so buy from a reliable specialist fruit nursery.

ROOTSTOCKS AND GRAFTING

The semi-dwarfing rootstocks 'Gisela 5' and 'Krymsk 5' are suitable for acid as well as sweet cherries and allow acid cherries to be grown in small gardens (*see facing page*). The semi-vigorous 'Colt' rootstock can also be used for acid cherries. While it produces a manageable bush tree, about 3–4m (10–12ft) tall, and a fan that is 2.2m (7ft) high and 4m (12ft) wide, it is too vigorous for the smaller trained forms used for plums.

Acid cherry pyramids are occasionally seen, but are mostly grown experimentally and need impractical levels of maintenance.

GROWTH AND FRUITING HABIT

Unlike most fruits, the acid cherry fruits almost exclusively on shoots that were produced the previous year. The aim of annual pruning, therefore, is to cut out some of the wood that has fruited each year to provide more space for existing young growth, and to stimulate further the production of new shoots.

Acid cherries can fruit in their third or fourth year, and it is important to bear this in mind when training young trees. Always cut to a pointed growth bud, rather than a fat fruit bud, to obtain a shoot growing from the intended point and in the planned direction. In the absence of a suitably placed single growth bud, a triple bud (a growth bud flanked by two fruit buds) will suffice (*see also* Peaches, *p.132*), though it is best to rub the fruit buds away to direct all available energy into the new shoot.

TIME OF PRUNING

As with other stone fruits, winter-pruned cherries are susceptible to silver leaf (*see* Plums, *p.122*), so pruning must be delayed

Harvesting cherries

Use scissors to snip off the fruit rather than pick by hand. The stalks are tough, and pulling them from the stem late in the season can leave many small tears in the bark that will be open to infection in autumn.

until bud-burst in spring when training a young tree, and spring and/or summer (*see below*) for established trees. Cut out diseased or damaged growth as soon as seen. In cooler climates, acid cherries may not be ready to harvest (*see above*) until very late summer.

ACID CHERRY BUSH

The aim is to create a well-structured, compact yet open crown on a short trunk. Cherries are spreading trees, and this needs to be borne in mind when pruning. Allow for a crown 4–5m (12–15ft) in width.

FORMATIVE TRAINING

As for a plum bush (*see p.123*), prune in spring. Take care to cut to growth or triple buds, not to fruit buds (*see* Growth and fruiting habit, *above*).

ESTABLISHED PRUNING

Prune partly in spring, as buds burst, and again after fruiting. On older trees, cut back one or two branches or sections of branches each year to encourage new growth, otherwise fruiting will gradually become limited to the periphery of the tree. This pruning is best done in spring, when growth buds can often be seen low down on shoots and branches. It can, however, be delayed until after fruiting (*see right*), when up to a quarter of the fruited shoots are also cut back to a new shoot. Leave those that have made plenty of fresh growth beyond the fruited portion, unless it spoils the shape of the tree: this growth will fruit well next year.

Newly established acid cherry bush, pruning after fruiting

1 Cut back one in four fruited shoots to a replacement shoot near their base.

2 Shorten to a side-shoot or leaf over-vigorous upright growth that will crowd the centre or, as it matures, put load-bearing stress on a spreading branch.

When deciding which shoots to prune, always remove growth that is downward-pointing on lower branches

Short, clear trunk of 75–90cm (2½–3ft)

ACID CHERRY FAN

An acid cherry fan, like a peach fan, is one of the more demanding fruit tree forms to develop and maintain successfully. It can be grown either on walls and fences equipped with horizontal wires, or on an open system of posts and wires. Because many of a fan's shoots need to be tied in at an angle, space wires closely (15cm/6in apart) or tie lengths of string vertically between wires to provide plenty of attachment points. Sunny sites are preferable but not essential, provided the site is airy, though a sunless site can increase the risk of disease in very wet years. Covering the fan with netting or muslin from late winter to bud-burst will protect buds from birds, and also to some degree against frost damage.

FORMATIVE TRAINING

Pruning and training to build up the framework of the fan is as for a peach fan (see p.134).

Acid cherry fan
A tree trained on a sunny wall can produce fruits ripe enough to be eaten raw, but even after a poor summer, in a less favoured site, the fruits will be excellent for cooking and preserving.

ESTABLISHED PRUNING

Pruning when established is also as for a peach fan, as both fruits crop on one-year-old shoots. The aim is to control growth to maintain the form, while maximizing crops in both the current and future seasons. The fan is pruned in late spring or early summer (see below) to favour, as far as possible, the one-year-old shoots on which fruits are developing. After harvesting, the fruited wood is removed (see facing page) to allow the following year's fruiting shoots to develop. On older fans, less productive, older parts of branches can be cut out in summer and new growth tied in to fill the gaps.

Established acid cherry fan, early summer

1 Remove shoots growing into the wall, or across other shoots.

2 Where necessary, thin the remaining new shoots until they are 10cm (4in) apart. On each shoot where fruits are forming, retain one sideshoot below the lowest fruits, and one further up. These will replace the fruited shoots when they are cut away.

Established acid cherry fan, pruning after fruiting

1 *Cut back each fruited shoot, either to the lower replacement shoot or, if there is room to tie in both, to the upper "reserve" shoot.*

2 *Tie in the replacement shoots to fill in the fan framework, spacing them evenly. These shoots should fruit next year.*

3 *Cut out any shoots growing towards the wall or fence, or across other shoots, that have grown since the spring.*

PERSIMMON *DIOSPYROS KAKI*

The Japanese or Oriental persimmon (the *Diospyros* species most widely grown for its fruits, sometimes known as Sharon Fruit) is hardy to -10°C (14°F), needing cold winter weather to set fruit, but also, for edible fruits, a long, hot summer. Persimmons fruit on the current season's shoots, so these must grow before the fruits can form. Cultivars are usually grafted; suckering from the rootstock can be a problem. Most cultivars bear only female flowers. Without a pollinator, fruits may be small and seedless.

TRAINING AND PRUNING
Fruiting persimmons can be trained as for ornamental species (*see Diospyros*, Dictionary of Ornamental Trees, *p.62*), reaching 12m (40ft) in height with a rounded canopy composed of upright branches. However, persimmons grown primarily for crops are usually trained as smaller, multi-stemmed trees on a short, clear trunk of about 60cm (2ft), as for an ornamental tree (*see Acer davidii, p.52*). Let dwarf cultivars develop naturally, but remove, in the early years, any badly placed shoots, or those making narrow angles with the trunk. Good formative

training is crucial for all persimmons; the branches tend to be brittle and may break under a heavy crop load. Branches with wide crotch angles are therefore essential: select only the strongest laterals making the widest angles with the main stem to form main branches. Remove all weak branches.

Because selection of shoots must be so rigorous, it can take five years to build up the framework of the tree. Routine pruning when established is not normally necessary

(nor does the tree tolerate heavy pruning well). They often produce an abundance of twiggy growth; if the centre of the tree becomes crowded, it may be thinned in winter to promote air circulation and to let more sunlight reach the fruits.

In cool climates, remove any growth damaged by frosts in summer. In warm areas, fruit thinning is normally essential to ensure a good quality crop. Thinning in the "on" year may solve any problems with biennial bearing (*see p.101*).

Persimmon
The persimmon makes a small tree in cooler regions with an attractive habit and dark shiny leaves that colour well in autumn. Although it cannot be wall-trained formally, this persimmon has been planted close to a wall for shelter, giving the fruits a better chance of ripening.

PEACHES AND NECTARINES *PRUNUS PERSICA*

Peaches and nectarines are downy and smooth-skinned forms of the same fruit, the latter preferring slightly warmer conditions. Nearly all cultivars are self-fertile. In warm temperate regions they are grown as bushes. In cool climates, a warm sunny wall or protection under glass is usually needed, and the fan is the most suitable trained form.

Triple bud
Some fruits, including peaches, often produce a growth bud that is flanked by two flower buds. The growth bud may not necessarily produce a shoot unless stimulated by pruning.

Fruit bud

Growth bud

Fruit bud

PEACHES IN COOL CLIMATES
Peaches flower in very early spring, and correct pruning is a vital factor in successful pollination. If growth is congested, the flowers are inaccessible to the few pollinating insects abroad at this time of year. In cool, wet climates, peaches are also vulnerable to peach leaf curl, a serious fungal disease prevalent in wet conditions. Control it by spraying, but if infection occurs, pick off and burn isolated affected leaves (new ones will grow). Repeatedly infected growth will become unproductive, and may have to be removed.

Fan-training allows peaches to be screened in winter with clear plastic sheeting on a wooden frame, protecting against frost but also excluding rain, so that peach leaf curl spores are denied the moisture they need to germinate. Hand-pollination, beneficial even to unscreened trees, will be necessary.

GRAFTING AND ROOTSTOCKS
Grafting is widely used, to obtain desired cultivars, to determine tree size and to give

Peach rootstocks

5.5 | 18

m | ft

'St Julien A'   'Brompton'

resistance (as with the Australian 'Nemaguard') to disease. Grafted trees will crop two or three years after planting. Plum rootstocks are widely used and, to a lesser extent, peach seedlings. There is as yet no compatible dwarfing rootstock, though double-working (*see p.95*) on the dwarfing 'Pixy' rootstock may prove successful. However, there are genetically dwarf cultivars, which fruit well in a warm, sunny site. These small trees can be protected in winter with a "hood" formed by stretching clear plastic over and around the top half of a frame made of wire or wooden battens.

Peaches and nectarines can produce worthwhile seedling trees, though fruits

will differ in quality from the parent. These trees usually grow vigorously, and take five to eight years to fruit.

FRUITING HABIT
Like acid cherries, peaches fruit on shoots that grew the previous year. The aim of pruning, therefore, is to remove fruited growth and encourage new shoots. When pruning to induce a new shoot, take care to cut to a pointed growth bud, and not a plump fruit bud. If necessary, cut to a triple bud (*see above*) and remove the two flower buds on either side of the growth bud. Unless many flowers have been damaged in bad weather, peaches almost always require some degree of fruit thinning (*see below*).

TIME OF PRUNING
Like plums, peaches are vulnerable to silver leaf (*see p.122*) and canker; do not prune in winter. Carry out formative pruning in early spring, as buds burst. Established trees are pruned in summer.

Dwarf peach
Dwarf peach cultivars such as 'Garden Lady' naturally make very small trees without grafting. Though the fruits resemble those of larger cultivars, the stems and foliage have a curious, congested growth habit that some find unattractive. Fruit thinning is particularly necessary on dwarf trees.

Fruit thinning, peaches and nectarines

1 *Where fruit set is heavy, make a preliminary thinning in mid-spring to one or two fruits per cluster.*

2 *If necessary, thin again when fruits are about the size of walnuts to leave fruits about 15–22cm (6–9in) apart (the closer distance for nectarines, and for peaches in warm climates).*

PEACH BUSH

Plant a feathered maiden in autumn or winter, but delay making any pruning cuts until early spring. Allow 4m (12ft) for the tree's spread. Seedling peaches may be allowed to develop naturally into an informal bush, but it is easier to control size and achieve a well-trained tree using a grafted cultivar.

FORMATIVE TRAINING

With a grafted cultivar, a bush is formed in much the same way as a plum bush (*see p.123*), aiming for a crown with 8–10 main branches on a short, clear trunk. If using a seedling, pruning should be minimal, removing only dead, diseased and damaged wood until cropping commences, and should then be as for an established bush (*see below*).

ESTABLISHED PRUNING

Once the bush is established, prune annually in early summer. The aims are first to maintain a healthy, strong, open-centred bush, then to maximize fruiting potential by removing older wood in favour of new growth. Keep the crown as open as possible while retaining some new growth in the centre of the bush, so that branches bent down by crop weight can be shortened to an upward-pointing replacement shoot.

Peach bush, year 1, early spring

1 *Select three or four laterals to form the main branches, and prune back the leader to just above the topmost one.*

2 *Prune the selected laterals by about two-thirds of their length, cutting to an outward-facing bud.*

3 *Remove any laterals below those chosen, close to the main stem.*

Clear trunk of 75–90cm (2½–3ft)

Peach bush, year 1, summer

1 *Pinch off or cut back to the stem any shoots growing from the clear trunk.*

2 *Remove any shoots growing into the centre of the bush, or downwards.*

Year 2, early spring

1 *On each main branch, select two or three strong, well-placed shoots and prune them to half their length. Cut just above outward-facing buds.*

2 *Cut back other laterals to two or three buds.*

Established peach bush, early summer

1 *Cut back one in four of the shoots that fruited last year to a replacement shoot, ideally upward- and outward-facing. Remove first those that have been bent down by cropping.*

2 *With fruits now developing, older, unproductive wood can be identified. Remove it, together with any crowded or crossing growth.*

PEACH FAN

A correctly trained peach fan has two short main arms, one on each side, from which ribs radiate outwards and upwards. To support it, equip the wall with the same arrangement of horizontal wires used for a plum fan (*see p.126*). In cool climates, a sunny outdoor wall is essential to produce regular, ripe crops. In glasshouses, support wires need to be held at least 22cm (9in) away from the glass to allow air to circulate and prevent sun scorch. Start with a young feathered tree of a grafted cultivar, planted in autumn or winter about 15–22cm (6–9in) from the wall. The wall needs to be at least 2m (6ft) tall, and 4–5m (12–15ft) wide for a peach on 'St Julien A'; 5–6m (15–20ft) on 'Brompton'.

FORMATIVE TRAINING

The fan's main branch structure is formed just as for a plum (*see p.126*). Use bamboo canes tied between the wires to "splint" young shoots securely at the desired angle. The angle can be adjusted temporarily if shoots are growing with unequal vigour (*see* Correcting uneven development, *p.98*). When branches are mature, remove the canes and tie in directly to the wires. As the framework of the fan fills out, tie lengths of tarred string or garden twine between wires to provide plenty of tying-in points for young shoots. Always keep the fan well tied-in to prevent growth shading the fruits. Pinch out surplus new shoots where the wires are well covered, to stimulate growth where there are gaps to be filled.

ESTABLISHED PRUNING

Once the fan framework has been established, the growth of all new shoots not required to fill in gaps in the framework needs to be controlled to avoid overcrowding. Starting in spring, the shoots are thinned when they are no more than a cluster of leaves. This thinning needs to be done systematically.

First remove shoots growing towards the fence, and any that seem excessively vigorous compared to the rest. Then, on each fruiting shoot (now in flower), select one strong sideshoot at the base, which will take the place of the fruited wood when it is cut back, and another shoot further up as insurance should the lower one fail. These shoots are retained (though later tip-pruned), while all others are pinched back to one leaf.

As the new shoots grow, shorten any that overlap fruiting wood and cannot be tied in where they will be out of the way. After the tree has cropped, each fruited shoot is cut back to its replacement, unless it is needed to fill a gap – in which case, tie it in to become part of the permanent framework. Older wood does tend to become bare, so if a branch in the framework produces few new shoots, it can be cut out providing there are some strong, young fruited shoots to tie in to take its place.

Peach fan, year 1, early spring

1 Select two laterals to form the main arms: one on either side, about 25–30cm (10–12in) from the ground. Cut out the leader just above the higher one.

2 Shorten each arm to about 38cm (15in), cutting to just above a strong, upward-facing bud.

3 Tie each arm to a bamboo cane attached at an angle of about 40° to the horizontal wires.

4 Cut back to one bud other laterals below the two main arms. (The remaining buds can provide reserve shoots should a main arm be lost.)

Year 1, summer, and year 2, spring

On each side, select "ribs": tie in the new branch leader in the same direction as the original arm and, ideally, two well-spaced shoots on the upper side of the arm and one below. Pinch or cut back all other shoots to one leaf. The following early spring, prune the ribs by a quarter of last year's growth to encourage further branching. Cut to a bud facing in the direction where there is space to be filled.

Year 2, early summer

1 Tie in well-placed sideshoots as they develop, adding canes where necessary, to build up an evenly spaced framework.

2 Cut out completely any badly placed or inward- or outward-growing shoots.

3 Now that the main arms are safely established, cut off previously shortened laterals below the main arms, close to the stem.

Year 3, early spring

Cut back each main branch leader by a quarter of last year's growth to stimulate further growth and extend the branch framework.

Year 3, spring

Thin young sideshoots to 10–15cm (4–6in) apart by pinching out unwanted shoots, removing first those growing towards the wall or across another shoot.

Year 3, early summer

Centre of framework is to be filled in last

1 *Where growth is crowded, shorten any shoots that overlap other stems to about four leaves above the basal cluster.*

2 *Tie remaining laterals in as they grow. They should fruit the following year. If any fruits are forming this year, thin to 22cm (9in) apart.*

Established peach fan, spring

1 *Remove completely shoots growing towards the wall, and those that will otherwise grow to cross other shoots.*

2 *Leaving a shoot below the lowest flower and another in reserve further up, pinch to one leaf all other sideshoots on flowering shoots.*

3 *Thin all other shoots to 10–15cm (4–6in) by pinching them out completely.*

Established fan, summer until after fruiting

When the replacement and reserve shoots on each fruiting stem are 45cm (18in) long, pinch out their tips, and pinch any sideshoots that form to one leaf. Shorten any other shoot that grows across another. Thin fruits if necessary (see p.132). After fruiting (see also Acid cherry fan, p.130), cut back each fruited shoot to its replacement near the base, and tie in the shoot. If there is room to retain and tie in the reserve shoot as well, cut to this shoot instead.

Reserve shoot
Lowest flower
Sideshoot will replace fruited shoot when latter is cut out

APRICOTS *PRUNUS ARMENIACA*

The apricot flowers very early in the spring, so while it makes an easily managed bush tree in warm climates (formed and subsequently managed as for a plum bush, *see p.123*), fan-training on a sunny wall, or under glass, is essential in cooler regions. Though self-fertile, apricots also benefit, in cool climates, from hand-pollination.

Always seek advice from a fruit nursery before buying. Apricots are fussy trees, and if they fail to do well this can be less to do with pruning, training or cultivation than to a dislike of some aspect of their site or the prevailing climate. This may manifest itself as dieback: pruning this away may cure the symptom but not the cause. Fruiting levels can also be affected by bad weather at pollination time: if the crop is sparse, much more growth will be made. This will need to be controlled by pruning, preferably at an early stage, or branches will become overcrowded.

GRAFTING AND ROOTSTOCKS

While a variety of rootstocks are used in countries where apricots are grown commercially, in Britain the plum rootstock 'St Julien A' is most suitable. In Australia, peach and apricot seedling rootstocks are used. Dwarfing rootstocks are not yet available.

FRUITING HABIT

Apricots fruit like plums: the crop is borne on two-year-old and older wood, but also at the base of one-year-old shoots. In warm climates, apricots crop prolifically and fruit thinning (*see p.101*), to 7cm (3in) apart, will be necessary.

TIME OF PRUNING

As with all stone fruits, prune as buds burst when training a young apricot, and in summer when the tree is established. Never prune in winter, when the risk of infection by disease (*see* Plum problems, *p.123*) is at its greatest.

APRICOT FAN

An apricot fan requires a wall or fence at least 2.5m (8ft) high by 5m (15ft) wide. The first years of training are as for a peach (*see p.134*). It is more likely, with apricots, that a selected shoot will be lost and a replacement, arising from the stubs of unwanted shoots that were pinched back, will need to be trained in.

Once established, prune as for a plum fan (*see below and p.126*). Shorten, rather than remove, shoots not needed to fill gaps, leaving their bases intact to fruit the following year. Relieve crowding by removing older sections of branches, filling gaps with strong new shoots.

Established apricot fan

Thinning shoots in spring
Pinch out young shoots to leave 10–15cm (4–6in) between those that remain.

Early summer

1 *To reduce overcrowding, cut small, older branches back to strong, young growth.*

2 *Where there are gaps in the framework, tie in well-placed new shoots on to the wires.*

3 *Cut or pinch out altogether any shoots pointing downwards or towards the wall or fence.*

4 *Cut or pinch back all other shoots to five or six leaves.*

Pruning after fruiting
Prune back to three leaves, shoots that were shortened to five or six leaves in early summer. If these shoots have produced sideshoots, shorten these also to one leaf.

MULBERRIES *MORUS* SPP.

Mulberries grown
for fruit include
Morus nigra, the
black mulberry,
M. rubra and
its hybrids,
and *M. alba,* the
white mulberry (*see also Morus*, Dictionary
of Ornamental Trees, *p.76*). Mulberries
are long-lived, slow-growing trees. They
need cold winters in order to crop well,
but start into growth late, so that frost
rarely damages flowers. The flowers are
self-fertile, and the fruits are borne on
second-year and older wood.

Mulberries are also sometimes grown
in containers, but cannot be allowed to
grow large enough to obtain a worthwhile
crop. Summer-pruning new shoots to five
leaves helps keep them compact, and
tying down branches to the horizontal
(*see p.99*) can increase crops.

WHEN TO PRUNE
Only in early to midwinter, when fully
dormant. Older trees, however, may
still bleed copiously (a red-hot poker is
traditionally used to cauterize wounds),
so only prune established trees if
absolutely necessary (to remove diseased
or damaged wood): remove dead wood in
summer. The roots also bleed, so do not
root-hybrids prune on planting.

TRAINING AND PRUNING
Later pruning can be kept to an
absolute minimum if the tree is well-
formed. Train a young tree (*see right*)
with a clear trunk of about 1.5m (5ft)
to accommodate the spreading branches
when mature. Unwanted laterals on the
main stem should be shortened in their
first year, then removed in the next. To
produce a structurally sound specimen
tree, retain a central leader to 6m (20ft)
if possible, by staking and removing
competing leaders, otherwise allowing
the crown to develop naturally. However,
if ease of maintenance and harvesting
is desired, a smaller, more compact tree
can be produced. Prune the leader to just
above the topmost of three or four strong
laterals, 1.35–1.7m (4½–5½ft) from the
ground. From these, develop a framework
of 8–10 branches as for an apple bush (*see
p.108*). Then allow the crown to develop
naturally, keeping pruning to a minimum.
Any unwanted new shoots are best rubbed
or pinched out promptly.

Mulberries have a tendency to lean
over, but crown lifting or reshaping is
not recommended. If possible, prop or
brace low branches where necessary rather
than removing them; combined with
the gnarled habit, this adds to the tree's
picturesque appeal.

Established mulberry tree
Though mulberries
are very long-lived,
their gnarled,
characterful habit
can make them look
prematurely aged,
increasing their
ornamental value.
The fruits ripen in
early to mid-summer.

Training a young mulberry
Young mulberries are not difficult to train.
Young whips are slow to develop "feathers",
or laterals, and the tree may be three or four
years old before pruning to clear the stem, as
for any ornamental standard tree (*see p.26*),
needs to start. Once a clear stem is achieved,
either let the crown develop naturally or, for
a more compact tree, prune the leader and
upper laterals (*see right*) as for an apple bush
in this and the subsequent year.

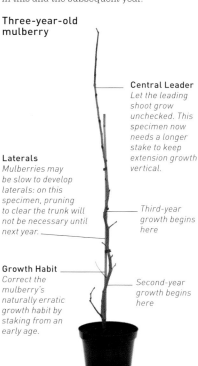

**Three-year-old
mulberry**

Central Leader
*Let the leading
shoot grow
unchecked. This
specimen now
needs a longer
stake to keep
extension growth
vertical.*

Laterals
*Mulberries may
be slow to develop
laterals: on this
specimen, pruning
to clear the trunk will
not be necessary until
next year.*

*Third-year
growth begins
here*

Growth Habit
*Correct the
mulberry's
naturally erratic
growth habit by
staking from an
early age.*

*Second-year
growth begins
here*

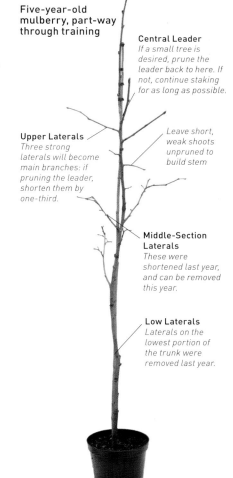

**Five-year-old
mulberry, part-way
through training**

Central Leader
*If a small tree is
desired, prune the
leader back to here. If
not, continue staking
for as long as possible.*

*Leave short,
weak shoots
unpruned to
build stem*

Upper Laterals
*Three strong
laterals will become
main branches: if
pruning the leader,
shorten them by
one-third.*

**Middle-Section
Laterals**
*These were
shortened last year,
and can be removed
this year.*

Low Laterals
*Laterals on the
lowest portion of
the trunk were
removed last year.*

FIGS *FICUS CARICA*

Figs ideally need a warm climate, with long, hot summers, to bear heavy crops. In warm countries, figs are grown as informal bush or half-standard trees, with trunks of about 60–120cm (2–4ft). In cool climates, unless they have a very favoured site and are pruned to be very open in habit (to let in light), trees or bushes seldom crop well. Growing under glass is difficult unless the root run is severely restricted. By far the most usual outdoor tree form for cool climates is the fan; even this may not crop well every year, and winter protection, in the form of netting filled with straw or bracken, is advisable.

ROOT RESTRICTION

Fig cultivars are raised from cuttings, not grafted, but a dwarfing effect can be achieved by restricting the root system, by

Summer pruning
Pinch out the tips of young shoots when they have made five or six leaves.

growing in pots or in open ground, planting in a brick- or concrete-lined pit, 60cm (2ft) square, with a layer of broken bricks at the bottom, not a solid base.

FRUITING HABIT

The fig has an unusual fruiting sequence and you may find figs present on a tree simultaneously at three distinct stages of development. First to ripen are figs that overwintered in leaf axils as "embryo" fruits from the previous season. Following these are fruits that form in the spring on new growth and, in hot climates, develop to ripeness as the main crop late in summer. Meanwhile, embryo fruits for the next year's crop are forming near the tip of the new shoots.

In hot climates, this cycle results in a long fruiting season. In cool climates, the summer season is not long or hot enough for fruits to develop and ripen in a single year. The only fruits to ripen fully will be those that overwintered as embryos from the previous year. Pruning is therefore concentrated on encouraging embryo figs to form, and giving these the best ripening conditions in their second year.

TIME OF PRUNING

Prune figs yearly in early spring, once any danger of prolonged frost has passed. In cool climates, pruning in early summer is also necessary: pinch back all new shoot tips to five or six leaves. This lets in more light and helps to reduce the production of the second crop of unwanted figs, but stop

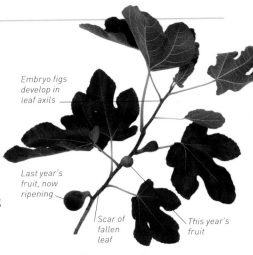

Embryo figs develop in leaf axils

Last year's fruit, now ripening

Scar of fallen leaf

This year's fruit

Fruit development, figs

On this unpruned shoot, a fig at the base that overwintered from last year is now ripening. Above it, figs that formed this spring will be the next to ripen, providing the summer is long and hot enough. Embryo fruits for next year are starting to form at the shoot tip.

pinching back before midsummer or you will remove the embryo fruits of next year's crop. With growth checked by tip-pruning, shoots will produce fewer fruits and will start into growth again, bearing sideshoots from leaf axils. At the end of the growing season, fruits in the leaf axils of these sideshoots will only be at an embryonic stage, and may overwinter successfully. Any larger, but still green fruits on the main shoot will not survive. Pick them off to direct the tree's energy into the more worthwhile fruits.

FIG BUSH

Start with a two-year-old fig with three or four well-spaced laterals of equal vigour arising from the main stem, at a height of 45–90cm (1½–3ft) from the ground. Planting and pruning in late winter/early spring (in cool climates, once severe weather is over), form a basic bush framework as for an apple bush (*see p.108*), with 8–10 main branches arising at or near the trunk.

Prune established fig bushes in spring and, in cool climates, in summer. In cool climates, spring pruning cuts should be made (*see right*) with the aim of keeping the bush as spreading and open in habit as possible. In warm climates, the reverse is true: cut spreading branches to upright shoots, and leave growth in the centre to give protection from sun scorch. In cool climates, pinch-prune new shoots in summer (*see Summer pruning, above*).

Established fig bush, spring (cool climate)

1 Cut back any frost-damaged shoots to healthy wood.

2 Thin out badly placed shoots and, to let in sunshine, overcrowded growth, particularly in the centre of the bush.

All pruning cuts have been made to encourage an open, spreading habit. In warm climates, denser growth is preferable

3 Cut any leggy, bare shoots or old branches back to one bud, or 5–8cm (2–3in), to encourage new growth.

Clear trunk of 45–60cm (18–24in)

Balanced crown with 8–10 well-spaced branches

FIG FAN

A fig fan has the same branch structure as other fruit fans, but its main ribs must be further apart to allow for the fig's much larger leaves. A wall at least 2.2m (7ft) high and 4m (12ft) wide is required, with strong horizontal wires.

FORMATIVE TRAINING

Start with a robust, two- or three-year-old fig. If its laterals are weak, badly placed or otherwise unpromising, by far the best course is to start again: remove them all and prune the leader to 40cm (16in), to stimulate strong lateral growth the following year.

Develop the branch structure as for a peach fan (*see p.134*). If the laterals are sturdy, prune away only a few inches; prune weaker ones harder, to about half their length. Aim to produce about six main ribs on either side over two or three winters, tying in laterals to fill out the framework. As soon as there are more laterals than are needed for tying in, start summer-pruning them to maintain the flat fan form and encourage fruit formation.

ESTABLISHED PRUNING

Fans must be routinely pruned in spring and, in cool climates, summer. When spring pruning, it is important to remove some older wood, and shorten a few young shoots back to one bud, in order to encourage new growth. However, any excessively vigorous, or in cool climates overcrowded, laterals should be removed.

Established fig fan, spring

1 Once any risk of prolonged frost has passed, cut any frost-damaged shoots back to their point of origin.

2 On each of the ribs, cut back two or three young shoots to one bud to encourage vigorous new shoots that will develop embryo fruits.

3 Tie the remaining well-positioned shoots in so that they are evenly spaced over the fan. In summer, pinch out new shoot tips to leave 5–6 leaves.

4 Prune shoots that grow towards the wall or across another shoot to their point of origin or to a well-placed sideshoot.

5 Cut back a proportion of old wood (perhaps one side branch on either side of the fan) to one bud or node and tie in newer shoots in its place.

GROWING FIGS IN CONTAINERS

Figs in pots, which can be moved into shelter for winter protection, can be grown as bushes, but with a clear trunk no more than 38cm (15in) high, to make them stable. They may also be grown in a multi-stemmed form, which is more compact. This is produced by cutting a two- or three-year-old fig down to ground level, once well-established in its pot, then selecting up to 10 of the best shoots that grow up from the base.

In subsequent springs, cut away three or four stems to the base (in later years, always removing the oldest or weakest), letting new growth replace them and removing any surplus basal growth. Shoots on these stems are summer-pruned as for any fig; remove only those that cross and rub against each other in the centre of the plant. These figs need light root-pruning every other spring (*see Root pruning a container-grown shrub, p.154*).

Container-grown fig
Prune at the base to maintain a multi-stemmed form. Summer-prune all sideshoots.

Tender fruits

Many of the frost-tender tree fruits need a completely frost-free climate. Others may survive light frosts, but will then fruit either poorly or not at all. Though all tender fruits benefit from initial training, regular pruning is not always needed (and can be inadvisable in hot, humid climates), and these trees are grown in much more free-growing forms than the hardy fruits. Training is more comparable to that of ornamental trees, and pruning when mature is often limited to the removal of dead, diseased or damaged wood, possibly with light pruning at or after harvesting. Most are better replaced than renovated.

Many tender fruits can be grown successfully under glass in cool climates. They may flower in a heated conservatory or glasshouse but, given the relative shortness of the summer season and reduction in hours of sunshine, fruits are unlikely to develop. The most satisfactory group to grow under glass is the citrus fruits (see p.142), highly ornamental plants that will tolerate pruning to size and shape and, given the right conditions, produce a small crop of fruits in most years. They make attractive container plants too, and if grown this way can be brought out of doors in summer to decorate terraces and patios.

ATEMOYA, CHERIMOYA & CUSTARD APPLE *ANNONA* SPP.

The cherimoya (*Annona cherimola*), the true custard apple or bullock's heart (*A. reticulata*) and the hybrid atemoya (called custard apple in Australia) are closely related. The atemoya and cherimoya thrive in tropical highlands and subtropical areas but will tolerate lower temperatures, shedding their leaves during dry or cool periods. The true custard apple prefers tropical, humid conditions with a cool but frost-free winter period.

Untrained trees may give good yields, but will be structurally weak. They fruit on both old and new wood.

■ **WHEN TO PRUNE** During the dormant or dry season; for custard apples, at the end of dormancy as buds break. Light pruning may also be needed during the growing season and after fruiting.

■ **TRAINING AND PRUNING** These fruits are best trained as multi-stemmed trees on a short trunk (see p.28). Prune the young tree back to about 1m (3ft), and let only three or four laterals develop. When these have grown to about 60cm (2ft), tip-prune them and let a new branch leader and two well-spaced sideshoots develop on each. These trees only develop shoots from buds just under the leaves once the leaf is shed, so removing strategically placed leaves, leaving the leaf-stalk on, can induce well-spaced laterals to grow where they are desired. Shorten vigorous, vertical shoots to an outward-facing bud or sideshoot.

When established, prune only to remove damaged, diseased, crossing or crowded growth; hard pruning stimulates excessive growth at the expense of flowering shoots. Atemoyas and cherimoyas may develop vigorous, non-flowering shoots; prune these by up to a third during the growing season to stimulate more flowering sideshoots.

Atemoya
Untrained trees grow with an erratic and weak branch structure; vigorous shoots tend to grow long and leggy, branching sparsely, and may break under the weight of crops.

Jackfruits
This jackfruit has been allowed to develop naturally into a tall tree that fruits all the way up the trunk and on main branches. A smaller, trained tree is easier to harvest.

BREADFRUIT, JACKFRUIT *ARTOCARPUS* SPP.

The breadfruit (*Artocarpus altilis*) grows best in wet, tropical lowland areas, while the jackfruit (*Artocarpus heterophylla*) tolerates a drier and cooler climate; it fruits well in many frost-free areas between the tropics but is very sensitive to soil waterlogging, cold and drought.

Breadfruit trees will grow to up to 30m (100ft), naturally developing a well-branched, spreading crown. The branches are brittle and easily damaged. The jackfruit grows to a height of 15–20m (50–70ft), with a dense, sometimes irregular crown that spreads with age.

Vegetatively propagated plants fruit in three or four years. Both trees crop better where two cultivars pollinate each other.

■ **WHEN TO PRUNE** When established, as fruits are harvested.

■ **TRAINING AND PRUNING** Once young plants are well established in their planting site, prune back the leader to the topmost of three or four laterals that will form main framework branches on a short clear trunk; remove all other laterals. Shorten excessively vigorous or leggy branch leaders by about one-third and, with the very upright breadfruit cultivars, bend and tie down laterals (see p.99) at an early stage to ensure an open crown.

Once the framework is established, shorten fruited shoots after harvesting to stimulate the growth of shoots that will flower the following year. Otherwise, keep pruning to a minimum. Mature trees sometimes require thinning to prevent leafy growth becoming too dense and shading the fruits; crowded branches restrict access for harvesting.

STAR FRUIT
AVERRHOA CARAMBOLA

The star fruit, or carambola, grows well in tropical and subtropical regions, although mature trees can withstand light frosts for short periods. Evergreen in the tropics, it is sometimes semi-deciduous in the subtropics, and is relatively slow-growing, with a short trunk and an initially pyramidal, then bushy, rounded crown; the branches of some cultivars have a drooping habit. Named cultivars, sometimes grafted, are preferable. They may flower within two or three years of planting. Fruiting is irregular but two main crops are obtained in some areas. Trees usually require pollination by another cultivar.

In warm temperate areas, with liberal feeding and watering plants may be grown in either containers or beds in full sun in a heated greenhouse or conservatory, with minimum summer temperatures of 22°C (72°F).

■ **WHEN TO PRUNE** After harvesting.

■ **TRAINING AND PRUNING** Train as a multi-stemmed tree (*see p.28*), pruning back to 30–45cm (12–18in) from ground level, then selecting four to six main stems. Some cultivars grow strongly upright and branch crotch angles may be narrow; to counteract this, tie down branches for a single growing season with twine pegged into the ground (*see p.99*) so that a more open crown is formed. As the tree develops, shorten very vigorous branch leaders by one-third to encourage a branching habit.

Little further pruning is needed. Low-hanging, weak and crossing growth should be regularly removed, together with any damaged or diseased wood.

Young star fruit trees
Most cultivars of these small, slow-growing, multi-stemmed trees need another cultivar planted nearby for pollination purposes.

PAPAYA *CARICA PAPAYA*

Though popularly referred to as a tree, botanically the papaya, pawpaw or tree melon is a tall, slender arborescent herb, with a single, thick, usually unbranched trunk, on which the fruits are borne. It has a productive lifespan of only four or five years. It is widely grown in subtropical to tropical regions. For fruits to form, both male and female plants are usually needed, although some self-fertile cultivars are available.

Papayas need a sheltered site in full sun, plentiful rainfall throughout the growing season and good drainage. A tropical climate is ideal, though some cultivars withstand minimum temperatures of 16°C (60°F): these may be grown in greenhouses in warm temperate regions. Plants under glass may not fruit reliably: high levels of light during the summer and temperatures that never fall below 20°C (68°F) are needed. Even self-fertile cultivars will need to be hand-pollinated. Papayas make attractive ornamentals, however; pruning back the leader will induce a less vigorous branched habit.

Papayas are usually propagated from seed. Young plants grow rapidly to a height of 4–6m (12–20ft), normally fruiting within two years. The fruits may be produced at any time of the year.

■ **WHEN TO PRUNE** After harvesting.

■ **TRAINING AND PRUNING** The single stem of the papaya rarely branches naturally, and initial training is therefore normally minimal. Branching may be induced, to restrict height and make harvesting easier, by removing the terminal shoot, tip-pruning the leader after the first harvest. Trees that have become too tall to harvest or have outgrown their space, for example under glass, may be cut back

Papaya flowers and fruits
The flowers are produced in the leaf axils; both the leaf and leaf-stalk are shed as the plant grows upwards and the fruits gradually increase in size.

to half their height or, to renovate completely, to within 80–90cm (32–36in) of ground level; they usually respond well, producing several shoots from dormant basal buds. Train the strongest stem vertically at first with a cane or short stake, and remove the others at the base (they can be used as cuttings for propagation). Male trees pruned in this manner sometimes produce female flowers and fruits in a form of sex reversion.

STAR APPLE *CHRYSOPHYLLUM CAINITO*

This large, evergreen tree prefers a humid, tropical environment with well-distributed rainfall and high temperatures throughout the year; in subtropical areas such as southern Florida, it requires protection from cold winds for the first two or three years after planting.

Star apples may grow to a height of 30m (100ft), developing a dense, broad canopy. Propagation is usually by seed but grafting (on to selected rootstocks of star apple) is successful, as is air layering. The flowers are insect-pollinated and are usually self-fertile. Star apples need minimal training and pruning. They usually develop naturally as multi-stemmed trees (*see p.28*) on a short trunk of 60–90cm (2–3ft); select only three main framework branches to allow light to penetrate the canopy. Thin inward-growing laterals if necessary to avoid a congested crown at maturity. Limit pruning of established trees to the removal of crossing or weak shoots, and any damaged or diseased growth. Remove any water shoots (*see p.30*) that develop at the sites of pruning cuts.

CITRUS FRUITS

The genus *Citrus*, like *Prunus*, contains a great many species grown for fruits, the most popular being oranges, lemons, grapefruits and limes. There are other citrus fruits from different genera, including kumquats (*Citrus japonica*) and calamondins (*C. × microcarpa*), both ideal for growing under glass, or in containers to be given winter shelter, in cooler climates. They are often grown purely for their ornamental value.

Citrus fruits grow well in almost any frost-free climate, and in areas with hot summers, as in Mediterranean countries, the well-ripened wood can survive light frosts. In cool climates, trees can be brought out into a sheltered spot for the summer months; cool night temperatures improve the fruit colour.

GROWTH AND FRUITING HABIT

In frost-free climates the growth cycles of most citrus trees usually last for four to six weeks, with up to five cycles per year under good growing conditions. It is therefore quite normal for flowers and fruits to be present on branches at any one time. Trees become dormant at temperatures below 13°C (55°F), or in dry or drought conditions (the onset of rain or resumption of watering usually results in flowering within four weeks).

TIME OF PRUNING

Prune at any time in warm, frost-free climates. Elsewhere, prune young trees from spring to late summer; spring gives regrowth time to ripen before cold weather sets in. Established trees can be pruned at or after harvesting.

FORMATIVE TRAINING

For ease of harvesting, cropping citrus trees are grown as bush trees (*see facing page*), with

Lemon fruits and flowers
While most fruits have distinct growth cycles, those of a lemon are much more likely to overlap, so that flowers and fruits may be present on the tree simultaneously.

a domed, open-centred crown on a clear trunk no shorter than 50cm (20in) to keep fruits from touching the soil. Where trees are grown as ornamentals, particularly in containers, they look better as small branched-head standards (*see p.144*), with a clear trunk of 1–1.5m (3–5ft). The trunk is cleared gradually of growth, as for any ornamental tree (*see p.26*), so that the foliage nourishes the stem and protects the young bark from sun scorch.

Once the desired height of clear trunk has been achieved, the crown is formed in much the same way. Select only three or four upper laterals as the main branches; these should be of about equal length,

making crotch angles of at least 40° to the main stem.

To develop a symmetrical and compact crown, shorten branch leaders again at the beginning of the growing season in spring or, alternatively, while the trees are semi-dormant during the winter period. The main branches should each give rise to two or three sublaterals that will, in turn, produce two or three shoots. Continued shortening of branch leaders promotes this neat, bushy habit. A second light pruning may be carried out during the growing season, if necessary, to remove any new shoots growing across other growth, or into the centre of the tree.

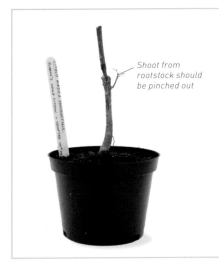

Shoot from rootstock should be pinched out

GRAFTING AND ROOTSTOCKS

Many citrus trees come true from seed and are easy to raise as seedlings. In general, these are more vigorous than grafted plants, lemons particularly so. They often have a greater degree of resistance to diseases such as root rot. However, seedling citrus are generally less productive, and do not start to crop until about six years old, whereas grafted trees may begin to flower within two or three years of grafting. Most citrus species and cultivars can be successfully bud-grafted onto a range of rootstocks that can be used to modify tree vigour, fruit

Recently grafted citrus

This young citron has been grafted on to Meyer's lemon, a useful rootstock that confers tolerance of lower temperatures.

yield and quality, resistance to disease and tolerance to low temperatures. Some combine several properties: the widely used Troyer citrange, for example, not only results in smaller trees but also confers some resistance to attack by root nematodes. Kumquat trees are usually grafted onto trifoliate orange (*C. trifoliata*) for its dwarfing effect and cold-resistance; this rootstock also reduces fruit acidity when used for grapefruits.

The chosen rootstock can affect the degree of pruning required, particularly where a dwarfing type of rootstock is used, and specialist advice is invaluable. Always choose a plant grafted onto dwarfing stock if the tree is to be grown in a container.

Training a citrus bush

Stage 1

When a young, unbranched plant is about 90–120cm (3–4ft) high, prune it to just above a leaf at about 60cm (2ft) from the ground.

Stage 2

1 *Select three or four strong laterals to form framework branches, shortening each to about 30cm (12in).*

2 *Pinch out any low shoots that develop on the stem, but retain single leaves.*

ESTABLISHED PRUNING

In general, prune mature trees as lightly as possible. An exception can be made for some cultivars of lemon grown on a vigorous rootstock. These cultivars have a predominantly upright habit and may require fairly severe pruning, when mature, to encourage lateral branching.

On grafted citrus, suckers are likely to arise from below the bud union. All citrus also tend to produce water shoots on their main branches. These should all be removed as soon as they appear. Inward-growing shoots should also be removed or cut back to an outward-facing bud since, shaded by other growth, they are unlikely to produce flowers. As with all fruit trees, diseased or dead branches should be regularly removed, and any crossing branches that could cause chafing damage.

Fruit thinning is rarely required, particularly with overlapping crop cycles when only a proportion of shoots are fruiting, while others are in flower. Remove the first-formed fruits from trees in containers, to promote growth.

When harvesting, prune each fruited shoot back to the next young shoot, since it will not fruit again. Always harvest with secateurs: citrus fruits pulled from the tree so that their calyx is damaged or left behind will quickly rot. Pulling fruit off may also bruise the rind.

RENOVATION

Citrus trees usually respond to hard pruning, if necessary. On older trees, an unproductive branch or section of branch can be removed. Do not remove more in any one year. Unlike many fruit trees, citrus trees, in general, have limited reserves of carbohydrates in their stem tissues and excessive pruning is therefore likely to set back growth and fruiting. If several shoots arise around a cut, select only one or two of the best-placed to develop as main branches.

Stage 3

1 *Shorten the new branch leaders by one-third of their growth, and tip-prune strong sideshoots by three or four leaves.*

2 *Remove sideshoots growing across other shoots or into the centre of the bush.*

3 *Remove any shoots on the clear trunk.*

Young established citrus bush

1 *Tip-prune vigorous branch leaders to maintain a balanced, compact crown.*

2 *Remove crossing shoots, especially those growing into the centre of the tree, to create and maintain an open branch structure.*

3 *When harvesting fruits, prune each fruited shoot back to a non-fruiting sideshoot.*

CITRUS FOR COOLER CLIMATES

Tangerines, mandarins and satsumas are, in general, more cold-tolerant than sweet oranges and also more drought-resistant. The lime *Citrus aurantiifolia* 'Tahiti' (syn. 'Persian') is more cold-tolerant than 'Mexican'. The Meyer lemon (now considered to be a cultivar of *C. × limon*) is a small, fairly cold-tolerant plant, very suitable for growing in containers. Kumquats are also excellent container plants. They usually remain semi-dormant during autumn and winter but grow vigorously during spring and summer. Though they normally make shrubby trees up to 4m (12ft) high, their size can be restricted

Frost damage

Prune back to completely healthy growth, cutting to a leaf so that a new shoot may develop from its axillary bud.

under cover by pruning in winter to remove much of the previous season's growth.

CITRUS IN CONTAINERS

When growing citrus trees in containers, feed young plants regularly each month during the growing season (*see p.13*). This is essential to promote strong and healthy branch development. During this period of active growth, any water shoots, or suckers growing from the rootstock, must be removed as soon as they develop.

Other pruning should take place in the early part of the year, particularly if the plants have been semi-dormant during the winter. At this time, shorten any shoots that have been cold-damaged (*see left*). For well-established plants, reduce watering to a minimum for three or four weeks during the early part of the summer, to promote flower initiation when watering resumes.

Make sure there is adequate ventilation, particularly during the summer months, and avoid excessive humidity, which could encourage disease. Shade and low levels of light reduce yields. Mature plants in containers may be transferred to a sunny outdoor site, protected from wind, during the summer.

Repotting should be carried out very carefully, in early spring, in order not to interrupt the growth cycle. Light pruning may follow repotting. Established trees grow best in large tubs.

Citrus standard in container

This calamondin has been trained as a standard largely for ornamental effect, though its small orange fruits can be crystallized or used in preserves.

Training a citrus standard

Stage 1

1 Lightly stake and tie in the leader to ensure straight, vertical growth.

2 Shorten all laterals by one-third of their length.

Stage 2

1 Once the desired height of stem has been exceeded, prune the leader back to a strong bud.

Leave new young laterals unpruned to thicken the stem

2 Remove the previously shortened laterals completely.

Leaves are shed naturally

Stage 3

1 Selecting four strong, well-spaced shoots from which to develop the head, tip-prune each by three to five leaves. Prune subsequently to develop a balanced crown as for a bush tree (see p.143).

2 Remove all other laterals and subsequent regrowth from the main stem. Remove stake and tie as soon as the tree is well established.

DURIAN *DURIO ZIBETHINUS*

Durians, grown chiefly in tropical South-east Asia, need high humidity and rainfall, with a definite dry season. A pollinating cultivar is usually required. Seedling trees may grow to 30m (100ft); grafted trees rarely achieve half this height. Young trees have a pyramidal shape that gradually becomes more irregular. Let trees develop naturally,

30 | 100

m | ft

pruning only to remove or shorten vigorous upright shoots, since vertical growth rarely fruits. Thin the more horizontally growing branches, on which most flowers form, to avoid crowding and crossing growth. Remove epicormic shoots (*see p.30*) on the trunk and main branches. Established trees need minimal attention. Thin fruitlets four to six weeks after flowering, to leave one or two fruits per panicle. Overlarge trees respond well to crown reduction (*see p.33*) to a height of about 10m (30ft).

Durian in fruit
The famously malodorous durian fruits form along the length of horizontal branches.

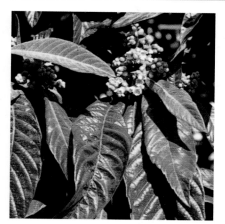

Loquat in flower
In suitable conditions, flowers, followed by fruits, are borne on the current year's growth, mainly in terminal clusters, from about four years after planting. For ease of harvesting, choose one of the more compact cultivars, grafted onto a dwarfing rootstock.

LOQUAT
ERIOBOTRYA JAPONICA

Loquats are hardy, though cold winters may reduce flowering. Many cultivars also require a pollinator. Train as a multi-stemmed tree (*see p.28*) on a short, clear trunk; shorten branch leaders by about one-third of their length, if necessary, to encourage branching. Prune just before trees start into growth. Established trees need no special pruning; to harvest, remove entire fruit clusters, cutting back to a bud or shoot. This may stimulate numerous sideshoots: thin by removing, not shortening, shoots if growth becomes crowded, particularly in the centre. Keep the short trunk clear of growth. If a heavy crop is set, thin fruit by removing the tip of each fruit cluster.

6 | 20

m | ft

LITCHI *LITCHI CHINENSIS*

The litchi, or lychee, is a slow-growing evergreen tree. It has a dense, symmetrical, domed canopy; some cultivars have branches with a spreading, semi-pendent habit. Most cultivars do not grow to more than 10–12m (30–40ft) tall. Lychees need a subtropical climate, with a cool, dry winter season and hot summers with relatively high humidity.

12 | 40

m | ft

■ **WHEN TO PRUNE** When harvesting.

■ **TRAINING AND PRUNING** Trees naturally branch from the base, but training is recommended to ensure a well-structured multi-stemmed tree. Choose a young feathered tree that has three or four well-spaced, wide-angled laterals between 30 and 60cm (1–2ft) from the ground and prune back the leader to the topmost. It is essential that laterals make wide V-angles with the main stem, otherwise mature branches may split away from the trunk. Remove any laterals less than 30cm (1ft) from the ground. Some cultivars develop long, semi-pendent branches and these should be shortened by about 30cm (1ft) to stimulate fruiting sideshoots.

Mature trees rarely need pruning. When the clusters of fruit are harvested, shorten the fruited shoots by about 30cm (1ft) to stimulate the growth of new laterals that will fruit the following season. Remove dead and weak branches within the crown at the same time.

Older trees, and particularly those that have been damaged by frost, will respond well to hard pruning; this will result in both increased fruit size and yield. In some regions, trees that are not cropping will, provided that they are well established, healthy and vigorous, respond to bark ringing (*see p.106*); always seek local expert advice before using this technique.

MANGOSTEEN *GARCINIA MANGOSTANA*

The mangosteen prefers the climate of its native Southeast Asia. Seedling trees are usually grown. Tree height is very variable, from 6 to 25m (20–80ft); crown reduction (*see p.33*) is often necessary.

Mangosteens are best pruned soon after harvesting; they may flower twice a year. Little training or pruning is required, except to remove inward-pointing and strongly upright branches, both on young and maturing trees, to encourage a tiered habit. Remove low branches that touch the soil. Overcrowded trees with very dense foliage fruit only at the tips of branches; thinning will increase light penetration into the tree canopy. Spread the work out over several seasons: heavy pruning at any one time is not recommended.

25 | 80

m | ft

Young mangosteen tree
Mangosteens grow slowly when young, with a straight trunk, symmetrically branched to form a pyramidal crown. Fruits are borne after 8–10 years at the tips of mature shoots.

MANGO *MANGIFERA INDICA*

Mangoes are well-branched, erect, evergreen trees with an oval, dome-shaped, open crown. The form develops naturally but training will ensure a strong branch structure. Mangoes need a tropical or subtropical, damp climate with a distinct dry or cool season. Wetter conditions encourage growth at the expense of fruiting. Seedlings take seven or eight years to fruit, but grafted cultivars usually flower in the third year after planting. Dwarfing rootstocks are available that restrict height to 7–10m (22–30ft), making it possible to grow mangoes under cover, given a warm, humid atmosphere.

■ **WHEN TO PRUNE** When young, between growth flushes, then after the main crop.

■ **TRAINING AND PRUNING** All mangoes benefit from formative training. Aim to form a bush tree, as for an apple (*see p.106*), with a clear trunk of about 1m (3ft) and a well-spaced crown formed by three to five framework branches with wide crotch angles. All weak laterals should be removed; mango fruits are heavy and will break branches that are not structurally sound. Fruits should be thinned for the first two years of flowering; later, fruit thinning is rarely necessary.

Established trees need no routine pruning. Remove any low or crossing shoots. Branch leaders may be shortened by one-third to promote branching, or to restrict the size of vigorous cultivars. Older trees can be reinvigorated by pruning out inward-pointing branches and thinning out crowded growth and some of the terminal shoots.

Mango fruits
Fruits are heavy and borne in drooping clusters; the branch framework must be strong.

RAMBUTAN
NEPHELIUM LAPPACEUM

The rambutan, native to Malaysia and Indonesia, is grown in many lowland tropical regions. Temperatures below 10°C (50°F) severely limit growth. Trees are prone to damage by strong winds.

Seedling rambutans grow to 12–20m (40–70ft) tall, with a canopy that spreads to about two-thirds of their height. Vegetatively propagated cultivars, which fruit earlier, are pruned and trained to grow only to 4–12m (12–40ft); they may have an erect, but more usually a spreading habit. Flowers are produced mainly at the shoot tips.

■ **WHEN TO PRUNE** After harvesting.

■ **TRAINING AND PRUNING** Trees tend to be dense and crowded if unpruned, so early training is essential to ensure a regularly spaced branch framework that lets in air and light. Aim to form a bush tree, as for an apple (*see p.106*). Prune a one- or two-year-old feathered tree on planting to 60–90cm (2–3ft) from ground level, just above three or four evenly spaced, vigorous laterals that make wide V-angles with the main stem. Three months later, shorten these laterals by about one-third of their length to encourage sideshoots.

Once the main framework has been established, minimal pruning is required. Remove water shoots (*see p.30*), diseased or dead wood, and any branches that are crossing or growing too close to the ground. After harvesting, the remains of the fruited panicles can be removed to stimulate new fruiting shoots.

OLIVE *OLEA EUROPAEA*

Olives are slow-growing evergreens, widely grown in Mediterranean-type climates. They need cool winters to crop, though they will be damaged by temperatures below -10°C (14°F). In temperate climates they need the protection of a sunny wall, and seldom grow taller than 4m (12ft). They can be grown as non-fruiting trees in cool climates, if brought under cover for winter. They tolerate pruning well, and their size can be restricted. Self-fertile cultivars are available. Trees normally fruit four or five years from planting, and may remain productive for 100 years or more. Fruits are borne on

one-year-old wood, often on the periphery of the tree canopy; trees should be given ample space, and have open crowns that allow sunlight to penetrate.

■ **WHEN TO PRUNE** Early spring.

■ **TRAINING AND PRUNING** Stake well on planting. In Mediterranean climates, train with a clear trunk of 1–1.2m (3–4ft). The crown often branches naturally: prune to induce branching at about 1.5m (5ft) if necessary, and select three or four well-spaced laterals to form framework branches. Then let the dense, twiggy crown develop with minimal pruning. Trees usually recover from light frost damage if cut back to live wood.

When established, remove only old and unproductive wood in order to stimulate new shoots that will flower the following year, and thin overcrowded growth in the centre of the crown to let in sun, if necessary. Trees can be maintained at a height of 4–5m (12–15ft) for ease of harvesting by pruning branch leaders to replacement shoots each year. Use the same technique to restrict growth of tub-grown trees. Olives respond well to hard pruning, and can be completely renovated by pruning to ground level; either select a new leader (*see Eucalyptus, p.64*) or allow a small, shrubby form to develop.

Olives can also be wall trained, tying in evenly spaced growth (*see also Magnolia, p.74*) to form a fan framework. Pruning back outward-growing and badly placed shoots will stimulate young, twiggy growth with attractive, fresh foliage.

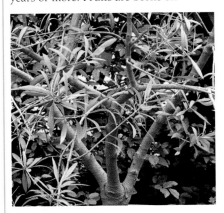

Olive tree
The central leader and branch leaders can be pruned low to form a smaller, branching crown, enabling olives to be grown in tubs.

AVOCADO PEAR (ALLIGATOR PEAR) *PERSEA* SPP.

The three types of avocado – Mexican, Guatemalan and West Indian – prefer, respectively, a semi-tropical, subtropical and tropical climate. All need plenty of light. Most form large trees, although size can be restricted by pruning and there are cultivars that do not grow to more than 5–6m (15–20ft) tall. Seedlings will not fruit until at least five years old, and their fruits are often poor. Grafted cultivars may flower in their third year; some rootstocks also give resistance to root rots and tolerance of lower temperatures.

Avocados generally have a spreading habit, although some cultivars have a more conical silhouette. Extension growth is made from terminal buds and there are two growth flushes per season. They are virtually evergreen. Lateral buds may be shed during dormant periods, often leaving flowers clustered at the tips of branches. Two or more trees often fruit better than single trees.

The Mexican cultivars are the most cold-tolerant and can grow well in sunny, open but sheltered sites where temperatures do not fall below 13–15°C (55–59°F). They will grow under glass in temperate areas, although light levels may still be too low for flowering (hand-pollination will be necessary). They dislike root disturbance.

■ **WHEN TO PRUNE** After fruiting.

■ **TRAINING AND PRUNING** Little initial training is needed; laterals may be shortened by up to half their length to induce branching, if needed; retain as much foliage as possible to protect the young bark from sun scorch. When established, prune only to remove damaged, diseased, crossing or crowded growth, or to tip-prune any vigorous upright shoots to encourage a more spreading, branching habit. Branches are brittle, and buds and shoots are

Avocado
Avocados tend to flower and fruit at the tips of existing branches, and then make new extension growth.

easily damaged; be extremely careful when pruning. Harvest fruits using a sharp knife or secateurs to cut the stalk about 1cm (½in) from the fruit.

Trees that have grown too large for comfortable harvesting may be "headed back" (*see* Crown reduction, *p.33*), preferably after harvesting.

GUAVA *PSIDIUM GUAJAVA*

A native of tropical America widely grown in tropical and subtropical regions, the guava is a multi-stemmed tree, often almost equal in height and spread, with a tendency to sucker and branch close to the ground. Grafted cultivars fruit more reliably than seedling trees. The guava may flower two or even three times per year. Fruits start to form two or three years after planting, on new shoots from mature wood. Regular, careful pruning keeps plants productive.

■ **WHEN TO PRUNE** After main harvesting periods.

■ **TRAINING AND PRUNING** The main aim is to allow full sunlight penetration to the centre of the canopy. Train as a multi-stemmed tree with four or five strong, well-spaced main stems; if the young tree reaches 1m (3ft) without branching, prune it back to 50cm (20in) to encourage low laterals (*see p.28*). Three months later, shorten each of these by about half its length, and thin inward-growing sideshoots to prevent overcrowding. When established, remove suckers from the rootstock and shoots on the clear stem. After harvesting, tip-prune branch leaders and vigorous laterals to encourage a compact habit and stimulate the growth of further flowering shoots.

POMEGRANATE *PUNICA GRANATUM*

A multi-stemmed or bush tree, probably native to Iran but very adaptable to a wide range of frost-free climates. It crops best in semi-arid climates with hot summers and cool winters. Here, trees are deciduous or semi-deciduous; they are evergreen in humid tropical areas.

Seedling pomegranates are very variable; choose trees grown from cuttings or lifted suckers. Fruits form four or five years from planting, ripening over five to seven months. Trees flower either once or twice a year, depending

Pomegranate
Harvest with secateurs to avoid damaging the spur, so that it may fruit the next year.

on climate. They are often self-fertile, but growing two together can improve fruit-set. Fruits are borne on short spurs that remain productive for three or four years. Remove a little old, unproductive wood annually to encourage new fruiting growth. Overpruning is likely to reduce crops.

Pomegranates will grow well and flower profusely, occasionally fruiting, in full sun in a heated glasshouse. They tolerate pruning to restrict size.

■ **WHEN TO PRUNE** In the dormant season.

■ **TRAINING AND PRUNING** Train as a multi-stemmed tree on a short leg (*see p.28*); if the young tree does not branch low, prune it to 60–75cm (24–30in) to encourage laterals to develop. Remove any less than 20cm (8in) from the ground, and select four or five of the remaining shoots, choosing the strongest and most widely spaced. For the next three years, shorten the leading shoots by about one-third of the previous season's growth, to develop a branched framework.

On established trees, annual pruning is mainly confined to shortening a small proportion of older branches to encourage the development of new shoots. Pomegranates have a strong tendency to sucker at the base of the stem; remove as seen unless a replacement for a main stem is needed, in which case train on a young, well-placed shoot.

Nuts

Most nuts are borne on trees or bushes. Some, such as walnut, chestnut and pecan, grow very large, forming handsome specimens suitable for big gardens or parkland. Cobnut and filbert bushes are more suited to the small garden. As with fruit trees, nut trees will only crop if successfully pollinated, sometimes by another cultivar; even nut trees that produce both male and female flowers on the same plant may not do so simultaneously.

Only cobnuts and filberts grow and crop well in any cool temperate region; sweet chestnuts, almonds and walnuts,

although hardy, need more favourable conditions to bear nut crops – although even then they may not do so regularly. In warm climates with hot summers pistachios and pecans can be grown, while the macadamia, brazil and cashew need tropical conditions.

Although cobnuts and filberts will crop more heavily if regularly pruned, nuts in general need minimal pruning. Early training will ensure well-shaped, sound trees, but subsequently little attention is essential beyond those routine tasks (*see p.29*) that keep any tree in good health.

CASHEW *ANACARDIUM OCCIDENTALE*

The cashew grows in tropical regions with definite dry seasons, such as India and East Africa. It is evergreen, with a wide, spreading crown. Lower branches, often nearly horizontal, may reach 6m (20ft), and are liable to break in high winds. Both seedlings and higher yielding grafted clones are used. Seedlings grow most rapidly, and quickly develop very long roots.

The aim is to develop an open-centred, multi-stemmed crown on a short, clear trunk of about 1m (3ft). Prune a young feathered tree back to a height of 1.2m (4ft), selecting four or five laterals to form the main branches (*see also Acer davidii, p.52*). These may be tipped back to induce further branching if necessary. Established trees have no special pruning needs.

Young cashew tree
Trees require a short, clear trunk to accommodate the low, spreading branches.

Cashews may also be pollarded (*see p.34*) at 50–75cm (20–30in) from the ground. The tree crops again in two or three years. In Australia, in commercial "hedgerow" plantings, when the foliage of trees in adjacent rows almost meets, alternate rows are pollarded.

BRAZIL *BERTHOLLETIA EXCELSA* (SYN. *B. NOBILIS*)

The Brazil or para nut grows wild in the Amazonian forests, and is also planted in south-east Asia where climatic conditions resemble those of the lowland rainforests. The trees are tall, and most densely furnished with branches about a quarter of the way up, giving a narrowly conical form. Fruiting

begins when trees are 10–20 years old; the fruits take a year to ripen. Wild trees are normally left unpruned, but young trees can be encouraged to branch lower, at a height of 1–2m (3–6ft), by pruning back the main leader and subsequently shortening the main framework branches at regular intervals.

PECAN *CARYA ILLINOINENSIS*

Many species of *Carya* make fine ornamental trees in cool climates (*see* Dictionary of Ornamental Trees, *p.56*). To crop well, however, the pecan, a vigorous, erect, deciduous tree, needs a fairly dry, subtropical or warm temperate climate with a hot summer and a distinct cold but frost-free season.

Choose a selected cultivar, grafted on to seedling stock, that will crop after about five years. Pecans quickly develop a long taproot: choose very young specimens sold in long pots or bags, and transplant carefully. Never buy an old containerized tree as the root system will not establish satisfactorily.

■ **WHEN TO PRUNE** From autumn to mid-winter. Trees bleed sap profusely if pruned in spring.

■ **TRAINING AND PRUNING** *Carya illinoinensis* looks best trained as a central-leader standard, although it may be kept as a feathered tree. Do not tip-prune laterals, either when training or as the tree matures; the separate male and female flowers are both borne on shoots that have grown from terminal buds in the previous growing season.

Established trees have no special pruning needs and dislike hard pruning.

SWEET CHESTNUT *CASTANEA SATIVA*

The sweet or Spanish chestnut matures into a stately tree prized as an ornamental specimen (*see* Dictionary of Ornamental Trees, *p.57*). If a nut crop is desired, remember that, while fully hardy, *C. sativa* is at its northern limit in cool climates such as that of the British Isles, where only in southern counties

and after a warm summer will it crop well. Always choose a cultivar selected for its nuts; such cultivars are grafted, and should crop after four years. Some require a pollinator.

Training and pruning are as for an ornamental tree (*see p.57*): train as a central-leader standard, selecting only laterals that will form well-placed framework branches making wide V-angles to the trunk. Heavy branches on old trees may become unsafe.

Sweet chestnuts
The spiny casings split when the fruits are ripe, revealing the dark brown, glossy nuts.

COBNUTS AND FILBERTS *CORYLUS AVELLANA, C. MAXIMA*

Cobnuts and filberts make attractive large, ornamental shrubs (*see* Dictionary of Ornamental Shrubs, *p.187*), but also crop well, even in cool climates. When trained and regularly pruned, their habit is more compact, and cropping improves markedly. There are many self-fertile cultivars available. Both cobnuts and filberts grow well from seed; suckers can also be carefully uprooted and used for propagation.

■ **WHEN TO PRUNE** Winter. When trees are cropping, this will coincide with pollen production from catkins; shaking the branches when pruning helps to pollinate the female flowers. Established trees are also "brutted" in summer.

■ **TRAINING AND PRUNING** Aim to form an open-centred bush on a clear stem of about 45cm (18in). Choose a young tree with three or four strong laterals at around this height. Prune the leader back to the topmost of these, as for an apple bush (*see p.108*), and shorten the selected laterals to 22cm (9in). Remove all other laterals. In the next two years, let 10–12 well-spaced shoots develop to form main branches, tip-pruning them if they are slow to branch. Remove any growth below the main branches.

On established trees, in late summer, partly break ("brut") long, vigorous shoots halfway along their length. Leave short, twiggy growth, as this usually carries the female flowers that will develop into nuts. The following winter, prune the broken ("brutted") shoots back to three or four buds. The year-on-year effect will be to build up spur systems, which will from time to time need reducing, with a saw or loppers, to a short stub on the main branch, from which new shoots should develop. As bushes age, also remove a worn-out branch or two where strong new growth exists to replace it.

Brutted cobnut shoots
Long, vigorous shoots often bear no female flowers, so will not crop. Breaking them partially (*see above*) retains their foliage to give the plant vigour, which is then diverted into female flower production on shorter, spur-like shoots.

WALNUTS *JUGLANS REGIA*

Walnuts, although fully hardy, may not crop in cool temperate regions unless conditions are favourable. Sites prone to late spring frosts should be avoided. Seedlings take 10 or more years to crop and nut quality is unpredictable, so always choose a named cultivar, grafted onto black walnut (*Juglans nigra*) or the Californian black walnut (*J. hindsii*). Although commercial growers, particularly in California, develop open-centred walnut bushes (using suitable cultivars), a central-leader tree with a clear trunk of 1.2–2m (4–6ft) looks far better in a garden setting. Train as for an ornamental tree (*see p.69*).

PISTACHIO *PISTACIA VERA*

This deciduous tree needs hot summers and cool, frost-free winters to crop. An open site is essential; lower branches die if shaded. It is much easier to train a grafted plant into a well-formed tree. Stake the leader carefully, maintaining it for at least 1m (3ft) before allowing the crown to branch and develop. Keep further pruning to a minimum. Cuts do not heal well or quickly, and pruning checks growth. To combat the straggly habit, growth may have to be thinned and branches shortened; do not remove too much in any one year. (*See also* Dictionary of Ornamental Trees, *p.79*.)

MACADAMIA *MACADAMIA* SPP.

Macadamias are native to the Australian tropical rainforest, and though they will tolerate light frosts, they need a hot growing season and plentiful rain. They are evergreen, with a dense, upright habit. Training should aim to produce a central-leader tree with a clear trunk of about 1m (3ft) and well spaced, spreading side branches. Young macadamias tend to produce leaves and shoots in whorls of three; if these develop, select one to form a main branch and cut the other two back to 1cm (½in); shoots from the buds on these stubs will develop into horizontal, flowering shoots. In South Africa growers repeatedly prune back the central leader of young trees at intervals of 40–50cm (16–20in) to produce tiers of horizontal branches. Established trees need minimal pruning.

Macadamia tree
Branches develop naturally with narrow crotch angles and may split in high winds.

ALMOND *PRUNUS DULCIS*

The almond is an attractive tree (*see* Dictionary of Ornamental Trees, *p.82*) that, although fully hardy, requires a Mediterranean-type climate to crop satisfactorily. To produce an easily maintained nut tree, choose a grafted cultivar and train as a bush tree or wall-train as a fan, just as for a peach or nectarine tree (*see p.134*). A suitable pollinating cultivar must be nearby. For an established bush, pruning should be minimal; remove a little unproductive wood in summer. Prune an established fan as for a peach fan (*see p.135*).

Ornamental shrubs

Attractive, well-shaped, healthy growth gives all shrubs greater ornamental value, in addition to flowering and fruiting displays that are enhanced by correct pruning at the right time.

Many of the most successful low-maintenance planting schemes rely on carefully chosen shrubs whose well-shaped forms and healthy growth give pleasure all year round. For these plants, light pruning to shape, and the routine removal of dead, diseased or damaged growth, is the only pruning necessary to maintain handsome, vigorous specimens. However, for many popular shrubs, proper care and cultivation involves not only training and maintenance, but also regular pruning to enhance ornamental characteristics such as flowering and fruiting. The aim of this pruning is to remove older, less productive wood in favour of that which will flower or fruit more profusely, while promoting healthy new growth for future displays – in effect, hastening and controlling the natural cycle of decay and renewal found in nature.

An enormous range of shrubs exists to fill any site or fulfil any requirement in the garden. They vary widely in size, vigour and growth habit, and also in productive lifespan – always a factor to bear in mind when deciding whether to renovate a neglected or overgrown plant. Because the

choice is so large, it should always be possible to select plants that not only are well suited to your climate and conditions, but that will also fulfil your ornamental requirements and expectations within the available space. Unless being trained for some special effect, in general shrubs always look best where their natural habit and vigour can be expressed to the full. Careful choice and siting of shrubs will ensure that pruning enhances, rather than restricts, their growth.

Euphorbia characias subsp. *wulfenii*
The long stems of this euphorbia grow in one year and flower in the next. While the shrub does not need pruning, its appearance is greatly improved if the old, flowered stems are removed in favour of the new basal growth.

◀ **Using structural plants**
Many shrubs used to form boundary or dividing hedges are also decorative with attractive foliage, flowers or fruits. Here the upright stems of *Berberis thunbergii* 'Helmond Pillar' provide a colourful and effective barrier in the garden.

Basic Techniques

The routine pruning of a typical selection of garden shrubs entails cutting through stems of all sizes, from pinching young shoot tips to removing old, woody stems. A range of good-quality, well-maintained tools (see p.14) – a knife, sharp secateurs, loppers and a pruning saw – is essential to maximize the benefits of pruning.

As with all plants, primary pruning tasks include the removal, as soon as seen, of dead, diseased and damaged growth, and of unwanted growth such as reverted shoots and suckers (see Routine tasks, facing page). Formative pruning not only gives a shrub a good start, but may also be desirable throughout its life. In ideal conditions, shrubs usually develop a balanced, even shape.

But many factors can unbalance growth: disease, damage or lop-sidedness caused by, for example, a shaded planting position, competition from other plants or a prevailing wind. Making well-positioned pruning cuts (and, if possible, removing the cause of the problem) is the key to restoring a balanced outline. Understanding flowering and fruiting habits, and how to maximize displays while maintaining health and vigour, gives an added dimension to the pruning of many shrubs. Pruning to enhance flowering or foliage effect should always respect the shrub's natural growth habit, and if possible improve it.

Types of cut

As a general rule, where possible, remove unwanted growth while still young. However, pruning shrubs often involves cutting woody growth, and cuts should be made with as much care as when pruning trees, giving the shrub the best chance of rapid recovery. Pruning cuts should always be clean; torn and bruised tissue heals slowly and is more likely to allow harmful organisms to gain entry, which may endanger the whole plant. Cuts should also always be as small as possible. Large wounds take longer to heal over, meanwhile remaining open to disease.

WHEN TO PRUNE
While formative and renovation pruning are usually best carried out while a shrub is dormant, the optimum time to prune an established shrub nearly always depends on its flowering habit. The age of the shoots on which flowering occurs is critical. Shrubs that produce flowers on the current season's shoots should be pruned before these develop, in late winter or early spring. Those that produce flowers on the previous season's growth, that is on older shoots, are best pruned after flowering, giving new growth time to develop before overwintering and flowering in the following year.

POSITIONING THE CUT
Shrubs with buds that grow opposite one another should be cut squarely across the stem (see above left). Stems with an alternate arrangement of buds or shoots should be cut at an angle (see above right). When cutting to a replacement stem or shoot, cut squarely across the stem parallel with the direction of the new stem.

Pruning cuts should be made as close to the bud or shoot as possible without physically damaging it. If made too close, a bud may become desiccated and die and a sideshoot might break off or crack in windy conditions. But if the cut is made too far away, the resulting

Cutting to opposite buds
On a shrub with opposite buds, cut squarely just above a pair of strong buds or shoots. If only one shoot is desired (for example, to form a central stem or an outward-facing branch) rub off the bud that is not facing in the desired direction of growth.

stub of stem without active buds will die back and become a site of infection. Sometimes the main stems of shrubs need to be cut near the base, where no buds are visible. However, the cut should stimulate dormant buds near the ground into life, and new shoots will emerge. If there is then a stub of wood left, it can be removed.

Always anticipate the kind of growth the shrub will make in response to the cut. As with all plants, hard pruning promotes stronger regrowth than light pruning. When correcting the shape of a shrub, cut back weak shoots hard, and strong growth lightly. When shortening growth, it is particularly important to envisage the direction of shoot growth that will result from the position of your pruning cut, or the result will be a poorly shaped plant with crossing stems and a crowded centre.

Cutting to an alternate bud
Select a healthy bud pointing in the direction in which you require a shoot to grow. From the side opposite a bud, cut at an angle to just above where the bud or shoot joins the stem. Do not angle the cut too steeply: this makes a larger wound that will take longer to heal.

Pinch out the shoot's soft growing tip to just above a leaf or pair of leaves

Pinching out shoot tips
Soft shoot tips can be pinched out cleanly with finger and thumb. Removing the terminal bud of the shoot (see p.11) stimulates buds lower down the stem into growth, to produce a bushy, well-branched plant.

Routine tasks

Minor pruning tasks to correct common problems may become necessary from an early stage. Dead, diseased and damaged growth and crossing stems (*see p.154*) should always be removed, as should reverted shoots and suckers on grafted plants, however much this appears to denude a young plant of growth. Always carry out routine tasks as soon as a problem is noticed.

DEADHEADING

Deadheading (*see right*) is not essential, but for some shrubs it can improve their appearance, stop them from self-seeding and, by preventing them from expending energy on setting seed, stimulate further growth and flowering.

REVERSION

Variegated cultivars occasionally produce shoots bearing plain green foliage. This may be a response to stress or to heavy pruning. Variegated growth tends to be less vigorous as the leaves contain less chlorophyll (essential in energy production); the more vigorous green-leaved growth should be removed or it will dominate the plant.

SUCKERS

The natural habit of many shrubs is suckering; new growth from ground level increases the plants' size and spread, and replaces stems that grow old and die. If the plant is congested or overgrown, it is the older stems that should be removed, not this vigorous young growth (unless, as is sometimes possible, the plant is being trained with a single stem). However, some shrubs are grafted, and shoots (continued on p.154)

Deadheading flowering shrubs

Spent flower clusters

Non-flowered shoot

Single flowers On some shrubs, such as rhododendrons, new shoots develop from buds just under the flowers, so pinch out only the flowerhead, taking care not to damage any growth below.

Flower clusters Use secateurs on shrubs such as buddlejas and lilacs (*Syringa*) to shorten flowered shoots to buds or young sideshoots: these should be stimulated into flowering, either later in the season or the following year, depending on time of pruning.

Removing reverted shoots

Cut out any plain green shoots on variegated shrubs as soon as they are noticed. If not removed, green-leaved shoots may quickly dominate the shrub, being more vigorous than variegated growth. Cut the entire reverted shoot back to its point of origin.

Identifying and removing suckers

Broadly oval, mid-green leaves on desirable cultivar

Smaller, unevenly margined, pale green leaves on the sucker

Normal growth   Sucker

Identifying suckers (*left*) A shoot from the top growth of a desirable cultivar of *Hamamelis mollis* is easily distinguished from a shoot that has been produced below the graft from the rootstock, the vigorous but aesthetically inferior *Hamamelis virginiana*.

Removing suckers (*right*) Ideally, suckers should be rubbed off by hand while they are still young and soft. If they have thickened, however, pull them off sharply at their point of origin, either on the stem or on a carefully uncovered root. Try to remove all growth with a single tug; if fragments remain, nip them off with a sharp knife (*see inset*), without enlarging the wound.

(*continued from p.153*) that emerge from below the graft union, either low on the trunk or from the roots, will be growing from the rootstock and not from the more desirable grafted plant (the scion). These must be removed if the usually weaker scion is not to be overwhelmed.

CROWDED AND CROSSING BRANCHES

Dense growth is desirable for barrier plantings of shrubs such as *Berberis*, and also for shrubs trained as hedges and topiary. However, for other plants, relieving congestion, by removing a few stems or taking out a whole branch, prevents the development of a dark, dank environment within a shrub that will encourage pests and diseases.

Do not let any shoots grow across and rub against other stems. Chafing damage provides a potential entry point for disease, and the plant may suffer structural problems when the stems develop and thicken (*see right*).

DEAD, DISEASED AND DAMAGED GROWTH

If there is a clear demarcation between live and dead wood, cut to just above this line. If, however, there is no clear distinction between healthy and unhealthy tissue, cut into completely healthy wood, to a suitable bud or shoot. If the cut surface is discoloured, cut further down until it is clean.

Jagged stem ends resulting from storm or other damage should be cut cleanly across to a bud or shoot. If damage is extensive, this might be the time to reshape or rejuvenate the shrub (*see Renovation, p.160*). Frost-damaged growth should not be removed until the risk of prolonged hard frost is over, because it provides some protection for the undamaged growth below.

Crossing branches

This well-established *Hamamelis* shows the dangers of allowing crossing branches to develop. Here, one branch is taking the weight of another, causing a split to develop on a main trunk. If the load-bearing branch breaks, the one resting on it is liable to break too, and the shrub will be badly damaged. Crossing branches should never be allowed to develop like this, but renovation (*see p.160*), or bracing or propping the load-bearing branch (*see p.30*) may help the plant to recover.

Branch crosses, touches and weighs down on branch beneath

Severe split developing at branch crotch

Removing dead wood

If the plant has formed a natural barrier to isolate dead wood (*see p.9*), it will continue to protect the rest of the plant; cut just above it to remove the bulk of the dead tissue.

Cut back to completely healthy growth

Frost damage

With this recent frost damage, there is no clear dividing line between affected and healthy growth. Cut well back to a bud, leaf or shoot on completely healthy growth.

GROWING SHRUBS IN CONTAINERS

Many shrubs grow well in containers; in cool climates, container-grown tender shrubs can be brought under cover for the winter. As they grow, these plants will need repotting in spring until they are in the largest practicable container, after which they should be top-dressed. After a few years, however, they may appear to be lacking in vigour. Lift the shrub carefully from its container (*right*) to check that the rootball has not become congested. If it has, both the top-growth and root system must be pruned; reducing the amount of top growth the roots must support will help the plant to develop new fine feeder roots.

Root pruning a container-grown shrub

1 If the plant is pot-bound (*inset*), using a hand fork, tease out the tightly packed rootball, working away as much of the old compost as possible without probing right into the centre of the root system.

2 Prune coarse and damaged roots by up to two-thirds, and repot using fresh compost. Prune the shrub to reduce top growth overall by one-third, either shortening growth or removing some stems.

Initial Training

Most shrubs are bought as young, partially trained plants from nurseries and garden centres (*see p.156*). They will have been propagated in a variety of ways. However, many gardeners propagate their own shrubs, most using simple vegetative methods such as taking cuttings and layering. It is never too early to start training the young plants in order to achieve strong, well-shaped mature specimens.

CUTTINGS

Like seedlings, softwood and semi-ripe cuttings tend to grow as single stems. Some branch naturally, while in others the apical bud is more strongly dominant and the shoot must be pruned to encourage side buds to develop into shoots (*see below*).

A hardwood cutting should develop several stems from buds along the length of the cutting. A root cutting may also develop several stems from adventitious buds along the portion of root. If the shrub is to grow with a single, central stem, and a conical form (as for *Abutilon vitifolium*), train the topmost shoot vertically, staking lightly with a split cane, and remove the other shoots, either by rubbing out as they emerge, or by cutting back. If, however, a bushy multi-stemmed form is desired, all well-placed healthy shoots can be retained.

LAYERING

The stems of some shrubs root naturally where they touch the ground; others may be more deliberately "layered", by nicking through the bark of a stem, then anchoring it under the soil, encouraging it to root at this point. When the latter method is used, the shoot tip should be trained more or less vertically up a light cane so that the new plant develops with an upright main stem. However, with naturally layered stems, the young plant is likely to have an obliquely growing main stem. This may be correctable by angled planting and light staking. If not, cut to a low, upward-facing bud and train the new growth vertically.

GRAFTING

Shrubs that are difficult to propagate in other ways may be grafted. Young bud-grafted plants will grow away with a single stem; if a section of stem is grafted, multiple shoots may develop from its several buds. These plants can be treated exactly like cuttings. However, any developing buds or shoots below the graft point must be rubbed off as soon as they are noticed.

PRUNING VERY YOUNG SHRUBS

As growth develops, young plants may be lightly pruned to influence their future shape. Tip-pruning – either pinch-pruning soft shoot tips, or cutting back long leading or lateral shoots by no more than one-third – can be used to encourage branching growth (*see below, centre*) that will result in a bushy habit.

Do not leave recently pruned young plants in hot sun, for example on a greenhouse bench; the previously shaded tender young bark may scorch.

In cool climates, do not prune plants that are out of doors after midsummer; the growth that is stimulated will not have time to ripen fully and will be particularly vulnerable to frost damage when winter sets in.

Deciduous cuttings

The young *Forsythia* (*below left*) is growing vigorously upwards as a single stem and may take some time to branch, which is ideal if a tall plant of upright habit is desired. However, if its growing tip had been removed early in the growing season, it would have developed as has the other young plant (*below right*): two vigorous sideshoots have grown, laying the foundations of a more branched, bushy habit. Because neither shoot has absolute dominance, other, lower buds are also stimulated, promoting further basal growth.

Evergreen cutting

Evergreens like this *Ceanothus* are much more likely to branch naturally low down, and form a balanced, in this case conical, shape. Such plants rarely need pruning in their first year.

Unpruned single stem

The cutting will branch, usually just below where it was pruned

Lower buds are also beginning to break

Single stem pruned to induce branching

Naturally branching cutting

Buying young shrubs

Young shrubs are increasingly sold as container-grown specimens, though bare-rooted and rootballed plants are available. Choose plants that have vigorous, healthy growth, and, if grafted, a strong, streamlined union (*see right*). The root system should also be large enough to support the top growth; an unbalanced root-to-shoot ratio is one of the principal reasons for poor growth after planting. Container-grown shrubs are particularly likely to have extensive top growth compared to their root system. Plants that have been encouraged to flower heavily as a sales feature should be avoided, or deadheaded as soon as possible.

BARE-ROOTED AND ROOTBALLED SHRUBS

These plants must only be planted in the dormant season; autumn is preferable, in order that the root system may become at least partly established before the next growing season. They should be planted as soon as possible after purchase. First inspect the roots, and cut any damaged portions cleanly away. This should always be done in the shade and out of the wind to avoid drying out fine fibrous roots, which die very swiftly when deprived of moisture.

CONTAINER-GROWN SHRUBS

Container-grown plants may be planted at any time of the year. However, make sure that the shrub has genuinely been grown in its container, and not just potted up for sale; such plants should only be planted in the dormant season.

Good container-grown plants should not usually require root pruning, but if any roots are damaged, cut them back. Light initial staking may also be necessary. These plants are often raised massed closely together, with pots touching, and so may develop long vertical stems. When sold individually, they lose their mutual support and the stems sometimes flop outwards.

PRUNING ON PLANTING

Do not buy plants that are generally in poor condition (*see below right*).

A well-chosen, healthy young plant (*see below left*) should need no pruning except perhaps to pinch prune or shorten any overlong shoots to encourage a balanced shape to develop, as for any young plant (*see p.155*). If there are one or two minor defects, however, they may be rectified on planting. Remove any damaged or weak shoots or dead tips, along with unnecessary canes and ties. Remove any flowered shoots to direct energy into new growth rather than seed formation. If the top growth seems too ample compared to the root system (*see right*), reduce it by up to 50 per cent. This can be done in two ways: by shortening all stems, which will result in a bushy habit, or by cutting stems to the base, to encourage taller, more upright growth.

Graft union
The union is the point at which rootstock and scion were joined

Grafted shrubs
Check grafted shrubs, such as this *Hamamelis*, for a sound union; the scion and rootstock should join smoothly, without forming a kink in the stem.

Top growth is ample and vigorous compared to small size of root system

Correcting root-to-shoot ratio
This plant will establish more quickly if its top growth is reduced, either by shortening all stems by half, or by removing the two shoots on the left.

Selecting shrubs for purchase

Shoot tips are healthy, with no sign of scorch or dieback

New foliage is abundant and vigorous

Older leaves remain, and are glossy and healthy

Good specimen This *Camellia* has all the prerequisites for a fine mature shrub: healthy growth, a good root-to-shoot ratio, and an attractive, well-balanced shape.

Leggy bare stems

Withered foliage

Dead growth

Congested rootball

Poor specimen This *Prostanthera* has been growing in its container for far too long. Its compacted rootball will not establish well, and the exhausted compost has been unable to sustain fresh, healthy growth.

Formative pruning

As young shrubs grow, any routine tasks, such as the removal of dead, diseased or damaged growth (*see pp. 153–154*), should be dealt with as needed. Once shrubs have had a growing season in which to establish in their planting site, and have become dormant, they may be pruned further to influence their future shape and the development of their ornamental features. On free-standing plants this could entail light corrective shaping, or pruning hard back to start developing a low framework, or tip-pruning to produce a dense bushy habit. Shrubs that are being grown for special effects have special training needs: for wall-training, coppicing, or training as a standard, *see pp.162–165*; for topiary, *p.48*, and hedging, *p.44*.

DECIDUOUS SHRUBS

Deciduous shrubs are much more likely to benefit from formative pruning than evergreens, which tend naturally to grow in an even, compact shape (*see below*). The pruning requirements of the shrub when mature should be anticipated when pruning young plants. It is important that shrubs that are to become permanent features of some stature (usually flowering on second-year or older wood, such as *Weigela* and *Philadelphus*) develop with an open centre. Overcrowding will restrict airflow and light penetration. Remove any crowded or crossing stems or shorten them to strong buds or young shoots that face in directions where growth can be accommodated.

Many shrubs that flower on the current season's growth are cut back to a framework each year, particularly in cool climates, and these shrubs (such as *Caryopteris*, *Buddleja davidii* and deciduous *Ceanothus*) should be pruned hard right from the start to build up a base of strong, woody stems that will support vigorous new growth each year (*see also Hydrangea paniculata, p.200*). This framework is usually near ground level, but if extra height is desired, a taller framework can be developed by more moderate pruning.

EVERGREEN SHRUBS

The object of formative pruning of an evergreen shrub is to ensure a healthy plant and develop its symmetrical shape, or whatever other outline is required, with the minimum amount of pruning.

Start by cutting out any cold-damaged growth, as well as any badly positioned stems. Then remove weak and straggly stems, and lightly tip-prune, if necessary, any overlong stems to balance the shrub's outline.

Young evergreen shrub

This young *Prostanthera* is in good condition. Though it is not necessary to prune further at this stage, the development of a balanced shape could be enhanced by pinching out the tips of the longer stems. Lower spreading shoots could also be removed if they will interfere with underplanting.

Developing a low framework, deciduous shrub

This young *Phygelius* will be pruned back hard each year, and it is important to develop a strong framework of well-ripened wood from the start. First remove any weak or badly positioned growth, then shorten all stems, either drastically, as here, or, if a taller framework is required, at least into strong, ripened growth (if this is not tall enough, the framework can be further developed next year). Try to form a framework that resembles an open hand, palm upwards, from which well-spaced growth will be produced.

Prune all stems back to outward-facing buds

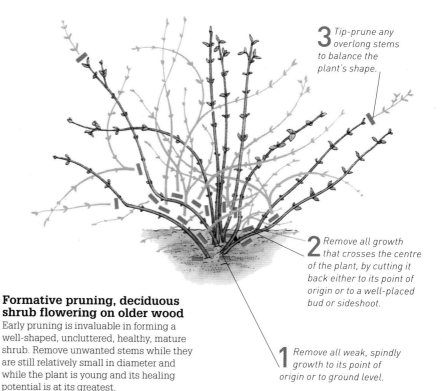

3 *Tip-prune any overlong stems to balance the plant's shape.*

2 *Remove all growth that crosses the centre of the plant, by cutting it back either to its point of origin or to a well-placed bud or sideshoot.*

1 *Remove all weak, spindly growth to its point of origin or to ground level.*

Formative pruning, deciduous shrub flowering on older wood

Early pruning is invaluable in forming a well-shaped, uncluttered, healthy, mature shrub. Remove unwanted stems while they are still relatively small in diameter and while the plant is young and its healing potential is at its greatest.

Pruning Established Shrubs

Without pruning, shrubs will deteriorate over the years; dead and congested growth will build up and encourage disease, and wayward growth will develop to result in a misshapen plant, perhaps prone to structural damage. Extensive renovation pruning (*see p.160*) can largely be avoided, however, if routine tasks (*see p.153*) are attended to promptly. These include the removal of dead, diseased and damaged growth, as well as crossing stems, reverted shoots and suckers.

SHRUBS WITH NO SPECIAL PRUNING NEEDS

Some shrubs, such as most daphnes, neither need nor will tolerate anything more than this minimal attention. Others, including many evergreens, need minimal attention but will tolerate harder pruning if necessary, for example to remove a branch that has grown across a path, or to renovate (*see p.160*). Some shrubs need minimal pruning when grown as "natural", free-standing specimens, but require extra pruning every year if being grown in

special ways. *Cornus alba*, for example, makes an attractive, branching shrub of some stature when allowed to develop with minimal pruning, but if being grown for the winter effect of its brightly coloured young stems (*see* Special stem and foliage effects, *p.164*), it is pruned hard each year to create a shrub of quite different habit, with a mass of vigorous, upright, unbranched stems.

The time taken to reach over-maturity is also important. Many shrubs, such as most *Berberis*, grow and flower well with only minimal pruning for several years, but then reach a stage where they would be strongly reinvigorated by hard pruning. Others will reach a point where no amount of pruning can encourage them to make vigorous young growth; these plants have simply reached the end of their productive lives, and should be replaced. Remember, too, that pruning cannot improve the growth of a plant that is not suited by the local climate and soil conditions.

However, in spite of all these qualifications, there are a great many

shrubs that benefit, in addition to routine attention, from regular pruning that removes a proportion of older wood in favour of new, vigorous growth, on which the best flowers and foliage are generally produced.

Although some general principles can be applied to broad shrub groupings (*see below and facing page*), most plants have needs relating to their individual growth habits (and individual specimens will not always conform to the general requirements for that plant). These individual requirements are given in the Dictionary of Ornamental Shrubs (*see pp.172–223*). When pruning, keep in mind that the way in which you position cuts will affect the future direction and vigour of growth. Always use the annual pruning of a shrub as an opportunity to restore, if necessary, a well-balanced framework and an open centre.

WHEN TO PRUNE

While routine tasks such as the removal of damaged growth should be attended to as soon as the problem is noticed, the timing

Pruning an established deciduous shrub that flowers on old wood

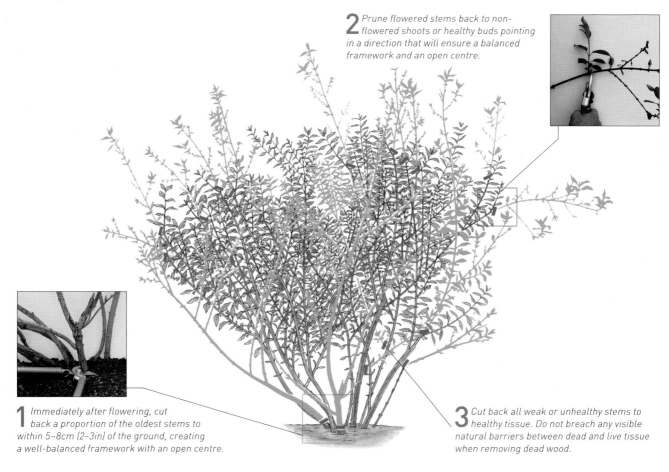

2 *Prune flowered stems back to non-flowered shoots or healthy buds pointing in a direction that will ensure a balanced framework and an open centre.*

1 *Immediately after flowering, cut back a proportion of the oldest stems to within 5–8cm (2–3in) of the ground, creating a well-balanced framework with an open centre.*

3 *Cut back all weak or unhealthy stems to healthy tissue. Do not breach any visible natural barriers between dead and live tissue when removing dead wood.*

of pruning to enhance ornamental features is critical. If you prune a shrub correctly, but at the wrong time, you may remove all the wood that would have flowered in the following season.

Where shrubs flower on new wood (mostly deciduous species, but including such grey-leaved evergreens as lavender), pruning in early spring will direct extra energy into the remaining buds, so that fewer but better flowers are produced. On deciduous shrubs that flower on the previous year's wood, pruning directly after flowering will promote the growth of strong flowering shoots for the following year.

Evergreens should generally be pruned in spring, after any danger of hard frost has passed; pruning scars are then easily disguised by growing foliage. Delaying pruning until summer may be necessary for shrubs that bleed sap profusely. Flowering evergreens may also be pruned lightly after flowering, to remove older flowered wood, to trim to shape or, in regions that experience heavy snow, to thin dense growth on which snow and ice could accumulate, and cause breakage.

Pruning an established shrub that flowers on new wood

Prune back all the stems to a low framework, taking care not to damage any promising new shoots at the base. This *Santolina* has already been trimmed over once, in the autumn, to remove straggly growth that wind and the weight of snow might force to splay outwards, causing damage in the centre of the shrub.

New growth at base

Cut squarely through stems close to the woody base

Pruning an established evergreen shrub

1 *Immediately after flowering, deadhead all flowering stems, cutting back to healthy, outward-pointing buds or non-flowered shoots.*

2 *Prune out any diseased, damaged or dead wood or straggly growth with sharp secateurs, loppers or a pruning saw.*

3 *Remove shoots to thin out congested areas and any badly positioned stems that spoil the balanced appearance of the shrub.*

Renovation

Many neglected and overgrown shrubs, typically producing few flowers and with crowded growth cluttered by accumulated dead wood, will respond well to hard pruning. Provided that the plants are healthy, hard pruning is an effective way of giving them a new lease of life. There are also several popular shrubs that tend to outgrow their space despite regular pruning – lilac (*Syringa*) and Portugal laurel (*Prunus lusitanica*), for example – but can be pruned hard to bring them back within bounds.

A surprisingly large number of plants will tolerate drastic renovation, in which all growth is cut back to near ground level or to a low framework of stumps (*see facing page*), and will respond rapidly with vigorous young growth. This is the most convenient way of dealing with shrubs such as *Berberis* that have a dense and tangled habit and spiny stems, and are difficult to thin out. However, other shrubs are slow to make new growth, and are better renovated in stages. Grafted plants require special care because the desirable grafted plant (the scion) will be lost if the cut is made below the graft union. Even if not all the scion is removed, severe pruning may stimulate the growth of vigorous shoots from the rootstock, and if these are not removed they will become dominant.

RENOVATION OR REPLACEMENT?

Deciding which plants to renovate very commonly forms part of a general garden renovation. It may be necessary to lift shrubs, either to remove perennial weeds and otherwise improve the soil, or to move them to preferred positions. This is best done at the beginning of the dormant season, and is generally much easier if the plants are cut back first.

It is not worth attempting to reinvigorate plants that are sickly. If a diseased shrub cannot be treated to bring it back to health, it is better to replace it entirely. It also has to be recognized that all plants have a finite life. Even plants that tolerate hard pruning when vigorous may not do so when old. It is thus a wise precaution to propagate from favourite plants so that you have replacements.

Although rare plants and particularly fine specimens are almost always worth salvaging, it is often more sensible to replace common, fast-growing shrubs than to attempt to rejuvenate them.

WHEN TO RENOVATE

Deciduous plants are normally best renovated in their dormant season, between autumn and early spring, and evergreens just as they are coming into growth in spring. The disadvantage of losing a season's display is offset by the more vigorous response that shrubs usually make in spring. However, pruning can also be carried out at the normal season for that shrub. Those that flower in spring and early summer, such as mock orange (*Philadelphus*) can be renovated immediately after flowering.

STAGED RENOVATION

If there is any doubt that a shrub will respond to drastic renovation, the operation should be carried out in two or three stages. Many evergreens, in particular, will often make only weak growth if all or most of the foliage is removed in a single pruning operation, and yet will respond well when the pruning is carried out over several years. Even plants that can tolerate heavy pruning in a single operation are sometimes worth renovating over two or three years simply for the sake of their appearance. The garden will continue to look reasonably well furnished if some growth is retained.

In the first year, remove up to half of the stems at ground level, or back to a framework of main branches, first removing dead, damaged and diseased wood and crossing and rubbing stems, then targeting the oldest, least productive growth. Any

Reinvigorating a neglected or overgrown shrub (*Philadelphus*)

1 First removing completely any dead, damaged or diseased stems, cut back up to half of the oldest stems to within 5–8cm (2–3in) of ground level.

2 Shorten the remaining stems by half, cutting to a healthy bud or vigorous sideshoot, aiming to produce a compact but open-centred plant.

3 Remove or shorten to a bud any sideshoots from main stems that are growing across the centre of the shrub, or crossing and rubbing against other stems.

remaining old stems may be shortened by up to a half, the cut being made to a well-placed bud or vigorous shoot, usually one facing out from the centre of the shrub. During the following growing season the shrub will probably produce a number of vigorous new shoots from below the main cuts, and these may need thinning. The following year, cut back half the remaining old stems to ground level or to framework branches, shortening the rest if appropriate; these last old stems should be cut back in the next year. Thereafter revert to the normal pruning appropriate to the individual shrub.

DRASTIC RENOVATION

Several, mainly deciduous, shrubs respond well when cut back drastically in a single operation. Unlike the regular hard pruning practised for ornamental effects on shrubs (see p.164) and trees (see p.34), where the aim is continually to renew fresh young growth, only strong stems should be carefully selected from the regrowth to redevelop a main framework of branches.

It is usually easier to manage cutting back the main branches if side branches are first removed. The main branches should be cut straight across, usually 30–60cm (12–24in) above ground level and always above any graft union (this slightly swollen area is generally around 15cm/6in above ground level). To avoid a heavy branch tearing and leaving a rough wound, cut first about 30cm (12in) above the desired final cut (see Removing a branch, p.20). Do not treat cut surfaces with preservative or with wound paint; these are not now generally recommended (see also p.20).

Staged renovation (year 2) of an evergreen shrub (*Rhododendron*)

Main stem cut back in first year

1 As in the first year, remove some old main stems, cutting back half of those that remain to just above ground level or the graft union. Repeat in year 3 so that all main stems are renewed.

2 As new shoots emerge around previous main pruning cuts, thin out surplus growth to leave only two or three of the strongest and best-placed young stems.

Shrubs should be well fed and mulched to ensure that they regrow vigorously.

Although at the time of pruning the buds from which regrowth will develop are not usually visible, a healthy shrub will produce numerous shoots from the pruned stumps in the growing season following drastic pruning. In the next dormant season, thin these to leave two or three strong, well-placed shoots per stump. Remove any further surplus growth from the base, and any suckers from the rootstock of grafted plants.

Drastic renovation of a deciduous shrub (*Syringa*)

1 When renovating a large shrub with heavy branches, reduce the top growth before cutting back main stems.

2 Cut back all main stems, making straight cuts across branches to form a low framework 30–60cm (12–24in) above ground level.

3 Remove all suckers from around the main stems or at their bases below graft unions.

Regrowth after hard pruning
Healthy and vigorous shrubs will produce many new shoots from the stumps in the first growing season after drastic pruning. In the following dormant season, thin these to two or three vigorous, well-placed stems per stump that will grow to form a new framework.

Wall Training

There are, in addition to climbing plants, a great number of shrubs that can be grown successfully against walls and fences. This not only gives an alternative form of display for the shrub, but can also increase the range of plants that may be grown. In a small garden, for example, training or tying in against a wall allows shrubs to be accommodated that would be too large grown as free-standing specimens. In cool climates, a great many shrubs that are not hardy enough to thrive in the open garden may be grown successfully close to a sunny, sheltered wall.

INFORMAL AND FORMAL WALL TRAINING

Some shrubs, including many of the slightly frost-tender plants, are best planted close to, but not hard up against, the wall, and allowed to develop naturally, with long stems tied in loosely at strategic points. This informal support enhances the ornamental value of many shrubs of naturally open and lax habit, often producing a cascading display of foliage and flowering shoots. Other shrubs lend themselves to more formal training and pruning, producing structured, fan-shaped or tiered arrangements of stems carrying blossoms or berries. To achieve a particular effect, however, account must

Wall-trained _Pyracantha_
The arching main stems of pyracanthas lend themselves to training in to a wall or fence, showing the berries off to maximum effect.

be taken of a plant's natural habit and the pruning that is used must relate to a shrub's specific needs. Individual pruning requirements are given in the Dictionary of Ornamental Shrubs (see pp.172–223).

Shrubs trained against walls or fences need similar supports to those used for climbing plants (see p.246). Plants will be in position for many years and, unlike flexible-stemmed climbers, they will

be difficult to detach to allow for maintenance. It is important, therefore, to ensure that walls and fences are in good condition before training shrubs on them. Use durable materials to provide a sturdy means of attachment for the plant, such as trellis or a system of wires to which stems can be tied, keeping them slightly away from the wall to allow free air circulation.

Initial wall training of a shrub (_Ceanothus_)

1 _Removing any original canes or ties, tie the plant in to the support, starting with main stems, then well-placed laterals._

2 _Remove, or shorten to one or two buds, stems growing directly outwards or inwards towards the wall that cannot be tied in._

3 _Pinch out the tips of young forward-growing shoots to encourage sideways branching._

4 _Shorten the longest laterals by a few buds, particularly where growth is gappy, to stimulate branching and balanced coverage._

PRUNING ON PLANTING

Plant at least 30cm (12in) from the base of the wall, avoiding the dry rainshadow area of soil. If the wall is old, it may have shed lime-rich mortar, making the site unsuitable for acid-loving plants. If planting a bare-rooted or rootballed shrub, position the plant so that the roots can be spread (not forced) to grow away from the wall. With a container-grown shrub, rotate it until you find the position where as much well-placed growth as possible can be tied in.

Initial pruning depends on the shrub's requirements and the desired effect. To make an informal fan of a lax shrub such as *Ribes speciosum*, little pruning may be required other than the removal of weak or badly placed stems before spacing out remaining stems and tying them in. For a more formal fan, of *Prunus triloba* 'Multiplex', for example, the ideal is to start with three to five strong stems radiating evenly from a main stem. Single-stemmed specimens of suitable plants should be cut back hard on planting to stimulate the growth of several stems that can be tied in to trellis, or to canes attached obliquely

to wires. It is also possible to train some single-stemmed shrubs in an espalier or palmette form, with tiered branches extending horizontally or obliquely on each side of a vertical main stem.

ESTABLISHED WALL SHRUBS

While individual shrubs will be pruned in different ways at maturity, some requirements are common to all wall-grown plants. Tie in new shoots promptly and check all ties regularly, loosening them before they become tight. Remove or shorten shoots growing into or away from the wall that cannot be trained in. Tie in laterals to fill gaps, stimulating growth by pruning if necessary. Where the form allows (as with a fan) aim gradually to replace old wood with vigorous new stems. Further pruning, perhaps to maintain close, formal coverage of the wall or to enhance flowering, may be possible or desirable (*see* Dictionary of Ornamental Shrubs, *pp. 172–223*). Some shrubs, including *Chaenomeles* and *Pyracantha*, can be spur pruned as for apples and pears (*see* Apples, *p.105*) to give a particularly dense display.

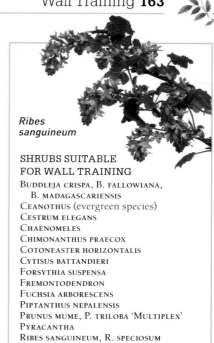

Ribes sanguineum

SHRUBS SUITABLE FOR WALL TRAINING

BUDDLEJA CRISPA, B. FALLOWIANA, B. MADAGASCARIENSIS
CEANOTHUS (evergreen species)
CESTRUM ELEGANS
CHAENOMELES
CHIMONANTHUS PRAECOX
COTONEASTER HORIZONTALIS
CYTISUS BATTANDIERI
FORSYTHIA SUSPENSA
FREMONTODENDRON
FUCHSIA ARBORESCENS
PIPTANTHUS NEPALENSIS
PRUNUS MUME, P. TRILOBA 'MULTIPLEX'
PYRACANTHA
RIBES SANGUINEUM, R. SPECIOSUM
VITEX AGNUS-CASTUS, V. NEGUNDO

Pruning an established wall-trained shrub (*Ceanothus*)

1 *Tie in new growth where possible (as shrubs mature, older, less productive framework stems may be removed to make way for younger growth). Shorten weak shoots (above) to stimulate stronger growth.*

3 *Shorten stems where the shrub is reaching the limits of its allotted space.*

2 *Prune flowered growth as appropriate to the shrub, removing some completely where there is congestion.*

4 *Check and reposition or replace any ties that are broken or constricting the stems, resulting in chafing damage (as above).*

Special Stem and Foliage Effects

A number of shrubs and trees, for example willows and hazels, have traditionally been pruned hard regularly for the practical purpose of obtaining a renewable supply of strong but pliable young stems for use in fencing and weaving. Coppicing, in which growth is regularly cut back to near ground level, and pollarding, cutting to the head of a single stem, are traditional techniques of woodland management that can be adapted to produce special ornamental effects in some trees (*see p.34*) and shrubs. Regular hard pruning, either to near ground level (as with the *Cornus, below left*) or to a low head or framework (as with the *Eucalyptus, below right*), can be used to renew young stems that are more colourful and decorative than older wood, as with willows (*Salix*). It may also perpetuate attractive juvenile foliage or induce extra-large leaves (as with the *Cotinus, above right*).

Only use shrubs for which hard pruning is recommended (*see* Dictionary of Ornamental Shrubs, *pp.172–223*). To produce a display from ground level, cut back hard each year while the shrub is young, so that a strong woody base is formed. If a taller plant is required, a clear stem, or even several clear stems, can be developed as for a standard (*see facing page*) and, at the desired height, a "head" or a stubby framework of older growth may be developed. Once the base or

Cotinus pruned for foliage effect
Cultivars of *Cotinus coggygria* and *C. obovatus* with purple foliage produce larger leaves when hard pruned, making their vivid orange-red autumn colour particularly striking.

framework is established, young growth may be cut back to it at intervals of between one and five years, depending on the plant. Many shrubs that may be pruned hard flower on old wood, so if the plant is cut back annually, the floral display will be lost; the stem or foliage effect is usually more than adequate compensation. However, the young growth of other plants, such as *Salix irrorata*, maintains its ornamental value for several years, allowing it to mature and flower before being pruned again. Alternatively, only one in two or three stems can be cut back each year, resulting in a mixture of growth of different ages.

SUITABLE SHRUBS
BERBERIS Several, such as *B. dictyophylla*, have attractive young stems with a white or purplish bloom.
CORNUS Red, yellow or bright green young stem colours; the red stems of *C. alba* 'Sibirica' are particularly vivid.
COTINUS Handsome foliage (*see above*).
PHILADELPHUS The yellow foliage of *P. coronarius* 'Aureus' is enhanced.
RUBUS White young stems of *R. thibetanus* are attractive in winter.
SALIX Strong young stem colours, some, as on *S. irrorata*, with attractive bloom.
SAMBUCUS Leaves are more finely cut and brightly coloured in, for example, *S. racemosa* 'Plumosa Aurea'.

Cornus pruned for stem effect
In early spring, just before growth begins, cut all shoots down to within 5–8cm (2–3in) of ground level with sharp secateurs or loppers (here on *Cornus stolonifera* 'Flaviramea').

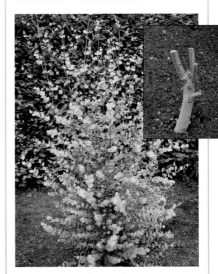

Eucalyptus, juvenile growth
Many *Eucalyptus* (*see* Dictionary of Ornamental Trees, *p.64*) make attractive shrubs if regularly pruned back hard.

Training Shrubs as Standards

Growing a shrub as a standard on a clear stem brings its decorative features up to eye level and often gives it a formal effect. Such shrubs are popular container plants, or are used to give height to a small border while allowing underplanting. Only certain plants are suitable (*see* Dictionary of Ornamental Shrubs, *pp.172–223*), although shrubs that cannot be trained in this way from the start are sometimes top-grafted onto the tall stem of a stock plant, giving the same effect. The head of both trained and grafted standards is developed and maintained in exactly the same way.

Top-grafting is a skilled job usually carried out in the plant nursery, and grafted standards are usually bought ready-formed. However, for other plants a leading shoot can be trained up to form a clear stem from an early age, following exactly the same principles as for an ornamental tree (*see p.26*).

Staking will be necessary, sometimes permanently. In the early stages, a cane will suffice; a mature standard needing support must have a wooden stake that reaches a point just below where the head branches. Use spacers (*see p.21*) to keep the stake clear of the stem.

TRAINING TO FORM A CLEAR STEM

Select a strong shoot as the leader (*see below*) and stake it to ensure straight, vertical growth. Just as for a tree, the central stem should be cleared in stages, first shortening, then removing laterals, so that some foliage is always retained. This will allow the plant to manufacture food that will help to build a strong central stem. Once the leader has reached the desired height, generally 1–1.7m (3–5½ft), allow three more sets of buds to develop above this height before pinching out the terminal bud. Removing the shoot's growing tip will encourage the growth of shoots from the lateral buds below that will form the main framework branches of the head.

DEVELOPING AND PRUNING THE HEAD

After the first growing season, or if a newly grafted shrub has been purchased, shorten laterals by about half. The aim when pruning subsequent growth should be to build up a dense, well-balanced head, by cutting to well-positioned buds and pruning weak shoots harder to stimulate stronger growth where necessary. Remove any badly placed shoots (although some crossing growth is unavoidable), and any growth from the clear stem or at the base of the plant. This is particularly important on top-grafted plants, when such growth will be from the more vigorous rootstock. Never remove too much growth from the head of such grafted plants at any one time because this could encourage the rootstock to sprout more vigorously.

As for any shrub, cut out any weak, dead or diseased stems as seen. Further pruning should be undertaken at the same season and broadly in the same manner as if the shrub had been grown as a bush, if necessary pruning harder to maintain a neat and balanced head.

Standard *Pyracantha*

Initial training and pruning

1 *Remove any competing leaders or strong, well-developed laterals to concentrate growth into a single, vertical leading shoot.*

2 *Shorten weaker laterals, removing them in the following year so that the portion temporarily retained feeds and builds a strong main stem.*

Leader has been pinched out just above desired height of clear stem

Forming a bushy head

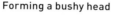

1 *As laterals are allowed to develop, tip-prune the young shoots to encourage a compact, branching habit.*

2 *Pinch out any shoots that grow on the clear stem. Single leaves may be left to nourish the plant; they will be shed naturally as the plant matures.*

Compact, bushy head maintained by pruning

Stem kept clear of growth

Established standard

Pyracanthas produce vigorous new shoots in summer, and these can be trimmed after the older shoots have flowered so that the developing berries are exposed and displayed, and the head maintains its compact form. After fruiting, further pruning can be undertaken if necessary to shape the head or relieve congestion by removing old, unproductive growth.

Bamboos, Grasses, and Perennials

Like most garden plants, perennials have growing tips on the ends of their shoots and may form new shoots on cut stems from areas of dividing cells or from dormant buds. As a result, cutting back perennials will cause many branching sideshoots to form, and since the shoots also possess flower buds (or cells that will form flower buds), any form of pruning will affect flower production.

By contrast, grasses and bamboos grow mainly from areas of dividing cells at the base of the bamboo shoot, grass leaf, or flowering spike. Pruning aerial parts therefore merely lowers the height of the plant and has limited effect on growth habit, which will continue from the base. Other garden plants that share this habit include agapanthus and phormiums.

BAMBOOS

Bamboos are often grown in gardens as long-lasting specimen plants or for an unusual permanent hedge-like screen. Garden lifespan can reach decades and each bamboo "culm" (jointed stem) has a life of up to 15 years. Established clumps can be very vigorous and where space is not available in smaller gardens, the excellent screening and ornamental properties of bamboo can be at the cost of excessive size and spread. A regular pruning regime can help restrict growth and keep plants looking attractive. For the best appearance and to avoid dieback, make cuts just above a node and use a saw or loppers if the stem is thick.

CONTAINING SPREAD

Bamboos can be classed as spreaders or clumpers, but these classifications are not always reliable and it is a sensible precaution to insert root control barriers for all types, preferably at planting time.

Pruning grasses
Shear the clump close to the ground, then pick out any debris to let light and air into the base of the plant. Many species have razor-sharp leaves, so always wear thick gloves.

Industrial vinyl flooring is often used, but similar flexible, very robust materials are offered specifically for the control of bamboo roots. The material should extend 10cm (4in) above the soil to prevent roots growing over the top, and to a depth of 1.4m (4ft), with joints overlapping by no less than 60cm (3ft).

PRUNING YOUNG PLANTS

Bamboo culms are superseded after a few years and newly planted younger plants will soon lose their original culms, which can be removed to better show off the mature culms. Some young bamboo plants may also produce undesirable arching stems and these can either be pruned out to allow more vigorous upright culms to develop, or shortened to encourage more vertical growth.

MATURE PRUNING

Thin out bamboos each year by removing any spent older canes and weak young canes. This will maintain an attractive density of canes and help to keep clumps healthy. Remove any older leaf blades at the same time to allow the colours and markings of the stems to be seen to best effect. Clumps can be renewed by cutting back to ground level in spring, though regrowth can be slow as food reserves are held in the older culms.

PRUNING FOR A "HEDGE"

While it is best to select plants for desired height, bamboo can be very variable and may not reach or may exceed the expected final height depending on the site. Where screening is required, it can therefore be a good idea to choose taller cultivars and

Thinning established clumps of bamboo

Before thinning Wearing thick gloves and using loppers, first remove dead and damaged canes, then cut out the oldest ones at the base until the desired effect is achieved.

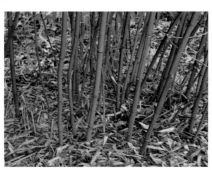

After thinning Without damaging new shoots, clear away debris at the base to relieve congestion further, let in light and air and allow young canes to grow unchecked.

Restricting the spread of bamboo

Dig a trench around the clump, deeper than the main body of the root system, chopping through and removing peripheral roots. Insert a barrier of, for example, slates or rigid plastic.

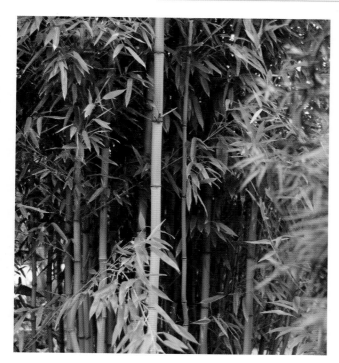

Phyllostachys aureosulcata* f. *aureocaulis
The canes of many bamboos are attractively coloured, such as the sulphur canes of this yellow groove bamboo. Thin out mature clumps and remove old leaf blades to really show them off.

PERENNIALS

Perennials die back at the end of the growing season to a permanent rootstock, from which new growth arises, and on the face of it do not seem to offer much scope for pruning. Pruning is needed merely to reduce the stems to a manageable and attractive height. This can be done with secateurs any time after flowering, but usually when stems die down and turn straw-like. The dried stems of some perennials, such as agapanthus and *Verbena bonariensis*, can be attractive in frost and are best removed in late winter.

PRUNING TO EXTEND FLOWERING
The flowering season of some perennials can be extended by severely trimming back a proportion of plants in late spring or early summer, using sharp shears or secateurs, while leaving others untrimmed. The flowering of trimmed plants is effectively "reset" and the plants grow new flowering shoots that will mature and flower later than the unpruned plants. *Echinacea purpurea*, *Helenium*, *Phlox paniculata*, *Sedum*, and *Solidago* are common plants that may be treated in this way.

PINCH PRUNING
Pinch pruning is commonly undertaken to make perennials more bushy. Any plants that are too leggy can be "pinched out" at the shoot tips using finger and thumb. Side shoots will then arise from below the base of the pinch point. In some cases pinch pruning can be repeated to build up very bushy plants in spring and to train plants into decorative shapes. See pages 168–71 for more information.

trim them on top to keep the screen to the desired height. A better "hedge effect" may also be accomplished by trimming the sides, which will result in more branching and leaf production.

BAMBOO FLOWERING
Contrary to popular myth, bamboos do not always die after flowering and though the chances of full recovery are not good, some steps can be taken to improve the odds. If you see a flowering shoot, cut it out promptly to discourage more from forming. If the whole clump begins to flower, allow it to do so undeterred and continue to feed and water. The following spring, cut the clump back to ground level and feed with a high nitrogen fertilizer, such as a spring lawn feed, to encourage new green growth from the base.

GRASSES, RUSHES, AND SEDGES

Grasses benefit from annual pruning, removing weather-buffeted old foliage and flower stems in favour of fresh, vigorous new growth. Deadhead annual grasses to prevent self-seeding, but leave the fading flowerheads of perennial species for winter display. As these die back or are broken by winter winds, they can be trimmed to tidy up the plant. In spring, cut the plant back to just above the ground; this work is best done with shears. When growing species that are not fully hardy in cool climates, leave this pruning until mid- to late spring so that the dead plant matter protects the new growth from any late frosts. When pruning, however, be careful not to damage the soft tips of young growth. Make a first shear 30cm (12in) from the ground and then clear away the shorn material, so that you can see into the heart of the plant clearly when making the final cuts.

To restrict spread, grasses are usually lifted and divided in spring when they exceed their allotted space. The split-off pieces can be used for propagation. Tufted grasses, that build up from a central crown, are the least invasive.

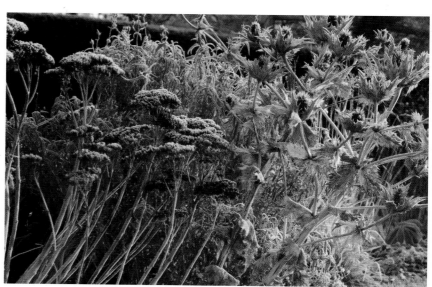

Flower heads touched by frost
The dried flower heads and stems of many perennials, such as sedums and sea holly (*Eryngium*), are decorative in their own right, adding interest over the winter months, and are best cut back in early spring.

Pinch Pruning

Pinch pruning is a technique occasionally used on a wide range of plants to produce bushy growth by nipping out soft shoot tips. When repeatedly applied to suitable plants, the technique can be used, particularly when combined with training on canes or wire frames, to produce many decorative shapes for flowering displays or foliage effect. With flowering plants, the repeated pinching effectively delays flowering, because the shoot never has time to form a flower bud at its tip; instead, energy is diverted into producing sideshoots. When pinching ceases (usually about two months before flowering is desired), the "last" set of shoots, because they all started into growth at the same time, all flower at the same time, giving a spectacular display. The plants that are used fall into the category known as subshrubs – short-lived plants, such as fuchsias, coleus (*Solenostemon*) and certain types of chrysanthemum, which become woody at the base with herbaceous top growth.

Basic techniques

Pinch pruning will be familiar to anyone who has grown chrysanthemums to obtain top-quality blooms timed for entering into exhibition (*see below*). No tools are generally required for pinch pruning, although on plants with hairy stems, such as helichrysums, a pruning knife can be used to make neater cuts.

CARE AND CULTIVATION
In general, always choose named cultivars bred for vigour and flowering performance, such as *Fuchsia* 'Swingtime', or for their attractive leaf colour, such as *Solenostemon* 'Pineapple Beauty' or *Helichrysum petiolare* 'Limelight'. Always use plants grown from cuttings, to obtain named cultivars and, in the case of *Solenostemon* (grown only for its leaves), to obtain plants that are more shy to flower than seedlings. Pot young plants on regularly, from 7cm (3in) to 12cm (5in) and then into at least 22cm (9in) pots to give the mature plant stability. Do not pinch prune a week or so before or after potting to enable root systems to re-establish well.

Site plants growing under glass in a well-lit, well-ventilated position, as the dense growth is vulnerable to mildew in a stagnant atmosphere. Pick off discoloured leaves as seen. Feed young plants with a high-nitrogen fertilizer to stimulate growth, then, when pinching stops, switch to a high-potash feed to stimulate flower development or, in *Solenostemon*, to allow the leaf colour to develop fully. Do not feed flowering plants when overwintering.

TRAINING FRAMES AND SUPPORTS
Bamboo canes, wire and wire netting, both large- and small-gauge, and soft twine or raffia for tying in young stems are the most commonly used materials for frames and supports. They can be used to create many variations on the shapes described on the following pages. The head of a pinch-pruned standard needs no frame, but is formed entirely by bushy growth, pinch pruned to create and maintain an even shape. However, no subshrub can, in one season, produce a stem sturdy enough to support the head, so staking with a cane is required.

Pinch pruning
Removing the shoot tip breaks its apical dominance (*see p.11*); side-buds, often latent in leaf axils, are stimulated into activity and develop into shoots. If these in turn have their tips pinched out, and so on, the effect is a proliferation of growth.

Pinching stimulates shoots from the top buds and further down the stem

1 With finger and thumb, pinch out the tip of the shoot just above an opened leaf. Remove only the very tip to stimulate the maximum number of buds into producing sideshoots.

2 Side buds will break and develop into shoots. When these have developed two to four leaves (or two pairs), repeat the process.

3 Further shoots will break from the original stem as well as from the sideshoots. The plant gets progressively bushier. It will not flower until you stop pinching and let shoots develop normally; shoots usually need 8–12 weeks of unchecked growth before producing a terminal flowering bud.

The next generation of shoots is pinched at two to four leaves

Site of second pinching

Site of first pinching

Single stem of original cutting

Show chrysanthemum blooms
To obtain flowers of this quality, growers pinch prune young plants, then allow shoots to develop, disbudding as buds form. For single blooms, all side buds are removed; for spray chrysanthemums, the strong central bud is pinched out so that side buds will develop evenly.

Pinch-pruned standard

Many subshrubs can be trained as standards, including those that do not naturally tend to form one single stem. Coleus (*see below*) are very easily trained, and cascade chrysanthemums and fuchsias are also popular; with the latter, young plants that have their leaves arranged in whorls of three, rather than in pairs, should always be used if possible, since they give much better, bushier results. More interest can be gained from experimenting with plants in addition to those mentioned on these pages. However, check examples before attempting to imitate them; some

of the more unusual standards seen, such as ivy-leaved pelargoniums, may have not been trained, but top-grafted.

The height of the clear stem and head will vary according to the plant used and, to a degree, on personal preference; the most pleasing appearance, in general, results if the depth of the head occupies one-third to half of the total height. The density of the head will also vary with the intervals at which growth is pinched, and also with the plant's size of leaf compared to its internodal distance; a vigorous coleus cultivar, with large, closely spaced leaves,

can be used to form a solid "lollipop" head, while a heliotrope will have a much looser, less formal head of growth.

In the early stages of training, growth is restricted to one single stem that will grow strongly upwards. If it breaks or otherwise fails, or (rarely) develops a flowerbud, before the desired height has been achieved, pinch or cut back to a healthy leaf and train in the resulting new shoot (there will be an unavoidable slight kink in the stem). Once the desired height is reached, pinch pruning is used to encourage growth at the top of the stem to bush out, forming the head.

Stage 1

Pot a vigorous, single-stemmed cutting into a 25cm (10in) pot, inserting a cane, and tie the young stem in vertically with soft twine or raffia, taking care not to damage either the stem or the leaves. Feed well, but do not remove any growth until the plant has had a week or so to re-establish.

Stage 2

Until the desired height is reached, pinch out all sideshoots that develop, but retain the large leaves from whose axils they sprang. This foliage will nourish the plant and thicken the stem. Keep tying in the main stem at regular intervals as it grows upwards.

Stage 3

When the leader is at least 20cm (8in) taller than the desired height of clear stem, pinch out the shoot tip.

Stage 4

At the head of the plant, pinch prune all new shoots when they have two to four leaves, until a bushy head is formed. Pinch out any shoots that develop on the main stem.

Finished standard

On flowering plants, stop pinching 8–12 weeks before flowers are desired. Foliage plants such as this coleus can continue to be pinched to maintain a neat shape. When plants start to deteriorate, use them to provide cuttings for next year's displays.

Leaves have been shed naturally from main stem; if not, they may be picked off carefully

Pillars and cones

Pelargoniums, fuchsias and even naturally spreading plants such as *Helichrysum petiolare* can be trained upright and pinch pruned to form dense cones and pillars that, with careful cultivation, can last for several years. While a single well-pinched plant will make a small, solid cone in a single season, three plants will result in a 1.2–1.5m (4–5ft) feature. A pillar of this height will need a little more attention to keep the sides vertical, and may need pinch pruning over two growing seasons in order to obtain the necessary density of foliage at the top. In cool climates, plants can be moved out of doors after the danger of frost has passed, either onto a patio or planted out as summer bedding, then brought back under glass to overwinter. In spring, trimming and pinching is resumed as new growth begins.

Stage 1, early spring

Starting with rooted cuttings or single-stemmed young plants, tie the leading shoot in vertically and let sideshoots develop

Spreading helichrysum stems must be drawn up carefully

Stage 2, six to eight weeks later

1 *Plant three young plants in their permanent 22cm (9in) pot and retie each to a new cane.*

2 *Pinch or cut back sideshoots to a bud or leaf, so that none extends beyond the width of the pot.*

Stage 3, throughout summer

1 *To produce a cone, tie the canes together to form a "wigwam". Keep tying in the leading shoots. If a leader breaks, choose a strong shoot below and tie that in. If desired, add extra height by sliding in longer canes or, for a cone, one long, central cane.*

Shoots on this side have been pinched

2 *Pinch all shoots back every week, developing a conical shape, or to a columnar outline for a pillar. Pillars must be pinched more often (every two or three days) on the top half to make the plant as bushy in the upper regions as it is at the base.*

Shoots on this side are yet to be pinched

Stage 4

Leaders now tied in to one central cane

When the plants reach the desired height and shape, pinch out the leaders. Then stop pinching flowering plants altogether, except to remove any vertical shoots that grow at the top, to allow flowering shoots to develop all over the plants.

Finished cone

This helichrysum *cone has been left to grow out for an informal display, and will flower. However, since* helichrysum *foliage is of more ornamental value than its flowers, the cone may be pinched further, or trimmed with shears, for a "topiary" effect.*

Leaves at base that discolour should be picked off

Pot has been placed in a 30cm (12in) clay pot for display and stability

Chrysanthemum sphere

Cascade chrysanthemums, which make plenty of growth, are the subshrubs most commonly used to cover large wire balloon frames, more commonly seen with climbing plants trained around them (*see p.246*). When in full flower a large sphere can be 2m (6ft) in diameter.

A big pot is needed to give stability. It is best to erect the frame around the young plants. A frame can be made in many ways; one of the easiest is made from large-mesh sheep or pig netting, with squares of about 20cm (7in). Cut eight strips from the wire, each one square across and six squares long, leaving prongs of wire at each end so that the strip forms a "ladder". The lower prongs can be pressed into the soil around the edge of the pot, and the ladders bent over to form the globe. The upper prongs can be twisted around each other and around stout central bamboo canes.

The most difficult part of the operation is drawing the plants' stems across to cover the framework evenly; they are fleshy, and snap very easily. While the main stems are trained upwards, their sideshoots are pinched to produce more and more lateral growth, which can be tied in where necessary to conceal the framework completely by late summer, after which shoots can be allowed to develop and flower.

Stage 1, late spring
Plant four 12-week-old cuttings, each with several main stems, in a 45cm (18in) pot, angling them slightly outwards.

Stage 2

1 *Using wirecutters, or the wirecutting notch on a pair of secateurs, cut eight "ladders" (see above) from sheep or pig netting.*

2 *Insert four canes vertically in the centre of the pot in a square. Insert the wire ladders around the pot, bringing them to the top in a curve and twisting the upper prongs around the canes.*

3 *Remove the plants' original canes, and very gently fan out and tie in the main shoots so that they are evenly spaced around the framework.*

4 *Very carefully, tease all loose shoots through the framework so that they can be tied to the outside of the sphere.*

Stage 3

Keep tying in the main stems, pinching their tips when they reach the top of the frame. Pinch out the tips of all other shoots once two leaves have unfurled, tying in growth laterally until the frame is well furnished with bushy growth. In early autumn, stop pinching to let flowering shoots develop. In cool climates, if plants are outdoors, bring them under cover.

Finished sphere
The sphere will flower in about eight weeks, and the display will last for about six weeks.

Dictionary of Ornamental Shrubs

A

ABELIA

Mainly evergreen or, in cool climates, deciduous shrubs of arching, twiggy habit that are hardy if given a warm, sheltered position. Most flower in summer on the previous year's wood and may flower again later in the season on the earliest of the current season's growth. Abelias regularly produce new growth from low down and thus benefit from moderate replacement pruning. All but dwarf forms are suitable for training against walls, especially *A. floribunda*.

■ **WHEN TO PRUNE** Spring, after the last frosts, and summer, after flowering.

■ **TRAINING AND PRUNING** If wall-training (*see p.162*), tie in branches promptly before they arch over. Spring pruning consists of removing dead or damaged growth. After flowering, remove some old wood (this is not as necessary for *A. triflora*), cutting back up to one in four flowered stems to strong new shoots or to the ground. To renovate, cut all stems to the base in early spring.

ABELIOPHYLLUM

Abeliophyllum distichum is a deciduous shrub with a lax and open habit, bearing white flowers in early

spring on the previous year's growth. Stems may root where they touch the ground. In cool climates it should be given a sheltered site; training against a sunny wall will encourage flowering.

■ **WHEN TO PRUNE** Spring, after flowering. Tie in wall-trained plants and prune to shape throughout the growing season.

■ **TRAINING AND PRUNING** Prune free-standing shrubs as for *Forsythia* (*see p.194*), cutting some old wood back to vigorous shoots low down. To renovate, cut back to a low framework of branches. To train on a wall (*see p.162*), select strong shoots to make an informal framework. Once established, cut back one in two or three of the flowered shoots to low replacement shoots or buds low down. As plants mature, remove entirely any old branches with few laterals and train in replacements.

ABUTILON

Evergreen, semi-evergreen and deciduous shrubs that in cool climates need a sheltered position and frost protection; several are best grown under glass. Some may be grown as standards. Abutilons flower on the current season's growth. They flower over a long period but are relatively short-lived.

A. MEGAPOTAMICUM

TRAILING ABUTILON

Evergreen, half-hardy shrub, flowering from spring to autumn; the cultivar 'Variegatum' has yellow-mottled

leaves. Its long, slender stems and readiness to produce growth from the base make it suitable for wall training.

■ **WHEN TO PRUNE** Early to mid-spring.

■ **TRAINING AND PRUNING** On free-standing shrubs, shorten the previous season's growth by one-third. Cut bare branches back to strong shoots or buds near the base. To produce larger leaves on variegated plants, prune hard each year (*see p.164*). Young, healthy plants respond well to hard cutting back. Wall-train (*see p.162*) as an informal fan, tying young growth to bamboo canes attached to wires (*see also* Tree fruits, p.98). Once a framework is established, occasionally remove old wood in favour of strong young replacement shoots, tying these in to fill in gaps.

A. x *hybridum* 'Souvenir de Bonn'

The natural habit (*left*) is tall and spindly. Pruning when young will encourage bushier growth (*right*).

Laterals have developed

Tip of shoot was removed here

***Abutilon* 'Kentish Belle'**
This hybrid can be treated as for *Abutilon megapotamicum*; wall training displays its flowers attractively, and the wall gives its slender growth shelter, warmth and support.

A. VITIFOLIUM

Fast-growing, evergreen shrub bearing masses of purplish-blue to white flowers in late spring and early summer. In

cool climates it may be damaged by severe frosts. It can be allowed to grow as a multi-stemmed shrub, but training with a central leader enhances the pyramidal form and gives it stature.

■ **WHEN TO PRUNE** Summer, after flowering.

■ **TRAINING AND PRUNING** Train initially with a central stem (*see p.155*). If this leader is broken, train in a replacement (*see p.24*) and cut back laterals by two-thirds. Do not prune established plants, except to remove dead, diseased or damaged growth. Hard cutting back spoils the plant's natural form by encouraging too much lateral growth, and should be avoided. Deadheading can increase the vigour of the plant.

OTHER ABUTILONS
A. × HYBRIDUM As for *A. pictum*. Many cultivars break readily from the base if pruned hard annually in spring.
A. × MILLERI As for *A. megapotamicum*.
A. PICTUM (syn. A. STRIATUM) In cool climates, ideal for a glasshouse or as summer bedding. Can be grown as an upright plant with a central leader; the stem may be cleared to form a standard (*see* Pinch pruning, p.169); can also be grown as a bushy shrub (*see left*); shorten the main stem by about half and laterals to 8–10cm (3–4in) in mid-spring.
A. × SUNTENSE As for *A. vitifolium*.

ACALYPHA

Evergreen shrubs and perennials with attractive foliage, some with interesting flowers. They may be grown outdoors only in tropical areas, either as free-standing bushes or as informal hedges. In cool climates they need a frost-free position, and are best grown in pots under glass. Acalyphas require little pruning except to remove wayward shoots, but can be cut back by up to a third in mid-spring to restrict growth. This will also result in larger leaves. They should not be cut back harder.

ALLAMANDA

Allamanda schottii (syn. *A. neriifolia*), the bush allamanda, is an evergreen shrub with dense growth and yellow, trumpet-shaped flowers from summer to autumn, followed by spiky seed capsules. It needs subtropical conditions. It responds well to pruning. Pinch-prune young plants (*see p.168*) to encourage bushy growth. Trim established plants from late winter to spring, cutting stems back by 5–12cm (2–5in) or more. During the growing season, shorten long stems to maintain a balanced plant. For other species, *see* Dictionary of Climbing Plants, *p.262*.

ALOYSIA

Aloysia triphylla (syn. *Lippia citriodora*), or lemon verbena, is a medium-sized evergreen grown more for its lemon-scented leaves than its white flowers, borne on the current season's growth. In cool climates it needs a sunny site and protection with a mulch in winter.

■ **WHEN TO PRUNE** Mid-spring, after any danger of frost has passed.

■ **TRAINING AND PRUNING** In cool climates prune main stems to strong buds about 30cm (12in) from ground level. In warm climates allow a woody framework to develop, then shorten growth to buds 5–10cm (2–4in) from the old wood. From spring to early summer pinch out shoot tips for leafy, bushy growth. May also be informally wall-trained (*see p.162*) or grown as a standard (*see p.165*).

AMELANCHIER

Large, deciduous, fully hardy shrubs or small trees. They bear white flowers in mid- to late spring and are noted for their beautiful autumn leaf colour. *A. canadensis* also produces edible berries. Amelanchiers may grow as multi-stemmed bushes (the natural habit of most species), or may sometimes be trained as a small tree. The spreading, vigorously suckering species, such as *A. stolonifera*, are grown as dense, thicket-like shrubs.

A. LAMARCKII

Deciduous, upright, multi-stemmed shrub that can be allowed to develop naturally with only minimal pruning. It may also be trained with a short trunk to form a small, branched-headed tree.

■ **WHEN TO PRUNE** Winter, when dormant, or after flowering in late spring.

■ **TRAINING AND PRUNING** If to be grown as a multi-stemmed bush, thin young plants lightly to create an open, informal vase shape: left unattended, main stems that are too close together tend to twist around each other as they mature. To renovate neglected, overcrowded specimens, cut congested, intertwined stems back to ground level. For a tree-like form, select the strongest, straightest stem and clear a short trunk of 0.6–1.5m (2–5ft) as for a central-leader tree (*see p.26*), then allow a

Amelanchier stolonifera
Prune in winter if growth is crowded, removing one in three stems.

Amelanchier lamarckii
A light, open form enhances the display of autumn colour in multi-stemmed specimens.

branched head to develop, selecting laterals to create an open, evenly spaced branch framework. In the dormant season, remove any shoots that have developed on the clear trunk.

A. STOLONIFERA

A suckering, woodland shrub, suitable for a large border or wild area of the garden. Unpruned, it tends to spread, and will eventually form an impenetrable thicket.

■ **WHEN TO PRUNE** Winter, when dormant.

■ **TRAINING AND PRUNING** No routine pruning is required. If established plants are congested, cut out up to one in three of the stems every two or three years, removing them to the base (*see left*). More drastic thinning, retaining only the strongest young shoots, can be used to renovate neglected specimens.

OTHER AMELANCHIERS
A. ASIATICA Train with a tree-like form as for *A. lamarckii*.
A. CANADENSIS As for *A. lamarckii*; if berries are desired, prune in winter only.
A. CONFUSA, A. × GRANDIFLORA As for *A. lamarckii*.

OTHER ORNAMENTAL SHRUBS
ACACIA *See* Dictionary of Ornamental Trees, *p.52*.
ACCA (syn. FEIJOA) No special needs; if necessary, prune ornamentals after flowering, and fruiting plants in winter.
ADENANDRA No special pruning needs. May be trimmed to shape after flowering.

AGAVE *See* Palms and palm-like plants, *p.41*.
ALANGIUM No special pruning needs. Will break from old wood if cut back hard.
ALOE *See* Palms and palm-like plants, *p.41*.
ALYOGYNE Frost-tender. Tip-prune young plants (*see p.155*) to encourage bushiness. Shorten main stems and laterals by one-third

in spring, keeping a woody framework.
A. huegelii (lilac hibiscus) may be cut back harder into old wood.
ANDROMEDA As for *Erica carnea* (see *p.191*).
ANISODONTEA Frost-tender. Regular pinch-pruning will keep them compact and bushy. Tolerates hard pruning to renovate.

ARALIA

Deciduous, hardy shrubs with very thorny stems, producing handsome pinnate leaves and showy panicles of white flowers. Aralias usually make large, suckering plants with upright stems and short laterals, but they sometimes naturally form small, sparsely branched trees. They should be pruned in early spring, before the onset of growth. Let young plants develop naturally, removing only dead, diseased, damaged or badly placed growth. When established, keep pruning to a minimum. The buds break late, and can appear lifeless until quite late in the season; do not mistake this for frost damage. If a late hard frost does damage the tip growth, prune back to a stubby lateral showing healthy growth. When grown with a single trunk, any suckers should be removed as they appear (*see p.153*). Reverted shoots on variegated cultivars (which may also appear as suckers) should also be promptly removed (*see p.153*). Old plants will not respond to hard pruning.

Aralia elata 'Variegata'

Reverted, green-leaved growth may appear as suckers, and these should be removed.

ARGYRANTHEMUM

Argyranthemum frutescens (syn. *Chrysanthemum frutescens*), the marguerite, is an evergreen subshrub with attractive white, yellow or pink daisy-like flowerheads all through summer. In cool temperate climates it is not hardy, but is often pot-grown for summer bedding, the young plants overwintered under glass. Increase the flowering potential and encourage a rounded shape by pinching out the tips of young shoots two or three times in spring (*see p.155*) and also by deadheading regularly. Argyranthemums are also suitable for growing as standards, formed and maintained by pinch pruning (*see p.169*). Train up a clear single stem, then form a bushy head by repeatedly pinching out the tips of lateral growths.

ARONIA *CHOKEBERRY*

Two species (and one hybrid between them) of medium-sized, hardy, deciduous suckering shrubs, related to *Pyrus* and *Sorbus*. They bear clusters of white flowers in spring on growth made the previous season, followed by fine autumn colour, often early in the season, and black or red fruits, according to the species; these often persist into mid-winter. Left unpruned, the shrub will not produce many new central growths to maintain a naturally rounded shape, and will gradually spread by suckering away from the main rootstock. When established, remove one in three of the older stems each year, pruning in winter to late spring. To restrict spread, prune off suckers around the shrub below ground level. Suckers can also be dug up and transplanted for propagation. Although old plants sometimes respond by producing vigorous new shoots when pruned hard, renovation is generally not worthwhile.

ARTEMISIA *WORMWOOD*

A genus that includes a number of hardy and half-hardy shrubs and subshrubs, grown for their attractive and aromatic foliage. They thrive in a sunny, well-drained site. Regular pruning is needed to prevent the plants becoming bare and leggy at the base and to promote bushy growth. Most can be cut back into old wood. The yellowish flowerheads are seldom attractive; pinch the inflorescences out as they develop to maintain the fine foliage.

A. ABROTANUM

LAD'S LOVE, OLD MAN, SOUTHERNWOOD

Deciduous sub-shrub with sweetly aromatic, grey-green foliage. Plants tend to become straggly; pruning them encourages bushy growth. Plants that have become leggy and bare at the base can be renovated by hard pruning.

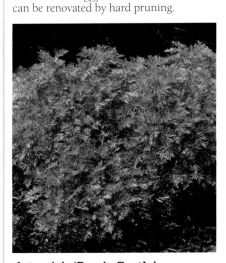

Artemisia 'Powis Castle'

Cut back to a low framework each year to renew the fresh, young foliage.

■ **WHEN TO PRUNE** Early spring, after any danger of severe frost is past.

■ **TRAINING AND PRUNING** The first spring after planting, cut all the stems back to 2.5–5cm (1–2in) from the ground to stimulate strong new growth. Encourage bushiness by regularly pinching out shoot tips. On established plants, clip the previous season's growth back by up to half every year. To renovate, cut all stems back hard.

A. 'POWIS CASTLE'

Mound-forming, evergreen shrub with filigree, silver-grey foliage. Since it is the young growth that is the most attractive, prune the plant annually to maximize the effect. It is pruned harder than *A. abrotanum*, because the foliage has a tendency to die back on older wood, leaving leggy bare stems.

■ **WHEN TO PRUNE** Early spring, after any danger of severe frost is past. In warm climates, can be pruned in autumn.

■ **TRAINING AND PRUNING** Pinch out the shoot tips of young plants to encourage bushy growth. Cut back annually to a low framework of main stems, as for other grey-leaved shrubs (*see p.158*). Discard old plants that cease to make vigorous new growth; they do not renovate well and are better replaced.

OTHER ARTEMISIAS
A. ARBORESCENS, A. LUDOVICIANA, A. NUTANS (syn. SERIPHIDIUM NUTANS), A. TRIDENTATA (syn. SERIPHIDIUM TRIDENTATA) As for *A. abrotanum*.

ATRIPLEX

Attractive foliage plants, including some annuals and perennials as well as a number of hardy, evergreen or semi-evergreen, grey-green shrubs that are noted for their tolerance of coastal sites. They tend to develop into straggly, open shrubs with age; keep them compact by annual pruning in spring. Either clip over the whole plant with shears, removing one-third of the previous year's growth, or, for a more natural outline, trim with secateurs. With trimming, *A. halimus* maintains a dense enough habit to be used as a hedge.

AUCUBA

Evergreen, rounded, hardy shrubs, several with variegated or spotted leaves; the female plants often bear showy fruits in autumn. The most commonly grown species is *A. japonica*, all of whose cultivars are similar in growth habit and are usually used in shrub borders or as specimens grown in tubs. They are also popular for dense, semi-formal hedging, particularly since they

tolerate heavy shade. Aucubas are naturally dense in growth and rounded in habit, but they are prone to dieback and also have a tendency to become bare at the base.

■ **WHEN TO PRUNE** Mid-spring, after the winter display of berries. Non-fruiting plants, or those on which berries are not desired, may be pruned in winter.

■ **TRAINING AND PRUNING** The first spring after planting, cut back the previous year's growth by one-third of its length to encourage a more bushy habit. As the plant becomes established, remove any over-vigorous, cane-like shoots that spoil its shape. Cut back any shoots that show signs of dieback (this may be caused by drought), either to strong, completely healthy buds, or to the main stem. Hedges should be trimmed with secateurs (*see p.46*), rather than clipped, to avoid unsightly damage to the large glossy leaves; shorten the previous year's growth by about one-third until the hedge is established, then trim over with secateurs each year to keep compact and to the desired height. Aucubas that have become bare at the base may be rejuvenated by hard pruning in stages (*see p.161*), cutting one in three of the main stems back to the base each year.

Aucuba japonica
Prune wayward stems to well within the plant's outline, so that cut marks are hidden.

BANKSIA

Australian genus of tropical and subtropical, evergreen shrubs or small trees with cylindrical or globe-like flower spikes. Banksias need frost-free conditions, but make good pot-plants under glass in cool climates. They need little pruning, but may be trimmed lightly to restrict size. Like *Eucalyptus* (*see p.64*), some banksias have a swollen base (lignotuber) from which new shoots grow if the shrub is pruned hard.

■ **WHEN TO PRUNE** After flowering.

■ **TRAINING AND PRUNING** Confine pruning of established plants to shortening the previous season's growth if this is necessary to limit size. *B. integrifolia*, *B. menziesii* and *B. spinulosa* should re-sprout if cut back into old wood, but *B. coccinea* and *B. ericifolia* will not respond well if cut back below green foliage. It is better to replace a plant that has become leggy or has outgrown its space than to attempt renovation.

Banksia ericifolia
The spikes of flowers and the needle-like foliage are popular with flower arrangers.

AZARA

Evergreen shrubs and trees grown for their leaves and their dense yellow flowerheads. In warm climates they may be grown as free-standing shrubs that need only minimal pruning. They are sometimes grown as hedging, in which case they may be trimmed over in autumn (or in mid-spring in cooler areas) as for *Escallonia* (*see p.192*). In cool climates they are only reliably hardy if given the protection of a warm wall; fan-train them (*see p.162*) and prune in late spring to remove any frost damage. Small-leaved species, such as *A. microphylla*, may be clipped into geometric shapes (*see Topiary, p.48*), but this will be at the expense of the flowers. Established azaras respond well to hard pruning in late spring, producing new growth freely from old wood.

BARLERIA

Barleria cristata, the Philippine violet, is a tropical, evergreen, medium-sized shrub with pale violet or white tubular flowers and a long flowering season. Pinch out shoot tips of young plants to encourage branching. Shorten long, flowered stems by about one-third to encourage future flowering growth. It may also be grown as a hedge (*see p.44*), in which case trim after flowering.

OTHER ORNAMENTAL SHRUBS
Arctostaphylos No special pruning needs. Prostrate species tolerate trimming in summer after flowering, but fruit is lost.
Ardisia Evergreen (*see p.159*), prune lightly in spring only if necessary.

Aristotelia No special pruning needs. Can be wall-trained, pruning in spring.
Asimina No special pruning needs.
Astartea No special pruning needs. Trim to shape if necessary after flowering.

Baccharis As for *Atriplex* (*see above*).
Bauera No special pruning needs. Trim lightly after flowering if necessary.
Beaufortia No special pruning needs.

BERBERIS *BARBERRY*

Hardy shrubs that vary in size from dwarf to large; some are semi-prostrate or mounding in habit while others are upright or arching. They have yellow or orange spring flowers followed by red or black fruits. Many deciduous species have fine autumn colour. Berberis are dense in habit, and tolerant of most situations and soils. The thorny evergreens are popular for barrier plantings, and for formal or informal hedges; they are most easily clipped with shears, because of the thorns, but look more attractive if pruned more selectively with secateurs. A few deciduous berberis, such as *B.* × *ottawensis* and cultivars of *B. thunbergii*, may be regularly coppiced or cut back to a low framework of permanent branches for larger and more vividly coloured leaves, and for attractively coloured young stems. Those grown for their autumn colour should not be pruned in this way, since the best leaf colour is usually produced on mature wood.

Berberis respond well to renovation, and even healthy plants that have not been neglected or become too large benefit from being cut back hard every seven years or so. When pruning, always wear thornproof gloves and clothing.

B. DARWINII

DARWIN'S BARBERRY

Evergreen, arching shrub, often used for informal hedging or in mixed shrub borders. Deep orange-yellow flowers, borne on the previous season's growth, are succeeded by bluish-purple berries. It has a naturally dense habit with arching stems, which is best preserved by minimal pruning. However, it can become very large, eventually flowering and fruiting only on the periphery of the plant; it responds well to drastic cutting back.

■ **WHEN TO PRUNE** After flowering, in early summer, provided that fruits are not required. Otherwise, prune in autumn or winter, after fruiting.

■ **TRAINING AND PRUNING** Specimen plants in shrub borders need minimal pruning. To renovate, cut back all stems to within 30cm (12in) of the base in late winter, though flowers will be lost the following season. Plants grown as an informal hedge should not be clipped, or the berries will be lost. Fruited stems can be shortened in winter to keep the hedge reasonably compact.

Berberis darwinii
Berberis that are outgrowing their site should grow back vigorously if cut back hard.

B. THUNBERGII

Deciduous shrub with many cultivars of varying habit, grown mainly for foliage that turns brilliant orange-red in autumn. It is popularly grown as a hedge, though at the expense of the flowers if clipped. It benefits from thinning each year, removing some growth to the base. Thinning dense growth also displays the foliage better. Some cultivars, such as 'Aurea' and 'Rose Glow', can be cut back hard each year to enhance the effect of spring foliage.

■ **WHEN TO PRUNE** Mid- to late winter. Remove dead wood in midsummer when it can be clearly distinguished.

■ **TRAINING AND PRUNING** Thin the plant and stimulate new growth by cutting out one in five of the stems each year, to the base or to a strong shoot low down. To cut back regularly for foliage effect, *see p.164*. Renovation is as for *B. darwinii*.

> **OTHER BERBERIS**
> B. ʙᴜxɪꜰᴏʟɪᴀ As for *B. darwinii*.
> B. × ᴄᴀʀᴍɪɴᴇᴀ As for *B. thunbergii*.
> B. ʜᴏᴏᴋᴇʀɪ As for *B. darwinii*. Neat, dense, upright habit.
> B. ʟɪɴᴇᴀʀɪꜰᴏʟɪᴀ As for *B. darwinii*.
> B. × ᴏᴛᴛᴀᴡᴇɴsɪs As for *B. thunbergii*. 'Superba' is vigorous, and recommended for regular hard pruning (*see p.164*), producing red young stems and purple-green leaves.
> B. × sᴛᴇɴᴏᴘʜʏʟʟᴀ As for *B. darwinii*. As an informal hedge it can be cut back hard in early summer, after flowering.
> B. ᴛᴇᴍᴏʟᴀɪᴄᴀ As for *B. thunbergii*. Cut hard back for the best stem effect.
> B. ᴡɪʟsᴏɴɪᴀᴇ As for *B. thunbergii*.

BORONIA

Mostly small, woody, evergreen shrubs, grown for their aromatic foliage and flowers. Some will survive light frost when mature, but are much better grown under glass in cool climates. Pruning helps to maintain vigour and bushiness and increases the number of flowers. Boronias are usually short-lived.

B. MEGASTIGMA

BROWN BORONIA, SCENTED BORONIA

Slender, evergreen shrub with powerfully fragrant, bell-like brown flowers borne along the stems in late winter and spring. Named cultivars with other flower colours are available.

■ **WHEN TO PRUNE** After flowering, in late spring.

■ **TRAINING AND PRUNING** Pinch out shoot tips on planting to encourage bushiness and flowering shoots. After the first flowering season, cut back flowered shoots hard, but do not leave any stems without foliage. In subsequent years shorten flowered shoots by about one-third. To renovate, cut back all stems by half in late spring; conditions need to be ideal for a good response.

> **OTHER BORONIAS**
> B. ᴅᴇɴᴛɪᴄᴜʟᴀᴛᴀ Intolerant of heavy pruning, but may be cut back lightly after flowering to maintain vigour.
> B. ꜰʟᴏʀɪʙᴜɴᴅᴀ As for *B. megastigma*: on established plants, reduce lanky flowered stems by half.
> B. ʜᴇᴛᴇʀᴏᴘʜʏʟʟᴀ As for *B. megastigma*.
> B. ᴍᴏʟʟɪs Requires minimal pruning.
> B. sᴇʀʀᴜʟᴀᴛᴀ As for *B. megastigma* but, once established, cut out one or two of the oldest branches. When shortening other stems, do not cut back beyond the foliage into bare wood.

BOUVARDIA

Deciduous, semi-evergreen or evergreen shrubs, grown mainly for their flowers, which are borne on new wood in terminal cymes. They are frost-tender, and should be grown under glass in winter in cool climates. Prune in late winter, removing dead and weak wood and cutting back stems that have flowered by half to three-quarters. Pinch-prune (*see p.168*) the resulting new growth until midsummer, to encourage bushiness. Cut any old, unproductive wood back to ground level.

BRACHYGLOTTIS

Evergreen, usually mound-forming, mostly hardy shrubs, formerly classified under *Senecio*; most have attractive silvery-grey foliage and bear terminal clusters of daisy-like, yellow flowerheads on the previous season's growth in summer. Hard pruning results in a finer foliage effect, but will be at the expense of the flowers. Most prefer a sunny aspect but tolerate windy coastal conditions. In shady or damp sites, however, they may become leggy. In cool climates plants are often damaged by frost, and a heavy fall of snow can break the rather brittle branches.

B. 'SUNSHINE' *(DUNEDIN HYBRID)*

Hardy, spreading shrub with grey leaves that are white beneath, and yellow flowerheads in summer.

■ **WHEN TO PRUNE** Mid-spring, when any danger of severe frost has passed and with the onset of new growth.

■ **TRAINING AND PRUNING** Plants grown on coastal sites and in warm climates tend to adopt a rounded habit without regular pruning. In cool climates growth may be spreading; cut back any wayward stems and frost-damaged growth. Established plants may also be clipped to shape after flowering. Prune hard to renovate damaged plants, cutting back to active buds on older wood. Plants must be in good health for renovation to be successful; old plants are best replaced.

OTHER BRACHYGLOTTIS
All other Dunedin Hybrids are pruned as for *B.* 'Sunshine'.
B. ELAEAGNIFOLIA Minimal pruning.
B. HUNTII Requires minimal pruning.
B. LAXIFOLIA As for *B.* 'Sunshine'.

Renovating *Brachyglottis* **'Sunshine'**
'Sunshine' will respond to drastic pruning, but the regrowth will be slow on old plants such as this one, shown here in midsummer after hard pruning in spring. It is usually preferable to replace an old plant with a young specimen, which will quickly make vigorous growth.

BRUGMANSIA *ANGELS' TRUMPETS*

Semi-evergreen or evergreen shrubs or small trees, formerly classified under Datura. They are grown for their exceptionally large, fragrant, trumpet-shaped flowers, which are borne in summer to autumn. They need frost-free conditions. In warm climates moderate pruning encourages plants to flower freely. Brugmansias grow well under glass in cool climates, as bushes or as standards (*see p.165*); they need regular pruning to restrict size while stimulating flowering growth. Softer growth may may die back in winter, but plants will usually regenerate the following spring. Wear gloves when pruning; toxic alkaloids are contained in the leaves and the flowerheads.

■ **WHEN TO PRUNE** Late winter, before the onset of growth.

■ **TRAINING AND PRUNING** Cut back the previous season's growth to within 15cm (6in) of ground level or to framework

Brugmansia pruned hard
Brugmansias make vigorous new spring growth after hard pruning, so their size can be restricted if required.

stems; these may consist of stubby branches on a clear trunk (*see above*). Deadhead faded flowerheads in summer. Brugmansias respond well to renovation, and a plant that has outgrown its allotted space may be cut back hard before spring growth commences.

BRUNFELSIA

Evergreen shrubs or small trees with glossy leaves, grown for their sometimes fragrant flowers, borne on the previous season's growth. The flowers are blue, often fading to lavender, then white (or sometimes yellow), so that flowers of several colours can be seen simultaneously. They will grow outdoors only in frost-free gardens, but grow well under glass.

B. PAUCIFLORA

YESTERDAY-TODAY-AND-TOMORROW

Spring-flowering, with a spreading habit, particularly when grown in shade. Suitable for wall training.

■ **WHEN TO PRUNE** Spring, after flowering.

■ **TRAINING AND PRUNING** To encourage young plants to branch and develop a more compact habit, pinch out the growing tips of shoots. Pruning should be light, to maintain bushiness; cut back straggling branches to shape the plants. To wall-train, *see p.162*.

OTHER ORNAMENTAL SHRUBS
BOENNINGHAUSENIA Subshrub that may be cut down by frost. Prune all growth to the base in spring.
BOWKERIA No special pruning needs.
BRACHYSEMA No special pruning needs.
BREYNIA No special pruning needs.

BRUCKENTHALIA Related to *Calluna* and *Erica*, but less vigorous. Pinch back shoots of young plants by about one-third in the first spring to promote denser growth. When established, cut back in late spring, after flowering, as for *Erica carnea* (*see p.191*).

OTHER BRUNFELSIAS
B. AMERICANA Dislikes pruning and should be left to develop naturally; it may form a small tree. Trim after flowering in summer if necessary.
B. LATIFOLIA As for *B. pauciflora*. Naturally more open in habit.

BUDDLEJA

Adaptable, mainly deciduous shrubs, grown for their fragrant flowers and elegant, often arching habit. They are usually grown as free-standing shrubs, but some species and cultivars look attractive grown as standards or trained against walls. Most are hardy. Some buddlejas flower on new wood, others on shoots from older wood, and this determines their pruning requirements: the former may be cut back hard each year, while for the latter a permanent branch framework (for example, fan-trained on a wall) should be developed.

B. ALTERNIFOLIA

Elegant, deciduous shrub with arching, pendent stems, along which, in early summer, clusters of scented, lilac flowers are borne on the previous season's wood.

■ **WHEN TO PRUNE** Midsummer, immediately after flowering.

■ **TRAINING AND PRUNING** Allow the plant to develop naturally, or train it as a standard (*see below and facing page*) or on a wall (*see p.162*). In all cases, the aim is to maintain a balanced shape and renew flowering wood. Cut back the flowered stems to healthy buds or non-flowering sideshoots. Neglected but healthy specimens can be cut back hard.

B. DAVIDII

BUTTERFLY BUSH

Vigorous shrub that produces terminal racemes of flowers on the current season's growth in summer. Unpruned, it tends to become a leggy, tangled mass of live and dead stems, flowering less freely. Hard annual pruning produces the best flowers, on vigorous stems that will grow to 2–2.5m (6–8ft) in height in a single season. It self-seeds prolifically, so it is best, although not essential, to remove spent flowerheads promptly (*see p.153*). This should also result in a second, smaller flush of flowers in late summer.

■ **WHEN TO PRUNE** Early spring, with the onset of new growth, and after any danger of hard frosts.

■ **TRAINING AND PRUNING** In the first spring cut out weak growth and shorten the main stems to start developing a low

Established *Buddleja davidii*, early spring (as growth begins)

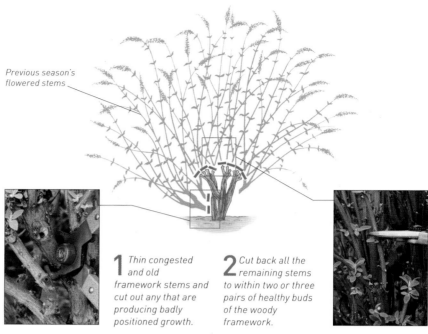

Previous season's flowered stems

1 Thin congested and old framework stems and cut out any that are producing badly positioned growth.

2 Cut back all the remaining stems to within two or three pairs of healthy buds of the woody framework.

framework 15–45cm (6–18in) high (*see also p.157*). For a plant positioned at the back of a border or elsewhere where extra height is needed, the framework may be taller, up to 1.2m (4ft) high. In the spring of subsequent years prune back to this framework, cutting back the previous season's growth to leave only two or three pairs of buds (*see above*). Shorten any new growth from the base by three-quarters or remove entirely if plants are too dense. As plants mature, remove with loppers or a saw any dead or old, unproductive sections of the stubby framework. Deadhead with secateurs as the flowers fade, cutting to a pair of strong

shoots. On windy sites, shorten the top growth by about one-third in autumn. Neglected plants usually respond well to hard pruning.

B. GLOBOSA

Medium to large, semi-evergreen shrub with orange, spherical flower clusters on terminal shoots from the previous season's wood. Shoots often retain their handsome foliage through the winter.

Initial training of *Buddleja alternifolia* as a standard

When purchased, most plants will have been pruned to develop a bushy habit (*left*). Remove up to three-quarters of the top growth (*right*) to leave a single stem, furnished with laterals to strengthen the leader as it grows upwards. Train on as a standard (*see p.165*).

Before pruning

Original leading shoot pruned back by nursery

Bushy growth from the base of the plant

After pruning

Cane assists vertical growth

Replacement shoot trained in as new leader

Single stem clothed in laterals remains

B. globosa is apt to become bare at the base, and is best grown towards the back of the border, with smaller plants in front. Pruning is seldom required; it may be needed to offset its naturally ungainly habit, but should be done selectively, or the next year's flowers will be lost.

■ **WHEN TO PRUNE** Late winter, before fresh growth commences.

■ **TRAINING AND PRUNING** Remove any dead or poorly growing shoots. Wayward stems can be shortened by about one-third (though this entails removing the flowering tip). Large branches that flower only very high up may be cut back into old wood. Although the next season's flowers will be lost, the plant will recover quickly and produce vigorous shoots that will flower the year after that.

B. MADAGASCARIENSIS

Frost-tender, vigorous, scandent, evergreen shrub. In cool climates it is best wall-trained in a very sunny, sheltered site, or grown under glass. Its trailing foliage is silvery on the underside, and panicles of small, yellow, fragrant flowers are borne in winter.

■ **WHEN TO PRUNE** Spring, immediately after flowering.

■ **TRAINING AND PRUNING** If grown as a free-standing plant, *B. madagascariensis* tends to develop into a large, spreading, untidy mound of shoots, and even in warm gardens is most commonly given support by wall training (*see p.162*). From early to mid-spring, cut back shoots that have flowered to a bud or vigorous young shoot.

OTHER BUDDLEJAS
B. AURICULATA Evergreen. In cool climates it benefits from wall training, as for *B. madagascariensis*. Prune free-standing shrubs as for *B. alternifolia*.
B. COLVILEI Prune after flowering, as for *B. alternifolia*, but more lightly.
B. CRISPA As for *B. davidii*; it looks better if a taller framework of stems is developed, rather than being cut down to near ground level. Also lends itself to wall training (*see p.162*).
B. FALLOWIANA As for *B. davidii*. In cool climates it benefits from being grown in the shelter of a sunny wall, or trained informally against it.
B. SALVIIFOLIA As for *B. davidii*.

Established *Buddleja alternifolia* standard, after flowering

1 Remove any old or weakened, unproductive growth, particularly where crowding the centre.

2 Cut back the long flowered stems, to non-flowering, preferably upward- and outward-growing, shoots where possible; otherwise cut to a healthy bud.

Clear trunk raises up trailing, flowering branches

BUXUS *BOX*

Tough, evergreen shrubs or small trees, with neat, small, rounded leaves, that are ideal as formal hedges (*see p.44*) or to use in topiary (*see p.48*). They respond well to clipping and break readily from old wood. All are hardy, though *B. balearica* may be damaged by hard frosts; heavy snow and ice, if allowed to accumulate, may damage large, dense specimens. The pruning of *B. sempervirens* cultivars should be guided by, and cannot alter, their habit of growth, which ranges from dwarf and prostrate to large and upright. *B. balearica* is large, with a more open habit, but may be kept compact by regular pruning.

■ **WHEN TO PRUNE** Mid- to late summer. Renovate in late spring.

■ **TRAINING AND PRUNING** Grown as an informal shrub, box requires little pruning, but cut back overlong growths to within the bush, so that the cut is masked. Keep plants at the desired height by trimming long shoots. Cut hedging plants and topiary specimens hard back while young to encourage bushy growth. Trim mature plants closely. Old or snow-damaged plants will make vigorous new growth if cut back to within 15–30cm (6–12in) of the ground. Remove any branches touching the ground that have rooted.

Buxus sempervirens
If using box for topiary or formal edging, plant young specimens to a depth slightly below the nursery soil mark; this will stimulate growth from the base of the plant.

OTHER ORNAMENTAL SHRUBS
BUPLEURUM Has no special needs, but tolerates pruning and makes a good informal hedge. Trim in late spring. Mature specimens can be cut back hard if they become too dense and twiggy.

C

CAESALPINIA

Shrubs and scandent climbers with attractive foliage and flowers, best wall-trained or grown under glass in cooler climates. Pinch out the main shoot tips of young plants to encourage bushiness. Prune free-standing specimens only to restrict growth after flowering. Prune established wall-trained plants in spring, cutting back the previous year's growth to 5–8cm (2–3in) of the framework.

CALLICARPA

Medium-sized, deciduous shrubs, grown for the clusters of bright violet fruits borne along the stems in autumn and through the winter. They sometimes flower on new as well as on second-year wood. Some are hardy, while others, such as *C. rubella*, need frost-free conditions. The plants are bushy, making plenty of growth from the base. They need regular thinning to prevent congestion, cutting older stems to the base.

C. BODINIERI VAR. GIRALDII

Hardy, bushy shrub with tiny lilac flowers in summer followed by dense clusters of violet fruits.

CALLISTEMON *BOTTLEBRUSH*

Bushy or lax and arching evergreen shrubs bearing distinctive red or yellow "bottlebrush" flowers on new growth. They will grow in open sites only in warm climates; in cool areas they need the protection of a sunny wall (species of arching habit may be loosely tied, but not rigidly trained, to the wall), or may be grown or overwintered under glass.

C. CITRINUS

CRIMSON BOTTLEBRUSH

Evergreen, arching shrub with long, red flowers that are borne at the ends of new shoots in summer.

■ **WHEN TO PRUNE** Summer, immediately after flowering.

■ **TRAINING AND PRUNING** Tip-prune young plants (*see p.152*) to encourage bushy growth. If planting in the shelter of a wall,

CALYCANTHUS

Fully hardy, deciduous, summer-flowering shrubs, with aromatic foliage and brownish-red or purplish flowers that have strap-shaped petals. None requires regular pruning other than to remove unhealthy, weak or wayward shoots. Calycanthus produce new shoots freely from the base. In spring, before growth starts, thin if necessary by cutting out up to one in three old stems at the base. Neglected specimens can be renovated by cutting out all but the youngest stems in spring.

■ **WHEN TO PRUNE** Early spring, after any danger of frost has passed, but while the plant is still dormant.

■ **TRAINING AND PRUNING** Each year, remove up to one in five of the stems completely, cutting them back to the base. Prune back any branches broken by the weight of fruit as soon as seen, either to a strong new shoot on the unbroken part of the stem, or to a shoot at the base of the plant. Callicarpas usually respond to hard pruning. Plants that appear to have been killed by frost may resprout if the dead growth is cut back to ground level in early spring.

> OTHER CALLICARPAS
> C. RUBELLA As for *C. bodinieri*.

no special pruning or training is required; simply tie in long stems at a few strategic points, where necessary, and allow the plant to grow upwards and outwards. Mature plants require little pruning, but to prevent them becoming straggly, older wood can be cut back to young shoots. These should usually be growing upwards or outwards, the aim being to enhance the naturally arching habit. Callistemons will respond well to the removal of some older wood, but such pruning should be staged over two to three years, and not more than one in two of the stems should be cut back in any one year.

> OTHER CALLISTEMONS
> C. 'HARKNESS', C. 'MAUVE MIST',
> C. PHOENICEUS, C. RIGIDUS As for
> *C. citrinus*.
> C. SIEBERI Minimal pruning required.
> C. VIMINALIS Larger, weeping habit,
> needs little pruning. Is also attractive
> tied loosely in against a wall.

***Camellia reticulata* cultivar**
This beautiful single-flowered camellia must be grown under cover in cool climates.

CAMELLIA

Long-lived evergreen shrubs, with often large, rose-like flowers in late winter or early spring. Many are hardy and can be grown in any climate, though the flowers are susceptible to damage by hard frosts; others are best grown under glass in cool climates. They may also be grown as wall shrubs, although sites exposed to morning sun should be avoided, as the sun's warmth early in the day may damage buds or flowers frosted overnight. Most benefit from formative pruning, since young plants often develop leggy shoots; pruning when established can also encourage a denser growth habit. Some camellia cultivars are genetically unstable and may "sport back", producing stems that bear flowers of a different colour. Young reverted growth, which may be useful for propagation, should be removed in spring but large, old branches (on, for example, inherited plants) may be left.

C. JAPONICA

COMMON CAMELLIA

The species itself is seldom grown, but there are many cultivars of very variable habit. Most need little attention.

CARAGANA

Deciduous shrubs with attractive pinnate leaves and usually yellow pea-flowers, borne on short shoots on second-year growth. Prune young plants lightly to encourage a bushy habit. No further pruning is required. *C. arborescens* can be trained up as a standard (*see p.165*); its weeping cultivar 'Pendula' is usually top-grafted onto a clear stem.

Young camellias

Young plants develop a great variety of forms; moderate pruning on planting will help to produce a balanced shape.

Bushy plant will develop compact form

Tall plant with central stem suitable for wall-training

Remove badly-placed dual leader

Shorten vigorous main stem to balance shape

Tip-prune longer shoots to encourage bushiness

Shorten overlong lateral to upward-growing sideshoot

Pinch shoot tips to encourage basal branching

■ **WHEN TO PRUNE** Spring, after flowering, but before growth buds break.

■ **TRAINING AND PRUNING** Prune young plants (*see above*) to shape and to encourage bushy growth, reducing thin, leggy shoots by two or three buds or cutting them out entirely. Established plants need minimal pruning, though the previous season's growth can be cut back to just above the old wood. This pruning encourages a bushy, free-flowering habit and can also be used to restrict size, for example of plants grown under glass. Deadhead after flowering: the flowers persist on the plant and are unsightly.

Camellias can usually be renovated by hard pruning. In early spring, cut large branches to 60cm (2ft) above ground level (or harder, if they are healthy). Spread the work over three years,

cutting back one in three main branches each year. The pruned growth may not show signs of new life until midsummer, but then a mass of shoots normally develops (*see below right*); these should be thinned to develop new framework branches (*see also p.30*).

C. SASANQUA

Shrub with fragrant flowers that needs frost protection (ideally under glass) in cool climates. It may be lax in habit and can be loosely or espalier-trained on a wall.

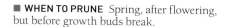

5 | 15

m | ft

■ **WHEN TO PRUNE** Spring, before growth buds break.

Camellia sasanqua

This fast-growing species may have a lax habit of growth, requiring it to be supported. Here it is tied in to a central post, the branches drawn up to display the flowers.

OTHER CAMELLIAS

C. CHRYSANTHA (syn.C. NITIDISSIMA) As for *C. sasanqua*.
C. × HIEMALIS As for *C. japonica*. This hybrid may also be used for hedging (see p.44).
C. LUTCHUENSIS As for *C. sasanqua*.
C. RETICULATA As for *C. japonica*. Prone to legginess, so benefits particularly from formative pruning.
C. × WILLIAMSII As for *C. japonica*. Deadheading is not necessary, since the spent flowers are shed naturally.

■ **TRAINING AND PRUNING** Unless it is intended to sprawl over a bank or low wall, *C. sasanqua* may benefit from the support of either a central stake around which branches can be "maypoled" (*see* Tree Fruits, *p.99*) or a wall (*see p.162*); to produce a formal espalier framework on a wall, *see Magnolia grandiflora, p.74*. Once this is formed, the plant needs minimal attention. Shorten any wayward branches that threaten the balanced shape of a specimen back to a healthy lateral. Remove entirely old branches that no longer flower. If renovation is needed, treat as for *C. japonica*.

Renovation of *Camellia japonica*

Camellias respond well, although slowly, if branches are cut back hard.

All stems have been cut back hard after flowering

By late summer the pruned branches are producing new growth

OTHER ORNAMENTAL SHRUBS

CALCEOLARIA Pinch out young shoot tips of *C. integrifolia* in spring to encourage bushy growth. Established plants may become open and straggly. This species breaks well from older wood if hard pruning is needed to rejuvenate old specimens, although it is usually best to renew such plants.
CALLIANDRA To contain the spreading

habit, cut stems back by up to two-thirds after flowering. Grows well in containers.
CALLUNA Single species of evergreen, bushy shrub (*C. vulgaris*), but with many cultivars, most pruned in the same way as *Erica cinerea* (see p.191). Dwarf cultivars such as 'Foxii Nana' should not need pruning, but any overlong shoots should be cut back to their point of origin as seen.

CALOTHAMNUS No special pruning needs.
CALYTRIX Tip-prune young plants. Lightly prune back flowered shoots after flowering.
CANDOLLEA See Hibbertia, p.198.
CANTUA For *C. buxifolia*, see Dictionary of Climbing Plants, p.267.

CARISSA

Evergreen, medium to large, often dense shrubs, with fragrant flowers in summer; *C. macrocarpa* (syn. *C. grandiflora*) bears edible fruits. They can be grown outdoors only in frost-free gardens, where thorny species are popular as barrier hedging, responding well to close clipping after flowering. *C. macrocarpa* and its cultivars may be grown in pots under glass in cool climates. Cut out weak, twiggy growth in early spring. Wayward shoots on free-standing shrubs may be cut out during the growing season as for *Aucuba* (*see p.175*).

CARPENTERIA

Carpenteria californica is an evergreen shrub with white flowers, borne in summer on the previous year's wood. Though hardy, it benefits from shelter in cool climates. It is an upright, leggy plant, and needs selective hard pruning to remove older wood that has become weakened by repeated flowering.

■ **WHEN TO PRUNE** Spring, immediately after flowering.

■ **TRAINING AND PRUNING** As plants mature, remove branches (no more than one in three) that have become exhausted by flowering, cutting them out at the base. More drastic pruning is possible, but recovery takes a long time, so it is better to replace old plants.

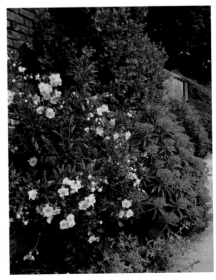

Carpenteria californica
Carpenterias are best grown against a wall in cool climates, but should be tied in loosely, rather than formally wall-trained.

CARYOPTERIS

Deciduous, hardy shrubs, with greyish foliage and blue flowers produced on the current season's growth in late summer and autumn. They are best pruned back annually to a low framework to prevent them from becoming bare at the base and to encourage the production of flowering shoots. In cold winters, most of the previous year's growth usually dies back.

C. × CLANDONENSIS

Upright, bushy shrub with bright blue flowers, produced at the ends of shoots and in leaf axils. The many cultivars are all pruned in the same way.

■ **WHEN TO PRUNE** Mid- to late spring, as the buds are breaking (when dead wood

Pruning *Caryopteris* in spring
Prune back nearly all of the previous year's growth, but do not cut into old wood.

is more obvious), and when severe frosts are no longer expected.

■ **TRAINING AND PRUNING** Develop a low framework (*see also p.157*) by pruning young plants hard in the first spring after planting. In subsequent years shorten all stems by at least three-quarters of the growth made the previous year, cutting to within 2.5cm (1in) of the older wood. Do not cut into the established framework, since plants will very rarely produce new shoots from old wood. To renovate neglected specimens, cut stems back in spring to the lowest active buds that can be seen. Plants are unlikely to survive more drastic pruning.

> **OTHER CARYOPTERIS**
> C. INCANA, C. MONGHOLICA As for *C. × clandonensis*.

Flowering in summer
These vigorous, arching shoots grow and bear terminal flowerheads in a single season.

CASSIA

Deciduous or evergreen, medium-sized shrubs (some now included in *Senna*), grown for their usually yellow pea flowers and handsome foliage. Few withstand frost; they should be grown under glass in cool climates.

C. CORYMBOSA SYN. SENNA CORYMBOSA

A semi-evergreen or evergreen shrub or small tree needing warm, frost-free conditions. Rich yellow flowers are borne in late summer on the current season's growth. In cool climates grow on a sheltered, warm wall or under glass.

■ **WHEN TO PRUNE** Spring, when growth is starting.

■ **TRAINING AND PRUNING** In warm climates keep pruning to the minimum. In cool climates establish a framework of stout growth as for *Caryopteris* (*see above*), then prune back to within two or three buds of this framework annually to encourage flowering shoots. The same applies to wall-trained specimens (*see p.162*); cut back the season's growth to within two or three buds of a permanent framework of branches.

> **OTHER CASSIAS**
> *See Dictionary of Ornamental Trees, p.56.*

CEANOTHUS

Deciduous and evergreen shrubs grown for their dense clusters of mainly blue flowers; they are often referred to as "California lilac". Those that flower on new growth are hardy enough to be grown in the open in cool climates. Evergreens are often wall-trained. The age of wood on which plants flower determines the time of pruning. Prostrate species need minimal pruning.

C. 'AUTUMNAL BLUE'

3 | 10
m | ft

Bushy evergreen with blue flowers, in late spring on the previous year's growth, and in autumn on the current season's shoots. It is best grown against a sunny wall where winters are severe.

■ **WHEN TO PRUNE** Spring.

■ **TRAINING AND PRUNING** Tip-prune young plants (see p.155). When established, lightly cut back the previous season's growth of free-standing specimens. Train plants on walls informally (see p.162), tying in shoots promptly. Prune the previous season's growth by one-third to half, and cut back or remove shoots growing into or out from the wall. Old or neglected free-standing specimens are best replaced. Gradually tie in new shoots to replace old branches on a wall-trained shrub, pruning back sideshoots on the replacement stem by one-third to a half.

C. 'GLOIRE DE VERSAILLES'

Deciduous, with pale blue flowers from mid-summer to early autumn on the current season's growth.

2 | 6
m | ft

■ **WHEN TO PRUNE** Early to mid-spring.

■ **TRAINING AND PRUNING** Shortening the previous season's growth each year (see above right), at first to establish a framework, then pruning back to these framework branches, produces the best flowering display. To renovate, cut all growth back to near ground level.

Training and pruning a deciduous *Ceanothus*

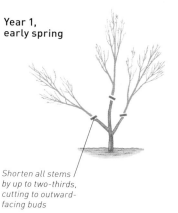

Year 1, early spring

Shorten all stems by up to two-thirds, cutting to outward-facing buds

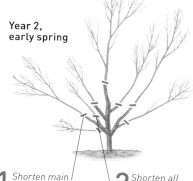

Year 2, early spring

1 Shorten main stems by up to two-thirds of the previous season's growth.

2 Shorten all sideshoots, cutting back to buds 10–25cm (4–10in) from the main framework.

Established plant, early spring

1 Cut back main flowered stems by half and weaker sideshoots to up to one or two buds from main branches.

2 Thin out congested areas by removing weaker growth completely.

3 Remove old, unproductive shoots to prevent crowded growth in the centre of plant.

C. ARBOREUS 'TREWITHEN BLUE'

6 | 20
m | ft

Vigorous evergreen with rich blue flowers in spring and early summer on the previous season's wood.

■ **WHEN TO PRUNE** Midsummer, after flowering.

■ **TRAINING AND PRUNING** Establish as for *C.* 'Autumnal Blue'. Thereafter, cut back longer flowered shoots by one-third to half after flowering. For more bushy growth, trim them again lightly later in summer. To grow as a wall shrub, see p.162. Neglected specimens are difficult to renovate, as growth does not break from older wood.

OTHER CEANOTHUS
C. 'Burkwoodii' As for *C.* 'Autumnal Blue'.
C. 'Concha' As for *C. arboreus* 'Trewithen Blue'.
C. × delileanus cultivars (inc. 'Marie Simon', 'Henri Desfusse', 'Perle Rose') As for *C.* 'Gloire de Versailles'.
C. dentatus and var. floribundus As for *C. arboreus* 'Trewithen Blue'.
C. impressus As for *C. arboreus* 'Trewithen Blue'. Popular for wall training, growing outwards from the wall to give a magnificent cascading effect (pruning back outward-growing stems too rigorously will spoil this); it therefore needs very sturdy support.
C. thyrsiflorus 'Skylark' As for *C. arboreus* 'Trewithen Blue'.

OTHER ORNAMENTAL SHRUBS
Carmichaelia No special pruning needs. Grow against a sunny wall in cool climates.
Cassinia No special pruning needs.
Cassiope As for *Erica carnea* (see p.191).

Castanopsis No special needs, but breaks from old wood if hard pruning is necessary.
Centradenia Pinch out shoots of young plants; trim to shape after flowering.

Cephalanthus No special needs.
Ceratopetalum If necessary to restrict growth, prune *C. gummiferum* in mid- to late summer.

CERATOSTIGMA

Deciduous, semi-evergreen or evergreen shrubs (and some perennials) grown mainly for their striking blue flowers, borne in late summer and autumn in terminal clusters on the current season's shoots. Most should be grown in a sheltered spot as they are not fully hardy in cold climates. In cold winters they will usually die back, sometimes to the ground, depending on the harshness of the winter. Prune in mid-spring: remove any dead wood and shorten all other stems to 2.5–5cm (1–2in) from the ground. In mild climates where plants retain a woody framework, prune as for *Caryopteris* (*see p.182*).

CESTRUM

Deciduous or evergreen shrubs with attractive flowers borne on the current year's growth, and sometimes on sideshoots from the previous season's wood. A few (such as *C. parqui*) are hardy enough to be grown outside in cool climates, in a sheltered site, and others may be grown in pots under glass. Cestrums usually have a lax habit, so when young, tip prune (*see p.155*) long shoots to encourage bushiness. May be wall-trained (*see p.162*). In early spring, thin by removing two- or three-year-old stems at the base. Top-growth of plants outdoors in cool climates is usually killed in winter; cut back hard in early spring and fresh growth will be produced from ground level.

CHAENOMELES FLOWERING QUINCE, JAPONICA

Deciduous, twiggy, hardy shrubs that flower in early spring and produce quince-like fruits in autumn. They may be grown as free-standing shrubs, but often flower better if trained as formal or informal fans against walls and spur-pruned. Pruning in summer helps limit damage by aphids and sooty mould, since any affected young leaves are removed. All chaenomeles are pruned in the same way. *C. speciosa*, which has a naturally dense habit, makes a good informal hedge, and clipping results in the formation of more flowering spurs. Some species are thorny.

Sideshoots left unpruned

Sideshoots pruned to two or three buds

Pruning for flowering
Unpruned *Chaenomeles* stems (*left*) produce few, if any, flowers; spur-pruning stimulates profuse flowering (*right*).

C. × SUPERBA

Deciduous, erect, spreading shrub, with many cultivars. The flowers – red, pink, orange or white – are borne in spring and followed by yellow fruits.

■ **WHEN TO PRUNE** Late spring, and early summer, after flowering.

■ **TRAINING AND PRUNING** Free-standing shrubs require little pruning beyond thinning once mature, but shortening new growth in summer to five or six leaves improves flowering performance. If grown against a wall, select five or six branches and tie in to form the main framework (*see p.162*). In summer prune back breastwood and remove crossing or badly spaced stems. Once established, cut back excess growth in late spring and summer, and form flowering spurs by cutting back all sideshoots to two or three leaves (*see left*). Any late-produced shoots should be pruned in winter to two or three buds. Spur systems will become congested and need reducing, as for apples (*see p.105*). prune hard in spring to renovate. Drastic cutting back is best done over two to three years.

OTHER CHAENOMELES
C. CATHAYENSIS Very vigorous, often of gaunt habit. As for *C. × superba*.
C. JAPONICA, C. SPECIOSA As for *C. × superba*.

CHIMONANTHUS
WINTERSWEET

Chimonanthus praecox is a deciduous or, in warm climates, semi-evergreen shrub, producing sweetly scented flowers in winter once plants are at least five years old. In cold areas the shelter of a warm wall or wall-training is advisable to protect flowers against frost.

■ **WHEN TO PRUNE** Late winter, after flowering.

■ **TRAINING AND PRUNING** Wintersweet is best left unpruned when young, so that mature flowering wood can develop. Once established, little or no pruning is required for a free-standing shrub. If necessary, shoots can be thinned, and older branches can be shortened by 15–30cm (6–12in).

On wall-trained shrubs (*see p.162*) cut back laterals that have flowered to two or three leaves. Cut old, weak or badly placed branches to the ground in winter or early spring. Renovate by cutting back all stems to 60cm (24in) from the base of the plant. The plant is slow to recover when renovated by hard pruning, and flowering will be delayed by several years.

CHOISYA

Dense, evergreen, medium-sized shrubs with aromatic foliage and clusters of strong-smelling white flowers in spring. Choisyas are usually hardy, and though prone to frost damage in

Choisya ternata
Pruning back flowered shoots will encourage a second, smaller flush of flowers.

CISTUS *ROCK ROSE*

Evergreen, small to medium-sized shrubs with flowers in a wide range of colours in midsummer. Pruning is best kept to a minimum except when young.

■ **WHEN TO PRUNE** Spring.

■ **TRAINING AND PRUNING** Prune young plants (*see below*) to encourage bushiness. Established plants need no special attention. Remove dead and frost-damaged wood in early spring. Old, straggly plants do not respond well to being cut back and should be replaced.

Before pruning

After pruning

Young *Cistus × purpureus*
Prune the leader and strong laterals back by two-thirds to produce a more bushy plant.

exposed sites they will usually survive. *C. ternata* (Mexican orange blossom) is very cold-resistant, and though it may show some dieback, will recover. Species that are less frost-resistant are better grown as pot-plants under cover in cold areas. Choisyas are fast-growing, and naturally form well-shaped bushes without pruning. Established plants need little attention, although cutting back flowered stems (*see left*) encourages a second flush of flowers in autumn. In a mild year, these will continue into the winter. Choisyas are apt to become unruly with age and top-heavy if their sideways spread is restricted. They respond well to hard pruning in spring.

■ **WHEN TO PRUNE** Spring, immediately after flowering.

■ **TRAINING AND PRUNING** On established plants, cut back the flowered stems by 25–30cm (10–12in) if a further crop of flowers is desired (*see left*). Any frosted shoots should be cut out entirely. If plants are old, misshapen, or badly frost-damaged, prune them hard.

CLERODENDRUM

Genus that includes climbers as well as tall, bushy, deciduous or evergreen shrubs that have showy flowers. Not all species are hardy.

C. BUNGEI

GLORY FLOWER

Evergreen or deciduous, upright, suckering shrub. It is frost-hardy, with heart-shaped leaves and fragrant, pink flowerheads borne in late summer and early autumn. In cool climates, where it tends to die back in winter anyway, it should be pruned hard to prevent the accumulation of dead wood that may harbour coral spot.

■ **WHEN TO PRUNE** Spring, when the buds begin to break.

■ **TRAINING AND PRUNING** In frost-free areas, cut back annually to a woody framework at a height of 60–90cm (24–36in). In cool climates remove all growth killed or damaged by cold; also cut out the oldest live stems completely.

C. TRICHOTOMUM

Deciduous, fully hardy shrub with heart-shaped leaves and fragrant white flowers followed by blue berries. It is best grown on a short, clear leg so that its suckering tendency can be controlled. Annual pruning reduces the number of flowers and fruit but increases their size.

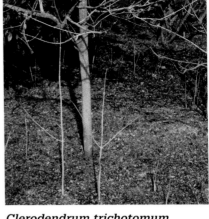

Clerodendrum trichotomum
The suckers that often emerge over a wide area around this species should be removed, or transplanted as new plants.

■ **WHEN TO PRUNE** Early spring, before buds break.

■ **TRAINING AND PRUNING** Train young plants with a single clear stem (*see p.26*), cutting back the leader anywhere between 60 and 180cm (2–6ft). Select five or six laterals to form a branching head. Little further pruning is needed. Injury to the root system can lead to suckers growing round the base. Prevent this by mulching and minimal disturbance of the soil. Remove suckers (*see p.153*) or transplant for propagation.

OTHER CLERODENDRUMS
C. SPECIOSISSIMUM, C. UGANDENSE
Bushy evergreens requiring minimal pruning.
For other species, see Dictionary of Climbing Plants, *p.269.*

OTHER ORNAMENTAL SHRUBS
CERCOCARPUS No special needs.
CHAMAEBATIARIA No special needs.
CHAMELAUCIUM Prune *C. uncinatum* after flowering, if necessary to restrict growth, shortening the flowered stems by half.
CHEIRANTHUS *See* Erysimum *(p.191).*
CHIONANTHUS No special needs.
CHORDOSPARTIUM No special needs, but cut out dead wood in spring.
CHORIZEMA Pinch-prune young plants (*see p.168*). Trim lightly after flowering.
CHRYSOLEPIS No special needs.
× CITROFORTUNELLA As for *Fortunella* (kumquat); *see* Citrus fruits, *p.142.*
CLETHRA Prune those species with a suckering habit as for *Amelanchier stolonifera* (*see p.173*). Other species should be allowed to develop unchecked; remove old branches in favour of younger growth only when weak and unproductive.
CLEYERA No special needs.
CLIANTHUS *See* Dictionary of Climbing Plants, *p.270.*
CODIAEUM Pinch out tips of shoots to encourage bushy growth. Tolerates being cut back if necessary.
COLEONEMA Heather-like. Trim over lightly in summer, after flowering.
COLLETIA Spiny shrubs with no special pruning needs. Will tolerate being cut back hard to rejuvenate.

COLQUHOUNIA

Evergreen or semi-evergreen, medium-sized shrubs with aromatic foliage, and attractive racemes of red, orange or yellow flowers in late summer that are borne on the current season's wood. Though frost hardy, they often die back in severe winters, so in cold areas they should be grown in a sheltered site. The habit is similar to that of *Buddleja davidii*, and in cool climates plants should be pruned in the same way (*see p.178*). They may also be wall-trained (*see p.162*), cutting flowered growth back to a framework. Pinch out young shoot tips in spring if a more bushy habit is desired.

COLUTEA

Hardy, deciduous, small to medium-sized, fast-growing bushy shrubs with pea-like flowers in summer borne on the current season's wood. They may be grown with minimal pruning, their size restricted if necessary by shortening long growths in spring. They may be trained on a short leg as low standards (*see p.165*), or, once plants are growing strongly, regularly cut back hard in the same way as *Cornus alba* (*see right*) to flower into late summer.

CONVOLVULUS

Convolvulus cneorum
is an attractive,
evergreen,
rounded subshrub
with silky, silvery-
grey foliage and,
through spring
and summer, yellow-centred white

flowers that are pink in the bud. It is the only commonly grown shrub in a genus that includes annuals, perennials and climbers. Frost-hardy, it requires a warm, sheltered situation to thrive. It is naturally mound-forming and needs little pruning. It occasionally produces elongated shoots that are best removed. It is also prone to dieback.

■ **WHEN TO PRUNE** Early spring, before buds break.

■ **TRAINING AND PRUNING** Allow plants to develop naturally with minimal pruning. Shorten overlong shoots, cutting them back either to the base or to a healthy sideshoot. Any shoots affected by dieback should be cut out to the base as seen. *C. cneorum* is not long-lived, and its response to hard pruning is poor, so it is better to replace old or neglected plants with new young specimens.

CORNUS *DOGWOOD*

Shrubby species, mainly deciduous and hardy, are grown mainly for the red, yellow or green winter colour of their stems, but in some cases also for their flowers, fruit and variegated foliage.

C. ALBA

RED-BARKED DOGWOOD, TATARIAN DOGWOOD

Vigorous, twiggy,
fully hardy shrub,
with heads of star-
shaped flowers in
late spring, which
are followed by

white or pale blue fruits. Young stems are bright red in winter. Hard annual pruning produces the best winter display of stems, but at the expense of flowering growth.

■ **WHEN TO PRUNE** Early spring, before bud break.

■ **TRAINING AND PRUNING** If growing for flowers and fruit or variegated foliage, allow it to develop unpruned. Restrict spread, if necessary, by cutting out one in four old shoots each year. This will also encourage new growth from the base. Neglected plants can be renovated by cutting out old wood at the centre of the bush. When cultivars are grown for their stem effect (*see also p.164*), allow the bush to grow unpruned in the first year after planting, then cut all stems back to 5cm (2in) from the ground. In subsequent years cut all stems back to two buds of the previous year's growth.

C. MAS

CORNELIAN CHERRY

Large, often multi-
stemmed, fully
hardy, deciduous
shrub that may also
be grown as a small
standard. Yellow

Staggered pruning, *Cornus alba*
Cut back to varying heights to create the effect of a sloping bank rather than a dense mass of regrowth.

Cornus stolonifera
The bright yellow colour of the young stems is striking when they are bare in winter.

flowers appear on the bare wood in winter and early spring. These are followed by rich leaf colour and bright red fruits in autumn.

■ **WHEN TO PRUNE** Early summer.

■ **TRAINING AND PRUNING** Keep pruning to a minimum on multi-stemmed shrubs. Thin if necessary to keep an open shape and display the flowers better. On variegated cultivars, limited renewal pruning will produce vigorous young shoots. Rejuvenate overgrown shrubs by cutting back to two buds of framework branches. To produce a standard, train with a clear stem (*see p.165*) to 60–150cm (2–5ft). Competing leaders often break from low on the stem; shorten these to four to six buds.

OTHER CORNUS
C. CHINENSIS As for *C. mas*.
C. OFFICINALIS As for *C. mas*.
C. SANGUINEA As for *C. alba*.
C. STOLONIFERA As for *C. alba*.
For other species, see Dictionary of Ornamental Trees, p.60.

CORONILLA

Small, deciduous or evergreen shrubs and perennials, grown for their attractive, in some cases blue-green, foliage and usually yellow flowers. They bloom in spring, or in some cases from late autumn to late spring. Some are not fully hardy, but may be grown in cool climates if given a sheltered site. Restrict pruning to the removal of old, unproductive wood at the base of the plant. Prune the hardier species in early spring, but in cool climates delay any pruning required of more tender species, such as *C. valentina* subsp. *glauca*, until they have finished flowering, cutting back any frost-damaged wood to healthy shoots. Coronillas are unlikely to survive drastic renovation.

CORYLOPSIS

Deciduous, fully hardy shrubs of twiggy habit with drooping, catkin-like yellow flowers borne in winter and early spring on the previous season's wood. They naturally form attractive shapes that are easily spoilt by pruning. If it is necessary to restrict size, take old branches out at the base in spring after flowering; trim flowered shoots of wall-trained plants (*see p.162*) at the same time. Otherwise, prune only to remove dead wood.

COTINUS

Deciduous shrubs and small trees grown for their foliage, smoke-like plumes of flowers in summer, and autumn colour. Flowers, produced on two- to three-year-old wood, are abundant only during hot summers, so in cool climates cotinus are more often grown for their foliage, the largest leaves being produced on plants that are cut back to a framework each year. Several cultivars with purple foliage are often hard pruned annually so that they produce much larger leaves than unpruned specimens.

C. COGGYGRIA

SMOKE TREE, VENETIAN SUMACH

Bushy shrub with many cultivars, all with spectacular autumn colour and smoke-like inflorescences. In the species, leaves are light green, often with a pink tinge; cultivars such as 'Royal Purple' have dark purple foliage and pink flower plumes.

■ **WHEN TO PRUNE** Spring, before growth begins.

■ **TRAINING AND PRUNING** To grow as a flowering shrub, keep pruning to a

***Cotinus* in bloom**
Left unpruned, cotinus will flower profusely; cut back annually, they produce larger leaves.

minimum. For a large-leaved effect (*see p.164*), in the first year select three to five strong stems as the main framework, pruning them to 60–90cm (24–36in). In subsequent years cut all the previous year's stems back by about three-quarters, but take care to leave at least two strong buds; harder pruning will produce less vigorous shoots.

> **OTHER COTINUS**
> C. OBOVATUS Needs minimal pruning. Hybrids of *C. obovatus* and *C. coggygria*, such as 'Flame', may be hard pruned.

CORYLUS *HAZEL*

Deciduous, hardy, suckering shrubs. Some have attractive foliage while others, such as *C. avellana* 'Contorta', are grown for their twisted stems; all have yellow catkins in late winter or early spring. They may be grown for nut crops.

C. AVELLANA

COBNUT

A large, multi-stemmed, cropping species, which is also an attractive ornamental shrub, especially in its yellow- or purple-leaved forms, if regularly pruned.

■ **WHEN TO PRUNE** Late winter.

■ **TRAINING AND PRUNING** Allow the multi-stemmed form to develop naturally.

Corylus avellana
Regrowth after hard pruning is strong: Coppicing of hazels (*see p.34*) is traditionally carried out on a seven-year cycle. First year growth is seen on the far right, second-year growth in the centre, and third-year growth on the left.

To maintain vigour and to balance mature and young growth, each year remove some older wood, occasionally cutting a branch right to the base. To renovate, cut back all stems in late winter. To grow as a cropping bush, *see p.149*. To prune 'Contorta', the corkscrew hazel, *see p.28*.

> **OTHER HAZELS**
> C. MAXIMA (filbert) Purple-leaved forms are best regularly pruned hard (*see p.164*) as for *C. avellana*. See also Nuts, *p.148*. For *other species*, *see* Dictionary of Ornamental Trees, *p.60*.

> **OTHER ORNAMENTAL SHRUBS**
> COPROSMA Evergreens with no special needs. Cut out any frost-damaged growth in mid-spring.
>
> CORIARIA Cut out dead wood in spring, to ground level if, in cool climates, plants have died back to a woody base.
>
> COROKIA Cut back frosted growth in spring, into old wood if necessary.
> CORREA No special needs.

COTONEASTER

Evergreen and deciduous shrubs, grown for their flowers and red fruits; those that are deciduous often have attractive autumn foliage. Fully to frost-hardy, they vary widely in habit, some being prostrate while others are large, arching bushes. Though most respond well to pruning, they generally need minimal attention.

C. HORIZONTALIS

FISHBONE COTONEASTER

Deciduous, fully hardy, spreading shrub; branches have a rigid habit and a characteristic herringbone arrangement of branchlets, covered in red berries in winter. In open ground it is a mounding, layered shrub, and grows well over low banks. It also looks very effective trained flat against a wall.

■ **WHEN TO PRUNE** Late winter.

■ **TRAINING AND PRUNING** On free-standing plants, remove only congested and old, sparsely furnished growth, cutting the branches right back to the main stem. To grow against a wall (*see p.162*), choose a young, pliable specimen, and provide initial support for the main branches; stems will then grow flat against the wall. Shorten outward-facing shoots to maintain this form. Fishbone cotoneaster does not respond readily when cut back hard.

C. × WATERERI

Evergreen or semi-evergreen shrub or small tree; its upright stems have arching laterals. Its small, white flowers are followed by clusters of spherical, red fruits.

■ **WHEN TO PRUNE** Winter or mid-spring.

■ **TRAINING AND PRUNING** For a multi-stemmed shrub, develop a framework of four to seven main branches, removing laterals crossing the centre of the shrub to reduce later congestion. Thereafter, keep pruning to a minimum. To renovate a neglected specimen, either cut any unwanted stems back to the main branches, or cut all stems back to the base.

Cotoneaster horizontalis

A species that is particularly effective grown against a wall; the flowers and autumn berries are displayed well by the flat branches with their regular arrangement of branchlets along the main stems. This pattern has gained it the name of fishbone cotoneaster.

OTHER COTONEASTERS

C. DAMMERI Small, prostrate shrub; trim wayward shoots in early spring. Responds to hard pruning if necessary.
C. DIVARICATUS Keep pruning to a minimum. Good for informal hedging.
C. FRANCHETII Keep pruning to a minimum.
C. FRIGIDUS As for *C.* × *watereri*.
C. FRIGIDUS 'CORNUBIA' As for *C.* × *watereri*.
C. 'HYBRIDUS PENDULUS' Minimal pruning. Maintain top-grafted standards as for any weeping standard (*see p.26*).
C. LACTEUS Keep pruning to a minimum. Informal hedges may be lightly trimmed.
C. MICROPHYLLUS As for *C. dammeri*.
C. SALICIFOLIUS As for *C.* × *watereri*.
C. SIMONSII Good for hedging (*see p.44*); can be clipped to a semi-formal outline without losing berries. Otherwise, keep pruning to a minimum.
C. STERNIANUS, C. WARDII Keep pruning to a minimum.

CYTISUS *BROOM*

Mainly deciduous shrubs, with yellow flowers in spring or summer. They are fast-growing, though often short-lived, plants that thrive in hot, dry conditions.

C. BATTANDIERI

MOROCCAN BROOM, PINEAPPLE BROOM

Semi-evergreen, frost-hardy shrub, flowering on the current season's shoots from early to midsummer. It freely produces growth from the base. Needs a warm, sheltered site and may be wall-trained.

■ **WHEN TO PRUNE** Summer, after flowering.

■ **TRAINING AND PRUNING** Free-standing specimens require little pruning, but old wood can be cut out. On wall-trained plants (*see p.162*), occasionally remove

an old framework branch and train in young replacement growth.

C. SCOPARIUS

Arching shrub, flowering in late spring on the previous year's wood. Although short-lived, annual pruning prevents the seed production that weakens it.

■ **WHEN TO PRUNE** Early or midsummer, immediately after flowering.

■ **TRAINING AND PRUNING** Pinch out the tips of young shoots for a bushy habit. When established, cut back flowered stems by about two-thirds of the previous season's growth, to a bud or shoot below the spent flowers. It does not break from mature wood; old specimens are best replaced.

OTHER CYTISUS

C. BEANII, C. × KEWENSIS No pruning required, but tolerate light shaping.
C. NIGRICANS Cut back all flowered shoots by about two-thirds in spring.
C. × PRAECOX As for *C. scoparius*.

Cytisus scoparius

Regular pruning prevents brooms from becoming too leggy.

After pruning

D

DAPHNE

Fully to frost-hardy, evergreen, semi-evergreen or deciduous shrubs, grown for their fragrant flowers in early spring. Most are best left unpruned: they are very susceptible to dieback, which pruning can encourage. *D. odora* tolerates light trimming to maintain a compact habit, as does *D. cneorum*. *D. mezereum* may withstand the removal of more wayward shoots. As a general rule it is better to layer a wayward shoot of a prostrate daphne than to remove it. In all cases, however, dieback must be removed as soon as it is seen. Remove the entire stem or branch, cutting back to its point of origin, and treat the plant with a fungicide. A few species, such as *D. jezoensis*, are summer-deciduous; their leaf-fall should not be mistaken for dieback.

DECAISNEA

Decaisnea fargesii is a deciduous, summer-flowering, upright shrub with racemes of greenish-white flowers and sausage-shaped fruits. It is fully hardy, but needs a sheltered site in areas where winters are very severe. Young plants require no pruning. Cut back any old, weak stems on established plants in spring, either to a healthy bud or, if none is available, to the ground. No other pruning is required. Fresh growth that is damaged by a late frost should be cut back in early summer to strong shoots further down the stems.

DENDROMECON

Frost-hardy to half-hardy evergreens with lax, erect to spreading branches, and grey-green foliage. fragrant, poppy-like, yellow flowers are borne on laterals from the main stems throughout the summer. *D. rigida*, the tree or bush poppy, is half-hardy, and may only be grown in cool climates if given a warm, sheltered site. Its arching habit makes it suitable for training formally or informally against a wall.

■ **WHEN TO PRUNE** Early spring, with the onset of fresh growth; prune wall-trained plants in summer after flowering.

■ **TRAINING AND PRUNING** After planting, pinch back young shoots to encourage a bushy habit. Once the plant is established, prune only to remove winter-damaged shoots or to shorten weak or bare shoots, cutting them back to a strong, outward-facing sideshoot. Prune wall-trained specimens after flowering, tying young shoots into the framework. Dendromecons may be cut to ground level to rejuvenate them.

DESMODIUM

Small, deciduous shrubs (and some perennials), grown for their foliage and racemes of lilac or deep pink flowers, which are borne on the current season's shoots. In cool climates their top growth is often cut back to ground level in winter by hard frosts, but plants will generally recover if they are grown in a sheltered site, preferably against a warm wall. In spring, prune all growth back hard close to ground level, as for *Indigofera heterantha* (see p.202). Neglected specimens will also generally respond to such treatment.

DEUTZIA

Medium-sized, deciduous shrubs bearing white or pink flowers in summer on new shoots from the previous year's growth. Like forsythias, they make new growth from the base, developing sturdy stems that support twiggy growth. Prune to encourage a bushy habit and to keep the plants well furnished with productive wood. Pruning should also be carried out to remove any damage by late spring frosts to species such as *D. gracilis* and *D.× lemoinei*. Branches whose buds open as small, shrivelled flowers due to the effects of frost will not recover satisfactorily, and should be pruned out.

D. SCABRA

Deciduous, upright shrub with white flowers in summer. The bark becomes attractively shaggy with age.

■ **WHEN TO PRUNE** After flowering.

■ **TRAINING AND PRUNING** Tip-prune on planting (see p.155). In subsequent years prune to young shoots below the flowered wood. As plants mature, cut out older branches to ground level, or to strong low shoots. To renovate, cut old main stems to the base and shorten others to well-placed sideshoots. Plants take a year or two to flower well again.

Deutzia scabra
As plants mature, remove some older stems completely to promote younger growth.

OTHER DEUTZIAS

D. crenata, D. gracilis, D. × hybrida, D. x lemoinei, D. pulchra, D. purpurascens As for *D. scabra*. D. monbeigii, D. setchuenensis Less vigorous and more compact, needing more moderate pruning. Cut back flowered sideshoots only to one or two buds after flowering. Can be wall-trained (see p.162).

OTHER ORNAMENTAL SHRUBS

Crinodendron No special needs.
Crossandra No special needs. Shorten flowered stems by half in late winter to promote new flowering growth.
Crotalaria Cut to the base in spring.
Crowea Prune lightly after flowering.
Cuphea Pinch-prune young plants to encourage bushiness, then clip over each spring to remove flowered shoots.
Cydonia See Quince, p.121.
Cyrilla No special needs.
Daboecia Trim lightly in spring to remove spent flowers.
Dais Prune lightly in autumn to shape.
Dampiera Prune lightly after flowering.
Danae Prune plants only once established, as for *Kerria* (see p. 202).
Daphniphyllum Pinch out the main shoot tips of young plants to encourage low branching. Can be cut back hard.
Darwinia Tip-prune after flowering to maintain a compact shape.
Datura See Brugmansia, p.177.
Dermatobotrys No special pruning required.
Desfontainea Do not prune.
Dichotomanthes As for *Cotoneaster* (see facing page).

DIERVILLA

Hardy, deciduous, suckering shrubs, similar to *Weigela*, with small, yellow flowers on the current season's growth in summer. They are best pruned hard each year, cutting stems back to a pair of buds about 30cm (12in) from the base in early spring, to stimulate the growth of vigorous young stems with attractive bronzed foliage. Neglected or overgrown specimens often respond well when pruned back hard, but old plants are better dug up and divided, and young, vigorous portions replanted.

DIPELTA

Large, hardy, deciduous shrubs, grown for their showy flowers in early summer and the peeling bark on mature plants. The natural habit is upright to arching, and strong, new shoots are often produced from the base. Prune after flowering, cutting one in five stems down to the base, selecting first the oldest and any with signs of dieback.

DODONAEA

Small to medium-sized evergreen shrubs, grown chiefly for their foliage. They may be grown outdoors only in warm climates, but make good pot-plants under glass. Pinch out the growing tips of young plants (*see p.155*) to encourage bushy growth well furnished with young leaves. Established plants may be pruned to shape in late summer and spring. Dodonaeas are good hedging plants for warm climates, tolerating windy situations (*see p.44*).

DURANTA

Evergreen shrubs with arching branches, sometimes spiny. They bear sprays of lilac, lilac-blue or white flowers from spring to autumn, and poisonous yellow berries. They are frost-tender, though *D. erecta* (syn. *D. repens*) tolerates light frost. Usually grown as open, multi-stemmed bushes, they are excellent informal hedging plants (*see p.44*). They may be trained as standards.

■ **WHEN TO PRUNE** Spring.

■ **TRAINING AND PRUNING** Let young plants develop unpruned, unless training as a standard (*see p.165*). Once established, cut out whole branches if necessary to restrict size. Do not shorten stems; this results in bushy growth below the cut and spoils the habit. Remove any shoots on the clear trunks of standards.

E – F

EDGEWORTHIA

Small, deciduous shrubs that are frost-hardy, and best given the protection of a warm wall in cool climates, since the fragrant, white or yellow flowers are susceptible to frost damage. The papery bark is attractive. The flowerheads form in autumn and the flowers open during late winter and spring. The stems, freely produced from the base, are so thin and supple that they can be tied in knots. Little pruning is needed. As plants mature, cut any old and unproductive stems out to the base after flowering.

ELAEAGNUS

Large, fully hardy, very vigorous, evergreen and deciduous shrubs, some with highly scented flowers. They make fine specimen plants, and are suitable for hedges or barrier plantings.

E. ANGUSTIFOLIA

OLEASTER

Large, spreading, deciduous shrub or small tree with silvery leaves. It bears fragrant flowers in early summer, which are followed by amber fruit in autumn.

7 | 22
m | ft

■ **WHEN TO PRUNE** Midsummer, after flowering.

■ **TRAINING AND PRUNING** Allow to develop naturally as a multi-stemmed bush, or train as a standard (*see p.165*) with a clear stem to a height of 1.2–1.5m (4–5ft). Tolerates hard pruning, so the head of the plant can be maintained in a compact and regular shape.

***Elaeagnus pungens* 'Maculata'**
Remove any shoots with plain green leaves on this variegated cultivar.

ELSHOLTZIA

Small, semi-evergreen or deciduous shrubs and subshrubs, often with aromatic foliage, grown for their two-lipped, tubular flowers, borne on slender panicles or racemes and usually produced in autumn on the current season's growth. In warm climates, in early spring cut out one or two old stems at the base, and shorten others to strong buds about 30cm (12in) from ground level. In cool climates they are best given a sheltered position. In severe winters the top growth is usually killed, and plants should be pruned annually in spring to a low framework of woody growth, as for *Perovskia* (*see p.209*).

***Elaeagnus
× ebbingei***
The young ever-green leaves have a natural silvery bloom that can be mistaken for disease; they should not be removed.

E. × EBBINGEI

Evergreen, fully hardy shrub with silver, scaly leaves and scented flowers in autumn. It does not require annual pruning, but pruning can be used to maintain plants as an informal hedge (*see p.44*). They tolerate coastal locations.

3 | 10
m | ft

■ **WHEN TO PRUNE** Late summer.

■ **TRAINING AND PRUNING** Free-standing specimens require only minimal pruning. To keep hedges in check, cut long shoots back to a bud with secateurs. Renovate by hard pruning back into old wood.

OTHER ELAEAGNUS

E. **COMMUTATA** Slow-growing, suckering habit; prune only to remove unwanted growth and excess suckers.
E. **GLABRA** As for *E. × ebbingei*; long, wayward shoots are frequently produced, especially by young plants.
E. **MACROPHYLLA** As for *E. × ebbingei*.
E. **PUNGENS** 'MACULATA' As for *E. × ebbingei*, additionally removing any reverted shoots (*see left*).
E. **UMBELLATA** As for *E. angustifolia*.

ERICA *HEATHER*

Large group of evergreens, ranging in habit from dwarf plants suitable as ground cover to large, tree-like plants. Most (but not all) are fully hardy. Flowering times occur throughout the year. Most will not break readily from old wood, so only the previous year's growth is usually pruned. Taller species ("tree heaths") may need harder pruning to encourage bushiness.

E. ARBOREA

TREE HEATH

Evergreen, frost-hardy, upright shrub that may become tree-like. Formative pruning establishes a good shape; thereafter only minimal pruning is required, except in cold areas where larger specimens are prone to damage by heavy falls of snow; regular pruning creates bushier, more resilient plants. Damaged or overgrown plants respond well to renovation.

4 | 12

m | ft

■ **WHEN TO PRUNE** Early spring, until established; thereafter, in late spring or early summer, after flowering.

Erica arborea
Unlike most heathers, this species responds very well to hard pruning into old wood.

■ **TRAINING AND PRUNING** In the first two or three years, cut back stems by up to two-thirds to promote bushy growth. In later years, pruning is largely unnecessary. Branches may be removed to restrict size, but there will probably be dense, bushy regrowth. In areas that are prone to heavy snow, cut back flowered shoots by about one-third, pruning to emerging shoots, to keep plants compact. Tree heaths will produce new growth if cut back into old wood in later years (*see below left*). It is best to stage renovation over two or three years (*see p.160*).

E. CARNEA

ALPINE HEATH, WINTER HEATH

Low-growing, evergreen, hardy shrub with bell-like flowers in colours that range from white through pink to red-purple. The flowers are borne in late winter and spring. Several have foliage that colours attractively in winter; some growers prefer to clip the flower buds off these plants in mid- to late winter, as the flower colours clash with the foliage. Annual pruning keeps plants compact, rounded in habit and free-flowering. They will not break readily from old wood, so only the previous year's growth is shortened.

0.6 | 2

m | ft

■ **WHEN TO PRUNE** Spring, as the last flowers fade and new growth appears.

■ **TRAINING AND PRUNING** Cut stems back to just below the old flower spikes, removing most, but not all, of the previous season's growth. Individual plants look better pruned selectively with secateurs, although for large heather beds shearing is much more practical; however, prunings should be cleared away. Old plants that have become straggly are best replaced.

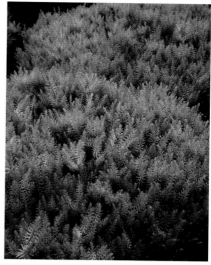

Erica carnea 'Westwood Yellow'
The golden-yellow foliage of this winter heath is attractive all year, with deep pink flowers in the dull days of late winter.

OTHER ERICAS
E. AUSTRALIS As for *E. arborea*, but renovation is likely to be successful only in mild climates.
E. CILIARIS As for *E. cinerea*.
E. CINEREA Prune or trim lightly in early spring, cutting back where possible to strong shoots below the flower cluster.
E. × DARLEYENSIS As for *E. carnea*.
E. ERIGENA Remove frost-damaged stems in spring, cutting back to new growth. Cut back flowered stems by one-third, to new shoots, after flowering. Should respond to hard pruning provided that some basal growth is retained.
E. LUSITANICA Minimal pruning, in spring if necessary, as for *E. australis*.
E. MACKAIANA As for *E. cinerea*.
E. SCOPARIA Minimal pruning only.
E. TERMINALIS As for *E. arborea*.
E. TETRALIX As for *E. cinerea*.
E. VAGANS As for *E. cinerea*.
E. × VEITCHII As for *E. australis*.

OTHER ORNAMENTAL SHRUBS
DILLWYNIA Trim lightly in spring after flowering.
DIOSMA As for *Agathosma* (*see p.173*).
DIPTERONIA No special needs. Remove any unwanted growth in spring.
DISANTHUS No special pruning needs.
DISCARIA No special needs. Remove any unwanted growth in spring.
DISTYLIUM As for *Hamamelis* (*see p.196*).
DORYCNIUM D. *hirsutum* (syn. *Lotus hirsutus*) is a subshrub; cut back dead and cold-damaged top growth in spring.
DRIMYS (syn. TASMANNIA) Remove

any unwanted growth in spring.
DRYANDRA As for *Banksia* (*see p.175*). Do not cut into old wood.
ECHIUM After flowering, remove spent flower spikes.
ELLIOTTIA No special pruning needs.
EMBOTHRIUM See Dictionary of Ornamental Trees, *p.63*.
EMPETRUM As for *Erica carnea* (*see above*).
ENKIANTHUS No special pruning needs. Responds well when cut hard back, as for *Rhododendron* (*see p.214*).
EPACRIS As for *Erica carnea* (*see above*).

ERANTHEMUM No special pruning needs.
EREMOPHILA No special pruning needs.
ERINACEA Minimal pruning only.
ERIOBOTRYA See Loquat, *p.145*.
ERIOCEPHALUS No special pruning needs.
ERIOGONUM No special pruning needs.
ERIOSTEMON May be clipped to shape.
ERYSIMUM Pinch out shoots of E. 'BOWLES MAUVE' (syn. *Cheiranthus* 'BOWLES MAUVE') to encourage bushy growth when young, then trim each year after flowering, cutting flowered shoots back to non-flowered sideshoots.

ESCALLONIA

Evergreen (except *E. virgata*), medium-sized to large shrubs with an arching habit, and white, pink or red flowers, borne mainly on year-old wood in summer and autumn. In cool climates they may suffer frost damage, but generally recover. Many are suitable as hedges, both formal and informal, although formal trimming reduces the floral display. A few can be trained successfully against walls.

E. 'LANGLEYENSIS'

Graceful, arching hybrid that is attractive as a free-standing specimen, though can also be trained against a sunny wall. Bears profuse, deep-pink flowers in summer.

■ **WHEN TO PRUNE** Summer, after flowering. Renovate in mid- to late spring.

■ **TRAINING AND PRUNING** Little formative pruning is required. If training against a wall (*see p.162*), tie in enough stems to form a framework of main branches, removing others. Each year cut back flowered shoots of wall-trained specimens to young sideshoots. Free-standing plants require less rigorous pruning, but cutting out a proportion of flowered wood keeps plants within bounds. Neglected plants usually produce vigorous new growth if pruned hard.

E. RUBRA

Medium-sized summer-flowering shrub. Cultivars such as 'Crimson Spire' are excellent for hedging.

■ **WHEN TO PRUNE** After flowering; if flowering finishes very late, prune in the next spring. Renovate in spring.

■ **TRAINING AND PRUNING** Little or no pruning is required, although plants will tolerate being cut back hard. To maintain an informal outline for hedges (*see p.45*), cut back selected stems to just above vigorous sideshoots.

***Escallonia* 'Langleyensis'**
Remove growth to well within the plant's outline; shortening spoils the arching habit.

OTHER ESCALLONIAS
E. ALPINA, E. BIFIDA, E. ILLINATA, E. 'IVEYI', E. RUBRA VAR. MACRANTHA As for *E. rubra*.
E. VIRGATA Keep pruning to a minimum. Other hybrids, such as 'Apple Blossom' and 'Donard Beauty', are treated as for *E.* 'Langleyensis', but most are too stiff in habit to be trained against walls.

EUONYMUS

Evergreen and deciduous shrubs. The evergreens, some of which are suitable as hedging in coastal areas, are grown for their foliage, while deciduous euonymus are popular for their autumn colour and fruits. Most are fully hardy, although some may be damaged by severe frosts. Training and pruning varies according to the species and whether plants are grown as free-standing specimens or as a hedge. Some cultivars of *E. fortunei* are effective ground cover and may climb against a support, while others are useful as wall shrubs. Remove plain green-leaved shoots that appear on variegated plants of any species, cutting them right back to their point of origin as soon as seen.

The evergreen species are the most popular as hedges; these should be trimmed with secateurs rather than shears (*see p.45*) for a less formal, more attractive outline, and to avoid cutting through leaves, which will turn brown and become unsightly.

To renovate, cut back neglected plants hard to 30–60cm (12–24in) above ground level; response is generally good.

E. EUROPAEUS

SPINDLE TREE

Shrub or small tree with fine leaf colour in autumn and conspicuous pink capsules that hold orange seeds.

■ **WHEN TO PRUNE** Late winter or early spring.

■ **TRAINING AND PRUNING** Minimal formative pruning is necessary. Prune established plants only to thin congested growth, cutting out older stems completely to the base to open up the centre of the bush.

E. JAPONICUS

Bushy, dense evergreen. Although hardy, its soft, young growth is sometimes damaged by frost. It may be wall-trained.

■ **WHEN TO PRUNE** Mid- to late spring.

■ **TRAINING AND PRUNING** Little formative pruning is required, but tip-prune hedging plants to encourage bushy growth. Use secateurs to cut back whole branches of hedges rather than trimming (*see p.45*). Wall-trained plants require only informal tying in. If necessary, cut out old wood and train in new growth.

OTHER EUONYMUS
E. ALATUS As for *E. europaeus*.
E. FORTUNEI Trim over for denser ground cover, or wall-train (*see p.162*) to exploit its creeping, climbing tendency.
E. HAMILTONIANUS As for *E. europaeus*.
E. MYRIANTHUS As for *E. japonica*.
E. NANUS, E. ORESBIUS Minimal pruning required.
E. PHELLOMANUS As for *E. europaeus*.
E. PLANIPES As for *E. europaeus*.

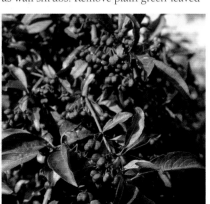

Euonymus europaeus
This reliable species needs pruning only to prevent congestion in the centre of the plant.

EUPHORBIA *MILKWEED, SPURGE*

A wide-ranging genus that includes perennials, annuals and succulents as well as a number of shrubs, most grown for their foliage and floral bracts. Some are hardy, others need winter protection in cool climates. Pruning needs vary according to the species, but should always be carried out with care and wearing gloves, since euphorbia stems exude an irritant, milky latex when cut.

E. CHARACIAS SUBSP. CHARACIAS

MEDITERRANEAN SPURGE

1.5 | 5

m | ft

Evergreen, frost-hardy subshrub, with large panicles of greenish-yellow bracts in spring and early summer. Stems are biennial, developing in one year and flowering the next. The flowers are terminal, so stems should not be shortened. Once a stem has flowered it will not flower again; remove it to accelerate the natural renewal cycle.

■ **WHEN TO PRUNE** Midsummer, after flowering.

Euphorbia characias subsp. characias
Prune after flowering to strong shoots low down.

■ **TRAINING AND PRUNING** Prune back flowered stems to a strong shoot or bud low down, or to the base of the plant. Strong, developing growth made during the current season that has yet to flower should be left unpruned. Although drastic pruning is rarely necessary, plants will usually regenerate vigorously if all stems are cut back to the base in late winter or early spring. The next season's flowers will be lost, but the plant should flower again in the following season.

E. PULCHERRIMA

CHRISTMAS STAR, POINSETTIA

3 | 10

m | ft

Deciduous or evergreen shrub with showy bracts in red, pink or white. It will grow to a substantial size in the tropics, but is widely grown as a houseplant in cool climates, where it is much less vigorous.

■ **WHEN TO PRUNE** Spring, after flowering.

■ **TRAINING AND PRUNING** Whether grown outdoors or as houseplants, cut back hard, removing faded flowered stems to encourage vigorous new growth.

OTHER EUPHORBIAS
E. CAPUT-MEDUSAE Needs no pruning.
E. DENDROIDES Dormant in summer. Minimal pruning needed.
E. INGENS Minimal pruning.
E. MELLIFERA In cool climates, pruning is best kept to a minimum.
E. MILII In warm climates, needs minimal pruning. If grown as an informal hedge, tip-prune all main stems and laterals to encourage branching growth.
E. MYRSINITES As for *E. characias*.

EXOCHORDA

Hardy, deciduous, medium-sized shrubs with a graceful, arching growth habit and racemes of showy, white flowers borne in late spring and early summer on the previous year's wood. Little formative pruning is necessary. Plants may produce numerous basal shoots. Prune established plants annually in late spring, after flowering, to remove weak growth or reduce overcrowding. Cut out to the base of the plant up to one in three old stems and any new shoots that are not required as replacements. Surplus stems can also be cut out in winter. Renovate by cutting out all old stems in spring.

× FATSHEDERA

Evergreen, medium-sized, sprawling shrub, grown for its large, attractive leaves. Though hardy, it benefits from shelter in cool climates. A hybrid of *Fatsia* and *Hedera*, it has characteristics of both a shrub and a climbing plant. If it is to be grown as a free-standing shrub, it needs staking when young; it makes a good standard. However, it is more commonly grown as a wall shrub (*see p.162*), though, unlike *Hedera*, it does not cling, and will need tying in to supports. It looks very attractive trained against a pillar. Its spreading habit also makes it a useful ground-cover shrub. In late summer cut back upright shoots to well within the plant's outline. Fatshederas may also be grown as houseplants, trained on canes as for *Hedera helix* cultivars.

FATSIA

The only species is *F. japonica*, the false castor oil plant, a medium-sized, spreading, architectural, evergreen shrub

6 | 20

m | ft

with large palm-like leaves and clusters of white flowers in autumn, naturally forming a rounded, billowing shape. It tolerates shady situations (or full sun in maritime gardens), but is best given a sheltered position in cold regions. It may be trained against a wall; otherwise pruning is required only to restrict the spread of the plant. Fatsia is also a popular houseplant.

■ **WHEN TO PRUNE** Mid-spring.

■ **TRAINING AND PRUNING** Formative pruning is not generally necessary, and established bushes usually need little attention. It is best to remove any gaunt or unwanted branches completely: shortening them spoils the plant's naturally graceful habit, and fresh growth will break freely from the base. If trained as a wall shrub (*see p.162*), cut stems growing too far outwards back to the main branch. Renovate by cutting out old stems completely and retaining only well-placed young growth.

OTHER ORNAMENTAL SHRUBS
EUGENIA Evergreen; minimal pruning.
EUPATORIUM (syn. AGERATINA BARTLETTINA) In cool climates cut back to the base in spring; otherwise, needs minimal pruning.
EURYOPS Pinch-prune young plants. When established, prune lightly after flowering.
FEIJOA See *Acca, p.173*.

FELICIA Pinch-prune to encourage a bushy, rounded habit. Pinch-pruning may also be used to form decorative shapes such as standards (*see pp.165–171*).
FICUS See Dictionary of Ornamental Trees, *p.66*, and Dictionary of Climbing Plants, *p.271*.
FONTANESIA As for *Ligustrum* (*see p.204*).

FORSYTHIA

Deciduous, medium-sized shrubs grown for their bright yellow flowers. These are borne in early spring, most profusely on mature, but not ageing, wood. Bushy forsythias, such as F. × intermedia 'Spectabilis', make effective informal flowering hedges. Others of lax, open habit, such as F. suspensa, are suitable for wall training. In large gardens F. suspensa may also be grown in closely-spaced groups, the stems of the several plants giving each other support.

Forsythias are very hardy and adaptable, but if not pruned regularly they tend to develop into ungainly bushes with long, vigorous shoots at the top, a congested twiggy centre and a bare base. Their flowering performance also deteriorates.

Pruning flowered shoots

On established plants, cut back some of the older flowered stems to vigorous, upward- and outward-growing shoots.

■ **WHEN TO PRUNE** Mid-spring, after flowering. Renovate in winter or early spring.

■ **TRAINING AND PRUNING** Allow young plants to develop with minimal pruning for the first three years after planting. Thereafter, annually thin out crowded shoots from the centre of the shrub, cutting back a proportion of the oldest flowered wood to vigorous shoots (*see left*). In addition, remove one or two old main stems at the base. To wall-train (*see p.162*), develop a framework, then cut the flowered shoots back to one or two buds of these branches. Occasionally train in young stems to replace older framework branches. Old and neglected plants can be renovated by hard pruning, staged over two years (*see p.160*).

FREMONTODENDRON

Large evergreens with spectacular, yellow flowers from summer to autumn on the current season's shoots. They need a sunny position, against a wall in cool climates. The stems and leaves are covered with irritant hairs.

7 | 22
m | ft

■ **WHEN TO PRUNE** After the first flush of flowers in midsummer.

■ **TRAINING AND PRUNING** Grow free-standing shrubs with a central leader, supported by a stake. Established plants need only minimal pruning. To wall-train (*see p.162*), tie in main stems to form a framework. Subsequently, only outward-growing shoots need to be shortened, cutting to sideshoots that grow parallel to the wall. Plants tend to be short-lived and dislike hard pruning.

Fremontodendron **'California Glory'**
Prune back flowered growth where strong shoots exist to replace it.

FUCHSIA

Usually small, deciduous or evergreen shrubs grown for their showy flowers, produced from summer to autumn on the current season's growth. Most are arching or pendulous in habit. They thrive in most soils and situations; some species and many hybrids are tender in cool climates, but are suitable for growing in pots under glass. Fuchsias are versatile plants: some are attractive border plants, while others may be used for an informal, flowering hedge; some may be wall-trained, and others pinch-pruned into decorative shapes.

F. MAGELLANICA

LADY'S EARDROPS

Deciduous, upright shrub with red and purple flowers followed by black fruits. As a specimen plant it is usually cut back hard annually, but it also makes an attractive, informal, flowering hedge.

2 | 6
m | ft

■ **WHEN TO PRUNE** Early spring, once growth commences. In cold, exposed sites bushes can be trimmed (shortening stems by one-third) in autumn to reduce the risk of wind damage.

■ **TRAINING AND PRUNING** Pinch out the tips of young plants to encourage bushy growth. The following spring, and in subsequent years, if top-growth has been killed by frost, cut old stems back to bare wood, being careful not to damage breaking buds at the base. Alternatively, if branches have survived the winter, cut back laterals to the lowest bud.

Fuchsia hybrid trained as a standard

Remove dead growth in spring as new shoots begin to break from the main stem.

On hedges, prune back laterals to healthy buds lower down. Straggly or gappy hedging plants may be rejuvenated by cutting right back in spring (*see p.47*). If an entire hedge needs renovating, stagger the pruning by cutting back every other plant one year, the remainder the next.

FUCHSIA HYBRIDS

The many named fuchsia hybrids vary in their hardiness. When grown in the open garden, they are treated as for F. magellanica. Others that are more tender are usually grown under glass. Many are densely bushy, and can be made more

0.6 | 2
m | ft

***Forsythia* 'Mini Gold'**
Many cultivars are selected for their profuse flowers, borne on bare branches.

so by pinch pruning, while some with lax stems, such as 'Golden Marinka' and 'Swingtime', are well suited to growing in hanging baskets and other containers. Vigorous growers, such as 'Tennessee Waltz', can be trained as standards or fans using pinch-pruning techniques (*see pp.168–171*).

■ **WHEN TO PRUNE** Pinch-prune throughout the growing season.

■ **TRAINING AND PRUNING** Trailing plants need little attention except to pinch out wayward growth. For a bush, regularly pinching out the tips of shoots (*see p.168*) enhances the development of a dense, well-balanced plant. To train as a standard, *see p.169*. Bush and hanging-basket fuchsias are often discarded after flowering, having yielded material for cuttings. Fans and standards are usually kept for several years. In cool climates they must be brought under cover for the winter. Trim the plants over to remove the flowered shoots, but do not prune again until growth begins in spring.

OTHER FUCHSIAS
F. ARBORESCENS Large, frost-tender evergreen; as for *F. magellanica*. Little pruning is necessary, but it will make vigorous regrowth if cut back.
F. BOLIVIANA Minimal pruning. Do not pinch out the tips of shoots.
F. EXCORTICA Large shrub or small tree requiring minimal pruning. Can be trained against a wall (*see p.162*), displaying its attractive bark.
F. FULGENS As for *F. magellanica*.

G

GARRYA

Evergreen, hardy, medium-sized to large shrubs with leathery leaves and attractive catkins (showier on male plants) in winter and spring. They can be grown as free-standing specimens or as informal hedges or windbreaks, or trained informally against a wall of any aspect (though frost may affect catkins).

G. ELLIPTICA

SILK-TASSEL BUSH

Bushy, dense shrub with grey-green catkins. The cultivar 'James Roof' has the longest catkins.

■ **WHEN TO PRUNE** Early spring, as the catkins fade, and before growth starts.

■ **TRAINING AND PRUNING** Allow free-standing shrubs to develop unpruned. To wall-train (*see p.162*), prune on planting to one or two framework stems, cutting back laterals growing away from the wall. Once established, cut back badly placed shoots. Renovate overgrown plants by cutting back to framework branches over three or four years (*see p.160*). Regrowth is vigorous.

GENISTA *BROOM*

Deciduous shrubs grown for their pea-like flowers, borne in spring or summer on second-year wood. Most are hardy, though some need a sheltered site, and all need full sun. Plant as young as possible and trim after flowering to keep plants bushy and compact. *G. aetnensis* is best grown as a standard (*see p.165*), with a well-staked clear main stem. Hummock-forming species such as *G. hispanica* may be clipped over after flowering in late summer. *G. lydia* dislikes any pruning. Most brooms do not make new growth when cut back into old wood and are better replaced.

OTHER ORNAMENTAL SHRUBS
FORTUNEARIA As for *Hamamelis* (*see p.196*).
FOTHERGILLA As for *Hamamelis* (*see p.196*).
FURCRAEA See Palms and palm-like plants, *p.41*.
GARDENIA As for *Camellia* (*see p.180*).
× GAULNETTYA See *Gaultheria*, below.
GAULTHERIA Little pruning is needed.

Garrya elliptica
The cultivar 'James Roof'; a free-standing specimen showing off its long catkins.

OTHER GARRYAS
G. FREMONTII As for *G. elliptica*.
G. × ISSAQUAHENSIS As for *G. elliptica*.
G. × THURETII Needs no pruning as a free-standing shrub; if grown as an informal hedge, trim with secateurs in late summer.

GREVILLEA

Evergreen, summer-flowering shrubs and trees (*see p.67*) with showy, yellow or red flowers over a long period. A few are hardy, such as 'Canberra Gem', and may be grown unprotected outdoors in cool climates if given the protection of a warm wall. In milder climates they make attractive specimen shrubs, and several are suitable for informal hedging. Tip-prune shoots of young plants (*see p.155*) to encourage bushiness. In cold areas cut out frost-damaged shoots in mid-spring. Remove stems to their point of origin if necessary to restrict size or when trimming hedges in late summer, after flowering.

Remove suckers (*see p.153*) to restrict spread. Cut back into old wood if plants become leggy.
GAYLUSSACIA As for *Gaultheria* (*see above*).
GEVUINA No special pruning needs.
GRAPTOPHYLLUM No special pruning needs.
GREWIA No special pruning needs.
GREYIA No special pruning needs.

GRINDELIA

The few shrubby species in this summer-flowering genus are hardy enough to be grown outdoors in sheltered locations in cool climates, but are generally cut back by hard frosts. They produce fresh growth each spring, however. In warm climates grindelias have a tendency to become leggy and flop over, and will benefit from pruning when young to encourage a branched, bushy habit from the start. Shorten the stems of young plants by one-third in the first spring after planting. Thereafter, keep pruning to a minimum in warm areas. In cool climates, cut hard back in spring, either to the base or to live wood.

GRISELINIA

Evergreen, medium-sized to large shrubs, hardy in coastal conditions, in which they thrive and where they are much used as windbreaks and informal hedges. They are vulnerable to frost in cold areas inland. They make new growth freely from the base and branch well, forming naturally rounded shapes, and need no formative pruning. Cut out damaged growth in spring, but otherwise keep pruning of specimen shrubs to a minimum. Clip over hedges in summer, using secateurs to prevent damage to individual leaves (*see also* Hedges, *p.44*). Plants make vigorous new growth if hard pruned.

GYNURA

Tropical, evergreen subshrubs and trailing plants (*see p.271*), grown for their foliage and winter flowers. In cool climates grow under glass, providing a high level of humidity and some shade in summer. Pinch out the growing tips of young plants to encourage bushiness. Cut all stems back to within 8cm (3in) of ground level in mid-spring.

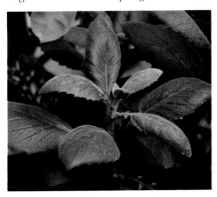

Young *Gynura* foliage
Pinch out young shoots to encourage a dense habit and fresh, attractive foliage.

HAMAMELIS *WITCH HAZEL*

Hardy, deciduous, large shrubs or small trees, most with good autumn colour and red or yellow flowers in winter. All have a similar habit, but some species are suckering, and others not. Many named cultivars are propagated by grafting, usually onto the suckering *H. virginiana*. Its suckers can be recognized, as they hold their leaves for longer. Witch hazels are slow-growing and respond slowly to pruning: this should only be necessary if mature plants have outgrown their allotted space.

H. MOLLIS

CHINESE WITCH HAZEL

Spreading shrub with yellow autumn foliage. Fragrant, yellow flowers are borne in winter.

■ **WHEN TO PRUNE** Early spring, as flowers fade but before leaves unfurl. Remove suckers on grafted plants as seen.

■ **TRAINING AND PRUNING** Pruning should be kept to a minimum. If it is essential to remove branches, cut back to healthy young growth. Plants are often grafted and

these tend to sucker. To remove suckers, *see p.153*. Plants recover only slowly from hard pruning, and on grafted specimens the rootstock may gain dominance.

H. VERNALIS

Suckering shrub with flowers in winter and spring and spectacular, vivid red autumn colour.

■ **WHEN TO PRUNE** As for *H. mollis*.

■ **TRAINING AND PRUNING** Keep pruning to a minimum. Suckers on plants growing on their own roots need only be removed if they become congested or are needed for propagation. Renovate plants by cutting out old wood over two years.

> OTHER WITCH HAZELS
> H. × INTERMEDIA cultivars, H. JAPONICA
> As for *H. mollis*.
> H. VIRGINIANA Autumn-flowering, but as for *H. vernalis*.

Pruning *Hamamelis mollis*

1 *Remove any crossing growth to avoid chafing damage, pruning where possible to a well-placed young shoot.*

2 *Remove any weak and unhealthy growth entirely.*

HEBE

Evergreen, prostrate to large shrubs, grown for their flowers and foliage. Some are suitable for rock gardens. They vary considerably in hardiness, the large-leaved hebes being vulnerable to frost damage. However, most hebes break readily from old wood and tolerate even hard cutting back to remove cold- or wind-damaged growth. Shortening lanky stems keeps plants neat, and for many hebes the removal of faded flower spikes helps to keep plants vigorous. Variegated hebes frequently develop green-leaved shoots, which will become dominant if not removed early.

H. CUPRESSOIDES

Evergreen shrub that is grown for its foliage, and for the rounded habit of the cultivar 'Boughton Dome', rather than for its sparingly produced, pale lilac flowers.

■ **WHEN TO PRUNE** Spring.

■ **TRAINING AND PRUNING** It is worth sacrificing the insignificant flowers for a compact neat shape, so trim the plant over lightly each year. In spring, stems

Frost-damaged *Hebe pinguifolia* **'Pagei'**
Cut out completely any localized patches of frost-damaged growth (*above left*), then trim the whole plant over lightly (*above right*) to stimulate vigorous regrowth.

may be pruned hard if new growth lower down is present. Plants hard pruned into old wood may not rejuvenate.

H. PINGUIFOLIA

Prostrate shrub popular as ground cover, with small, glaucous leaves, bearing flowers from late spring to summer. It is best known in the white-flowered 'Pagei'.

■ **WHEN TO PRUNE** Spring, and in summer after flowering.

■ **TRAINING AND PRUNING** In mid- to late spring cut out growth that has been damaged during the winter and any stems that have died back. Use shears to clip over plants in summer to remove dead flowers and keep growth compact.

H. SPECIOSA

Medium-sized shrub with large, glossy leaves and spikes of purplish flowers in summer and autumn.

***Hebe* 'Great Orme'**
Prune in spring as for *Hebe speciosa*, so that there is then time for shoots to grow and flower, from midsummer to mid-autumn.

In cool temperate regions it is often damaged by frost. It is a parent of many of the finest hybrids, most of which require similar pruning.

■ **WHEN TO PRUNE** Mid- to late spring, as the plant begins to make active growth.

■ **TRAINING AND PRUNING** Little formative pruning is required, except to ensure balanced growth (*see p.157*). Prune established plants to remove frost-damaged stems and to keep plants within bounds, cutting stems back to shoots low down if necessary. Plants do not always tolerate heavy pruning, so it is best to replace old specimens rather than attempt renovation by drastic pruning.

OTHER HEBES
H. ALBICANS As for *H. pinguifolia*.
H. ARMSTRONGII As for *H. cupressoides*.
H. BRACHYSIPHON As for *H. pinguifolia*.
H. DIEFFENBACHII As for *H. speciosa*.
H. × FRANCISCANA As for *H. speciosa*.
H. HULKEANA As for *H. speciosa*.
H. MACRANTHA As for *H. speciosa*.
H. OCHRACEA As for *H. cupressoides*.
H. RAKAIENSIS As for *H. pinguifolia*.
H. SALICIFOLIA As for *H. speciosa*.

HELIANTHEMUM *ROCK ROSE*

Evergreen, prostrate shrubs for rock gardens or sunny borders, producing cup-shaped flowers in summer. Many named hybrids are available in a range of colours. Unpruned, they become straggly, with a build-up of old stems under younger growths.

■ **WHEN TO PRUNE** Mid- to late summer, after flowering.

■ **TRAINING AND PRUNING** Pinch prune young plants (*see p.168*) to establish a compact habit. Keep plants neat and encourage repeat flowering by cutting back lightly, pruning stems individually rather than shearing over the whole plant. Plants are short-lived; replace rather than attempt renovation.

OTHER ORNAMENTAL SHRUBS
HAKEA Pinch prune young plants; apart from occasional shaping cuts, mature plants have no special needs.
× HALIMIOCISTUS As for *Cistus* (*see p.185*).
HALIMIUM As for *Cistus* (*see p.185*).
HALIMODENDRON Minimal pruning.
HEIMIA As for *Fuchsia magellanica* (*see p.194*) but pruning less hard, to 15cm (6in) above ground level.

HELICHRYSUM

Evergreen shrubs and subshrubs that are grown mainly for their foliage. In cool climates several species are hardy enough to be grown outdoors, although they often suffer frost damage. The half-hardy *H. petiolare* is often used for summer bedding or in containers, and is overwintered as cuttings with protection from frost. All helichrysums respond well to light pruning, which is carried out chiefly to enhance the foliage effect, but not all break readily from old wood.

H. ITALICUM

CURRY PLANT

Hardy, bushy sub-shrub with silver-grey, distinctively aromatic foliage and yellow flower-heads in summer. *H. italicum* subsp. *serotinum* has densely felted leaves.

■ **WHEN TO PRUNE** Spring.

■ **TRAINING AND PRUNING** Remove frost-damaged growth and cut back leggy shoots to old wood. Little further pruning is generally needed. Neglected plants usually make vigorous growth if hard pruned in spring.

H. PETIOLARE

Half-hardy shrub with trailing, silver-grey stems and felted, grey leaves; usually grown as a

Helichrysum petiolare

Although most frequently grown as a trailing plant, *H. petiolare* can also be trained, for example, as a standard. Throughout summer pinch out the tips of shoots to maintain dense growth and a compact form.

foliage plant, though cream flowers are produced in summer. It can be allowed to trail, or may be staked and pinch-pruned to form decorative shapes such as standards, cones and pillars.

■ **WHEN TO PRUNE** Spring. Pinch back long growths to encourage bushiness throughout the growing season.

■ **TRAINING AND PRUNING** Pinch out shoot tips regularly to make a bushy plant, removing unwanted flower buds if they form. For training in special forms such as standards, *see* Pinch pruning, *pp.168–171.* Plants are not worth renovating.

> **OTHER HELICHRYSUMS**
> H. SPLENDIDUM As for *H. italicum*.
> H. PLICATUM, H. STOECHAS As for *H. italicum*, but less likely to respond well to hard pruning.

HELIOTROPIUM

Heliotropium arborescens and hybrids of which it is a parent are evergreen shrubs bearing fragrant flowers on the current season's wood throughout the growing season. They are tender, but are suitable for summer bedding or growing in pots outside or under glass. They are usually replaced after one, or sometimes two, years. In warm climates keep pruning to a minimum. Pinch out the growing tips of young plants to encourage bushiness. Large plants may need staking. Use pinch-pruning techniques to grow as a standard (*see p.169*); stake a young plant and train up a clear stem, removing all lateral shoots. Pinch out the growing tip at three leaves above the height of clear stem required. Pinch out laterals at the head to encourage bushy growth. If standards are to be kept for a second year, trim over the head in autumn.

Bushy head developed by pinch pruning

Clear stem

Heliotropium hybrid

Although often grown as an annual bedding plant, heliotrope can be trained up as a standard.

HETEROMELES

The single species is *H. arbutifolia* (syn. *Photinia arbutifolia*), the Christmas berry or California holly, a large, hardy, evergreen shrub or tree that produces white flowers in late summer, followed by red fruits. It is frost-hardy, and needs some shelter in cold areas. Bushy and spreading in habit, it is very tolerant of pruning, and may be grown as a multi-stemmed shrub or with a single trunk. Prune from late winter to early spring. Tip-prune young plants to promote bushy growth. When established, thin twiggy growth lightly and, if necessary to shape or restrict size, cut branches back to suitably placed laterals. To rejuvenate old plants, cut them back hard to a framework of main branches in late winter or early spring, before growth begins. Heteromeles also makes a good informal hedging plant (*see p.44*).

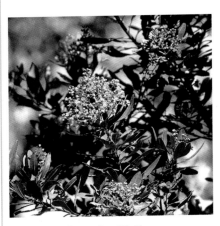

Heteromeles arbutifolia

This adaptable flowering shrub may be trimmed to shape as required.

HIBBERTIA *GUINEA FLOWER*

Small to medium-sized, evergreen shrubs with attractive, yellow or orange flowers, usually in spring and summer (some species flower most of the year). Some tolerate light frosts, but others need a completely frost-free climate. Prostrate and semi-prostrate species (which are suitable for growing in pots) need minimal pruning. Other species may be pinch-pruned when young to promote bushiness. To keep them compact, prune after flowering or between flowering flushes by removing shoot tips and spent flowerheads. Thin out any congested growth in spring. *Hibbertia* also includes a number of climbers (*see p.273*).

HIBISCUS

Genus that includes annuals and perennials, as well as a number of deciduous and evergreen shrubs and small trees. They are grown for their large, mallow-like flowers that are borne on the current season's wood in late summer. They need a warm, but not exposed, site, and full sun in order to bloom well. Not all can be grown outdoors in cool temperate climates, but tender species may be grown successfully under glass.

H. ROSA-SINENSIS

CHINESE HIBISCUS

2.5 | 8
m | ft

Evergreen, rounded shrub, of which there are many named selections, grown for its showy flowers, which may be produced throughout the growing season. It needs warm, frost-free growing conditions when grown outside, where it may be used as a hedge or screen, and can make a fine specimen plant for pot culture under glass in cool climates. Prune to restrict the size and spread of pot-grown specimens and to encourage flowering.

■ **WHEN TO PRUNE** Late spring.

■ **TRAINING AND PRUNING** Prune young plants lightly if necessary (*see p.157*) to ensure a well-balanced framework of branches. Prune established plants by cutting back main shoots by as much as one-third, and shorten laterals, leaving two or three buds. Dead wood attracts coral spot, so it should be removed promptly. To renovate completely, remove older branches entirely and cut the remainder back hard. The response is usually good, but if most stems have died back, it is best to replace the plant.

Renovating a poorly shaped *Hibiscus syriacus*

2 *Prune the remainder of the plant lightly, removing any weak or unhealthy-looking growth.*

1 *Remove badly placed and sprawling growth, either to the base or to strong, upward-growing stems.*

H. SYRIACUS

Fully hardy, deciduous shrub with flowers in a range of colours. It is prone to dieback and is unsuitable for exposed sites; the root system sometimes provides an inadequate anchor and plants may become lopsided and sprawling.

3 | 10
m | ft

■ **WHEN TO PRUNE** Late spring.

■ **TRAINING AND PRUNING** Prune young plants hard to encourage branching at the base. On established plants pruning is best kept to a minimum, though any shoots that show signs of dieback should be cut back to live wood. Renovation is as for *H. rosa-sinensis*. Lopsided plants respond well to reshaping (*see above*) if then sheltered from any prevailing wind; otherwise the problem will recur.

OTHER HIBISCUS
H. DIVERSIFOLIUS, H. HETEROPHYLLUS, H. MUTABILIS As for *H. rosa-sinensis*. H. SINOSYRIACUS As for *H. syriacus*. H. TILIACEUS, H. WAIMEAE As for *H. rosa-sinensis*.

HIPPOPHAE

Fully hardy, deciduous trees and shrubs, bearing male and female flowers on separate plants. They are grown for their foliage and for the showy fruits on female plants, and do best in an open site. Their natural habit is to form suckering clumps, but they can be trained as standards. They may also be used as hedging (*see p.44*), for which they are useful in coastal areas; they tolerate strong, salt-laden winds well.

■ **WHEN TO PRUNE** Summer, when it is easiest to distinguish between live and dead wood.

■ **TRAINING AND PRUNING** Little pruning is needed, either at the formative stage or when plants have become established. Mature specimens often have numerous twisted branches. If growth becomes crowded, cut unwanted stems to ground level and remove superfluous suckers from around the perimeter of the plant. However, drastic pruning is likely to stimulate the production of numerous suckers. Although plants can be trained as standards (*see p.165*), they tend to develop an irregular head and need careful attention to shaping. Trim hedges in late summer, if needed.

OTHER ORNAMENTAL SHRUBS
HELWINGIA Minimal pruning.
HEPTACODIUM Minimal pruning in spring if necessary.
HERMANNIA No special needs. Tolerates trimming if required.
HOHERIA In warm climates can be lightly trimmed after flowering. In cool climates delay pruning until spring and cut out any frost-damaged growths.
HOLODISCUS No special needs. Can be rejuvenated by cutting out one in three stems, as for *Spiraea* 'Arguta' (*see p.219*).
HOVEA Tip-prune young plants, and trim or thin the flowered, twiggy growth lightly after flowering.

HYDRANGEA

Fully to frost-hardy, deciduous, medium-sized to large shrubs that flower in late summer to autumn. All respond well to pruning. Some species are woodland plants that require little attention; cultivars of garden origin can be left unpruned, but flower better if pruned correctly. Some can be wall-trained, though choosing a climbing species (*see p.273*) is a simpler option.

H. MACROPHYLLA

Bushy shrub with many cultivars, bearing terminal summer flowers. Some have domed heads of mainly sterile flowers (hortensias or mop-head hydrangeas); others have flat heads with large, sterile flowers on the outside and smaller, fertile flowers in the centre (lacecaps). Flowers are borne on the previous season's wood, often satisfactorily with little attention, but regular pruning nearly always enhances flowering.

■ **WHEN TO PRUNE** In warm climates prune after flowering. In cool climates leave the old flowerheads on over winter to protect the new growth beneath, and prune in mid-spring.

■ **TRAINING AND PRUNING** Little formative pruning is needed. On established plants (*see above right*) cut back weak, thin shoots and one or two of the oldest stems to the base of the plant. Prune the previous year's flowered branches by up to 30cm (12in) to fat buds; these will produce flowering shoots. Neglected or badly cold-damaged plants may be cut to the base in spring, but there will be no flowers the following summer.

Pruning *Hydrangea macrophylla* in spring

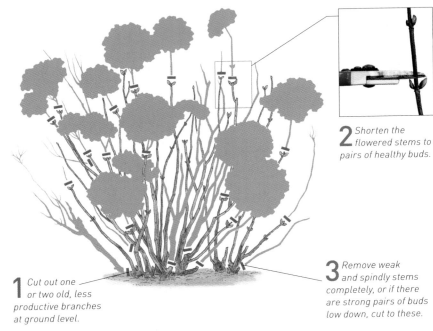

2 Shorten the flowered stems to pairs of healthy buds.

1 Cut out one or two old, less productive branches at ground level.

3 Remove weak and spindly stems completely, or if there are strong pairs of buds low down, cut to these.

H. PANICULATA

Upright shrub with large panicles of flowers in late summer on the current season's growth.

■ **WHEN TO PRUNE** Early spring, before plants start into active growth.

■ **TRAINING AND PRUNING** Pruning is not essential, but plants flower much better if pruned back annually to a woody framework (*see below*), as low as 25cm (10in) in exposed positions, but 60cm (2ft) tall or more at the back of a border. In the spring of subsequent years cut all growth back to the lowest pair of buds above this framework. Neglected plants usually respond well if cut back hard to recreate a low framework.

OTHER HYDRANGEAS

H. ARBORESCENS Minimal pruning, or can be treated as for *H. paniculata*.
H. ASPERA, H. HETEROMALLA, H. QUERCIFOLIA, H. SARGENTIANA, H. VILLOSA Minimal pruning, in spring if necessary; *H. villosa* wall-trains well (*see p.165*).
H. SERRATA As for *H. macrophylla*.
For other species, see Dictionary of Climbing Plants, *p.273*.

Pruning *Hydrangea paniculata* to a low framework

First spring after planting Cut out all but three or four strong stems, and shorten these to 25–60cm (10–24in).

Established plant Each year, cut the previous season's growth to its lowest pair of healthy buds. Remove any lifeless stubs.

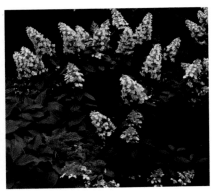

Established plant in flower Hard pruning each year results in fewer, but much larger, flower clusters.

HYPERICUM

Large, diverse genus, containing mostly hardy, vigorous, deciduous and evergreen shrubs of varying sizes, with bright yellow flowers borne over a long period in late summer and autumn. Some make effective ground cover; larger hypericums may be used for an informal flowering hedge. The pruning method depends on the species grown and the purpose for which it is used.

H. CALYCINUM

AARON'S BEARD, ROSE OF SHARON

Evergreen, low-growing shrub which spreads by means of long stems that creep across or just under the surface of the soil, producing new plantlets. It is suitable for use as ground cover even in dry shade, though it needs to be kept under control. Flowers are borne on the current season's growth, most profusely in a sunny site; annual pruning will produce a fresh crop of leaves and keep the plant within bounds.

1.2 | 4
m | ft

■ **WHEN TO PRUNE** Early spring.

■ **TRAINING AND PRUNING** Cut back all the previous year's growth, either with shears or, for large areas of ground cover, a hover mower on the highest setting, or a nylon-line trimmer. To control spread, chop through peripheral roots; this may yield new plantlets.

Hypericum forrestii

Remove some older wood (*below*) to leave an open, well-shaped plant (*right*).

H. FORRESTII

Evergreen or semi-evergreen, bushy shrub with nearly erect, then arching branches. It can be pruned annually to increase the flowering potential, and benefits from harder pruning every few years. This hypericum and other species of similar habit may be used as hedging plants.

1.5 | 5
m | ft

■ **WHEN TO PRUNE** Spring.

■ **TRAINING AND PRUNING** On free-standing plants remove any old, weak or thin growth, then shorten the remaining stems back to the base or to strong shoots to keep growth compact. For use as a hedge, *see p.44*. To reinvigorate old or neglected specimens, prune all stems to ground level in spring; plants usually produce vigorous growth in response.

OTHER HYPERICUMS

H. AEGYPTICUM, H. BALEARICUM Rock plants that require no pruning.
H. ANDROSAEMUM As for *H. calycinum*, but cut back only every two or three years.
H. BEANII, H. BELLUM, H. 'HIDCOTE' As for *H. forrestii*.
H. × INODORUM As for *H. androsaemum*.
H. KOUYTCHENSE, H. × MOSERIANUM As for *H. forrestii*.
H. 'ROWALLANE' As for *H. forrestii*, but cut to ground level if damaged by frost.

I – K

ILEX *HOLLY*

Mostly evergreen trees (*see p.68*) and shrubs, fully to half-hardy, with male and female flowers usually carried on separate plants. They are grown for their foliage and the berries borne on female plants in autumn and winter. They are generally tolerant of pollution and maritime conditions, and will grow in sun or shade. Fairly slow-growing, they make fine free-growing specimen plants but also respond well to pruning, and can be clipped to a formal shape; some species may be used for a formal or informal hedge.

I. OPACA

AMERICAN HOLLY

Erect, evergreen shrub or small tree with red berries (yellow in *I. opaca* f. *xanthocarpa*) and oval leaves that are a matt light green and more or less spiny. Fully hardy, but needs a continental climate to grow well. In temperate climates it is unlikely to make a good hedge, nor will it bear good crops of berries.

14 | 46
m | ft

■ **WHEN TO PRUNE** Late summer, when the new growth is ripe but not woody.

■ **TRAINING AND PRUNING** Little formative pruning is needed, except to encourage a single main stem. Established specimens tolerate pruning, but little is required for plants grown informally. Use shears to trim formal hedges from an early age (there is an inevitable loss of berries). Free-standing specimens and hedges tolerate drastic pruning if renovation is necessary (*see p.160*). Stage hard pruning over two or three years.

OTHER HOLLIES

I. CRENATA Hardy, bushy, dense species with black fruits. Grown as a specimen shrub, it requires minimal pruning, but is also suitable for topiary and hedging, when it is treated as for *I. opaca*.
I. × MESERVEAE Dark foliage with blue tints; young foliage is most attractive, so it is attractive as a clipped hedge. Prune as for *I. opaca*.
I. PERNYI Best grown as a specimen shrub or small feathered tree (*see p.25*) with only minimal pruning.
I. VERTICILLATA Deciduous; minimal pruning required.
For other species, see Dictionary of Ornamental Trees, p.68.

INDIGOFERA

Small to medium-sized, deciduous, multi-stemmed shrubs that produce pea-like flowers on the current season's growth in summer and early autumn.

I. HETERANTHA SYN.
I. GERARDIANA

Medium-sized, arching shrub with racemes of purple-red flowers in summer. Although hardy, it reaches its full potential height only in warm climates. In cool climates it may be damaged by hard frosts, and is best pruned hard each spring to stimulate strong young growth.

■ **WHEN TO PRUNE** Early to mid-spring, before the onset of fresh growth.

■ **TRAINING AND PRUNING** In warm climates, keep pruning to a minimum. In cold areas, remove weak stems and cut back all others to just above ground level. Neglected specimens will make vigorous new growth if all stems are cut back drastically in spring.

OTHER INDIGOFERAS
I. AMBYLANTHA As for I. heterantha. The woody base can be built up into a low framework to give the plant height.
I. AUSTRALIS, I. DECORA, I. KIRILOWII Small shrubs; prune as for I. heterantha.

Indigofera heterantha
Like other indigoferas, this species is best cut to near ground level in spring when grown in cool climates.

IXORA

Small, tender, evergreen shrubs that need a warm, frost-free climate. Flowers are borne on the current season's stems. Ixoras form twiggy plants that can be made bushier by regular pruning. Pinch out the tips of young shoots when they are about 15cm (6in) long. After flowering, remove about half the current year's growth, shaping the plant. Rejuvenate old plants by thinning, then cutting all remaining stems back to about 30cm (12in) from the ground in late winter or early spring.

JASMINUM *JASMINE*

Vigorous, deciduous or evergreen, small to medium-sized shrubs (for climbers, see p.274) with an arching habit. All of the shrubby species, such as J. humile and J. parkeri, bear yellow, star-like flowers in terminal clusters in summer on the previous season's wood. All need pruning to prevent a build-up of old wood. In cool climates more tender jasmines benefit from the protection of a warm wall. Young plants require little pruning. When established, remove one or two old stems after flowering. More drastic pruning of neglected plants is best carried out in spring, but there will be few flowers the following summer.

KALMIA

Evergreen, small to large shrubs that, given a sunny site, flower attractively, mainly in early summer. They require very little pruning, but it is worth deadheading where this is practicable. Specimens that have outgrown their site can be cut back, staging hard pruning over two or three years (see p.160).

KERRIA

Deciduous, fully hardy, vigorous, suckering shrub of medium height with an arching habit, flowering in spring. There is one species in the genus, K. japonica, of which the double-flowered form tends to be the more vigorous. Each year, new cane-like shoots are produced from ground level which will flower the following year. Prune to prevent a build-up of old wood and to remove the unsightly faded flower stems.

■ **WHEN TO PRUNE** Late spring, after flowering.

■ **TRAINING AND PRUNING** Prune the flowered stems either to strong sideshoots or to ground level, aiming to produce a balanced, open shape. Cutting the stems back to different levels encourages new flowering shoots at different heights. If plants are spreading too widely, chop peripheral canes out with a spade: the unwanted suckers can be used for propagation. To renovate, cut all stems back to ground level in spring.

KOLKWITZIA

Genus of one species, K. amabilis, the beauty bush, a medium-sized, deciduous shrub with pink flowers in late spring or early summer on second-year wood.

■ **WHEN TO PRUNE** Midsummer, after flowering.

Pruning *Kerria japonica*

1 To maintain vigour, cut out up to one in three stems at ground level in spring each year.

2 Cut back other flowered stems to vigorous young sideshoots where these exist.

■ **TRAINING AND PRUNING** Keep pruning of young plants to a minimum, letting the arching habit develop. Established plants may sucker, and freely produce basal shoots. Thin each year to maintain vigour: prune back one in three or four stems, always removing the oldest, cutting either to a low sideshoot or to the base. To renovate, cut old growth hard back to ground level, leaving five to seven strong, young upright stems.

L

LANTANA

Evergreen shrubs with heads of tubular flowers. The best known, *L. camara*, is a weed in some tropical and subtropical regions, but it and other species are widely grown as bedding or greenhouse plants in temperate areas. They may be trained as standards.

■ **WHEN TO PRUNE** Spring; standards under glass may need autumn trimming.

■ **TRAINING AND PRUNING** Pinch out the shoot tips of young plants to encourage bushy growth. Use pinch pruning to train as a standard (*see p.169*); train up a single clear stem and pinch out its tip just above the desired height of clear stem, then pinch-prune laterals to form a bushy head. Plants are often discarded after one season; if standards are to be overwintered, prune laterals at the head back to about 8cm (3in) in autumn.

LAVATERA *TREE MALLOW*

Very vigorous, deciduous shrubs flowering on the current season's growth over a very long period from summer until autumn. They are fully to frost-hardy, but prefer a warm, sunny site. The wood is not strong, and old, heavy branches may split or crack. Lavateras are thus vulnerable to frost and wind damage, but all tolerate hard pruning, which helps to keep bushes tidy and improves flowering performance.

Lavatera 'Barnsley'
Prune hard to the base each year once fresh shoots are growing strongly.

■ **WHEN TO PRUNE** Spring, after the buds begin to break, and after the last severe frosts. In exposed positions, shorten stems in autumn. During the growing season, cut out any damaged wood.

■ **TRAINING AND PRUNING** In spring cut out weak growths and prune all other stems to within 30cm (12in) of ground level (*see below*). During the growing season remove all damaged growth. In autumn shorten stems by up to half their length where there is danger of wind damage. Plants are not long-lived; replace old or neglected specimens.

LAVANDULA *LAVENDER*

Fully to half-hardy, small, evergreen shrubs with aromatic, often grey-green foliage and scented flowers, usually mauve or purple but sometimes white or pink, in summer. Lavenders are best grown in sunny positions, and are useful planted in rows to form a low, flowering hedge. To use as a hedge or as edging, plant 23–30cm (9–12in) apart. Annual pruning keeps specimen and hedging plants compact and clothed with foliage to ground level.

L. ANGUSTIFOLIA

ENGLISH LAVENDER

Bushy, evergreen shrub with spikes of fragrant flowers in summer. There are many cultivars and hybrids, including 'Hidcote' and the dwarf lavender 'Munstead'.

Lavandula angustifolia
In cool climates, deadhead in autumn to tidy the plant (or harvest the last of the flowers), then prune harder in spring after any danger of frost.

■ **WHEN TO PRUNE** In warm climates prune in autumn, but in cool climates only deadhead in autumn to tidy plants, delaying pruning until spring.

■ **TRAINING AND PRUNING** Prune young plants hard to encourage bushy growth. Clip over established plants, removing most of the previous season's growth. If deadheading in autumn, simply remove the long, bare flower stems; leave foliage on the plant over winter to protect young growth buds. Prune hedges in the same way. Plants do not break freely when cut back into old wood. Replace old and neglected specimens.

OTHER LAVENDERS
L. DENTATA, L. × INTERMEDIA As for *L. angustifolia*.
L. STOECHAS, L. STOECHAS subsp. PEDUNCULATA As for *L. angustifolia*, although not as hardy.

OTHER ORNAMENTAL SHRUBS

IOCHROMA *I. cyaneum* is tender, but tolerates light frosts. Prune in late winter or early spring, cutting into old wood, reducing growth by one-third to half. Isopogon As for *Kalmia* (*see facing page*), but do not deadhead.
ITEA In warm climates *I. virginica* needs little pruning. Wall-train informally as for *Escallonia* 'Langleyensis' (*see p.192*) in cool climates.
JAMESIA No pruning required.
JUANULLOA Scandent shrub; in warm climates, train on a wall or support. As a pot-plant, treat as for *Justicia*.

JUSTICIA Remove dead growth or cut back flowered stems at the end of winter. In warm areas where all growth survives, shorten all stems by half every two or three years.
KUNZEA Trim lightly after flowering.
LEDUM Minimal pruning.

LEONOTIS *LION'S EAR*

Leonotis leonurus, also known as wild dagga or the minaret flower, is an evergreen subshrub grown for its aromatic leaves and whorls of bright orange-red flowers in summer and autumn. It can grow 2m (6ft) in a year in good conditions. It is not fully hardy, but with protection may survive mild winters in cool climates. It is also suitable for growing under glass, in full sun, but keep cool in winter.

■ **WHEN TO PRUNE** Autumn in warm climates; in cool climates spring, after flowering.

■ **TRAINING AND PRUNING** Tip-prune young shoots to encourage branching. In warm climates cut back the previous season's growth to a low permanent framework. In cool climates cut all growth to within 15cm (6in) of ground level. Renovate neglected specimens by this method.

LESPEDEZA

Small to medium-sized shrubs, some of which are evergreen in warm climates. The attractive, white to purple, pea-like flowers are borne on the current season's wood in late summer or autumn. In warm areas remove some of the old wood each spring. In cool climates plants are usually cut to the ground by hard frosts, even with the protection of a warm wall. Use a straw or similar mulch to protect the roots in winter and cut down the old stems after any danger of frost has passed.

LIGUSTRUM *PRIVET*

Evergreen and deciduous, medium-sized to large shrubs, fully to frost-hardy, grown for their foliage and flowers. Their vigour, tolerance of pollution and a wide range of sites and good response to clipping make them popular as formal hedging plants. Some species, such as *L. confusum* and the deciduous or semi-evergreen *L. sinense* (Chinese privet), are decorative enough to be grown as free-standing shrubs. Privets are also suitable for use in topiary (*see p.48*) or to be grown as standards.

L. OVALIFOLIUM

OVAL-LEAFED PRIVET, PRIVET

Vigorous, fully hardy, evergreen or semi-evergreen, large shrub with glossy leaves, and white flowers in summer followed by black fruits. Some cultivars have attractive variegated foliage.

■ **WHEN TO PRUNE** Spring.

■ **TRAINING AND PRUNING** Keep the pruning of free-standing shrubs to a minimum; no pruning is necessary at planting. Watch variegated cultivars for reverted shoots, removing them as seen (*see p.153*). Cut back young hedging plants on planting to 30cm (12in) above ground level, and cut back new growth by half in each of the following two or three years to ensure dense growth at the base. To train as a standard, *see p.165*. Trim hedges

Ligustrum sinense 'Pendulum'
The deciduous Chinese privet is densely branching, with pale oval leaves and large panicles of fragrant white flowers in summer.

and topiary two or three times between late spring and late summer. Old and neglected privet bushes and hedges can be renovated by hard pruning in spring, but this may cause variegated cultivars to revert.

OTHER PRIVETS

L. DELAVAYANUM As for *L. ovalifolium*.
L. JAPONICUM As for *L. ovalifolium*.
L. LUCIDUM As for *L. ovalifolium*, or grow as a standard (*see p.165*) on a single short stem, no taller than 60cm (2ft).
L. OBTUSIFOLIUM As for *L. ovalifolium*.
L. SINENSE As for *L. ovalifolium*.
L. VULGARE As for *L. ovalifolium*.

LEYCESTERIA

Frost-hardy to half-hardy, clump-forming, deciduous shrubs. New stems grow and flower in a single season. The green bamboo-like hollow stems of *L. formosa* are attractive in winter. The plants need a sunny position and also shelter, since the stems are often broken in strong winds. Plants left unpruned will become congested.

■ **WHEN TO PRUNE** Spring.

■ **TRAINING AND PRUNING** Thin out clumps annually, cutting old and weak stems down to near ground level. Neglected specimens can be renovated by drastic pruning, cutting back all stems to within 5–8cm (2–3in) of the base. Feed well to aid recovery.

Leycesteria formosa
These shrubs form attractive, arching clumps. Cut some stems back to ground level in spring, as unpruned plants become congested and produce weak growths.

LONICERA *HONEYSUCKLE*

Fully hardy to frost-tender, deciduous and evergreen shrubs, some large, and others low-growing. They often bear strongly scented flowers on second-year wood, followed by showy fruits in some species. They are mostly vigorous and adaptable, usually responding well to pruning. Many are of arching habit, and these may become unruly if left unpruned. Others, such as *L. nitida* and *L. xylosteum*, are more compact and are useful as hedging. Timing of pruning depends on the flowering season and the purpose for which the plant is grown. The genus also includes a number of attractive climbers (*see p.276*).

L. NITIDA

Evergreen, fully hardy, bushy shrub with small, creamy flowers. Its dense habit makes it a useful plant for low formal hedges. Popular cultivars in varying leaf colours include 'Aurea' and 'Baggesen's Gold'.

■ **WHEN TO PRUNE** Trim hedges at least three times between spring and autumn.

■ **TRAINING AND PRUNING** Specimen shrubs need minimal pruning. Cut back hedging plants by at least half at planting time, and trim two or three times in the first season. Then cut back annual growth by half until the hedge attains the desired height. Plants that become bare at the base can be renovated by cutting back to 15cm (6in) of the ground in early spring.

L. TATARICA

Vigorous, fully hardy, deciduous, arching shrub that bears fragrant white to pink flowers on the previous season's shoots in early summer. The flowers are followed by colourful berries.

■ **WHEN TO PRUNE** Midsummer, after flowering.

Lonicera xylosteum
The fly honeysuckle is a less well-known but neat and attractive species. It is easy to keep in order as an informal screen or hedge.

■ **TRAINING AND PRUNING** Cut old and weak stems back to the base of the plant to encourage growth low down that will keep the base well furnished. Shorten up to one in three of the other branches, cutting them back to just above fresh, upright shoots, keeping a balanced shape: try not to spoil the natural outline of the plant. Old and neglected specimens can be renovated by being pruned back to a low framework in winter or early spring.

OTHER LONICERAS
L. FRAGRANTISSIMA Prune as for *L. tatarica*, but in late spring, after flowering. Can be wall-trained (*see p.162*).
L. KOROLKOWII As for *L. tatarica*.
L. MAACKII As for *L. tatarica*.
L. PILEATA Minimal pruning.
L. × PURPUSII As for *L. tatarica*, but prune in late spring after flowering.
L. SYRINGANTHA (syn. L. RUPICOLA VAR. SYRINGANTHA) As for *L. tatarica*.
L. XYLOSTEUM As for *L. tatarica*.
For other species, see Dictionary of Climbing Plants, *p.276*.

LOTUS

Genus that contains a few subshrubs, notably the low-growing *L. berthelotii* (coral gem, parrot's beak, pelican's beak), with trailing, silvery stems and striking red flowers in summer. It is tender, needing frost-free conditions, but is widely grown in cool climates, planted out in containers in summer; it may be overwintered under cover. In warm climates it is used in rock gardens or to cover banks. Pinch out the shoot tips of young plants. To encourage fresh growth of established plants and keep the plant tidy, cut out some of the old stems in late summer after flowering. Plants overwintered under cover can be cut back hard in spring.

LUCULIA

Tender, evergreen, medium-sized to large shrubs with scented, phlox-like, white or pink flowers in winter. Hard pruning encourages plants to flower freely. As soon as flowers fade, cut back flowered wood to within 8cm (3in) of a framework of main branches. Cut hard back in spring to rejuvenate.

LYCIUM

Medium-sized, hardy, deciduous and evergreen shrubs of untidy habit and with ornamental berries. Those species that are spiny are often used for formal and informal hedging. In some countries *Lycium ferocissimum* (African boxthorn) is an invasive weed.

■ **WHEN TO PRUNE** Winter. Trim hedges in spring and summer.

■ **TRAINING AND PRUNING** Remove dead wood annually and shorten overlong stems, pruning to upright shoots. Plants grown as informal hedges need little pruning. For formal hedges (*see p.45*), cut back at planting to 15–30cm (6–12in) and in subsequent years cut back half the annual growth in mid- to late summer until the desired height is reached. Harder pruning may be needed every three or four years; prune growth close to the base in winter to rejuvenate.

OTHER ORNAMENTAL SHRUBS
Leptospermum Minimal pruning. Trim young growth in spring to encourage bushiness, avoid cutting into old wood.
Leucadendron May be moderately pruned, if necessary, after flowering.
Leucaena No special needs, but tolerates pruning if necessary.

Leucopogon Minimal pruning.
Leucospermum As for *Leucadendron*.
Leucothoe Minimal pruning. If necessary, cut out at the base one or two old stems in late spring, after flowering.
Lomatia Minimal pruning, but old wood can be cut out in spring.

Loropetalum No pruning required, but pinch out shoot tips and trim after flowering if a bushy habit is desired.
Lupinus Cut off seedheads of *L. arboreus* to stop self-seeding and keep compact.
Lyonia Prune lightly after flowering if necessary.

M

MAGNOLIA

A genus that consists mainly of trees but includes a number of usually large, deciduous and evergreen shrubs. They are fully to frost-hardy, and are grown for their waxy, often fragrant flowers and the graceful habit that normally develops without extensive pruning. They can be grown in sun or semi-shade, but need some protection from strong wind.

M. × SOULANGEANA

Large, deciduous shrub, popular for its white to purple flowers, borne from mid-spring to early summer.

10 | 30
m | ft

■ **WHEN TO PRUNE** Midsummer, when in full leaf. Avoid pruning in spring or early summer, when the wounds will bleed, and in the dormant season, as dieback often affects growth pruned at this time.

■ **TRAINING AND PRUNING** After light formative pruning (see p.157) little other pruning is needed, unless the brittle wood suffers wind damage. Heavy flowering followed by production of copious seed can reduce the plant's vigour. If possible, remove flowers when faded. Badly shaped specimens can be renovated by hard pruning, staged over two to three years (see p.160).

OTHER MAGNOLIAS
M. GLOBOSA, M. SIEBOLDII SUBSP. SINENSIS, M. WILSONII Only minimal pruning required.
M. LILIIFLORA As for M. × soulangeana.
M. STELLATA Allow young plants to develop naturally. Renovate as for M. × soulangeana, but plants are slow to recover from hard pruning.
For other species, see Dictionary of Ornamental Trees, p.74.

Magnolia × soulangeana
These fragile flowers need shelter from the damaging effect of wind.

MAHONIA

Fully to half-hardy, medium-sized to large, evergreen shrubs. Some are low-growing, spreading plants that make good low cover. The taller-growing species make fine architectural plants. Most mahonias thrive in shade.

M. AQUIFOLIUM

OREGON GRAPE

Vigorous, low-growing, suckering shrub; the yellow flowers are followed by blue-black berries.

1 | 3
m | ft

■ **WHEN TO PRUNE** Spring, after flowering.

■ **TRAINING AND PRUNING** This species spreads by means of suckers, so remove any unwanted growth at the edge of the plant. Shear ground-cover plants to just above ground level annually or every two years, to keep them thick. Taller-growing specimens need little pruning, except to remove unwanted suckers. To renovate neglected shrubs, cut old branches back to ground level, leaving young ones unpruned.

M. × MEDIA

Group of upright shrubs, valued for their whorls of dark, spiny foliage and the yellow flowers produced in autumn and winter. They make large,

4 | 12
m | ft

Mahonia × media
Where stems are overlong, shorten to a sideshoot or a whorl of foliage after flowering.

sometimes strikingly gaunt, shrubs, but will tolerate being cut back hard.

■ **WHEN TO PRUNE** Spring, after flowering.

■ **TRAINING AND PRUNING** No regular pruning is required, but long or old stems that are bare at the base can be cut back to strong growth lower down. Old and neglected plants usually respond slowly, but satisfactorily, when cut back to a low framework 30–60cm (12–24in) from ground level.

OTHER MAHONIAS
M. JAPONICA As for M. × media.
M. LOMARIIFOLIA As for M. × media.
M. PINNATA As for M. aquifolium.
M. × WAGNERI As for M. aquifolium.

MALVAVISCUS

Tender, evergreen, sometimes sprawling shrubs, flowering on the current year's wood. M. arboreus (sleepy mallow, wax mallow) has tubular red flowers. In cool climates they may be grown in pots under glass. In late winter or early spring cut back the previous year's growth by a half to two-thirds. If the plant is crowded, remove twiggy or old, unproductive stems, but keep the plant's natural, rounded shape. Tolerates harder pruning if required. In warm climates it can be wall-trained (see p.162), or used as an informal or clipped hedge (see p.44).

MELASTOMA

Medium-sized, tender, evergreen shrubs and trees, grown for their foliage and white, pink or purple flowers. Some have edible fruits. M. affine is considered a weed in parts of the tropics. Pruning improves the overall appearance and keeps the plants well furnished with new wood. Tip-prune young plants to make them bushy. Prune established specimens, if the fruits are not required, lightly in late winter. Removing some older wood will encourage the production of vigorous new shoots.

MIMOSA

This varied, frost-tender genus includes small to medium-sized, evergreen shrubs with attractive leaves, some of which, including M. pudica (the humble or sensitive plant), may be grown as annuals in cool climates; they are also suitable for growing in pots. Growth habits vary: the prostrate species should be left to develop naturally, while the bushy types may be pinch-pruned (see p.168) when young to encourage dense growth, and may also be trained as standards (see p.165).

MIMULUS *MONKEY FLOWER*

Evergreen shrubs with snapdragon-like flowers in a range of colours borne on new wood from spring to autumn. They are tender, but generally survive the winter in cool climates if grown against a warm wall or in a cool glasshouse. Pinch out the shoot tips of young plants to encourage branching. After the first flush of flowers, cut back flowered stems by 10–20cm (4–8in) to encourage further flowers. In late spring shorten all growth by at least half, to a framework for wall-trained plants (*see p.165*).

MUSSAENDA

Tender, evergreen shrubs and climbers that from spring to autumn have striking flowers with colourful bracts at the ends of stems. They require frost-free growing conditions, but may be grown in pots under glass in cool climates. Prune to maintain the production of fresh growth and flowers. Cut off the old flower clusters throughout the flowering season; in winter or spring, when flowering has finished, cut back hard, removing most of the growth made in the previous season. In warm climates mussaendas are often planted en masse or used for an informal hedge.

MYRICA

Deciduous or evergreen shrubs grown for their aromatic foliage and, in some cases, for their berries. *M. gale* (sweet gale, bog myrtle) is a hardy, deciduous, compact shrub of suckering habit. It needs little or no pruning, but cut any leggy stems to ground level in spring and trim plants lightly. *M. californica* (California wax myrtle, California bay berry) is a compact evergreen, valued for its wax-bloomed, purple fruit and aromatic foliage. It needs no regular pruning, but it is susceptible to cold and may be badly frost-damaged. In spring cut back damaged growth to live wood or to ground level.

N

NANDINA

Evergreen, frost-hardy, medium-sized shrub with an elegant, bamboo-like habit of growth. *N. domestica* (heavenly bamboo, sacred bamboo) bears small, white, star-shaped flowers in summer, followed, in warm climates or under glass only, by red berries. Several cultivars, such as 'Firepower', have fine spring and autumn colour: Vigorous specimens freely produce new growth from the base. If young plants are spindly, cut back on planting to stimulate growth. Further pruning is needed only to keep the plant tidy.

NERIUM *OLEANDER*

Nerium oleander, the most widely grown species, is a large, evergreen shrub with periwinkle-like flowers. There are many cultivars with flowers in a range of colours, some double. It is tender, and in cool climates needs a very favoured site, but will also grow well under glass. The habit is upright, and can be ungainly. Oleanders make excellent standards, or can be wall-trained or used for informal hedges. The sap is toxic, so gloves should be worn when pruning.

■ **WHEN TO PRUNE** Late summer to autumn.

■ **TRAINING AND PRUNING** Tip-prune shoots of young plants. In warm climates specimen plants require little pruning; shape lightly after flowering, if needed. Prune pot-grown or trained plants annually, cutting back flowered shoots by half and laterals to 10cm (4in). Plants tolerate hard pruning, but may take two years to flower freely again.

Plaited stems
Oleanders make ideal conservatory plants in cool climates, and can be trained as highly ornamental standards (*see p.165*). The stems may be plaited (*see p.51*) while they are still young and pliable.

Nerium oleander
In cool climates, oleanders often flower well if grown in the shelter of a sunny wall.

OTHER ORNAMENTAL SHRUBS

MACKAYA Prune lightly in winter, after flowering. Can be pruned hard.
× MAHOBERBERIS Cut straggly stems back to strong shoots in late spring, after flowering.
MALPIGHIA Trim lightly after flowering.
Malvastrum As for *Anisodontea* (*see p.173*).
MEDICAGO Minimal pruning.
MEDINILLA Prune *M. magnifica* after flowering to shape. In suitable climates it makes a good hedge (*see p.44*).
MELIANTHUS In warm climates cut

flowered stems out in autumn. In cool climates cut back old growth in spring.
MELICYTUS Minimal pruning.
MENZIESIA Minimal pruning.
MICROCITRUS As for *Citrus* (*see p.142*).
MITRARIA Minimal pruning.
MONTANOA Minimal pruning.
MURRAYA After flowering, trim lightly, removing flowered growth.
MYRCEUGENIA If necessary to limit size, prune in spring.
MYRICARIA Shorten flowered shoots

to 5cm (2in).
MYRSINE Minimal pruning.
MYRTUS COMMUNIS Minimal pruning.
NEILLIA See *Stephanandra, p.220.*
NEMATANTHUS As for *Justicia* (*see p.203*).
NEMOPANTHUS As for *Ilex* (*see p.201*).
NEVIUSIA Cut out old wood in summer after flowering.
NICOTIANA Cut back to the base or a low framework after flowering.
NOTELAEA Tolerates shaping.
NOTOSPARTIUM Tolerates renovation.

O – P

OCHNA

Tender, evergreen or semi-evergreen, medium-sized shrubs and trees, grown for their flowers and ornamental fruits. *O. serrulata*, the Mickey-mouse plant, is the most commonly grown; it has yellow flowers in spring and summer, followed by red calyces on which a ring of glossy, black fruits forms. The berried branches are good for cutting. Ochnas need full sun and frost-free conditions (though established plants tolerate light frost), where they may be grown as specimen plants, but they may also be grown under glass in pots. Pinch out the shoot tips of young plants to encourage a bushy habit. Prune established plants lightly in early spring, cutting flowered stems back to strong laterals. At the same time remove dead, damaged or unproductive wood, and weak, twiggy shoots. In warm climates ochnas may be espalier-trained on walls (*see p.162*), or used as an informal hedge (*see p.45*).

OLEARIA *DAISY BUSH*

Evergreen shrubs of varying size, grown for their foliage and daisy flowerheads, mainly produced in summer. Although Australasian in origin, most olearias are hardy enough to be grown in cool climates, where they are often planted in front of a sunny wall (they are not suitable for wall training). They thrive in windy coastal sites, where they usually form compact bushes. Pruning is required only to remove frost damage or to keep plants within bounds, but olearias make vigorous new growth when cut back. *O. macrodonta* and *O. × haastii* make good informal hedges.

■ **WHEN TO PRUNE** Spring, but not before fresh growth emerges.

■ **TRAINING AND PRUNING** On young plants shorten the longest shoots to encourage bushiness. Cut young hedging plants back hard (*see p.44*) to encourage dense growth. Once established, allow free-standing specimens to develop unpruned, apart from cutting back any frosted stems beyond the point of damage to healthy, outward-facing buds. To restrict size, prune stems by one-third to half of the previous season's growth, cutting to outward-facing buds. If removing larger sections of branches, cut to well within the body of the plant to hide cut marks. For the pruning of hedges, *see p.45*.

Renovate by cutting back hard into old wood. Response is usually good.

OSMANTHUS

Large, evergreen shrubs, grown for their foliage and small, but fragrant, flowers. Most are hardy. Free-standing specimens do not require regular pruning, but from time to time it may be necessary to keep them within bounds. All tolerate being cut back, even into old wood, but timing depends on the flowering season. Some osmanthus are suitable for hedging, although trimming reduces the floral display.

O. DELAVAYI

Bushy shrub with glossy leaves and very fragrant, white flowers from mid- to late spring on wood made the previous season. Frost damage is likely in cold climates; plants benefit from the protection of a warm wall, but are too stiff and slow-growing to train formally.

WHEN TO PRUNE Late spring, after flowering. Hedges may be clipped over several times during summer, but in cool climates do not trim them any later than midsummer, or the resulting fresh growth may be vulnerable to frost damage in winter.

■ **TRAINING AND PRUNING** Little formative pruning is required (*see Evergreen shrubs, p.157*). Prune established specimens only to keep them within bounds and enhance the shape, cutting overlong stems back to a shoot within the body of the plant to hide the cut marks. When given the protection of a warm wall, plants are best allowed to grow naturally, tying in loosely only if necessary. Clip hedges to shape once or twice in a season (*see Hedges, p.46*). Rejuvenate old, neglected plants by cutting hard back into old wood; they should respond well.

OTHER OSMANTHUS

O. ARMATUS, *O. FRAGRANS VAR. AURANTIACUS*, *O. × FORTUNEI* Prune in late spring as for *O. delavayi*.
O. × BURKWOODII As for *O. delavayi*. Trim hedges in midsummer.
O. DECORUS As for *O. delavayi*.
O. HETEROPHYLLUS Prune in late spring. Not suitable for wall training.
O. YUNNANENSIS As for *O. delavayi*.

PAEONIA *PEONY*

Peonies fall into two groups, the herbaceous perennial peonies, and the medium-sized, hardy, deciduous shrubs known as "tree peonies". The two groups bear similar types of flower. The shrubs include *P. delavayi* var. *lutea*, larger than most, with fine, dense foliage, and *P. suffruticosa*, or Moutan peony, which has many beautiful cultivars. Tree peonies are long-lived plants that may be slow to establish. The habit is upright, and older stems may become leggy. Peonies require little pruning, but judicious cutting out of old wood encourages bushier growth. Named cultivars are usually grafted.

■ **WHEN TO PRUNE** In summer, after flowering, and in autumn after leaf-fall.

■ **TRAINING AND PRUNING** Plants require little formative pruning (*see p.157*). Remove the dead flowers in summer or, if seeds are wanted, the fruiting heads in

Paeonia delavayi* var. *lutea
The flowered shoots will die back to new growth below after fruiting. Prune back to these shoots in autumn.

autumn. Occasionally cut old leggy stems of mature plants back to ground level. Avoid more drastic pruning, especially of grafted plants.

PAVONIA

Evergreen shrubs grown mainly for their attractive flowers. Some need tropical or subtropical conditions, but others tolerate light frosts. The natural habit is open and spreading, so tip-prune young plants (*see p.155*) to make them bush out. Prune established plants lightly in early spring, cutting back any straggling stems. Rejuvenate old, neglected plants by removing some old wood and cutting back the rest by up to half, to well-placed young shoots.

PENSTEMON

Some shrubs in this genus are dwarf or prostrate rock-garden plants that need minimal pruning. The more commonly grown species (sometimes included in *Keckiella*) are woody-based subshrubs bearing attractive flowers in early summer, with an upright habit that is best encouraged by cutting back each year. Most are hardy, but may suffer frost damage in cool climates.

■ **WHEN TO PRUNE** Spring, after any danger of severe frost has passed, and after flowering.

■ **TRAINING AND PRUNING** In spring, prune any winter-damaged stems back hard to encourage fresh growth from the base. After flowering, shorten flowered stems by half to prevent seed production and encourage further flowering. Cut any stems showing dieback right back to the base: if dieback spreads, plants are usually best replaced, since penstemons do not renovate well.

PEROVSKIA

Fully hardy, deciduous shrubs with aromatic, grey-green foliage and spikes of blue flowers, borne at the ends of new stems from late summer to mid-autumn. The top growth dies back in winter but new shoots are produced from the woody base the following spring. In cool climates the dead top growth provides some protection in winter. Annual hard pruning keeps the plants tidy and can produce larger, though fewer, flower spikes. Left unpruned, plants become leggy, and old dead wood accumulates.

■ **WHEN TO PRUNE** Mid-spring, as new growth is breaking.

■ **TRAINING AND PRUNING** From the first year onwards, prune all the previous season's growth back hard, to within

Pruning an established Perovskia

1 Cut all flowered stems back to within three or four buds of the old wood, varying the height at which you cut.

2 Cut away old sections of the framework that produced no new growth last year.

Perovskia atriplicifolia
If regularly pruned, perovskias will produce vigorous flowering shoots from a basal framework for many years.

5–10 cm (2–4in) of the ground initially, and then to the framework of old wood that will gradually develop (*see below*). Old and neglected plants should also respond well to this treatment.

PERSOONIA

Large, evergreen shrubs of Australian origin, with pine-like foliage, terminal spikes of saffron-yellow flowers in summer, and pendulous clusters of edible, green to plum-purple fruits in winter. They will withstand light frosts if grown in a sunny position in well-drained soil. Persoonias may be grown as small trees by training a young plant with a central leader.

■ **WHEN TO PRUNE** Autumn, after fruiting.

■ **TRAINING AND PRUNING** Do not prune when young, to allow the plant's natural habit to develop. Only light trimming of established plants is needed to thicken the foliage. Wayward shoots may also be shortened to improve the shape. Remove the spent flowerheads if fruits are not required; otherwise, prune after fruiting. To grow persoonia as a standard, train up a vigorous stem, removing competing shoots, and then cut back laterals to form a branching head (*see p.165*).

OTHER ORNAMENTAL SHRUBS

OEMLERIA (syn. **OSMARONIA**) *O. cerasiformis* is of suckering habit; cut back flowered shoots, and chop round edges to restrict spread if necessary.
OPLOPANAX Spiny. Minimal pruning, if necessary, in spring.
OSBECKIA In spring cut back by half shoots that flowered the previous summer.
× OSMAREA See *Osmanthus × burkwoodii* (*facing page*).
OSMARONIA See *Oemleria*.
OSTEOMELES Free-standing specimens require little pruning. On wall-trained specimens gradually train in young stems to replace old wood, pruning in midsummer.
OXYLOBIUM No special needs. Flowered shoots can be trimmed lightly after flowering. Remove some old wood occasionally.
OZOTHAMNUS Little pruning needed, except to remove frost-damaged growth in spring. Tolerates hard pruning.
PACHYSTACHYS As for *Justicia* (*see p.203*).
PACHYSTEGIA Minimal, as for *Olearia* (*see facing page*).
PALIURUS Minimal pruning as a free-standing shrub. May also be grown as a standard (*see p.165*), and tolerates being cut back hard in the spring.
PARAHEBE Little pruning needed; trim over lightly in summer after flowering.
PARROTIOPSIS Minimal. If necessary, prune lightly in early summer.
PAVETTA Little needed; remove some old wood, after flowering or fruiting.
PENTAS Deadhead and trim lightly in spring. Tolerates hard pruning if necessary.
PERNETTYA See *Gaultheria* (*p.195*).
PETROPHILA No special needs.

PHILADELPHUS

Medium-sized to large, hardy, deciduous shrubs, mainly grown for their highly fragrant, white flowers, usually in midsummer, that are produced on the previous season's wood. They produce new stems from the base that branch and, after about four years, can become congested, and flowering performance declines. Most philadelphus respond well to pruning, and need regular pruning to maximize their flowering potential. Those grown for their flowers are pruned in the same way, but a few, especially *P. coronarius* 'Aureus', that are grown more for their foliage, are often additionally pruned to enhance this effect, at the expense of the flowers. To encourage young plants to make fresh growth from the base, plant 5cm (2in) deeper than the nursery soil mark.

P. CORONARIUS

MOCK ORANGE

Medium-sized shrub. The species itself is seldom grown, but it has several popular cultivars with attractive spring foliage. This species can be pruned in several ways, either for flowers or to enhance and prolong the foliage display, which is particularly effective on the gold-leaved 'Aureus', the foliage of which turns green in midsummer.

■ **WHEN TO PRUNE** Late summer, after flowering, or for the best leaf effect, prune in late spring, immediately before flowering. Renovate in winter or early spring.

■ **TRAINING AND PRUNING** For a flowering shrub, treat as for *P.* 'Virginal'. To enhance and prolong the foliage effect (though this will inhibit flowering), trim over lightly to remove flower buds and to promote further leaf growth. Plants can also be pruned back to a framework in early spring as for *Hydrangea paniculata* (*see p.200*), feeding the plant generously to maintain vigorous growth. Renovation is as for *P.* 'Virginal'.

P. MICROPHYLLUS

Small shrub of twiggy habit, with white flowers in early summer. It generally needs little pruning.

■ **WHEN TO PRUNE** Summer, after flowering. Renovate in spring.

***Philadelphus* 'Virginal'**
Cut several stems to the ground each year to promote fresh growth with abundant flowers.

■ **TRAINING AND PRUNING** Extensive annual pruning is not desirable, but cut back any wayward branches to healthy lower shoots. If the shrub becomes congested, thin growth by cutting some stems down to the base. To renovate, cut back hard to a low framework in spring.

P. 'VIRGINAL'

Medium-sized shrub, with masses of double, white flowers in early summer. Prune to thin out crowded growth and to maintain peak flowering performance.

■ **WHEN TO PRUNE** Late summer, immediately after flowering. Renovate in winter or early spring.

■ **TRAINING AND PRUNING** Aim to stimulate young, flowering growth while keeping a shrub of balanced proportions. Cut back one in four stems, choosing the oldest, to ground level or to a low shoot. To renovate, cut down all old stems to ground level and shorten any younger vigorous stems by one-quarter to half. If the shrub does not respond with new growth, replace it.

OTHER PHILADELPHUS
P. 'Avalanche', P. 'Belle Etoile' As for *P.* 'Virginal'.
P. delavayi As for *P.* 'Virginal'.
P. mexicanus As for *P.* 'Virginal', but in cool regions best grown with the shelter of a warm wall (do not wall-train). Cultivars of *P.* × *lemoinei* and *P.* × *purpureo-maculatus* are all treated as for *P.* 'Virginal'.

PHLOMIS

Small, evergreen shrubs and perennials native to the Mediterranean region, with grey-green, sage-like foliage and whorls of hooded, yellow or lilac flowers in summer. *P. fruticosa*, the Jerusalem sage, is a spreading species; *P. italica* is more upright, with pink flowers. most species are quite hardy; they may suffer some frost damage, but they usually recover well, making new growth from the base. Regular attention to the removal of damaged and wayward growth helps to keep plants neat and compact. Young, vigorous specimens tolerate being cut back hard.

■ **WHEN TO PRUNE** Mid-spring, when the shrub is in active growth.

■ **TRAINING AND PRUNING** Plants require little formative pruning except to remove weak growths and to shorten straggly stems. Established plants need no annual pruning, but benefit from occasional shaping cuts. Shorten any frost-damaged stems, cutting to just above healthy buds. Cut out any weak and old shoots entirely. When branches become leggy and untidy-looking, cut them back to a shoot or bud well within the bush; if this is done regularly, a good shape will be maintained.

Renovate neglected specimens by cutting hard back into the old wood, either to within 8–10cm (3–4in) of the ground or, for a bigger plant, to a taller framework of branches. Recovery is usually good, but phlomis are relatively short-lived: very old specimens are better replaced.

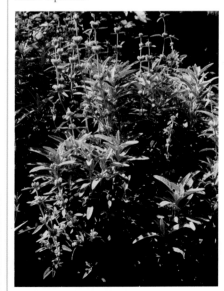

Phlomis italica
Only light pruning to remove damaged or wayward growth is needed.

PHOTINIA *INCL. STRANVAESIA*

Fully to frost-hardy, medium-sized to large, deciduous and evergreen shrubs and trees, usually of bushy, upright habit, with white flowers in spring or summer. Some of the evergreen photinias have brightly coloured young leaves in spring. The deciduous species, which tend to be intolerant of lime, have showy fruits in autumn and attractive leaf colour. Photinias do not require regular pruning, but they can be trained as standards, and pruning can also be used to enhance the effect of the striking spring foliage of some of the evergreens.

Photinia x fraseri

P. × FRASERI

Group of evergreen hybrids with brilliant red young foliage, which pruning can enhance. The hybrids may be used as formal or informal hedging.

■ **WHEN TO PRUNE** Spring. Clip hedges in spring and summer.

■ **TRAINING AND PRUNING** Like many evergreens, needs only minimal formative pruning (*see p.157*). To encourage more bright young leaves, when established, shorten stems by up to 15cm (6in), cutting just above an outward-facing bud. Tip-prune young shoots on hedges to encourage leafy growth. Clip hedges two or three times a year (*see p.46*). To renovate, cut hard back into the old wood. Response is usually good.

P. VILLOSA

Deciduous shrub, flowering in late spring or early summer, with red fruits and orange-red autumn colour.

■ **WHEN TO PRUNE** Winter, while dormant.

■ **TRAINING AND PRUNING** For a multi-stemmed shrub, allow to develop with minimal pruning. If growth becomes overcrowded, cut stems back to a low shoot where needed. To train as a standard, *see p.165*. Renovate an overgrown shrub by cutting back to a low framework. Thin subsequent growth if shoots are congested.

> OTHER PHOTINIAS
> P. ARBUTIFOLIA *See Heteromeles, p.198.*
> P. BEAUVERDIANA As for *P. villosa.*
> P. DAVIDIANA Minimal pruning.
> P. GLABRA, P. SERRATIFOLIA As for *P. × fraseri.*

PHYGELIUS

Evergreen and semi-evergreen shrubs or subshrubs, with tubular flowers on the current season's growth in summer to autumn. In cool climates they are usually cut back by severe frosts, but generally recover in spring. Plant in a sheltered spot or train on a warm wall.

■ **WHEN TO PRUNE** Spring, after the danger of frost has passed.

■ **TRAINING AND PRUNING** In warm climates, trim lightly in spring. In cool climates, cut back all frosted stems to healthy buds on live growth, or to the base of the plant. More growth is likely to survive if stems are tied in loosely on a warm wall. To renovate, cut all stems to the ground in spring.

***Phygelius* 'Winchester Fanfare'**
In cool climates, cutting back old stems will stimulate the fresh growth already appearing at the base of the plant.

PIERIS

Small to medium-sized, fully to frost-hardy, rounded, evergreen shrubs, with pink or white flowers in spring and, in some species, brilliant young foliage.

P. JAPONICA

LILY-OF-THE-VALLEY BUSH

Spring-flowering shrub with many cultivars that have brightly coloured young leaves; they can be grown in pots.

■ **WHEN TO PRUNE** Spring, after flowering.

■ **TRAINING AND PRUNING** Like many evergreens, needs minimal formative pruning (*see p.157*). Deadhead annually, and cut out frost-damaged growth promptly. To correct an uneven shape, cut back overlong branches to upright shoots; prune harder on the weaker side. To renovate a neglected specimen, cut back to a low framework. Plants usually recover, even when cut into old wood.

> OTHER PIERIS
> P. FLORIBUNDA As for *P. japonica.*
> P. FORMOSA As for *P. japonica.*
> P. FORMOSA VAR. FORRESTII cultivars As for *P. japonica.*

> OTHER ORNAMENTAL SHRUBS
> PHILESIA No pruning required.
> PHILLYREA Allow to grow freely or use to make topiary shapes, pruning as for *Buxus sempervirens* (*see p.179*), but in summer after flowering.
> PHILODENDRON Prune only to restrict size (for example, if growing under glass). *See also* Dictionary of Climbing Plants, *p.280.*
> PHORMIUM *See* Palms and palm-like plants, *p.41.*
> × PHYLLIOPSIS Minimal pruning, if necessary, as for *Erica cinerea* (*p.191*).
> PHYLLODOCE Minimal pruning, if necessary, as for *Erica cinerea* (*p.191*).
> PHYLLOTHAMNUS Minimal pruning, if necessary, as for *Erica cinerea* (*p.191*).
> PHYSOCARPUS Remove up to one in four of the oldest stems in summer after flowering, as for *Philadelphus* 'Virginal' (*see facing page*).
> PIMELEA Minimal pruning, if necessary, in spring.
> PIPTANTHUS Cut out frost-damaged wood in spring, and up to one in four old stems in summer, after flowering. May be wall-trained (*see p.163*).
> PISONIA Tolerates pruning, but little is generally needed.

PITTOSPORUM

Medium-sized to large, evergreen shrubs and trees with attractive leaves and fragrant flowers in spring or summer. They are usually neat, rounded and erect in habit, needing little pruning, and thrive in coastal conditions, where they grow even more dense and bushy. Most are suitable only for warm climates, but tender species may be grown under glass. *P. tenuifolium* and *P. ralphii*, among the hardiest species, are excellent for hedges or screens. Many cultivars of *P. tenuifolium* are available.

P. TENUIFOLIUM

TAWHIWHI, KOHUHU

Frost-hardy shrub or tree, with black stems, wavy-edged leaves and honey-scented, maroon flowers in spring.

■ **WHEN TO PRUNE** Mid-spring, when growth has started. Trim hedges again in midsummer (*see p.44*).

■ **TRAINING AND PRUNING** Maintain a single main stem. Established plants require little pruning; trim or thin growth only if necessary. They usually recover well if pruned hard in mid-spring.

> OTHER PITTOSPORUMS
> P. CRASSIFOLIUM, P. EUGENIOIDES, P. UNDULATUM As for *P. tenuifolium*.
> P. RALPHII As for *P. tenuifolium*, but more regular pruning is needed to keep it compact.
> P. TOBIRA As for *P. tenuifolium*, but response to renovation is slower. Can be trained as a standard (*see p.165*).

Pittosporum trained as a standard
Most pittosporums grow naturally with a single main stem or "central leader", making them suitable for training as standards (*see p.165*).

POTENTILLA

Fully hardy, deciduous, small to medium-sized shrubs of dense, rounded habit. The wiry stems of the current season's growth are covered with wild-rose-like flowers over a long period in summer. The many cultivars of *P. fruticosa* and several hybrids range widely in colour. Some look well in rock gardens, while others may be used for a low, informal hedge. Potentillas tend to accumulate old and twiggy shoots; pruning helps to keep them tidy and maintains their flowering performance.

■ **WHEN TO PRUNE** Mid-spring; trim in autumn.

■ **TRAINING AND PRUNING** Shorten vigorous young shoots by up to half. To tidy plants, trim over lightly after flowering. Cut back the oldest wood to the base and remove weak, twiggy growth. Prune hedges in the same way. Old shrubs sometimes respond well when cut back to a low framework of robust branches, but may be better replaced.

PROTEA

African genus of evergreen, frost-tender shrubs and trees, grown mainly for their large, striking flowerheads. They make handsome specimens in containers or under glass in cool temperate regions. They require minimal pruning unless it is necessary to restrict their size (for example, when growing under glass); shorten growth in early spring.

Protea cynaroides
The king protea may withstand light frosts when established.

PRUNUS *CHERRY*

Small to large, hardy shrubs, grown for their flowers and, in some cases, autumn colour and fruits. The evergreens make good hedges. Members of this genus are susceptible to various diseases, including silver leaf, which can gain entry through pruning wounds (*see also* Plum problems, *p.123*). With some exceptions, pruning is best kept to a minimum. Plants are least vulnerable in early summer, when in full leaf. The genus includes many trees (*see p.82*).

P. GLANDULOSA

Small, deciduous shrub with upright stems bearing pink or white flowers in late winter to early spring on the previous season's wood. It is best known in cultivars that have double flowers. Plant in a sunny site for the flowering wood to ripen well, otherwise dieback may occur in cold winters. Regular pruning is necessary to maintain the flowering performance. Free-standing specimens should be cut back annually to a low framework. Plants can also be trained against walls.

■ **WHEN TO PRUNE** Early spring, immediately after flowering.

■ **TRAINING AND PRUNING** In the first year after planting prune stems back to near ground level. In subsequent years, cut all stems hard back. To train against a wall (*see p.162*), develop a fan of framework stems. Cut out wood that has flowered as soon as blossom fades and tie in replacement shoots. Remove outward-growing shoots annually in midsummer. To renovate, cut all stems back to the ground in early spring. Old plants may not respond well, however, in which case they are best replaced.

P. LUSITANICA

LAUREL, PORTUGAL LAUREL

Large, evergreen shrub that may become tree-like if left unpruned. Slender spikes of small, fragrant, white flowers are produced in summer amid glossy, dark green leaves. It is suitable as a screening plant or an informal hedge and may be grown as a standard on a short clear leg.

Potentilla hedge
Trimmed plants have a neat, dense habit.

PTELEA

Large, fully hardy, deciduous shrubs and trees, which are grown mainly for their foliage and winged fruits. Pteleas generally require little pruning, but they will tolerate hard cutting back if required. Prune in early to mid-spring. They have weak root systems, and initial staking of plants is often advisable. *P. trifoliata*, the hop tree or water ash, is a low, spreading plant that may be trained as a small standard, with a single clear stem no more than 60–90cm (2–3ft) high (*see p.165*).

■ **WHEN TO PRUNE** Late spring or early summer.

■ **TRAINING AND PRUNING** Needs no special pruning, except to restrict size if needed: cut overlong shoots well back, to the trunk or a main stem. Specimens trained as standards (*see p.165*) are often trimmed to a rounded shape. Plants break readily from old wood, so if overgrown can be pruned hard back to a framework, or even almost to ground level. One season's new growth is usually enough to hide pruning wounds.

PYRACANTHA *FIRETHORN*

Fully to frost-hardy, evergreen, medium-sized to large shrubs, grown for their small, white flowers in early summer, and showy, red, orange or yellow fruits, borne on spurs from the old wood. They may be grown as specimens in a border, but make effective wall shrubs, trained as fans or espaliers. They are dense and spiny, making them also suitable for formal or informal hedging or barrier planting. The close pruning needed to maintain plants as wall shrubs can also be adapted to other formal shapes. Pyracanthas are prone to fireblight (*see p.117*), which must be cut out, though there are disease-resistant cultivars. Wear gloves when pruning; the thorns are long and sharp.

■ **WHEN TO PRUNE** Mid-spring. Wall-trained shrubs can also be pruned in late summer, shortening some new growth to expose the berries. Prune formal hedges in spring, then clip two or three times during the growing season.

■ **TRAINING AND PRUNING** Specimen shrubs need little pruning at the formative stage or when established. If wayward or over-vigorous branches spoil the shape, remove them completely. On wall-trained espaliers or fans, form a framework of permanent branches (*see p.162*). Cut back outward-growing shoots and shorten other shoots in spring, although this will mean losing some flowers and berries. In late summer cut back young shoots not needed for tying in to two or three leaves, to expose the next crop of ripening berries. Formal hedges need pruning two or three times during spring and summer. Hard pruning can be used to renovate plants, but it may make them more vulnerable to fireblight.

Pruning a wall-trained pyracantha, summer

1 *Remove completely any weak, damaged or unhealthy growth.*

2 *Shorten vigorous new shoots to two or three leaves.*

OTHER PRUNUS
P. LAUROCERASUS As for *P. lusitanica.*
P. MUME Allow to develop as a large shrub or small tree with minimal pruning. Remove any dieback promptly.
P. PUMILA Minimal pruning.
P. SINENSIS As for *P. glandulosa.*
P. TENELLA Minimal pruning except to control suckering; usually responds to hard pruning if flowering deteriorates.
P. TRILOBA Minimal pruning. If trained on a warm wall, laterals need to be pruned back to the framework.
For other species, see Dictionary of Ornamental Trees, p.82, *and* Tree Fruits, pp.122–136.

OTHER ORNAMENTAL SHRUBS
PLECTRANTHUS In warm climates *P. ecklonii* can be cut back hard in early spring, though pruning is not necessary.
PODALYRIA Prune in summer, after flowering, only if necessary.
POLYGALA Cut back long growths in late winter, if necessary.
POLYSCIAS No special needs.
POMADERRIS Tip-prune when young. Trim, if necessary, after flowering.
PONCIRUS Cut back young plants to encourage bushiness. Avoid pruning once established. Trim hedges twice in summer.

PORTULACARIA No special needs.
PROSTANTHERA Tip-prune young plants. Prune established plants after flowering if necessary, but do not cut into old wood.
PSEUDERANTHEMUM Prune in summer after flowering, only if necessary.
PSEUDOPANAX No special needs.
PSEUDOWINTERA Tolerates pruning, although it is rarely needed.
PSORALEA Tip-prune when young. When established, shorten flowered shoots by half after flowering. Do not cut into old wood.
PTEROSTYRAX Prune in summer after flowering, only if necessary.

R–S

RHODODENDRON

Small to large, evergreen, semi-evergreen and deciduous shrubs, which include azaleas. They have spectacular flowers, usually in spring; those that are deciduous often have attractive autumn leaf colour. Dwarf rhododendrons make good rock garden shrubs, while larger ones may become tree-like with age; many are woodland plants and some are suitable for informal hedges. Most are hardy; the tender species and hybrids may be grown under glass, and some are suitable as flowering house plants.

Most rhododendrons need little pruning, though many tolerate being cut back hard. However, rhododendrons can also be moved, in autumn or spring; transplanting is often a better course than renovation. Many rhododendrons are grafted and suckers should be removed. Older plants may become congested and suffer dieback through lack of light to the centre.

R. AUGUSTINII

Upright evergreen with lavender-blue flowers in spring. Lack of light may lead to dieback in the centre.

■ **WHEN TO PRUNE** Late spring or early summer, after flowering.

■ **TRAINING AND PRUNING** Little formative pruning is necessary. The natural habit of established plants is easily spoiled by pruning; remove only dead, diseased and damaged wood. Deadhead if practicable. Renovate by cutting back hard, leaving a balanced framework of old wood. Response is generally good.

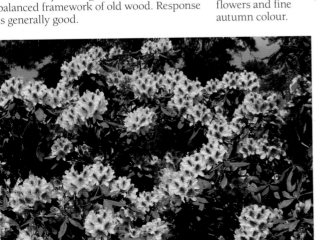

Clipped kurume azaleas in japan
R. kiusianum is a parent of these slow-growing, small-leaved hybrids, which in traditional Japanese gardens (*left*) are often trimmed to form bun shapes. They are sometimes grown as container plants and bonsai.

R. KIUSIANUM

A compact, semi-evergreen azalea with mauve or purple flowers in late spring. It tolerates clipping.

■ **WHEN TO PRUNE** Summer, after flowering. Renovate in spring.

■ **TRAINING AND PRUNING** Unless they are to be trimmed closely, plants require little pruning. Tip-prune young plants that are to be clipped, to promote dense growth. Clip over established plants with shears in early summer when flowers fade and, for a formal effect, once more in midsummer. Neglected plants can be renovated by shortening all growth by about half in spring, but old plants are better replaced.

R. LUTEUM

Hardy, deciduous, suckering azalea, with fragrant yellow spring flowers and fine autumn colour.

Rhododendron 'Mrs G. W. Leak'
Most of the large-flowered hybrids, including this magnificent example, require minimal pruning and are best treated as for *R. rex*.

■ **WHEN TO PRUNE** Summer, after flowering.

■ **TRAINING AND PRUNING** Prune young plants lightly to promote a balanced shape. Annual pruning of established plants is not necessary, but to prevent congestion and stimulate flowering, occasionally cut out completely, or to low shoots, one or two of the oldest stems. To renovate, cut back all but young stems in spring.

R. REX

Large evergreen with red, pink or creamy flowers in spring. The dark leaves have a buff felted underside.

■ **WHEN TO PRUNE** Early summer, after flowering.

■ **TRAINING AND PRUNING** Lightly prune young plants to form an evenly-shaped bush. Established specimens will require little to no pruning for many years, but deadhead where practicable. Old plants become leggy; this is not easy to rectify by hard pruning, as new growth does not break freely from old, thick branches.

OTHER RHODODENDRONS
LARGE-LEAVED HYBRIDS As for *R. rex*, but hard pruning may be successful provided that a good length of stem is left above the graft union.
KURUME AZALEAS As for *R. kiusianum*.
R. ARBOREUM As for *R. rex*.
R. CALOPHYTUM As for *R. rex*.
R. HIPPOPHAEOIDES As for *R. augustinii*.
R. MACABEANUM As for *R. rex*.
R. OCCIDENTALE As for *R. luteum*.
R. PONTICUM As for *R. augustinii*. Suitable for an informal hedge.
R. SINOGRANDE As for *R. rex*.
R. THOMSONII As for *R. rex*.
R. YAKUSHIMANUM HYBRIDS Avoid pruning except to deadhead.
TRIFLORUM SERIES As for *R. augustinii*.

Rhus typhina
Hard pruning produces a display of larger, showier leaves.

RHUS *SUMACH*

Hardy, deciduous shrubs, many of suckering habit, mainly grown for brilliant autumn leaf colour. Some can be regularly hard-pruned to enhance the foliage effect. Wear gloves to prune, since the sap is potentially harmful.

R. TYPHINA

STAGHORN SUMACH

Spreading, suckering shrub that may also be grown as a small standard. The cultivar 'Dissecta' (syn. 'Laciniata') has fine, fern-like foliage, which is enhanced by regular hard pruning.

■ **WHEN TO PRUNE** Early spring. Remove unwanted suckers as they appear.

■ **TRAINING AND PRUNING** For a shrub, allow to develop naturally. To grow as a standard, train with a clear stem about 1.2m (4ft) in height (see p.165). Remove any suckers (see p.153). Cut back plants grown for foliage effect (see p.164) either to about 10cm (4in) from the ground or to a low framework of woody stems each year. To renovate, cut to the ground, and thin out subsequent new shoots.

> OTHER RHUS
> R. COPALLINA, R. GLABRA, R. POTANINII, R. × PULVINATA As for *R. typhina*. R. × VERNICIFLUA *See* Dictionary of Ornamental Trees, p.86.

RIBES *CURRANT*

Fully to frost-hardy shrubs, grown for their attractive spring flowers (other species are grown for their fruit). Unpruned plants accumulate old wood and flowering performance declines.

R. SANGUINEUM

FLOWERING CURRANT

Fully hardy, deciduous shrub with white, pink or red flowers in spring, borne on the previous year's wood. Grow as a free-standing shrub, or use for an attractive, informal flowering hedge. Regular pruning encourages the production of fresh, young growth.

■ **WHEN TO PRUNE** Mid- to late spring, after flowering. Renovate in late winter.

■ **TRAINING AND PRUNING** Cut to the ground one in three or four of the oldest branches, leaving the remainder unpruned. Prune hedges selectively in the same way (shearing hedging plants will impair flowering). Neglected specimens can be renovated by cutting all stems to ground level.

ROSMARINUS *ROSEMARY*

Frost- and half-hardy evergreen shrubs, grown for their aromatic, grey-green leaves and blue spring flowers. *R. officinalis* has many cultivars of varying habit. Upright cultivars can be grown as formal or informal hedges.

■ **WHEN TO PRUNE** Early summer, after flowering. Renovate in mid-spring.

■ **TRAINING AND PRUNING** Allow young plants to develop unchecked. Established plants need little pruning except to cut lanky growth back to a main branch or low shoot. Formal hedges should be trimmed twice in the season (see p.46). Old, neglected plants are best replaced, but an overgrown, vigorous specimen can be renovated by cutting all stems back by at least half.

R. SPECIOSUM

FUCHSIA-FLOWERED CURRANT

Medium-sized, deciduous, spiny shrub with drooping, red flowers in mid- to late spring. It is frost-hardy, but in cool climates it flowers better if grown against a warm wall.

■ **WHEN TO PRUNE** Late spring, after flowering.

■ **TRAINING AND PRUNING** Prune a free-standing shrub as for *R. sanguineum*, but more moderately. To grow against a wall, train as a fan (see p.162); once the framework is established, plants need little pruning except, occasionally, to remove an old framework branch and train in young replacement growth. To renovate a neglected plant, cut all main stems back to about 30cm (12in).

> OTHER RIBES
> R. ALPINUM Minimal pruning required. R. ODORATUM As for *R. sanguineum*. *See also* Soft Fruits, pp.232–238.

Rosmarinus officinalis
With patience, rosemaries can be trained on cane frames – for example, to site container-grown plants against a wall in confined areas.

> OTHER ORNAMENTAL SHRUBS
> REINWARDTIA Remove shoot tips for a bushy habit. Prune hard after flowering.
> RETAMA Deadhead only.
> RHAMNUS No special needs. To prune evergreen hedges, clip the previous year's growth back by one-third in spring.
> RHAPHIOLEPIS No special needs, but tolerates pruning to shape if necessary.
>
> RHODOTYPOS Prune out some flowered wood in summer, after flowering. In warm climates can be pruned in winter.
> RICHEA Very slow-growing; needs minimal pruning. Spent flowerheads may be removed.
> RICINUS In cool climates, often grown as an annual, but may also be overwintered under glass. No special pruning needs
>
> when young, but support with canes. Treat mature specimens as for *Fatsia* (see p.193).
> ROMNEYA Prune in spring. In warm climates, remove up to half of the stems close to ground level; in cold climates, cut all winter-damaged growth back to live wood or to the ground.
> RONDELETIA If necessary, prune lightly in spring.

RUBUS *BRAMBLE*

Fully to frost-hardy scramblers and shrubs, producing cane-like growth from the base of the plant. Some are grown for their decorative young stems and foliage; others for the rose-like flowers. Some species have edible fruits. Most *Rubus* are prickly, so wear gloves when pruning.

R. 'BENENDEN' SYN. R. × TRIDEL

Vigorous, fully hardy, deciduous, arching shrub with peeling bark and large, white flowers in spring.

■ **WHEN TO PRUNE** Summer, after flowering.

■ **TRAINING AND PRUNING** Requires less drastic pruning than *R. thibetanus*, but annual removal of flowered growth and some old wood (*see below*) is needed to maintain the plant's vigour. To renovate, cut all stems to the ground in spring.

R. THIBETANUS

GHOST BRAMBLE

Vigorous, fully hardy, deciduous, arching shrub, whose young stems are most attractive when bare in winter. The stems flower in the second year, after

Rubus cockburnianus
Second-year stems are removed in summer after flowering (*inset*), to leave only the young, white stems for winter display.

which they are best removed, retaining only the youngest growth for a winter display of ghostly white stems.

■ **WHEN TO PRUNE** Summer, after flowering.

■ **TRAINING AND PRUNING** Each year, cut all of the flowered stems to the ground, leaving the current season's new canes unpruned (*see above*).

OTHER RUBUS
R. BIFLORUS, R. COCKBURNIANUS, R. ODORATUS As for *R. thibetanus*.
R. SPECTABILIS Suckers freely and can be invasive. As for *R. thibetanus*.
See also Soft Fruits, pp.228–231;
Dictionary of Climbing Plants, p.282.

Pruning an established *Rubus* 'Benenden'

2 *Shorten other stems by about one-third, to a vigorous young replacement shoot that enhances the shape.*

1 *Remove one in three or four stems, choosing the oldest and cutting to the base of the plant.*

3 *Tip-prune to remove dead flowerheads.*

RUTA *RUE*

Small, hardy, evergreen subshrubs, grown more for their blue-grey foliage than their unexciting heads of yellow summer flowers. Pruning keeps the plants compact, and can be used to enhance the foliage effect, at the expense of the flowers. Wear gloves for pruning, since the sap is potentially harmful. Prune in early spring: cut back all growth by at least half, to old wood, and remove any weak stems. Neglected plants often respond when cut back to within 15cm (6in) of ground level, but old specimens are best replaced.

SALIX *WILLOW*

Hardy, deciduous shrubs (some dwarf) and trees, grown for their habit, foliage, catkins and, in some cases, coloured stems. Regular pruning of those with attractive young growth ensures a supply of new, strongly coloured stems. If the plant is vigorous, all stems can be cut back, as for those large tree willows (*see p.86*) that can be grown as shrubs by coppicing. Other willows need lighter, less regular pruning. Dwarf willows require no special pruning.

S. HASTATA 'WEHRHAHNII'

Small, upright shrub with deep purple stems and silver-grey catkins in spring. Prune to maintain a balance between young stems (which usually have the best winter colour) and older wood with catkins.

■ **WHEN TO PRUNE** After planting, then occasionally in spring after the catkins have faded.

■ **TRAINING AND PRUNING** Let young plants develop with minimal pruning. On established plants, occasionally remove one or two of the oldest branches. To renovate, cut all stems back hard.

OTHER SALIX
S. FARGESII, S. MAGNIFICA As for *S. hastata* 'Wehrhahnii'.
S. ELAEAGNOS SUBSP. ANGUSTIFOLIA (syn. S. ROSMARINIFOLIA), S. GRACILISTYLA, S. PURPUREA No special needs. Prune lightly in winter if necessary.
S. HELVETICA, S. LANATA No special needs.
S. IRRORATA No special needs, but cut back older stems regularly to the base for a display of young, glaucous shoots.
S. REPENS, S. RETICULATA Dwarf species needing only minimal pruning. *See also* Dictionary of Ornamental Trees, p.86.

SALVIA *SAGE*

Small, evergreen shrubs and subshrubs in a genus that also includes annuals, biennials and perennials. The shrubs and subshrubs are grown for their flowers and aromatic foliage, of culinary value in some salvias. Some are hardy, while others may only be grown in cool climates in the shelter of a warm wall, though they are not suitable for wall-training. Regular pruning produces strong young growth on shrubby sages.

S. MICROPHYLLA SYN. S. GRAHAMII

Half-hardy shrub with bright red flowers in late summer and autumn. In cool climates it may survive winters as a small shrub at the base of a warm wall.

■ **WHEN TO PRUNE** Spring, when growth begins.

■ **TRAINING AND PRUNING** In warm climates keep pruning to the minimum. In cool climates tip-prune shoots of young plants to encourage branching. When the shrub is established, cut back annually to the framework of woody stems. Neglected plants may respond if cut back hard to near ground level, but it is not long-lived in cool climates.

S. OFFICINALIS

COMMON SAGE

Hardy shrub with racemes of blue-purple flowers in summer. This culinary herb has various cultivars with purple, variegated or golden leaves. Unpruned, they become leggy and lose their compact habit.

■ **WHEN TO PRUNE** Mid-spring, and in summer to remove flowers.

■ **TRAINING AND PRUNING** Tip-prune after planting (*see p.155*). If older plants become bare at the base, cut back into the old wood, in effect a form of renovation. Forms grown chiefly for their coloured foliage give a better display if trimmed in spring, this regular pruning resulting in neatly rounded bushes. If flowers are produced in summer, trim them off.

> **OTHER SALVIAS**
> S. FULGENS, S. GREGGII, S. LEUCOPHYLLA, S. SESSEI As for *S. microphylla*.

SAMBUCUS *ELDER*

Hardy, medium-sized to large deciduous shrubs, some of which are coarse and weedy. Other elders, however, are grown for their flowers and fruits; some also have highly ornamental foliage. Most respond vigorously to pruning; regular hard pruning also enhances the effect of cultivars grown for their foliage. They are most commonly grown as multi-stemmed bushes, which tend to become tall and leggy unless pruned. Some strong-growing elders will make good standards when trained with a clear trunk.

■ **WHEN TO PRUNE** Winter, while dormant. Remove suckers at the base of standards as they appear.

■ **TRAINING AND PRUNING** For a large shrub, allow to grow unpruned for a season. Then cut down half the stems to ground level and shorten the remainder by half. Thereafter, shorten one-year-old wood by half and cut back older stems to the ground. More severe pruning, carried out regularly, can be used to enhance the foliage effect of purple and cut-leaf elders, such as *S. canadensis* 'Acutiloba' and 'Aurea', and *S. nigra* f. *laciniata*, and the purple-leaved *S. nigra* 'Guincho Purple'. They can be cut back annually (*see p.164*) to ground level or to a low framework, as for *Buddleja davidii* (*see p.178*). If the resulting shoots are congested, thin them early in the growing season.

Use only vigorous species such as *S. sieboldiana* to train as standards (*see p.165*), clearing the stem to a height of 1–2m (3–6ft). These vigorous elders tend to produce numerous suckers and shoots on the clear stem, which should be removed promptly. Elders are generally short-lived, in spite of the rejuvenating effects that hard pruning can have. Old and neglected specimens are best replaced.

Santolina splayed out by snow
Prune back hard into old wood to stimulate fresh, bushy growth.

SANTOLINA

Small, evergreen, frost-hardy shrubs with aromatic, finely divided grey-green leaves, and yellow to white, button-like flowers in summer. Unless regularly pruned, plants become straggly.

■ **WHEN TO PRUNE** Autumn, after flowering. Prune hard in early spring.

■ **TRAINING AND PRUNING** Shorten stems on newly planted santolinas to encourage bushy growth. Trim off faded flowers and long shoots annually in autumn. Every two or three years, as plants become more open and straggly, cut hard back into old wood. Young plants usually respond well, but old specimens are better replaced.

> **OTHER ORNAMENTAL SHRUBS**
> RUELLIA No special needs. Prune lightly to shape after flowering if necessary.
> RULINGIA No special needs. May be tip-pruned to encourage a bushy habit.
> RUSCHIA Minimal pruning.
> RUSSELIA Prune some of the oldest stems to the base in winter.
> SARCOCOCCA Minimal pruning, if necessary, in spring.
> SELAGO Minimal pruning.
> SENECIO *see Brachyglottis* (p.177), *also* Dictionary of Climbing Plants (p.283).
>
> SENNA *see Cassia* (p.182).
> SERISSA Trim after flowering, in autumn.
> SERRURIA As for *Protea* (see p.212).
> SESBANIA As for *Cassia* (see p.182).
> SHEPHERDIA Minimal pruning.
> SIBIRAEA As for *Spiraea* 'Arguta' (see p.219).
> SIDERITIS No special needs.
> SIMMONDSIA No special needs. May be trimmed as a hedge.
> SINOJACKIA Minimal pruning.

SKIMMIA

Small to medium-sized, hardy, evergreen shrubs, grown for their neat habit, fragrant spring flowers and long-lasting red fruits. Fruits are produced on female plants usually only if a male is sited nearby, though a few skimmias are hermaphrodites. Skimmias are naturally compact shrubs, requiring little pruning, but if overvigorous shoots spoil the outline, these can be cut back to well within the bush (to hide the cut) in spring, after flowering. Skimmias will tolerate harder pruning but old plants are better replaced than cut back hard in an attempt to renovate them.

Skimmia japonica
Cut back overlong shoots that unbalance the neat, rounded shape.

SOLANUM

Large genus containing many scandent or scrambling species (*see* Dictionary of Climbing Plants, *p.283*), and a number of evergreen, semi-evergreen or deciduous small shrubs with attractive flowers and, in some cases, fruits. Most of the shrubs are rather tender. In cool climates they are grown under glass; some, such as the bushy, half-hardy, evergreen *S. pseudocapsicum*, the scarlet-fruited Jerusalem cherry, and its cultivars are treated as annuals. The smaller evergreen, *S. capsicastrum*, the winter cherry, has ovoid, not rounded, orange-red fruits. Those not grown as annuals, whether outdoors or under glass, benefit from being cut back to a low framework in spring.

SOPHORA *KOWHAI*

Genus that includes not only trees (*see p.88*) but also medium-sized to large, deciduous or semi-evergreen shrubs, grown for their foliage and pea-like flowers. They are fully to frost-hardy, but require sun; some benefit from shelter and in cool climates are best planted against a warm wall. Allow plants to develop their naturally elegant habit without extensive pruning. Pruning cuts, especially if they are made in late winter or spring, are likely to bleed sap, and for this reason pruning is best delayed until midsummer.

Sophora davidii
Minimal pruning allows mature, flowering growth to develop.

S. TETRAPTERA

Large, evergreen or semi-evergreen shrub with golden-yellow flowers in late spring. The buds form in winter, so may be damaged by severe weather. Grown as a free-standing specimen, it may reach tree-like proportions. It may also be wall-grown for protection in cool climates. Flowers are borne on mature wood, so pruning is best kept to a minimum.

■ **WHEN TO PRUNE** Midsummer, when cuts are least likely to bleed.

■ **TRAINING AND PRUNING** Allow free-standing shrubs to develop naturally. Tie in shrubs planted against a wall informally and allow to develop with minimal pruning, or train more formally as fans (*see p.162*), though the pruning necessary may delay flowering for five years or more. Hard pruning is likely to be successful only in warm climates.

OTHER SOPHORAS
S. DAVIDII, S. MACROCARPA,
S. MICROPHYLLA As for *S. tetraptera*.
For other species, see Dictionary of Ornamental Trees, *p.88*.

SPARRMANNIA

Sparrmannia africana is a large, tender, evergreen, erect shrub or small tree with white and yellow flowers in late spring and summer. It responds well to pruning to restrict size under glass.

■ **WHEN TO PRUNE** Summer, after flowering; winter if pruned back hard.

■ **TRAINING AND PRUNING** In warm climates, allow free-standing shrubs to develop with minimal pruning. Under glass in cool climates, cut back the flowered growth to sideshoots for a more compact habit. For larger leaves and flowers, cut back hard annually or biennially (*see p.164*). To renovate, cut all growth back to near ground level.

SPARTIUM

Spartium junceum (Spanish broom) is the only species, a hardy, medium-sized, deciduous shrub with erect, rush-like stems, bearing fragrant, yellow flowers from summer to autumn on the new growth. Left unpruned, it tends to become top-heavy. Prune to keep compact and promote a long flowering season.

■ **WHEN TO PRUNE** Early spring, when growth commences.

■ **TRAINING AND PRUNING** In the first two years, cut back the main stems by half to promote a dense habit. Subsequently every two or three years reduce the previous season's growth to within 2.5cm (1in) of the old wood. Plants may be rejuvenated by hard pruning but replacement is preferable.

SPHAERALCEA

Small, half-hardy, deciduous subshrubs (evergreen in warm climates), flowering in summer on the current season's growth. may be grown outdoors in cool climates if in a sheltered, sunny site, but the top growth is usually killed by frost. They can also be grown under glass. In warm climates, little pruning is generally needed; cut back any overlong stems in spring. In cool areas prune annually to a woody framework or to the base. Replace old plants rather than attempt renovation.

SPIRAEA

Small to medium-sized, hardy, deciduous or semi-evergreen shrubs, some suckering freely, with attractive flowers and, on some cultivars, foliage. Some spiraeas are large and arching in habit, flowering on either old or new growth; others are small and twiggy, flowering on the current season's shoots. Regular pruning, to which all respond well, maintains flowering performance. Timing depends on whether the species flowers on new or old wood.

S. 'ARGUTA'

BRIDAL WREATH, FOAM OF MAY

Medium-sized shrub with clusters of small, white flowers from mid- to late spring on the previous season's growth. Prune to prevent an accumulation of old, dead wood, and to encourage the production of new stems that will flower the following year.

■ **WHEN TO PRUNE** Early summer, just after flowering.

■ **TRAINING AND PRUNING** On young plants, cut back flowered stems to strong buds and remove any weak growth entirely. Once established, thin growth by cutting back to ground level one in four of the oldest stems. Remove any weak growth, and shorten the flowered stems by up to half, cutting back to strong shoots. Neglected specimens may respond slowly to drastic pruning. Leaving two or three strong stems unpruned, cut the others back to ground level.

Pruning *Spiraea* **'Arguta'**
Thin these dense, twiggy bushes annually by removing some stems at the base, and by shortening flowered stems back to healthy buds or well-placed sideshoots.

S. DOUGLASII

Vigorous, upright, medium-sized shrub that suckers freely. It produces purplish-pink flowers in mid-summer on the current season's growth. Annual pruning keeps it healthy and encourages new flowering stems.

■ **WHEN TO PRUNE** Early spring; deadhead after flowering.

■ **TRAINING AND PRUNING** Cut all weak and very old wood back to ground level. Shorten one in three or four (depending on the plant's vigour) of the remaining stems to within two to four buds of the previous year's growth; remove some stems entirely where necessary to maintain an open habit. When clumps decline in vigour, use young rooted stems as replacements; cut these back to near ground level on planting.

S. JAPONICA

Small shrub with small heads of usually pink flowers on the current season's shoots in summer. There are many cultivars, some, such as 'Goldflame', with attractive young leaves. Annual pruning keeps plants free-flowering with fresh young foliage.

■ **WHEN TO PRUNE** Early spring; deadhead after flowering.

■ **TRAINING AND PRUNING** On planting, cut out all weak and old wood. Prune back remaining stems to leave a framework 10–15cm (4–6in) high, and prune to one or two buds of this every year (*see also Perovskia, p.209*). Dwarf cultivars need only be clipped over to shape after flowering. Renovate as for *S. douglasii*.

> **OTHER SPIRAEAS**
> S. CANTONIENSIS, S. NIPPONICA, S. PRUNIFOLIA, S. THUNBERGII, S. × VANHOUTTEI, S. VEITCHII As for S. 'Arguta'.
> S. DOUGLASII SUBSP. MENZIESII, S. JAPONICA 'BUMALDA' (syn. S. × BUMALDA) As for S. japonica.
> S. SALICIFOLIA As for S. douglasii.

STACHYURUS

Medium-sized to large, hardy, deciduous shrub with an open, spreading habit, flowering in early spring on buds produced the previous autumn. It does not require regular pruning, but can be lightly renovated by cutting out old, thin growth at the base, and shortening overlong branches by up to a third. Prune in spring after flowering; plants break readily from the base.

Stachyurus chinensis **'Magpie'**
The pendent clusters of bell-shaped, pale yellow flowers of this variegated cultivar, here seen informally wall-trained, open before the leaves in early spring. Buds may be affected by severe winter cold.

OTHER ORNAMENTAL TREES
SORBARIA Prune in late winter, removing one or two old stems and cutting back flowered shoots close to main stems. Remove unwanted suckers (*see p.153*).

SORBUS Remove unwanted suckers from *S. reducta*. See also Ornamental Trees, *p.88*.

STEPHANANDRA

Fully hardy, deciduous, medium-sized shrubs. They are grown more for their autumn leaf colour and the effect of their rich brown stems in winter than for their summer flowers, which are insignificant. They form suckering clumps in maturity. In summer, after flowering, thin plants by removing about one in four old stems to the base, then cut back the remaining flowered stems to strong sideshoots, aiming to maintain the natural arching habit. Renovate by cutting all stems back to the base in winter or early spring.

SYMPHORICARPOS

Fully hardy, deciduous shrubs, with dense, twiggy growth and clusters of showy fruits. Most are suckering plants, useful for low barrier planting and as ground cover. For dense cover, prune on planting to 30cm (12in) high. No further pruning is necessary, though old, twiggy growth can be thinned in early spring. If spread needs restricting, in early spring either remove surplus growth to the base or chop it away at the edges with a spade. Renovate by cutting all stems to ground level; on large areas, a nylon-line trimmer may be used.

SYRINGA *LILAC*

Fully hardy, small to large deciduous shrubs, becoming tree-like with age, grown for their attractive, usually scented flowers borne in spring and early summer.

S. VULGARIS

Vigorous shrubs with white, pink, lilac or purple flowers on the previous season's wood. They need minimal attention until stems become old and lanky, when they respond well to renovation. Cultivars are often grafted and may sucker freely.

5 | 15

m | ft

Syringa meyeri 'Palibin'
This lilac is usually grown naturally as a densely twiggy bush, but it can be trained into an attractive standard shrub, as here.

■ **WHEN TO PRUNE** Midsummer, as the flowers fade. Renovate in winter.

■ **TRAINING AND PRUNING** Young plants often need light formative pruning (*see p.157*) to encourage the development of a balanced shape. Established plants should be deadheaded carefully, where practical, with secateurs (*see p.155*) to avoid damaging the young shoots which will flower next year. Remove suckers as seen (*see p.153*). To renovate, cut back main stems to within 30–60cm (12–24in) of the ground (*see also p.161*). Response is good, and regrowth should be thinned, but flowering will be delayed by up to three years. It is preferable to stagger hard pruning over two to three years.

S. MEYERI

Syringa meyeri is a twiggy shrub grown for its panicles of fragrant purple flowers, which are borne in early summer; there is sometimes a second flush of flowers later in the season.

2 | 6

m | ft

■ **WHEN TO PRUNE** Midsummer, after flowering.

■ **TRAINING AND PRUNING** Bushes are naturally twiggy, and require minimal pruning. *S. meyeri* may also be trained as a standard (*see left, and p.165*).

OTHER LILACS
S. × JOSIFLEXA As for *S. vulgaris*.
S. MICROPHYLLA 'SUPERBA' As for *S. meyeri*.
S. × PERSICA, S. × PRESTONIAE, S. REFLEXA, S. YUNNANENSIS As for *S. vulgaris*.

T – V

Tamarix parviflora
This spring-flowering tamarisk should be pruned in summer, to prevent it from becoming straggly.

TAMARIX *TAMARISK*

Fully to frost-hardy, deciduous or evergreen shrubs and trees, grown for their feathery, plume-like branches and pink flowers. In gardens they usually require pruning to keep them compact; they are suitable for an informal hedge, particularly in coastal sites.

5 | 15

m | ft

■ **WHEN TO PRUNE** Tamarisks flowering in early summer, such as *T. parviflora*, are pruned in summer, after flowering. Prune those flowering in late summer, such as *T. ramosissima*, in early spring.

■ **TRAINING AND PRUNING** To grow as a well-branched, multi-stemmed shrub, cut back stems by half on planting and again in the following year. Prune established plants annually, removing weak growth and cutting back flowered stems to strong sideshoots. *T. ramosissima* can be hard-pruned annually to encourage flower production and keep the plant bushy. To use as an informal hedge, cut back plants to 30cm (12in) on planting and tip-prune new shoots in summer to encourage dense growth. Cut back the previous season's growth on established hedges in late winter (*see also* Hedges, *p.45*). To renovate overgrown specimens and hedges, cut back hard into the old wood. They may not flower again for at least two years. Plants grown as standards (*see p.165*) need staking and the head needs hard pruning at the appropriate time to keep it compact. The new stems will arch gracefully.

THYMUS *THYME*

Fully to half-hardy shrubs and sub-shrubs grown for their aromatic leaves. Some are used as culinary herbs. All thymes are small plants (some are prostrate), requiring full sun; they are suitable for rock gardens or for cracks in paving. Regular pruning keeps them neat and maintains the production of fresh leaves. Cultivars are available that have gold, silver or variegated foliage. These may produce shoots with plain green leaves.

■ **WHEN TO PRUNE** Late summer.

■ **TRAINING AND PRUNING** The very prostrate cultivars need no pruning. Lightly trim other thymes with shears or secateurs in summer to remove all dead flowerheads. On forms with coloured or variegated leaves, remove any reverted shoots (*see p.153*) throughout the growing season, cutting them right out to their point of origin. Fresh growth will not break from old wood, so old, neglected plants are best replaced.

***Thymus vulgaris* 'Silver Posie'**
Lightly trim or clip over this variegated thyme in summer, after flowering.

TIBOUCHINA

Large, tender evergreens, grown for their foliage and summer flowers borne on new wood. They may only be grown as free-standing shrubs in warm climates. In cool climates they may be grown under glass.

ULEX

Small, hardy shrubs with vicious spines and yellow flowers. Although virtually leafless, their green stems and spines make them appear to be evergreen. They thrive in windy, exposed sites and on poor soil; *U. europaeus* (gorse) is a serious weed in some countries, including Australia and New Zealand. Planted in rich garden soil they may become leggy, with straggly stems that become bare at the base. Pruning keeps plants compact and shapely.

■ **WHEN TO PRUNE** The first spring after planting, then in late spring to early summer, after flowering. Renovate in early spring.

■ **TRAINING AND PRUNING** If young plants are straggly, encourage them to bush out by shortening all stems by a quarter to half in early spring (on the small species *U. minor*, just pinch out the tips of the stems). Once established, clip over lightly after flowering to keep growth compact. Shorten wayward stems, if necessary. Renovate plants that have

Pinch out the tips of young shoots to encourage bushiness. Cut back flowered shoots to two pairs of buds in spring. They can be cut back to a framework and are suitable for wall training (*see p.162*).

Ulex europaeus
In favoured garden conditions, gorse often becomes spreading and leggy if not regularly clipped over after flowering.

become leggy by cutting back hard (*see p.160*) into the old wood, to within 15cm (6in) of the ground if necessary. Response is usually very good.

VESTIA

Medium-sized, fast-growing, evergreen shrub, grown for its pale yellow flowers and berries, borne on the current season's wood, and also for its foliage. The single species, *V. foetida*, is usually cut to the ground by hard frosts; it needs a sheltered position in cool climates. Pinch out the growing tips of young plants (*see p.152*) to encourage branching. In warm climates, prune in late summer

as for *Cestrum* (*see p.184*), cutting back growths that have flowered by about half. Each year, cut to the base one or two of the oldest stems so that old growth does not accumulate and crowd young, flowering shoots. To renovate neglected specimens, cut back to ground level or a low framework in early spring. In cool climates, cut all stems back to the ground in spring.

OTHER ORNAMENTAL TREES

STAPHYLEA As for *Sambucus* (*p.217*). Large species, such as *S. holocarpus*, can be trained as standard trees (*see p.26*).
STRANSVAESIA, × STRANVINIA *see Photinia* (*p.211*).
STREPTOSOLEN *See Dictionary of Climbing Plants, p.284.*
SUTERA Minimal pruning only.
SUTHERLANDIA Prune lightly if necessary after fruiting. Short-lived; straggly plants are best replaced.
SWAINSONA Cut back each spring to within 30cm (12in) of the ground.
SYCOPSIS Minimal pruning.

SYMPLOCOS No special needs. Shorten over-long stems; when mature, some unproductive old growth may occasionally be removed.
TECOMA *See Tecomaria, Dictionary of Climbing Plants, p.285.*
TELOPEA Tip-prune young plants (*see p.155*). After flowering, prune flowered stems to leave 25cm (10in) of the previous year's growth. May be cut back hard to renovate.
TERNSTROEMIA No special needs. Shape lightly in spring if necessary.
TETRAPANAX Deadhead, and remove any suckers; no other special needs.
TEUCRIUM Prune in spring as growth begins,

removing frost damage and trimming to keep compact. Responds well to hard pruning if necessary. *T. chamaedrys* can make a low hedge, clipped in summer.
TURRAEA No special needs. Can be trimmed as a hedge.
UGNI No special needs. Shorten any overlong shoots.
VACCINIUM No special needs; if necessary, trim deciduous species in winter, and evergreens in spring.
See also Blueberries, p.239.
VALLEA Lightly prune in summer after flowering.

VIBURNUM

Hardy, small to large, deciduous, semi-evergreen and evergreen shrubs. Some are grown for their fragrant flowers; others have attractive berries in autumn. Habits vary, but all make new growth from the base. Pruning requirements depend on the purpose for which the shrub is grown. Some make fine specimens; others that benefit from cross-pollination to produce berries, such as *V. davidii*, are best planted in informal groups. A few lend themselves to formal training and trimming. The timing of pruning depends on the flowering season. All mature viburnums (with the exception of *V. plicatum*) usually respond well to hard pruning.

V. × BODNANTENSE

Belongs to a group of deciduous, medium-sized, upright shrubs with fragrant, white or pink flowers at the ends of the bare stems in autumn and winter. New stems are regularly produced from the base. Pruning is usually restricted to the removal of old, unproductive wood.

■ **WHEN TO PRUNE** Early spring, immediately after flowering. Renovate in late spring.

■ **TRAINING AND PRUNING** Allow young plants to develop unpruned. On established bushes, cut out up to one in five branches to the base, removing the oldest and weakest. Leave the remainder unpruned: shortening them may affect flowering the following year and spoil the shape of the shrub. To renovate, cut all branches down to the base. New shoots are usually freely produced.

Viburnum × bodnantense
Remove up to one in five of the oldest stems at the base to thin this dense, erect shrub.

V. PLICATUM

JAPANESE SNOWBALL TREE

Stately, deciduous shrub, with branches held in horizontal tiers. Showy, white, "lace-cap" flowers are borne in late spring and early summer on the previous season's wood. A spreading habit normally develops without extensive pruning, but vigorous, upright shoots that spoil the outline may need to be removed.

■ **WHEN TO PRUNE** Summer, after flowering. Renovate in late spring.

■ **TRAINING AND PRUNING** On young plants, keep pruning to a minimum. Strong, upright growths will develop at the centre of the bush, and then branch to form the characteristic tiers. On mature plants, new vertical shoots growing through the tiers may spoil the form and can be removed at their point of origin, unless it is preferable to let them develop and replace old, damaged or unproductive branches. If reasonably young and vigorous, plants may respond to drastic cutting back to a branch framework in spring, but such pruning usually spoils the form.

V. TINUS

LAURUSTINUS

Medium-sized, evergreen shrub with heads of star-shaped, white flowers in winter and spring. More compact than many viburnums, it responds well to pruning and can be trained and clipped. It may be grown as a specimen shrub, a standard, or a formal or informal hedge.

■ **WHEN TO PRUNE** Early summer, after flowering. Renovate in late spring.

Viburnum plicatum* var. *tomentosum
Once the mature form is well-established, remove any strongly growing vertical shoots that spoil the distinctive tiered form.

■ **TRAINING AND PRUNING** When grown as a specimen shrub, it may require some formative pruning (*see p.157*) to ensure that the developing shape is well balanced. Once plants are established, keep pruning to a minimum, but remove any overvigorous shoots that spoil the shape, cutting them back to well within the plant's outline to hide where the cuts have been made. To train as a standard, *see p.165*. Hedges (*see p.44*) should be trimmed with secateurs to avoid unsightly damage to individual leaves. To renovate a specimen plant, cut back hard (*see p.160*) in late spring. Treat a neglected hedge in the same way.

Viburnum tinus
All viburnums tend to make new growth from the base; if trained as standards, rub out any emerging shoots on the clear trunk as soon as seen.

OTHER VIBURNUMS

V. BETULIFOLIUM As for *V. × bodnantense*, but prune in late winter, after fruiting.
V. × BURKWOODII, V. CARLESII, V. × CARLCEPHALUM Minimal pruning, in midsummer if necessary.
V. DAVIDII Spreading, dense habit, good ground cover. Minimal pruning; to keep ground-cover plants neat, cut back to strong shoots or base of plant. Deadhead male plants; they do not set fruit.
V. FARRERI As for *V. × bodnantense*.
V. LANTANA, V. RHYTIDOPHYLLUM As for *V. × bodnantense*, but prune late winter.
V. OPULUS As for *V. × bodnantense*.

VINCA *PERIWINKLE*

Evergreen, hardy subshrubs of indefinite spread that make excellent ground cover. The stems are initially upright, then trail, rooting at their tips or where they touch the ground. Blue, white or purple flowers are produced at varying times of the year. Prune to maintain dense growth, to keep the plants within bounds and to expose the flowers. Occasional hard pruning makes it possible to clear out debris and can improve flowering performance.

■ **WHEN TO PRUNE** Spring.

■ **TRAINING AND PRUNING** Prune annually to cut back excess growth and any long, straggling stems. When growth becomes congested, trim the whole surface with shears or a nylon-line trimmer.

VITEX

Medium-sized, deciduous shrubs and trees grown for their flowers, borne in summer and autumn on the current season's growth. In cool climates, they require a sheltered position, and do well fan-trained against a warm wall (*see p.162*). Free-standing shrubs require only minimal pruning when young. When established, prune flowered shoots back to spurs or young shoots on main stems in spring and remove one or two old stems completely. On a wall-trained fan of permanent branches, cut back the previous season's growth to short spurs. Occasionally train in a young shoot to replace an old framework stem.

OTHER ORNAMENTAL SHRUBS

VIMINARIA Prune *V. juncea* as for *Cytisus scoparius* (*see p.188*); take care when pruning not to spoil the natural habit.
WEINMANNIA Prune lightly in spring if necessary.
WESTRINGIA No special needs. If necessary, prune lightly in summer after flowering.
WIGANDIA Prune in spring, cutting out growth that has flowered.
WITHANIA Prune in spring, cutting out growth that has flowered.
XANTHOCERAS No special needs. Tolerates thinning if required.
XANTHORHIZA Suckering and naturally untidy in habit. No special needs.
XANTHOSOMA Minimal pruning needed.
XYLOSMA No special needs, but suitable for wall-training or clipping as a hedge or shaped specimen.
YUCCA See Palms and palm-like plants, *p.43*.
ZANTHOXYLUM Pruning in spring is necessary to remove accumulated dead wood. Some species are spiny.
ZAUSCHNERIA Subshrub; cut back to the woody rootstock in spring.

W–Z

WEIGELA

Small to medium-sized, fully hardy, deciduous shrubs, grown for the tubular, red, white or pink flowers borne in summer on the previous year's wood. Some also have attractive foliage. All respond well to pruning, which should be used to divert the plant's energy away from seed production and encourage strong new growth.

W. FLORIDA

Medium-sized shrub with flowers in a range of colours in spring or summer. Regular pruning benefits flower production. Harder pruning can be used to enhance the foliage effect of those cultivars with attractive bronze, purple or variegated leaves.

3 | 10

m | ft

■ **WHEN TO PRUNE** Midsummer, after flowering. Renovate in early spring.

■ **TRAINING AND PRUNING** Young plants require little formative pruning. When established, each year cut back flowered stems to strong, usually upright, shoots below the faded flowers. Cut out at the base one or two old stems, aiming to maintain a balance between mature and young wood, and remove or shorten overlong new growth that spoils the plant's shape. Yellow and purple-leaved cultivars may be cut back harder: remove about three-quarters of the old wood entirely and shorten the remaining stems by three-quarters. Cut out any reverted shoots on variegated cultivars (*see p.153*). To renovate, cut all stems to ground level. Thin the new shoots in midsummer.

OTHER WEIGELAS

W. 'BRISTOL RUBY', 'EVA RATHKE' and other hybrids As for *W. florida*.
W. HORTENSIS, W. MIDDENDORFFIANA, W. PRAECOX As for *W. florida*.

Pruning an established *Weigela florida*

1 Remove one or two of the oldest stems completely, cutting to within 5–8cm (2–3in) of the base.

2 Remove over-vigorous upright new growth, or shorten to a sideshoot (though these shoots are often unbranched).

3 Prune back flowered stems to healthy buds or a well-placed sideshoot.

ZENOBIA

Genus of one species of medium-sized, fully hardy, deciduous or semi-evergreen shrub, *Z. pulverulenta*, grown for its fragrant, white summer flowers. Pruning promotes vigour and benefits flowering in subsequent seasons. The plant's habit is arching and suckering, and new shoots are freely produced from the base.

■ **WHEN TO PRUNE** Midsummer, as the flowers fade. Renovate in mid-spring.

■ **TRAINING AND PRUNING** Young plants require little formative pruning. Once plants are established, prune annually. Cut back the flowered stems to strong shoots. Cut out weak growths completely and, over a period of three years, take out one or two old branches completely, but without spoiling the plant's natural habit. To renovate old or neglected, overgrown plants, cut all old wood back to ground level. Response is usually very good.

Soft fruits

Whether grown as bushes or standards, trained as fans or cordons against sunny walls, or forming a decorative fruiting screen, bush and cane fruits need annual pruning to crop well.

A crop of fresh summer fruits is a pleasure that even a small garden can afford. A well-tended, traditional "model" fruit garden may for many gardeners be the ideal, but soft fruits (sometimes called berry fruits) can also be used to great effect in the ornamental garden. Indeed many soft fruits, such as raspberries (*Rubus idaeus*) and blackcurrants (*Ribes nigrum*), have purely ornamental counterparts that are among the most popular of garden plants.

Soft fruits are, generally, cool-climate plants that enjoy sun but dislike humidity and stagnant air. All are self-fertile, and are propagated by suckers, layers or cuttings. None requires grafting, but some can be grafted – for example, to form standards. Most are prone to viruses, and a specialist fruit nursery is always the best source for healthy stock. For some fruits, certification schemes ensure that plants are virus-free.

The soft fruits requiring pruning fall into two groups: cane fruits and bush fruits. The cane fruits – raspberries, blackberries, and hybrid berries such as the tayberry – are closely related, as are the bush fruits gooseberries and currants; the acid-loving blueberry bush belongs to the heather family. The aim of pruning and training is not only to develop and maintain healthy, well-shaped plants, but also to establish a gentle cycle of pruning from season to season, removing old or otherwise unproductive wood to encourage young, strong, fruitful growth to take its place. Left unpruned, all soft fruits will crop, but fruit quality and size decline steeply. Understanding and using the correct pruning and training techniques is the essence of success, ensuring the best possible quantity and quality of fruit and encouraging strong new growth that will crop in future years. It may seem daunting at first, since incorrect pruning could result in the loss of a season's crop. However, a basic grasp of the fruiting habits of each type is not hard to achieve, and makes the various tasks simple and satisfying.

Standard gooseberry
Gooseberries are particularly amenable to pruning and training. A standard bush, as shown here, has ornamental value and raises the fruit-bearing branches to a level at which harvesting becomes less of a back-breaking task.

◀ Bountiful blueberries
With their white, bell-shaped flowers, succulent blue fruits and vivid red and orange autumn leaf colour, blueberries are attractive ornamental as well as productive shrubs.

Soft Fruit Forms

The cane fruits (raspberries, blackberries and hybrids such as the loganberry) each year throw up strong new vertical shoots – canes or "rods" – from the base, and these replace older, fruited canes as they die. Pruning speeds up this natural process, and is made easier by careful training of the long, whippy growths. The bush fruits – currants, gooseberries and blueberries – are naturally shrubby and compact. Most can also be readily trained into a number of forms to take advantage of favoured sites. Wall-training suits them well, though the wall must first be correctly wired (*see p.228*) to let air circulate behind the plants.

Both training and correct pruning can increase yields and also make cultivation easier, particularly for the thorned plants.

Matching the choice of cultivar and trained form to the site is important, particularly for the cane fruits, as they dislike being moved once established.

Pruning must also be tailored to the vigour and growth habit of the chosen cultivar (these vary widely) and its performance on your soil and site. Indiscriminate hard pruning encourages vegetative growth at the expense of fruiting wood. Under-pruning results in weak, crowded growth, which leads to increased pest and disease problems, especially if dead wood (such as old raspberry canes) is not removed. The benefits of choosing a trained form are also lost as the shape deteriorates. The longer the neglect continues, the more difficult rescue will become.

Single cordon

A single stem clothed in fruiting spurs gives a high yield of good-quality gooseberries, red currants or white currants for the space occupied. Cordons can be grown against a wall, but are more usually seen in rows on posts and wires. They may be trained vertically or at an oblique angle. A row of cordons is easily draped with netting, or a block of rows sited within a fruit cage. Measures such as these are essential to protect soft fruits, which are all attractive to birds.

Multiple cordon

Double ("U"-shaped), triple, and four-armed (double-"U") cordons are popular and ornamental trained forms for red and white currants and for gooseberries. Wall-training is necessary for support and to minimize the risk of damage by wind.

Multi-stemmed bush

Blackcurrants and blueberries produce new shoots from the base of the plant each year, forming an upright, multi-stemmed bush.

Bush

Red and white currants and gooseberries are grown as bushes with a crown of framework branches on a short trunk or "leg".

Standard

A bush on a tall clear stem is produced by grafting a selected gooseberry or red currant cultivar onto vigorous *Ribes* stock.

Fan

Fan-training red currants and gooseberries against a wall not only provides shelter and warmth but also creates a decorative feature.

Raspberry canes

Raspberries sucker freely, and new canes emerge each year over a wide area around the original planting site.

Blackberry and hybrid berry canes

Canes develop from a more or less central point. They should be separated and trained apart to receive air and light.

Basic Techniques

With the exception of autumn-fruiting raspberries (*see p.231*), all soft fruits crop on wood that is at least a year old. With some – the cane fruits and, to a degree, blackcurrants – wood is routinely cut out after it has fruited once, and on others – red currants and gooseberries – it is shortened ("spurred back") to a branch framework, so as to encourage the formation of new sideshoots that will fruit the following year. On these spur-pruned fruits, the branch framework and spur systems thus build up over the years, and need thinning if growth is not to be crowded.

There are two main pruning periods for soft fruits: winter and summer. Winter is the time to develop and improve the plant's shape, remove badly placed or old, unfruitful wood in favour of younger growth, reduce overcrowding and open up the centre of a bush. Winter pruning should ideally be left until as late as possible in the season, so that bird damage to buds can be taken into account when deciding what to cut out. Badly bird-damaged growth, which may not crop well again for two years, should be completely removed. Summer pruning is necessary only for trained forms, to restrict vegetative growth and maintain their shape and structure.

Soft fruits are particularly prone to serious virus diseases. Dig up and burn affected plants before starting to prune other plants. Remember that secateurs and other tools can spread viruses. Disinfect tools by dipping them in a solution of household disinfectant, ideally when moving from plant to plant, and always once the job is done.

Routine tasks, bush fruits (winter)

Spur pruning
While gooseberries, red currants and white currants can be grown as a loose, multi-stemmed bush like a blackcurrant (*see below*), it is better to develop a permanent framework on which growth is pruned to create short, fruiting spurs, rather like those on an apple or pear tree.

Cut branch leader to a bud here, to shorten it by about a third of the previous season's growth

All sublaterals are cut to a few buds from base

Renewal pruning
With bush fruits (particularly blackcurrants and blueberries, which are not spur-pruned), a proportion of older wood must be taken out each winter to keep the centre open and increase the proportion of the plant formed by one- and two-year-old shoots. These will fruit in the summer, while new shoots that will fruit the following year are developing.

Routine tasks, cane fruits

Cane pruning Removing fruited canes is the key pruning principle for raspberries, blackberries and hybrid berries such as tayberries and loganberries. Cut them straight across at ground level, being careful not to damage young growth that is being retained.

Figure-of-eight tie

Tying in Canes need secure tying in, particularly if, like those of blackberries and summer-fruiting raspberries, they must survive a winter's winds. Regular spacing of the canes improves ripening and makes harvesting and cane pruning (*left*) easier.

Suckers All canes begin as suckers developing from adventitious buds on the roots of, or at the base of, the plant. Lightly hoe out those that are too far from the row, or remove them carefully with a portion of root, as above, if wanted for propagation.

Cane Fruits

Raspberries, blackberries and the many hybrid berries bear fruit on short, young sideshoots that develop on long, vigorous, whippy canes that, with the exception of autumn-fruiting raspberry cultivars, grew the previous year. Annual pruning consists of removing old fruited canes so that they can be replaced by new shoots.

All cane fruits are cool-climate plants. Though descended from woodland natives, to produce a fine crop they need a sunny site (blackberries will tolerate some shade). To achieve maximum exposure to the ripening sun, they must be well trained using a method that suits the varying vigour of individual cultivars.

Berry fruits

There are numerous hybrid berries, including the loganberry, tayberry, boysenberry, sunberry and tummelberry. Some hybrids are crosses between other recognized fruits – the tayberry, for example, is a cross between a blackberry and a raspberry. Others have a more mixed parentage within the genus *Rubus*.

Tayberries

Blackberries

Boysenberries

Loganberries

BLACKBERRIES AND HYBRID BERRIES *RUBUS FRUTICOSUS, RUBUS* HYBRIDS

Blackberries and hybrid berries can all be cultivated, trained and pruned in the same way. The aims are always to encourage vigorous, healthy growth; to separate the fruiting canes from the new shoots that appear throughout the growing season; to splay out the fruiting canes to enable the fruits to

ripen well and be harvested easily; and to keep the canes clear of the ground to prevent layering. Always buy plants from a reliable nursery; these fruits are not normally certified, as raspberries may be, against viral diseases. Avoid plants showing signs of infection, such as mottled leaves or dwarfed growth.

■ **TRAINING METHODS** A stoutly-wired wall or fence is the simplest support, though a robust system of posts and wires, open on both sides, will suffice. The weaker-growing cultivars, such as the loganberry 'Thornless', can also be trained around a single stout post. The simplest and most manageable training methods (*see below*) keep fruiting

Training methods for berry fruits

Fan A compact system for less vigorous cultivars, especially those with more rigid canes. The fruiting canes are spread out, and new canes tied in to the central space as they grow. These are lowered and tied into position once the fruited canes have been cut away (*see facing page*).

Rope Suitable for cultivars with many pliable canes, such as loganberries. Fruiting canes are twisted into "ropes" and tied along the lower wires; the new canes up the middle and along the top. When the fruited canes are cut out, the new ones are divided between the lower wires.

Alternate bay Ideal where several plants grow along a long wall. Fruiting canes are trained towards each other in the spaces between plants, or bays, as are the young canes as they grow. All the canes in any bay are therefore fruiting or not fruiting in alternate years.

Weaving A space-saving method for vigorous cultivars with pliable canes. Fruiting canes are trained in a serpentine manner on the lower wires, new ones up the middle and along the top wire. When the fruited canes are cut away, the new ones are lowered and woven into position.

and new canes separate; some allow
the new canes to be trained directly
into their final position as they grow,
minimizing handling of prickly stems.
Walls and fences should be at least
1.5–2m (5–6ft) high, and wired using
either bolts or battens and staples to keep
the wires a little distance away from the
wall. For posts and wires, use 2.5m (8ft)
posts sunk 60cm (24in) into the ground,
with diagonal support struts. Space three
or four horizontal wires about 45cm
(18in) apart. Depending on the training
method, allow at least 3m (10ft) between
plants; very vigorous cultivars, such as
'Himalaya Giant', will need space for
canes 5m (15ft) or more in length.

■ **WHEN TO PRUNE** After planting,
then in autumn after fruiting and
again in late winter or early spring.
Unwanted canes and suckers can be
removed at any time. Always wear
gloves for thorned cultivars.

■ **FORMATIVE TRAINING** Plants are
bought as one-year-old rooted tips (a type
of layering). Plant them, ideally, in early
winter or, if the weather is very severe,
in early spring. Shorten the original cane
to 20–30cm (8–12in) from ground level
when first planted to stimulate new basal
growth, then cut it out entirely in the first
summer. Raising the soil level slightly by
mulching also encourages the growth of
strong new canes. Tie these in firmly as
they develop, using a suitable training
method (*see facing page*).

■ **ESTABLISHED PRUNING** The aim is
to maintain an annual succession of
year-old, heavy-cropping canes. Once
the last berries have been harvested,
all the fruited canes are cut out and, if
required by the training method used,
the new canes retied into position. If
there are not enough new canes to fill
the available space, keep a few old ones,
cutting sideshoots back to 2.5cm (1in).

As the new canes develop, any weak
ones can be removed, particularly if
overcrowding seems likely. Pull out any
growth springing up too far from the row
as soon as seen, or it will quickly become
a nuisance. At the end of the winter,
tip-prune all canes by 15cm (6in) or
so, though if frost damage is severe you
may have to remove more (sometimes
the entire cane). Canes may be untied
and retied in a single bundle on the lowest
wire for protection in hard winters, then
trained out again in spring.

Neglected plants are not easy to deal
with. Dig out suckers and rooted growth,
and cut away old and tangled canes.
Some young canes may be salvageable,
and retrained to the support; otherwise,
carefully uprooted suckers or layers may
be usable as new plants.

New growth after planting

The plant's original cane is not used for fruiting. Shorten it to 20–30cm (8–12in) to stimulate new basal shoots. These shoots will fruit in their second season. Remove the stump of the old cane in midsummer.

New canes are supple and green — Previous year's cane is woody and dark

Established blackberry, pruning after fruiting

1 Cut out the fruited canes at ground level.

2 Separate and tie in (see below) the new canes according to the training method used (see facing page).

Tying in new shoots

Use figure-of-eight knots to secure the canes firmly to the wires. Choosing a smooth-stemmed cultivar, such as 'Oregon Thornless', makes tying in a less difficult task.

RASPBERRIES *RUBUS IDAEUS*

Raspberries produce numerous canes that grow directly from a mass of fibrous roots just below soil level. For the best crops, old canes should be cut out after fruiting and replaced by the strongest of the new ones.

There are two distinct types of raspberry: summer- and autumn-fruiting. Cultivation is identical, except for pruning. The canes of summer-fruiting cultivars grow one year and crop the next – after which they are removed at ground level. Autumn-fruiting cultivars, with a longer cropping season – late summer to the first frosts – are treated rather like herbaceous plants: the whole plant is cut back to the ground in late winter, then canes grow and fruit in a single season.

A sheltered site is advisable, and good support is essential for summer-fruiting cultivars, which must survive winter weather. There are variations on an open posts-and-wires system that are widely used (*see right*). Growing against walls or fences is not ideal: the poor air circulation encourages mildew on the fruits, and it is also difficult to tend the row on the wall side. Single posts are not recommended: sun exposure may be poor and harvesting awkward.

Raspberries are very prone to viral diseases, for which there is no cure. Plants showing symptoms – short, weak canes, yellow-blotched foliage and sparse, small or distorted fruits – must be dug up and burned. Any suckers that grow from overlooked root fragments must be watched for and removed. Do not replant raspberries for several years where virus-infected ones grew.

SUMMER-FRUITING RASPBERRIES

These are bought as single canes, usually shortened in the nursery to about 60cm (24in). Having set up a support system (*see above right*), plant at any time from late autumn to early spring, fanning the roots out in a shallow hole to encourage new canes to grow from them.

■ **WHEN TO PRUNE** On planting, thereafter in late winter and after fruiting.

■ **TRAINING AND PRUNING** Prune the cane on planting, but leave a portion of it intact until early summer so that the foliage it carries helps nourish the new shoots. As the growing season progresses, tie new canes into position. If the odd flower appears this year, pinch it out. Make sure the canes are well supported over winter, tip-pruning them (*see facing page*) as winter ends (unless using the Scandinavian system, *above*). A crop will be borne the following summer.

Training methods for raspberry canes

Canes woven around each other and the wires

Low, stout, strutted post takes the strain of the single wire

Scandinavian system (*above*) Ideal where a large, sheltered area can be devoted to a quantity of plants, this method is used for less vigorous summer-fruiting cultivars. The canes will not require tip-pruning. Once the system of keeping fruiting and new canes separate is established, it is easy to maintain. Make two parallel rows of low posts 90cm (36in) apart, with about 3m (10ft) between posts in the rows. Use 1.5m (5ft) posts driven 60cm (24in) into the ground, with diagonal support struts, then stretch a single wire between the tops of the posts. The new canes, while still pliable, are brought to one side or the other and gently woven along the wires and around each other. No more than three or four canes from any one plant should join each "rope", so use only the strongest ones and remove any surplus. Tie in if and where necessary. In the second season, new young canes are left to grow up in the central space between the wires, where they are sheltered and protected from possible damage during harvesting. When the fruited canes are cut away, the replacement canes can be woven into place.

Posts and wires (*below*) This is a compact, secure method for windy areas. The fruits receive maximum sun. Stretch three wires at heights of 75cm, 1m and 1.6m (2, 3 and 5ft), either strained between two endposts or stapled along a line of four or five posts. Tie canes in on one side of the wires; do not weave them in and out or they may chafe. New canes may need holding up with string at first (*see* Supporting young shoots, *facing page*).

Posts and nylon string (*above*) The simplest method (here seen from above) is to guide the canes within a loop of nylon string, 45cm (18in) from the ground, stretched and nailed between 2m (6ft) posts. Add an extra loop at 1.2m (4ft) in windy sites or conditions. Add connecting ties between the parallel strings at intervals to stop the canes slumping or being blown towards one end.

Raspberry, year 1, summer

1 *Tie the new canes to support wires as they grow (see Spacing new canes along a wire, facing page).*

2 *The original cane was shortened to 25cm (10in) on planting. Prune out its stump in midsummer.*

As soon as cropping has finished, the fruited canes are cut out at the base and the new season's canes tied in. Where there is lots of new growth, retain only the strongest young canes. During the ensuing winter, soft cane tips may be damaged by frost, so in late winter tip-prune to remove any damaged growth.

Canes emerging more than about 20cm (8in) from the row should be removed as seen. Cutting them away at ground level or tracing them back to their point of origin (disturbing the root system) will only encourage more to appear. Instead, hoe them away lightly while they are still young and soft. The exception to this rule is when the suckers are required as new plants; these should be carefully lifted with a substantial portion of root.

Raspberries can be renovated, but they have a useful life of only 12 years or so. If neglected rows seem relatively young and healthy, cut out the oldest canes and tie in the rest. If the crop next summer is small, the plants are probably not worth keeping: they may be too old, or may be fruiting poorly because of viral infection, so site new canes elsewhere.

AUTUMN-FRUITING RASPBERRIES

Autumn-fruiting cultivars are bought as single canes and planted as for summer-fruiting cultivars (*see left*). In summer the new canes will both grow and bear their first crop. An annual cycle is maintained by pruning all of the canes to ground level each winter. If they are not cut back, they fruit again, but only on the portion of the cane that did not fruit the previous year. A much bigger crop is gained from strong new canes.

■ **WHEN TO PRUNE** On planting, then in late winter when the plants are fully dormant. Do not remove fruited canes after cropping as for summer-fruiting cultivars, or new growth will appear before the frost, which may destroy it.

■ **TRAINING AND PRUNING** Plant and prune initially as for summer-fruiting cultivars (*see left*). As the new canes grow, shorter cultivars such as 'September' will require no support, but more vigorous ones such as 'Autumn Bliss' need training to guard against wind damage. Since there is no need to keep new and fruiting canes separate, a simple system such as posts and nylon string is suitable (*see above left*).

At winter's end, but before any sign of growth, all canes are cut to the ground. As the next year's young canes grow, remove weak or damaged growth. Do not tip-prune, since much of the fruit is borne at the top of the canes. Replace old plants when cropping declines.

Routine tasks, established raspberries

Cutting out weak shoots Most cultivars will produce canes surplus to requirements. Removing the spindly ones will concentrate vigour into the canes that remain. Retain about eight strong new canes per plant, pruning out any surplus at the base.

Supporting young shoots Emerging new canes may need extra support before they reach the lowest wire of the system, or because they are too numerous to tie in. Loop string around the support structure and the canes to hold them up.

Cutting out fruited canes Prune out all fruited canes at ground level, being careful, with summer-fruiting cultivars, not to damage the current season's new shoots. With autumn-fruiting raspberries, all growth is cut down.

Spacing new canes along a wire Tie canes no closer than 10cm (4in) apart using a continuous length of string, which is looped around the cane and the wire, then taken on to the next cane, holding each in position.

Looping over extra-tall canes Bend very long canes over and tie in again to the top wire while still pliable. At the same time, tip-prune weaker canes to stimulate growth.

Tip-pruning summer-fruiting cultivars Unless using the Scandinavian system (*see facing page*), at winter's end prune canes by about 15cm (6in), to roughly the same height.

Bush Fruits

Although blackcurrants, red and white currants, gooseberries and blueberries can all be managed simply by removing, each year, some older, less productive wood in favour of young fruiting growth (rather like many flowering shrubs), it is worth using different methods for red and white currants and gooseberries, which can be spur-pruned to a framework each year, not only resulting in heavier-cropping bushes, but also enabling many decorative trained forms to be produced.

BLACKCURRANTS *RIBES NIGRUM*

The blackcurrant is grown as a "stooled" bush – with as many young shoots as possible originating at or near ground level. The bulk of the crop is carried on shoots that grew the previous summer. Some fruit is also borne on two-year-old wood, but a proportion of this crop is worth sacrificing, with older wood, to make room for new shoots.

Blackcurrants are very prone to viral diseases, and to blackcurrant gall mite, which spreads reversion virus, so always buy certified plants where available. The easily visible "big buds" containing gall mites must be picked off and burned (no spray is really effective); badly infested bushes must be dug up and burned.

BLACKCURRANT BUSH

Blackcurrants are purchased as two-year-old bushes that will crop in the second summer after planting. Choose a healthy specimen that has three or four strong, vigorous shoots. Plant at any time during late autumn and winter, setting the bushes slightly below the nursery soil mark and mulching after planting to encourage basal growth.

■ **WHEN TO PRUNE** Winter, as buds begin to burst. Delay the initial pruning of containerized bushes bought and planted in leaf until after leaf-fall. On well-established bushes, "winter" pruning can in fact be started in summer when the fruits become ready to pick. Cutting out whole shoots bearing ripe fruit makes picking easier, and the bush will also benefit from the increased light and air circulation. Winter pruning then consists of tidying up what is left.

■ **FORMATIVE TRAINING** The aim is to create a strong, upright, productive bush. First, prune all of the shoots hard back,

The newest shoots, which will fruit the next year, have smooth bark the colour of strong tea

Shaggy grey wood is in its second year and has fruited once, but will bear another, smaller crop. It may also bear strong new shoots for cropping next year

New and old growth
Blackcurrant wood changes colour as it ages, providing a valuable recognition aid when pruning. Younger wood, which can be retained, is smooth and pale; older wood, which can be removed, is rough and dark.

Remaining stalks of the characteristic long, loose bunch, or "strig", of blackcurrant fruits

Year 1, winter

Well-grown two-year-old plant has several strong shoots

Plant so that nursery soil mark is a thumb's width or so below ground

Immediately after planting, cut back all shoots to one bud above soil level.

Year 2, winter

Strong new shoots have developed

Remove completely only those shoots that are very weak, or are growing horizontally or downwards

Established blackcurrant bush, pruning after fruiting

1 *Using loppers or a pruning saw, cut out older wood right down to the base, to a bud where one is visible.*

Strong, two-year-old wood with plenty of new sideshoots is retained

2 *Remove any weak or crossing stems.*

Low, horizontal branch pruned to a strong upward-growing shoot to restrict spread

Less productive two-year-old wood with few sideshoots is removed

almost to ground level, to encourage strong young growth in the summer. The next winter, only weak or badly placed shoots should be removed. The remaining strong shoots should bear their first crop the next summer.

■ **ESTABLISHED PRUNING** An established bush can be pruned at any time between cropping and late winter (*see* When to prune, *facing page*). The aim is to cut out as much dark, three-year-old or older wood as possible in favour of young growth with better fruiting potential,

while maintaining the bush's upright habit and shape. Some new growth will originate from near the base of the bush, and some from grey, two-year-old wood. On strong bushes, it may be necessary to cut out up to one-third of this two-year-old wood to reduce overcrowding. On weaker bushes, more of the two-year-old wood with its young shoots should be retained to fill out the bush. No tip pruning is necessary. Remove low shoots to restrict spread and avoid fruit touching the soil, where it will be damaged by rain and pests.

Neglected blackcurrants can often be renovated successfully, although if the bush is more than 10 years old, or seems generally weak or unhealthy, it is best to replace it. Otherwise, in winter, cut out as much old wood as possible, keeping only the best strong young shoots – or, if no new wood seems promising, cut all growth down to about 5cm (2in) from the ground. In both cases feed and mulch after pruning and, the following year, thin out the new shoots to 8–12 of the strongest and best. No fruit will be produced until the following year.

Pruning an established blackcurrant bush

Before pruning This unpruned bush is crowded; the stagnant atmosphere caused by poor air circulation within the bush's centre will encourage disease, especially in a damp year. Light levels will also be low, to the detriment of the fruits.

After pruning One or two of the oldest branches have been removed at ground level, and the remaining growth thinned to relieve overcrowding. The bush is left with a good balance of one- and two-year-old wood.

RED- AND WHITE CURRANTS *RIBES RUBRUM* (SYN. *R. SYLVESTRE*)

These fruits are comparatively simple to train and prune, particularly in bush form. Because they are spur-pruned to a permanent framework of branches, they are also easy to train and maintain as cordons and fans. Both redcurrants and white currants (the same fruit in terms of cultivation) fruit at the base of one-year-old laterals. These laterals are hard-pruned in winter to form spurs, which will then fruit annually. Unlike blackcurrants, there is no need to replace the fruiting wood each year, and whole branches are taken out only in cases of disease, old age or the overcrowding that results as the bushes age and spur systems develop.

Red- and white currants do not suffer from reversion virus, as blackcurrants do, and certification is unnecessary. They are, however, susceptible to dieback, particularly when old: if this affects a branch, prune it back until a completely clean, white cut surface is exposed. Burn the prunings, and let a suitably placed strong, young shoot grow on to fill the gap. If successive cuts reveal that dieback has affected the main stem, the whole bush must be destroyed.

Ripe redcurrants
Redcurrant bushes need good formative training and regular pruning to prevent weak and congested growth and ensure good-quality fruits.

REDCURRANT BUSH

The aim of formative pruning is to produce an upright bush with 8–10 main branches, its centre open to let in sun and air. Red- and white currants are usually bought as one-year-old plants grown from cuttings, which will crop in the second season after planting. Two- and three-year-old bushes are sometimes available and will crop sooner. Plant in late autumn or winter in well-manured ground, providing shelter from strong winds that may damage new shoots.

■ **WHEN TO PRUNE** Winter, as late as possible before bud-burst so that bird damage can be taken into account.

■ **FORMATIVE TRAINING** A well-grown one-year-old bush should have three or more vigorous shoots on a short, clear stem, known as a leg. Buds or shoots on this clear leg should be removed, though are likely to have been rubbed out already in the nursery. The shoots are cut back by half in winter to encourage further strong growths from which the framework of branches can be developed in the second year. The young branches should be staked initially for protection on exposed, windy sites.

Redcurrant bush, pruning after planting

1 Remove shoots within 10cm (4in) of soil level, cutting them back to the main stem, to make a short, clear leg.

2 Prune each shoot to an outward-facing bud (upwards, on a drooping shoot) about half-way along its length.

Year 2, winter

Centre of bush is left open

1 Shorten by half new leading shoots on existing branches.

2 Select up to six other well-placed, strong shoots and shorten these by half.

3 Cut any weak sideshoots back to one bud to encourage stronger growth.

Badly placed shoots are cut back to one outward-facing bud

■ **ESTABLISHED PRUNING** Each winter, the year's new growth is shortened so that, after pruning, the bush consists solely of its main branches, clothed with short spurs. An old, less fruitful branch may be taken out occasionally; unless the bush seems overcrowded, prune to a new low shoot that will grow to replace it. Choose a replacement shoot that will maintain the open-centred but upright bush shape: low, spreading branches are liable to expose fruits to rodents and other pests on the ground. If growth is vigorous, bushes may also be summer-pruned by shortening the new laterals to five leaves, as for cordons (see p.236) but this is not essential.

A neglected but still young red currant bush can usually be regenerated, but a bush more than 15 years old, sickly-looking or infested with perennial weeds, is best dug up, and its replacement planted on a fresh site. To renovate, first remove dead, diseased or damaged wood, then remove old or badly placed branches, if necessary, to open up the centre of the bush. Cut overgrown sideshoots and spurs back to one or two buds. The treatment is best spread over two winters, the eventual aim being to create a bush with a well-spaced structure of 8–10 strong, young branches, whereupon routine pruning as above can begin once more. Always feed and mulch well after renovation.

Established redcurrant bush, winter

1 Prune to one bud all shoots that grew from framework branches or spurs in the previous growing season.

2 While there is still space for the bush to fill, cut 5–7cm (2–3in) from the tips of branch leaders to stimulate new growth.

3 Remove an older, unproductive or unhealthy-looking branch, cutting to a vigorous shoot that will take its place. Leave this shoot unpruned.

4 Remove low branches: when carrying a crop, their fruits will be vulnerable to rodents and other pests on the ground.

REDCURRANT FAN

A redcurrant fan takes three years to establish. Laterals on its framework of ribs are pruned to form fruiting spurs. Wire walls and fences as for a cordon (see p.236).

2.5 | 8

m | ft

■ **WHEN TO PRUNE** Winter, as for a bush, and also midsummer, to restrict growth.

■ **TRAINING AND PRUNING** In winter, plant a one-year-old currant, 15cm (6in) from the wall or fence. Cut the leader back to the topmost of two strong laterals about 15cm (6in) from the ground that can be trained to the left and right, and tie them to two bamboo canes tied to the wires at a 45° angle. Cut each back by half to a downward-pointing bud; remove all other shoots. If one arm grows more vigorously than the other, retie the weaker one nearer to the vertical and the stronger one more horizontally to balance their growth rates (see Correcting uneven development, p.98).

During the summer, select three or four well-spaced shoots on each arm (at least one on the underside) to train

on canes as the fan's ribs. Remove vigorous surplus shoots, but keep weaker ones, shortening them to three leaves.

The following winter, shorten the ribs by about half their length and cut their sideshoots back to one bud. During the third summer, fill in gaps, usually in

the centre, by tying in young shoots. Shorten all sideshoots to five leaves in summer, then to one or two buds in winter. In subsequent years, spur-prune each rib as for a cordon (see p.236). For step-by-step illustrations of forming a fan framework, see Peach fan, p.134.

Redcurrant fan

Redcurrant fans do best with the support and protection of a wall or fence, rather than of posts and wires. This method of training not only ensures maximum sunlight falls on the ripening fruit but also, in the spring, exposes the flowers well to pollinating insects. Wall- or fence-trained fruits are also easy to net against birds.

REDCURRANT CORDONS

A single cordon has one vertical main stem with fruiting spurs along its length. Multiple cordons branch at the base from a short stem, with several upright arms, rather like a candelabrum. All require a wall, fence or 2m (6ft) posts with horizontal wires at 30cm (12in) intervals. Single, double, triple and four-armed cordons should be spaced, respectively, 40cm, 80cm, 1.2m and 1.5m (16, 32, 48 and 60in) apart.

■ **WHEN TO PRUNE** The first spring after winter planting, thereafter in winter, as for bushes (see p.235), and midsummer.

■ **FORMATIVE TRAINING** Plant a year-old, single-stemmed currant in winter, staking it with a cane tied to the wires. For a single cordon, proceed as shown right.

For a double cordon, in the first spring, cut the leader back to the topmost of two nearly opposite laterals of comparable vigour. Cut any other laterals back, first to two leaves, then later in the summer to the base. Train the two arms first on canes fixed at about 30° to the ground – one to the left, one to the right. When their tips are 30cm (12in) apart, start training them vertically on canes tied to the wires.

For a triple cordon, the leading shoot is trained vertically, and two sideshoots, shortened by half, are trained outwards at 30° until the tips are 30cm (12in) from the central shoot, then vertically.

A four-armed (double-"U") cordon needs an extra year's training to produce the branching structure at the base. Using the same method as for a double cordon, train two shoots as near to horizontal as possible before training them vertically when they are 45cm (18in) long. In the winter, cut sideshoots back to one bud, and shorten the vertical portion of each arm to two buds. Train the resulting pair of shoots on each arm as if each were a double cordon.

Thereafter, the arms of all cordons continue to be shortened and trained on as for a single cordon (right) until the arms reach their desired height. This gives a firmer, more vigorous main stem. All other shoots are shortened, and the shoots that grow during the summer are then pruned back (shown top right) to form spurs that will fruit the next year.

■ **ESTABLISHED PRUNING** All cordons are summer- and winter-pruned each year as for a single cordon. In time, older spur systems will need thinning (see Apples, Spur pruning, p.105). The leading shoot must also be cut back to a bud to restrict height. Pinch out or shorten shoots growing inwards towards the wall.

Single redcurrant cordon, pruning on planting, winter

1 Cut back the leading shoot by half its previous year's growth. If a lower shoot is stronger, train this in instead, cutting the main stem back to just above it in the summer.

Top of original cutting

2 Cut back other shoots to one bud.

Year 1 onwards, summer

When new shoots have at least seven or eight leaves, prune back to five leaves. If they have developed any sideshoots, pinch or cut these back to one bud.

Year 2 onwards, winter

1 As the cordon grows, prune new growth on the leading shoot by a quarter each winter, always cutting to a bud on the opposite side to last year's cut. When the cordon has reached the top wire, prune back new growth to one bud.

2 Cut back all the summer-pruned shoots, and any new sideshoots, to one bud. As the plant ages and spur systems become more complex, cut away old and unproductive sections to relieve overcrowding.

3 Cut back to the point of origin any shoots on the main stem less than 10cm (4in) from the ground.

GOOSEBERRIES *RIBES UVA-CRISPA*

The gooseberry fruits on year-old shoots and older spur systems. The growth habit of the various cultivars varies between pendent and upright. They are usually grown as open-centred bushes, which can be pruned in two ways: either on a loose renewal basis, or spur-pruned to a permanent framework. This second option makes possible such trained forms as cordons, fans and standards, which make picking easier. Gooseberries are usually viciously spiny, though near-thornless cultivars are now available. Many newer cultivars are also resistant to American gooseberry mildew.

Do not grow gooseberries in frost pockets as the early spring flowers are liable to be frost-damaged. A sheltered but airy site, shaded for part of the day, is ideal. As with redcurrants, dieback may be a problem. If it reaches the main stem, the bush must be uprooted and burned. Otherwise cut affected growth back to completely healthy wood, if possible to a replacement shoot.

One-year-old, fruiting wood

This season's growth

Two-year-old wood

Three-year-old wood

Spur pruning
The pruning and fruiting pattern of the gooseberry can be seen from this section of stem.

GOOSEBERRY BUSH

Gooseberries are most often bought as one-year-old rooted cuttings, although older plants are sometimes available.
The aim is to produce a bush 1.2–2m (4–6ft) tall, with a strong framework of 8–12 main branches on a short leg. Branches should be well-spaced, and the centre as open as possible, to aid air circulation and to make picking easier. Choose a strong specimen with at least three good shoots, and plant in autumn or winter, staking initially in exposed sites as the new shoots are fragile.

■ **WHEN TO PRUNE** Late winter or just as buds are beginning to burst in early spring; earlier pruning will increase the impact of bird damage. In areas where American gooseberry mildew is troublesome, summer-prune young shoots too, as for cordons and fans. Removing the tips of the shoots, which are most likely to be affected, reduces the spread of the disease.

■ **FORMATIVE TRAINING** In late winter after planting, shorten all shoots by about three-quarters of their length (this may already have been done in the nursery, in which case trim by 2–3cm/1in). If the cultivar has a pendent habit, always prune to an upward-pointing bud. Sideshoots should then develop in the following season, from which 8–10 are selected to form the main branches.

Gooseberry bush, year 1, winter

Prune back each shoot by three-quarters to an outward-facing bud. (Prune to an upward-facing bud on a cultivar with pendent branches.)

Year 2, winter

1 *Select 8–10 well-spaced strong shoots and shorten each by up to a quarter.*

2 *Shorten remaining shoots to four buds. Remove any that are crossing.*

■ ESTABLISHED PRUNING Established gooseberry bushes can be pruned in two ways. Spur pruning (*right*) – shortening all new growth on a permanent framework of branches – gives a smaller crop of large fruits, while less labour-intensive "regulated" or renewal pruning (*below*) – removing older branches entirely – encourages a heavy crop of small fruit, ideal for preserving. With either method, if larger fruits are required, remove every other fruit in late spring or in early summer, when the thinned fruits may already be large enough to be of culinary use.

A neglected bush less than 12 years old may well repay renovation. In winter, remove strong, vertical shoots from the base of the bush, and shorten trailing growth (which may have layered) to an upward-facing bud. Remove the oldest branches – up to one in four – to reduce overcrowding. After fruiting in summer, you will be able to see which older, less fruitful branches should be removed the next winter, allowing strong, well-placed new growth to take their place.

Established gooseberry bush, spur pruning in winter

1 To form spurs, prune all new shoots to a bud about 8cm (3in) from their base.

2 To restrict size, tip-prune branch leaders to three or four buds of the new growth.

Established gooseberry bush, regulated pruning in winter

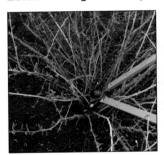

Before pruning Older, less productive or weak branches must be removed to prevent overcrowding and to maintain an open centre.

After pruning Branches are well-spaced after the removal of overcrowded growth, allowing light to penetrate and air to circulate freely.

1 Remove older branches, following the natural growth habit of the cultivar to maintain an upright but open bush.

2 Remove all growth arising from less than 10cm (4in) from the ground.

GOOSEBERRY STANDARD

The selected cultivar is grafted on to vigorous American *Ribes* stock at 1–1.2m (3–4ft), and must be firmly staked. Formative pruning of the head should be as for a bush, aiming to create a balanced, compact yet open-centred crown. This is then pruned as for an established gooseberry bush, using the spur-pruning method to maintain a compact head of branches. Any shoots growing from the clear stem should be rubbed out as seen. Both stake and tie need to be checked regularly, loosening the tie if it is constricting the stem.

GOOSEBERRY CORDON

Gooseberries can be trained and maintained as single, double or multiple cordons, just as for redcurrants (*see p.236*). The winter pruning, however, is less severe, shortening side shoots to about four buds. As the plants age, spur systems will become overcrowded and thinning will be necessary (see Apples, Spur-pruning, *p.105*).

A row of single cordons that consists of a mixture of cultivars, alternating fruits that ripen to different colours (red, yellow and green are available), makes a striking display.

GOOSEBERRY FAN

A gooseberry fan against a sunny wall should produce large fruits of dessert quality, especially if they are thinned, removing every other fruit when they are the size of a hazelnut. However, a fan will also produce fruits ripe enough for culinary or preserving purposes on a cool, partially shaded wall. Training and pruning is as for a redcurrant fan (*see p.235*). Good control of gooseberry mildew is essential when plants are trained close to a wall or fence, rather than as freestanding bushes in well-circulating air.

BLUEBERRIES *VACCINIUM* SPP.

The most widely grown blueberry is the highbush type (*V. corymbosum*), which in shape and habit is rather like a blackcurrant bush. However, blueberries can be allowed to develop more of a branched framework, since the wood is fruitful for several years.

The dusky navy-blue berries ripen from midsummer, so a sheltered sunny site and an open, well-ventilated bush are essential in cool climates for fruits to ripen satisfactorily. Though self-fertile, blueberries will crop better if grown together to allow cross-pollination.

Highbush blueberries require acid soil (pH 5.0) but can make successful container-grown shrubs, given only non-alkaline water and repotted every two to three years (*see p.154*).

The smaller, more spreading rabbit-eye blueberry (*V. ashei*) tolerates slightly higher pH conditions, but still requires acid soil. This species does not produce such fine fruit, but named cultivars and hybrids with *V. corymbosum* bear very palatable berries, and can also be grown in warmer, drier climates. They too are attractive plants, particularly since, like the highbushes, they provide a fine display of autumn colour. *V. ashei* and hybrids are pruned as for a highbush.

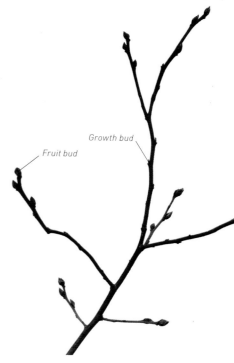

Growth bud

Fruit bud

Cropping blueberry

Blueberry branches with the potential to crop heavily can be identified at an early stage. When pruning in late winter, this can be taken into account when selecting what to remove. The fruit buds are distinctly fatter compared to the relatively insignificant growth buds.

HIGHBUSH BLUEBERRY

Highbush blueberries are sold as two-year-old cuttings. Plant while dormant, from late autumn through winter. The principle of pruning is the same as for blackcurrants (*see p.232*), though wood will fruit well from one year until at least four years old, after which it should be removed in favour of younger, more productive growth.

■ **WHEN TO PRUNE** Late winter, when fruit buds are readily distinguishable.

■ **FORMATIVE TRAINING** The only pruning necessary in the first two years will be to encourage the formation of a strong, well-shaped, open-centred bush. Prune back shoots growing out horizontally and any weak growth, cutting to an upright shoot or low bud where visible.

■ **ESTABLISHED PRUNING** Prune out the oldest and weakest wood, always as near to the base of the plant as possible to encourage strong new growth. Remove, also, any growth spreading out towards the ground. Remove no more than a quarter of the bush annually. Renovate as for a blackcurrant (*see p.233*).

Established highbush blueberry, winter

1 Remove unproductive wood close to ground level.

2 Cut back weak growth to a strong, young shoot.

3 Either remove any low growth completely or cut it back to a strong, upward-pointing shoot.

HONEYBERRIES *LONICERA CAERULEA*

Honeyberries are the fruit of *Lonicera caerulea*, a very hardy, deciduous, shrubby species of honeysuckle. They are a typical fruit of East Asia and Russia, but plants can be found growing in all subpolar regions. The oblong, white-frosted, blue-black berries are borne in early summer and have a flavour similar to blueberries and raspberries. Honeyberries happily grow in alkaline soil and are a useful alternative for people who struggle with acid-loving blueberries. Plants are not self-fertile and two or more bushes must be grown to ensure good pollination, though it is not necessary to grow "male" and "female" bushes; all bushes carry fruit and are pruned in the same way.

BUSH HONEYBERRY

Since flowers and fruit are borne on one-year-old wood or older, and the most vigorous stems produce the largest crops, the basis of pruning honeyberry is to maintain a good supply of productive shoots and replace older shoots with younger ones. Honeyberry has the habit and shape of a blackcurrant bush at first, but can develop into a small tree. Cropping on trees is likely to be light, however, and gathering fruit would be difficult. By removing older, more substantial shoots, honeyberry can be kept to the size of a small bush of about 1.5m (5ft) in height and spread. Some cultivars tend to spread and others are naturally more upright, but this does not require correction by pruning.

■ **WHEN TO PRUNE** From late autumn to late winter, while plants are dormant.

■ **FORMATIVE TRAINING** For the first 3 to 5 years, while the young bushes are establishing themselves, prune only to remove any dead or diseased material.

■ **ESTABLISHED PRUNING** Honeyberries produce many strong shoots from near the base of the plant. These should be thinned out to encourage bud formation, allow the free circulation of air, and facilitate fruit-picking. Remove older and less vigorous shoots, up to a one quarter of the total, cutting stems 5–10cm (2–4in) above soil level. At the same time prune out any weak and damaged growth. Where growth is sparse, some shoots can be shortened by one third to encourage lateral cropping shoots. However, this will eliminate some flower buds and therefore reduce the crop in the short term. Removal of too many shoots will also reduce the crop until resultant regrowth becomes fruitful.

Honeyberries ready for picking
The commonest form of honeyberry in cultivation is *Lonicera caerulea* var. *kamtschatica*; var. *edulis* is also available, but named fruit-bearing cultivars, such as 'Indigo' and 'Blue Velvet', are most likely to provide rewarding crops.

Established honeyberry, late autumn to late winter

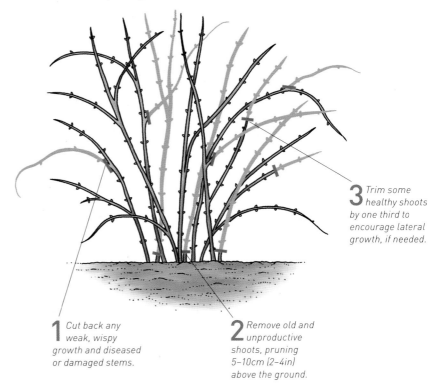

3 Trim some healthy shoots by one third to encourage lateral growth, if needed.

1 Cut back any weak, wispy growth and diseased or damaged stems.

2 Remove old and unproductive shoots, pruning 5–10cm (2–4in) above the ground.

GOJI BERRIES *LYCIUM BARBARUM*

Also known commonly as wolfberries and boxthorn, goji berries are somewhat spiny, deciduous shrubs grown for their aromatic and highly nutritious, sweet-savoury red fruits. Cropping does not require that goji be pruned, but they can grow into sizeable shrubs, up to 2.5m (8ft) high and 4m (13ft) wide, which can be hard to manage in gardens without a degree of control. Their lax, arching stems will also develop an "untidy" congested form unless pruned and trained.

BUSH GOJI BERRY

Goji can be grown as lank bushes and kept within bounds by annual pruning. Neglected bushes can easily get out of hand and if this is the case, they can be cut right back to ground level and the pruning and training of new growth started again. Cropping will recommence after a year or two.

■ **WHEN TO PRUNE** Flowers and fruits are borne on shoots that grow the same spring and summer. Bushes should therefore be pruned in late winter to avoid removing any new fruiting wood and to encourage new shoots that will crop that year.

■ **TRAINING** Some form of training or support will be required in most gardens to keep the lax habit within bounds. Typically, this will involve tying stems to wires strung between stakes or against a wall or fence. Remove any shoots that grow inwards, outwards, or in other ways that do not lend themselves to being tied in. It is possible to train goji berries as single stem cordons (*see pp.226 and 236*) or espaliers (*see pp.114–15*), with a permanent framework of older branches from which young shoots grow and bear the crop.

■ **ESTABLISHED PRUNING** Wear gloves to protect against spines. The main arching stems carry many sideshoots and these should be shortened to one bud in late winter to induce numerous new shoots with cropping potential. Bushes can be kept productive and restricted in size with the removal of typically one third of the main arching mature shoots, which should be cut out 5–10cm (2–4in) from ground level. Shorten the longest shoots and remove some of the oldest, woodiest stems to relieve congestion. Removal of entire shoots will reduce the cropping potential of the bush and should be done gradually, taking out no more than 20 per cent of stems in any one year. Plants sucker freely and can become invasive unless suckers are removed (*see p.227*).

Ripening fruits of *Lycium barbarum*

Look out for less vigorous cultivars of *Lycium barbarum*, such as 'Lifeberry', which will require less pruning than the species. *Lycium chinense* and *L. europaeum* are also grown under the name of goji and can be cultivated and pruned as for *L. barbarum*.

Established goji berry, late winter

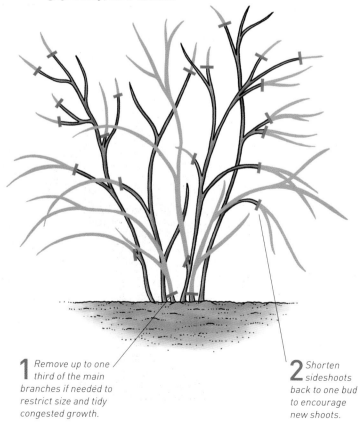

1 *Remove up to one third of the main branches if needed to restrict size and tidy congested growth.*

2 *Shorten sideshoots back to one bud to encourage new shoots.*

Climbing plants

Climbers are one of the most rewarding plant groups; with careful and imaginative training, they can provide year-round displays and combinations of foliage, flowers and fruits.

In the wild, climbing plants evolved their growth habit in order to compete with other plants, scrambling up and over obstacles (including rival plants) in search of air and sunlight. Their energies are concentrated on producing long, fast-growing shoots rather than robust, self-supporting stems, which is why support and training are so important to the successful use of climbers in the garden. While some climbers develop thick, woody stems with age (when the heavy growth needs substantial support), in general they are unable to support their young growth in an upright position. Unless climbers are to be used as ground cover, they need something to grow up, through or against.

Climbing plants greatly extend the possibilities of shape, colour and foliage in garden design. They are used particularly to give the dimension of height. In small gardens or confined sites where trees and large shrubs cannot be grown, they can be trained along walls and fences to provide a backdrop to other plantings. Free-standing focal points, such as tripods, arches and pergolas, arbours and shady bowers, give a new dimension to the garden. Climbers can also be grown over existing garden features: on the walls of a house, up into a tree, or over a hedge. More practically, they can cover an ugly shed or other eyesore, or form a "natural"

screen on economical materials such as chainlink fencing or breezeblock walls. Climbers can also be chosen to set off decorative materials, such as stonework, rustic poles and wrought iron, and there is enormous scope for associating them with other plants, both climbing and otherwise.

◀ *Clematis alpina* 'Ruby'
Clematis are among the most ornamental and versatile of all climbing plants, ideal for training on walls, fences and pergolas. They are also very effective grown on tripods or obelisks to add height to beds and borders of lower growing herbaceous plants.

Topiary effect
Not all climbers are rampant in growth. Training these small ivies over a wire seahorse frame produces a decorative "topiary" effect. Small-leaved climbers are best suited to this type of training, where a neat outline is desirable. A frame also enables a climbing plant to be grown as a free-standing specimen, forming a focal point.

Types of Climbing Plants

Climbing plants have developed a variety of methods by which to support themselves. At the simplest level, they resemble lax shrubs with very long, flexible stems that drape themselves over neighbouring objects and plants; some have thorns on their stems that act as anchors. At a more specialized level, the growth habit of the stems or leaf stalks (petioles) has adapted to twine around other stems and branches. The shoots usually extend rapidly before leaves develop, so that stems are not weighed down as they seek their next point of anchorage. The most sophisticated climbers have developed additional adaptations that enable them to climb. Some grapple with tendrils onto other stems or branches; others develop adhesive stem roots or suckering pads with which to cling to a sheer surface. It is important to understand the way in which your chosen plants grow in order to provide appropriate support. Other aspects of growth habit must also be taken into account: whether the plant, when fully trained, will be accessible for any necessary pruning (or the support for any maintenance it may need); whether it is of a type where a permanent woody framework can be developed, or whether some or even all growth should be removed at the base each year; and of course the vigour of the plant, and whether this is appropriate to the site and support.

Matching climbers to supports

The method by which plants climb is not directly linked to their pruning needs, but does affect training. Choose climbers whose growth habit complements their intended support. An attractive wrought iron obelisk will be so swamped by a vigorous climber such as *Parthenocissus* or hop (*Humulus*) that the purchase cost of such a decorative feature is wasted. If a fuel tank or tree stump is to be masked, a densely growing, permanent evergreen is, generally, a better choice than a deciduous or herbaceous climber.

It is equally important to choose methods of support, and give additional attention where necessary, that will enable the plant to climb or be trained successfully. For example, whereas ivy will creep up a bare stone wall, a honeysuckle will simply mound up in a heap at the base. However, if the wall is equipped with wires or trellis, the honeysuckle will, with initial guidance, twine around the wires or struts and climb the support. This is not the case with winter jasmine, which will never make its own way up a vertical support unaided: each stem must individually be tied in to achieve height and coverage.

The Dictionary of Climbing Plants (*see pp.262–287*) contains symbols that indicate by which method plants climb.

SCRAMBLING PLANTS
Many climbers do not twine or cling, but simply throw out long shoots that fall or scramble over obstacles. They are ideal for ground cover (*see p.253*), and for smaller host plants (*see p.255*), since they will not wrap and smother the host's stems too closely. They produce a cascading effect (for example, over the top of a wall), because they do not creep back into and around their own growth. Many continually throw up new basal shoots to replace stems or canes that eventually die. In nature the plant uses its own dead stems to climb higher, but in the garden these should be removed because of the risk of disease.

Clinging climbers
Ivy (*left*) will cling to any rough surface with aerial stem rootlets, while *Parthenocissus tricuspidata* (*above*) holds on with touch-activated adhesive pads. Both roots and pads continue to adhere after the death of the stem.

Hooked thorns
Some climbers, such as bougainvillea (*right*), brambles and, of course, climbing roses (*see p.316*), have thorns, sometimes hooked, that support scrambling stems by catching on the plant's support.

Twining stems
The stems of climbers such as wisteria (*left*) twine around any support that they touch. The stems twine clockwise or anti-clockwise, depending on the species. Climbers with twining stems can grow very rapidly, with vigorous laterals that branch out in search of other supports. Young stems may need to be guided towards supports.

SCANDENT PLANTS

It is difficult to draw a sharp distinction between scrambling climbers and lax, long-stemmed shrubs – a habit that is described as "scandent". Some argue that if a plant is unable to twine or cling by itself, it is not a climber at all but simply a very lax or prostrate shrub, while some shrubs are so universally wall-trained that in many nursery catalogues they are included as climbing plants. Plants such as *Cantua buxifolia*, *Tecoma stans* and *Streptosolen jamesonii* are the subject of regular debate about their categorization. They have more robust growth than, say, *Jasminum mesnyi* (*right*), a scandent plant whose long, thin stems, although tough, are not rigid enough to be self-supporting. What is certain about these plants is that they all benefit from training. Wall-training is the most suitable method; those that can be spur-pruned will create a more formal effect, with dense, two-dimensional coverage. All will need initial training and regular tying in thereafter.

Jasminum mesnyi

True tendrils

True tendrils are modified shoots that grow out from a stem, as seen in *Passiflora* × *violacea* (*left*). These tendrils will twine around any thin support, and then coil up and shorten to tighten their grip. Some tendrils branch and twist in different directions. Many thicken to form a long-lasting hold.

Leaf tendrils

Climbers such as *Cobaea scandens* (*right*) and perennial peas (*Lathyrus*) have leaf tendrils – leaves, or parts of leaves, that have become modified into twining tendrils that reach out in search of support. These plants usually rapidly climb unaided.

Twining petioles

On a few climbers, such as *Clematis montana* (*left*), the leaf stalks, or petioles, will wind round each other, or any support they meet. Even if the plant is deciduous, the petioles remain on the stem after the leaves are shed. Tying in is needed only to guide and direct growth.

TWINING AND TENDRIL CLIMBERS

Twining and tendril climbers must be given something to wrap their stems and tendrils around. Walls, fences, posts and pillars need to be equipped with wires, netting or trellis. On a wired wall or fence, tie vertical lengths of string between wires to give more anchorage points and hence achieve denser coverage. Trellis or wide-gauge pig or sheep netting, whether attached to a wall or between posts, are ideal for twining climbers. Tendrilled climbers will quickly camouflage plastic netting, chicken wire or peasticks.

For informal training these climbers are also ideal for growing up into a tree, or into other plants: they support themselves and need no tying in. Herbaceous climbers can be given light, seasonal support such as beanpoles or peasticks. The more vigorous and long-lasting plants that develop thick woody stems (such as wisterias) need robust supports; they can also be trained as standards.

CLINGING CLIMBERS

Some climbers develop adhesive roots and pads that cling unaided to masonry, wood and tree trunks. Adhesive roots form along stems; they do not take in nourishment or water. They are distinct from the long aerial roots formed by many tropical climbers, which do not adhere (though with age they may harden to prop the plant). Adhesive pads form at the tips of branched tendrils that develop at leaf nodes.

Clinging climbers are best grown directly up or along flat surfaces such as walls and fences, but should be used with caution on house walls. They may loosen old, crumbling mortar; shoots may penetrate under house eaves, or leaves may block gutters and downpipes. The stems often become thick, woody and heavy with age. Because stem roots develop only where the plant is in contact with a surface, several of these climbers can be trained as standards.

Fixtures and fittings

A wall- or fence-trained climber is likely to be in position for many years, during which time it will be difficult to do any painting, cleaning or maintenance of the support. Therefore, any structures must be in good condition before planting; fences, for example, must be treated with non-toxic preservative. It is also essential to ensure that the support is capable of bearing the full weight of your chosen climber when mature. Wires and fixings must be resistant to corrosion and be able to outlast the plant. In areas of high air pollution, wires should be plastic-coated, and fixings should be made of non-ferrous metal or plastic. All fixings should be in position before planting.

COVERING WALLS AND FENCES

In sheltered sites, plastic or wooden trellis can be erected between posts to form free-standing screens, or fixed above or against walls and fences. Netting is available in a range of gauges, from the open-weave heavy-duty wire known as pig or sheep netting to fine-mesh plastic suitable for lightweight annual or herbaceous climbers. Flexible chicken wire can be used to mould shapes, to soften outlines (to make plants appear to "billow" over a step, for example) or to train for a topiary effect.

Trellis or netting must not be fixed directly onto the surface of a wall or fence; plant stems cannot then twine around it, and a stagnant atmosphere will be created, an ideal environment for disease organisms. The wall or fence may also deteriorate. In order to allow some airspace between the plant and the wall, nail wooden battens to the wall and then fix the trellis panels to them, either with screws or, to allow access to the wall by lifting away both plant and support, with hinges and hooks. The base of wooden trellis should be at least 30cm (12in) from the ground, to prevent it from rotting.

Wires stretched along a fence or wall should be held about 5cm (2in) away from the surface. They are best spaced 23–30cm (9–12in) apart, depending on the vigour of the climber, and attached by vine eyes or rustproof nails. Vertical wires or twine may also be added, to form a squared framework that will improve the plant's coverage of the area.

VERTICAL FEATURES

A permanent structure must be constructed of durable materials. The width and height of an arch or pergola need to be generous, because the space under an archway is reduced once plants are established on the framework. In a bed or border, wooden supports should be set in free-draining gravel, not bare soil, to stop the bases from rotting.

Using wire netting

Here, a clematis has been trained on a spherical wire "balloon", formed by strips of wire netting, one square wide and eight squares deep, that have been buried in the soil around the pot's edge, then brought over and joined at the top. Wide-gauge galvanized wire netting (often called pig, deer or sheep netting) is one of the most versatile of supports. It can be stapled to wooden battens on a wall as an economical "trellis", and will quickly be disguised by a dense climber.

Fixings for wires and trellis

Wiring walls and fences Vine eyes (*above*) are the simplest way to hold wires away from the surface of a wall or fence. Use galvanized straining bolts for preference, or (*top*) tighten with pliers to tauten wires.

Raising the height of a fence A strip of trellis on top of a fence is held by metal plates screwed into the fence posts. Short posts with taut or looping wires between them can also be fixed along the top.

Fixing trellis panels to a wall or fence

The easiest way to fix trellis panels is to screw 5cm (*2in*) battens to the fence or wall (*left*), then screw trellis to the battens. This leaves airspace behind the plant. If you want to take down the plant and trellis together – for example, from a wall or fence that is painted regularly – use hooks-and-eyes at the top and hinges at the bottom (*centre and right*).

Basic Techniques

Early training and, often, pruning is essential to encourage climbing plants to produce plenty of strong shoots that will grow to cover the available space. Guiding or tying in stems to best utilize, direct and display the available growth according to the training scheme is crucial to the achieved effect. Time and effort spent developing a good basic framework of stems for permanent climbers will be amply repaid as the plant matures.

From then on, some climbers need only minimal attention, and these should be selected for sites where the mature plant will be difficult to attend to regularly – in the branches of a tree, for example, or high up a wall. However, climbers may also be pruned to control growth and restrict size, to remove old, less productive growth in favour of young stems, or to increase flowering potential. The amount of time spent cutting overlarge plants back can be minimized if the vigour of the plant is well matched to the site. Pruning to enhance flowering performance is an annual or sometimes twice-yearly task. It must be carefully timed to complement the flowering habit of the plant. In some genera, such as *Clematis*, different species flower, and thus must be pruned, at different times.

Neglected climbers soon become overgrown and tangled. Old specimens of relatively short-lived plants are best replaced. Otherwise, many plants can be selectively renovated so that the plant is retained as a garden feature. Climbers that respond well to hard pruning may be cut to near ground level, and the resulting new growth trained in again.

Types of cut

The majority of pruning work on climbers can be done with secateurs or with shears, because the stems tend to remain small in diameter. However, some climbers do develop thicker, woody growth that will need cutting with loppers or a saw. Climbers with a permanent framework of woody stems, such as *Wisteria* and vines (*Vitis*), should have each stem spur-pruned individually with secateurs. Climbers that produce a dense mass of spindly growth, such as honeysuckle (*Lonicera*), are often clipped with shears because it is impractical to prune so many stems individually. The exact pruning and training methods depend on the growth and flowering habit of individual species (*see* Dictionary of Climbing Plants, *pp.262–287*), as does the time of year in which pruning takes place. Always feed and mulch well after pruning.

WHEN TO PRUNE
Overall shaping of deciduous climbers is best done in the dormant season, while evergreen climbers should be pruned in spring, when the cut ends will be quickly disguised by new growth. Those grown for their flowers are additionally pruned either in early spring or after flowering, depending on the age of the wood on which they flower and their season of flowering. In tropical conditions, where climbers may grow continuously, prune during the growing season as necessary to shape them and keep them manageable. More drastic cutting back of climbers can be carried out when plants are dormant, or nearly so.

POSITIONING THE CUT
Climbers that do not lend themselves to overall clipping should have individual stems cut back just above a healthy bud or shoot facing in the direction growth is desired. On stems with alternate buds, always cut at an angle (*see above right*).

Base of cut is opposite base of bud

Alternate buds
On stems with an alternate arrangement of buds or shoots, make an angled cut just above the bud, parallel to its angle of growth, starting from the opposite side.

Opposite buds
Prune stems with opposite buds straight across the stem just above a pair of healthy buds or shoots. Never leave a budless stub of stem that will die back and invite disease.

Cutting to a replacement shoot
Unless you require the stem to follow a radically different direction for training purposes, pruning to shoots that follow the line of the older stem gives a more natural effect.

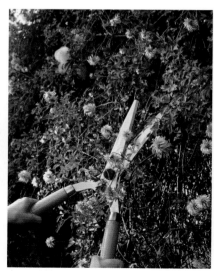

Pruning dense climbers
Climbers that produce a dense mass of thin, twiggy stems may have their growth routinely pruned and generally shaped with shears, as here, rather than secateurs.

Routine tasks

As with all other plants, the pruning of climbers can be divided into essential and non-essential tasks. Some problems will crop up at any time and should be dealt with as soon as they are noticed, while other jobs become necessary as the plant matures: tying in, for example, and thinning crowded growth.

Dead, diseased and damaged growth should always be removed as soon as seen. Burn diseased prunings, and dip the tools used in household disinfectant. Some climbers flower for a longer season if deadheaded, though this is often impractical where climbers are large or trained up high. Like all pruning that enhances flowering, deadheading is not essential, but should always be undertaken to improve the display if possible. Do not deadhead plants whose fruits are ornamental.

Guiding in
Guide young, flexible stems of tendril and twining climbers, like this hop, between netting or wires; they will then climb in the desired direction. Shoots are often very fragile.

Very few climbers are grafted, so the attendant problem of suckering from the rootstock is rarely encountered. There are, however, variegated cultivars of many plants, and on these any shoots with plain green leaves should be promptly removed, or they will come to dominate growth that has the desired foliage variegation.

TRAINING IN STEMS
Guiding and tying in is crucial to climbing plants, particularly wall-trained specimens, both to obtain the desired direction of growth and to encourage maximum coverage of the support. Unless a special effect such as a standard climber (*see p.260*) is being created, the stems of young climbers should be fanned or spread out as much as possible at first. This will encourage twining and tendrilled plants to climb up the whole width of the allotted space, rather than straight up the middle. Further growth can be guided or tied in as necessary. With climbers that need regular tying in (those that do not twine with stems or tendrils), early training lays the foundations of an attractive, well-balanced framework, such as a fan. Always train some shoots horizontally or spiralled around the support. Such horizontal training stimulates the production of flowers and fruit (*see* Horizontal training, *p.11*). The shape and structure of the climber is then maintained by pruning and further tying in as needed. Neglected plants will revert very quickly to vertical growth.

Training for good coverage of a framework or support also involves cutting out shoots growing in unwanted directions (for example, inwards towards

Strong new growth

Dead wood

Removing dead wood
This jasmine shoot has died back to buds that have developed into a pair of vigorous shoots. They are completely healthy, so it is safe to assume that the natural chemical barrier (*see p.9*) that isolates dead from live wood has formed. Cut back to just beyond the visible line between live and dead wood.

a wall), to stimulate growth in desired directions. Similarly, weak or straggly shoots should be pruned, to concentrate the energy of the plant into young, strong, vigorous shoots.

CHECKING TIES
Ties must be checked regularly to ensure that they are intact and that they are not constricting any stems. Temperate-climate climbers increase their stem diameter rapidly each spring; the stems of tender plants expand gradually and continuously. Ties should be loosened before they constrict stems or the stem will become damaged and

Tying in

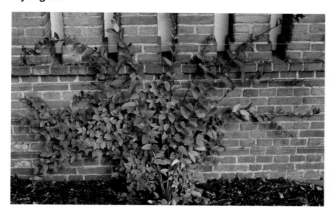

Achieving maximum coverage Early training is essential to obtain good coverage. Where the lower area of a support is to be covered, always fan some shoots out towards the horizontal from the start; gaps at the base can be difficult to fill later.

Figures-of-eight Using twine tied in figures-of-eight allows for some stem expansion and buffers the stem against hard surfaces.

Checking ties Neglected ties can constrict and eventually bite into stems, and may permanently damage the plant.

thus more susceptible to disease, or will die above the tie. Chafing can often be avoided by adding extra ties, even on climbers that do not require them for support, to minimize the movement of the stem.

CROSSING AND CROWDED GROWTH

Congestion and crossing growth, always to be prevented with trees and shrubs, are difficult to avoid with climbing plants. If the climber is cut back hard each year, problems are unlikely to accumulate. However, where a permanent framework of woody growth is developed it is vital that main stems are evenly and well-spaced (see facing page, below left), or they will chafe and eventually become damaged. Shorten excess growth in crowded areas rather than tying it in across other stems.

Once the framework is formed, plants with light, slender stems can be allowed to develop unchecked, since their profusion of stems and density of habit is often precisely the effect that is wanted. Climbers such as honeysuckle and *Clematis montana* that produce a thick blanket of tangled stems over a period of years may be completely "cropped" back to the wall or support to relieve congestion and stimulate vigorous regrowth. Always prune at the correct time for the individual plant, to avoid cutting out growth that will flower in the coming season.

With other climbers of sturdier growth, thinning of the stems that develop from the framework is necessary to prevent the plant from becoming extremely heavy and growing too far outwards from its support, and to prevent a dank, lightless environment within the plant. With some plants, thinning may be achieved by the routine pruning that enhances their flowering performance; on plants that are not pruned regularly in this way, it will

Deadheading

The dead flower heads or stalks of some climbers, such as this bougainvillea, are unsightly. Where possible, pick or snip them off, taking care not to damage any new growth.

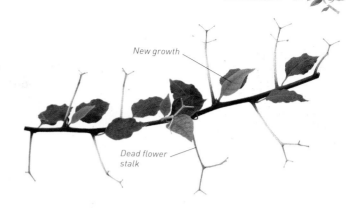

New growth

Dead flower stalk

have to be a job in its own right. The aim should be to prevent congestion building up, not to wait until extensive pruning is necessary, as this will spoil the plant's appearance. Plants that become mildly congested may be thinned by cutting some stems back either to their point of origin, to a young replacement growth, or to near ground level to encourage new stems to develop. Some wall and tripod plants can be taken down, laid flat on the ground, selectively thinned and retrained. If this is not possible, a practical, if unpredictable, method for tangled growth is to cut a few stems, then wait two or three days for their severed top growth to wilt. It is then easier to see and remove the dying stems, then make further cuts as needed.

CLIMBERS UNDER GLASS

It is always important to thin climbers grown under glass in greenhouses or conservatories, as they can be very vigorous. Thinning will increase airflow around the plant, as will training the stems along wires and canes to keep them from touching the glass. Clear debris such as fallen leaves and flowers regularly, and

keep walls and supports clean and dry. Plants that can be taken outside in warm weather are at less risk of problems arising from lack of air circulation or moisture. More delicate species must be kept under cover all year in cool climates. Despite the fact that they require high temperatures and humidity levels, conservatories and glasshouses should always be ventilated because of the increased risk of pests and mildew in closed environments.

CLIMBERS IN CONTAINERS

Only a relatively small number of true climbing plants are native to temperate regions. Many attractive plants come from tropical and subtropical parts of the world. In cool climates, many tender climbers are popularly grown under cover, often in containers. In these conditions, growth is usually less vigorous and these plants, often very large in their native habitat, are kept to a manageable size. Plants need regular feeding, and repotting when necessary (see p.154). Containers can be moved outside in summer if the plants are not too tender, and brought inside in winter.

Thinning growth

Flowered stems

Replacement stems

Thinning flowered shoots The routine pruning for flowering of many climbers involves removing flowered shoots, which is often enough to prevent congestion.

Tracing stems It may not be easy to trace stems to their point of origin. One method is to cut a main stem near the base, then cut and tease out the growth that subsequently wilts.

Shearing Crop densely growing, vigorous climbers back to their support. Once new growth begins, any severed growth that has been overlooked can be seen and picked out.

Initial Training

Wall- or fence-training, as shown on these pages, is the most popular and basic way of training climbers, and many of the principles apply to all types of training. Different plants, however, vary in their individual pruning needs; these are given in the Dictionary of Climbing Plants (*see pp.262–287*).

BUYING AND PLANTING

Choose young plants with sturdy stems and healthy leaves and buds. Remove any dead, damaged or weak and spindly stems. If only one stem is needed, remove all but the strongest. If strong stems are sparse and more are required, pinch out their tips to encourage branching near the base. However, if there is only one stem (as with many *clematis*) it is best not to check its growth until after the first growing season. Then, in late winter or early spring, cut it back almost to ground level to encourage new basal growth.

If the climber is to be trained against a wall or fence, plant it at least 20cm (9in) from the structure, if necessary using angled bamboo canes to lead the shoots towards their support. Climbers can be planted near the base of a post, pillar or tripod leg, and trained vertically or around the support. It is important to tie in all newly planted climbers, whatever their method of climbing: any twining or clinging habit does not develop until the plant has acclimatized to its new home, and young stems may be damaged by wind if not tied in. Little or no pruning should be needed in the first growing season. As growth proceeds, train shoots to the support in the desired direction. To cover a flat surface, fan them out evenly (*see right*); on a three-dimensional structure, there are several options (*see* Special training, *pp.253–259*).

FORMATIVE TRAINING AND PRUNING

Provided that the climber is not one that is cut down every year, the next few years should be spent developing a sound and well-spaced framework. Sometimes a young stem will break when being trained, so tie in the selected stems before cutting out surplus growth. Where growth is sparse, stems can be shortened to stimulate branching. Shoots growing in undesirable directions (for example, across another stem or outwards from a wall) can be carefully repositioned and tied in to spaces while the shoots are still young and supple, or shortened or removed. Regular guiding and tying in of growth is essential in the early years to cover the support well; plants will always naturally grow upwards rather than sideways.

Pruning and training on planting

1 Cut any badly placed, weak or damaged shoots back to their point of origin (here on Jasminum mesnyi) to encourage the development of the strongest stems.

2 Secure the young stems to the support, using twine tied in figures-of-eight (see p.248). If using guiding canes, tie the shoots to the canes and secure the canes to the wires or trellis.

Pruning to develop a framework

1 Where leading shoots grow vigorously without developing sideshoots, shorten them to stimulate branching growth that will cover the allotted space evenly.

2 Shoots that are not required for tying in to develop the main framework may be shortened to three to six buds; this will encourage fresh young sideshoots that, in many plants, will bear flowers.

3 Shorten shoots where growth is sparse, particularly at the base of the wall, to encourage branching.

Pruning Established Climbers

Those climbers that are trained as permanent features against a wall or any other support need a certain amount of maintenance if they are to remain healthy and vigorous. Many tasks should be undertaken as seen (*see* Routine tasks, *p.248*). Others, such as thinning (*see p.249*) and replacement pruning (removing an older section of the framework and tying younger growth into the gap) become necessary as the plant matures. Flowering and fruiting climbers may benefit from additional pruning to enhance their performance. Pruning may also be needed to keep a plant within its allotted area, or to maintain the shape of supports such as arches (*see* Special training, *pp.253–261*).

MAINTENANCE PRUNING

Basic, maintenance pruning (*see below*) will keep plants in good condition and encourage vigorous growth, while keeping the plant within bounds. The general principles are illustrated here, but the degree to which the plant is pruned will depend on the individual plant and its vigour and condition. Avoid overzealous pruning; it may result

Summer pruning

Climbers that flower on the previous season's wood benefit from pruning after flowering, cutting flowered shoots back to buds or new sideshoots that will become the next year's flowering growth.

in excessive growth and few flowers or fruits. Maintenance pruning is generally best undertaken in the dormant season, though the timing varies; evergreens are often pruned in summer, when growth will soon disguise cut marks.

PRUNING FOR FLOWERS AND FRUIT

The pruning of climbers to increase production of flowers and fruits falls broadly into two categories, depending on the age of wood on which flowers are produced. Plants that flower on the previous year's ripened shoots should be pruned, unless fruits are required,

immediately after flowering (*see above*) to allow new shoots to develop before the onset of winter. Vigorous climbers may also be summer-pruned to restrict growth. Plants that flower on the current season's shoots can be pruned in late winter or early spring, at the same time as any maintenance pruning (*see below*). Their shoots are usually spur-pruned – shortened to between three and six buds (depending on the plant), which then develop into flowering shoots.

To prune individual plants correctly and at the best time, *see* Dictionary of Climbing Plants, *pp.262–287*.

Maintenance pruning, dormant season

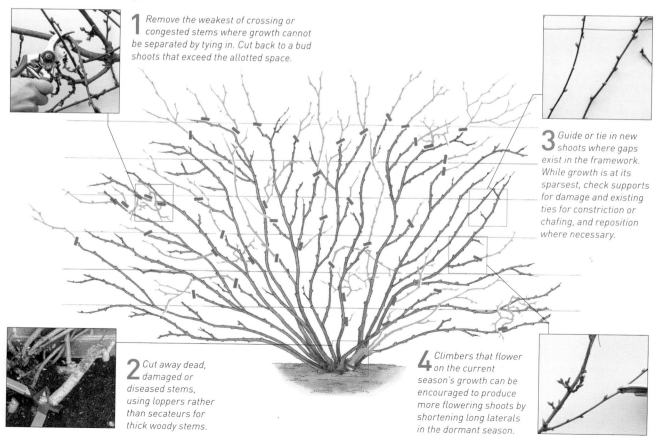

1 *Remove the weakest of crossing or congested stems where growth cannot be separated by tying in. Cut back to a bud shoots that exceed the allotted space.*

3 *Guide or tie in new shoots where gaps exist in the framework. While growth is at its sparsest, check supports for damage and existing ties for constriction or chafing, and reposition where necessary.*

2 *Cut away dead, damaged or diseased stems, using loppers rather than secateurs for thick woody stems.*

4 *Climbers that flower on the current season's growth can be encouraged to produce more flowering shoots by shortening long laterals in the dormant season.*

Renovation

Neglected climbers soon become overgrown. They also tend to revert to upward growth, which, if it has become woody, may be difficult to retrain. Dense, tangled growth may be pulling down supports, and is likely to be full of dead shoots and foliage. Flowering and fruiting are likely to have declined.

A plant that is moribund, or is suffering badly from disease or pest infestation, is usually not worth renovating. It is best removed and replaced by a vigorous young plant. This may take time to establish, but in two or three years it will make a much better specimen.

Plants that are basically sound, however, can often be renovated. Such work is best done in the dormant season. By far the easiest way to renovate, provided that the plant will tolerate drastic pruning, is to cut the entire plant down (*see right*). Check first that the plant is likely to respond well (*see Dictionary of Climbing Plants, pp.262–287*). Mulching afterwards is helpful, but do not overfeed the plant as

regrowth is likely to be vigorous. Tie in the new shoots as they develop.

If the plant will not tolerate drastic treatment (as with many evergreens), or if you are unwilling to sacrifice the effect of the climber for the time needed for it to grow back, stage the pruning over two or three years. In each year, cut only one in two or three of the main stems back to ground level (*see below*).

Detaching a climber from its support and laying it flat on the ground often makes it easier to sort out the tangle of live and dead shoots. This also enables maintenance work on walls, fences and wooden supports to be carried out. The disentangling needs to be done with care, as stems are often very stiff or brittle. Many plants wrap themselves so firmly around supports that it is impossible to remove some stems intact.

Clear away debris behind the support, which could harbour pests or diseased material, and tie the climber back onto it, spacing out the remaining shoots and securing them in position.

Drastic renovation

Climbers that respond well to hard pruning can be cut back almost to ground level. For many, such as this honeysuckle, it is best not to cut right to the ground, but to leave 30–60cm (1–2ft) of main stem, with plenty of dormant buds that should be stimulated into life and produce strong new stems. These buds will rarely be visible, so simply cut stems across, making clean, angled cuts with loppers or a saw, at the appropriate height.

Renovating an overgrown climber

1 With long-handled loppers (right), cut back one in three of the main stems, selecting the weakest and oldest to remove. Tease out the severed top growth.

2 Now that it is more visible, look for dead (right), diseased and damaged growth and remove it.

3 Tie in strong young growth to fill gaps in the framework, shortening stems if necessary. Where growth is still crowded, relieve congestion by removing weak stems.

Special Training

While the shape of a tree or shrub is enhanced largely by well-judged pruning cuts, climbing plants are more versatile in that they can be trained not only on vertical surfaces but also to take on the form of all manner of supporting structures. The following pages explain and illustrate how to create striking displays by training climbers through host trees and shrubs (*see p.255*); on vertical features and arches (*see p.256*); and up and over pergolas (*see p.258*). It is possible, however, to train climbers into three-dimensional features on much simpler supports, such as basic wire frameworks, or even, as ground cover, with no support at all.

USING CLIMBERS AS GROUND COVER

The dense, trailing growth of many climbers makes ideal ground cover, and is particularly effective over banks and slopes. Their flowering, fruiting and foliage displays make a welcome change from the more usually seen range of low-growing shrubs and perennials.

Ground-cover plants should provide thick cover yet need little maintenance, because, once established, they can be difficult to reach without stepping onto, and so damaging, the long stems or foliage. Laying down a plank to work from makes tasks such as clearing dead matter and prunings easier.

Ground coverage is most simply achieved by allowing suitable species to trail on the ground, guiding them if necessary with pegs. Pegging down prompts many climbers to root, increasing their vigour and spread. To peg down a climber, space its stems evenly around the planting site and anchor them with short lengths of heavy-gauge wire bent into hoops, looped over each stem and then pushed into the ground. If the pegged stems root they will become firmly anchored and the pegs can be moved elsewhere.

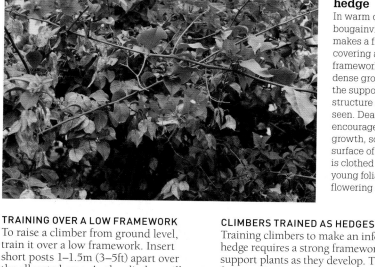

TRAINING OVER A LOW FRAMEWORK

To raise a climber from ground level, train it over a low framework. Insert short posts 1–1.5m (3–5ft) apart over the allocated area. As the climber will become heavy, the posts must be well driven in; try to have as much post below ground as above. Treat wooden posts with non-toxic preservative. Attach wires or, more simply, wire netting between the posts. Use a wide-gauge sheep or pig netting, with squares large enough to allow you to step into the bed. Staple it to the post tops, not too tightly. (Never rig wiring in cold weather: when the weather warms up, it will expand and go slack.) Tie the stems onto it evenly around the plant using twine in figures-of-eight (*see p.248*), then guide or tie new shoots into place.

Varying the heights of the posts, or using crumpled masses of wire netting at intervals, will create a more interesting "landscaped" effect. The wire structure can readily be extended to provide "seamless" cover over garden features such as low buildings, or a fuel oil tank.

Bougainvillea hedge

In warm climates bougainvillea makes a fine hedge, covering a low framework with dense growth until the supporting structure cannot be seen. Deadheading encourages new growth, so that the surface of the hedge is clothed with fresh young foliage and flowering shoots.

CLIMBERS TRAINED AS HEDGES

Training climbers to make an informal hedge requires a strong framework to support plants as they develop. The framework should have ample vertical and horizontal struts or tightly stretched wires. The best climbers to use are those that in time make thick, woody stems. Ivies (*Hedera*) are ideal, as are *Campsis* (these need a sheltered, sunny site in cool climates) and climbing roses (*see p.316*); in subtropical climates, bougainvilleas and allamandas make fine hedges.

To keep hedges neat in outline, tie in or shorten overlong shoots throughout the growing season, in addition to any regular pruning the plant may require.

CLIMBERS IN CONTAINERS

Small frameworks improvised from wire or wire netting make ideal supports for container-grown climbers. Many climbers are suitable for growing in containers, both outdoors and under glass – generally light, non-woody, short-lived plants with growth that is not too vigorous. (*Continued on p.254.*)

Ivy as ground cover

Any wall or sloping feature is easily covered by ivy (*left*). This evergreen, stem-rooting climber is popular because it is so easy to maintain; it may take a year to establish, but thereafter is likely to need only occasional trimming to keep it to its allotted area.

RECOMMENDED FOR GROUND COVER

AKEBIA
AMPELOPSIS
ANTIGONON LEPTOPUS
CLEMATIS (especially VITICELLA GROUP)
DECUMARIA
HEDERA ZORICA, H. CANARIENSIS,
   H. COLCHICA, H. HELIX (vigorous cvs.)
HYDRANGEA (climbing species)
LONICERA (climbing species)
RUBUS HENRYI, R. LINEATUS,
   R. TRICOLOR, R. PENTALOBUS
   (syn. R. CALYCINOIDES)
SCHISANDRA
SCHIZOPHRAGMA
TRACHELOSPERMUM JASMINOIDES
VITIS

(Continued from p.253.) The climbers need support, which can be provided by wire shapes such as hoops, rings and spheres, or bamboo-cane tripods.

Initial training of climbers on such supports is relatively easy. Pinch out the shoot tips of annual plants such as rhodochitons and tropaeolums to encourage several stems to form. The leading shoots are guided or tied into place until the structure is covered. Climbers with only one main shoot may be cut back hard on planting to encourage new basal growth to train in.

Climbers that produce aerial roots, such as epipremnums, philodendrons, *Manettia luteorubra* and *Syngonium podophyllum*, should be trained around moss poles, to which they must be tied. The long roots that grow from their stems have little function as supports.

Once plants have reached their desired size or extent, shorten shoots to keep the required shape. Pot-plants do not tend to reach the size of those in open ground, so pruning is scaled down accordingly. Many conservatory plants have tropical origins and in a warm environment may grow continuously, with no specific dormant season; they may be pruned as needed, taking care not to remove future flowering growth.

Flowers can be encouraged on climbers that flower on the previous season's shoots by immediately pruning flowered wood back to replacement shoots that will flower the following year. Plants that bloom on the current season's wood should be pruned back to a framework before growth begins.

Climbers that have become too large for their pots can be repotted and root-pruned if necessary *(see p.154)*. If too large for their support and situation they may be planted out, if climate permits, or used as propagation material.

PLANTS SUITABLE FOR TRAINING ON MOSS POLES

CISSUS ANTARCTICA,
  C. RHOMBIFOLIA
EPIPREMNUM
HEDERA HELIX CVS.
MANETTIA
  LUTEORUBRA
MONSTERA DELICIOSA
PHILODENDRON SCANDENS
SENECIO
  MACROGLOSSUS
STEPHANOTIS
  FLORIBUNDA
SYNGONIUM PODOPHYLLUM

Training on a moss pole
Long stem roots from plants such as this epipremnum will probe into a moss pole, which must be kept damp by misting.

Pruning a container-grown *Jasminum polyanthum*

Before pruning Jasminum polyanthum *grows vigorously in warm climates, but in cool climates makes a small pot-plant. It benefits from annual pruning after flowering.*

1 *Untie and gently untangle all of the stems, spreading them out around the pot. Take the opportunity now to inspect the frame for damage or instability, or insert a new frame* if a different form is desired for next year's display. Repot the plant, or top-dress by carefully scraping away a shallow layer of soil and replacing it with fresh compost.

2 *Prune all the long flowered shoots back to non-flowering sideshoots, or to a pair of healthy buds.*

3 *Carefully retrain the plant over the frame, gently tying in stems as evenly as possible around the wire form.*

Regrowth after pruning *Feed the plant to obtain vigorous new growth. Guide it in horizontally around the frame for maximum coverage and to stimulate flowering sideshoots.*

Training climbers through host plants

A climber growing through a host plant can create striking visual effects. An evergreen climber will give year-round colour and foliage contrast to a deciduous host tree; a summer-flowering climber in a spring-flowering host shrub gives twice-yearly value.

Host plants must be healthy, strong and well established. The vigour of the climber and its weight when mature must also be able to be supported by the host. Trees, shrubs and hedges are all suitable hosts, provided that the climber complements their growth habit and vice versa. Do not choose a shrub that needs extensive annual pruning, because the presence of the climber will make this awkward – unless host and climber are pruned at the same time. Hedges are best interlaced with light annual or herbaceous climbers, which will die down and so allow access for clipping. Climbers with tendrils or twining stems are most suitable, because they will attach themselves to the stems of the host. Vigorous plants with adhesive stem roots or pads should be avoided on all but large trees: they blanket the host too closely with growth and can smother it.

Clematis in host
This vigorous clematis, 'Comtesse de Bouchaud', has been encouraged to grow up into a sturdy tree. Host and climber must be well matched in vigour; when two plants grow in such close proximity, one must not dominate the other.

PLANTING AND INITIAL TRAINING
Climbers planted too close to the host will be slow to establish, and may lack vigour because of root competition and shading from both light and rain. Plant, ideally, at the perimeter of the crown of the host plant, and on its windward side, so that the prevailing wind blows shoots into, rather than out of, the host. The climber will make its way towards the sunnier side, so the garden's aspect should be borne in mind when planting.

The climber can be trained up a stout rope running up into the host, or be trained up a supporting stake beside the host, then across into its upper branches (this relieves smaller hosts of some of the weight of the plant). Continuing guidance will probably be needed for the first two or three years after planting, simply by guiding and tying in main stems.

Little pruning may be possible once the climber is fully established, but where feasible any weak, dead, damaged or diseased wood should be removed, and crowded growth thinned.

MATCHING HOST PLANTS AND CLIMBERS
Provided that host and climber are matched in vigour and cultivation needs, the final considerations when matching plants are aesthetic ones. Colours of flowers and foliage should complement each other, though what constitutes a pleasing contrast or a colour clash is a matter of personal taste. The "style" of the two plants must also be in keeping. For example, while in warm climates monsteras and bougainvilleas climb into lofty, tropical trees to spectacular effect, an exotic-looking evergreen such as *Berberidopsis* might look incongruous trained into an apple or pear tree. On these trees, a *Clematis montana* or honeysuckle would provide the classic "English cottage garden" effect. Vividly coloured flowers on a dark background (*see right*) have a sophisticated, urban look, while ivies and climbing hydrangeas clambering up wide-trunked trees invoke a more sylvan, woodland mood. Seasons of interest may differ or coincide. A summer-flowering honeysuckle bridges the gap between an apple tree's blossom and its ripening fruits, for example, while the split, orange and scarlet fruits of *Celastrus scandens* give an added dimension to the autumn colour of *Cornus kousa*.

Tropaeolum in yew hedge
Given acid soil conditions, *Tropaeolum speciosum* and *T. aliatum* will clamber over hedges, contrasting vividly with dark-leaved conifers. These plants "run" underground, so the flowering stems will emerge and climb at different spots along the hedge from year to year.

Training climbers on vertical features

A strong vertical emphasis is introduced into the garden by training climbers on pillars, arches, tripods or four-legged structures such as obelisks. Even a simple tripod of three rustic poles provides a strong architectural feature in garden design. Vertical features are especially effective in a border or other open part of the garden away from walls and boundaries.

CHOOSING SUITABLE CLIMBERS

All types of climber are suitable, provided that their vigour is appropriate to the size of the structure. The selected species should be capable of reaching the top of the structure, and, if vigorous, tolerant of annual pruning to restrict size. Some, such as *Cobaea scandens*, are easily trained in close to a support, while others, such as honeysuckle, develop into a cascading feature.

If the winter appearance of the plant is immaterial, ideal choices for easily maintained plants are herbaceous species, or those climbers that tolerate severe pruning once their roots are established, then produce numerous vigorous basal stems that will grow to the height of the structure in one

VIGOROUS HERBACEOUS AND ANNUAL CLIMBERS	
ADLUMIA	LABLAB
CANARINA	LATHYRUS ODORATUS, L. LATIFOLIUS
CARDIOSPERMUM	MAURANDYA BARCLAYANA
CIONURA	MENISPERMUM
CLEMATIS VITICELLA HYBRIDS	MINA LOBATA
COBAEA SCANDENS	MOMORDICA
CODONOPSIS	PHASEOLUS
DIOSCOREA	THLADIANTHA
ECCREMOCARPUS	THUNBERGIA ALATA
HUMULUS LUPULUS 'AUREUS'	TRICHOSANTHES
IPOMOEA COCCINEA, I. PURPUREA	TROPAEOLUM MAJUS, T. PEREGRINUM

growing season – for example, *Clematis viticella* hybrids. Provided that supports are well equipped with attachment points, in the shape of wiring, netting wrapped around the posts (or even the entire structure), or strips of trellis on wide pillars, some of these climbers will, with minimal guidance, make their own way to the top. One disadvantage, compared to plants that are cut back to framework stems each year, is that all of the growth must be untangled and removed. It is much easier to remove support such as wiring from the structure with the plant still on it, then remove the plant material at ground level.

A solution is to use plastic netting on the structure, then both netting and plant can be cut away and disposed of. However, this should not be done if you intend to compost the material.

If you want a more permanent planting, then, even if the climber is vigorous enough to reach the top in one season, it is worth spending two or three years spiralling shoots gradually around the structure to develop a well-spaced framework of stems. Because they are trained towards the horizontal, these stems will produce flowering shoots along their length. These sideshoots will need pruning according to the needs of the individual

Mixing climbers with different training and pruning needs

The requirements of passion flowers (*Passiflora*) and late-flowering clematis complement each other well. The first is spur-pruned to permanent framework stems, while the second is cut back close to the base. Both are pruned in spring.

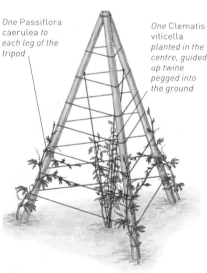

One Passiflora caerulea *to each leg of the tripod*

One Clematis viticella *planted in the centre, guided up twine pegged into the ground*

Prune all trailing passion flower shoots back to within two buds of the horizontal stems

Cut the Clematis viticella *back to 15cm (6in) from the ground*

Initial training *Tie or guide in clematis stems at first (they will soon climb unaided). Train and tie in laterals from the passion flowers to make permanent horizontal arms along the wires. When they reach the next leg, cut to a bud to stimulate sideshoots.*

Summer flowering *By the time the passion flowers have developed curtains of flowering sideshoots from their horizontal arms, the clematis has grown out and over the top, so it will not be affected adversely by the shade cast on its main stems.*

Early spring *Spur-prune the passion flowers first, because it will not matter if, while doing so, you cut through any clematis stems as well. Once the framework is clear, cut through the base of the clematis stems and tease (never pull) the top growth out.*

plant (*see* Dictionary of Climbing Plants, *pp.262–287*). For quick results while long-term planting matures, choose annual or herbaceous climbers, such as *Ipomoea* or *Asarina*. Tender species that can be used as half-hardy annuals greatly broaden the range of climbers that can be grown in cool climates. Choosing different annuals each year will vary the effect.

TRAINING OVER AN ARCH

An arch – framing a recess, marking a boundary or covering a path – can be covered in many ways. Scented climbers can be fully appreciated over arches and arbours. Plants can be mixed to give a succession of flowers and scents, and non-climbing shrubs introduced to bulk out the lower part of the arch. A woody climber can be trained up one side and over the top of the arch while an annual or herbaceous one climbs up the other. To make the best of the feature, the climbers used must tolerate regular trimming to keep the passage clear. Avoid thorny-stemmed plants.

It is inadvisable to spiral shoots around the sides of an arch; it restricts the gap within and produces a rather clumsy "sleeve" effect. Plant climbers on the outside of the arch and space their shoots out to cover the sides, tying them into position. Train laterals sideways to fill in any gaps.

As the climber becomes established, continue to tie in the laterals sideways and extend the main stems across the top of the arch. Once the arch is covered, vigorous vertical shoots must be shortened or tied in.

MIXED PLANTING EFFECTS

Vertical features are ideal structures on which to combine two or more climbing plants to provide either a longer season of interest, or eye-catching contrasts of foliage or flowers. Plants can be sited on different sides of a structure and then trained so that their stems entwine, or several plants can be used, one at the base of each leg. With this arrangement, a vigorous climber can also be planted in the centre of the structure and trained rapidly up a central, vertical wire or tall cane. Its stems will then cascade from the top of the structure as those of the other plants are climbing up to meet them (*see left*).

It is all too easy to cut the wrong stem when trying to prune one of two intertwined plants, so use climbers whose pruning needs are similar or complementary; for example, herbaceous or annual plants on one side and a woody-stemmed, spring-pruned climber on the other. In the latter category, roses (*see p.320*) should not be overlooked; they can provide some of the most charming and floriferous effects, whether alone or combined with other plants.

Training climbers on an arch

Arch of metal with plastic coating is rot- and rust-proof

Training *Humulus lupulus* 'Aureus' on an arch
Plant climbers on both sides of the arch, as stems should not be trained downwards. This illustration shows golden hops at two different stages of growth, to demonstrate the changing pruning and training needs.

Plastic netting on the frame is soon disguised by foliage

Established pruning
Long shoots must be shortened to maintain the arch's form. Flowering plants should be carefully pruned according to their individual needs, or flowering may be impaired. On this vigorous foliage plant, wayward shoots can be trimmed at any time.

Climber planted on outside of arch

Initial training *Given adequate support, twining and tendrilled plants will climb unaided. To direct their growth, guide young shoots into the wires or netting. Young hop shoots are fleshy and fragile, and must be handled with extreme care.*

RECOMMENDED CLIMBER COMBINATIONS
ASARINA with a white-flowered clematis or rose
CLEMATIS VITICELLA with PASSIFLORA CAERULEA
JASMINUM POLYANTHUM with HOYA CARNOSA
LONICERA PERICLYMENUM 'SEROTINA' or 'BELGICA' with CLEMATIS 'JACKMANII' or 'MADAME JULIA CORREVON'
LONICERA with perennial climbing peas (LATHYRUS LATIFOLIUS, L. NERVOSUS)
RHODOCHITON (annual) through HUMULUS LUPULUS 'AUREUS'
SOLANUM JASMINOIDES with CLEMATIS 'LASURSTERN' or a blue C. VITICELLA HYBRID
SOLLYA or BOMAREA with SOLANUM JASMINOIDES 'ALBUM'
TRACHELOSPERMUM JASMINOIDES with ECCREMOCARPUS SCABER
TROPAEOLUM PEREGRINUM through PLUMBAGO AURICULATA
VITIS VINIFERA 'PURPUREA' with annuals growing through it: sweet peas (LATHYRUS ODORATUS) in pale shades or, for a more vivid colour contrast, nasturtiums (TROPAEOLUM) or black-eyed Susan (THUNBERGIA ALATA)
WISTERIA SINENSIS with a pink-flowered rose, for example 'NEW DAWN'

Training climbers on a pergola

A pergola consists of either a series of posts or pillars linked by crossbeams, or a row of linked arches. It needs to be sturdy, and made of durable materials. A well-placed, well-constructed pergola can be a valuable and integral part of a garden design. Half-pergolas may be butted up to a wall to form a walkway or, against a house wall, a verandah. Climbing plants are trained up the pillars and along the top, where those with trailing stems or pendent flowers are particularly effective.

It is advisable to allow 3m (10ft) of headroom, especially if you intend to use plants with trailing stems. The structure will need wiring or, for wider pillars, stapled strips of wire netting or narrow panels of trellis. Equip the pergola liberally with supports at the start; it can be a fiddly and awkward job to add more when plants have grown.

CHOOSING SUITABLE CLIMBERS

Choose climbers that will enhance the structure and complement the materials of which it is made, not obscure it entirely. The objective is to create an open feature, not a tunnel of vegetation. Depending on the size of the pergola, one very vigorous climber, such as a wisteria, may cover the entire structure, or several less vigorous climbers may be planted, one to each upright. If the pergola is of uneven aspect, plant more shade- or cold-tolerant climbers on the less favoured side to match the vigorous growth of plants on the sunny side.

TRAINING AND PRUNING

There are two ways of training the climbers up the pillars: straight up, or spiralled. Choose the former if you want plants to cover the canopy rapidly, although their stems will become bare at the base. If you wish the plants to flower on the pillars as well as over the top, then spiral the stems. Bare stems at the base of established climbers may be concealed by underplanting with shrubs or with light annual climbers, such as nasturtiums and sweet peas.

Once the stems have reached the tops of the posts, spread them evenly over the crossbeams, tying them in position. Prune them according to the individual needs of the plants (*see* Dictionary of Climbing Plants, *pp.262–287*). Long-handled tree pruners are invaluable for snipping off, or hooking down, vigorous stems. If climbing a ladder, make sure it is firmly positioned, and resist the temptation to overreach, particularly above your head or behind you; the job may take longer, but will be much safer, if you climb down and move the ladder whenever necessary.

VERY VIGOROUS CLIMBERS
ACTINIDIA ARGUTA
BIGNONIA CAPREOLATA
CLEMATIS MONTANA
LONICERA
 HILDEBRANDTIANA
POLYGONUM
VITIS COIGNETIAE
WISTERIA SINENSIS

Quick coverage

Very vigorous climbers will clothe a pergola quickly but their exuberant growth often needs to be checked. Some plants can simply be cropped back to the pergola framework with shears (*above*) but others need more precise pruning.

Long shoots can be snipped back or tucked into other growth

FREE-FLOWERING CLIMBERS
BOUGAINVILLEA
CAMPSIS
CLEMATIS
LONICERA
PYROSTEGIA VENUSTA
THUNBERGIA
 GRANDIFLORA
WISTERIA

Pruning for flowers

Although some climbers require little, if any, attention to flower freely, others, including *Clematis* and *Wisteria*, perform best if regularly pruned.

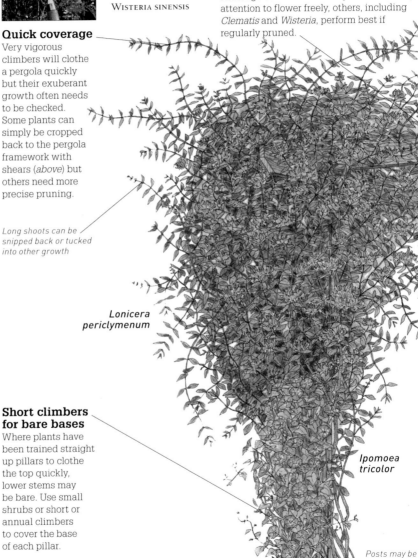

Lonicera periclymenum

Ipomoea tricolor

Short climbers for bare bases

Where plants have been trained straight up pillars to clothe the top quickly, lower stems may be bare. Use small shrubs or short or annual climbers to cover the base of each pillar.

Posts may be of brick, metal, hardwoods or pressure-treated softwood

FOR PILLAR BASES
HARDENBERGIA VIOLACEA
IPOMOEA TRICOLOR,
 I. LOBATA
LATHYRUS ODORATUS
MANETTIA
RHODOCHITON
SOLLYA
THUNBERGIA ALATA (*left*)
TROPAEOLUM MAJUS,
 T. TUBEROSUM

Wires
Equip all pillars and crossbeams with plenty of attachment points. Wires can also be stretched between crossbeams.

CLIMBERS FOR FOLIAGE
ARISTOLOCHIA
  MACROPHYLLA
BOUGAINVILLEA GLABRA
  'VARIEGATA'
HEDERA COLCHICA
  'DENTATA VARIEGATA'
VITIS VINIFERA
  'PURPUREA', V. 'BRANT'
WISTERIA

Foliage plants
Climbers grown for their foliage are often allowed to romp unchecked, but a rigorous pruning regime, for example spur pruning of *Vitis* (*above*), may be used on many plants to keep growth in check so that other plants are not overwhelmed.

CLIMBERS WITH
FLOWERS AND
FRUIT
ACTINIDIA DELICIOSA
CELASTRUS
CUCURBITA
PASSIFLORA (*right*)
PERIPLOCA
SINOFRANCHETIA
  CHINENSIS
VITIS

Fruit display
Edible and ornamental fruits, in the case of the passion fruit (*above*) preceded by unusual flowers, are often only produced in quantity when plants are grown in very favourable conditions.

Climbing roses are ideal pergola plants (see p.322)

Shortening flowered shoots, as on this Solanum, maintains the pergola's form

Vitis vinifera
'Purpurea'

Solanum crispum

Rosa
'New Dawn'

Clematis viticella

Passiflora caerulea

Clematis
'Hagley
Hybrid'

Jasminum polyanthum

Planting distance
Plant a little distance from the pillar or post, guiding and tying in the young stems. Plant either on the outside of the structure or on each side – not within the pergola.

Training climbers as standards

Most climbers used as standards can never be completely free-standing. They need a permanent stake of wood or a durable material such as wrought iron, or one of the umbrella frames used for weeping rose standards (*see p.311*).

Climbers that can be spur-pruned to a framework, such as *wisteria*, are ideal as standards, as are those that tolerate regular pruning, such as honeysuckles and, especially, those climbers with dense, evergreen foliage that can be trimmed without revealing bare growth beneath, such as ivy. Do not use climbers with wispy or wiry stems, particularly strongly twining or tendrilled climbers, as they will become tangled and unmanageable. Plants with aerial roots can be used; the roots normally develop only when the stem touches a suitable surface.

FORMATIVE TRAINING

Plant and stake a young plant with one sturdy stem, removing others if necessary, although several stems can be twisted or braided together (*see* Topiary, *p.48*). Training (*see right*) initially aims to form a strong, thick trunk, so laterals are cleared only gradually, just as for a standard tree (*see p.26*); the remaining foliage "feeds" and thickens the main stem. Annual shortening of the main stem, and training on the new topmost shoot as the new leader, also encourages vigorous, robust growth. If the leader is damaged, train in a replacement as for a standard tree (*see p.24*). Once the desired height of clear stem has been achieved, shorten laterals and their sideshoots to develop a strong, compact, well-structured framework, with bushy growth, for the head.

PRUNING AN ESTABLISHED STANDARD

Adapt the routine pruning for the individual plant as necessary to maintain the form. In winter, prune to enhance the shape of the head (pruning harder on a weak side), and remove older wood to reduce congestion. In summer, shorten long shoots to restrict size and encourage dense foliage and, if appropriate, flowers.

Training a climber (wisteria) as a 1.5m (5ft) standard

Year 1, pruning on planting

1 *Shorten leader by at least one-third, to a strong bud where the stem is thick.*

2 *Holding the stem straight, tie it to the stake. Tree ties are adjustable and will protect the bark.*

Stout stake

Choose a young plant with one strong main stem

3 *Pinch out any sideshoots.*

Year 1, summer

1 *Shorten the leader again, to a strong bud.*

2 *Leaving shorter upper laterals unpruned, shorten laterals midway up the stem by two-thirds. Remove those less than 30cm (1ft) from the ground completely.*

3 *Check and, if necessary, loosen ties.*

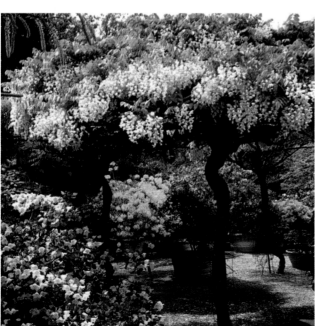

Wisteria standard

Today, standards 1.5–2m (5–6ft) tall are popular for patios and borders, but in the past standards were made much taller, with heads above top-hat or parasol height. Most of the great Victorian wisteria standards still in existence in British gardens have fragments of metal embedded in them that were once part of their supporting pillars.

CLIMBING PLANTS SUITABLE TO TRAIN AS STANDARDS

ACTINIDIA ARGUTA, A. KOLOMIKTA
BAUHINIA CORYMBOSA
BEAUMONTIA GRANDIFLORA
BIGNONIA CAPREOLATA
BOUGAINVILLEA GLABRA, B. PERUVIANA
CAMPSIS RADICANS
CLERODENDRUM THOMSONIAE
COMBRETUM GRANDIFLORUM
HEDERA HELIX
HYDRANGEA PETIOLARIS, H. SEEMANNII
JASMINUM POLYANTHUM
LONICERA PERICLYMENUM, L. JAPONICA
MANDEVILLA × AMOENA, M. SPLENDENS
MUSSAENDA ARCUATA, M. ERYTHROPHYLLA
PANDOREA JASMINOIDES, P. PANDORANA
PETREA VOLUBILIS
PLUMBAGO AURICULATA (SYN. P. CAPENSIS)
PYROSTEGIA VENUSTA
SCHIZOPHRAGMA HYDRANGEOIDES
SOLANDRA GRANDIFLORA, S. MAXIMA
SOLANUM CRISPUM, S. JASMINOIDES
STEPHANOTIS FLORIBUNDA
STREPTOSOLEN JAMESII
TECOMARIA CAPENSIS
VITIS AMURENSIS, V. VINIFERA
WISTERIA FLORIBUNDA, W. SINENSIS

Year 1, winter

1 *Shorten the new leader again. Remove all secondary growth stimulated by the summer pruning, and one-third of the previously shortened growth.*

2 *Spur-prune all of the laterals to two or three healthy buds.*

Summer pruning cut was made here

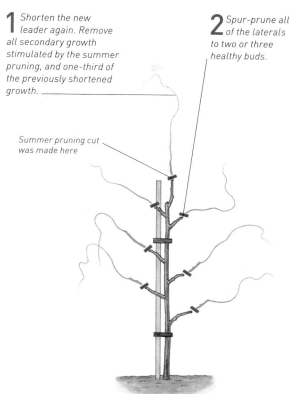

Year 2, summer

1 *Pinch out the leader at the desired height. The leading shoot will become indistinguishable as the head develops.*

2 *Restrict growth by shortening laterals by one-third to a half, to encourage sideshoots and the thickening of the main stem and framework.*

3 *Check and, if necessary, loosen ties.*

Year 3, winter

1 *Shorten new laterals on the main stems back to two or three buds, beginning the formation of spur systems.*

2 *Shorten all shoots from existing laterals to two or three buds to encourage spur formation.*

3 *Spur-prune the lower shoots on the trunk, rather than removing them now, so that the stem will continue to benefit from the food manufactured by their leaves.*

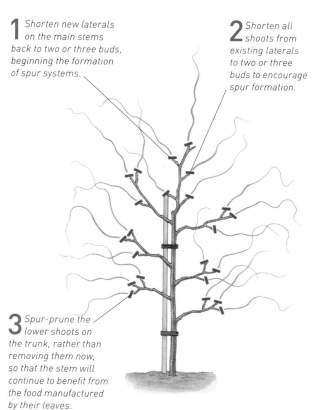

Year 3, summer

1 *Shorten all new shoots by half to two-thirds for compact, bushy growth.*

2 *Remove low laterals to clear the trunk. Rub or cut off any new shoots that emerge.*

Dictionary of Climbing Plants

A

ACTINIDIA

Mainly hardy, deciduous, twining climbers valued for their alternate, oblong to heart-shaped leaves, in some species splashed with colour. Foliage colour is best when plants are trained up into the sun, though the base of the plant should be in semi-shade. They have white, cream or buff flowers; where plants of both sexes are grown, females produce large, sometimes edible fruits (*A. deliciosa* is the Chinese gooseberry or kiwi fruit). Most species need ample space and the support of robust fences, pergolas or stout tripods, or large trees; *A. kolomikta* is a less vigorous species.

Actinidia kolomikta
Trained on a fully sunny wall, the leaves of *A. kolomikta* will colour well.

A. KOLOMIKTA

Fully hardy climber grown principally for its large leaves, attractively splashed with creamy-pink and white.

■ **WHEN TO PRUNE** Late winter or early spring, before growth begins. Remove or shorten over-vigorous or badly placed shoots in summer.

■ **TRAINING AND PRUNING** Cut young plants back to strong buds about 30–40cm (12–16in) above ground level to encourage basal growth. Select five to seven strong shoots, tying in as growth proceeds. In the second season, cut back strong laterals by two-thirds of their length, and weaker shoots to one or two buds. Remove any very weak growth. Once established, to keep within bounds, shorten growth by one-third to half of its length, cutting back to a healthy bud. Remove an old main stem at the base occasionally, to encourage new growth. Renovate by cutting all tangled growth back to the framework of main stems in spring.

> OTHER ACTINIDIAS
> A. DELICIOSA (syn. A. CHINENSIS) *See* Kiwi fruit, *p.297.*
> A. ARGUTA As for *A. kolomikta.* Much more vigorous, and particularly suitable for training through large trees. Pruning established plants trained in this way may prove impractical.
> A. POLYGAMA As for *A. kolomikta.*

Akebia quinata
Train the chocolate vine where its small, brownish-purple flowers and their vanilla scent can be appreciated close at hand.

AKEBIA

Vigorous, hardy, deciduous or semi-evergreen twiners, with elegant divided foliage and maroon to chocolate-purple flowers followed, after long, hot summers, by pendent, sausage-shaped, violet to grey-purple fruits. Tolerant of sun or semi-shade, akebias are suitable for walls, fences or pergolas. Plant them as young as possible, as they resent disturbance. Guide young stems into the support, and tie in until they begin to twine. Train and prune as for *Actinidia kolomikta* (*see left*), but prune in late spring, after flowering.

ALLAMANDA

Evergreen scramblers with large, paired, glossy leaves and showy flowers. They prefer subtropical conditions; while mature specimens may survive light frost, they are better grown under glass (or in pots that can be brought under cover in winter) in cooler areas. Grow against pillars, walls or strong trellis.

■ **WHEN TO PRUNE** Late winter, before active growth begins.

■ **TRAINING AND PRUNING** After planting, pinch back young shoots to encourage bushy growth, and tie in new shoots to form a framework as growth proceeds. Once established, prune annually by shortening sideshoots to within two or three pairs of buds of the main framework stems. Remove weak, dead or unwanted growth at the same time. They respond well to hard pruning.

AGAPETES

Agapetes (syn. *Pentapterygium*) are scandent, semi-scrambling evergreens bearing pendent flowers from winter to spring beneath branches that often have a delightful zigzag growth pattern. All are frost-tender. In frost-prone climates, grow them in a humid conservatory, in dappled shade. Train young plants against a wall or trellis. Space out the main shoots to give even coverage and tie in as growth proceeds. Prune in late winter or early spring to remove badly placed growth if necessary. *A. macrantha* looks better with slightly more formal training than *A. serpens*. Established plants need little pruning, other than to remove weak, dead or badly placed growth. *Agapetes* do not respond well to hard pruning.

KEY
Throughout this section, these symbols are used to indicate the plant's method of climbing

 Scrambling (scandent)

 Stem tendrils

 Loosely twining

Leaf tendrils

Strongly twining

 Clinging stem roots

Twining leaf-stalks

 Adhesive pads

AMPELOPSIS

Deciduous, woody-stemmed, tendrilled vines with handsome, pinnate or lobed leaves. The insignificant flowers are sometimes followed by attractive berries, usually reliably only during long, hot summers. Vigorous and hardy, *Ampelopsis* are generally too large for small gardens, but are ideal for sheltered pergolas or fences and, with initial support, will scramble through trees. If grown on house walls, cut back in winter to prevent rampant growth clogging gutters and dislodging roof tiles. Provide initial support by tying in strong young shoots. Subsequent training and pruning is as for *Vitis* (*see p.286*).

ANEMOPAEGMA

Evergreen tendrilled climbers with trumpet- or bell-shaped flowers, borne during summer at the leaf axils of the current season's growth. Frost-tender, they need a humid glasshouse or conservatory in cool climates. After planting, tip-prune all shoots to encourage strong growth. Tie shoots in as they grow to develop a framework. In later years, shorten all laterals to within two or three buds or nodes of the main stems, and remove weak shoots, pruning in late winter or early spring. If the plant becomes congested, prune also during summer, thinning out surplus stems. Responds well to hard pruning.

ANREDERA
MADEIRA VINE, MIGNONETTE VINE

Twining evergreens with racemes of small, fragrant flowers and heart-shaped leaves, often herbaceous, dying down in winter and regenerating from the base in spring. Ideal for pergolas and fences in warm, dry climates; in cooler regions, grow against a conservatory wall or pillar. Training consists only of guiding growth to the support. In late winter or early spring, cut back all of the previous year's growth by one-third to half of its length, or if growth has died back, cut almost to ground level.

ANTIGONON

Perennial, scrambling evergreens with slender stems, sometimes developing tendrils, and racemes of coral-pink to red flowers, mainly in summer, but all year in tropical conditions. They will clothe buildings, arbours or large pergolas in tropical and subtropical gardens, but in cooler areas they must be grown under glass. Little training is needed other than to guide new growth in to supports. In early spring, cut over-vigorous growth back hard, removing weak, congested or damaged shoots at the same time.

ARGYREIA

Vigorous, woody-stemmed climbers, producing soft annual shoots that die back to a woody framework during winter. The flowers, which open in sunshine from late summer to autumn, are funnel-shaped, pink to lavender or maroon, with distinctive hairy outer bands. Suitable for arbours, pergolas and trellis in tropical gardens; in cooler climates, plant in a conservatory border in full sun. Provide strong support with wires or trellis.

ARISTOLOCHIA *BIRTHWORT, DUTCHMAN'S PIPE*

Vigorous, deciduous or evergreen, twining climbers grown for their extraordinary siphon-shaped, often unattractive-smelling flowers. Most species, such as *A. littoralis* (syn. *A. elegans*), are subtropical and in cooler areas need warm glasshouse conditions, but *A. macrophylla* and the evergreen *A. sempervirens* tolerate short spells of light frost, and are suited by sunny or part-shaded sheltered walls. Plant hardy species in late spring or early summer.

■ **WHEN TO PRUNE** Late winter or early spring, or in midsummer after flowering.

■ **TRAINING AND PRUNING** After planting, select the strongest shoots and train in to the support. Remove weak and straggly growth completely, cutting out close to the base. Once established, remove weak

ASARINA

Asarina (syn. *Maurandya, Maurandella*) are scandent to twining, evergreen perennials with soft, diamond- or heart-shaped leaves and pouched, usually pink or purple flowers. Most, including *A. barclayana*, are frost-tender; some may survive very light frosts, dying back to the base. Scrambling species, such as *A. antirrhinifolia*, *A. erubescens* and *A. scandens*, need tying to lightweight support such as wires, bamboo canes or twiggy branches. They need no pruning, other than to cut back dead or damaged growth in spring before growth begins.

■ **WHEN TO PRUNE** Late winter, before new growth begins.

■ **TRAINING AND PRUNING** Tie in young growth to give well-spaced coverage of the support, and remove excess growth carefully during the growing season, if necessary. In subsequent years, if the previous season's growth has been very vigorous, thin surplus shoots by cutting back to within one or two buds or nodes of the main framework. Responds well to hard pruning if necessary.

Twining aristolochia stems
Aristolochias respond well to hard pruning, producing new shoots that will twine around wires and develop trailing sideshoots.

growth and cut back long shoots or stems to two or three nodes of the main stems. This can be done annually, in midsummer after flowering or in early spring. Aristolochias respond well to hard pruning.

OTHER CLIMBING PLANTS

ADLUMIA As for *Asarina* (*see above*).
ARAUJIA Guide twining stems in to the support. Prune only to remove dead or badly placed growth in spring. Responds reasonably well to hard pruning.

ASPARAGUS Treat *A. scandens* as for evergreen *Bomarea* species (*see p.264*).
ASTERANTHERA As for *Berberidopsis* (*see p.264*).
BAUHINIA On planting, select four or five

strong shoots from which to develop a framework on wires or trellis. Once established, after flowering, spur-prune laterals to four or five buds of the framework stems. Do not prune hard.

B

BEAUMONTIA

Beaumontia grandiflora (herald's trumpet, Nepal trumpet flower) is a vigorous, evergreen, woody-stemmed twining climber, grown for its handsome paired leaves and fragrant flowers, borne at the tips of the previous season's growth. It needs a frost-free, warm temperate climate, or protection under glass, and substantial support, such as thick wires or pillars or a large tree. After planting, select four or five strong shoots and tie in to the support to give well-spaced coverage. Cut the remaining shoots back to their bases. Once established, prune annually after flowering to thin the plant out; remove weak growth, and prune strong laterals to within two or three nodes of the main framework stems. It responds well to hard pruning.

Berberidopsis corallina
Glossy green leaves set off the pendent clusters of fleshy, red, globular flowers.

BERBERIDOPSIS

Berberidopsis corallina, the coral vine, is a woody-stemmed, twining and scrambling evergreen. It needs a sheltered, shaded or semi-shaded wall with wires or trellis, or will scramble through other plants. It is hardy, but may die back in hard winters; established plants usually resprout from below ground if protected with a winter mulch.

On planting, remove only dead or damaged growth. Guide and tie in young shoots at first; they usually become self-supporting once the plant is established. Cut out weak or dead growth from the base of established plants, pruning in spring after any danger of severe frost has passed. If the interlocking stems become congested, remove the weakest growth, cutting back to a main stem or strong bud. Does not respond well to hard pruning.

BERCHEMIA

Scrambling climbers, with oval alternate leaves and panicles of white or greenish-white flowers, followed by attractive berry-like fruits, blue-black in the vigorous *B. scandens*. They are hardy if sheltered from cold winds. On walls and fences, provide the support of stout wires or trellis, or grow through large shrubs or over tree stumps.

B. RACEMOSA

Deciduous scrambler with heart-shaped leaves that turn yellow in autumn. The late summer flowers are followed by red berries that turn black when ripe. The cultivar 'Variegata' has leaves that are attractively marked with creamy-white.

BIGNONIA

Bignonia capreolata (cross vine, trumpet flower) is a vigorous evergreen with orange flowers, climbing by leaf tendrils. In a sunny, sheltered site it will tolerate light frost. Suitable for tall posts; wall-grown specimens need strong wires or trellis. After planting, select two or three strong shoots as the main framework stems and tie in. In subsequent springs, before growth begins, shorten the previous season's laterals by up to two-thirds, cutting to a strong, well placed bud. Tie in or remove surplus shoots. To renovate, cut back hard into old wood once any danger of frost has passed.

BILLARDIERA

Slender-stemmed, evergreen twiners with attractive flowers and fruits. They need shelter from hot sun and cold winds, and although they tolerate very light frost they grow best in a completely frost-free climate. In cool climates, they are ideal for a shaded conservatory or greenhouse. Provide support with light trellis or netting, or grow through shrubs or other, more vigorous climbers.

■ **WHEN TO PRUNE** Early spring, or late summer, after fruiting.

■ **TRAINING AND PRUNING** Keep pruning to a minimum. Tie in young shoots to provide even coverage of the support. Once established, plants usually need pruning only to remove dead or badly placed growth, but if congested, cut back surplus shoots to within two or three buds or nodes of a main stem.

■ **WHEN TO PRUNE** Late winter or very early spring.

■ **TRAINING AND PRUNING** Tie in young shoots as growth proceeds, until even coverage of the support is achieved. Once plants are established, prune annually to remove dead or damaged growth, thin out congested shoots, and shorten any stems that have outgrown their allotted space. Responds well to hard pruning.

> OTHER BERCHEMIAS
> **B. SCANDENS** As for *B. racemosa*, but prune in spring, immediately after flowering.

BOMAREA

Herbaceous or evergreen, tuberous-rooted, scrambling and twining climbers. They are grown for their clusters of brightly coloured, alstroemeria-like flowers. They need a position in full sun and a frost-free climate. Provide upright supports, with wires or trellis, or allow plants to clamber up and through shrubs or other climbers. Bomareas need no formative pruning. Herbaceous species, such as *B. caldasii*, die back completely during winter. In spring all dead growth can be cut back to the base. With evergreen species, remove the old, flowered stems after flowering, as the leaves begin to turn yellow.

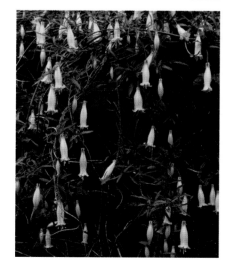

Billardiera longiflora
The narrowly bell-shaped, greenish-yellow (sometimes purple-tinged) flowers are followed by large, glossy, purple-blue fruits.

BOUGAINVILLEA

Vigorous, deciduous or evergreen, often spiny, woody-stemmed climbers, with ovate or elliptic bright green leaves. The insignificant flowers are surrounded by brilliantly coloured bracts, mostly in white and shades of magenta, crimson, violet or purple, but occasionally yellow or apricot. They flower on the current season's growth. In warm climates bougainvilleas are very effective grown up large trees, or on walls. They need full sun, and tend to flower most freely in tropical or sub-tropical conditions, growing very well under glass. In cool climates, grow in large tubs or bricked-in beds in a warm conservatory; they usually flower better if their roots are confined. *B. glabra* and *B. × buttiana* are best for containers, since they flower even when young. All need the support of trellis or pillars. They may be trained as standards and spur-pruned annually to restrict size.

Basal buds stimulated into growth by pruning

Spur-pruned bougainvillea
All sideshoots have been pruned hard to two or three buds.

■ **WHEN TO PRUNE** Late winter or early spring, just before growth begins.

■ **TRAINING AND PRUNING** It is essential to develop a well-spaced, strong framework of stems. To train as a climber, prune back hard at first to stimulate strong growth from the base, then tie in shoots as growth proceeds. Tie in only the strongest shoots, removing others; if too many stems are trained in initially, plants will be overcrowded at maturity, especially when confined against a wall (*see below*). In subsequent years, reduce leading shoots by two-thirds to three-quarters of the previous season's growth, cutting back to a strong bud. Cut back laterals and sideshoots that are not needed to tie in to extend the framework to within two or three buds of the main stems; the shoots that develop will bear the current year's flowers. Once the framework is established, cut back all the previous season's lateral shoots to two or three buds, to leave spurs about 2–3cm (¾ –1¼in) in length. During the growing season, remove weak growth as necessary. Old plants should respond to hard pruning, but are better replaced.

To train as a standard, *see p.260*. Once a balanced head is formed, cut back all the previous season's laterals to within two or three buds of the branch framework each year.

Wall-training a bougainvillea

Pruning on planting, spring

1 *Fan out strong shoots and tie in to form an evenly spaced framework.*

2 *Shorten all shoots to 15–20cm (6–8in), cutting to just above a healthy bud pointing in such a direction that the new shoots will not cross each other.*

Year 2 until allotted space is covered, spring

1 *Prune back the previous season's growth by three-quarters, then tie in new leading shoots as they appear.*

2 *Cut any sideshoots back to one or two leaves or buds to start encouraging the development of flowering spurs.*

Established *bougainvillea*, spring

1 *Where shoots exceed the allotted space, cut back to a healthy bud or sideshoot.*

2 *Where growth is crowded, cut out some older stems, tying in a young sideshoot to fill any gaps in the framework.*

3 *Spur-prune all other sideshoots to 2–3cm (¾ –1¼in), leaving two or three leaves or buds.*

Established *bougainvillea*, summer

1 *Deadhead as flowers fade, cutting entire flower clusters back to a young, non-flowering sideshoot.*

2 *As growth develops, tie in new shoots where there is space to do so.*

C

CALCEOLARIA

Calceolaria pavonii is the only commonly grown climbing species in this varied genus; a robust, evergreen scrambler with a woody base and rather triangular, dark green leaves. It bears showy trusses of pouched, sulphur-yellow flowers, sometimes banded with brown-purple, from late summer through to winter on the current year's growth. It makes good ground cover, and will also grow well in containers. It needs a completely frost-free climate, though with sufficient rainfall it will flower well in relatively cool summers; in these conditions it may adopt the habit of a semi-woody subshrub. Provide light support if grown on a wall or in a conservatory.

■ **WHEN TO PRUNE** Early spring, before new growth begins.

■ **TRAINING AND PRUNING** After planting, pinch back young shoots to encourage the production of vigorous sideshoots that will form framework stems. Train in the new stems to the support, either vertically or over a horizontal framework as ground cover. Subsequently prune established plants annually: trim out weak, dead or unwanted growth, and reduce the remaining shoots by up to two-thirds of their length, cutting back to a strong healthy bud. Calceolarias respond reasonably well to hard pruning, but old plants are better replaced by strong young ones.

CALOCHONE

Calochone redingii is a moderately vigorous, evergreen, scrambling climber with hairy, elliptical leaves and trusses of handsome, salver-shaped, red or orange-pink flowers, borne in midwinter on growth made during the previous growing season. It must be grown in full light, and in warm tropical conditions. Provide the support of wires or trellis.

■ **WHEN TO PRUNE** After flowering, in late winter or early spring.

■ **TRAINING AND PRUNING** Pruning is best kept to a minimum other than to remove weak or unwanted growth. Tie in all shoots to the support as growth proceeds. Once the plant is established, prune annually by thinning out overcrowded shoots, cutting back to main stems. It dislikes hard pruning.

CAMPSIS

Vigorous, deciduous, woody-stemmed climbers, often clinging by means of small aerial stem roots. They are grown for their handsome, pinnate leaves and the bold terminal trusses of orange to red, trumpet-shaped flowers, produced on the current season's growth from late summer to autumn. Although hardy, they need shelter from cold winds, and full sun to ripen the wood if they are to flower freely. Grow against a high sunny wall; in Mediterranean-type climates, they thrive on fences or when grown up stout trees.

C. GRANDIFLORA

CHINESE TRUMPET CREEPER, TRUMPET VINE

Campsis grandiflora (syn. *C. chinensis, Bignonia grandiflora, Tecoma grandiflora*) is the hardiest species, with trumpet-shaped, deep orange flowers, yellow within, that can be 8cm (3in) across. It forms few aerial roots, so tie in the main stems to a strong support.

■ **WHEN TO PRUNE** Late winter or early spring.

■ **TRAINING AND PRUNING** It is essential to establish a strong woody framework. After planting, prune all stems back

hard to about 15cm (6in) above ground level to promote vigorous growth. Select two or three of the strongest shoots and remove the rest. Train in to the supporting wires or trellis and tie in as growth proceeds, until shoots extend fully over the allotted space. In most cases, an area at least 4m (12ft) high is needed. It may take two or three seasons to complete the framework. Once it is established, prune the plant annually, spur-pruning all lateral shoots back to within two or three buds of the main stems. Remove weak or diseased growth entirely. *Campsis* respond well to hard pruning. If a main framework branch is damaged, cut it back to the base, and train in the strongest of the resulting replacement shoots. Renovate by cutting back all growth to within 30cm (12in) of the ground to encourage strong new shoots to break from the base.

> **OTHER CAMPSIS**
> **C. RADICANS** As for *C. grandiflora*, but produces small stem roots more freely and is completely self-clinging once established.
> **C. × TAGLIABUANA** As for *C. grandiflora*.

Campsis × tagliabuana
After spur-pruning in winter (*below*), new shoots grow and flower in a single season.

CANARINA

Herbaceous, scrambling climbers or trailing perennials, with large, pendulous, bell-shaped flowers of yellow or orange-yellow, handsomely marked with green or reddish lines. They have a tuberous root that can be lifted, removing all top growth, and stored over winter, as for dahlias. They are frost-tender, preferring a Mediterranean-type climate with dry winters; they may be grown under glass in cooler climates, trained on supports. They flower from late summer to early winter, after which the top growth dies back. Each year, cut back dead growth close to the ground in spring, being careful not to damage any emerging new growth. Once new shoots are growing strongly, their tips may be pinched out to encourage branching. Guide and, if necessary, tie stems into the support as growth proceeds.

CANTUA

 Cantua buxifolia (syn. *C. dependens*) is a scandent evergreen with slender stems that look well arching over and through other shrubs, or tied in informally to a wall or pillar. It bears drooping clusters of trumpet-shaped, magenta-red flowers in spring, on the previous season's wood. Frost-tender, it prefers a Mediterranean-type climate.

■ **WHEN TO PRUNE** After flowering, in late spring or early summer.

■ **TRAINING AND PRUNING** Needs little training or pruning. Tip back the shoots after planting to encourage strong new growth. Once established, prune only to shape or remove weak growth. Reduce overcrowding, if necessary, by thinning out old flowered shoots. Does not respond well to hard pruning.

Cantua buxifolia
Sometimes known as the sacred or magic flower of the Incas, this South American native needs hot, sunny conditions.

CARDIOSPERMUM

 Cardiospermum halicacabum (balloon vine, heart pea, winter cherry) is a deciduous, perennial, scandent climber with slender, woody-based stems and dissected leaves. It is grown mainly for its curious inflated, yellow-green fruits that follow the small greenish-white summer flowers. The flower clusters produce clinging tendrils. It needs warm, frost-free conditions, but in cool climates can be grown outdoors in full sun, as an annual. Provide support with trellis or twiggy branches, or grow as ground cover. When grown as a perennial, cut back all the previous year's growth by two-thirds to three-quarters of its length in spring.

CELASTRUS *BITTERSWEET*

  Deciduous twiners or scramblers grown for their spectacular autumn displays of fruits. Plants of both sexes must be grown together to produce fruit (though hermaphrodite forms of *C. orbiculatus* are available). The bittersweets are fully to frost-hardy and tolerate semi-shade. Most are vigorous, needing ample space and stout supports. Although generally unsuitable for house walls, they look well on large garden walls, or festooning garden buildings or large tree stumps. They can also be trained on stout pillars or tripods.

C. ORBICULATUS
SYN. C. ARTICULATUS

ORIENTAL BITTERSWEET

Celastrus orbiculatus is a vigorous, deciduous twining climber with deep yellow fruits in autumn that split to reveal pink or red seeds.

■ **WHEN TO PRUNE** Winter or early spring.

■ **TRAINING AND PRUNING** After planting, guide in new growth to the support as growth proceeds. Established plants need little regular pruning, but remove old or badly placed growth and any that arches out too far from the support, cutting shoots back to their base. Trim back overlong laterals to within three or four buds of the main stem, if needed. Over-pruning leads to the production of many vigorous, leafy shoots, with fewer flowers and fruits. However, large, old branches can

Celastrus orbiculatus
Both male and female plants must be grown to obtain these decorative fruits.

be cut back hard to within 30–40cm (12–16in) of ground level and will usually resprout. Train in the strongest new shoots to fill any gaps in the framework, and remove the rest.

OTHER CELASTRUS

C. ANGULATUS, C. RUGOSUS, C. SCANDENS As for *C. orbiculatus*.
C. GLAUCOPHYLLUS Scandent in habit rather than twining, and thus needs more tying in to its support. Otherwise, as for *C. orbiculatus*.

CIONURA

 Cionura erecta (syn. *Marsdenia erecta*) is a deciduous twiner with heart-shaped, grey-green leaves and fragrant, five-petalled white flowers during summer. Its fruits split to reveal silky seeds. It grows best in full sun and must have frost-free conditions. The milky sap may cause skin blistering, so avoid contact. No formative pruning is needed. Tie young shoots in loosely until they begin to twine. Once established, prune after flowering, or in early spring in cool areas, to remove weak or dead growth. Thin overcrowded shoots by cutting them back to their base in early spring. Suitable for use as ground cover. Does not respond well to hard pruning.

CISSUS

 Evergreen, woody-stemmed vines, most of which are tendrilled climbers. Grape ivies are grown mainly for their lush foliage. *C. discolor*, the rex begonia vine, needs tropical conditions, but *C. antarctica* (kangaroo vine) and *C. rhombifolia* (Venezuela treebine) will tolerate cooler frost-free conditions and may be grown in a conservatory in cool climates, or as houseplants. They look well trailing from hanging baskets. The near-hardy *C. striata* may be grown against a sunny wall with minimal winter protection. All need semi-shade in summer. Pinch out the growing tips of young plants at intervals to promote bushy growth. They need little pruning once established but, if necessary to restrict size, in spring or summer long growths may be cut back to a healthy bud close to a main branch. *Cissus* respond well to hard pruning.

CLEMATIS *OLD MAN'S BEARD, TRAVELLER'S JOY*

Evergreen and deciduous climbers, most with twining leaf-stalks. Flat, cupped or bell-shaped flowers may be followed, especially in small-flowered species, by silky seedheads. *Clematis* are best sited so that, while their roots are in cool shade, the top growth can be trained into full sun. It is essential that they are pruned according to the season of flowering and the age of wood that bears flowers; the many species, hybrids and cultivars fall into three distinct groups (*see below and facing page*).

C. MONTANA (GROUP 1)

Clematis montana with its cultivars, such as 'Elizabeth' and 'Tetrarose', is the most vigorous of the fully hardy, deciduous species that bear small, flattish, usually single flowers in late spring to early summer on the previous season's ripened growth. They will cover large walls and old buildings or clamber up large trees. When established they need pruning only when overgrown.

■ **WHEN TO PRUNE** Immediately after flowering, if necessary.

■ **TRAINING AND PRUNING** Provide robust support well equipped with trellis or wires. Pinch out young shoot tips. Young growth is brittle, so tie it in carefully. Keep pruning of established plants to a minimum. Cut back overlong shoots to healthy buds. Remove winter-damaged growth only after any danger of frosts has passed. Old, congested plants can be thinned (*see above*) or, if total

Overgrown *Clematis montana*, after flowering

1 *Thin where growth is dense, or exceeding the allotted space, cutting individual stems back to a pair of healthy buds or to their point of origin.*

2 *Cut any weak or damaged growth to strong buds or to its base.*

renovation is necessary, cut back almost to the base, just after flowering. Do not repeat for at least three years.

C. 'NELLY MOSER' (GROUP 2)

'Nelly Moser' (*see below*) is typical of most large-flowered, deciduous hybrids that have two flushes of flowers, first in early summer on the previous year's wood, then in late summer on new shoots. With careful pruning, the two can virtually overlap, providing a long, uninterrupted flowering season.

Established *Clematis* 'Nelly Moser', late winter/early spring

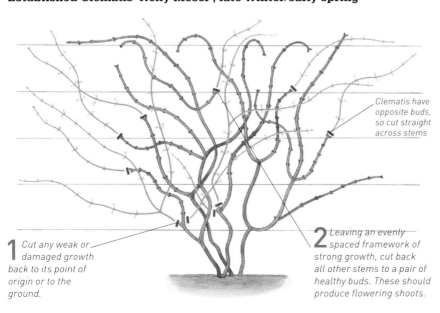

Clematis have opposite buds, so cut straight across stems

1 *Cut any weak or damaged growth back to its point of origin or to the ground.*

2 *Leaving an evenly spaced framework of strong growth, cut back all other stems to a pair of healthy buds. These should produce flowering shoots.*

■ **WHEN TO PRUNE** Late winter or early spring, before new growth begins.

■ **TRAINING AND PRUNING** Early pruning and training is as for *C. montana*. When established, pruning (*see left*) aims to retain a framework of old wood and also to stimulate new shoots, to maximize flowering. Staggering the pruning, cutting back some shoots to healthy buds later than others, prolongs flowering still further. However, these plants can be grown with minimal pruning, cutting hard back every three or four years, as for *C. montana*; the first flush of flowers is lost after hard pruning, but the second is greatly enhanced.

C. VITICELLA (GROUP 3)

C. viticella and its cultivars and hybrids, like some large-flowered hybrids (*see facing page*), flower in late summer on growth made in that season. They make new growth from the base each year, so can be cut back hard on a regular basis.

■ **WHEN TO PRUNE** Late winter or early spring, when buds show signs of growth.

■ **TRAINING AND PRUNING** Early pruning and training is as for *C. montana*. Established plants must be pruned hard each year (*see facing page*), or vigour and flowering performance will dwindle. Cut back to strong pairs of buds about 15–30cm (6–12in) above ground level. If any main stems have been killed by frost, cut them right out; new ones will usually develop from ground level.

Established *Clematis viticella*, late winter/early spring

New shoots, though growing vigorously, are fragile

1 Remove any dead growth (on which buds are not visibly breaking).

2 Cut the remaining stems just above a pair of healthy buds, about 15–30cm (6–12in) above ground level.

OTHER CLEMATIS

GROUP 1

Clematis in this group, like *C. montana*, flower early in the year on wood produced in the previous growing season.

C. ALPINA (inc. 'Columbine', 'Frances Rivis', 'Ruby'), C. 'BLUE BIRD', C. CIRRHOSA (inc. VAR. *balearica*), C. MACROPETALA (inc. 'Markham's Pink'), C. 'ROSIE O'GRADY', C. × VEDRARIENSIS
Not over-vigorous and rarely need any pruning. If overgrown, thin as for *C. montana*.

C. ARISTATA, C. ARMANDII, C. MARATA, C. PANICULATA, C. PETRIEI
Evergreens whose leaves are prone to wind-scorch; they need a sheltered site. *C. armandii* can become heavy and needs substantial support. Train and prune as for *C. montana*. Prune established plants only if necessary to restrict growth.

GROUP 2

Clematis in this group, all large-flowered hybrids, flower first on wood produced in the previous year, then, in late summer and autumn, on the new growth.

C. 'BARBARA DIBLEY', C. 'BARBARA JACKMAN', C. 'BEE'S JUBILEE', C. 'BELLE OF WOKING', C. 'BEAUTY OF WORCESTER', C. 'CARNABY', C. 'COUNTESS OF LOVELACE', C. 'DANIEL DERONDA', C. 'DUCHESS OF EDINBURGH', C. 'EDITH', C. 'ELSA SPÄTH', C. 'GENERAL SIKORSKI', C. 'HENRYI', C. 'H. F. YOUNG', C. 'JOHN WARREN', C. 'LASURSTERN', C. 'MARIE BOISSELOT', C. 'PROTEUS', C. 'RICHARD PENNELL', C. 'THE PRESIDENT', C. 'VYVYAN PENNELL', C. 'W.E. GLADSTONE', C. 'WILLIAM KENNET'
Prune as for *C.* 'Nelly Moser'.

GROUP 3

Clematis in this group flower late in the season on the current year's growth.

C. 'ABUNDANCE', C. 'ETOILE VIOLETTE', C. 'ERNEST MARKHAM', C. 'DUCHESS OF ALBANY', C. 'GRAVETYE BEAUTY', C. 'LADY BETTY BALFOUR', C. 'MADAME JULIA CORREVON', C. 'ROYAL VELOURS', C. 'VILLE DE LYONS' and other clematis in the Texensis and Viticella Groups
Prune as for *C. viticella*.

C. 'BILL MACKENZIE', C. 'BURFORD VARIETY', C. 'CORRY', C. 'HELIOS', C. 'ORANGE PEEL', C. ORIENTALIS, C. SERRATIFOLIA, C. TANGUTICA, C. TIBETANA SUBSP. VERNAYI
Prune as for *C. viticella* to grow in small gardens and restricted sites; however, they can also be allowed to develop into large, permanent plants with minimal pruning. If overgrown, they can be thinned as for *C. montana*, but in spring, because they flower late in the summer on new shoots.

C. 'COMTESSE DE BOUCHAUD', C. 'GIPSY QUEEN', C. 'HAGLEY HYBRID', C. 'JACKMANII', C. 'JACKMANII SUPERBA', C. 'JOHN HUXTABLE', C. 'NIOBE', C. 'PERLE D'AZUR', C. 'ROUGE CARDINAL', C. 'STAR OF INDIA' and other clematis in the Jackmanii Group
Can be pruned either as for *C. viticella* or as for *C.* 'Nelly Moser'. The latter method retains a framework of growth on which new shoots grow and flower, somewhat earlier in the season than if the plant is pruned hard back. Combining the two methods, retaining some growth while cutting other stems to the base to stimulate new basal shoots, effectively extends the flowering season.

CLERODENDRUM

Genus that includes trees and shrubs (popularly grown as pot-plants), as well as woody-stemmed, evergreen, scandent or twining climbers; these are grown for their sprays of flowers, borne in summer on the current season's shoots. Like the shrubs, they grow well under cover, in heated glasshouses or conservatories. They need a position in full sun, but with part-shade in summer.

C. THOMSONIAE

BLEEDING HEART VINE, BAG FLOWER

Vigorous, scandent evergreen, bearing clusters of flowers with white, heart-shaped calyces and dark red corollas during summer.

■ **WHEN TO PRUNE** After flowering.

■ **TRAINING AND PRUNING** After planting, tip back weaker shoots to promote strong growth, and tie in strong shoots as growth proceeds to form the framework. Established plants need little further pruning, other than to remove weak or overcrowded growth by cutting back to healthy, well-placed buds. Where breastwood (growing away from the wall) cannot be tied in and is shading plants below, cut back to one pair of buds from the main stem. Replace old plants rather than attempt hard pruning.

OTHER CLERODENDRUMS

C. BUNGEI, C. TRICHOTOMUM See Dictionary of Ornamental Shrubs, p.185.
C. × SPECIOSUM As for *C. thomsoniae*.
C. SPLENDENS As for *C. thomsoniae*.

Clerodendrom thomsoniae
In this glasshouse, wires are arranged to keep the plant off the glass, where it might scorch.

CLIANTHUS

 Clianthus puniceus (glory pea, lobster claw, parrot's bill) is a handsome, evergreen or semi-evergreen scrambling shrub with arching stems, glossy leaves, and striking flowers, borne on the previous year's wood in spring or early summer. In a sunny, sheltered site *Clianthus* may stand light frost; otherwise, grow in a cool conservatory.

■ **WHEN TO PRUNE** After flowering.

■ **TRAINING AND PRUNING** Pruning is best kept to a minimum. After planting, pinch out shoot tips to encourage the production of sideshoots. Carefully tie in the slender, brittle stems to wires or trellis as growth proceeds, to create even coverage. Once established, train in new shoots to complete the framework. Plants will not tolerate severe pruning and do not renovate well, but dead or weak growth should be removed. If it is necessary to restrict growth or relieve overcrowding, shorten healthy stems by no more than one-third of their length.

Clianthus puniceus
Drooping clusters of bold, claw-like, scarlet or pink flowers are best displayed if this shrubby plant is trained up against a wall.

CLYTOSTOMA

 Evergreen, frost-tender, tendrilled climbers, flowering on the previous season's wood, needing strong support. At planting, select two or three strong shoots to develop a framework. When established, thin out tangled excess growth in early spring, removing stems or shortening them by up to two-thirds of their length. Unpruned plants become congested, which can lead to dieback. To renovate, cut back all main stems by up to two-thirds, after flowering.

CONGEA

 Congea tomentosa (shower orchid) is an unusual, frost-tender, semi-climbing evergreen, with small flowers set off by white or pink bracts. It needs little formative pruning, other than to pinch-prune, if necessary, to encourage new growth. Keep pruning of established plants to a minimum. Older plants may need encouraging to produce new growth from the base; after flowering, cut back one or two main stems to within 30cm (12in) of the ground.

COBAEA

 Cobaea scandens, the cup-and-saucer vine, is a vigorous, semi-shrubby, evergreen, tendrilled climber, grown chiefly for the large, bell-shaped flowers borne in summer and early autumn on the current year's growth. It is frost-tender, needing full sun and shelter from wind, so is commonly used as a fast-growing annual in temperate gardens, but will survive for several years under glass, or outdoors in warm climates. After planting, pinch out the growing tips of young plants to encourage the development of lateral shoots. These rapidly attach themselves to their supports. Prune established plants annually: cut back hard in early spring, removing up to three-quarters of all the previous year's growth.

Cobaea scandens
These striking flowers turn from greenish-cream to purple as they develop.

D

DECUMARIA

 Woody-stemmed climbers, related to *Hydrangea*, with clinging stem rootlets and flat-topped clusters of honey-scented cream flowers in early summer. *D. barbara* is fully hardy, while *D. sinensis* may be damaged by hard frost; it will be adequately protected on an east- or west-facing wall. Train and prune as for climbing hydrangeas (*see p.273*).

DISTICTIS

 Evergreen, woody-stemmed, tendrilled climbers with showy, tubular or bell-shaped flowers, borne during late spring and summer. Given a warm, sunny, sheltered wall, *D. buccinatoria* tolerates light frost, but grows best in completely frost-free conditions, which are essential for *Distictis* such as *D. lactiflora*, *D. laxiflora* and *D.* 'Mrs Rivers'; in cool areas these are suitable for pillars or trellis in a conservatory.

■ **WHEN TO PRUNE** Early spring.

■ **TRAINING AND PRUNING** After planting, cut back the entire plant to within 15cm (6in) of ground level. Retain only two or three of the resultant strong shoots to form the main framework and tie them in to a support. In subsequent years, thin out weak or crowded growth, disentangling branches as necessary. Retain only the strongest shoots, cutting them back to a strong, well-placed bud if necessary to restrict growth. Old plants respond well to hard pruning: cut main stems back to within 1m (3ft) of the ground, either gradually or all at once.

DREGEA

 Dregea (syn. *Wattakaka*) *sinensis* is a frost-hardy, evergreen, twining climber, related and similar to *Hoya* (*see p.273*), with paired, ovate leaves and fragrant, star-shaped white flowers with red spots and streaks in summer. Like hoyas, dregeas need minimal pruning. Tie in young shoots until they begin to twine. When established, prune only to remove frost-damaged growth in spring, or to thin after flowering. Dregeas do not always respond to hard pruning. An older branch can occasionally be cut back to the base to encourage new growth, but this may not always succeed.

E – G

ECCREMOCARPUS

Eccremocarpus scaber (Chilean glory flower) is a tendrilled, evergreen climber with slender stems and finely divided, grey-green leaves. Its scarlet to orange flowers are borne on new shoots, especially in full sun. In cool climates frost may cut it down, but it usually re-sprouts from the base if protected with a winter mulch. It may also be grown as a half-hardy annual.

■ **WHEN TO PRUNE** Spring.

■ **TRAINING AND PRUNING** Pinch out growing tips after planting, to create a bushy specimen with several shoots springing from its base. In subsequent years, cut back all the previous season's growth to within 30–60cm (12–24in) of the base in spring. In temperate areas, plants may die back to ground level in winter. As new growth sprouts again, cut back all shoots to a strong, healthy bud to ensure dense, bushy growth. Replace old plants rather than attempt renovation.

EPIPREMNUM

Tropical, evergreen, woody-stemmed climbers with adhesive aerial roots, grown for their attractive foliage. They seldom flower in cultivation. In tropical climates, they are very vigorous and need minimal attention; they are particularly effective if allowed to scramble through large trees. In cool climates, although often grown as houseplants, epipremnums usually grow better in a warm, humid conservatory. Provide strong support, such as a sturdy moss pole. Train and prune as for *Monstera* (*see p.277*). Once established, pinch out growing tips from time to time to encourage branching. Restrict growth, if necessary, by cutting over-vigorous shoots back to a well-placed bud. Renovate by cutting old plants back to within 1m (3ft) of the base to stimulate strong new growth.

***Epipremnum pictum* 'Argyraeus'**
These attractively patterned, fleshy leaves are well displayed on a moss pole.

***Ficus pumila* 'Dorthe'**
The creeping fig will cling to rough stone and brickwork without encouragement. It can be rampant in growth but is much less vigorous grown in cool climates under glass.

FICUS *FIG*

A large genus of deciduous and evergreen trees (*see p.66, also* Figs, *p.139*) and shrubs, and evergreen, scrambling or self-clinging climbers. The climbing species (usually tropical or subtropical) are invasive in the wild; *Ficus pumila*, the creeping fig, is most commonly cultivated, and even this can be a nuisance. It is an evergreen stem root climber, grown for its foliage; juvenile leaves are small, glossy green, heart-shaped and somewhat puckered. Frost-tender, it usually only reaches the adult stage in warm climates or in a heated glasshouse; it then produces larger, leathery oval leaves, with rooting stems that spread over a large area. In warm climates, train on walls and tree trunks. In cool climates *Ficus pumila* is often grown as a conservatory or house plant, in hanging baskets or with support. It tolerates partial shade. Train and prune as for *Epipremnum* (*see left*).

GELSEMIUM

Gelsemium sempervirens is an evergreen, twining climber with lustrous green leaves, and jasmine-like flowers borne on the previous season's growth in late spring and early summer. Though frost-hardy it will not survive prolonged cold. It looks well on trellis or pergolas. After planting in spring, pinch back young shoots to encourage a bushy habit. As growth proceeds, tie in to the support. Established plants need only trimming, after flowering, to keep within bounds and to remove weak or overcrowded growth. To rejuvenate old plants, cut back the oldest flowered wood to the base to encourage strong new shoots.

GYNURA *VELVET PLANT*

Evergreen perennials, shrubs (*see p.196*) and semi-scrambling climbers with velvety foliage and daisy-like flowers. The most commonly grown climbing species, *G. scandens* (syn. *G. aurantiaca*), needs subtropical conditions and light shade in summer. After planting, pinch out shoot tips to encourage a bushy habit. Prune established plants in spring before new growth begins, only to remove crowded, weak or damaged growth. Gynuras do not respond well to hard pruning. If grown as a houseplant, flowers should be removed due to their unpleasant smell.

OTHER CLIMBING PLANTS

CLITORIA *C. ternatea* is a small, evergreen scandent trailer needing little attention.
CODONOPSIS Scandent herbaceous climbers; cut to the base in spring.
COMBRETUM Treat *C. grandiflorum*, an evergreen scrambler and twiner, as for *Hardenbergia* (*see p.272*).
DOLICHOS See Lablab (*p.275*).
ERCILLA Evergreen, stem-root climber suitable for walls or fences, but needs tying in to wires or trellis; the aerial roots will not support the weight of mature branches. Needs little formative pruning; established plants can be thinned out or cut back after flowering.
EUSTREPHUS Evergreen scrambler, best grown through host plants or as ground cover; tip-pruning reduces its straggly growth habit and tendency for stems to become bare at the base.
FALLOPIA See Polygonum (*p.281*).
FARADAYA SPLENDIDA Vigorous, frost-tender, evergreen climber suited to growing through host trees.

H–I

HARDENBERGIA *CORAL PEA*

Handsome, evergreen, twining climbers grown for their fine stems with simple or pinnate leaves and long racemes of small pea-like flowers, borne during late spring and summer. They are frost-tender and need full sun for vigorous growth; in warm climates grow them on a wall, fence or pergola; in cool climates, grow in a glasshouse border or in large tubs in a conservatory, with trellis or wires for support. As with passion flowers, the new shoots trail downwards to form a loose, flowering curtain.

■ **WHEN TO PRUNE** After flowering.

■ **TRAINING AND PRUNING** Tie in young growth to the support until it begins to twine. Established plants need little further pruning other than to remove overcrowded, weak, dead or damaged growth. Hardenbergias do not respond well to hard pruning.

Hardenbergia violacea
The delicate stems of the new growth are studded with compact racemes of rose-pink or purple flowers, giving rise to the common name of vine lilac.

HEDERA *IVY*

Evergreen, woody-stemmed, trailing shrubs and self-clinging climbers with adhesive roots, grown for their decorative foliage. Numerous forms and cultivars are available, with variously shaped leaves, many variegated in shades of yellow, grey or white. The upper stems of mature plants of many cultivars are non-clinging, with usually unlobed leaves and clusters of greenish-yellow flowers in autumn and winter. Ivies range from half-hardy to fully hardy, and in height from 1m (3ft) to 15m (50ft) or more, so match the plant carefully to the space available. In general, those with plain green leaves are hardier and more shade-tolerant: those with variegated leaves need more light. Although the latter are more prone to frost damage, they generally recover in spring. Ivies are useful for ground cover, and for covering walls, fences and tree stumps, but plants

Creeping stems
Never train ivies on lapped fencing; their questing shoots will penetrate between the boards, as here, and, as they mature and thicken, eventually prise them apart.

may become top-heavy at maturity. Although they generally do no harm to well-maintained brickwork, the stem roots may dislodge old mortar and block gutters. Less vigorous cultivars can be kept small by trimming as necessary, making them ideal for containers.

■ **WHEN TO PRUNE** Early spring, before new growth begins.

■ **TRAINING AND PRUNING** After planting, pinch back weak or spindly shoots to encourage strong young growth. Young plants may be slow to establish and attach themselves to their supports. This can be overcome by pegging down stems horizontally, close to the support base, encouraging the laterals to grow upwards. Small-leaved cultivars of *H. helix* look well trained as standards (*see p.260*) or over wire shapes.

Prune established plants to restrict height and spread, if needed, by cutting back stems to a well-placed bud within the plant's outline to make cut marks less obvious. Cut out excess or outward-pointing growth, particularly from ivies on walls and fences. To renovate, cut back to within 1m (3ft) of the base; they will resprout readily from old wood.

Training ivies as free-standing features

Training on a small tree trunk or post
Lift up the attractive, fresh trailing stems and trim older growth beneath to restrict size.

Training as a standard Use a cultivar whose leaf size is proportionate to the size of standard you wish to create.

Training for "topiary" effects For a formal effect, ivies will quickly cover, as here, a "diamond" made from a trellis square.

HIBBERTIA *BUTTON FLOWER, GUINEA GOLD VINE*

Hibbertia scandens (gold Guinea plant) is a vigorous, evergreen, twining climber with glossy leaves, grown for its saucer-shaped, bright yellow flowers, borne during the summer months. Suitable for walls, fences and pergolas, it thrives in dappled shade. It requires a completely frost-free climate.

■ **WHEN TO PRUNE** Early spring.

■ **TRAINING AND PRUNING** After planting, pinch out the growing tips to encourage strong sideshoots, and tie in new growth until the plant begins to twine. Once established, prune only to thin out congested branches. Does not respond well to hard pruning.

HUMULUS *HOP*

Fully hardy, herbaceous, twining climbers with lobed leaves; female plants bear pendent clusters of greenish-yellow bracts ("hops"). They are vigorous, forming an effective seasonal disguise for unsightly structures, or they can be grown on stout arches (*see p.257*) or tripods. Shoots are fragile. Hops die back in winter; in early spring, cut the dead growth down to ground level.

HYDRANGEA

Climbing hydrangeas (for shrub species, *see p.200*) are grown for their heads of creamy-white flowers, borne in summer on the previous year's ripened lateral shoots. They are useful for shaded and semi-shaded walls and for growing up into trees. The deciduous *H. anomala* subsp. *petiolaris* is fully hardy, but unripened wood may be damaged by hard frost. The evergreen *H. serratifolia* (syn. *H. integerrima*) tolerates light frosts, particularly with shelter.

■ **WHEN TO PRUNE** After flowering.

■ **TRAINING AND PRUNING** No formative pruning is needed. Tie in young shoots to their supports until they form aerial roots. This may take two or three seasons. Once firmly attached, plants will climb vigorously. Pruning of established plants is best kept to a minimum, but as plants fill their space, shorten overlong shoots and outward-growing laterals by cutting them back to a healthy bud. Wall-trained plants flower most abundantly at the top, so retain as much upper growth as

IPOMOEA *MORNING GLORY*

Genus of mainly evergreen twining climbers, perennials, annuals and shrubs, generally half-hardy to frost-tender. They are grown for the large, tubular flowers, in various colours, that are produced in succession during summer; several species are useful for their late-summer flowering. The fragrant, white flowers of *I. alba* open at night. Tender climbing species that are perennial in tropical or subtropical areas may be grown in pots under glass, or out of doors as annuals, in temperate regions, given a warm, sheltered site. They need the support of trellis or a wired wall, or will climb into sturdy host plants or over unsightly structures. Little training is required except to tie in young shoots to the support as they grow. The more vigorous species can be trimmed back with shears during the growing season. Old and congested growth should be cut out in late winter or early spring.

Hoya carnosa
Do not deadhead hoyas: the "pegs" on which the flowers form will often bloom again.

HOYA
PORCELAIN FLOWER, WAX FLOWER

Genus of rather fleshy, lax shrubs and woody-stemmed, twining climbers, sometimes developing clinging aerial roots. They have paired, glossy leaves, and are valued for their waxy, white or pink flowers. All are frost-tender, requiring humidity, semi-shade in summer and strong support. Used for clothing walls, fences or large trees in subtropical gardens, they may be grown as house plants (particularly *H. carnosa*) in cool climates. Wear gloves to prune: cut stems exude a latex that can cause allergic reactions.

■ **WHEN TO PRUNE** Spring, before new growth begins, or after flowering.

■ **TRAINING AND PRUNING** No formative pruning is needed. Tie in young shoots to their support until they begin to twine or cling. Established plants need little pruning other than to cut back or thin congested growth. If this is done after flowering, do not remove the flowered "pegs", since more flowers are often borne on the stumps of previous clusters. Hoyas do not respond well to hard pruning, and are best replaced with young, vigorous plants.

Climbing hydrangea
You may need to shorten outward-growing stems, so that they do not shade plants below.

possible. Old plants tolerate hard pruning: cut back hard in early spring to leave only the framework branches. Drastic pruning may reduce flowering for a year or two, and is best spread over three or four years.

OTHER CLIMBING PLANTS

HIDALGOA Evergreen scrambler; handsome on walls or pergolas in subtropical gardens. Prune and train as for *Congea* (*see p.270*).
HOLBOELLIA As for *Stauntonia* (*see p.284*).
HOLMSKIOLDIA Evergreen leaf-tendrilled climber for training on wires or trellis. Tie in young shoots loosely. Prune established plants in early spring, only to thin out weak or crowded growth. To rejuvenate old main stems, prune to within 30cm (12in) of the base.

J

JASMINUM *JASMINE*

Woody-stemmed, scrambling and twining climbers with paired, usually divided, leaves and often highly scented flowers. Most are heavy when mature.

J. NUDIFLORUM

WINTER JASMINE

 Deciduous, scandent shrub, bearing primrose-yellow flowers on bare stems in winter and early spring, on the previous summer's shoots. Fully hardy, it thrives in sun or shade, but flowers best in sun. It looks best when tied in close against a wall, or sprawling unsupported over a bank or terrace. If not pruned annually, new growth covers older growth, leading to untidy amounts of dead wood.

■ **WHEN TO PRUNE** Spring, immediately after flowering.

■ **TRAINING AND PRUNING** After planting, cut back young shoots by up to two-thirds of their length, to encourage strong growth from the base. To wall-train, space and tie in the resulting shoots evenly across the support, to create a framework of branches (*see below*). In subsequent seasons, continue tying in shoots as necessary to extend or fill in the framework, and cut back other flowered shoots to within two or three pairs of buds of the main branch, leaving the framework intact. Winter jasmine tolerates hard pruning, as described for *J. officinale*, but old plants are usually better replaced.

J. OFFICINALE

COMMON JASMINE, JESSAMINE

 Deciduous, woody-stemmed, twining climber flowering on laterals from the previous year's wood and terminally on new growth through summer and early autumn. It is fully hardy, but may be shy to flower in cold gardens or on rich soil.

■ **WHEN TO PRUNE** After flowering.

■ **TRAINING AND PRUNING** Prune on planting as for *J. nudiflorum*. Lead young shoots to the support, tying loosely at first, and spacing to provide even coverage. Plants begin to twine quickly. In subsequent years, prune to thin out overcrowded growth, removing weak shoots and cutting flowered shoots back to strong buds or to their bases. They tolerate being cut back hard, to within 60cm (24in) of the base if necessary. However, while new growth will be vigorous, it may not flower well for several years.

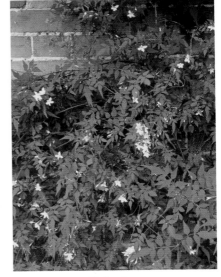

Jasminum officinale
Given a wired wall, this twining species, with its very fragrant flowers, will climb unaided.

J. POLYANTHUM

 Half-hardy, evergreen twiner with dark green leaves and, from late spring (earlier under glass) to early summer, very fragrant white flowers. On a warm, sunny wall it tolerates light frosts, but prefers frost-free conditions. It grows well in a cool conservatory or as a houseplant (though it dislikes heated rooms), trained over wire hoops or on trellis.

■ **WHEN TO PRUNE** After flowering.

■ **TRAINING AND PRUNING** Prune on planting as for *J. nudiflorum*. To train on a wall or pillar, form a framework of branches as described for *J. officinale*, then spur-prune flowered laterals back annually to two or three buds. To prune pot-grown plants, *see p.254*. It responds well to hard pruning, as for *J. officinale*.

OTHER JASMINES
J. BEESIANUM As for *J. officinale*.
J. GRANDIFLORUM (syn. **J. OFFICINALE** *f.* GRANDIFLORUM) As for *J. officinale*.
J. HUMILE, J. PARKERI See Dictionary of Ornamental Shrubs, *p.202*.
J. MESNYI (primrose jasmine) As for *J. nudiflorum*, but prune after flowering in summer.
J. REX Vigorous, half-hardy twiner. Train and prune as for *J. officinale*.
J. × STEPHANENSE Vigorous hybrid, needs ample space, suitable for clothing unsightly garden buildings, walls and fences. Train and prune as for *J. officinale*.

Developing a framework, *Jasminum nudiflorum*

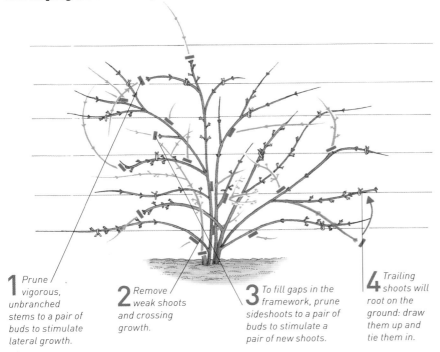

1 Prune vigorous, unbranched stems to a pair of buds to stimulate lateral growth.

2 Remove weak shoots and crossing growth.

3 To fill gaps in the framework, prune sideshoots to a pair of buds to stimulate a pair of new shoots.

4 Trailing shoots will root on the ground: draw them up and tie them in.

K–L

KADSURA

Kadsura japonica is a twining evergreen, closely related to *Schisandra*, grown primarily for its large, lustrous green leaves and scarlet berries. Small, scented cream flowers are borne in summer, with males and females on separate plants. (For fruits, both must be grown together.) It is frost-hardy, if sheltered from cold winds. Train and prune as for *Schisandra* (*see p.282*).

Kennedia rubicunda
K. rubicunda is one of the fastest-growing and also most drought-resistant kennedias.

KENNEDIA *CORAL PEA*

Mainly woody-stemmed and evergreen, but occasionally herbaceous, twining and trailing climbers with brightly coloured, pea-like flowers, useful on trellis or pillars or for scrambling through other plants. Shoots that trail on the ground may root, providing ground cover. They need a frost-free climate. In cool areas, grow in a cool conservatory with full light.

■ **WHEN TO PRUNE** After flowering.

■ **TRAINING AND PRUNING** When grown through host plants or as ground cover (*see p.253*), little pruning and training is needed. To train plants to climb, select two or three strong shoots, and tie in loosely until they begin to twine. If there is only one shoot, cut it back by half its length to encourage lateral shoots to break. Keep pruning of established plants to a minimum. Thin out crowded growth and remove weak or damaged shoots. Does not respond well to hard pruning.

LABLAB *AUSTRALIAN PEA, HYACINTH BEAN*

Lablab purpureus, the only species in this genus, is a deciduous, woody-stemmed, twining climber, bearing purple, pink or white pea-like flowers in summer, followed by long, dark purple pods. It will grow out of doors only in warm, frost-free climates. In cool areas, it is grown as a half-hardy annual, or is suitable for a conservatory, trained on wires or pillars. Prune and train as for *Kennedia* trained as a climber.

LAPAGERIA

Lapageria rosea (Chilean bell flower) is a spectacular, long-lived, evergreen climber for shaded or semi-shaded walls. It is grown for its large, waxy, bell-shaped flowers of rose-crimson or, in var. *albiflora*, ivory-white. Given shelter from cold, dry winds, it will survive light frosts. Keep pruning to a minimum, removing dead or damaged shoots in early spring. It is better to replace old plants than to prune hard.

LARDIZABALA

Vigorous, evergreen, twining climbers, of which the best known is *L. biternata*, grown for its handsome, leathery leaves and extraordinary sausage-like, dark purple fruits. Though frost-hardy, it fruits well only in Mediterranean-type climates. Provide strong support, and train in young shoots to form a well-spaced permanent framework. Once the plant is established, prune in early spring to thin crowded growth and remove or reduce weak growth. On wall-trained plants, cut back outward-facing shoots to within two or three buds of their base. To rejuvenate old plants, cut main stems back to within 30cm (12in) of the ground. Train in new growth to re-create even coverage of the support.

LATHYRUS
VETCHLING, WILD PEA

The perennial peas are mainly leaf tendril climbers, with winged stems, widely grown for their showy racemes of often scented flowers in summer, followed by slender seed pods. They are excellent plants for walls and fences, for trellis, or for growing on pillars, wigwams or tripods. All grow best in full sun. Herbaceous species suitable for cool climates, such as *L. latifolius* and *L. grandiflorus*, die back in winter, and are cut back to ground level annually. In warmer climates, species such as the frost-hardy *L. nervosus* (Lord Anson's blue pea) may be semi-evergreen.

L. LATIFOLIUS

PERENNIAL PEA

Fully hardy, herbaceous perennial that can be trained on fences, trellis or wigwams, or allowed to scramble over and through other plants.

■ **WHEN TO PRUNE** After flowering in autumn, or in early spring.

■ **TRAINING AND PRUNING** After planting, pinch out the growing tips to encourage the production of strong lateral shoots. In warmer climates, prune established plants after flowering only to remove weak, damaged or dead growth. In cooler climates, cut back all dead growth to the base in spring, before new growth begins. Old plants are best replaced.

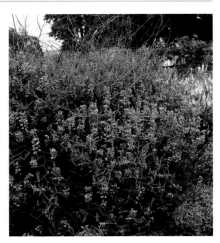

Lathyrus latifolius
Informal or rustic supports such as pea-sticks enhance the old-fashioned appeal of this plant.

OTHER LATHYRUS
L. GRANDIFLORUS As for *L. latifolius*.
L. NERVOSUS (syn. **L. MAGELLANICUS**) Herbaceous, tendrilled climber. Cut out only dead or damaged shoots in spring.
L. PUBESCENS As for *L. nervosus*.

LONICERA *HONEYSUCKLE*

Deciduous, semi-evergreen or evergreen, woody-stemmed, mostly twining climbers. They have often fragrant, funnel-shaped or two-lipped flowers and, in some species, bright berries. They are excellent plants for walls, fences, trellis and pergolas. Most commonly grown species are fully hardy, and some will thrive in shade. The half-hardy *L. etrusca* and frost-tender *L. hildebrandtiana* prefer sun.

L. JAPONICA

JAPANESE HONEYSUCKLE

Vigorous, woody-stemmed, evergreen, twining climber with white and cream flowers all summer and autumn, borne on the current season's growth.

■ **WHEN TO PRUNE** Early spring.

■ **TRAINING AND PRUNING** After planting, cut young plants back by up to two-thirds to encourage strong basal shoots. Select the best to form the framework, and tie them in until they begin to twine. Tip back shoots when they have reached the required height. Mature plants usually need pruning to restrict size; thin out congested growth and cut back over-long shoots to suitable buds. To renovate, in late winter or early spring cut all stems back to within 60cm (2ft) of the base. Thin the resultant vigorous shoots as necessary.

L. PERICLYMENUM

COMMON HONEYSUCKLE, WOODBINE

Vigorous, deciduous twiner, flowering from early to late summer at the tips of short laterals produced on the previous season's growth. Many forms are grown, including 'Belgica' and 'Serotina', the early and late Dutch honeysuckles.

■ **WHEN TO PRUNE** After flowering.

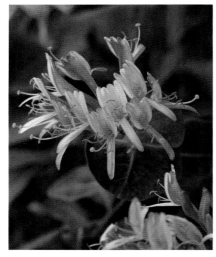

Lonicera × heckrottii
This brilliant-flowered hybrid can be trained up shady walls and fences.

■ **TRAINING AND PRUNING** Prune on planting and train as for *L. japonica*. Once established, cut back flowered shoots by up to one-third. Healthy, dense plants tolerate clipping over with shears; on small areas such as pillar or post sides, cut back laterals to within two or three buds of a main stem. Where space allows, honeysuckles may be allowed to scramble naturally with little or no pruning, although plants will eventually become bare at the base. Renovate as for *L. japonica*.

OTHER HONEYSUCKLES
L. ALSEUOSMOIDES, L. HENRYI, L. HILDEBRANDTIANA As for *L. japonica*. L. × AMERICANA, L. × BROWNII, L. CAPRIFOLIUM, L. ETRUSCA, L. × HECKROTTII, L. SEMPERVIRENS, L. × TELLMANNIANA, L. TRAGOPHYLLA As for *L. periclymenum*. *For other species, see* Dictionary of Ornamental Shrubs, *p.205.*

Lonicera japonica 'Halliana'
The flowers grow in pairs, in the leaf axils; though small, they are numerous and very fragrant. It is always worth planting and training honeysuckle where its beautiful scent can be fully appreciated.

M

MACFADYENA
CAT'S CLAW CREEPER

Macfadyena unguis-cati is a frost-tender evergreen with branched leaf tendrils, grown for its showy, tubular, yellow flowers. It can be grown in a conservatory in full sun in cool climates, with the support of wires or trellis. Train in the strongest shoots of young plants to an upright support. Prune established plants immediately after flowering to thin out congested growth and remove weak and damaged shoots. If grown against a wall (*see also p.250*), shorten outward-growing shoots to within two or three buds of a main stem. All growth on old plants may be cut back to within about two buds of the framework, preferably over two or three years (*see also p.252*).

MANDEVILLA

Deciduous, semi-evergreen and evergreen, woody-stemmed, twining climbers with dark, lustrous leaves, grown for their showy, trumpet-shaped flowers, usually borne in summer and autumn on the current season's shoots. Most are frost-tender; *M. laxa*, with very fragrant, white or cream flowers, is half-hardy. Grow in good light, but provide shade from the hottest sun in summer.

M. × AMOENA

Evergreen with large, pale pink blooms in summer; those of its free-flowering cultivar 'Alice du Pont' are bright pink.

■ **WHEN TO PRUNE** Late winter or early spring.

■ **TRAINING AND PRUNING** After planting, select three to five strong young shoots to form the framework. Tie them in until they begin to twine. Remove the remaining shoots. If young plants have only one main shoot, shorten it by up to one-third to encourage growth from the base. Once established, prune to thin out overcrowded growth and remove weak shoots. Tip-prune shoots that have filled their allotted space to keep plants within bounds. Established plants resent drastic pruning and are best replaced.

OTHER MANDEVILLAS
M. × AMABILIS, M. LAXA, M. SANDERI As for *M. × amoena*.
M. SPLENDENS As for *M. × amoena*, but prune immediately after flowering.

MERREMIA

Vigorous, evergreen, twining climbers, related to *Ipomoea*, with lobed leaves and showy, funnel-shaped flowers. All need a completely frost-free climate, but they grow best in subtropical conditions. *M. tuberosa*, the wood rose or yellow morning glory, is extremely vigorous, with bright yellow flowers in summer, followed by pretty, semi-woody fruits. In warm climates it will cover large fences or clamber up trees. *M. aurea*, rarely more than 3m (10ft) high, with large, golden flowers, is better suited to a conservatory.

■ **WHEN TO PRUNE** Immediately after flowering.

■ **TRAINING AND PRUNING** Needs no formative pruning. Guide vigorous young shoots in the required direction, aiming to create even coverage. Once established, prune the plant annually to reduce congestion and remove unwanted growth. Prune lateral shoots back to within a bud or two of the main framework. Tip back the main stems as necessary to restrict the size of the plant. *Merremia* tolerate being cut back to within 60–90cm (24–36in) of the base.

METROSIDEROS

Evergreen woody-stemmed climbers, some with aerial roots, which are grown for their handsome, leathery foliage and often brilliantly coloured flowers in early or midsummer. In warm climates, they are suitable for clambering up stout pergolas or mature trees, and in cool regions are beautiful conservatory plants. Grow in full sun.

■ **WHEN TO PRUNE** Immediately after flowering.

■ **TRAINING AND PRUNING** Needs little formative pruning other than to train in the strongest shoots to the support, and remove the remainder. Once established, prune only to thin out weak, old or overcrowded growth; overpruning will reduce flowering. Replace old plants.

MONSTERA

Monstera deliciosa, the ceriman or Swiss-cheese plant, is a heavy, evergreen climber, with long, non-clinging aerial roots and handsome, lobed, leathery foliage. In tropical and subtropical climates, mature plants reliably produce creamy white, arum-like flowers, followed by large, oval, edible fruits, which are, however, very poisonous when unripe. This species will climb tall trees, and is effective tied in to cover large areas of wall. In cool climates, monsteras grown as house or conservatory plants, although less vigorous, are best given the support of a stout moss pole, into which the aerial roots may burrow.

■ **WHEN TO PRUNE** Early spring.

■ **TRAINING AND PRUNING** Needs little formative pruning other than tying in growth as necessary, and tipping back shoots of established plants to restrict size or to encourage lateral branching. Remove overlong aerial roots if desired. Hard

***Monstera deliciosa* 'Variegata'**
The aerial roots that develop from the stems of monsteras do not adhere to surfaces like those of ivies; however, they will bore into moss or soft, old bark to give some support.

pruning of plants that have outgrown their allotted space will stimulate the production of vigorous new shoots.

MUCUNA

Vigorous, evergreen, sub-tropical and tropical twining climbers, usually bearing pendent racemes of large, often brilliantly coloured, pea-like flowers in summer or late summer, followed by velvety or bristly fruits. The plant and fruit hairs can cause irritation, so wear gloves when handling, and clean any clothing that comes into contact with the plant. All need partial shade in summer, and most need ample space to climb, with the strong support of wires or trellis.

■ **WHEN TO PRUNE** Early spring, or after flowering if fruits are not required.

■ **TRAINING AND PRUNING** Needs little formative pruning. Train young shoots in the required direction to give even coverage of the support. Once the plant is established, thin out crowded growth as needed and remove weak or damaged shoots. To stimulate flowering shoots, spur-prune laterals to within two or three buds of the main stems. It usually responds to hard pruning.

MUEHLENBECKIA

Deciduous or evergreen, slender-stemmed, twining or scrambling climbers or shrubs, grown for their delicate tracery of subtly coloured, interwoven branches and tiny, sweetly scented, star-shaped flowers. Most are frost-hardy; *M. axillaris* and *M. complexa* are both fully hardy if sheltered from cold, dry winds. They are best grown to cover tree stumps, rough posts or low frameworks, or allowed to scramble up through other shrubs.

■ **WHEN TO PRUNE** Early spring.

■ **TRAINING AND PRUNING** Need no formative pruning. Young plants tend to produce several stout, straight shoots which should be tied to a suitable support. These eventually branch to form the characteristic mass of delicate interwoven branches. Prune established plants only to restrict the size of plants that have outgrown their allotted space. It is difficult to prune without spoiling the delicately branching habit. Replace old plants rather than attempt to renovate by hard pruning.

OTHER CLIMBING PLANTS

MANETTIA As for *Mussaenda*, (see p.278).
MENISPERMUM Herbaceous twiner; cut back hard each spring.

MIKANIA Train in strong young shoots and remove weak growth. Established plants need pruning only to thin out. Do not prune hard.

MILLETTIA As for *Hardenbergia* (see p.272).
MITRARIA As for *Hardenbergia* (see p.272).
MOMORDICA As for *Hardenbergia* (see p.272).

MUSSAENDA

Mussaenda erythrophylla is a tropical, sun-loving, scrambling or twining evergreen, with brightly coloured flowers that have one enlarged, leaf-like sepal in a contrasting colour. In cooler climates it can be grown in a sunny conservatory, with the support of trellis or wires.

■ **WHEN TO PRUNE** Early spring.

■ **TRAINING AND PRUNING** Cut back hard after planting to within 15–30cm (6–12in) of the base, to encourage vigorous basal shoots. These may take a year or two to adopt a climbing habit, so tie them in to the support as the plant extends to form the main framework. Prune established plants to thin out and remove weak growth. Reduce laterals to within two or three buds of the framework branches. Do not prune harder; it does not respond well.

MUTISIA

Frost-hardy or half-hardy, evergreen, flexuous-stemmed climbers with leaf tendrils, grown for their long-lasting, usually brightly coloured flowerheads. All grow best with their top growth in sun, and their roots in moist shade. They may prove difficult to establish.

M. OLIGODON

Frost-hardy climber with brilliant salmon-pink, daisy-like flowerheads produced during summer.

■ **WHEN TO PRUNE** Spring, when any danger of frost has passed, or, in warm climates, immediately after flowering.

■ **TRAINING AND PRUNING** Little formative pruning is needed, but pinch out the growing tips of young plants to encourage a bushy habit. Shoots soon begin to cling and will quickly support themselves; use twiggy branches initially to guide the stems in to the support. Mutisias will not tolerate heavy pruning, so once established, prune only to remove weak or dead stems. Living wood often appears to be dead at the end of the winter, so delay removing any dead growth until it is more easily distinguished, once new growth has begun to sprout in spring.

OTHER MUTISIAS
M. DECURRENS, M. ILICIFOLIA As for *M. oligodon*.

N–P

NEPENTHES *PITCHER PLANT*

Tropical, evergreen, climbing or scrambling, insectivorous perennials, mostly epiphytic. It climbs by means of leaf tendrils, some of which enlarge to form pendulous, lidded "pitchers", mottled green and red or purple, which trap and ingest insects. All require warm, partially shaded conditions but have no special pruning needs. Overlong growth can be cut back in early spring.

PANDOREA

Half-hardy, evergreen, woody-stemmed twiners, related to *Campsis*, with glossy foliage and scented, trumpet-shaped flowers, borne on the previous summer's growth. In warm climates they are useful for walls, fences or pergolas, and as ground cover on sloping banks; in cool regions, for high conservatory walls.

■ **WHEN TO PRUNE** After flowering.

■ **TRAINING AND PRUNING** Need little formative pruning, but train and tie in vigorous young shoots to create even coverage. Established plants can be pruned to remove unwanted growth and thin out overcrowded shoots by cutting stems out close to the base. Cut overgrown plants back hard to encourage strong new growth from the base; very old specimens are best replaced.

PARSONSIA

Parsonsia capsularis is a frost-hardy, evergreen, twining climber, grown mainly for its young leaves, pink-flushed and overlaid with buff and chocolate-brown. It bears small, white, bell-shaped flowers in summer. It looks most attractive on sunny fences and pergolas.

■ **WHEN TO PRUNE** After flowering.

■ **TRAINING AND PRUNING** Needs little formative pruning other than to remove weak growth. Prune established plants to remove dead or weak growth, and to relieve congestion. The remaining shoots can be cut back by up to one-third of their length, if required to keep plants within bounds. Old plants will shoot vigorously if cut back hard, but this will inhibit flowering for a year or so; replacement with a vigorous young plant is preferable.

Nepenthes in a hanging basket
Hang plants where the pitchers can be appreciated at eye level.

PARTHENOCISSUS

Vigorous, mostly deciduous climbers with suckering pads, grown for their handsome foliage and autumn colour. Most are fully hardy; all grow well in shade or semi-shade. They require ample space and are ideal for lofty walls, unsightly buildings and banks, or for clambering up large trees. Supports must be strong and structurally sound. Keep growth away from window frames, eaves, cladding, roof tiles and gutters.

■ **WHEN TO PRUNE** Autumn or early winter; can be lightly pruned in summer.

■ **TRAINING AND PRUNING** Need no formative pruning. Guide and tie in young shoots to their support until they begin to cling. Prune established plants to keep them within bounds, and to shorten or remove shoots that have become detached or are growing away from their support. Large specimens can be trimmed with shears. The suckering pads make thinning impracticable. To renovate, cut back to within 1m (3ft) of the base.

Parthenocissus in winter
These clinging creepers can be cropped so that growth is kept flat against a wall.

PASSIFLORA *PASSION FLOWER*

A large genus of mostly tropical and subtropical, evergreen or semi-evergreen, woody-stemmed tendrilled climbers. They have handsome foliage, but are grown mainly for their complex, often spectacular flowers in a variety of colours. Some also produce edible fruits. In warm climates, they are excellent for training on walls and fences, or for covering trellis and pergolas; the larger species can become bulky and may need strong supports. The majority flourish in full sun or partial shade. Training displays the flowers to best effect, and regular pruning not only increases flowering potential, but also prolongs the flowering lifespan.

In cool temperate climates most climbing species need conservatory or glasshouse protection. *P. antioquiensis*, *P. edulis* and *P. quadrangularis* will tolerate slightly lower temperatures than *P. coccinea* and other tropical species. *P. caerulea*, *P. incarnata* and *P. lutea* are hardy in temperate conditions.

P. CAERULEA

BLUE OR COMMON PASSION FLOWER

Fast-growing, evergreen or semi-evergreen, woody-stemmed, tendrilled climber. In late summer, it bears white, sometimes pink-flushed flowers, green on the outside, with the crown banded with blue, white

and purple. Given shelter from cold, dry winds it is fully hardy.

■ **WHEN TO PRUNE** Spring, and after flowering.

■ **TRAINING AND PRUNING** All training methods should aim to develop a permanent framework to which flowered shoots can be pruned back. To fan-train on a wall, remove growing tips after planting to encourage branching from the base. Select three to five of the strongest resulting shoots and tie them in to develop a framework. If training up and along high wires, train the single stem vertically, pinching back sideshoots until the plant reaches the height where laterals can be allowed to develop and be trained horizontally to form permanent main stems along the wires.

Once established, prune in spring to remove dead, weak and overcrowded growth, and shorten shoots to keep within bounds. After flowering, cut back flowered shoots to within two or three buds of the framework branches. Harder pruning often results in excessive vegetative growth and, in some instances, reduced flowering for a year or two. Replace old specimens with young, vigorous plants rather than attempt renovation by drastic pruning.

Passiflora × violacea

One of the hardiest of the passion flowers, this beautiful hybrid of *P. caerulea* and *P. racemosa* has elegant purple flowers.

> **OTHER PASSIFLORAS**
> All climbing species are pruned and trained as for *P. caerulea*, but where growth is vigorous the tropical species may need additional thinning out immediately after flowering.
> To grow passifloras for fruit, *see* Passion fruit and granadillas, *p.297*.

Training passiflora on a pergola

Permanent stems trained horizontally overhead will produce flowering shoots that hang down to display the flowers to great advantage, and create a "tropical" effect. The shoots must be spur-pruned after flowering, to within two or three buds of the main stems.

Main stem is trained horizontally under beam

Wires stretched tightly between cross beams

Laterals are allowed to develop as permanent framework stems along wires

Trailing flowered shoots cut back to two or three buds of main stems

Plant is trained straight up pillar

Other climbers can be planted to cover pillars

PETREA

Petrea volubilis (purple wreath or sandpaper vine) is a tropical, semi-deciduous or evergreen, woody-stemmed, twining climber, grown for its arching racemes of lilac and amethyst flowers. An excellent climber for pillars, walls and tree trunks (provided that it can climb into full sun), it can also be trained as a standard (*see p.260*).

■ **WHEN TO PRUNE** After flowering.

■ **TRAINING AND PRUNING** After planting, pinch out growing tips, and select three to five strong shoots to form the main framework. Tie in young shoots until they begin to twine. Prune established plants annually, aiming to maintain an open framework. This will discourage scale insects, sooty mould and mealy bugs, to which petreas are susceptible. Thin out congested growth and cut back laterals to within two or three buds of the framework branches.

Petrea volubilis
The purple wreath, *P. volubilis*, bears cylindrical, lilac spikes of flowers over a long season. It can only be grown in a heated glasshouse or conservatory in cool climates.

PHASEOLUS

Vigorous, annual or perennial twining climbers, some of which, such as *P. coccineus* (the runner bean) and *P. vulgaris* (French bean), are grown as vegetables. Most, however, can also be grown for their ornamental pea-flowers. All will provide rapid cover during the growing season on any support. They grow readily from seed and are usually treated as annuals, though both *P. coccineus* and *P. lunatus* are half-hardy to frost-hardy, tuberous-rooted perennials that die down to ground level in winter. They need no pruning, other than to cut old, dead stems of perennial species back to the base in early spring.

PHILODENDRON

Evergreen, woody-based climbers grown for their handsome, often beautifully coloured foliage. They produce stem roots which, though not adhesive, will twine to give the plant support. They occasionally produce arum-like flowers, usually in shades of green or yellow. In tropical gardens, philodendrons are usually long-lived and require little maintenance. They are ideal to grow through large trees. In cooler areas, they are suitable for the home or warm conservatory: *P. scandens* (the heartleaf or sweetheart plant) is a popular house plant. Grow it in partial shade, and provide the support of a stout moss pole.

■ **WHEN TO PRUNE** Spring or summer.

■ **TRAINING AND PRUNING** Pinch out the growing tips of young plants to encourage a bushy habit. Train young shoots by tying in at first in the required direction. Once established, prune only to remove excessive or unwanted growth. If necessary, shorten main stems before the new leaves emerge in spring. Philodendrons respond well to hard pruning.

Climbing philodendron (*right*)
Many philodendrons produce twining aerial roots that will make use of any support to further the plant's upward progress.

PLUMBAGO

A varied genus that includes several slender, evergreen or semi-evergreen, woody-stemmed, scrambling climbers, all frost-tender to varying degrees. They are grown primarily for their terminal racemes of salver-shaped flowers, borne on the current year's growth throughout summer and sometimes into early winter. Plumbagos are ideal for walls, fences and pergolas, but can also be trained as standards and over wire hoops; they are beautiful specimens for conservatory walls. All prefer dappled shade rather than full sun.

P. AURICULATA SYN. P. CAPENSIS

CAPE LEADWORT

Plumbago auriculata is an evergreen or semi-evergreen, woody-stemmed, scrambling climber, producing trusses of pale Cambridge-blue flowers from summer to autumn or early winter. It is the hardiest plumbago, tolerating temperatures of 5°C (41°F). In these conditions it is not over-vigorous, and makes an ideal conservatory or glasshouse plant. The blue of its flowers look particularly attractive when seen against a white-painted wall. *P. auriculata* f. *alba* has pure white flowers.

Plumbago trained over a wire balloon
Plant within the balloon, spreading the shoots out evenly around the structure. Prune them to stimulate laterals, pruning harder in areas where more growth is needed. Spiral the leading shoots around the globe, so that their laterals can be tied in to criss-cross and thus cover the entire structure. The display can be maintained for several years by deadheading; once growth becomes overcrowded, plants are best renovated by being taken off the wires, unravelled, pruned to strong young shoots and retied, as for *Jasminum polyanthum* (*see p.274*).

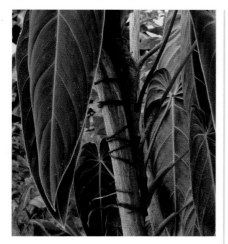

■ **WHEN TO PRUNE** Late winter or early spring.

■ **TRAINING AND PRUNING** To train against a wall (*see also p.250*), pinch out the growing tips of young plants after planting, and select three or four of the strongest resulting shoots to form the main framework. Plumbagos will not cling to supports by themselves, and their stems must be tied in regularly as growth proceeds. Once the main stems have reached the required height, pinch out their tips to encourage the production of laterals.

Once established, aim to maintain the primary branch framework, and spur-prune all laterals to within two or three buds of their base. Remove all weak or badly placed shoots completely, cutting back to a main framework branch. To renovate, cut back all branches to within 30cm (12in) of the base of the plant, and tie in strong new shoots to the support as growth proceeds. If new growth is not strong, the plant may be too old and is best replaced.

To train as a standard, *see p.260*. Once the head is established, spur-prune all laterals annually to the main framework. To grow over a wire balloon or other shape, after initial planting and pruning (*see facing page*) tie in as many shoots as possible around, not up, the wires; this not only provides even coverage but also encourages more sideshoots to break (*see Horizontal training, p.11*). Maintain by deadheading (*see facing page*) until dense growth requires renovation.

OTHER PLUMBAGOS
P. INDICA, P. SCANDENS As for *P. auriculata*.

POLYGONUM

Vigorous, fully hardy, twining climbers frequently included in *Fallopia*. The most popular, *P. aubertii* (Russian vine) and *P. baldschuanicum*, both deciduous, bear small white or pale pink flowers all summer. They are invaluable for masking large unsightly buildings and fences, but being fast-growing and invasive they are unsuitable for confined spaces.

■ **WHEN TO PRUNE** Late winter or early spring. Excess growth can be trimmed at any time of the year, except during frosty or snowy weather.

■ **TRAINING AND PRUNING** Polygonums need no formative pruning, but guide young stems into the support to provide evenly spaced coverage. Established plants form a mass of intertwined stems that is difficult to prune methodically. In large, open areas, plants can be left unpruned. Otherwise, cut all stems back by one-third of their length, with shears or secateurs. To renovate, cut the plant back to within 1m (3ft) of ground level, and re-train the resulting strong growth to cover the support.

Polygonum baldschuanicum
The extraordinary vigour of this plant gives rise to its common name, mile-a-minute.

PORANA

Vigorous, evergreen, sun-loving twiner, useful for trellis and pergolas; if wall-grown, it needs the support of vertical wires. Frost-tender, in cool temperate regions it will only flower in a heated conservatory. Needs no formative pruning; guide young stems in to the support. Once established, in late winter to early spring, cut back laterals to within one or two buds of a main stem. Does not respond well to hard pruning.

PUERARIA

Pueraria lobata (syn. *P. hirsuta*, *P. thunbergiana*), the Japanese arrowroot or kudzu vine, is a deciduous, twining climber with hairy stems, bearing scented, purple, pea-like flowers on new growth. It is quite hardy and will resprout from the base if cut down by frost. In cold areas, it is also grown as an annual.

■ **WHEN TO PRUNE** Early spring.

■ **TRAINING AND PRUNING** Needs no formative pruning, but train shoots as required to establish a framework. In subsequent years prune annually to remove weak stems and thin out congested growth; stems may be cut back to the framework branches to control spread. To renovate, cut back all growth to within 30cm (12in) of the base; the plant should respond well.

PYROSTEGIA

Pyrostegia venusta (syn. *P. ignea*) is a woody-stemmed, evergreen, tendrilled climber, grown for its long display of tubular orange flowers. In tropical and subtropical gardens it is ideal for arches, pergolas, trellis or host plants. In cold areas, grow in a heated conservatory.

■ **WHEN TO PRUNE** Late winter to early spring.

■ **TRAINING AND PRUNING** After planting, select one or two strong shoots to form a framework and remove the remainder. Under glass, tip back when they reach the required height, usually at about 3–4m (10–12ft). Once established, cut back all lateral shoots annually to within two or three buds of the framework branches, and remove unwanted growth. Responds well to hard pruning.

OTHER CLIMBING PLANTS
PERIPLOCA Vigorous twiner for wired walls or fences, pergolas and trellis. Needs no formative pruning, except to guide young shoots. Prune established plants in early spring only to remove weak growth or to keep within bounds. Trim with shears or secateurs.
PHILAGERIA As for *Lapageria* (*see p.275*).
PILEOSTEGIA (syn. SCHIZOPHRAGMA VIBURNOIDES) Self-clinging, for large walls or tree trunks. Prune in early spring, as for climbing hydrangeas (*see p.273*).
PODRANEA As for *Pandorea* (*see p.278*).
QUISQUALIS Tropical scrambler; no special pruning needs.

R

RHODOCHITON

Rhodochiton atrosanguineus (syn. *R. volubile*) is an evergreen, perennial climber with twining leaf-stalks and slender, eventually woody stems, grown for its tubular, deep maroon-purple flowers set off by showy, expanded, bell-shaped calyces of a similar, though paler, colour. Grow in sun or light shade, in completely frost-free conditions; the roots must be in cool moist shade. It is a short-lived perennial, often grown as a half-hardy annual, flowering readily in the first year from seed.

■ **WHEN TO PRUNE** Early spring.

■ **TRAINING AND PRUNING** Needs permanent support, but little formative pruning, other than to pinch out the growing tips to encourage a bushy habit. Provide initial light support of twiggy sticks or netting, until plants attach themselves to the permanent support of wire or trellis. Established plants need pruning only to remove dead or damaged shoots. Does not tolerate hard pruning.

RUBUS *BRAMBLE*

Genus containing plants grown for their fruits (*see* Cane Fruits, *pp.228–231*), and also several shrubs (*see p.216*). *Rubus henryi* var. *bambusarum* is a fully hardy, evergreen, scrambling climber to 6m (20ft), grown primarily for its handsome, pleated, three-lobed leaves, glossy deep green above and white beneath. During summer, it bears slender racemes of bramble-like, pink flowers, followed by small, shiny, blackberry-like fruits. It is useful for fences and old tree stumps, or as ground cover, as is the graceful *R. flagelliflorus*.

■ **WHEN TO PRUNE** Late winter or early spring.

■ **TRAINING AND PRUNING** After planting, shorten the main stem to within 30cm (1ft) of the base, to encourage strong shoots. Tie these in as growth proceeds, to give even coverage of the support. Prune established plants annually, to ensure continual production of new stems. Remove several of the shoots that flowered in the previous season, cutting out close to the base of the plant. The new basal shoots will flower in the following year. When the production of new shoots slows down, the plant is probably ageing and is best replaced.

S

SCHISANDRA

Handsome, deciduous or evergreen twiners bearing striking clusters of scented flowers and, where male and female plants grow together, curious "string-bead" fruits. Frost-hardy to fully hardy, schisandras are useful on shady, sheltered walls, fences and trellis, and in mild areas may be trained up into trees.

■ **WHEN TO PRUNE** From late winter to early spring.

■ **TRAINING AND PRUNING** Need no formative pruning if grown up into trees, but if grown on walls, trellis or fences, select five to seven strong shoots to form the main framework, and tie them in to provide well-spaced coverage of the support (*see also p.250*). Continue tying in as growth proceeds. Prune established plants to remove shoots that shade out lower growth, and to keep within bounds. Cut back overlong or outward-growing laterals to within two or three buds of the framework to encourage more flowering shoots, or tie in to fill gaps. Drastic pruning is best staged over several seasons, to maintain flowering. Each year, cut back one old woody branch to the base, and train in strong replacement shoots.

SCHIZOPHRAGMA

Deciduous, woody-stemmed climbers with clinging aerial roots, related to *Hydrangea*. Schizophragmas are hardy and will tolerate part shade, but need shelter from wind. Ideal for lofty walls, they are very effective trained up large tree trunks, or as ground cover.

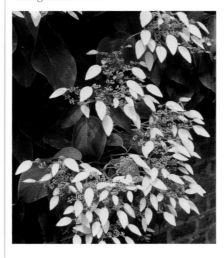

■ **WHEN TO PRUNE** After flowering, if necessary.

■ **TRAINING AND PRUNING** Need no formative pruning, but tie in young shoots close to the support to encourage them to anchor themselves. On smooth surfaces additional ties may be needed. Established specimens need little further pruning, other than to remove excess or unwanted growth. If gaps occur as plants extend, secure young branches in place with an occasional tie, so that they fill the space. Mature plants will sometimes produce long, soft, leafy growths; shorten these by up to two-thirds, as they are unlikely to flower.
Schizophragmas should not be drastically pruned. Renovate gradually, removing one or two main branches each year to try to stimulate new growth from close to the base (*see also* Renovation, *p.252*).

Schizophragma integrifolium
The white or cream "lacecap" flowerheads resemble those of climbing hydrangeas; schizophragmas have a similar growth habit.

SEMELE

Semele androgyna (climbing butcher's broom) is a vigorous, frost-tender, evergreen perennial. The rigid, twining stems bear deep green, leaf-like cladodes on which small, star-shaped, cream flowers are produced in summer, followed by orange-red berries. It is a robust plant for a conservatory or, in warm climates, for a wall or tree trunk.
It needs no formative pruning, but guide and tie in young stems to the support. The shoots take two or three years to develop fully and the fruits often take a full 12 months to mature. When fruiting is over, in winter or early spring, remove the entire shoot at the base, leaving younger shoots intact. Otherwise, prune only to restrict the height of stems, if necessary: any pruning will reduce the potential display of fruit. Plants are long-lived, but can be cut entirely to ground level, for example if wall maintenance becomes necessary.

***Senecio macroglossus* 'Variegatus'**
The ivy-like leaves are broadly edged with cream in this variegated cultivar, echoing the buttery yellow of the flowers.

SENECIO

A large genus that includes several leaf-twining climbers, particularly useful for growing among wall shrubs, hedges or other climbers outdoors in warm climates, or in heated conservatories. *Senecio scandens* is frost-hardy.

S. MACROGLOSSUS

NATAL IVY, CAPE IVY, WAX VINE

Evergreen, woody-stemmed, frost-tender twining climber with triangular leaves and yellow flowers, mainly in winter.

■ **WHEN TO PRUNE** After flowering.

■ **TRAINING AND PRUNING** After planting, pinch out growing tips to encourage branching from the base, and tie in to the support to form a framework. Prune established plants only to remove weak shoots, or cut flowered shoots back by up to one-third, if becoming too long. Does not respond well to hard pruning, which will reduce flowering.

> **OTHER SENECIOS**
> S. MIKANIOIDES (syn. DELAIREA ODORATA),
> S. SCANDENS As for *S. macroglossus*.
> Shrub species are now included in *Brachyglottis* (see Dictionary of Ornamental Shrubs, *p.177*).

SMILAX

Frost-hardy to frost-tender scramblers with wiry, prickly stems that will scramble over tree stumps or through shrubs and trees. Need no early pruning; guide young shoots over the support. Once established, thin in late winter or early spring, cutting out old shoots at the base; wear gloves, and cut stems out in sections. May be cut back completely to renovate.

SOLANDRA *CHALICE VINE*

Subtropical, evergreen, woody-stemmed, scrambling climbers with handsome, trumpet-shaped flowers that are sweetly fragrant, especially at night. They require warm conditions and a dry winter season, and may be grown under glass. Growth can be very vigorous. Prune after flowering. Need little formative pruning, but remove the growing tips to encourage a bushy habit. Restrict pruning of mature plants to the removal of weak or excess growth; unduly vigorous shoots can be shortened by up to one-third. A plant that is pruned harder will respond, but only slowly regains its shape. Flowering will be affected for a year or two.

SOLANUM

A large genus that includes several woody-stemmed climbers, scrambling or with twining leaf-stalks. They are grown for their broad clusters of star-shaped flowers, in shades of pale grey-blue to blue-violet or white, borne on the current year's shoots. *S. wendlandii* and *S. seaforthianum* are frost-tender; *S. jasminoides* and *S. crispum* will tolerate light frost. The sap can cause allergic reactions; wear gloves to prune.

S. CRISPUM

Vigorous, evergreen or semi-evergreen scrambling climber. It will usually survive light frost in a sheltered, sunny site. Provide the support of wires or substantial trellis.

■ **WHEN TO PRUNE** Early spring, or after flowering in warm, frost-free gardens.

■ **TRAINING AND PRUNING** After planting, remove the growing tips to encourage branching from the base, and select three or four strong shoots to form a framework. Tie in to the support as growth proceeds. Once established, prune annually to remove unwanted growth, and cut back lateral shoots to within two or three buds of the main framework. Plants do not respond well to severe pruning and renovation should be spread over two or three years. Remove one old stem at its base each year, training the strongest of the new stems as a replacement. Very old specimens are best replaced.

> **OTHER SOLANUMS**
> S. JASMINOIDES As for *S. crispum*.
> S. SEAFORTHIANUM, S. WENDLANDII
> As for *S. crispum*, but in all climates prune after flowering.

***Solanum crispum* 'Glasnevin'**
The most commonly grown cultivar of *S. crispum*, 'Glasnevin' has golden-yellow stamens that are in vivid contrast to the deep violet-blue petals of the flowers.

> OTHER CLIMBING PLANTS
> RAPHIDOPHORA *R. glauca* is a large, stout-stemmed, evergreen climber with aerial roots, closely related to *Monstera*; most effective in tropical climates when allowed to clamber up tall trees. Needs humid conditions. Prune and train as for *Monstera* (see *p.277*).
> RHOICISSUS Evergreen, tendrilled climber, shade-tolerant, for posts or tree trunks in warm gardens. As for *Cissus*, *p.267*. Old plants often become dense and congested, so thin out excess growth by removing it close to the base.
> SINOFRANCHETIA As for *Stauntonia, p.284*.
> SOLLYA Slender-stemmed, evergreen twiners, may need protection under glass in very cold regions. Need no special pruning.

STAUNTONIA

Stauntonia hexaphylla is a frost-hardy, vigorous, evergreen twiner, grown for its glossy leaves and sweetly fragrant, lilac-tinted white flowers in spring. Male and female flowers are born on separate plants. When both are grown together female plants produce edible, fleshy, egg-shaped, purple fruits, up to 5cm (2in) long, during summer; females may also occasionally produce fruit without a male pollinator. *S. hexaphylla* is frost-hardy, but if grown outside in cooler regions it needs a warm, sunny, sheltered site. Fruits will not set if the flowers have suffered frost damage. In colder areas it may be grown in a cool greenhouse or conservatory. It needs the support of trellis, or a wired wall, or may be grown on a pergola. Spur-pruning encourages the production of flowering shoots and helps to keep the plant within bounds.

■ **WHEN TO PRUNE** Late winter to early spring.

■ **TRAINING AND PRUNING** Needs no formative pruning, but grows rapidly, so guide the young shoots in to the support as they develop to build up even coverage. Once a framework is established, shorten lateral shoots back to six to eight buds of the framework branches during summer, and then spur back the same shoots to two or three buds in early spring, as for *Wisteria* (see p.286). The main stems can be shortened to encourage new growth but severe pruning is not recommended.

STEPHANOTIS

Stephanotis floribunda is a rather fleshy, evergreen, twining climber with leathery leaves, grown chiefly for its powerfully fragrant, waxy, salver-shaped white flowers, produced from spring to autumn. It can grow to 4–5m (12–15ft) in tropical gardens, making a handsome specimen for trellis or pergolas, but is less vigorous as a house or conservatory plant in cool climates.

■ **WHEN TO PRUNE** Late winter to early spring.

■ **TRAINING AND PRUNING** After planting, pinch out the growing tips to encourage a bushy habit, and train in the resulting shoots to the support. Prune established plants to remove weak shoots and thin out congested growth. Tip back over-long shoots if necessary, and continue spacing and tying in new shoots to extend coverage of the support. Replace old plants rather than attempt to renovate by hard pruning.

Stephanotis floribunda
Its handsome evergreen foliage makes stephanotis an attractive house or conservatory plant, even when not in flower.

Streptosolen jamesonii
With a similar habit to winter jasmine, streptosolen has long, straight shoots that tumble over, rather than cling to, supports. On a wall or fence, a well tied-in framework of stems is essential.

STREPTOSOLEN *FIREBUSH, MARMALADE BUSH*

Streptosolen jamesonii is a fast-growing, evergreen, loosely scrambling plant, bearing rounded clusters of funnel-shaped, orange flowers mainly in spring or summer. It is frost-tender and needs sun; it grows well under glass.

■ **WHEN TO PRUNE** Late winter to early spring.

■ **TRAINING AND PRUNING** After planting, pinch out the growing tips of young plants to encourage a bushier habit. Select three or four of the strongest shoots to form the main framework and tie in at intervals. *Streptosolen* does not cling or twine and shoots need regular tying in. It is a good choice to cover a wire balloon (see *Plumbago, p.280*). Once established, cut back all lateral shoots annually, to within 15cm (6in) of the main framework. Remove weak stems at the same time. Plants can be renovated by cutting back all shoots to within 30cm (12in) of ground level.

STRONGYLODON

Strongylodon macrobotrys (the emerald creeper or jade vine) is a rare, vigorous evergreen, grown for its spectacular waxy, luminous, jade green, claw-like flowers, borne in pendent racemes in winter and spring. Needs partial shade in summer, and tropical conditions. Train and prune as for *Wisteria* (see p.286), reducing laterals in two stages; harder pruning results in weak growth and reduced flowering.

Strongylodon macrobotrys
Training over pergolas or roof beams allows these striking flowers to hang freely.

T

TECOMANTHE

Evergreen, twining climbers, grown for their shiny, pinnate leaves and trumpet-shaped flowers, borne in pendent racemes in late summer or autumn. They are tropical plants that in temperate climates require a heated glasshouse, with light shade in summer. *T. speciosa* may be shy to flower under glass.

■ **WHEN TO PRUNE** Early spring.

■ **TRAINING AND PRUNING** Needs no formative pruning, but tie in young shoots as growth proceeds. Once established, prune annually to remove weak shoots and thin out congested growth. If necessary, shorten back leading shoots to restrict the plant's size. Replace old plants rather than attempt renovation by hard pruning.

TETRASTIGMA
JAVAN GRAPE, CHESTNUT VINE, LIZARD PLANT

Tetrastigma voinierianum is an evergreen, woody-stemmed, tendrilled climber with lustrous foliage. It is closely related to *Cissus*, and is often grown as a house or conservatory plant, where it tolerates deep shade. In tropical gardens, it and other species are useful for shaded or semi-shaded walls and banks, or can be grown up large trees. Plants grown under glass need warm and not too dry conditions.

■ **WHEN TO PRUNE** Late winter to early spring.

■ **TRAINING AND PRUNING** Pinch out the growing tips of young plants at intervals to promote bushy growth. They need little pruning once established, but if necessary to restrict size, cut back over-long growths to a healthy bud close to a main branch. Remove weak stems or thin out congested growth at the same time. To renovate, cut back to within 1m (3ft) of ground level to encourage strong new growths, or replace with new plants raised from semi-ripe cuttings.

THUNBERGIA

Perennials in this genus (which also includes half-hardy annuals) are mainly tropical and subtropical twining evergreens, with funnel-shaped flowers borne on the current season's growth. They are ideally trained high on walls, trellis and pergolas, or grown through shrubs and trees (they prefer some shade in summer). Thunbergias grow well in heated glasshouses and conservatories where there is room for ample vertical growth.

T. MYSORENSIS

Evergreen, woody-stemmed, twining climber, bearing long, pendent racemes of tubular yellow flowers with reddish-brown lobes and greenish-purple bracts, from spring to autumn.

■ **WHEN TO PRUNE** Late winter to early spring, or after flowering.

■ **TRAINING AND PRUNING** After planting, pinch out the growing tips to encourage a bushy habit, and tie in young shoots to provide even coverage of the support. Keep pruning of established plants to a minimum; remove weak stems and thin out congested growth by removing it at the base. Hard pruning results in excessive leafy growth and reduced flowering; old plants are best replaced.

TRACHELOSPERMUM

Frost-hardy, evergreen, woody-stemmed, twining climbers. They are grown for their glossy, leathery foliage and sweetly scented jasmine-like flowers, borne in lateral clusters in summer and early autumn. They are suitable for trellis, pergolas, arbours and walls, in sun or semi-shade. The most commonly grown is *T. jasminoides*, the star or Confederate jasmine. Like many other twining to scandent climbers, it looks best, and to a degree supports itself, if allowed to climb over the top of its support and mound up upon itself, so that the shoots cascade downwards.

■ **WHEN TO PRUNE** Early spring.

Thunbergia mysorensis
The flowers hang down on long stalks, so *T. mysorensis* is best trained up high.

OTHER THUNBERGIAS
T. ERECTA, T. GRANDIFLORA As for *T. mysorensis*.
T. GREGORII As for *T. mysorensis*. Grown as an annual in warm temperate areas.

■ **TRAINING AND PRUNING** Needs no formative pruning, but guide young growth in to the support, tying in until it begins to twine. Flowers are produced on laterals on old wood, and pruning of established plants is best kept to a minimum. Remove weak shoots, and thin out old or badly congested growth, bearing in mind that the plant's habit is naturally to form a rather dense entanglement. Train outward-growing shoots back in to the support, and tip back any that exceed their allotted space by cutting them back to just above a flowering spur. To renovate, cut back up to two-thirds of all growth to encourage strong new shoots to break. Very old plants are best replaced.

OTHER CLIMBING PLANTS
STIGMAPHYLLON Needs little pruning, other than to restrict size, remove weak shoots, or thin out congested growth, in autumn or winter.
SYNGONIUM As for *Philodendron* (see p.280).

TECOMARIA *T. capensis* (syn. *Bignonia capensis*, *Tecoma capensis*) is an evergreen, shrubby scrambler, suitable for a cool conservatory, or outdoors in almost frost-free gardens; treat as for *Tecomanthe* (see above). Prune back overlong shoots if using as a hedge or ground cover.
THLADIANTHA As for *Humulus* (see p.273)
TROPAEOLUM As for *Humulus* (see p.273)
WATTAKAKA See *Dregea*, p.270.

V

VIGNA

 Vigna caracalla (snail flower) is a vigorous, evergreen twiner, useful for trellis, pergolas or pillars in subtropical or tropical gardens, or for a warm conservatory in cold regions. Young shoots need guiding but no pruning. Once established, prune in late winter to early spring to remove dead shoots and thin out crowded growth, or cut all the previous year's growth back hard in spring.

VITIS *VINES*

 Genus of hardy, deciduous, woody-stemmed, tendrilled climbers that includes the grape vine, *V. vinifera* (*see* Grapes, *p.288*). All have handsome, generally lobed leaves that usually take on rich autumn tints; some also produce attractive bunches of bitter or edible fruits. *V. coignetiae*, the crimson glory vine, can be relied upon for spectacular autumn colour; the foliage of *V. vinifera* 'Purpurea' is always purple-tinged.

Provide a warm, sunny site for vines, with shelter from wind to avoid foliage scorch. Vines are particularly attractive on wires on old walls, and can be grown up stout pergolas and arches, or allowed to scramble into large trees. They can also be trained as standards.

■ **WHEN TO PRUNE** Mid-winter, before sap begins to rise.

■ **TRAINING AND PRUNING** After planting, pinch out the growing tip and select two or three of the resulting strong shoots to form the primary framework. Guide in to the support to provide well-spaced coverage. Over the next two to three years continue tying in shoots as growth proceeds, aiming to extend the main framework to cover the allotted space. To train as a standard, *see p.286*.

Once the framework, or head of a standard, is established, shorten all laterals to within two or three buds of the main branches. In subsequent years the spur systems will become increasingly complex and gnarled; a well-trained vine is attractive even in winter. Excessive growth of lateral shoots can be trimmed back to a strong bud during the summer. Vines in large trees require very little pruning.

Vines can be kept for many years and rarely require renovating. If wall maintenance is necessary, plants may be cut back almost to ground level, and will generally sprout freely from the base.

W

WISTERIA

 Deciduous, woody-stemmed, twining climbers, usually vigorous, with pinnate leaves, grown for their beautiful pea-flowers, borne in pendent racemes in late spring and early summer. Flowers may be white, blue-violet or deep purple, pink or apricot, and are borne on lateral spurs on ripened wood. These very ornamental plants are ideal for high walls and fences, for stout pergolas or arches, where the flowers can hang down, or for clambering up large trees. Most are fully hardy, but flower best in a warm, sunny, sheltered site. Wisterias may take seven years or more to begin flowering, and plants on nitrogen-rich soils may produce excessive vegetative growth at the expense of flowers.

Wisterias can be trained against walls and fences in a variety of shapes. The espalier form is one of the best suited to display the flowers. They can also be trained as standards. To maintain trained forms and enhance flowering, wisterias must be rigorously spur-pruned in two stages, in summer and winter. Even wisterias that are allowed to ramble informally flower markedly better when spur-pruned.

■ **WHEN TO PRUNE** Mid-winter, and again in summer, about two months after flowering.

■ **TRAINING AND PRUNING** To grow as an espalier, *see right*. To train as a standard, *see p.260*, and on a pergola, *see p.258*. Whichever system of training is chosen, it will take three or more years to build up the basic framework of the plant. Once established, the aim of pruning is to control extension growth and to encourage the production of lateral flowering spurs. The current season's shoots are cut back in two stages (*see right*) to within two or three buds of their base. These will bear the coming season's flowers. Growth and flower buds are easily distinguished in late winter, the former being narrow and pointed, the latter plump and blunt.

Wisterias are long-lived and, if pruned annually as described, seldom need renovation. If necessary, however, it is best done in stages over several years, removing one main branch at a time and tying in a suitable replacement shoot. If wall maintenance is needed, wisterias may be cut back almost to the base, and will normally re-sprout vigorously. It will take a number of years, however, for a plant that has been pruned hard to flower freely again.

Training wisteria on a wired wall

Pruning on planting

1 Cut back the leader to a strong bud about 75–90cm (30–36in) above ground level, taking care not to cut below the graft union on grafted cultivars.

2 Remove any existing laterals to stimulate a strong new leading shoot.

Year 1, summer

1 Tie in the leading shoot vertically.

Surplus laterals can be removed

2 Select two strong laterals and tie them in at 45° angles. Prune any sideshoots to about 15cm (6in), or three or four buds, to begin the formation of flowering spurs.

Year 2, winter

1 Cut back the leading shoot to about 75cm (30in) above the topmost of the laterals.

2 Lower the pair of laterals and tie in to the lowest horizontal wires. Prune them back by about one-third of their length, to strong ripe growth.

Year 2 until allotted space is covered, summer

1 *Continue to tie in the leading shoot.*

2 *Select the next pair of strong laterals and tie them in at a 45° angle.*

3 *Remove unwanted growth at the base or from the main stem, cutting out completely to its point of origin.*

4 *Tie in the new leading shoot of each lateral, and spur-prune any sideshoots back to about 15cm (6in), or three or four buds.*

Year 3 until allotted space is covered, winter

1 *Cut back the leading shoot to about 75cm (30in) above the topmost of the laterals.*

2 *Lower the topmost pair of laterals and tie in to the nearest horizontal wire.*

3 *Prune all of the laterals back by about one-third of their length, to strong ripe growth.*

Established *wisteria*, summer

1 *Continue to tie in the main lateral growths and cut them back when allotted space has been covered.*

2 *About two months after flowering, cut back laterals and sideshoots to within five or six buds, or 15cm (6in), of a main branch.*

Established *wisteria*, winter

Cut back the laterals and sideshoots pruned in summer to within two or three buds of their base. These will bear the coming season's flowers

Site of summer pruning cut

Wispy regrowth

Several tiers of laterals now tied in horizontally

Once plant is well established, cane and ties may be removed

Fruiting Vines

The term "vine" is usually used to describe a climber with vigorous growth and strongly twining or tendrilled shoots, and fruiting vines are no exception. All are characterized by rampant and, when bearing crops, heavy growth that requires substantial support. In the open, free-standing systems of posts and wires must be as robust as those used for fruit trees; when in full leaf, a mature vine offers considerable resistance to wind.

The vines most prized for their fruits are the grape, the kiwi fruit, and the various types of passion fruit and granadilla. The genera to which they belong – *Vitis, Actinidia* and *Passiflora* – also contain many ornamental plants (*see pp.287, 262*, and *279*, respectively). Fruiting vines are also highly decorative trained

over pergolas or arbours, and some cultivars, such as the grape 'Brant', display superb autumn colour. In cool climates, however, cropping will be sparse and unreliable, and no *Passiflora* grown outdoors will produce edible fruits. The use of alternative training methods and additional pruning techniques to those used for ornamental vines will increase fruit size and quality and make maintenance and harvesting easier in all climates.

To obtain worthwhile crops the growth of fruiting vines must be well trained and restricted by hard winter pruning and, often, some summer pruning. Without training and pruning, the vigorous, wayward shoots soon become tangled, with consequent reduction in light levels and fruiting.

GRAPES *VITIS VINIFERA, V. LABRUSCA*, AND HYBRIDS

The grape is probably the most widely grown fruit, and was certainly one of the earliest to be cultivated. Progress in breeding and cultivation has opened up new grape-growing areas across the world. Only in tropical and subtropical regions is it rare to be able to grow grapes. In cool climates, grapes grow well under glass (*see p.296*). Both for dessert fruits and for wine-making, it is important that cultivars are chosen for their suitability for the prevailing climate.

BREEDING AND ROOTSTOCKS
Vitis vinifera is noted for the quality and flavour of its fruit, and breeders usually try to incorporate it in any new cultivars. Hybridization with the American vine, *Vitis labrusca*, has improved the prospects for grape growing in relatively cold and wet regions. *V. labrusca* used as a rootstock for *V. vinifera* also confers resistance to the phylloxera aphid; in countries where phylloxera still exists, vines must be grafted. Choice of rootstock and cultivar should be guided by local conditions and by local expert advice.

GROWTH AND FRUITING HABIT
Pruning is imperative to keep grape vines under control and fruiting well. Training is equally necessary, on stout posts and wires, on horizontal wires on a wall, or in a greenhouse. The fruit is borne on new growth arising from wood of the previous year, so most pruning methods involve cutting fruited shoots back in winter to permanent stems ("rods"). Grape vines are very long-lived: the rods, which soon become thick and gnarled, can produce strong, new, fruit-bearing shoots for decades.

The size and quality of crops is determined by the climate coupled with the health and vigour of the vine. However, for dessert grapes in particular, vines should not be allowed to fruit prolifically. Pruning restricts vegetative

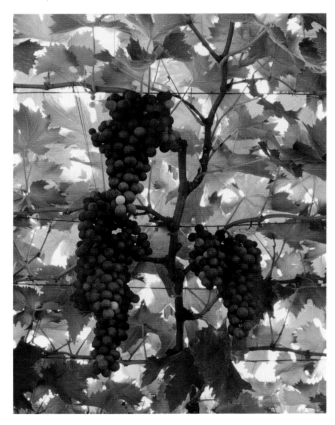

growth so that fewer but finer bunches of grapes are produced. In addition, the bunches and, for dessert grapes, the individual fruits are often thinned.

Vines should not be allowed to fruit until at least their third year so that vigour is channelled into producing a fully established plant capable of bearing increasingly heavy crops.

TRAINING METHODS
Most cultivars respond to training methods that involve spur-pruning fruited shoots back to one or two basal buds, from which the next

Grape vine trained under glass
The simplest methods of training and pruning vines entail developing a strong, permanent, central stem, or rod, on which, each year, shoots develop and bear fruit, and are then pruned back. Here, the central rod has been trained up and then along the roof of a conservatory, giving the fruits maximum exposure to sunlight. This is one of the most attractive and productive ways of using the often underemployed upper levels of a glasshouse.

year's fruiting shoots will develop (*see* Rod- and-spur method, *p.290*; Curtain method, *p.294*). Standards can also be formed and pruned in this way (*see p.296*). A few cultivars, however, do not readily produce growth that will fruit from these buds. For these it is better to use "rod-renewal" systems, such as the Guyot (*see p.292*) or Kniffen (*see p.295*), that allow a shoot to develop in one year, then fruit in the next; fruited shoots are removed completely each year, and strong, young shoots that were specially selected during the growing season and reserved as replacements are tied in. These shoots will develop fruiting sideshoots along their length in the coming season.

WHEN TO PLANT AND PRUNE

Plant vines in autumn or early winter. From then on, prune only in midwinter when the risk of sap bleeding from cuts is at a minimum; any later, and bleeding may be difficult to stop (cauterization with a red-hot poker is the traditional remedy). Of equal importance is the control of unwanted shoots during the growing season.

MAKING CUTS

Vine stems have a cane-like structure, and are soft and pithy in the middle. Buds occur at visibly swollen nodal areas. When cutting to buds, always cut beyond the swollen node to prevent structural damage to the stem. On upward-facing shoots, angle each cut so that water will run off it; horizontal shoots can be cut straight across.

On rod-renewal systems, remove the entire stem, either cutting straight across at the stem base, or also removing the stub from which the stem grew (provided that this does not also bear the replacement shoot). On spur-pruned cultivars, the permanent rods carry spurs all along their length, and it is the growth from these that is shortened each winter after bearing the crop. Extensive spur systems are thus built up over many years. These will need to be reduced in size; if very overcrowded, some weaker spur systems should be sawed out completely.

"Summer" pruning – shortening or removing young shoots – is an ongoing exercise throughout the growing season. Without it, an indiscriminate tangle results. It is most effectively done when the shoots are still young, removing soft shoot tips by pinching them out.

Spur pruning
Cut to one or two strong buds, and select the strongest of the shoots that develop to become the fruiting shoot. Always cut beyond the swollen nodal area where buds form.

Rod renewal
On some cultivars, entire fruited stems are cut away, leaving strong young replacements to be trained in, usually horizontally. Always remove any unproductive stubs as well.

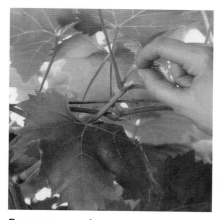

Summer pruning
Restrict vigorous growth by pinching or pruning back surplus shoots as they develop. This directs energy into fruit development and prevents crowding and shading.

Thinning foliage
Ripening grapes need maximum exposure to sunlight, particularly in cool climates: as well as summer-pruning new growth, remove individual leaves that cast shade on the fruits.

Fruit thinning
Fruit thinning is unnecessary for wine grapes (though bunches should be at least 30cm/12in apart), but improves the quality of dessert grapes. Remove one in three or four fruits.

Harvesting dessert grapes
Where only one bunch of fine fruits has been allowed to develop per stem, leave a "handle" of stem on the bunch to carry the grapes without touching and spoiling their bloom.

Harvesting wine grapes
Simply cut the bunches off using secateurs. It is not necessary to make precise cuts, as the fruited stem will be removed anyway in the following winter.

ROD-AND-SPUR (CORDON) SYSTEM

This method can be used for all cultivars that are spur-pruned. It is particularly suitable for growing dessert grapes, because the fruiting shoots are kept short, each developing only one or two fruit trusses: thin these to one truss for finer fruit.

FORMATIVE TRAINING

The permanent rod, to which fruited shoots will be pruned back each year, needs careful initial pruning to ensure that it is built up only of fully ripened wood. Prune the newly planted vine back hard before midwinter by two-thirds, or more if the wood is not fully hardened, and remove any laterals. During the following summer let the new leading shoot grow unchecked, tying it in, but pinch laterals back to five leaves, and their sideshoots back to one leaf. In winter, again shorten the leader, and prune back all laterals to one or two buds, forming the first spurs. Repeat this annual treatment until the rod consists of fully ripe wood up to the top wire. Then shorten it to below the wire, from then on treating the new leading shoot as for all other laterals.

ESTABLISHED PRUNING

To encourage even shoot development along the whole rod length, untie the upper half from its support and lower it to a horizontal position well before any growth begins, raising it again once young shoots emerge. In spring thin these shoots to two per spur, one as the fruiting shoot, the other as a reserve in case the selected shoot is damaged. Let only one or two bunches develop on each fruiting shoot, pinching the shoot out to two leaves beyond the last bunch. Pinch out sideshoots to direct energy into the developing fruits and prevent excessive growth shading the ripening bunches: remove any leaves that shade fruits (*see* Thinning foliage, *p.289*).

As the vine matures the knobbly spur systems to which fruited shoots are annually pruned back will gradually become larger and more congested. In later years they will need to be reduced in size, or removed completely to avoid overcrowding, using loppers or a saw.

Year 1, winter

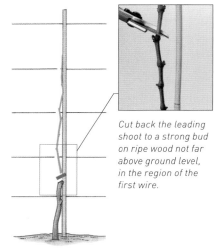

Cut back the leading shoot to a strong bud on ripe wood not far above ground level, in the region of the first wire.

Year 1, summer

1 Tie in the new leading shoot vertically.

3 Pinch back to one leaf any sideshoots on the laterals, including those that grow after the laterals have been shortened.

2 Cut back each lateral that has grown from the central stem to five or six leaves.

Year 2, winter

1 Cut back the leading shoot by two-thirds of the summer's growth, or further if necessary, to leave only brown, ripened wood.

2 Prune back laterals to one bud if this looks strong, or to two buds if not.

Year 2, summer

1 Tie in the new leading shoot vertically.

2 Cut back each of the laterals to five or six leaves of the current season's growth.

3 Pinch back to one leaf any sideshoots on the laterals, including those that grow after the laterals have been shortened.

4 Pinch out any flower trusses that form.

Year 3, winter

1 Cut back the leading shoot by half to two-thirds of the new growth, or further if necessary, to leave only brown, ripened growth.

2 Prune back laterals to one bud if this looks strong, or to two buds if not.

Bud faces in opposite direction to the one pruned back to the previous year

Last year's pruning cut

Spring pruning, year 3 onward

As shoots develop at each spur, pinch out all but the strongest two. Aim to use the stronger one as the fruiting shoot, and keep the other in reserve in case the first one fails. Shorten the reserve shoot to two or three leaves so that it does not cause overcrowding.

Established rod-and-spur system, summer

1 If any laterals are without flower trusses, prune back to five or six leaves.

Spring pruning has allowed only one pair of shoots to grow at each spur; the reserve shoot is pinched back

2 Cut back each of the laterals bearing flowers to two leaves beyond the last truss.

New leading shoot is tied vertically

3 Pinch out flower trusses to leave one per lateral for dessert grapes, one every 30cm (12in) for wine grapes.

4 Throughout the summer, pinch back to one leaf any sideshoots that grow from the laterals.

Established rod-and-spur system, winter

1 Cut back the leader to a bud below the top wire.

2 Untie and gently lower the leader and tie it in to one of the horizontal wires; this will encourage shoots to break on the lower part of the main stem. The leader is retied vertically when buds break in spring.

3 Prune back laterals to one bud if this looks strong, or to two buds if not.

4 If spurs become congested, saw off an old section of the system with a pruning saw.

GUYOT SYSTEM

This is the system most often used for growing wine grapes in an open site in the garden. It allows longer fruiting shoots (bearing several bunches of grapes) to develop, and suits cultivars that cannot be spur-pruned, but must be pruned using a rod-renewal method (*see p.289*).

Strong support is essential. Give endposts extra support with struts or guy ropes. Posts should be 6m (20ft) apart at most, with wires at 40cm (16in) intervals. Some growers use pairs of wires, one stapled to each side of the posts, so that shoots can be tucked between them, reducing the need for tying in. Letting the double wires cross over between posts prevents bunching of new growth. Space the vines 1.5–2m (5–6ft) apart.

FORMATIVE TRAINING

The vine takes two years to train, producing its first crop in the third summer. Initially, training and pruning aim to build up a strong, low trunk, then to develop, in the second summer, only three strong shoots. In the second winter, two are brought down and tied in to form horizontal arms from which shoots will grow upward and fruit. The third is the source of the next year's three strong shoots; it is pruned hard to encourage strong basal shoots to grow.

ESTABLISHED PRUNING

Shoots from the two horizontal stems are trained vertically. Any sideshoots must be kept under control. Remove leaves that shade developing fruits from the sun (*see* Thinning foliage, *p.289*). On the shortened stem, three strong shoots are retained in order to repeat the procedure in the following year, when the existing arms and their fruited shoots are completely removed, and the replacements shortened and tied in horizontally on the bottom wire. The third new cane is pruned hard, as before, and so the process of rod renewal can be repeated each year.

For a vine that takes up less space (or to create space for extra vines in a row), use only one shoot trained horizontally, to the left or to the right. Two replacement shoots are needed annually, one to be tied down for fruiting, the other cut back to two or three good buds to produce the next pair of replacements.

Pruning on planting

On planting in winter, insert a cane and tie it vertically to the wires. Prune the vine back to about 15cm (6in) from soil level, leaving at least two strong buds. Make the cut well clear of the nodal swelling.

Year 1, summer

1 *Tie the leading shoot to the stake using a loose figure-of-eight tie.*

2 *Prune laterals back to five leaves.*

3 *Remove any over-vigorous upright shoots that may compete with the leader.*

4 *Remove any low shoots that develop on the original stem by pinching out when young.*

Year 2, winter

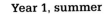

Prune the leading shoot to the topmost of three good buds below the lowest wire.

Year 2, summer

1 *Select three strong main shoots and loop string around them and the stake to give them some support.*

2 *Cut or rub any other shoots back to the main stem throughout the summer.*

Vine shoot begins to support itself with tendrils

Year 3, winter

1 Prune each of the two outer shoots to leave about 60cm (2ft) of stem, with 8–12 strong buds.

2 Prune the central shoot to leave three or four good buds. The aim is to allow only three strong shoots to develop from this portion of stem.

3 Gently bend the two outer shoots and tie them to the bottom wire, one on either side. This will stimulate sideshoots all along the stem.

Year 3, summer

1 Tie in shoots from each arm vertically on the wires (or guide through double wires), pinching out the tips at the top wire.

2 As sideshoots develop on the vertical shoots, pinch them out completely to prevent their leaves shading the developing fruits.

3 Allow only three shoots to develop from the central arm, removing any others.

4 Cut or pinch any sideshoots on the three central shoots back to one leaf.

Year 4 and onward, winter

1 Shorten the middle shoot of the three that were allowed to develop from the short, central stem, pruning to leave three or four strong buds.

3 Shorten the two outer shoots of the central three shoots to leave about 60cm (2ft) of strong growth, with 8–12 healthy buds.

2 First untying all ties and detaching tendrils, remove the two outer arms, with all their fruited shoots, entirely.

4 Gently bring the two outer, replacement shoots down to the horizontal and tie in to the bottom wire.

Established double Guyot, summer

1 Train new shoots in vertically, pinching out the tips when they reach the top wire. Thin bunches of fruits to 30cm (12in) apart.

2 As before, allow only three strong shoots to develop from the central arm, and pinch any sideshoots that develop back to one leaf.

3 Once vertical shoots are tied in at about 15cm (6in) intervals, remove any more that develop from the main arms.

4 Pinch out completely any sideshoots that develop on the vertical, fruiting shoots.

CURTAIN METHOD

This is a simple method for all grape cultivars that can be spur-pruned, used by many commercial growers and easily adapted for the garden. It saves on labour where several rows of vines are to be grown (for example, for amateur winemaking). Commercial rows are usually spaced 2.5–3m (8–10ft) apart to let vehicles pass, but, in a sunny site, 1.5–2m (5–6ft) is adequate spacing. A vine could also be sited against a wall, either outdoors or under glass; inward-growing shoots must be carefully pinched out.

The method is derived from the more complex Geneva Double Curtain, an innovative system (*see facing page*) which

established that the fruiting shoots of a vine may hang downward without affecting fruit quantity or quality, provided that growth is not allowed to become too dense and shady.

The fruiting shoots are selected to be well spaced, hanging freely from permanent rods trained horizontally at head height. Pinching out the shoot tips, if necessary, at about 20 buds long (1m/3ft) makes harvesting comfortable. Choose shoots that originate growing upwards and outwards, rather than down: a cascading habit allows more light and air circulation around the shoots than a flat "fringe" of growth.

The fact that the shoots hang downwards means they are less vigorous,

which is desirable: fruit is finer, and summer pruning is less of a chore. Some commercial growers do not carry out summer pruning, but the vine will be more manageable for it, and fruits ripen better if it is done.

FORMATIVE TRAINING
Train the vine as a single stem up to the top wire as for a rod-and-spur system (*see p.290*). Then, select either the leader and a strong lateral or two strong laterals (pruning the leader to the topmost one) and train them horizontally along the top wire. It is best for the shoots to form a wide-angled "Y" shape rather than a "T" so that there is no danger of load-bearing stress on the fork, at least until the main stem is woody and thick. Over the following growing season, tie in the two arms along the wire until the desired spread has been reached. Meanwhile, let shoots develop from upward and outward-facing buds, at approximately 30cm (12in) intervals. As these shoots flower, allow one truss every 30cm (12in) to develop. As the fruits increase in weight, the shoots will arch over and hang down. Summer-prune sideshoots, pinching back to one leaf to restrict growth and prevent shading.

ESTABLISHED PRUNING
Each winter, spur-prune the fruited shoots back to two or three buds from the permanent rods. In summer, select the best-placed shoot of those that develop, keeping one other, pinched back to five leaves, as insurance should the selected shoot be damaged. As the vine ages, spur systems will become more knobbly: relieve congestion by sawing off an older section (*see also p.291*), trying to keep spur systems facing in a generally upward direction.

Year 3, winter

Laterals selected to become permanent horizontal rods form a wide fork below the top wire

Taut wires are stretched at 45cm (18in) intervals between sturdy posts no more than 6m (20ft) apart

Vertical main stem trained on cane tied to the wires

1 Cut the leader back to the uppermost of a pair of strong laterals.

2 Tie the laterals on to the wires, and continue tying in once growth begins, allowing sublaterals to develop and hang freely.

3 Remove lower laterals completely.

Year 4 and onwards, winter

1 Spur-prune the fruited shoots, cutting them back to two or three buds.

2 Cut out all downward-growing shoots completely.

Fruiting shoots at intervals of 30cm (12in)

Central stem kept clear of shoots

OTHER TRAINING METHODS

MULTIPLE CORDON (RIGHT)
Grape vines are so vigorous that the single rod-and-spur system can be extended to form multiple cordons, with fruiting shoots spur-pruned each year to several vertical rods. It is a particularly decorative form; the rods may also be angled for a "chevron" effect. Multiple cordons are particularly suitable for dessert grapes because many short fruiting shoots are developed, each bearing one bunch of grapes. Train the vine with two low horizontal arms, as for the Guyot system (*see p.292*), then let vertical rods develop, no closer than 1.2m (4ft) apart.

KNIFFEN (LEFT)
This follows the same principles as the Guyot system (*see p.292*), but the rods are trained horizontally in pairs from one central stem, then pinched out at 10 buds (allowing 10 fruiting shoots to develop). An additional replacement shoot is allowed to develop parallel to each rod from a shoot spur-pruned to two buds; this shoot is tied to the wires when the fruit-bearing growth is cut away completely, thus renewing the rod. Crops are heavy, but fruits may be shaded, particularly by the replacement shoot, so this system is suitable only for wine grapes in regions with hot summers.

GENEVA DOUBLE CURTAIN (RIGHT)
This more complex form of curtain-training is popular commercially, but is usually impractical in gardens, requiring a large, well-constructed support system of two rows of posts (*as right*), or single posts with "T-bars" across their tops, between the ends of which two parallel wires are stretched. Its advantage is that twice the number of vines can be grown, while needing only another 60cm (2ft) or so of space. Training and pruning are as for a single curtain, but the vines have one horizontal rod on each wire (resembling a queue of people, each with their right arm reaching to the shoulder of the person in front, and their left arm to the shoulder of the person behind).

LYRE (LEFT)
This earlier version of the Geneva Double Curtain is, basically, the same training and pruning method, but upside down. It is still popular in cooler regions such as northern France because the fruiting shoots are tied in, well-spaced, at a level where they receive all the available sun. Because the fruiting shoots grow upward they are vigorous and are pinched back when they shade fruits below. The fruited shoots are spur-pruned back to the rods each year. Unlike the Geneva Double Curtain method, the lyre allows cultivars requiring rod-renewal to be used; replacement shoots can develop and hang downwards until required.

TRAINING GRAPES UNDER GLASS

In cooler, more unreliable climates, the only certain way of obtaining consistently good dessert grapes is with the aid of a glasshouse. If the house can be heated, so much the better, though good ventilation is essential – grape vines do not like humid conditions. To simplify watering needs, or if you do not have a bed of soil in your glasshouse, plant the vine just outside and lead it through a purpose-made hole in the base of the wall (this must be able to be enlarged as the trunk thickens). Cut the vine back so that two buds are inside, and train in a new leading shoot, pinching back the other as a reserve.

The dimensions of the house will dictate the ultimate size of the vine and how it may be trained. A single rod-and-spur system (*see p.290*) is usually most suitable: the vine can be trained up and along the apex of the roof, or along the angle of the eave should this be high enough. Where the vine grows against glass, support wires or struts must be at least 22cm (9in) from the glass, or fruits and foliage will be scorched. In a lean-to structure, the vine may be trained into a multiple cordon (see *p.295*) against the back wall. The reflected heat from the wall will benefit fruit ripening.

Regular pinching out of surplus shoots throughout the growing season is essential for vines under glass, not only because space is limited but also because growth will cast dense shade on the fruits and other plants below.

STANDARD GRAPES

Where less space is available, or for a free-standing vine under glass or out of doors, training as a standard (*see right*) is an attractive way of obtaining a few bunches of fine fruit. If grown in a pot, the vine can be moved outside. It should not stay in a heated glasshouse in winter; chilling is necessary to initiate flowers. Use a 45cm (18in) pot for stability, and top-dress and feed each spring.

Training a standard vine

Forming the main stem

It is vital to allow several years for a robust trunk to develop. Starting with a vine that is cut back hard, each winter shorten the previous season's growth by at least half, to where it is brown and ripened. Do not retain any green wood. Pinch sideshoots back to six leaves in summer, and remove in winter.

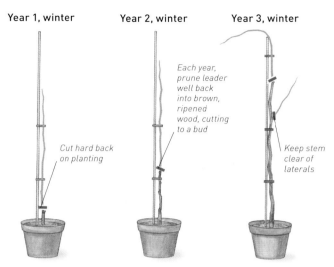

Year 1, winter   Year 2, winter   Year 3, winter

Cut hard back on planting

Each year, prune leader well back into brown, ripened wood, cutting to a bud

Keep stem clear of laterals

Forming the head

When you have the desired height of clear stem, let a cluster of laterals develop at the top, pinching out any lower shoots. In winter, spur-prune them to two or three buds. Repeat each winter, gradually building up spur systems; when these become congested, thin by sawing sections away (*see p.291*). In summer, pinch out shoots that develop from these spurs when they reach 45–60cm (12-18in). As fruits form, "maypole" the stems (*see p.99*), tying them up to the top of the stake with string for support when they are heavy with fruit.

Year 4, winter   Year 5 and onwards, winter

Fruiting shoots pinched out in summer at 30–45cm (12–18in)

Spur-prune fruited shoots to two strong buds

Allow a cluster of well-spaced laterals to develop, then prune back to two buds

Thin spur systems as they build up and become congested

Scraping
Careful removal of the outermost layers of old bark with a knife assists in the control of some pests.

CARE AND CULTIVATION UNDER GLASS

Grape vines have exacting watering needs, and a glasshouse border will need to be deep, fertile and well drained; considerable attention is needed to ensure that soil conditions are always neither too wet nor too dry.

Good ventilation is crucial to keep pest and disease problems to a minimum. Both side and top ventilation is desirable, allowing fresh air to circulate freely and avoiding excessive humidity.

Hand-pollination is essential, either by tapping the stems sharply or by carefully drawing cupped hands down over the flower trusses. The best time to do this is around midday on a sunny day, when the most pollen is being released.

Where fruits develop next to or directly underneath glass, be careful, if thinning foliage (*see p.289*), to leave the bunch in the shade of a leaf or two, or the fruits will scorch.

Scraping stems clean of old strips of bark (*see left*) after winter pruning will help to reduce pest levels, particularly of mealybugs, as it leaves them with no convenient nooks and crannies in which to shelter.

Kiwi fruit (Chinese gooseberry) ACTINIDIA DELICIOSA

The kiwi fruit is a handsome, deciduous, twining climber with thick, fleshy shoots that ripen to form substantial woody stems. The weight of the plant and its vigorous growth habit (shoots can be 9m/28ft long) mean that plants need strongly constructed supports. It is important not to allow shoots to twine around supporting poles, struts, or battens; they will constrict and thicken to cause distortion or damage.

A warm, temperate climate is ideal, but several cultivars crop well in cool areas, though the late-ripening fruits may be damaged by early frosts. Training against a wall gives more protection. An espalier form (*see p.95*) is suitable, with a vertical central stem, and tiers of horizontal arms trained on wires 30cm (12in) apart. Alternatively, train across the top of a sturdy pergola or on a tripod of stout poles.

The fruits are borne in clusters at the leaf-joints on one-year-old wood and at the bases of new shoots. Both female and non-fruiting male plants are usually necessary for a crop, although there are a few self-fertile cultivars. Male plants are generally more vigorous than female ones; where space is limited, the male plant can be cut back severely after flowering. One male plant will pollinate up to eight or nine females.

■ **WHEN TO PRUNE** Late winter or spring, before growth starts. Pinch-prune during the growing season to restrict growth.

■ **TRAINING AND PRUNING** On planting in winter, cut the (usually) single stem back to 30cm (12in). On walls, posts and wires or a pergola, tie in the new leading shoot to a cane tied vertically to the wires or pillar, and let it grow upwards. Allow pairs of laterals to develop that will form permanent, fruiting arms where desired (either along each horizontal wire, or once the top of the pergola is reached). On a tripod, select two shoots, and spiral them around the structure in a double helix.

When these arms are about 1m (3ft) long, pinch out their tips and train in a new leading shoot. Allow laterals to develop at 50cm (20in) intervals along the arms, pinching out their tips once five leaves have formed. Throughout the growing season, pinch out any sideshoots they develop and any new shoots from the main arms.

In the next year the plant will fruit on these short shoots and at the base of their sideshoots. Pinch out the tips of these sideshoots once six or seven leaves have developed beyond the cluster of developing fruits. Pinch back shoots on

Cut to buds showing signs of growth

Frost-damaged buds

Spur-pruned kiwi fruit
Cut shoots back to two active buds to stimulate fruiting growth. In time, spur systems will build up and need reducing, using loppers or a saw.

which no fruits develop to five leaves. After harvesting, the fruited shoots are pruned back to two healthy buds beyond the last fruit. This builds up spur systems; once they are three years old, cut right back to dormant buds near the main arm. The shoot that grows is then pinched at five leaves to begin reforming spur systems.

To renovate overgrown or neglected specimens, cut back hard into old wood in spring. Plants usually respond well.

Passion fruits, granadillas PASSIFLORA SPP.

Passion fruits
Train fruiting shoots to climb along or down strings to keep them separate and give them some support, particularly necessary when the shoots are heavy with fruits.

Many species of *Passiflora* are cultivated for their fruit, largely in tropical regions. None tolerates frost but many can be grown under glass. Cultivars selected for their fruit quality are often grafted; their pollination needs vary. The fruits are produced on the current year's growth.

■ **WHEN TO PRUNE** After fruiting.

■ **TRAINING AND PRUNING** Fruiting plants can be grown as for ornamental *Passiflora* species (*see p.279*). Under glass, given full sun, they fruit well on a wired wall, along wires on the roof, or trained around a tripod in a pot. In the garden, a simple system resembling the curtain method used for grapes (*see p.294*) will make harvesting less awkward than when plants are grown on more ornamental structures, such as pergolas. Wire netting or chain-link fencing also makes a good support, provided that both sides are accessible.

To grow plants up and then along horizontal wires or beams, whether outdoors or under cover, first train the leader and, if the plant is to be trained in two directions, one strong lateral (which can be allowed to develop at any point)

to grow up a post, pillar or wall, pinching out sideshoots. Once the top is reached, train the two stems along the wires: laterals should develop and hang down to form a fruiting curtain. If no strong laterals have developed by the time a shoot is 60–90cm (2–3ft) along its wire, pinch out its growing tip, allow laterals to develop and train in the last along the wire as the new leader. If the laterals do not develop flowers, prune them back to two or three buds to encourage flowering regrowth.

If the fruiting shoots are allowed to hang down freely they tend, because they produce vigorous tendrils, to become tangled together. One way to avoid this is to stretch strings from the horizontal wires to the ground; the shoot will then be guided by the string instead of entwining itself with its neighbours. This also stops the fruiting shoots from blowing against each other in exposed areas: the fruits bruise easily.

The shoots will fruit only once, so after harvesting, prune them back to 20cm (8in), or two buds. Repeat in subsequent years. Plants more than six years old may become unproductive, and are then best replaced.

Roses

Roses are among the most versatile of garden plants, the many species and hybrids varying greatly in size, habit and flowering performance. Most need some pruning to achieve their best.

The great appeal of roses is that they may be used in a wide range of situations, and for many purposes, in the garden. They are extremely adaptable, tolerating a wide variety of soil types, and there are roses to suit almost any climate throughout the world. In height they range from low ground-cover plants to large, multi-stemmed shrubs. In growth, habit and form they vary from tiny, compact bushes to rampant ramblers with stems up to 20m (70ft) long. Some roses are suitable for growing grouped together in traditional rose beds; others can be used as hedges, and many make superb specimen plants. Miniature roses look splendid and grow well in pots, tubs, troughs and other containers, while climbers and ramblers can be trained to cover walls, fences, arches, pillars and pergolas. Roses can be used to create any mood in the garden, from the artless informality of wild roses, with sprawling stems and masses of single flowers, to the regimented symmetry of a row of standards or flower-clad obelisks.

Employing the correct pruning and training methods to achieve these different effects not only results in sturdy, healthy and well-shaped plants but also encourages the maximum number of flowers, especially when combined with generous feeding. For climbers and ramblers, in particular, skill and imagination when training can transform a plant from being merely attractive to becoming a truly striking display.

When deciding how best to prune a rose, the enormous range of recognized groups and cultivars, and their varying requirements, may initially seem daunting. The key to successful pruning and training is to identify the manner in which each rose grows and flowers, and match it to a training programme or pruning routine that will best exploit its vigour, habit and flowering performance.

Miniature rose
Modern roses are available in an ever-broadening range of colours, sizes and habits. With annual pruning, these tiny bushes maintain a neat and compact shape and will flower all summer long.

◀ Elegant border rose
Shrub roses derived from wild species, such as the white-flowered *R. sericea* and the yellow-flowered *R. xanthina* that require minimal pruning, are very useful in borders, as they provide an attractive contrast with the more brightly coloured, often double, blooms of many modern cultivars.

Rose Types and Forms

The popularity of the rose since ancient times has ensured that many species and an astonishing number of hybrids are cultivated today. Although some retain the habit of many roses in their wild state, making lax, free-standing shrubs with long, arching stems, studded with single flowers in summer, roses are extremely varied in the way they grow. Some produce only one, often sensational, flush of blooms in summer, usually on older wood. Many others are repeat-flowering, producing two or more flushes, sometimes in almost unbroken succession, from early summer until autumn (even, in mild climates, into winter), the flowers being borne on wood produced in the current season. A large number bear semi-double or double flowers rather than the single flowers of their wild relations.

Pruning plays an important part in the cultivation of this major group of ornamental plants, speeding up the natural process by which old wood that has flowered is replaced by new, vigorous shoots. Although the aim of pruning is the same for all roses – to maintain a healthy, well-shaped plant that achieves its full ornamental potential – the extent and timing of pruning is not. The pruning regimes recommended here are generally appropriate to broad categories of roses. However, their complex parentage means that some roses do not conform in habit and pruning requirements to the groups to which they are conventionally assigned; if a rose seems uncharacteristic of its group, try adjusting its pruning to that of roses in a group that it seems to resemble more.

Major groups of roses

Any method of grouping roses to determine their pruning and training requirements must take account of broad characteristics of growth, and important stages in the history of rose breeding. Because of the very complex hybridization this has involved, a great many roses have no easily attributable species or hybrid name, unlike most other shrubs and climbing plants, and are known simply by their cultivar name. It is important, in order to prune correctly, that you know to which grouping and sub-grouping a rose conventionally belongs. Those roses to which it is possible to assign a species name are largely grouped together, for pruning and training purposes, into a single category, the "species roses".

SHRUB ROSES

The shrub roses, useful in borders and mixed plantings, form a disparate group, although in general requiring only light pruning. They include several species roses, such as *Rosa glauca* (syn. *R. rubrifolia*), outstanding for its blue-green foliage, and a number of roses close to their species parents, and like them flowering once in summer. Several have highly ornamental hips.

The old garden roses are a major category. Many are of great beauty, as well as having considerable historical interest. They all belong to groups that existed before the introduction in the late 19th century of the large-flowered bush roses (hybrid teas). Most have semi-double or double flowers but their colour range is limited, in some groups, to white and shades of pink. The earliest historically – the albas, damasks, gallicas, Provence roses (centifolias) and mosses (sports of the Provence roses with mossy growth on sepals and flower stalks) – with few exceptions have a single flush of flowers in summer. The repeat-flowering characteristic, found in the China roses

Rose groups and growth habit

Old roses of upright habit
Among the old roses are a number of medium size and upright growth, often forming dense, twiggy shrubs. Like other old roses, they do not require heavy pruning, but some thinning and occasional removal of entire older stems will relieve congestion and stimulate the production of vigorous new growth that will flower well in future summers. Many gallicas, a group of old garden roses that bear a single flush of flowers in midsummer, have this habit.

Old roses of spreading habit
A large number of old garden roses have an arching habit, and when placing them in the garden allowance must be made for their spread and for their long, thorny stems, which may encroach on neighbouring plants. Shortening these stems to restrict size and spread will spoil this graceful, informal habit. However, light annual pruning, removing some of the older flowered wood, can keep them under control and enhance their flowering performance.

Modern shrub roses
The modern shrub roses are very diverse in size, growth habit and manner of flowering. Some resemble species roses, bearing single flowers on arching stems. Others are more upright, and some have flowers that equal those of a modern bush rose in fullness. Whether flowering in a single flush or repeat-flowering, however, they do not need the heavy pruning that is used to maximize the flowering performance of modern bush roses, and their character is easily spoiled by severe pruning.

ENGLISH ROSES

These roses, many with evocative names such as Gertrude Jekyll and 'The Wife of Bath', are the result of hybridizing modern and old shrub roses to create new cultivars that combine the advantages – disease resistance, compact habit, wide colour range – of modern roses with the nostalgic flower shapes and scents of older roses. Their growth habits, and hence pruning method, vary so widely that no universal rules can apply. In general, however, they should not be pruned as hard as the modern large-flowered or cluster-flowered bush roses, but benefit from light cutting back in the dormant season. Prune cultivars according to the rose group they most resemble, as advised by stockists.

Graham Thomas

late last century, was passed to the Bourbons, hybrid perpetuals and Portland roses, which are important precursors of the modern, freely repeat-flowering bush roses. None of these roses usually requires heavy pruning but the regime depends on the scale and vigour of the plant and whether it is repeat-flowering.

In this century, growers have continued hybridizing roses to produce modern shrub roses, combining desirable characteristics of modern roses with old and even species roses. Some modern shrub roses, for example 'Golden Wings', produce at least two flushes of flowers in the summer; others of compact habit are increasingly popular as ground-cover plants.

Modern bush roses

All modern bush roses are repeat-flowering, bearing their flowers on the current season's growth. They are pruned the most heavily of all roses (*see pp.306–308*); a large proportion of flowered wood is removed in order to stimulate growth the following year.

BUSH ROSES

Since the late 19th century much effort in rose breeding has concentrated on producing reliably repeat-flowering bush roses that are compact and suitable for bedding displays. The large-flowered bush roses (hybrid teas) are remarkable for the shapely, high-centred flowers, double or single, and available in a wide colour range. Even more dramatic for massed displays are the cluster-flowered bush roses (floribundas), with their large trusses of flowers. The range of small bush roses – miniature roses, patio roses and polyanthas, the last a group that preceded the cluster-flowered bush roses – is increasing all the time in response to growing demand for roses intended for restricted sites and container planting.

Small bush roses

Patio and polyantha roses (*see p.308*) are small cluster-flowered bushes, pruned in a similar way. Miniature roses (*see p.309*) are dwarf counterparts of large-flowered and cluster-flowered bushes, usually no more than 25cm (10in) tall. Their twiggy growth does not require severe pruning.

Standard roses

Bush roses are top-grafted on to clear stems of varying heights to form bush standards (*see p.310*); other roses with long shoots, such as ramblers, can also be used to form weeping standards.

CLIMBERS AND RAMBLERS

Many roses have long stems that are flexible, at least when young, allowing them to scramble through shrubs and into trees to reach for the light, their thorns giving them a powerful hold among other vegetation and on uneven surfaces. The ramblers, including several species, usually bear clusters of small flowers in a single flush, and are very vigorous, some, such as *Rosa filipes* 'Kiftsgate', overwhelmingly so.

The climbing roses are on the whole more moderate in growth, have larger flowers and offer a wider colour range. They include a few old garden roses, such as boursaults and noisettes, as well as many modern hybrids, among them climbing sports of modern bush roses. The most recent area of interest for rose breeders has been in developing the so-called "pillar roses" of short stature that bear flowers in succession at all levels.

Ramblers and climbers can be allowed to grow freely into strong host plants but are most commonly grown on man-made supports, where they need training and pruning to flower well.

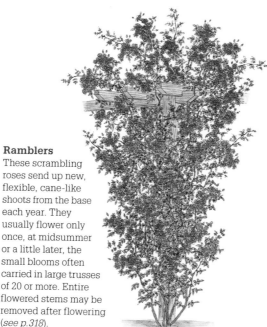

Modern climbers

These roses should be trained (*see p.316*) to form frameworks of fairly stiff, long shoots, which usually require tying in to supports. Their flowering laterals should be pruned annually to stimulate further flowering growth.

Ramblers

These scrambling roses send up new, flexible, cane-like shoots from the base each year. They usually flower only once, at midsummer or a little later, the small blooms often carried in large trusses of 20 or more. Entire flowered stems may be removed after flowering (*see p.318*).

Basic Techniques

The principal reason for pruning roses, as for any plant, is to maintain health and vigour. The removal of dead, diseased and damaged wood as soon as it is noticed is particularly important for roses. They are prone to a variety of ailments, and are often planted *en masse* in traditional rose beds, increasing the dangers of disease spreading.

Shaping the plant, preventing over-crowding and, if necessary, restricting its size are also routine tasks that are important aspects of rose pruning. In comparison with an unpruned plant, a rose that is open-centred, with well-spaced shoots that do not cross and rub against each other, is more pleasing to the eye and less prone to disease.

However, although a healthy rose will flower freely, much of the annual task of rose pruning is devoted simply to encouraging more, or finer, blooms. It is the strong new shoots on a rose that flower best. As they age, these shoots become woody and usually produce fewer blooms of lesser quality. If a rose is left to itself, the old stems will die and eventually be shed, to be replaced by new ones. In the meantime, however, a tangle of dead, old and new growth builds up, increasing the risk of disease. Annual pruning, therefore, aims to speed up the natural process by removing old, moribund wood and stimulating the growth of vigorous new shoots that will flower well in following summers. With

climbing and rambler roses, in particular, these pruning cuts complement training, so that the rose clothes its support well with both foliage and flowers.

Though many routine tasks (*see facing page*) are common to most rose groups, pruning techniques used to enhance flowering vary with the type of rose, its situation, and the climate in which it grows. In warm climates where roses flower almost continuously, gardeners may choose to prune very lightly – not much more than continual deadheading – to avoid interrupting the display. Bush roses will, however, benefit from heavier pruning to renew the flowering growth every two or three years.

Making cuts

All roses have alternate buds (*see p.8*). Make angled cuts just above a healthy bud (*see right*) that faces in the direction in which you want a new shoot to develop. To maintain an open-centred and rounded shape on bush roses, prune to an outward-facing bud. On roses with arching shoots, where inward- or upward-growing new shoots are needed to fill in the centre, prune to an inward-facing bud. If no bud is visible, prune the stem at the appropriate height, and when dormant buds start into growth, cut the stem back again to a shoot growing in the required direction.

All roses benefit occasionally from renewal pruning: the complete removal, in the dormant season, of an older, less productive main stem. If a strong, well-positioned shoot has already emerged near the base of an old main stem, cut to this shoot (*see far right*).

WHEN TO PRUNE

Roses planted in the dormant season are pruned on planting; container-grown roses planted during the growing season are best left unpruned until their first spring. The degree of pruning varies depending on the type of rose.

Once established, roses with a single flush of flowers in early to midsummer – mainly species roses, some old garden roses and ramblers – should be pruned soon after flowering. Repeat-flowering roses may also be pruned once the last flowers have faded in autumn, although many growers in cool climates delay pruning bush roses, in particular, until spring, once the harshest weather is over but while the rose is still dormant or nearly so. In warm climates, prune after flowering, often at its peak in the coolest part of the year.

Angled cut 5mm (¼in) above the bud

Healthy bud in leaf axil

Older, less productive wood

Strong young growth

Straight cut

Cutting to a bud

With a pair of sharp secateurs, angle the cut cleanly across the stem not more than 5mm (¼in) above a bud either on the stem or in a leaf axil, sloping gently away so that the lower end of the cut is opposite the bud.

Renewal pruning

Using loppers or a pruning saw, cut squarely through the old stem at the base or, as here, 5mm (¼in) above a strong young shoot, neither leaving a stub nor damaging the structure of the stem where the shoot joins it.

Good and bad cuts (below)

A rough cut (*far left*) is slow to heal and is often an entry point for disease. Angling the cut wrongly (*centre left*) will allow water to collect near the bud, encouraging rotting. A cut too high (*centre right*) leaves a stub that will die back, possibly affecting the whole shoot. A correct cut (*far right*) gives the best chance of a strong, healthy shoot developing in the desired direction.

Bruised tissue will be slow to heal; if disease enters, the bud may die

Water will collect at shoot base

Stub above the active bud will die back

Rough cut **Badly angled cut** **Cut too high** **Correct cut**

Routine tasks

Although pruning to stimulate new flowering growth differs in both method and timing according to the type of rose, there are many tasks that are common to all roses. Though some have positive benefits, such as deadheading and tying in, others are preventive measures or a response to localized problems.

DEADHEADING

A rose's energies are diverted into seed production if hips are allowed to develop. Roses that flower only once are usually pruned after flowering, removing the spent flowers. Species and other roses that are grown for their decorative hips should not be deadheaded. On repeat-flowering roses, cutting back faded flowers to a bud will stimulate new shoots that will bear a second or even third crop of blossoms. For strong new shoots, always cut well back to the second or third bud down the stem, rather than just nipping off the flower heads. In a truss, the central flower will open and fade first; it can then be pinched out if desired. Once the whole truss has finished flowering, it can be removed entirely.

TYING IN

The long shoots of climbers and ramblers, and of tall shrub roses grown up against a wall, need to be tied in to their support, both to protect them from wind damage and to display their flowers to maximum effect. They may be secured to horizontal wires strung between vine eyes on a wall or fence, or to supports such as arches, pillars, pergolas and tripods. Use garden twine tied in figures-of-eight or, preferably, purpose-made ties. These short, narrow, adjustable straps have a buffer, which is positioned between the rose stem and the support to prevent chafing.

DAMAGED AND CROSSING SHOOTS

A clean cut is less likely to encourage disease than a torn or grazed rose stem, so always cut out damage, pruning stems back to just above a bud to stimulate a replacement shoot. Also, remove or shorten to a bud or sideshoot any stem that is rubbing, or will grow to rub, against another. This should minimize damage by chafing or thorns.

DEAD WOOD AND DIEBACK

With roses it is particularly important to distinguish between wood that has been dead for some time, where a "natural barrier" (see p.9) has been formed between dead and live wood, and growth that is suffering from the progressive condition known as dieback. Wood that is obviously dead (continued on p.304)

Deadheading repeat-flowering roses

Large-flowered roses Cut to a strong, outward-facing bud (*see facing page*) or shoot below the faded flower to stimulate the production of a new flowering shoot.

Cluster-flowered roses Prune away the whole flowering truss once the flowers have finally faded, by making a correctly angled cut just above a healthy bud (*see facing page*).

Tying in

Secure long shoots by tying them to their support, either with garden twine in a figure-of-eight, or with purpose-made ties. Ties should be loose enough to allow room for the shoots to expand as they grow.

Dead, damaged, crowded and crossing stems

When pruning roses, take out damaged and diseased stems, remove crossing stems that clutter the centre of a bush or cause rubbing, and cut out completely old wood that is past its flowering best. Cut or saw away any old stubs that have failed to produce shoots and died.

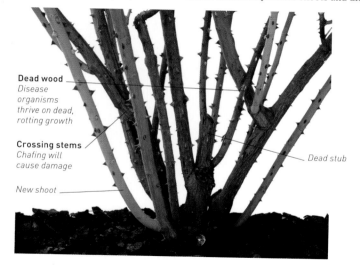

Dead wood *Disease organisms thrive on dead, rotting growth*

Crossing stems *Chafing will cause damage*

New shoot

Dead stub

(*continued from p.303*) and terminates in a clear demarcation line should be removed as soon as seen, cutting back to just above the natural barrier so as to keep it intact. However, if shoots appear dried-up and light brown, and no clear demarcation between dead and live wood can be seen, dieback is probably the cause, and pruning cuts must be made well below the affected area. Dieback travels down the centre of stems, and may be detected when you cut back into an apparently healthy part of the stem and find that the cut surface has a brown patch in the centre. Cut to buds further down the stem until healthy, white pith is reached.

BLIND SHOOTS
A rose will sometimes produce a shoot with no sign of a flower bud at its tip (*see below left*). Such "blind" shoots occur more often on some cultivars than others – the large-flowered bush 'Peace', for example, being particularly prone. The most likely cause is frost damage to the shoot tip. Shortening the blind shoot will stimulate a lower bud into growth, and this shoot should produce flowers, although slightly later in the season.

REMOVING SUCKERS
For roses, bud-grafting (budding) is the simplest and most widely used method of vegetative propagation. Some of the older roses, such as gallicas, albas, and *R. pimpinellifolia* and some of its hybrids, sucker very freely if grown from cuttings, and must be grafted onto other rootstocks to reduce the problem. Most modern roses are grafted onto rootstocks of certain selections of wild rose in order to increase their vigour and longevity. During the growing season, shoots, or suckers, may grow from these rootstocks, usually a short distance from the base of the rose. Their leaves are often smaller and of a different

Removing rose suckers

1 *Gently scraping away soil, trace the sucker back to the stem or root (below the bud-graft union) from which it has developed.*

2 *Pull the sucker away sharply from the root. This is not easy, but is far less likely to cause suckers to regrow than cutting it off.*

green to those of the scion. Suckers should be removed (*see above*) as soon as they appear, as they will initially weaken, then eventually replace the grafted cultivar. Cutting them off at ground level only encourages more growth: trace them to their point of origin on the roots and carefully pull them off at the root. This will remove dormant buds clustered at the base of the sucker that might, if left, be stimulated into growth.

Standard roses, which are top-grafted, may also produce suckers on their stems, and these too must be pinched off (*see p.311*) or cut cleanly back to the stem.

PESTS AND DISEASES
Pruning can supplement the use of insecticidal and fungicidal sprays in the control of pests and diseases. Shoots severely affected by mildew (*see below*

centre) should be cut out, and leaves affected by blackspot are best plucked off and burnt. The activities of the leaf-rolling sawfly (*see below right*) are not particularly harmful to the plant, but may leave growth so disfigured for the rest of the summer that pruning it out is preferable.

CARE AFTER PRUNING
All roses benefit from spring feeding and mulching, but those that are pruned hard, such as large- and cluster-flowered bush roses, need additional feeds throughout the growing season to maintain strong growth. Many specially-prepared rose fertilizers are available. In cool climates, do not apply fertilizer after mid- to late summer; it will stimulate soft growth that will not have time to ripen sufficiently before winter, and will be vulnerable to frost damage.

Shoot with no terminal flower bud

Bud concealed in leaf axil

Blind shoot
Cut back to a bud in the axil of a healthy, outward-growing leaf. The bud should be stimulated to develop into a flowering shoot.

Mildew
Shoots that are badly affected by the greyish bloom of mildew are unlikely to recover and should be removed and burned.

Damage by leaf-rolling sawfly
This characteristic damage does not harm the plant but can be removed if found unsightly. Cut the shoot back to where leaves are intact.

Renovation

In a newly acquired garden, neglected roses, particularly bush roses, often look as if they are hardly worth keeping, but in general it is worth trying to renovate them. Some may prove to be roses of quality and, in any case, you should not plant new roses in the same position without completely replacing or sterilizing the soil, such are the replant problems associated with this group of plants.

Climbers and ramblers are often neglected even in the best-kept gardens, simply because they are difficult to get at; moreover, most will flower well for years without attention. The time will come, however, when they will become so overgrown and vulnerable to disease that action must be taken.

When renovating roses trained on supports, always take the opportunity, once growth is cut away, to inspect the wall, fence or other structure on which the rose was trained. This is the ideal time to carry out maintenance work such as repainting, or repairing broken fixtures such as trellis or wires.

WHEN TO RENOVATE

The dormant season is generally the most suitable time to carry out drastic pruning to renovate roses, even of categories, including the ramblers, that are normally pruned after flowering, although this may mean a season without flowers. Follow any renewal and renovation work on roses by feeding and mulching well (see p.13) in spring.

BUSH AND SHRUB ROSES

For these roses, hard cutting back is the simplest, if sometimes risky, renovation method. At worst, it will kill a rose that would very likely have lingered only a little longer anyway. More often, it will stimulate dormant buds at the base of the plant into growth and completely reinvigorate the rose.

First cut away all dead stems and stumps at the base of the plant. Use loppers or a pruning saw if necessary, although long-dead material may well just break away. Remove any suckers (see facing page, top). The remaining growth should then be cut to within 2.5–4cm (1–1½in) of ground level. Do not worry about trying to cut to a bud: you will probably not be able to find one.

A less drastic treatment is to combine the elimination of all unproductive wood with overall shortening and renewal pruning (see right). This gradual renovation can be spread over two years if you are particularly anxious not to lose the rose.

CLIMBING ROSES

Neglected climbers are characteristically bare at the base, with excessive top growth. Cut back to within 30cm (12in) of ground level a proportion of the main stems (as many as one in three in any one year). This should encourage new growth from low down. If the rose does not respond (and some cultivars are reluctant to do so) the only solution is to plant a low-growing, dense plant in front to hide the bare stems.

With a climber that has outgrown its space and become top-heavy, shorten all main shoots until the rose occupies not more than two-thirds of the allotted space, and prune all laterals on the main stems by two-thirds of their length, cutting to a healthy bud or shoot.

Gradual rose renovation

This 'The Queen Elizabeth' rose is a valuable taller feature in a border planting, but it has been neglected for several years, resulting in a build-up of dead and unwanted growth. Mild renovation measures should invigorate it without leaving a gaping hole in the planting scheme over the following growing season. Next winter, provided that new growth has developed, the thick, old stems at the centre and on the far left of the bush should be cut to the base, and so on in subsequent years until all the main stems are renewed.

RAMBLER ROSES

Old, overgrown ramblers are a mass of tangled stems, some of which may have died right back to the base. To simplify the removal of pruned wood, cut stems in sections. Cut out dead wood and thin and feeble-looking stems, together with any showing signs of disease. Cut out completely or to near ground level all old stems to leave only three or four strong young canes. Prune all laterals on these stems by 8–10cm (3–4 in).

Ramblers that are impossibly tangled and unhealthy-looking may be cut down completely to ground level in late summer. Most ramblers not only spring back to life remarkably quickly, but also seem to benefit all round from this drastic treatment.

4 Shorten the remaining strong, healthy stems to reduce the overall height of the bush by at least half. Cut to a range of heights to stimulate new growth at all levels.

3 Where possible, cut older main stems back to strong new shoots arising low down, cutting cleanly and squarely across the stem.

1 Saw away dead stumps at the base of the plant, where rain is collecting and encouraging rot.

2 Remove completely any very old, unhealthy or spindly stems, cutting back to the point of origin.

Modern Bush Roses

The aim of pruning all modern bush roses is to encourage plenty of new growth that will bear a succession of flowers throughout the growing season. These roses are therefore pruned back annually to a low framework of main stems. This prevents the base of the bush from becoming bare, and encourages the growth of strong, vigorous shoots bearing good-quality flowers; even harder pruning, as practised by rose exhibitors (*see right*), will result in fewer but finer flowers.

Never be afraid to prune bush roses hard. Underpruning, year after year, is the most common cause of an unproductive bush rose, with bare, leggy "stepped" stems, spindly leafless shoots and stubs of dead wood.

In recent years, trials have been conducted to investigate the theory that bush roses can be pruned much less systematically (even using a hedge trimmer) than is traditionally recommended. While the results so far are intriguing (*see p.309*), it is too early to draw firm conclusions.

ROSE BEDS

Routine annual pruning to a specified height encourages uniform growth, which is ideal for roses massed together for display in a traditional rose bed, as all bushes of the same cultivar will flower at about the same time and height. With this type of close planting, it is vital to ensure that air can circulate freely around the plants. When pruning roses in rose beds, it is more important to ensure that stems do not crowd or cross those of neighbouring bushes than to create a balanced shape for each individual plant.

BUYING AND PLANTING

Modern bush roses benefit from initial hard pruning. This stimulates vigorous growth from low down, which is desirable for a strong and well-shaped rose bush. Bare-rooted roses are available during the dormant season, the traditional time for planting roses, allowing the root system to become established before vigorous young shoots appear. Prune the roots, shortening any overlong, coarse roots and trimming away any damage. After planting, prune the top growth (*see facing page, top*).

Containerized plants can be planted at any time. Prune as bare-rooted roses if planted in the dormant season, but if planted while in growth, remove open flowers and cut out any damaged growth, then prune hard in the early spring of the next year.

PRUNING FOR SHOW ROSES

Modern bush roses that are pruned for show blooms are cut back very hard, almost to ground level, letting the plant produce only a small number of main stems. These will bear a very few individual large blooms, or clusters of blooms. In addition, disbudding (*see below*) enhances the show qualities of the flowers. Large-flowered roses produce blooms of maximum size and good form if only one flower is allowed to develop per stem. Remove surplus flower buds as soon as they develop. With cluster-flowered roses, the central bloom normally opens and fades before the lowest have started to unfurl. More even flowering is achieved if the central bud is removed.

Disbudding

Large-flowered roses Carefully pinch off any side buds that form below the large, terminal flower bud.

Cluster-flowered roses Pinch out the central bud in a cluster at an early stage, removing all of its flower stalk.

WHEN TO PRUNE

The main time for pruning modern bush roses is while the roses are dormant, or nearly so – between late autumn and early spring. In cooler climates, pruning is better left until as late as possible. However, harsh winter winds may damage tall, upright rose stems. Wind-rock may loosen the roots, and also create a gap in the soil at the base of the plant. Water that collects here may freeze and damage the graft union, the plant's most vulnerable spot. To reduce wind-rock, cut rose bushes taller than 1m (3ft) back in autumn (*see below*). The rose can then be pruned normally, depending on its type, in the following spring, once any danger of prolonged frost has passed.

During the growing season confine pruning to deadheading (*see p.303*) – nearly all modern bush roses are repeat-flowering – and the removal of diseased or damaged growth, as well as any other necessary routine tasks (*see p.304*), such as removing suckers.

Autumn trimming

In cool climates, roses are often damaged by winter weather, particularly in exposed sites. To protect the roses, shorten their stems by half to one-third of their height. After severe winds or frosty weather, carefully firm the soil around the base of the plant.

Before trimming

After trimming

LARGE-FLOWERED BUSH ROSES

These roses, often called "hybrid teas", are usually sold as one-year-old plants. They must be pruned hard on planting, cutting stems back close to the ground (*see right*). They need no further formative pruning or training; after their first full growing season, treat for pruning purposes as established plants.

ESTABLISHED PRUNING

During the growing and flowering season remove as necessary any dead, diseased or damaged growth and any suckers, and deadhead regularly to encourage a continuous show of flowers (*see* Routine tasks, *p.303*).

During the dormant season (*see* When to prune, *facing page*) the main, annual pruning of bush roses consists of removing all unproductive and unhealthy shoots, and shortening what remains. Only strong, healthy growth is retained to supply vigorous shoots in the following growing season. Most large-flowered bush roses are naturally upright, and this often leads to overcrowded stems in the centre of the bush. By selectively shortening stems to healthy, outward-pointing buds, a well-shaped and open-centred bush can be

Pruning a newly planted bush rose

Shoot tip is slightly damaged

Growth is already crossing and rubbing

Before pruning *These long shoots should be pruned hard to stimulate vigorous growth from low down, where it is wanted, and also eliminate any defects or nursery damage.*

After pruning *Each shoot is pruned to 7–15cm (3–6in) above ground level. Angled cuts just above outward-facing buds encourage open, well-spaced new growth.*

formed, allowing free air circulation and reducing the risk of disease.

First remove dead or diseased wood, and any stumps left from the previous year's pruning that did not produce worthwhile shoots. Cut away spindly shoots of less than pencil-thickness; they are unlikely to flower and will be the first to succumb to blackspot. Remove entirely any shoots growing into the centre of the bush or, if this will denude the bush too much, cut to a low, outward-facing bud. Shorten or remove one of any pair of crossing shoots. Finally, shorten the remaining stems, to approximately

20cm (8in) from the ground in cool and temperate climates. In warmer climates, cut back less severely, to 25–30cm (10–12in). The exact height will have to vary from stem to stem, as it is impossible to keep cutting to exactly the same point. Cut to a suitable, preferably outward-facing, bud 5–8cm (2–3in) above last year's cut, but when the stem in question has three or four "steps" in it, then cut well back into the older wood, if possible to a strong basal shoot; shorten this to 5–8cm (2–3in). Rotate this renewal pruning between the stems of the rose. For renovation, *see p.305*.

Pruning an established large-flowered bush rose

1 Remove any shoots that are dead, diseased or damaged, and cut back to healthy wood any showing signs of dieback.

Position cuts to encourage outward growth that will not cross the centre or other stems

2 Shorten the remaining stems, making an angled cut to 5mm (¼in) above an outward-facing bud 20–22cm (8–9in) above ground level.

EXAMPLES OF LARGE-FLOWERED BUSH ROSES (HYBRID TEAS)

ALEC'S RED
ALEXANDER
BLESSINGS
'DEEP SECRET'
ELINA
'ERNEST H. MORSE'
FRAGRANT CLOUD
FREEDOM
JUST JOEY
PAUL SHIRVILLE
PEACE
PICCADILLY
'PRECIOUS PLATINUM'
REMEMBER ME
ROSEMARY HARKNESS
ROYAL WILLIAM
'RUBY WEDDING'
SAVOY HOTEL
SILVER JUBILEE
THE LADY
TROIKA

'Ruby Wedding'

CLUSTER-FLOWERED BUSH ROSES

Cluster-flowered roses, also called "floribundas", are pruned on planting as for large-flowered bush roses (*see p.307*). When established, the only difference between pruning large-flowered bush roses and these is that, after unwanted growth has been cut away, the remaining stems are not shortened so drastically. The charm of these roses lies in their mass of flowers, so more buds are retained on a longer length of stem in order that they may develop into flowering shoots.

A problem characteristic of cluster-flowered roses, also encountered when deadheading (*see p.303*), is that there may appear to be no buds to cut to on shoots that have carried large trusses of flowers. Cut to the approximate desired height. This should stimulate a dormant bud into life. Should a stub be left above this new shoot, cut it away later.

Neglected and old cluster-flowered bushes usually respond well to gradual or complete renovation (*see p.315*).

EXAMPLES OF CLUSTER-FLOWERED BUSH ROSES (FLORIBUNDAS)

ANISLEY DICKSON
ANNE HARKNESS
'ARTHUR BELL'
HANNAH GORDON
ICEBERG
'KORRESIA'
MARGARET MERRIL
MATANGI
MOUNTBATTEN
'THE QUEEN ELIZABETH'
REGENSBERG
'SOUTHAMPTON'

Pruning an established cluster-flowered bush rose

1 *Cut out all dead or diseased stems back to healthy wood or to the base of the bush.*

2 *Remove any stems that are rubbing or likely to rub against one another.*

3 *Shorten the remaining stems to within 25–30cm (10–12in) of ground level, making a correctly angled cut just above a healthy, outward-facing bud or shoot.*

4 *Shorten any laterals back to two or three buds from the main stem, cutting to an outward-facing bud.*

PATIO AND POLYANTHA ROSES

Patio roses are simply small cultivars of cluster-flowered roses; Anna Ford, Sexy Rexy, Cider Cup, 'Top Marks' and 'The Times' are among the best-known. Polyanthas, such as 'White Pet' and 'Nathalie Nypels', are compact bushes with tight clusters of small flowers. The growth habit and therefore the pruning of both these rose types is the same as for full-sized cluster-flowered bush roses (*see above*), though on a smaller scale.

After all unproductive wood has been removed, their main stems should be reduced by about two-thirds to a healthy bud or lateral. This regular pruning will also keep patio and polyantha roses that are growing in containers, for which they are ideal, compact and free-flowering.

Both patio roses and polyanthas can be renovated in the same way as other bush roses (*see p.305*).

MINIATURE ROSES

These appealing, tiny bush roses have flowers or clusters of flowers that are scaled-down versions of those borne by large-flowered or cluster-flowered bush roses. The principles and timing of pruning are similar to those of their full-sized counterparts – deadheading during the flowering season, followed by annual pruning when dormant.

Prune miniatures hard on planting, in the same way as full-sized large-flowered bushes (*see p.307*), cutting back to a height of 5–8cm (2–3in). In subsequent years, there are two methods by which they may be pruned. If they are growing and flowering well, light pruning (*see right*) will suffice, removing only dead, diseased and damaged growth and any crossing or congested stems (some miniatures, such as Baby Masquerade, produce much twiggy growth in the centre and need quite drastic thinning), and tip-pruning the remaining stems.

If the rose is growing poorly or is in need of renovation, or if you find by trial and error that it responds better, prune harder, retaining and drastically shortening only strong stems, as for larger bushes. It is difficult to prescribe exact heights to which main stems should be shortened. Bush size varies between cultivars – a satisfactory rule of thumb is, whatever their flowering type, to shorten by two-thirds.

Light pruning of an established miniature rose

2 Tip-prune main stems to remove any last spent flowers.

1 Remove any dead, diseased or damaged growth. Relieve congestion by cutting out the oldest stems entirely.

3 Prune any laterals back to within one or two buds of the main stem.

EXAMPLES OF MINIATURE ROSES

ANGELA RIPPON	'JUDY FISCHER'	'POUR TOI'	'STACEY SUE'
'ARIZONA SUNSET'	MAGIC CAROUSEL	RED ACE	STARINA
BABY MASQUERADE	MINNIE PEARL	'RISE 'N' SHINE'	'SWEET FAIRY'
DARLING FLAME	'PARTY GIRL'	SNOWBALL	TEENY WEENY
'EASTER MORNING'	'PEACHES 'N' CREAM'	'SNOW BRIDE'	'YELLOW DOLL'

ALTERNATIVES TO TRADITIONAL ROSE PRUNING

The traditional techniques for pruning modern bush roses require a degree of judgment that some gardeners find difficult; they can also be time-consuming. In recent years, the question has arisen as to whether using the traditional method really is worthwhile. A British programme of pruning trials has, since 1990, been comparing traditional with quite revolutionary rose-pruning methods. The most spectacular, and probably best known, of the findings is that rose bushes that are simply cut down to knee height with a hedge trimmer flower as well, if not better, than those that are painstakingly pruned on traditional lines.

Hedge-trimmer pruning, with no attempt made to remove dead wood, is, therefore, now being recommended by some writers, though not by the body that hosted the trials, the Royal National Rose Society. Many growers believe that leaving jagged cuts and dead or unhealthy wood

on a rose bush cannot be good practice in the long run, and that the bushes on which it is left will eventually succumb to disease.

The results of another of the trials seem more promising and more practical. In this, the roses were roughly pruned, with no attempt to make angled cuts or indeed to cut to specific buds. Dead wood was removed but, as with the lighter method of pruning miniature roses (*see above*), the weak, twiggy stems that would normally have been removed were left on the bush. This produced new growth that was actually better than that of the conventionally-pruned roses, and on cluster-flowered roses also resulted in more flowers.

Until the trials have been running a good deal longer, this method cannot be officially recommended. In the meantime, however, there is no harm in experimenting with one or two bushes, pruning lightly as for the miniature rose (*see above*), to see if it suits your roses.

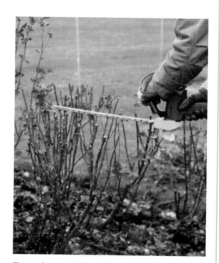

Pruning with a hedge trimmer
This crude approach appears to work in the short term, but its long-term effects are as yet unknown. A pair of shears will do the same job as a hedge trimmer, and more safely.

Standard Roses

Standard roses range from miniatures, ideal for a pot or tub, through half- and full-standard bush roses, with overall heights of about 1.1m (3½ft) and 1.35m (4½ft) respectively, to, tallest of all, weeping standards. All are formed by top-grafting the desired scion onto a tall, clear stem of, usually, *R. rugosa*, though growers are experimenting with other types, such as *R. laxa*, that live longer and are less prone to sucker. Standards must be permanently staked. Use a cane for miniature standards, but a preservative-treated wooden stake for larger types. The stake should reach up to the graft union (the weakest point on the stem) but not rub against it.

All standard roses must be pruned annually. Their specific pruning requirements depend on which type of rose forms the head. Pruning prevents the rose from becoming top-heavy, maintains a compact, symmetrical shape and improves flower quantity or quality.

TIME OF PRUNING
This varies according to the type of rose forming the head: repeat-flowerers in the dormant season, to encourage a continuous show of blooms on new growth, and after flowers have faded for those with a single flush of flowers.

Throughout the growing season, the routine tasks appropriate to all roses (*see p.303*) should also be carried out, particularly the removal of suckers at an early stage. Suckers may emerge from below the ground or on the clear stem; rub them from the stem when young whenever possible.

Patio rose grown as a standard
This small cluster-flowered rose (Little Bo Peep) grafted onto a tall, clear stem makes a charming container plant.

BUSH STANDARDS

Many cultivars of large-flowered and cluster-flowered bush roses are available trained as half- or full-standards, with clear stems of 75cm (2½ft) and 1.1m (3½ft) respectively. Standard patio, polyantha and miniature roses, usually with clear stems no taller than 50cm (20in), are also increasingly popular.

TRAINING AND PRUNING
Prune on planting and when established as for a normal bush, according to the type of rose that forms the head, whether large-flowered (*see p.307*), cluster-flowered (*see p.308*), patio, or miniature (*see p.309*). When shortening stems to a specified height, treat the graft point of the standard as if it were at ground level.

It is particularly important to maintain a balanced head; to achieve this, prune harder on the weaker side of the plant. Light pruning on the more vigorous side will keep the head in shape but discourage the production of strong shoots.

In regions with hard winters, autumn trimming (*see p.306*) is advisable to reduce the risk of long stems being buffeted and damaged by strong winds.

RENOVATION
A neglected standard rose (for example, in a newly acquired garden) should be pruned hard (*see p.305*) in winter or early spring. Do not waste further effort in attempting to rescue it if it does not make strong new growth in the following flowering season.

Established standard rose, early spring

Before pruning
The stems of this standard large-flowered bush rose were shortened in the autumn to prevent wind damage in winter. Now all danger of frost has passed, the rose should be pruned again to eliminate unproductive wood, create a balanced, open head and encourage vigorous new flowering growth.

Crossing shoot that may damage another stem should be removed

Remove dead, damaged and diseased growth

Sideshoots cut back to a healthy bud

Main stems shortened to suitably-placed buds and shoots

After pruning
Remaining healthy main stems have been cut back to about 20cm (8in) from the graft union, and their sideshoots shortened to two or three buds. Pruning has been slightly harder on the left side, with the aim of stimulating some new, strong shoots to create a better-balanced head.

WEEPING STANDARDS

A weeping rose standard is formed by top-grafting a rambler, climber or trailing ground-cover rose on to a clear stem, usually 1.5–2m (5–6ft) tall. When buying one, it is important to know which type forms the head; it will affect the look of the rose, the amount of pruning and training required and the time of pruning.

Only ramblers, with their long, flexible shoots, will weep naturally. The spreading ground-cover roses will not so much weep as droop from the graft point. Climbers need to be trained to overcome their natural tendency to grow upwards; only cultivars with flexible shoots are really suitable.

TRAINING AND PRUNING

Weeping standards are best left unpruned on planting and for their first couple of years to develop their form. Prune only to remove dead, diseased or damaged growth or to shorten weak, spindly shoots to a strong bud, encouraging fresh, vigorous shoots. The stems of

Umbrella frame
This proprietary frame, made of plastic-covered metal, acts as both stake and training frame to which shoots can be tied in. The resulting shape is more compact and formal than a free-growing weeping standard.

Tie in stems to create a well-balanced head

climbing cultivars are best trained downwards while still young, by tying them down evenly around a wire "umbrella" frame (*see above*).

Once established, prune according to the rose type: rambler (*see p.318*), climber (*see p.317*), or ground-cover rose (*see p.315*). Vigorous ramblers, such as 'Dorothy Perkins', can (if fed well) produce so many new stems that all flowered shoots can be removed each year, cutting back to the new basal shoots. On less vigorous roses, remove only one in two or three flowered stems, perhaps only every

other year, depending on how congested the head has become. Cut to shoots or buds facing upwards and outwards to produce a cascading effect. Ramblers easily weep to ground level, and stems may need to be shortened.

With climbers, prune to buds facing outwards and downwards to improve the shape of the plant. Ground-cover roses probably require least work of all, though they benefit from thinning if very twiggy and congested.

Renovate according to rose type (*see p.305*); ramblers usually respond best.

Pruning a rambler trained as a weeping standard after flowering

1 Cut the oldest flowered stems back to just above the graft union.

2 Prune other flowered stems to an outward-growing replacement shoot.

3 Prune any sideshoots to three or four buds.

4 Tip-prune stems that touch the ground.

5 Throughout the growing season, remove as seen any suckers on the rose's stem, preferably pinching them out at an early stage.

Shrub Roses

The shrub roses form a diverse group that spans the entire history of the genus *Rosa*, from species roses to modern shrubs developed in this century. Unlike bush roses, shrub roses, in general, flower on older wood, so they should be allowed to develop into

Upright habit

Spreading habit

permanent features, maintained by light, but regular, renewal pruning that keeps them shapely and with a healthy balance of older wood and young, vigorous growth. In their pruning requirements they are more similar to many deciduous flowering shrubs than to other rose groups.

While broad generalizations can be made about the various groupings, the exact pruning required depends much more on the individual cultivar's growth and flowering habit.

SPECIES ROSES

The truly wild roses and the hybrids close to them require very little pruning. Formative pruning, in the dormant season, consists of tipping back lightly any overlong stems. Once established, prune also in the dormant season, only to remove dead, damaged or weak shoots and, if necessary, correct an unbalanced shape. Cut weak stems back harder than those that are growing strongly, with the aim of stimulating vigorous regrowth. After reshaping, a rose may produce few flowers in the following year. Species roses that are performing poorly or have become an

EXAMPLES OF SPECIES ROSES AND CLOSELY RELATED HYBRIDS

ROSA NUTKANA 'PLENA'
   (syn. R. CALIFORNICA 'PLENA')
R. 'DUPONTII'
R. ECAE
R. FEDTSCHENKOANA
R. FOETIDA 'BICOLOR'
R. FORRESTIANA
R. GLAUCA (syn. R. RUBRIFOLIA)
R. HARISONII
R. MOYESII 'GERANIUM'
R. 'PAULII ROSEA'
R. VIRGINIANA
R. 'WOLLEY-DOD' (syn. R. POMIFERA
   'DUPLEX')
R. XANTHINA 'CANARY BIRD'

Rosa moyesii

unhealthy tangle of old growth may be rejuvenated by pruning; renovate as for gallicas (*see facing page*).

OLD GARDEN ROSES

Most of these roses may be pruned by one of two methods (*see facing page*). Other techniques are used for hybrid musks (*see p.314*), boursaults, noisettes and climbing bourbons (*see p.316*) and for hybrid perpetuals (*see p.320*).

Pruning an established gallica rose after flowering

1 *Completely remove one or two old, very woody, stems at the base.*

2 *Shorten laterals to a sideshoot or bud 5–15cm (2–6in) from a main stem.*

3 *Remove all dead, damaged or weak stems, as well as any rubbing against another stem, to keep the rose healthy.*

ALBAS, DAMASKS, MOSSES AND PROVENCES

Most of these rose groups should be pruned as soon as their single flush of summer flowering is over. One or two moss roses, however, do have a rather fitful second blossoming and so pruning for these should be slightly delayed.

On planting, lightly tip back long shoots. Once established, cut out dead, diseased and damaged wood and thin crossing stems. Then cut back main shoots and laterals by one-third of their length. In autumn, extra-long, whippy shoots may be shortened (*see below right*) so that they are not damaged if blown about in winter winds.

Old specimens can be renovated by thinning, cutting out all but the most vigorous young stems; these should be cut back by one-third. Renovate either after flowering or in the spring.

BOURBONS, CHINA ROSES AND PORTLANDS

These are pruned as for albas (*see above*) but in the dormant season, because they are repeat-flowering. Deadhead regularly in summer.

GALLICAS

These fairly dense old garden roses (which make excellent hedges) need only light prunin on planting. Tip back lightly any overlong stems and cut out one or two stems if growth is crowded. On established plants take out all dead, diseased and damaged stems in spring. Just after midsummer, when flowering has finished, thin growth by cutting back laterals to a main stem or to a shoot close to a main stem. Every one to three years, depending on the vigour of growth, take out at or near ground level one or two old main stems. In winter, use shears to clip over lightly gallicas grown as hedges. No attempt should be made at formal shaping.

Old and neglected gallicas will often respond well if pruned drastically in early spring, all but the most vigorous young stems being cut out completely.

Pruning an established alba rose after flowering

1 Cut back old main stems by about one-third.

2 Reduce laterals by about one-third to a strong, healthy, outward-facing shoot or bud.

Remove low-growing shoots that will arch over to touch the ground

Trimming alba roses, autumn
Shorten vigorous, overlong shoots protruding above the main outline of the shrub to avoid wind damage.

EXAMPLES OF OLD GARDEN ROSES

Alba roses
ROSA × 'ALBA MAXIMA'
R. × 'ALBA SEMIPLENA'
'BELLE AMOUR'
'CÉLESTE'
  (syn. 'CELESTIAL')
'FÉLICITÉ PARMENTIER'
'GREAT MAIDEN'S BLUSH'
'KÖNIGIN VON DÄNEMARK'

Bourbon roses
'BOULE DE NEIGE'
'MADAME ISAAC PEREIRE'
'SOUVENIR DE LA MALMAISON'
'VARIEGATA DI BOLOGNA'

China roses
'CÉCILE BRÜNNER'
R. × ODORATA 'MUTABILIS'
R. × ODORATA 'PALLIDA'
  (syn. 'OLD BLUSH CHINA')
'PERLE D'OR'

Damask roses
'ISPAHAN'
'MADAME HARDY'
'OMAR KHAYYAM'
'DE RESCHT'

Gallica roses
'ALAIN BLANCHARD'
'BELLE DE CRÉCY'

'CHARLES DE MILLS'
'DUC DE GUICHE'
'R. GALLICA 'OFFICINALIS'
'PRÉSIDENT DE SÈZE'
R. GALLICA 'VERSICOLOR'
  (syn. 'ROSA MUNDI')
'TRICOLORE DE FLANDRE'
'TUSCANY SUPERB'

Moss roses
'CAPITAINE JOHN INGRAM'
R. × CENTIFOLIA CRISTATA
  (syn. 'CHAPEAU DE NAPOLÉON')
'GÉNÉRAL KLÉBER'
'HENRI MARTIN'
'JAMES MITCHELL'

'JEANNE DE MONTFORT'
'WILLIAM LOBB'

Portland roses
'COMTE DE CHAMBORD'
'JACQUES CARTIER'
R. PORTLANDICA

Provence (centifolia) roses
'DE MEAUX'
'FANTIN-LATOUR'
'PETITE DE HOLLANDE'
'ROBERT LE DIABLE'
'SPONG'
'THE BISHOP'
'TOUR DE MALAKOFF'

MODERN SHRUB ROSES

This group covers a number of rose types developed over the last 100 years or so. Many combine the vigour of a species rose with the repeat-flowering characteristic of modern roses, so they are pruned during the dormant season, most usually in early spring. Most are upright, bushy and robust, reaching heights of 1.2–2m (4–6ft), and make impressive specimen plants. Others have more dense and spreading growth, and are commonly referred to as "ground-cover roses" (see facing page).

Some modern shrubs, such as 'Nevada' and 'Marguerite Hilling', need only light pruning (see below). The cluster-flowered modern shrubs are simply large cultivars of cluster-flowered bush roses, and can be pruned similarly (see p.308), shortening main stems by only one-third, to keep the plant's stature; cut back laterals by two-thirds. Other named groups of modern shrubs require slightly different approaches.

HYBRID MUSKS

These vigorous, repeat-flowering, leafy shrubs and others of similar habit (see right) require little or no formative pruning. Prune established plants in the dormant season, removing dead, diseased and damaged wood and removing one to three of the oldest, least productive stems. Cut back main stems by up to one-third, and laterals by half.

Supporting shrub roses

Two low stakes with strong twine or plastic chainlink nailed between them form a useful support for the stems of lax shrub roses, giving them a more upright habit. Underplanting can help disguise the support.

RUGOSAS

These are mostly turn-of-the-century selections or hybrids of *R. rugosa*; upright, thorny, repeat-flowering shrubs with bright green, wrinkled (rugose) foliage that colours well in autumn. Some have bright red, tomato-shaped hips.

They require little or no formative pruning. Prune established plants in the dormant season, tipping back long stems and occasionally taking out an old stem completely. To renovate, thin more drastically, taking out several old stems and cutting back one in two or three that remain by up to half (see p.305).

EXAMPLES OF MODERN SHRUB ROSES

Cluster-flowered-type
CHINATOWN
EYE PAINT
'FOUNTAIN'
FRANCINE AUSTIN
'FRED LOADS'
'FRITZ NOBIS'
JACQUELINE DU PRÉ
WESTERLAND

Hybrid musks and others resembling them in habit
'BUFF BEAUTY'
'CORNELIA'
'GOLDEN WINGS'
'KATHLEEN FERRIER'
'PENELOPE'
ROSY CUSHION
SMARTY

Rugosas
'AGNES'
'BELLE POITEVINE'
'BLANCHE DOUBLE DE COUBERT'
'FIMBRIATA'
'F.J. GROOTENDORST'
'FRU DAGMAR HASTRUP'
'PINK GROOTENDORST'
'ROSERAIE DE L'HAŸ'
R. RUGOSA 'ALBA'
'SCABROSA'

Light pruning of an established modern shrub rose

1 When growth becomes crowded, remove one or two old unproductive stems at the base.

2 To maintain a compact habit and encourage flowering, tip-prune a proportion of sideshoots at the periphery of the plant.

3 Remove any dead, diseased or damaged growth, cutting to a healthy bud.

GROUND-COVER ROSES

There are two kinds of ground-cover roses: the modern shrubs, and the creeping ramblers. Each has a distinctive growth habit. Both need pruning mainly to keep them to their allotted space. They may also be used to form weeping standards (*see p.311*).

MODERN SHRUB TYPE

These low-growing, spreading roses – generally less than 60cm (2ft) tall – offer dense leaf coverage in summer, providing good weed suppression, but, being deciduous, they are bare in winter. They can also be grown in containers. Prune those that are repeat-flowering in spring, the rest in summer, after flowering.

Little or no formative pruning is required. Once established, cut out any dead or diseased stems and tip-prune main stems – or shorten them if they extend over their intended boundary. Open up the centre of the bush a little by shortening laterals. If practicable, deadhead in the flowering season. These roses usually respond well to hard cutting back if necessary.

CREEPING RAMBLER TYPE

These roses are closely allied to ramblers such as *R. wichuraiana*. Their long, flexible stems hug the ground, making them ideal for an awkward bank, for example. The stems root where they touch the ground, and may reach 3m (10ft) or more in length, the laterals forming a substantial mound.

Lightly prune in summer after flowering, only to cut stems back to upright shoots to keep them within bounds. To increase flower production, spread and peg down stems (*see* Pegging down, *p.320*). If more drastic pruning becomes necessary, renovate as for ramblers (*see p.305*).

Rambler-type ground-cover rose

The vigorous, scrambling, rambler type of ground-cover rose is ideal for wilder areas of the garden. Stems will root into the ground, increasing the rose's spread. Little pruning is needed except to keep the rose within bounds.

Vigorous first-year stems can be pegged down

Second-year stems become prostrate with the weight of flowering shoots

Shrub-type ground-cover rose

The neat modern shrub type of ground-cover rose (*left*) is a small, compact bush with a spreading rather than upright habit, ideal for planting in groups for low-maintenance beds or to cover awkward slopes.

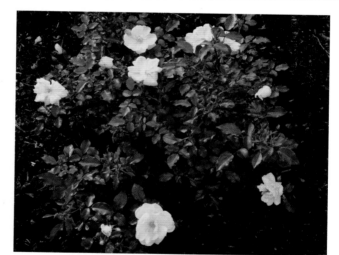

EXAMPLES OF GROUND-COVER ROSES

Modern shrub type
AVON, KENT, SURREY & SUSSEX
BONICA
FERDY
FIONA
FLOWER CARPET
PINK BELLS
'RAUBRITTER'
'THE FAIRY'

Creeping rambler type
CHILTERNS
GROUSE, PARTRIDGE, PHEASANT
R. × JACKSONII 'MAX GRAF'
'NOZOMI'
SNOW CARPET
SWANY

Roses for hanging baskets

The "county" series of shrub-type ground-cover roses, such as Avon, will trail attractively when planted in a hanging basket or a manger on a wall. Although roses generally make good container plants, they should not be kept in a container as shallow as this one for more than two growing seasons.

Climbing and Rambler Roses

These roses can be trained to create a wide range of effects (*see* Special Training, *pp.319–325*) but are most commonly grown against walls and fences. The aim when pruning is to create a strong, well-shaped plant that will bear many healthy new flowering shoots each year. How this is done depends on whether the rose is a climber or a rambler: they differ in their growth and flowering habits, and thus in their pruning needs.

The main aim when training climbers and ramblers against a flat surface is to train as much growth as near horizontal as possible. Initial fan training of the main stems allows flexible shoots to be trained horizontally, giving maximum coverage and an even distribution of flowers (*see* Horizontal training, *p.11*). If the stems were all allowed to grow directly upwards they would flower only at their tops. For awkward spaces where horizontal training is not possible, such as a narrow area of wall between two windows, choose either a large shrub rose or a climbing rose suitable for pillars, as recommended for vertical features (*see p.320*).

Before the rose is planted, provide a system of horizontal wires to which the shoots can be tied. Set the lowest wire

Wall-trained climbing rose
Horizontal training is the key to maximizing the flowering potential of wall-trained roses.

45cm (18in) off the ground, and space subsequent wires 30cm (12in) apart. Use strong, galvanized wire, strung through vine eyes to hold it about 8cm (3in) from the surface. This will allow space for air to circulate between the rose and wall or fence, and so help to keep disease at bay.

Plant climbers and ramblers at least 30cm (1ft) from the wall, with roots spreading away from the wall, so they are not in a rain shadow. Their shoots will probably reach the lowest wire but if not, bamboo canes can be used to guide and support them; remove the canes in the second year.

MODERN CLIMBERS

4 | 12

m | ft

Modern climbers are no more than very tall bush roses, with fairly stiff shoots that need support and tying in. Although they lend themselves well to many different training methods (*see pp.319–325*) they are most commonly grown against fences and walls. The aim here must be to fan out the main stems so that laterals can be trained sideways.

WHEN TO PRUNE

Like modern bush roses, climbers are mostly repeat-flowering, so the main pruning season is also the same – from autumn, after the sequence of flowering has finished, to early spring. It is as well to prune in autumn, so that any long, whippy shoots can be shortened or tied in before strong winter winds can blow them about and damage them; in cool climates, the extra protection afforded by the wall should minimize any frost damage. Deadhead and tie in growth throughout the growing season.

EXAMPLES OF MODERN CLIMBERS

'ALOHA'
ALTISSIMO
BANTRY BAY
'COMPASSION'
'DANSE DU FEU'
DUBLIN BAY
'GLOIRE DE DIJON'
GOLDEN SHOWERS
HANDEL
'MADAME ALFRED CARRIÈRE'
'NEW DAWN'

'PARADE'
'PINK PERPÉTUÉ'
'SCHOOLGIRL'
SUMMER WINE
SYMPATHIE
'WHITE COCKADE'
'WILLIAM ALLEN RICHARDSON'
'ZÉPHIRINE DROUHIN'

FORMATIVE TRAINING

Climbers are sold with much longer shoots than those of bedding roses, and these should not be pruned (except to tidy up minor damage), leaving plenty of buds from which new shoots can break when growth begins. It is particularly important to leave stems intact where the rose is a sport of a bush rose (for these, the cultivar name will be prefixed by the word "climbing", as in 'Climbing Iceberg'), because pruning at this stage may encourage it to revert to its original bush form.

Once growth begins, if the main stem or stems are slow to branch, tip-prune them to the first strong bud (outward-facing on outer stems) to encourage laterals to develop. Fan out the main

stems from the start (*see facing page, above*), spacing them evenly, and tie in laterals, training them to the horizontal, as they develop. Always cover the lower parts of the wall or fence from the beginning; while new shoots will nearly always break from horizontal stems to grow upwards into gaps, it is difficult to fill in gaps lower down.

The stems must be guided while still young and pliable and tied in, well spaced, to form a strong, well-structured framework. Until this is established no other pruning is necessary, except to remove dead, damaged, diseased or spindly, leafless growth and any suckers, and to deadhead repeat-flowering climbers to encourage subsequent flowering (*see p.303*).

ESTABLISHED PRUNING

Once the rose has filled the allotted space, its framework branches are regularly renewed, removing old growth in favour of vigorous young stems. At the edges, growth that needs shortening back can be pruned at any time, along with any other routine tasks and the tying-in of new growth to the wires. Deadhead (*see p.303*) to extend the flowering season. Once this is over, prune flowered sideshoots to stimulate the remaining portion to develop new flowering shoots in the next year. Once the stem itself becomes less productive of flowers, usually after no more than three years, cut it to a lower new shoot (*see* Renewal pruning, *p.302*), tying this in to fill the gap. Remove completely any growth that is weak or diseased.

On a mature climber, an entire main stem that is old and unproductive can be cut to the base, to stimulate new growth. If the climber becomes bare at the base, or has been neglected, more extensive renovation (*see p.305*) may be necessary.

Wall-trained climber, year 1, summer

1 *Tie in new growth to build up the framework, training sideshoots near-horizontally along the wires where possible.*

3 *Tip-prune vigorous non-branching main shoots by 5–8cm (2–3in) to encourage branching. Make an angled cut just above a leaf or bud.*

Canes tied in to wires guided the original stems to wall

Stems were tied to canes

Rose planted 45cm (18in) from wall

2 *Remove any dead, diseased or damaged growth.*

Established modern climber, pruning in autumn

1 *Prune flowered shoots by two-thirds of their length, making angled cuts just above a healthy shoot or bud.*

3 *Check new growth tied in throughout the season. Reposition or shorten any shoots that have grown to rub against others.*

2 *Cut out completely any unhealthy or spindly and leafless growth.*

4 *Where an old stem has become less productive, prune it back to a healthy shoot, tying this in, or to a low bud.*

5 *Shorten stems where they have overgrown the rose's allotted space.*

RAMBLERS

5 | 15

m | ft

EXAMPLES OF RAMBLER ROSES

'Albéric barbier'
'Bobbie james'
'Emily gray'
'Félicité perpétue'
'François juranville'
'Goldfinch'
'Paul's himalayan musk' (syn. 'Paul's himalayan rambler')

'Rambling rector'
R. multiflora 'grevillei' (syn. Seven sisters rose)
'Seagull'
'Silver moon'
'The garland'
'Veilchenblau'
'Wedding day'

Rambler roses, whether species or hybrids close in character to their wild forebears, are vigorous, regularly producing new flexible stems at or near ground level, and flowering most freely on wood produced in the previous year. They are pruned in summer, once their single flush of flowers is over.

With their wild, rampant habit, ramblers are generally used for informal effects. While they often flourish and flower perfectly well without pruning, if a rambler is to be a prominent feature in any but the wildest of gardens, training and pruning will be required to avoid a hopeless tangle of stems. However, it is because their stems are so long and flexible that ramblers can be trained to create such a variety of effects (*see* Special Training, *pp.319–325*). Their stems are easily trained horizontally on a fence or to form a screen. A chainlink or other openwork fence is preferable to a solid fence or wall; ramblers are very prone to mildew, which is encouraged by poor air circulation.

FORMATIVE TRAINING

Ramblers should be pruned on planting to stimulate growth from the base. Remove dead, damaged or weak and twiggy growth, and cut the main stems back to about 40cm (16in) from the ground. Fan out the shoots and tie the stems in near the horizontal as they grow to cover the allotted space evenly.

ESTABLISHED PRUNING

Once the allotted area is well covered, thin and shorten excess growth after the summer flowering. Ramblers make much more new growth from the base of the plant than climbers, and this should be encouraged by cutting out one in three main stems to the base. Remove the oldest stems, cutting them in several places and teasing small sections out: pulling an entire stem right through the remaining plant will cause damage.

It is often recommended that all flowered stems should be cut down and new ones tied in their place. This is not necessary, since ramblers will flower very well on the same wood for several years, and it will also prevent the rose ever becoming a large and established garden feature. However, it is a useful technique either for renovating a rambler (*see p.305*) or for growing one (particularly vigorous cultivars like 'Dorothy Perkins') in a small space. Feed the rose well in the spring following hard pruning.

Established rambler rose, pruning after flowering

4 Tip-prune the remaining leading shoots by 5–8cm (2–3in) to encourage branching.

1 Cut one in three of the old flowered stems back to ground level, removing them in short sections.

2 Shorten sideshoots by about two-thirds to encourage them to develop flowering sideshoots for the following season.

3 Throughout the growing season, secure new shoots to wires with garden twine or ties, allowing room for the shoots to expand.

Special Training

One of the great attractions of roses, particularly the climbing and rambling cultivars, is that they can be grown in so many different ways. They will not only cover walls and fences, but also grow as hedges or screens on a rigid framework, on vertical structures such as tripods and obelisks (*see p.320*), on pergolas and arches (*see p.322*), along ropes to form swags (*see p.324*), and, for the most artless of all effects, through trees or other host plants (*see p.325*). As with all climbing plants, careful training is nearly always the foundation of the best results. It ensures that a structure is densely and evenly covered not only with foliage but also with flowers, and that the trained form is not lost through rampant growth. A rose arch over a path, for example, can become a hazard, not a feature, if the archway is filled with long, whippy rose shoots.

A rose cannot use its thorns to hook and grip on to artificial supports such as arches, tripods and struts, so shoots must be tied into position. Do not tie them directly to supports, particularly to brick or concrete pillars, as the shoots will be damaged by rubbing. Knock in nails or staples or insert vine eyes where ties are needed – or, on a large support such as a pillar, attach vertical wires or a narrow strip of trellis or netting. Around thinner supports such as ironwork, use twine tied in figures-of-eight around the stem and support, or purpose-made ties, to prevent the stems chafing.

Rose swags
One of the most popular features for adding height and graceful curves to formal rose displays, swags and catenaries (rows of swags) are produced by training roses along thick rope.

With frequent tying-in, shoots can be directed to grow exactly where they are needed, and to maximize their flowering potential where it is wanted. Where the flowering display is required high up, for example on the roof of a pergola or in a host tree, train the shoots directly upwards, pruning sideshoots to direct energy into vertical growth until the objective has been reached; then allow the rose to branch naturally.

When shoots are trained directly upwards, they flower largely at the top: a natural inhibitor (*see also p.11*) prevents buds lower down from forming flowering shoots. Training shoots horizontally breaks this habit, and

sideshoots will develop and bloom along the stem's length.

Horizontal training is easy against a large, flat surface, where shoots can be fanned out, but on a narrow surface (a small screen, or the side of a deep arch, for example), some ingenuity is needed. One approach is to train shoots in a serpentine or "pretzel" shape, bringing them back on themselves to maximize horizontal growth (*see below left*). Alternatively, wind shoots round in a spiral up the support. This encourages uniform flowering all the way up, and is the best way of covering three-dimensional structures such as tripods or obelisks.

Spiral training
Spiral training of roses on vertical supports will encourage flowering at all levels. Train the shoots when young and still pliable.

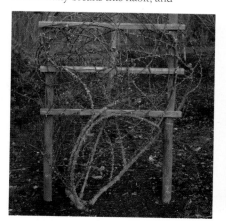

Rose screen
Training shoots in serpentine fashion on a narrow flat surface will produce a better display than will a narrow fan.

Edging for paths and beds
Rustic poles, bent canes (*as above*), or even lengths of netting stretched between posts can provide support for rose stems.

Pegging down roses

Rose stems can be trained completely horizontally at ground level using a technique known as "pegging down". This was popularly used in Victorian England for the tall and leggy hybrid perpetual roses, which tend to flower only at the tips of shoots if allowed to grow freely. Any rose with flexible shoots is suitable for pegging down.

Pegging down produces a low, dense mound of flowers without restricting choice only to those roses recommended for ground cover (see p.315). The main stems are fanned out like the spokes of a wheel, resulting in masses of vertical flowering shoots. The stems are pegged to the ground, or tied to wires pegged into the ground, either criss-crossing the bed or in a cartwheel pattern; the latter is ideal for covering a manhole cover with growth; entire wire "spokes", with the rose attached, can be lifted clear.

Give the rose a growing season to become established. After flowering, carefully bend the stems down to near ground level and either peg them down (see below left) or tie them to wires. Cut back all laterals (see below) to 10–15cm (4–6in). If starting with a mature rose, some of the older flowered stems should be removed (or even all of them, if there are plenty of new stems).

In following summers, deadhead repeat-flowering roses regularly. In autumn, cut out all weak growths and two to three older main stems, pegging or tying down vigorous young stems as replacements. Shorten flowered laterals to 10–15cm (4–6in).

Pegging down
The simplest method is to peg down shoots directly using hoops made from galvanized wire. Stems can also be tied to low wires fixed to pegs.

Pegging down a hybrid perpetual

1 Trim back the leading growth on each pegged-down stem to confine to the allotted space.

2 Shorten all the upward-growing laterals to 10–15cm (4–6in).

Training roses on vertical features

Rose-covered tripods or obelisks give height and colourful focal points to planting schemes. The need for access to train and prune should be borne in mind when siting such features. Roses suited to this form of training are the less vigorous climbers, usually less than 3m (10ft) in height when mature, that are often sold as "pillar" roses. Bourbon roses, which can be unruly if left to their own devices, are also suitable, as are some large, vigorous, old and modern shrub roses; these often grow even taller against a support than when in open ground. Most ramblers are too vigorous for narrow, free-standing features.

Careful training is needed (see right). Spiralling the shoots either around individual "legs" or the entire structure will encourage flowering laterals to develop at all levels. Where only one or two sides of a pillar can be used, and shoots have to grow upwards, choose a cultivar known to flower well at all levels (for example, Golden Showers). If stems become bare at the base, they can be masked by another plant.

A single plant will take several years to establish fully, the time varying according to the cultivar. For a quicker and attractive effect, use several roses on one structure – for example, one up each leg of a tripod. The roses should be matched for vigour, and pruning will

Horizontal training on vertical features

Without horizontal training The stems of this climbing rose have simply been tied into the framework of this rustic tripod as they extend vertically. The result is that flowers are, with few exceptions, clustered at the top, and main stems are bare of sideshoots and flowers lower down.

With horizontal training The main stems of this rose have been wound around and tied into this ironwork obelisk in spirals. Bringing them down more towards the horizontal has stimulated buds to break and develop into flowering laterals all along their length (see also Horizontal Training, p.11).

be simpler if they require the same regime. Alternatively, use climbing annuals or other climbing plants that either die back, or are cut back, each year, leaving the rose stems clear for pruning.

WHEN TO PRUNE

Prune roses that have a single flush of flowers in summer, once they have finished flowering. Prune repeat-flowering roses during the dormant season, between autumn and early spring. Pruning in autumn has the advantage that long growths can be shortened or tied in before any risk of damage by winter winds.

FORMATIVE PRUNING AND TRAINING

Plant the rose about 25cm (10in) from the base of the structure, and splay the stems out around it. Climbers and shrub roses need not be pruned on planting except to trim off any dead, damaged or spindly wood. If a rambler is being used, cut its stems back on planting (*see p.318*). Throughout the growing season, train in growth while it is young and pliable; modern climbers in particular develop stout inflexible shoots quite quickly. Tie them in evenly spaced spirals up the structure. Avoid, where possible, tying shoots so that they cross.

PRUNING ESTABLISHED ROSES

With climbers, maintain a permanent framework of spiralled main stems just as on a wall-trained climbing rose (*see p.317*); cut back flowered shoots to an outward-facing bud or shoot. When growth becomes crowded, older stems can be cut back to vigorous new replacement shoots lower down or removed completely, with new stems growing from ground level being trained in as replacements. With ramblers, cut back flowered sideshoots by two-thirds of their length, and tip back the main stems. Every year remove one or two of the oldest main stems (*see also p.317*).

Old and neglected roses often need more drastic pruning. The best course is to take the entire rose down, lay it on the ground and unravel it. Once the rose has been pruned (*see Renovation, p.305*) its stems can be wound back around the support and tied in.

Pruning an established climber on a tripod

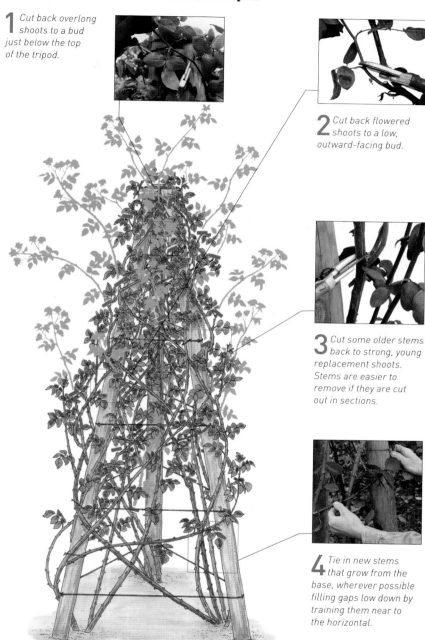

1 Cut back overlong shoots to a bud just below the top of the tripod.

2 Cut back flowered shoots to a low, outward-facing bud.

3 Cut some older stems back to strong, young replacement shoots. Stems are easier to remove if they are cut out in sections.

4 Tie in new stems that grow from the base, wherever possible filling gaps low down by training them near to the horizontal.

RECOMMENDED FOR VERTICAL FEATURES

ALCHYMIST (modern climber)
'ALOHA' (modern climber)
ALTISSIMO (modern climber)
'AMERICAN PILLAR' (modern climber)
BANTRY BAY (modern climber)
'BOULE DE NEIGE' (Bourbon)
CHINATOWN (cluster-flowered shrub)
'CLIMBING CÉCILE BRÜNNER'
CONSTANCE SPRY (large-flowered shrub)
DORTMUND (modern climber)

DUBLIN BAY (modern climber)
'GLOIRE DE DIJON' (climbing noisette)
GOLDEN SHOWERS (modern climber)
'GRUSS AN TEPLITZ' (China)
HANDEL (modern climber)
JOSEPH'S COAT (cluster-flowered shrub)
LAURA FORD (modern climber)
'LOUISE ODIER' (Bourbon)
'MADAME ISAAC PEREIRE' (Bourbon)
'MADAME PIERRE OGER' (Bourbon)

'MAIGOLD' (modern climber)
'PINK PERPÉTUÉ' (modern climber)
'REINE VICTORIA' (Bourbon)
R. × ODORATA 'MUTABILIS' (China)
SUMMER WINE (modern climber)
'SWAN LAKE' (modern climber)
WARM WELCOME (modern climber)
'WHITE COCKADE' (modern climber)

Training roses on a pergola

The choice of rose or roses to clothe a pergola will depend on the structure's size and strength. Ramblers are obvious choices for large pergolas, and those with stout oak posts or brick pillars supporting strong wooden crossbeams can comfortably accommodate even the most vigorous, such as 'Seagull' or 'Bobbie James'. If climbers are preferred for their long, repeat-flowering season, a large pergola may need one rose planted at every post. One or two plants, however, will be quite sufficient for pergolas no more than 2m (6ft) in length, particularly if they are of the "rustic pole" variety, as these will not bear the weight of a large rambler.

If the rose is to be grown over the top, its stems must be trained to turn almost at right-angles at the top of the pillars; ramblers, or the climbing cultivars with more flexible stems, are much easier to use. For large pergolas, use any of the roses recommended for growing up large host trees (*see p.325*); for small pergolas, use those roses suitable for smaller trees.

Since the main aim is to obtain a display of flowers along the crossbeams, this is most quickly achieved by training the stems straight up the pillars (*see below*). It is unlikely, however, that these vertical stems will bear many flowers after the first few years.

Combining roses on a pergola
A combination of ramblers, climbers and pillar roses has been used to clothe this large pergola, whose open roof allows sunlight to reach the inner and under sides of the structure.

Flexible-stemmed climbers and ramblers can be spiral-trained around a pillar just as for a tripod (*see p.320*), but if stems are then trained on across the top, it is probable that, with its energies directed into

blooming profusely across the top, the rose will also become bare at the base. The most reliable way to obtain flowers on both the pillar and the top is to plant another rose at the base of the pillar. To clothe a pillar, use one of the roses recommended for vertical features (*see p.321*): they are usually less than 3m (10ft) in height and flower well on their lower stems.

Alternatively, use other plants: herbaceous climbers that will die back, or can be pruned back, in winter (for example, some clematis) give access to the rose stems for pruning. Climbing annuals enable different combinations to be tried each year (*see also* Training climbers on a pergola, *p.258*).

FORMATIVE TRAINING

Fix staples, wires or strips of trellis to the framework of the pergola to give plenty of attachment points for ties. If you are aiming for a solid "roof" of greenery and flowering stems, attach battens or string wires between the crossbeams.

Plant the rose about 25cm (10in) from the foot of the pillar, and tie in its shoots. If you are planting two roses, place them at each side of the pillar, not one inside and one outside the pergola, or the inner rose may be too shaded to flourish. With climbers, no pruning is necessary, except to trim away any damaged growth. Ramblers should be pruned to encourage strong basal growth (*see p.318*). Tie in growth as it develops. Once the rose reaches the top of the pillar, start guiding the shoots across the crossbeams, spacing

Training a rose up a pergola pillar

Main stems will reach canopy most quickly if sideshoots are removed

Stems on far right and left can be taken round and tied in to pillar's sides

1 *Remove any weak shoots, cutting them out at ground level, to encourage stronger shoots to grow rapidly.*

2 *Space out and tie in the remaining stems, attaching them with figure-of-eight ties to wires or struts held slightly away from the pillar's surface. Remove any sideshoots to encourage vertical growth.*

them evenly and tying them in. To make the necessary right-angles and achieve even coverage, it is often impossible to avoid crossing stems: check them occasionally and reposition if necessary to avoid or minimize chafing.

ESTABLISHED PRUNING

Particular care must be taken when pruning roses on pergolas; the work often has to be done from a ladder. Follow the guidelines for pruning climbers (*see p.316*) and ramblers (*see p.318*) but prune less hard. Plentiful, billowing growth is more desirable on free-standing structures than it is on walls, and will soften the regular lines of the pillars and beams.

A neglected or overgrown rose trained on a pergola is difficult to renovate *in situ*. Cutting out a number of entire main stems to encourage new basal growth will be a formidable task, and will create gaps that may take several years to fill satisfactorily. Although the procedure is laborious, the easiest way to renovate a neglected specimen involves untying the rose, laying it out on the ground, pruning it selectively, then tying the remaining stems in again, evenly spaced.

Training over an arch

Arches can be made from a variety of materials, ranging from rustic poles and trellis fixed to a wooden framework, to lightweight metal tubing, which is sometimes plastic-covered. When training a rose to cover an arch, the main aims are to achieve even coverage (to avoid all the flowers and growth being "bunched" at the top) and, if the arch is to be walked through, to keep growth to the outside.

Pruning a climber on a pergola, autumn

1 Deadheading where practical will improve flowering: cut to a low bud (in leaf axil).

2 As the rose matures, and new basal stems develop, cut out oldest stems at the base, teasing them out in sections.

3 Tie in new shoots. Wire staples make useful attachment points: do not tie twine around the entire beam and stems, or they will rub.

New stem has developed from near base of pillar

Although the rose can be trained up and over the top of the arch, it cannot easily be trained down again on the other side, so two roses should be planted. The choice of cultivars is partly governed by the size of the arch. Any of the cultivars recommended for vertical features (*see p.321*) will grow well up the sides of an arch, although the modern climbers with more inflexible stems may be harder to train across the top. 'Climbing Iceberg'

Rose arches
A series of arches draws the eye to a gateway that acts as a focal point: it is important that the roses clothing the arches do not become overgrown, obscuring the perspective and making it difficult to walk down the path without being snagged by thorny stems.

or 'Compassion' both have pliable stems. Thornless cultivars, such as 'Zéphirine Drouhin', are good choices for arches spanning paths. An alternative is to use one of the smaller traditional ramblers, such as 'Albéric Barbier', recommended for growing into smaller host trees and shrubs (*see p.325*). They are not over-vigorous and make plenty of growth from the base, although they flower only at midsummer. At all costs, avoid large ramblers such as 'Seagull', as they will swiftly engulf the structure.

TRAINING AND PRUNING
Roses should always be planted and trained on the outside of the supports so that access beneath the arch is not restricted by thorny stems. If it is difficult to tie the rose directly to the framework, provide extra anchorage points by attaching netting or mesh to the structure.

If the sides of the arch are wide, fan the shoots out at first as on a wall or fence (*see p.317*); on a simple, narrow structure, let all the stems grow vertically, then draw them and their laterals over the top of the arch.

Once established, prune and, if necessary, renovate as for wall-trained climbers and ramblers (*see pp.218–220*). Throughout the growing season, tie in or, if growth is crowded, shorten vigorous upright or outward-growing shoots that spoil the form of the arch.

Training roses along ropes

A rose trained along a heavy rope hung between two posts makes an attractive swag. A row of swags, often seen each side of a path, is known as a catenary. Traditional ship's rope looks best, dipping by about 60cm (2ft) midway between the posts. With a single rope, 2.1–2.4m (7–8ft) posts produce the best effect at eye level. The rope should be 1.2–1.5m (4–5ft) longer than the distance between posts. For "double-decker" swags, use posts 30–60cm (1–2ft) taller, attaching the second rope 60cm (2ft) below the topmost one.

Vigorous roses with flexible stems are needed. Almost all ramblers are suitable, as are climbers with pliable stems (*see box on facing page*). When using several cultivars, match them for vigour as well as colour, so that there is an even distribution of flowers and foliage.

FORMATIVE TRAINING
Plant one rose at the base of each post. On a single swag, their shoots will be trained to meet at the middle of the rope. With catenaries, each rose is usually trained in the same direction except for the one planted at the last post, whose shoots are trained to meet the preceding rose. Plant the roses 30cm (1ft) from the posts, and prune on planting according to the rose type, trimming climbers (*see p.316*) and cutting ramblers back harder (*see p.318*). To produce flowers quickly

Ropes and wires
The most secure method of attachment for the rope is to drill a hole at the top of the post, thread the rope through and nail its end firmly down. Attach vertical wires to each side of the post, using vine eyes to keep the wires about 5cm (2in) from the post's sides.

along the rope, train the roses straight up the post. When they reach the top (this may take two growing seasons), bend the shoots over and tie them on to the rope. Where two ropes have been used, allocate half the main stems to one rope, and half to the other. If there are insufficient main stems (as may be the case with climbers), guide laterals along the lower rope and allow the leaders to grow up, then along the upper one.

While ties should not constrict the rose stems, they should be tight around the rope so that they do not swivel and allow the rose to "slump" under its own weight beneath the rope. Tying in with garden twine is time-consuming but is the most effective way of attaching stems inconspicuously.

Guiding shoots along the rope
The shoots will need not only winding around but also attaching to the rope. Always tie shoots to the rope, not to other shoots, to avoid damage by chafing.

ESTABLISHED PRUNING
For the first few years, prune as recommended for the type of rose. As the rose develops, wayward shoots will spoil the line of the swag. More systematic treatment, perhaps every two years, will be needed, particularly for ramblers. Untie and unravel the rose from the rope (*see below*) and cut back the oldest stems to strong new shoots. If it is impractical to unravel the swag, trace older stems through the tangle, cutting at intervals and teasing out the cut sections until a strong new shoot is reached. Then tie the remaining growth back in position. If a swag is overgrown, remove one or two of the oldest main stems at the base, cutting to a younger stem if one exists. For more drastic renovation, *see p.305*.

Pruning an established swag rose

Before pruning
Vigorous new shoots, encouraged by the horizontal training of the rose's main stems, are growing upright, then arching over, spoiling the line of the swag. If simply tied down, growth around the rope will be too congested.

1 *Wearing stout gloves (if thorned stems are very long and whippy, safety goggles are also advisable), carefully detach the rose stems from the rope and unwind them until each main stem with its sideshoots can be distinguished from the others.*

2 *Prune each of the flowered main stems back to a vigorous shoot. This will usually create an "L"-shape in the direction of growth. Sideshoots growing in the direction of the rope will be easier to manage when tying in.*

3 *Taking care not to damage growth at the junction between the sideshoots and the main stem, gently straighten the "L"-shaped stems and wind them around and attach them to the rope.*

Training roses up a host tree

Roses with long, arching stems tend to scramble over and through nearby plants with no encouragement, but more deliberate training is needed to produce the spectacular effect of a climber or rambler that has colonized a "host" tree.

SITING AND PLANTING
The host must be healthy and strong to bear the weight and the added wind resistance of the rose's stems and foliage. It must be of a size and vigour not to be overwhelmed by the choice of rose – a moderately vigorous climber such as 'New Dawn', for example, would be suitable for an apple tree, while rampant ramblers such as 'Rambling Rector' need much larger trees.

Position the rose on the windward side of the host, so that the prevailing wind blows any wayward shoots into, rather than out of, the tree. The shoots will make their way towards the sunnier side of the crown, so do not choose a host on the sunny boundary of your garden if you want to fully appreciate the rose in flower. Do not plant the rose near the base of the trunk, where the ground is dry and shaded.

FORMATIVE TRAINING
A stout rope, anchored to a peg in the ground and tied either to the tree's trunk or to a low branch, may be used to guide the rose shoots until they are long enough to tie to the lower branches of the host. Thereafter, ramblers should clamber unaided towards the upper branches. Climbers, with stiffer shoots, may need

Climbing rose in a host tree
Careful siting and initial training are needed to guide the rose up to a tree fork; it will then follow the natural tendency of plants to grow upwards towards the light.

more guidance, and are also more likely to be damaged by wind: in autumn, when leaves are shed and you can see the rose clearly, secure loose whippy shoots to branches, wherever it is possible to do so.

ESTABLISHED PRUNING
It is extremely difficult – but fortunately unnecessary – to regularly prune the very vigorous ramblers that are favourites for growing up trees.

If you do need to tackle a rose that has got out of hand, prune hard either after flowering or in winter, when it may be easier to tackle the job because the leaves of the tree have fallen. Removing entire main stems at the base is the best course, cutting them out in sections; if this is impractical, judiciously shorten top growth to strong replacement shoots. A well-established, vigorous rambler will recover well from almost any amount of trimming and pruning.

Length of rubber hose threaded onto rope protects branch fork

Planting and initial training
Plant the rose at least 1–1.2m (3–4ft) away from the tree base, so that it does not have to compete with the tree for moisture, nutrients and light. The denser and lower the tree's crown, the further from the trunk the rose must be planted in order to receive enough light to thrive in its early years. Twist or tie all the shoots around a stout rope, then the lower branches of the tree, for the first two or three years.

VIGOROUS ROSES SUITABLE FOR TRAINING UP LARGE TREES
'BOBBIE JAMES'
'BRENDA COLVIN'
R. FILIPES 'KIFTSGATE'
'KEW RAMBLER'
'PAUL'S HIMALAYAN MUSK' (SYN. 'PAUL'S HIMALAYAN RAMBLER')
'RAMBLING RECTOR'
'SEAGULL'
'SIR CEDRIC MORRIS'
'SUPER EXCELSA'
'WEDDING DAY'

LESS VIGOROUS ROSES FOR SMALL TREES OR LARGE SHRUBS
'ALBÉRIC BARBIER'
'CLIMBING CÉCILE BRÜNNER'
'COMPLICATA'
'GOLDFINCH'
'NEW DAWN'
'SANDERS WHITE RAMBLER'
'VEILCHENBLAU'

Glossary

The glossary explains horticultural terms that are used in this book. Fuller explanations and illustrations may be found elsewhere by looking up the term in the index.

ADHESIVE PADS Suckering tips of tendrils that grip surfaces for support.

ADVENTITIOUS BUD Latent or dormant bud on the stem or root, often invisible until stimulated into growth.

AERIAL ROOT A root produced from a stem above ground level, sometimes able to cling to or twine around supports.

ALTERNATE Single buds, leaves or stems alternating at different levels on opposite sides of a stem.

ANGLE OF ATTACHMENT Angle at which a shoot develops from main stem.

APEX The tip of a stem.

APICAL BUD The bud at the tip of a stem.

APICAL DOMINANCE Controlling influence of the apical bud over the growth of a stem, which restricts the development of lateral buds. If the tip is removed apical dominance is broken and a shoot below will become the leader.

AUXINS Synthetic or naturally-occurring substances in plants controlling shoot growth, root formation and other physiological processes.

AXIL The upper angle where a leaf stalk joins a stem.

AXILLARY BUD One that occurs in an axil.

BALLED ROOTS *See* Rootball.

BARE-ROOTED Plants sold with their roots bare of soil.

BARK The surface layer of the trunk and branches of woody plants, protecting the tissue within; usually composed of dead corky cells.

BARK-RINGING The controlled removal of a ring of bark from the trunk or branches of certain fruit trees, to reduce vigorous growth and to encourage fruit cropping.

BASAL Growing at the base of a plant.

BASAL CLUSTER The lowest cluster of leaves on a shoot, around its point of origin.

BASAL SHOOTS Those rising from near or at ground level.

BIENNIAL BEARING The production of a heavy fruit crop in alternate years, with little or no fruit in the intervening years.

BLEEDING The oozing of sap through a cut or wound.

BLIND SHOOT A shoot that does not form a terminal flower bud, or one where the growing point has been destroyed.

BLOSSOM THINNING Removing a proportion of blossom from a fruit tree, often to correct the problem of biennial bearing.

BOLE The trunk of a tree; sometimes used to describe the thicker base.

BRACT A modified leaf, usually at the base of a flower, which may be coloured, resembling a petal, or small and scale-like.

BRANCH BARK RIDGE Fold in bark where branch joins trunk, sometimes visible.

BRANCH COLLAR The thickened ring at the base of a branch.

BRANCH LEADER The leading shoot of a branch, extending its length.

BRANCHED-HEAD STANDARD A tree with a clear trunk and a branched crown.

BREAK Often used to describe the process of a shoot emerging from a bud.

BREASTWOOD Shoots growing forward from trees or shrubs trained flat against a wall.

BRUTTING A technique commonly used for nut trees, which involves fracturing, but not severing, longer sideshoots half-way along their length to encourage more female flowers to form, and to restrict late growth.

BUD A condensed shoot containing an embryonic leaf, leaf cluster or flower.

BUD-GRAFTING A form of grafting in which a bud is taken from one plant and inserted under the bark of another.

BUDDING Bud-grafting.

BURR On a tree trunk, a raised, thickened, corky area that sometimes produces shoots.

BUSH TREE A branched-headed tree with a short trunk, often formed by pruning.

CALLUS TISSUE Protective tissue formed by plants over a wounded surface, particularly in woody plants.

CALYX Ring of sepals beneath flower or fruit.

CAMBIUM LAYER The layer of tissue capable of producing new cells to increase the girth of stems and roots.

CATENARY A row of swags joined together.

CENTRAL LEADER The central, usually upright, stem of a plant.

CENTRAL-LEADER STANDARD A tree with a clear trunk that persists as a central leader through the crown of branches.

CHILLING REQUIREMENT The requirement of some plants for a specific period of dormancy below a particular temperature in order to initiate flowering.

CLADODE A stem which functions as a leaf, but which carries flowers.

CLIMBER A plant that climbs using other plants or objects as support. Self-clinging climbers climb by means of aerial roots or adhesive tendril tips. Tendril climbers coil their leaf stalks or tendrils, while twining climbers coil their stems. Scandent and trailing climbers produce long flexible stems that grow over or through their support.

CLONE A group of plants produced by vegetative propagation or asexual reproduction to be genetically identical.

COLLAR *See* Branch collar.

CONTINENTAL CLIMATE Characterized by hot summers and cold winters, with rainfall spread through the year.

COOL TEMPERATE CLIMATE Climate with warm summers and cold winters, intermediate spring and autumn seasons, and rainfall throughout the year.

COPPICING The regular pruning back of trees or shrubs close to ground level to stimulate the growth of vigorous shoots.

CORAL SPOT A fungal disease; affected shoots die back and the dead bark becomes covered in orangey-pink pustules.

CORDON A trained plant consisting of one main stem clothed in short growths, produced by rigorous pruning.

CROTCH The angle between two branches, or between a branch and a trunk.

CROWN The branched part of a tree above the trunk.

CROWN LIFTING The removal of low branches to produce a taller clear trunk, usually best undertaken by a professional arboriculturist.

CROWN REDUCTION Making the crown of a tree smaller by cutting back the longest branches.

CROWN THINNING Removing crowded growth from the crown of a tree to allow more light in and promote healthy growth.

CULTIVAR A distinct plant variation which has originated in cultivation, not in the wild.

DEADHEADING The removal of spent flowers or flowerheads.

DECIDUOUS Plants that shed leaves at the end of the growing season and renew them at the beginning of the next.

DEFOLIATION Loss of leaves.

DIEBACK The death of tips of shoots, spreading down the stem, caused by damage or disease.

DIOECIOUS Bearing male and female organs in flowers on separate plants. Males and females must thus be grown together for pollination.

DISBUDDING The removal of surplus buds to promote finer flowers or fruits.

DIVISION A method of increasing a plant by cutting sections from it, each with part of the root system and one or more shoots.

DORMANCY The state of temporary cessation of growth in plants, and slowing down of other activities, usually during winter.

DORMANT Alive but inactive.

DOUBLE CORDON A plant trained so that it has two parallel main stems.

"DOUBLE-U" CORDON *See* Four-armed cordon.

DUAL LEADERS Competing leaders of equal strength. The narrow crotch angle between rival leaders is a source of structural weakness in a tree, so one leader should be removed.

DOUBLE-WORKING Technique of grafting together plants that are naturally incompatible. A cultivar compatible with both the rootstock and the scion cultivar is used as an "interstock" between the two.

DWARF Naturally small-growing mutation of a plant, often vegetatively propagated to produce a named dwarf cultivar.

DWARFING ROOTSTOCK In grafting, using the roots of a smaller-growing plant than the plant which is grafted on to it, in order to limit the latter's size.

EPICORMIC SHOOTS Shoots that develop from latent or adventitious buds under the bark of a tree or shrub; they frequently arise close to pruning wounds on tree trunks or branches. *See also* Water shoots.

ESPALIER A plant trained with a vertical central trunk and tiers of branches growing horizontally on either side in a single plane; often applied to fruit trees.

EVERGREEN Plant that retains its foliage for more than one growing season.

EXTENSION GROWTH New growth made during a season.

EYE A dormant or latent growth bud that is visible at a node.

FAMILY In plant classification, a grouping of related plant genera.

FAN An intensively pruned tree trained with the main branches radiating in a flat fan shape from a short trunk.

FASTIGIATE Trees or shrubs with branches growing vertically and almost parallel with the main stem.

FEATHERED MAIDEN One-year-old tree that has developed lateral shoots (feathers).

FESTOONING A technique for training fruit trees, where branches are tied down to a more horizontal position to stimulate fruiting growth.

FIREBLIGHT A bacterial disease which results in blackened blossoms and stems.

FLUSH CUT Complete removal of growth at its point of origin, leaving no stub. Now not generally recommended.

FORMA (Lat.) Form (f.). Applied to plants within a species which differ in some minor character: *Clematis montana* f. *grandiflora* is a larger-flowered form of *C. montana*.

FOUR-ARMED ("DOUBLE-U") CORDON A plant trained with four parallel upright main stems.

FRAMEWORK The permanent branch structure of a tree or shrub; the main branches that determine its ultimate shape.

FROST HARDY A plant able to withstand temperatures down to −5°C (23°F).

FROST TENDER A plant vulnerable to frost damage.

FRUIT BUD A bud from which a flower, followed by a fruit, develops.

FRUIT SET The successful development of fruits after pollination and fertilization.

FRUIT THINNING The removal of some developing fruits after natural fruit drop has occurred, to improve the growth and quality of the remainder.

FULL LORETTE SYSTEM See Lorette system.

GENUS (pl. genera) A group of related species linked by common characters. A category in plant classification between family and species.

GRAFT UNION The point at which scion and rootstock are joined.

GRAFTING Making an artificial union between the top growth of one plant (the scion) and the roots of another (the rootstock) so that they eventually function as one plant.

GROWING POINT Topmost bud of a shoot.

GROWTH BUD A bud from which leaves or a shoot develop, not flowers.

GUMMING A physiological disorder of stone fruit trees. A translucent amber-coloured liquid is exuded from the bark and may also occur around fruit stones.

HABIT Characteristic, natural form of growth of a plant – upright, prostrate, weeping, etc.

HALF-HARDY Plants not able to tolerate frost, but generally able to withstand lower temperatures than frost-tender plants.

HALF-STANDARD A tree or shrub that has a single clear stem of 1–1.5m (3–5ft).

HEADING BACK See Crown reduction.

HERBACEOUS A non-woody plant in which the part above ground dies down to the rootstock at the end of the growing season.

HYBRID The offspring of genetically different parents, usually of distinct species.

INTERNODAL CUT A cut made between two nodes or growth buds.

LAMMAS GROWTH A second flush of growth which may occur in mid- to late summer.

LATENT BUD A bud that fails to develop in the season it was formed, but remains dormant and may later be stimulated into growth.

LATERAL Side growth that arises from any shoot or root.

LATERAL BUD Bud that will form a sideshoot.

LATEX A fluid produced by many plants, containing substances such as starch, alkaloids, mineral salts and sugars; often white in appearance.

LAYERING A method of propagation by which a shoot is pegged into the ground so that it roots while still attached to the parent plant.

LEADER The main, usually central, stem of a plant.

LEADING SHOOT The main central shoot of a plant, or of a main branch.

LEAF SCAR Point on a stem where a leaf was attached. It can usually be seen as a crescent or horseshoe shape just under a bud.

LEG Clear length of main stem on a shrub or tree before branching begins.

LIGNIFY Turn woody.

LIGNOTUBER Woody, swollen tuberous root from which growth emerges, as in *Eucalyptus*.

LIMB A branch of a tree.

LORETTE SYSTEM Method of summer-pruning apples and pears, designed to restrict vegetative growth and encourage fruiting growth. The Modified Lorette System is used in temperate climates; the Full Lorette System is used in warmer climates.

MAIDEN A tree in its first year. *See also* Feathered maiden.

MAIDEN WHIP A tree in its first year, without lateral branches.

MARITIME CLIMATE A damp climate moderated by a nearby sea mass that prevents severe seasonal temperature fluctuations.

MAYPOLING A method by which branches heavily laden with fruit are prevented from breaking. Lengths of strong twine are tied to laden branches of the tree to hold them up, and are attached to the top of the trunk or the tree's stake.

MEDITERRANEAN CLIMATE Sunny climate with hot dry summers and mild winters; rainfall is generally in winter.

MICROCLIMATE Localized climatic conditions, from those in a garden to a particular geographical area.

MODIFIED LORETTE SYSTEM *See* Lorette System.

MONOECIOUS A plant bearing separate male and female reproductive organs on the same plant.

MONOPODIAL Growing indefinitely from an apical or terminal bud on a stem.

MULCH A material applied in a layer to the soil surface to suppress weeds, conserve moisture, and maintain a cool, even root temperature. In addition to organic materials such as manure, bark and garden compost, polythene, foil and gravel may also be used.

MULTIPLE CORDON A trained plant, usually a fruit tree, with three or more vertical stems.

MULTI-STEMMED Tree or shrub with several main stems arising either directly from the ground or from a short main stem.

NATURAL BARRIER An internal chemical barrier produced by a plant in order to stop the spread of infection from one area to the rest of the plant.

NICKING The removal of a small triangle or semi-circle of bark below a dormant bud, inhibiting the bud's development (*see also* Notching).

NODE The point on a stem from which leaves, shoots or flowers arise.

NON-RECURRENT Plants which only produce one flush of flowers, as with many roses.

NOTCHING The removal of a small triangle or semi-circle of bark above a dormant bud, stimulating the bud to grow (*see also* Nicking).

OCCLUSION Process by which a pruning cut or wound closes over with callus tissue.

OPEN CENTRE On branched-headed trees or bushes, an open centre in the crown of growth, achieved by pruning.

OPPOSITE BUDS Buds at the same level on opposite sides of a stem or other axis.

PALMETTE An espalier with arms raised up at an angle of about 45° to the horizontal.

PANICLE A branched raceme of clustered, stalked flowers, as in lilac (*Syringa*).

PARING Trimming with a pruning knife.

PATHOGENS Micro-organisms that cause disease.

PETIOLE The stalk of a leaf.

PHOTOSYNTHESIS The production of organic compounds required for growth in plants by a complex process involving chlorophyll, light energy, carbon dioxide and water.

PINCH PRUNING Method of pruning whereby shoot tips are removed, to influence growth and flower or fruit production.

PINCHING BACK pinching out soft shoot tips to shape growth.

PINCHING OUT The removal of the growing tip of a stem (with finger and thumb) to induce the production of sideshoots or the formation of flower buds.

PINNATE Of a leaf, a compound form in which leaflets grow in a row on each side of a midrib.

PLEACHING A technique whereby branches from a row of trees are woven together and trained to form a screen or canopy of foliage.

POLLARD A tree which is cut back at regular intervals to the head of the main trunk.

POLLARDING The regular pruning back of the main branches of a tree to the head of the main stem or trunk, or to a short branch framework. The effect is to maintain a compact head of fresh young growth.

POLLINATION The transfer of pollen so that sexual reproduction may occur in plants.

POLLINATOR The agent or means by which pollination is carried out. Of fruit trees, a cultivar required to ensure fruit set on a sterile or partially sterile cultivar.

POME FRUIT A firm, fleshy fruit, with seeds enclosed in a central core, as in apples, pears.

POT BOUND A condition resulting from a plant's growth being restricted by growing for too long in the same container, so that the roots become congested and begin to coil round and round.

PRIMARY BRANCH One growing directly from the main stem or trunk of a woody plant.

PROSTRATE With stems growing along the ground.

PRUNING Removing growth from a plant or tree to maintain its health and vigour, regulate its shape and size, and control its flowering and fruiting.

PYRAMID A method of training a fruit tree in which each tier of branches is composed of shorter branches than the tier below.

RACEME An unbranched flower cluster with, usually, many small stalked flowers borne on a long stem.

RAMBLER *See* Climber.

RECURRENT, REMONTANT *See* Repeat-flowering.

REGULATED PRUNING The occasional removal of sections of branches, or whole branches, from large, woody plants to prevent congestion and stimulate younger growth.

REMEDIAL PRUNING The removal of dead, damaged or diseased wood to protect the plant's health.

REMONTANT *See* Repeat-flowering.

RENEWAL PRUNING A system in which older growth is regularly removed in favour of younger.

REPEAT-FLOWERING Plants that flower more than once during the growing season, for example most modern roses.

REPLACEMENT SHOOT A strong, young shoot that is retained in such a position that it may develop to replace older growth removed by pruning.

REVERSION The production of shoots with plain green leaves on variegated plants.

RIB Main branch of a fan-trained tree.

RIPE WOOD Dark, mature, hardened wood.

ROD A main stem of a grapevine.

ROOTBALL The roots and accompanying soil visible when a plant is removed from a container or lifted from the open ground.

ROOT BOUND See Pot bound.

ROOT PRUNING The removal of part of the root system of a fruit tree to restrict growth and induce fruiting.

ROOT RUN The area of soil into which a plant's roots extend.

ROOT-TO-SHOOT RATIO The proportional size of the root system to the top growth.

ROOTSTOCK A plant used to provide the root system for a grafted plant.

RUBBING OUT The removal of unwanted new shoots by rubbing them off by hand.

SAP Plant fluid contained in the cells and vascular tissue.

SCAFFOLD BRANCHES The main framework branches on a tree.

SCANDENT Scrambling or loosely climbing. See also Climber.

SCION Plant, usually a desirable cultivar, that is grafted onto the rootstock of another plant.

SECONDARY BRANCHES Those arising from primary branches.

SECONDARY GROWTH Growth that appears after pruning in summer.

SELF-CLINGING CLIMBER See Climber.

SELF-FERTILE A plant that produces viable seed when fertilized with its own pollen.

SEMI-EVERGREEN A plant that retains only a proportion of its leaves for more than one season, depending on climatic conditions.

SEPAL Outer whorl of calyx, usually small and green, but may be coloured and petal-like.

SHRUB A woody-stemmed plant, usually lacking a single trunk, branching from or near the base.

SIDESHOOT A shoot growing out from a stem.

SILVER LEAF A disease attacking a wide range of trees and shrubs, but particularly *Prunus* and *Malus*, where leaves take on a leaden or silvery appearance.

SINGLE CORDON Form of training where a plant is restricted by rigorous pruning to one main stem clothed in short growths.

SNAG An overlong stub or frayed end left after incorrect pruning.

SOIL MARK The usually noticeable point on a plant's stem showing the original soil level before the plant was lifted in the nursery.

SPACER Small piece of padding used in conjunction with a plant tie to hold a trunk or branch away from its stake or support, preventing chafing damage.

SPECIES A category in plant classification, denoting closely-related similar plants.

SPECIMEN PLANT A striking plant, usually a well-shaped tree or shrub, grown in an open site where it can be seen clearly.

SPINDLE BUSH High-yielding fruit tree form.

SPORT Natural mutation of a plant or part of its growth, or a plant propagated from this growth, that differs from the normal characteristics of habit, size, shape, form or colour of foliage, flower or fruit.

SPROUT A shoot emerging from a clear trunk, often unwanted.

SPUR A short shoot or branchlet bearing flower buds, as on fruit trees.

SPUR BEARING Plant which produces its flowers and fruits on short shoots along the length of stems. See also tip bearing.

SPUR PRUNING Shortening shoots to stimulate flower or fruit bud production.

SPUR SYSTEM Clusters of shortened, jointed shoots, built up by spur pruning, producing more short, fruiting shoots each year.

SPUR THINNING Removing sections of spur systems to reduce overcrowding.

STAG-HEADED DIEBACK Antlered appearance of trees caused by dead branches protruding from the tree canopy.

STANDARD A tree with a clear length of trunk below a head of branches.

STEM BUILDER Shoot on a main stem retained temporarily so that its leaves can nourish the stem's vertical growth.

STEPOVER Low horizontal cordon, which can be stepped over.

STOCK See Rootstock.

STOCK PLANT A plant used to produce propagating material, whether seed or vegetative material.

STOLON A horizontally spreading or arching stem, usually above ground, which roots at its tip to produce a new plant.

STOLONIFEROUS Bearing or producing stolons.

STOOL A number of shoots arising, more or less uniformly, from the base of a plant, often as a result of pruning.

STOOLING The regular pruning back of woody plants to ground level.

STOPPING See Pinching out.

STUB Portion of stem remaining between the point where a cut is made and the next area of active growth (as when cutting a shoot above a bud, or a branch back to a main stem).

SUBLATERAL Sideshoot from a lateral shoot.

SUBSHRUB A low-growing plant that is woody at the base and with soft, usually herbaceous, growth above.

SUBSPECIES A subdivision of a species.

SUBTROPICAL Hot in summer with a cool winter season; rainfall seasonal or all year.

SUCKER A shoot that arises at or below ground level from a plant's root or underground stem; on grafted plants, any shoot that arises below the graft union (from the rootstock).

SUMMER PRUNING Pruning in summer to restrict or control vegetative growth.

SWAG Climbing plant (often a rose) trained along a rope hanging between two posts.

TAP ROOT Single, downward-growing root of a plant (especially a tree).

TARGET PRUNING Removing growth with as small a pruning cut as possible.

TAXON A group of living organisms at any botanical level; applied to groups of plants that share distinct, defined characters.

TENDRIL A modified leaf or stem, usually long and slender, capable of attaching itself to a support.

TERMINAL At the tip of a stem or branch.

THINNING The removal of a proportion of shoots, woody growth, flowers or fruit buds

to improve the vigour and quality of the remainder.

TIP BEARING Carrying much of the crop at or near shoot tips. See also Spur bearing.

TIP PRUNING Pinching out or cutting back the growing tip of a shoot to encourage sideshoots to develop or to remove damaged growth.

TIPPING See Tip pruning.

TOP-GRAFTING Grafting onto the top of a Length of clear trunk.

TOP-WORKING See Top-grafting.

TOPIARY The art of clipping and training trees and shrubs into various geometric or free shapes.

TRANSPIRATION Loss of water by evaporation from the leaves and stems of plants.

TREE A woody, perennial plant, usually with a well-defined trunk or stem having a head or crown of branches above.

TREE PRUNERS A pruning tool, usually 2–3m (6–10ft) long, suitable for cutting branches up to 2.5cm (1in) thick that would otherwise be out of reach. The blade is operated by a lever system or a cord, and may have a saw or fruit-picker attachment.

TRIPLE CORDON See multiple cordon.

TROPICAL High year-round temperatures. Rainfall may be high, seasonally or all year, except in arid tropics, where it is low.

TRUE Of plant breeding, plants that when self-pollinated reliably produce offspring very similar to their parents.

TRUNK Thick, woody, main stem of a tree.

TRUSS A compact cluster of flowers or fruits.

"U" CORDON See double cordon.

UNION See Graft union.

UNRIPE WOOD Young, green wood.

V-ANGLE Crotch angle between branch and main stem.

VARIEGATED Irregularly marked with various colours; particularly of leaves that are patterned with markings in white, yellow or other colours.

VARIETAS, VARIETY Naturally-occurring variant of a wild species, ranked botanically between subspecies and forma.

VEGETATIVE GROWTH Non-flowering, usually leafy growth.

WARM TEMPERATE CLIMATE Rainy climate with a fairly narrow temperature range; warm to hot summers and mild winters.

WATER SHOOTS Sappy, fast-growing epicormic shoots, usually arising around damage or sites of pruning cuts.

WEEPING Growing with slender branches that hang down.

WHIP A young tree, consisting of a single stem that has not yet developed lateral branches.

WHORL The arrangement of three or more organs, frequently leaves or shoots, arising from the same point.

WIND-PRUNING Distortion of a plant or tree's shape through the stunting of growth by prevailing winds.

WIND-ROCK The destabilizing of a plant's roots by strong wind.

WINTER PRUNING Thinning a plant in winter to encourage better quality fruit or flowers.

WOUND PAINT A specialized paint applied to a cut surface of a plant after pruning; not generally now recommended.

X Sign denoting a hybrid, produced from crossing two genetically distinct plants.

XYLEM Vascular tissue under bark taking water and nutrients up a stem.

Index

Acknowledgments

PHOTOGRAPHY
The publishers are grateful to the following for permission to
reproduce illustrative material:
Deni Bown: 81, 221 *left*; Christopher Brickell: 113 *right*, 214 *top*;
Neil Campbell-Sharp: 319 *bottom right*; Eric Crichton: 78, 160, 316;
Gap Photos/Neil Holmes: 2, J.S.Sira: 38 *top*; Garden Picture Library:
322 top; Garden World Images/Alain Guerrier: 85; Jerry Harpur: 187 *top*,
255 *bottom*, 260, 319 *top*, 323, 325; Holt Studios International: 117 *bottom*;
Stephen Josland: 9 *top left*, 277; Andrew Lawson: 36 *main*, 60 *top*,
130 *top*, 255 *top*; David Paterson: 36 *inset*; Photolibrary/Mark Bolton: 6;
Photos Horticultural: 235 *bottom*; Royal National Rose Society: 309;
Professor H. Don Tindall: 140 left and *right*, 141 *top main picture*, *top inset*,
bottom, 145 *top*, *centre* and *bottom*, 146 *top*, 147 *top*, 148 *top*, 149 *bottom*,
297; John White: 10 *top right*, 29 *bottom centre*, 33
Photographs taken at the 1995 Chelsea Flower Show by Steve Gorton,
with thanks to: Ben Loseley Williams of Greens Garden Furniture
(braided *Ficus*) Harpers & Queen/Cartier garden (pleached limes);
Mattocks Roses (rose in hanging basket, standard Bo Peep rose);
Rosemary Verey (standard-trained *Syringa meyeri*); Rayment Wirework
(ivy-covered seahorse frame). All other photographs by Peter Anderson

ARTWORK
Step-by-step artworks: Karen Cochrane
Plant silhouettes: Karen Cochrane, John Hutchinson
Chapter opening motifs:

PROPS AND LOCATION PHOTOGRAPHY
Secateurs by Felco; all other tools by kind permission of Spear &
Jackson. Other items courtesy of Agriframes, Marshalls Seeds.
Many thanks for their valuable time and advice to: Reads Nursery,
Hales Hall, Norfolk; The Romantic Garden Nursery, Swannington,
Norfolk; and Piers Greenwood of Newhall Vineyard, Essex

ADDITIONAL DESIGN ASSISTANCE
Sasha Kennedy and Rachael Parfitt; thanks also to Gillian Allan,
Steve Crozier, Nicola Erdpresser, Bob Gordon and Ina Stradins.

Rob Nunn and Emma Shepherd for picture research; and John
Goldsmid for production assistance.

ADDITIONAL EDITORIAL ASSISTANCE
Candida Frith-Macdonald, Linden Hawthorne, Laura Langley,
Martha Swift and Melanie Tham; thanks also to Jane Aspden,
Lynn Bresler, Joanna Chisholm, Tracie Lee, Andrew Mikolajski,
Laraine Newberry and Anne Reilly

INDEX
Dorothy Frame

Dorling Kindersley would also like to thank:
In the United States, Paul W. Meyer of the Morris Arboretum and
American Horticultural Association; Dr Alexander Shigo; and
Ray Rogers, Mary Sutherland and Will Lach at DK Inc., New York
In Australia, Frances Hutchison for much invaluable advice
For plant-finding and location research: Diana Mitchell
For additional text inputting: Colin Belton, Royal Botanic Garden
Edinburgh; Audrey Longhurst, RHS Vincent Square

All the staff of the Royal Horticultural Society for their time
and assistance, in particular: at Vincent Square, Susanne Mitchell,
Karen Wilson and Barbara Haynes; at Hyde Hall, Tom McMasters,
Tom Angus, Chris White and Eileen Mackenzie: at Wisley, Mike
Honour, Haden Williams, Jim Arbury, Ray Waite, Andy Hart,
Carol Howat, Roma Sinclair, Nancy Hopper and Sue Burnham,
and the ever-patient staff in Glass, Propagation and the Plant Centre